T0367660

Complexity-Intelligence Strategy
A New Paradigmatic Shift

Complexity-Intelligence Strategy
A New Paradigmatic Shift

Thow Yick Liang

Singapore Management University, Singapore

NEW JERSEY · LONDON · SINGAPORE · BEIJING · SHANGHAI · HONG KONG · TAIPEI · CHENNAI · TOKYO

Published by

World Scientific Publishing Co. Pte. Ltd.
5 Toh Tuck Link, Singapore 596224
USA office: 27 Warren Street, Suite 401-402, Hackensack, NJ 07601
UK office: 57 Shelton Street, Covent Garden, London WC2H 9HE

Library of Congress Control Number: 2016040296

British Library Cataloguing-in-Publication Data
A catalogue record for this book is available from the British Library.

COMPLEXITY-INTELLIGENCE STRATEGY
A New Paradigmatic Shift

ISBN 978-981-3200-63-0

Desk Editor: Alisha Nguyen

Typeset by Stallion Press
Email: enquiries@stallionpress.com

Printed in Singapore

Dedicated to

Char Hoon

Zhen Ning (Justin)

Wei Ning (Nicole)

Organizing around individual intelligence/consciousness, and nurturing intense collective intelligence/org-consciousness is the new intelligence paradigmatic shift that drives a redefined human complex adaptive, self-organizing, and more sustaining dynamic that is greatly needed by all competitive organizations in the present rapidly changing, knowledge-intensive, and highly interconnected and interdependent environment — the surfacing of a new niche, the intelligence advantage.

Contents

Preface

The Newtonian mindset (order, linearity, determinism and predictability) has dominated the entire human world for more than three centuries. It has provided the knowledge/theories and conceptual foundation (including deterministic laws, mechanistic thinking, Laplace belief, design paradigm, Cartesian belief, reductionist hypothesis/fundamentalism, deliberate planning and mapping techniques, and certainty) that supported the industrial revolution, and operational control (exploiting hierarchical/bureaucratic leadership and governance, deliberate planning and strategy, transformational leadership, regularity, functional cohesion, static equilibrium and forecasting) of all organizations (corporations, communities, nations and regional/global institutions) in humanity. However, over the last few decades, constraints and incoherency are emerging due to new accelerants and elevating complexity density. The new situation and dynamics, and the multi-dimensional changes require a fresh thinking and deeper comprehension that is beyond the boundaries of the exact sciences. As the continuality of human existence requires a new global order to be established (nurtured and emerged), a paradigmatic shift is essential.

This book is an attempt to provide the foundation for nurturing the intelligence mindset (encompassing the complexity mindset and Newtonian mindset selectively) that is critical in the present rapidly changing, high interconnectivity and interdependency, and knowledge-intensive environment, in particular, with the more frequent appearance of new unknowns and surprises. Fundamentally, the intelligence mindset and its paradigmatic shift encompasses intelligence/consciousness-centricity, complexity-centricity, network-centricity and stability-centricity, as well as the constructionist thinking as its foundation pillars leading to a fresh intriguing pursuit (constructionist effect <=> innovation and creativity) in the human world. This transformation in thinking and paradigm is inevitable as additional profound changes in humanity, including modified principles, values, expectations and perception (perceived 'rights' and other construal aspects) of human agents; nonlinear organizational relational friction and dynamics; as well as in-complete phase space are greatly redefining the attributes of human interdependency, leadership, governance, strategy, management and operations. The conceptual foundation of this new thinking has been conceived as the intelligent organization theory, and the theory of relativistic complexity.

In the visible world, intelligence and stability-centricity are mutually correlated. The formation of the physical matter world and biological world is fundamentally determined by this highly significant attribute of stability-centricity. This attribute allows a 'small' segment of the Universe to reverse its universal expanding dynamic. It is the presence of proto-intelligence that initiated the formation of physical structures — physical self-organization and localized (atomic/subatomic) order. More directly, the inference is that it is the proto-intelligence embedded in the physical matter world that drives its own physical stability-centric dynamic — towards more and more robust order/structure. Atoms that are stable do not react. While, atoms that are not stable combined to form more complex molecules that are stable. These stability-seeking processes continue and increase in complexity, and at a vital threshold life emerges. This is a constructionist phenomenon as a new attribute, life and its associated consciousness (awareness, self-awareness) that is not present at the lower level (physical matter world) emerges. Concurrently, the astonishing new strengths of biological stability-centricity also surface.

Biological stability (associated with the evolution of genes, chromosomes, cells, organs, organisms, and more complex species with the trait of independency) is much more sophisticated relative to physical stability — also vastly due to the emergent of new dimensions at the macro level (locomotion, audio space, visual space and mental capacity). A biological organism (from single cell to trillion cells) that learns, adapts and evolves to the changing environment is a localized order that is created by intelligence that also drives its autopoietic processes. The intrinsic intelligence that sustains biological stability is the basic life-intelligence, and it is from the latter that consciousness emerges. In this respect, the Universe is conscious. Thus, the biological world (Gaia and its ecosystems) encompasses a space of consciousness that greatly redefines its dynamics. This new dimension also creates a new intangible world that is totally different from physical matter (alone). The primary mental functions of awareness (at least responding to the changing environment), and self-awareness (recognizing the existence of the 'self') emerge. At the peak of this evolution process are human beings (Homo sapiens sapiens), each encompasses a complex thinking system. Primarily, the unique capacity of the human thinking systems is associated with the relatively 'advanced' development of the human cerebral cortex.

Apparently, the consciousness of different species in the global ecosystem is highly diversified. The human thinking systems (complex neural networks) are the most intense intelligence/consciousness sources on this planet. The intensity of consciousness is closely associated with the intensity of intelligence source from which it emerges. For more 'intense' intelligence, the presence of the brain (a collection or network of neurons) is a pre-requisite. Human brains are each a complex neural network (an intense integrated network of networks) with approximately a trillion neurons. These intense and nonlinear intelligence/consciousness sources each projects a complex abstract mind encompassing a cognitive space, (subjective) knowledge, and possessing the unique capability of utilizing character sets and physical symbols systems, that leads to the emergent of sophisticated written languages (a phenomenon unknown to other biological species). No other species in Gaia has ever created a written language or exploited technologies (advanced knowledge creation).

In addition, a new consciousness function, namely mindfulness (core of the self-awareness function — an inwards focusing capability) emerges from human consciousness. It enables a human being to observe and control the mind. With the presence of this additional capability (the recognition of 'I'), human consciousness is significantly beyond that of all other biological species. Therefore, human stability-centricity (associated with self-centricity, α-state, self-powered capacity, intrinsic leadership capacity and independency) is significantly different, encompassing an integrated physical, biological and mental space. In particular, the presence of the mental space redefined human interdependency (versus independency) and existence. Therefore, current leaders must recognize that better management, ambidexterity, social consensus and conformity, high relational capacity and integration of the human thinking systems (appropriate intelligence-intelligence linkages) in an organization is a critical requirement associated with its success — a strategic path towards new competitiveness, resilience and sustainability. In this respect, intelligence/consciousness-centricity is a significant attribute of intelligent human organizations (the presence of an orgmind), and organizing around intelligence is a new basic strategic approach (rather than around functions or processes) that must be well exploited.

Over the last few decades, swift changes in the human environment have elevated complexity density in an unprecedented manner creating intense new differentials. Apparently, orderliness, linearity, equilibrium, determinism and predictability are not the only characteristics that define the human world. Instead, order and complexity (stasis and turbulence) co-exist inherently, and nonlinearity, in-determinism and limited predictability are vital new attributes that must be better comprehended. The entire humanity and their organizations, including human beings are intrinsic complex adaptive systems (and composite systems). Succinctly, the complexity theory must be better comprehend and effectively exploited, as characteristics such as sensitive dependence on initial conditions, dissipation, nonlinearity, adaptive tension, cascading chain, space of complexity, punctuation point, rugged/fitness landscape, far-from-equilibrium, red queen race, self-organization (self-transcending constructions), self-organizing capability, basin of attraction, attractor' (in-complete) phase space and emergence are all natural characteristics of humanity and all its subsystems. Hence, in the current environment where the human world and its microcosms is continuously changing (gradual and sudden), change is the only attribute that never change. In this respect, complexity theory is also a theory of change.

Fundamentally, complexity has always been around. This attribute is an inherent component of this Universe, as well as our biosphere since the beginning. However, the study of complexity both in the natural sciences, and its extension to humanities (social, economic, political, military, and environmental perspectives) is relatively new (despite the presence of some historical roots). Currently, recognizing and exploiting the co-existence of order and complexity in humanity and its organizations is not a strategic norm, although, it has been observed that the Newtonian mindset and thinking is exhibiting constraints and disparities because human organizations are nonlinear, open, complex, dissipative and adaptive. Many traditional attributes and concepts are revealing escalating incoherency — indicating that even entrenched norms are not permanent. With the present multi-dimensional and multi-perspective accelerating changes (especially, due to numerous technological advancement and integration, including mobile/social media) and deeper globalization, the human world has 'shrunk' (space-time compression), human interdependency has intensified and transformed, spaces of complexity and punctuation points are emerging more frequently (physical and mental) due to higher wider causal chain effect (for instance, the last global financial crisis), and competition has been transformed (higher complexity <=> higher interdependency).

In the new emerging context, human organizations are manifesting more and stronger properties/characteristics of complex adoptive systems (CAS) and the complex adaptive dynamics (CAD) — their inherent status. The significance of intrinsic complexity in all human systems is becoming highly apparent and cannot be suppressed or ignored. This observation leads to the conceptualization of the complexity-intelligence strategy — the holistic/global strategy of the intelligent organization theory. As absolute order, linearity, determinism and high predictability associated with traditional thinking, leadership, governance, strategy, and management is no longer sufficient, complexity and its associated attributes have to be better explored and exploited. Certain spaces of complexity are new unexplored territories embedded with 'gold nuggets', awaiting the right innovative explorers. Hence, towards complexity-centricity is a significant and inevitable inclusion. In this respect, a new primary focal point is recognizing the strengths of human agents (intense intelligence/consciousness sources, organizational assets), and the constraints of human organizations (in-complete phase space due to the presence of unknown unknowns, the states of a preferred attractor may not be totally known) — recognizing the close correlation between intelligence/consciousness and complexity (complexity-intelligence linkages) and introduces a new strategic path.

In this context, the presence' of intense intelligence/consciousness-centricity and third order stability-centricity in the human world also renders complexity relativistic. The impact of the human mental space is so intense that 'complexity is in the mind of the beholder', and predictability becomes significantly subjective. In such a situation, the state of relativistic static equilibrium may be beneficial. Certain spaces of complexity appear as spaces of relativistic order with surface patterns becoming more apparent (the presence of a prepared mind). Such spaces must be creatively explored and exploited (elevating exploratory capacity) leading to a more advanced level of intelligence advantage. In this respect, effective self-transcending constructions, higher self-organizing capacity and emergence-intelligence capacity are vital attributes that the new leadership must focus on. In intelligent organizations, the intelligence leadership strategy adopted exploits the significant positive correlation of intelligence/consciousness-centricity and relative complexity, and optimizes the more comprehensive coverage and contributions of the integrated deliberate and emergent strategy. In addition, subjectivity may be a positive attribute.

The holistic exploitation of an integrated deliberate and emergent strategy in human organizations is a new necessity. Concurrently, these are two broad paths that allow human organizations to exploit order and complexity (as indicated by the autopoiesis theory, network theory and power law) more effectively, comprehensively and innovatively. The emergent component emphasizes that strategic planning cannot be totally mapped out, structured and predicted, although, being futuristic is still highly significant. Rather, an emergent path must always be nurtured to encompass and exploit the complex and nonlinear perspective continuously. The emergent component allows a new direction that manages nonlinearity and complexity more constructively to emerge. In particular, nurturing collective intelligence with a high self-organizing capacity and better network integration is vital to all current human organizations, as it supports positive spontaneous processes (that are particularly vital at punctuation points).

Hence, the interconnectivity of intense individual intelligence/consciousness sources, and nurturing high collective intelligence/org-consciousness (higher structural capacity, adaptive capacity, collectiveness capacity, relational capacity, self-organizing capacity, emergence-intelligence capacity and unifying capacity; agent-centricity, network-centricity, intra-system order and intra system order) is a new critical niche. Fundamentally, new distinctive leadership (lateral/collective leadership, consultative leadership, learning leadership and latent leadership), and governance (self-organizing governance, e-governance, network-centric governance and adaptive governance) attributes are necessary for providing the fresh unifying impetus — ideally towards an 'everybody is in charge' situation (if needed).

Thus, the above introduction illustrates the merits of the intelligence paradigmatic shift that provides a more comprehensive path into the human world of complexity and network organizations. All human organizations (corporations, communities, economies, education institutions, military units, nations and regional/global institutions) are inherently CAS driven by complex adaptive dynamics, as well as possessing a multi-layer structure, and engulfing complex networks (network of networks). More networks (formal and informal) have been emerging due to more 'intelligent' agents, intense self-organizing communications, and the accelerated formation of localized spaces and/or networks. The intelligent organization theory and its complexity-intelligence strategy that focuses on intelligence-intelligence linkages, high finite dimensional in-determinism and unpredictability, biotic multi-layer structure and dynamics, positive relational parameter, new leadership attributes and fresh basis for governing (ambidexterity, coherency, synergy, constructionist effect and organizational mental cohesion) introduced an essential new conceptual foundation. A deeper and more complete analysis of the new situation (raplexity) with the intelligence mindset and its theory/strategy will be covered in this book.

However, it is vital to recognize that our knowledge (cognition) is a subjective construction and not an 'absolute' reflection of realty due to the constraints of our sensory systems and thinking systems. In realty, 'realty can never be known'.

Anyway, an important factor is an inquisitive mind (a key necessity) that always takes on new challenges is a pre-requisite for emergent of new order. Happy reading!

Liang Thow Yick
(May 2016)

Foundation Topics of the IO Theory

Complexity will be the science of the 21st century.

Stephen Hawking

Chapter 1

Humanity into the Intelligence Era

"Subtle insight and premonition are intelligence dependent,
in particular, intense nonlinear intelligence"

Summary

This chapter highlights the impact and manageability of rapid, constantly/continuously and unique changes taking place in humanity that are affecting the existence individuals, as well as all categories of human organizations. It has been observed that the traditional Newtonian mindset, and its associated reductionist hypothesis and design paradigm that have served humanity 'well' are manifesting their limits/constraints, vulnerability and disparities. The crux of the issue is escalating complexity density, incoherency, greater mismatch among current thinking, principles, values, structure, dynamic, and hierarchical dominance, limited predictability, and the overall changing 'reality'.

Vividly, order and linearity are not the only inherent attributes of humanity. Consequently, the significance, appropriateness and exploration of certain properties of complexity theory are introduced, partially to better identify, analyze, comprehend and manage the accelerating gaps of inconsistency — in particular, to nurture a new mindset. Arising from the new mindset, human organizations/systems are confirmed as intrinsic composite complex adaptive systems (composite CAS, nonlinear adaptive dynamical systems) comprising human beings/agents that are CAS. In this respect, leadership, governance, management, and strategic approaches adopted by all human organizations must be redefined.

Concurrently, a special focus on intelligence (and its associated consciousness), the first inherent strengths of all human agents, and its role as the key latent impetus/driver, is vital. This recognition indicates that a change in era is inevitable. Humanity is entering the new intelligence era — the core of the knowledge-intensive and complexity-centric period. Overall, an integrated intelligence/consciousness-centric, complexity-centric and network-centric approach is essential. It adopts a complexity-intelligence-centric path that focuses on the optimization of all intense intrinsic intelligence/consciousness sources (human thinking systems), better exploitation of the co-existence of order and complexity, and integration of networks in human organizations — (certain spaces of complexity must be better utilized, coherency of network of networks must be achieved, and preparation for punctuation point must be elevated).

The new holistic (multi-dimensional) strategy of the intelligent organization theory (IO theory) is the complexity-intelligence strategy, and the new mission focuses on the new intelligence advantage.

Keywords: Newtonian mindset, reductionist hypothesis, design paradigm, fundamentalism, intelligence era, order, exactness, linearity, predictability, deterministic, stability, Cartesian belief, Laplace belief, hierarchical decomposition, functional cohesion, self-powered, self-organizing capability, self-organization, self-transcending constructions, adaptation, connectivity, engagement, intelligence/consciousness-centric, intelligence, consciousness, awareness, mindfulness, complexity, complexity mindset, complexity-centric, co-existence of order and complexity, raplexity, networks, self-organizing networks, network-centric, coherency, tipping point, space of complexity, punctuation point, interdependency, holism, self-organizing communications, butterfly effect, *i*-space, *i*-empowerment, hysteresis, complexity theory, systems thinking, evolution thinking, cybernetic thinking, intelligence mindset, intelligence paradigm, global mindset, human thinking systems, ordered systems (OS), complex adaptive systems (CAS), intelligent biotic macro-structure, rugged landscape, emergence, interconnectedness, interdependency, space of complexity, cosmic mind, intelligence spectrum, autopoiesis, symbiosis, self-centric, stability-centric, org-centric, uncertainty, unknown unknowns, first mover advantage, dimensionality, stasis, punctuated equilibrium, static equilibrium, dynamical equilibrium, far-from-equilibrium, systemic transformation, organizing around intelligence, governance, governance systems, social conformity, intelligence leadership strategy, complex adaptive dynamic (CAD), biosphere, emergent of order, Gaia, intrinsic intelligence, basic life-intelligence, collective intelligence, orgmind, swarm intelligence, complexity-intelligence linkage, autonomous, ambidexterity, unifying capacity, intelligence advantage and complexity-intelligence strategy.

1.1 Introduction: The World of Change

1.1.1 *The Newtonian mindset and reductionist hypothesis*

The **Newtonian mindset** has dominated all individual and organizational perspectives (scientific, technological, social, economic, management, political, education, environmental) of humanity for over the last three centuries — from the late 17th century to the late 20th century (**Isaac Newton**, 1642–1727). It provided the knowledge and supported the dynamics of the industrial revolution and planned economy. It believes that the Universe and its subsystems are mechanistic (most prominent in non-living machine and the physical matter world) and possess clockwork characteristics, and are governed by the deterministic laws of nature. The systems involved are **linear, orderly,** and **predictable** (leading to the practice of mapping and exploiting deliberate strategy, and forecasting in most operations), and driven by **equilibrium dynamics** (always leading to **static equilibrium**). Most people today, consciously or subconsciously still encompass such a mindset (generally due to the contents of the education systems/materials, and the culture/belief of humanity).

This thinking (encompassing order, simplicity, regularity, reversibility, gradualism, reductionism, mechanistic design, static equilibrium, and the inertia of status quo) approach (general linear realty) have been 'imported' and exploited by many disciplines beyond the natural/exact sciences. For instance, **Frederick Taylor** (1856–1915), had exploited this mindset in the business/management domain, establishing a sub-domain known as scientific management in 1911 (the 'principles of scientific management'). Similarly, **Henri Fayol's** (1841–1925) planning, organizing, directing, and controlling, as well as forecasting, are also Newtonian-oriented thinking and applications in management (including the **design paradigm** — see Appendix 7). Over time, forecasting becomes a common and significant activity in many other disciplines, including finance, economics, sociology, and politics. Thus, in the non-sciences, the thinking, strategies, theories, models, frameworks, and decision making focus on linearity, equilibrium, certainty, and determinism. Systems constructed and exploited in this 'Newtonian world' are normally closed, linear, orderly, hierarchical, and could be better understood and controlled by **hierarchical decomposition, functional cohesion**, and can be completely captured as a mathematical model.

Hierarchical decomposition is associated with the **reductionist hypothesis**, and the reductionist thinking of the **Cartesian belief** (see Appendix 7). This hypothesis assumes that entities, properties, and processes at one level are just a manifestation of entities, properties, and processes that occur at a lower level ('absolute' functional cohesion). More basically, it assumes that 'everything' at every levels obey the same fundamental laws. For instance, Maxwell's electrodynamics (**James Clerk Maxwell**, 1831–1879) can be 'reduced' to optics and electromagnetism; and Kepler's law (**Johannes Kepler**, 1571–1630), and Galileo's law (**Galileo Galilei**, 1564–1642) can be derived from the Newtonian laws. This is the traditional fundamentalist thinking of the exact sciences. Beyond the exact sciences, order, exactness, linearity, and predictability are also the characteristics of current thinking, leadership, governance, strategy, management, operations, and productions in humanity. To a great extent, its dominance has an intense and significant impact on human existence, and provides the fundamental foundations of confidence and comfort in the human world.

However, over the last three decades, the entire human world has been drifting from a machine-based setup to an information-based and knowledge-intensive environment (intensive organizational learning is elevating). In addition, more recently in the 21st century, **self-powered self-organizing capability (self-transcending constructions)**, **autonomous adaptation**, and **self-organizing networks** are becoming more apparent. Consequently, a glaring mismatch in numerous aspects as well as many new unfamiliar problems is surfacing. The current mindset and its thinking and associated knowledge are underperforming due to their own constraints and ambiguity. Its dysfunction, futility, and vulnerability are becoming overwhelming. Apparently, there is a significant incoherency/ in-congruency between present thinking, and the emerging structural and dynamical aspects, and operational environment (including redefined expectations and values of agents, obsolete governance strategy of organizations, and diminishing sustainability of the environment and humanity) that have to be more deeply analyzed, comprehended, and rectified.

1.1.2 *General shift in structure and dynamic*

The post-2000 landscape possesses significantly transformed attributes resulting in higher complexity density. Over the last few decades, all highly developed organizations/economies/nations have been re-directing their attention and resources gradually towards establishing a knowledge-based structure with a significant focus on technological developments, including social media and military technologies (**exploitation of technologies is unique to humanity — no other species possess this capability**). More recently, the development of social/ mobile/wireless technologies has redefined human awareness, information access, connectivity, communication, learning, and engagement. Consequently, a more nonlinear technology-based (intangible) structure is also surfacing. As the impact and reward from swift communication, action and reaction; high-value-added knowledge; and information-intensive activities is much greater, inevitably in the new millennium, the entire humanity has been gravitating gradually towards the nucleus of the knowledge/ technology era, the **intelligence era**. This development further broadened the diverging gap identified (a significant proportion of human 'reality' does not occur in a 'linear' manner anymore). The sophistication of a knowledge-based, technology-based, and complex structure and dynamic can only be constructively managed with higher **intelligence/ consciousness-centricity**.

Apparently, changes happening in the human world are accelerating at a pace never observed previously (**change is the only attribute that does not change**). This is a new sophisticated challenge to human intelligence and consciousness. The rampant (rapidity) and enormous changes (increases in complexity density) sweeping across the whole of the humanity are so intense that a new term 'raplexity' has been coined (rapidity + complexity => **raplexity**). Modifications (with the present mindset) to present thinking and practices are also failing. For instance, leadership, governance, and structural issues (high skepticism, **incoherency**) are emerging in the political, social, and education systems in many countries. The human adaptability to slow changes is still fine but confusion suddenly emerges at certain intermediate threshold. The immense and unprecedented impacts experienced due to the high frequency of **tipping points** and **punctuation points** (sudden, unforeseen spaces of high complexity) surfacing, coupled with the emergent of the '*i*-space' (wireless connectivity, *i*-technology, social media; profound shift resulting from *i*-empowerment), require more than just some ad hoc structural alterations.

Meanwhile, an additional contemporary issue is that the economic, social, political, educational, and environmental perspectives of humanity are becoming more closely interconnected and interdependent — towards a more prominent surfacing of **holism**. Spaces of high complexity that critically encompass more than one of those perspectives are emerging more regularly — for instance, massive regional/global financial crisis, more complicated and interdependent international relationships, more frequent large-scale political conflicts, global organizational and new environmental crisis, new knowledge-intensive R&D spaces, and constant upgrading of certain technologies. Nonlinear dynamics usually exist both within and without the human organizations, and are consistently spreading over space-time — also history dependent (**hysteresis**). Most of the present global/regional/organizational activities and crises manifested apparently redefined economic, social, political and environmental volatility, interconnectivity and interdependency — a new multi-dimensional space-time compression, and a profound transition.

Thus, to accommodate the rapid formidable happenings and developments (partially known or totally unknown), a compelling need to exploit new knowledge (in particular, those associated with **complexity theory** — see Chapter 2) that better comprehends the escalating high nonlinear dynamics of human organizations/systems is inevitable — the constraint of the reductionist thinking paradigm is apparent, and must be transformed or supplemented. Fundamentally, all human organizations (including businesses, education systems, economies, military units, nations, and regional/global institutions) and their interacting agents (human beings/**human thinking systems**) are nonlinear **ordered systems (OS)** but inherently **complex adaptive systems (CAS)**. Therefore, nurturing a new mindset and a paradigmatic shift is necessary and crucial (see Chapter 3).

1.2 Some Significant World Changes

With the above recognition, it is imperative and beneficial to more closely identify, rigorously examine, and deeply comprehend the key factors and developments that initiated the observed transformation. More specifically, some of the crucial organizational/societal/global events/problems identified to have constantly exerted unprecedented incoherency and pressure on our current existence are more deeply examined as follows (also illustrated in Figure 1.1):

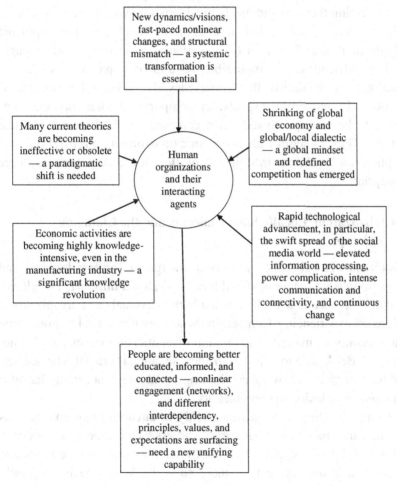

Figure 1.1 Some significant changes affecting humanity and its organizations.

a. The New Dynamic/Vision and Structural Mismatch

The entire humanity has drifted rather deeply into the information/knowledge/media era but many of the existing socio-economic-political systems/nations, structured like machines that support the requirements of the industrial era, are still intact. Thus, there is a severe ambiguity between the new dynamics, leadership, governance, and visions, and the present structure and systems design in human organizations — resulting in more frequent political and societal crisis/discontentment in certain countries, and the underperformance of some business organizations.

Expecting the old rigid mechanical structure with hierarchical/ control dominance to accomplish new visions and exploit the new rapid and volatile nonlinear dynamics (in governance, leadership, and management) is difficult, if not impossible. As a great disparity exists, a new (intelligence) revolution that supersedes the industrial revolution is essential. In numerous aspects, contemporary human organizations appear to be semi-paralyzed when compared to intelligent biological systems. Thus, to begin with, a systemic transformation is essential, and adopting an evolving **intelligent biotic macro-structure** is more appropriate.

b. Globalization, Local/Global Dialectic, and the Changing Landscape

In addition, a global economy has been emerging (for a few decades), and competition is no longer confined locally — **global mindset**. The global/ local dialectic is a new challenge that both individuals and organizations/ nations are experiencing. Competition is no more localized. Environmental issues, economic matters, and cultural diversification issues are also not localized. Being able to adjust to the new situation is crucial. The accelerated pace of global environmental changes and interconnectivity has also increased complexity and nonlinearity.

Comprehending and reacting swiftly to environmental changes has become a transnational/global critical success factor. (Speed is associated with the ability to recognize the shortest path but knowing the landscape of the path is also critical — more so if the landscape is constantly changing — see **rugged landscape** in Appendix 7.) Thus, being able to be environmentally proactive, that is, being able to influence the environment is a new challenge and advantage. Today, many human organizations are still not intelligent/consciousness enough to act and respond in the desired manner. In addition, an integrated globalized system may also introduce higher complexity density and cascading disasters. Therefore, nurturing and developing a new mindset, collective intelligence, leadership, governance, strategies, and management with a high intelligence/consciousness-centricity and **unifying capability** is a significant first step.

c. Better Interconnectivity, Engagement and the Redefined Interdependency

Next, the rapid advancement of technological developments, in particular, the integrated information and communications technology (ICT — digital revolution), has substantially increased the potential of better connectivity, higher speed of interactions, and more extensive communications and engagement in the human world. Quality connectivity is a significant property of intelligent systems (both natural and artificial). Understanding connectivity, and establishing well-connected networks (natural and artificial) spreading across an organization or geographical boundaries is a new challenge (initial possesses of **emergence**).

The present focus on connectivity is very much restricted to the level of the physical structure. Many human organizations are still ignorant as to how deeper interconnectivity, **truthful engagement**, **self-organizing communications**, **interdependency**, and **self-organizing networks** of the deep structure (intangible — biological possesses) can be better established, and how well-integrated virtual teams can be more constructive (media as a medium of interaction). They are not fully aware of the implications and significance of effective localized and global **interconnectedness,** and the redefined interdependency with respect to sociality — encompasses both positive and negative effects (that 'explosive'/unpredictable consequences that could surface because of minute differences — **butterfly effect**). Currently, almost the entire human is interconnected by Internet and its WWW.

d. Better Education, Extensive Information Access and Transformed Values/Expectations

Next, people (especially the younger generations, gen Y and gen Z) are also becoming better educated and informed, more so in highly developed countries. The quality of the knowledge structures in their thinking systems has been greatly enhanced. Their awareness has also been significantly elevated. They are more complex, heterogeneous, interconnected, and also autonomous. The better education, economic affluence, emergence of the e-landscape, and impact of the integrated wireless communication technology have redefined their mindset. Consequently, their logic, principles, normative beliefs, expectations, outlook, values, and behavior in life are constantly changing and different (beyond monetary centricity) from their ancestors (which are more simplistic). In general, agents with more intensive knowledge tend to challenge governance and leadership more frequently.

This new and sophisticated set of intangible assets is penetrating and transforming the economy and humanity. A broad consensus is that organizational dynamic (social, economic, and political) with the younger generations as interacting agents is rather dissimilar. In this respect, they will have to be managed and led rather differently. Thus, a transformed governance, leadership, and management approach is necessary for better nurturing of **collective intelligence,** and accommodating their greater differentiated norms and needs. Hierarchical empowerment (structuralism), control, and elitist/aristocratic leadership/ governance are losing its effectiveness — a new **social conformity** is needed.

e. Increasing Knowledge-intensive Economics Activities

Currently, economics activities are escalating and becoming highly knowledge-intensive (into the core of the knowledge era). Even at the extreme, in manufacturing intensive organizations, a whole new areas of production concept develops around the knowledge gained by cross-fertilization of new sciences is moving production standard from mass production to custom-built products. Computers, automation, and robotics based on new knowledge change the ways of production — high elevation in nonlinearity and complexity. Thus, even very mechanistic activities such as manufacturing are beginning to rely heavily on intelligence (natural and artificial) and knowledge (subjective) to enhance its innovative perspective. Inevitably, intangible assets such as intellectual capitals and social capitals are becoming the new valuable assets of businesses/economics activities.

f. Weaknesses/Constraints in Certain Current Theories and Knowledge Domains

Besides, many contemporary theories, concepts, and thinking are no longer able to handle or explain certain current changes and dynamics — for instance, the economic theories of equilibrium, perfect rationality, decreasing returns, and reductionist method are incapable of explaining the highly complex dynamic global economy (no theory or concept lasts forever — recognizing relative truth is significant — all theories are only useful for a certain time-space). The existing organization and decision theories that concentrate on linear high deterministic models, and depend on high forecasting precision, such the deliberate strategy and business process re-engineering are revealing in their distortions and inadequacy. In general, the utilization and domination of the standard reductionist analytic approach (**Cartesian belief**, **reductionist hypothesis**, and **fundamentalism**) of the contemporary Newtonian deterministic science (exact sciences) is manifesting its limits. At the minimal, intangible properties such as human intellectual capital and social capital must be recognized as crucial organizational assets — thus, a paradigmatic shift is essential.

1.3 Two Unique Critical World Changes

Concurrently, there are two special recognitions in the human world (illustrated in Figure 1.2) that is the crux of the issue and emerging threats. Their emergence is partially associated with the accelerated increase in human world population (over dominance) and its consumption rate; more intensive economic activities; accelerating human-created environmental changes; modified global military intelligence, dynamics, and destruction; higher human migration/integration rate; greater nonlinear organizational/societal/

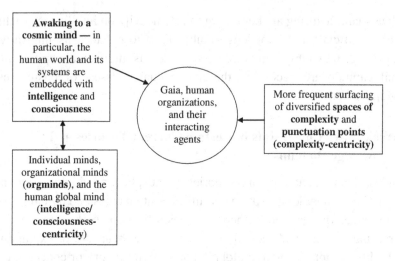

Figure 1.2   Two other special factors/recognitions affecting humanity and its organizations.

global interconnectivity; redefined interdependent new spaces of complexity; and changing human thinking, mental, and knowledge analysis.

a. More Frequent Surfacing of Diversified Spaces of Complexity and Sudden Appearance of Punctuation Points

Humanity is currently encountering **spaces of complexity, tipping points,** and **punctuation points** (sudden and unexpected high complexity spaces) much more frequently than any periods of human history (in the intelligent human organization theory not all spaces of complexity are punctuation points). For instance, the 2008 world financial crisis; the recent widespread socio-political unrest in numerous countries; the natural massive physical destructions in several geographical regions (large-scale tsunami and land-slide); the accelerated pace of military technological developments (unmanned weapons); the escalating environmental issues due to human over-dominance (enormous typhoon, rising world temperature); and the large numbers of knowledge-intensive R&D spaces (technospheres) are some prominent examples. These nonlinear physical and mental spaces of high complexity are causing the human world to change in a more unpredictable way. The levels of certainty in human organizations (including global/ regional organizations, nations, economies, communities, and business organizations) are diminishing tremendously. The weak 'exactness abilities' have threatened to undermine the sustainability of many human organizations — many stable (perceived) systems collapsed. Simultaneously, the stress level, complexity density, and nonlinearity of individual human beings' mental space have also heightened — leading to more unpredictable individual and collective behavior and responses. Apparently, the intense presence of complexity, and the constraint in forecasting cannot be ignored. Instead, certain spaces of complexity must be more comprehensively explored and exploited (that is, towards **complexity-centricity** and better complexity management is inevitable).

b. Existence of the Cosmic Mind — Presence of Intelligence and Consciousness in the Universe

The final and extremely important factor selected for illustration is the **awakening to a cosmic mind** and its nonlinear dynamics (see core properties of complexity/chaos theory in Chapter 2). Humankind is beginning to realize and understand that **the Universe and its subsystems is more a mind than a machine** — manifesting consciousness. The entire cosmic world and its microcosms, including all human organizations, ecosystems, and the atomic/physical world, are driven by certain levels of intelligence (intelligence is perceived as a spectrum — see **intelligence spectrum** in Chapter 3). In this respect, the Universe is a mysterious space (including the recent discovery of a huge percentage of dark energy and matter that form the Universe — see Universe in Appendix 7) embedded with infinite localized structures created by sources of proto-intelligence. In particular, the living world is dominated by different levels of intelligence and consciousness sources — **basic life-intelligence** and **human intelligence**.

Interestingly, the entire humanity, including its social, economic, and political systems and networks, congruous with the natural biological/ecological and physical systems, possess both linear and nonlinear components. They are intrinsic CAS in which **order and complexity co-exist**. Such systems are driven by human intelligence and consciousness (**awareness, mindfulness**). These systems consume new information, update knowledge structure, and learn to adapt and change continuously — a natural evolution dynamic. Otherwise, the system will self-destruct due to complacency and low competitiveness (that is, towards intelligence/consciousness-centricity and its management is highly crucial).

In this respect, conceptualizing a fresh viable alternative thinking is essential. The Newtonian mindset, thinking, and paradigm have manifested its controversies and constraints. 'New' scientific concepts in the complex adaptive (and Einsteinian/ quantum) domains (**Ralph Kilmann**, 'Quantum organizations' published in 2001) must be utilized to explore, manage, and optimize social, economic, political, and environmental phenomena in the human world. Ironically, in the natural sciences, some of these 'new' concepts have been emerging and developing over the last couple of decades. For instance, beyond physics, complexity theory and quantum-relativistic theory are still fresh and unexplored knowledge domains (in human daily activities).

1.4 Towards Complexity-Intelligence-Centricity

1.4.1 *Necessity for systemic transformation and a new thinking*

The above discussion vividly indicates the close association between complexity and intelligence, and the significance of a **complexity-intelligence-centric** foundation in the rapidly changing environment. Thus, there is a compelling need to change our current entrenched Newtonian mindset if humanity is to remain as the most dominant species on this planet (however, many of our devastating problems are due to our over-dominance).

First, a **systemic transformation** is essential. Basically every human organization is a living biological system — not a machine-like system (**living => biological => intelligence and consciousness => intelligence/ consciousness-centricity**). Some of the industrial era concepts and practices such as linearity, order, mechanistic structure, forecasting, domain specialization, and reductionism are manifesting their limitations. Leaders and managers are not merely controllers of mechanistic systems and their hierarchical dynamic. The increasing recognition of the presence of complexity as an integrated part of our existence, and the better comprehension of complexity itself must be achieved. Thus, in many contemporary issues, complexity cannot be ignored or 'deleted'. Contradictory, certain spaces of complexity in creative economies, social systems, and other human organizations may be unexplored territories that could be embedded with new opportunities and niches (gold nuggets).

Since the 1980s, the **complexity mindset** has been emerging in many complexity research institutions [including Santa Fe Institute (US, 1984), New England Complex Systems Institute (US, 1996), Complex Systems Research Center (UK, 1999), Australia Research Council Center of Complex Systems (Australia, 2004), and The Institute Para Limes (Holland, 2005)], and some other organizations. Complexity researchers and research organizations are emerging, and gradually spreading worldwide. Conceptual foundation from the self-conscious science of complexity with high practical utility is a new vital path. Some business organizations, military units, and nations are beginning to take a more serious view on the studies and knowledge associated with complexity theory. Soliciting and exploiting complexity knowledge in leadership and governance is a new advantage. A primary significant focus of the intelligent organization (IO) theory is recognizing and exploiting the co-existence of order and complexity in all human organizations through the correlation of complexity density and intelligence/consciousness-centricity.

1.4.2 *Recognizing the co-existence of order and complexity*

Order and complexity co-exist in all human organizations at all time (see Figure 1.3). With escalating changes, the levels of order and complexity will fluctuate/ oscillate with time — including a mental dimension/phenomenon. This oscillation is continuous over the entire lifespan of the **organization — a continuous-time dynamical nonlinear system**. In this respect, the study of complexity is closely associated with the **study of change** and its management (that is, complexity and rapid change are correlated).

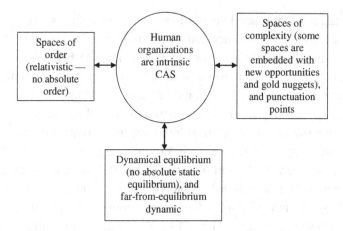

Figure 1.3 Better exploitation of co-existence of order and complexity in humanity is a new critical recognition.

At the extreme, order (absolute order) indicates that there is no change to an agent/system or the environment — static equilibrium. This property is also closely linked to linearity, predictability, and the Newtonian world. In human organizations, the three properties (order, linearity, and predictability) are interconnected, and are observed/perceived/construed by the intrinsic intelligence of the interacting agents. In this respect, order defines the levels of comfort of the interacting agents. In reality, absolute order does not exist. CAS do not exist in such a space as change is their inherent characteristic. Very often, 'manageable rate of change may be perceived as orderly'. Hence, both order and complexity are relativistic in the human world (due to the high mental dimension of human agents). Many other properties such as autopoiesis, symbiosis, self-centricity, stability-centricity, awareness, mindfulness, self-organization, emergence (order-centric or order-seeking — new order out of complexity) are also present. In addition, changes continue after the new order has been achieved.

According to the complexity theory, complexity indicates that the details of the agents (microscopic aspect) cannot be comprehended or identified but the surface pattern (due to potential emergence) that enables the system as a whole to be understood is/may be present. Thus, associated with certain spaces of complexity there is a critical **first mover advantage**. Primarily, all CS/CAS are **high finite dimension** systems with known variables, and also encompassing **'known**

unknowns' and **'unknown unknowns'** (see **uncertainty** in Appendix 7). Hence, all CS/CAS, including human organizations/nations/civilizations fluctuate between **stasis** and **punctuated equilibrium**. As stipulated, there is no absolute **static equilibrium** in the human world (only **dynamical equilibrium**), and all human organizational dynamics are also **far-from-equilibrium** (see Appendix 7).

1.4.3 *Correlation between complexity and intelligence*

Due to higher complexity density, the present strategies that assumed an orderly, linear, and highly predictable internal and external environment is no longer effective at all time. In this respect, ensuring resilience and sustainability can only be partially fulfilled (at most). The presence of complexity, nonlinearity, and unpredictability in the human world can only be better managed by first focusing on the intense human intelligence/consciousness sources, and their collectiveness — moving even beyond traditional natural/biological evolution. Hence, there is a significant correlation between complexity and intelligence (see Figure 1.4) — a **complexity-intelligence**

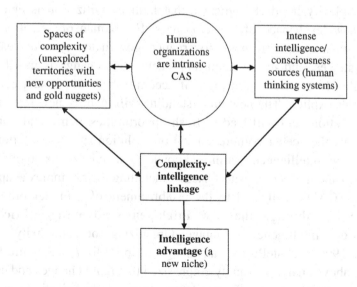

Figure 1.4 Relationships between complexity and intelligence (complexity-intelligence linkage) in human organizations.

linkage (see Appendix 7) — a vital integration that must be an organizational key focus point (complexity density <=> intelligence intensity).

Consequently, for all human organizations (businesses, economies, social communities, education institutions, military setups, medical institutions, nations, and regional/world institutions), the fundamental change in thinking indicates that **organizing around intrinsic intelligence** (rather than around machines, functions or processes) is the new basic interesting path identified. Complexity, evolution, and human thinking systems are new knowledge domains that need to be better scrutinized, and more optimally exploited. This recognition leads to the emergence of a complex-adaptive and intelligence/consciousness-centric paradigmatic shift, a new direction and a fresh path for human advancement.

1.5 The Intelligence Era and Its Criticality

A shift in mindset is an extremely important phenomenon in human history. Such a transformation marks the end of an existing belief, and the beginning of a new understanding. It is also tantamount to a change in era. The change from a machine-based mindset to the more holistic intelligence mindset and paradigm (encompassing the Newtonian mindset, and complexity mindset) indicates that human civilization is entering into a new level/space of consciousness. For human organizations to enhance their competitiveness, governance, governance systems, leadership strategies, and management approaches this change is inevitable. The higher level of consciousness, if accomplished, will render certain obscurities explicit. The new understanding will identify new territories for exploration, and will lead to fresh opportunities/niches and norms. Eventually, the deeper comprehension of evolution and co-evolution of CAS (living, intelligence, learning, knowledge acquisition, adaptive and changing) and their composite systems [including their complex adaptive dynamic (CAD)] will lead to the establishment of a higher order of existence — through the new **intelligence advantage** (**Michael McMaster**, 'Intelligence advantage: Organizing for complexity' published in 1996; see intelligence advantage in Appendix 7; see Figure 1.4).

The above analysis strongly emphasized that rapid changes and escalating complexity density affecting humanity and its organizations vividly confirmed that the dominance of the current Newtonian mindset is diminishing. The latter mindset that focuses on order, linearly, determinism, and predictability cannot explain and manage the highly nonlinear dynamic of complex adaptation. Thus, a significant anomaly exists as more unfamiliar problems are surfacing. Hence, nurturing a new consensus and understanding is critical. Conceptually, with overwhelming complexity, very often the present state of human organizations/systems cannot be precisely comprehended and measured, and the developmental path cannot be accurately determined [as a (set) simple mathematical equation — see Appendix 2, and **Laplace belief** in Appendix 7]. With diminishing insights, forecasting is not always accurate or possible. In such a situation, complexity can best be accommodated and exploited with the presence of intense intelligence/consciousness, and human collective intelligence/org-consciousness — which is also beyond traditional biological evolution (see **swarm intelligence** in Appendix 7).

Consequently, humanity has to drift into and exploit complexity-intelligence-centricity — a new environment/space that requires a redefined conceptual foundation. Hence, humanity is entering the intelligence era (core of the knowledge era). Briefly, the changing sequences are illustrated below (see Figure 1.5):

Industrial era => Information/Knowledge era => Intelligence era

and

Newtonian mindset => Complexity mindset => Intelligence mindset

The above transformation in mindset is essential and critical. The higher complexity density must be counteracted by higher intelligence/consciousness intensity. The contents, boundaries, and implications of the complexity mindset and intelligence mindset will be discussed more deeply in Chapters 2 and 3. Briefly, the complexity mindset encompasses **systems thinking, evolution/biotic thinking**, and **cybernetic/connectionist thinking,** while the intelligence mindset (a highly intelligence/consciousness-centric thinking) encompasses part of the earlier mindsets, as order is still significant in the human world (**the science of complexity**

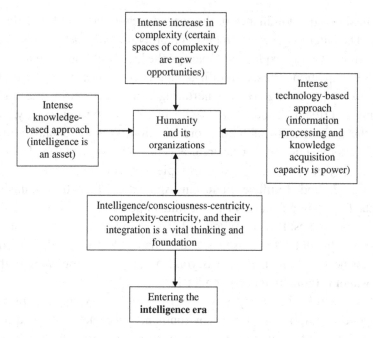

Figure 1.5   Humanity into the intelligence era.

concentrates on the emergent of new order), and a deeper comprehension of the complex world. In summary, ideally and simplistically, the following situation must be sustained:

Increase in intelligence intensity > Increase in complexity

Summary

The basic steps into deeper intelligence/consciousness-centric and complexity-centric comprehension, exploration, integration, and exploitation encompass the following necessities:

• Nurturing the new intligence mindset so that fresh intelligence/consciousness-centric thinking emerges — intelligence/consciousness is the key driver/impetus of all human organizations and the entire humanity.

- Recognizing the presence of complexity, and attempt to better comprehend and exploit (establishing complexity-intelligence linkages) it (focusing on certain spaces of complexity).
- Nurturing the new paradigmatic shift as it allows certain existing problem spaces, as well as new unexplored spaces to be better comprehended so that more strategic paths are accessible, and dysfunctions to be minimized.

1.6 Conclusion

The above discussion succinctly endorses that the entire **biosphere, Gaia (Jim Lovelock**, 1919–present) and its microcosms (ecosystems, organizations, networks, and agents) on this planet are intrinsically complex, nonlinear, and adaptive, as well as intelligent and conscious. Over time, these systems/subsystems constantly or continuously increase in complexity and exploit it with self-organizing capabilities (for instance, for a human community from village to small town to cosmopolitan city) — **emergent of new order**. Thus, a deeper understanding of complexity theory (in particular, CAS, CAD, and their attributes), and being able to adopt and apply some of the concepts of complexity theory and IO theory (and relativistic complexity) to leadership, governance, strategy, and management of human organizations are crucial in the present highly interconnected, interdependent, fast-changing, and complex environment (see Figure 1.6).

The IO theory advocates that organizing around intrinsic intelligence sources (will be further analyzed in subsequent chapters) and nurturing high collective intelligence is a new fundamental principle/strategy for elevating **unifying capacity**, and organizational resilience and sustainability (see unifying capacity in Appendix 7). Consequently, intelligence/consciousness-centricity coupled with complexity-intelligence-centricity is the fresh critical strategic thinking direction (see Figure 1.7). Apparently, human intelligence/consciousness is a vital entity/asset of human organizations as it is the internal latent impetus (driving force) of intelligent complex adaptive dynamic (iCAD), and certain spaces of complexity that encompass new opportunities (stimulates innovativeness) are highly

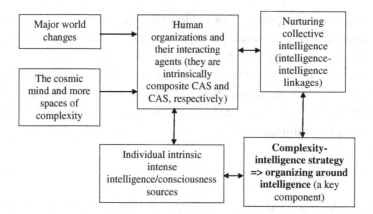

Figure 1.6 The new paradigm focuses on intelligence/consciousness and complexity, and adopts the complexity-intelligence strategy.

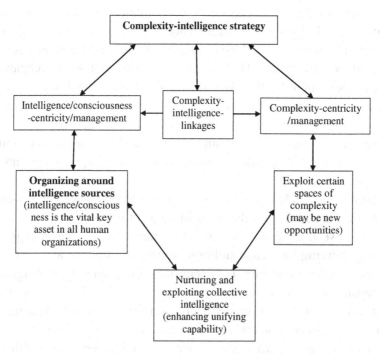

Figure 1.7 Organizing around intelligence is a key sub-strategy of the holistic complexity-intelligence strategy of the IO theory.

valuable. In addition, it is significant to recognize that human agents are not fully autonomous (independency versus interdependency, autopoiesis versus symbiosis, self-centric versus org-centric, and **ambidexterity**). Hence, the human thinking systems must also be better comprehended. Finally, the holistic strategy of the IO theory is the **complexity-intelligence strategy** that encompasses numerous components will be gradually explained in subsequent chapters (see complexity-intelligence strategy in Appendix 7).

Inherently, the entire biosphere on this planet (Gaia) and all its sub-ecosystems are highly intelligence/consciousness-centric to a varying degree. Thus, the new critical sustainable niche with better sustainability is the intelligence advantage.

I am convinced that the nations and people who master the new sciences of complexity will become the economic, cultural, and political superpowers of the next century.

Heinz Pagels, The Dreams of Reason

Where chaos (complexity) begins, classical science stops.

James Gleick, Chaos

Chapter 2

Fundamentals of Complexity Theory and Human Complex Adaptive Systems

"Complexity theory is a nascent field that points towards
accelerative resilience and sustainability"

Summary

This chapter is an introduction to complexity theory (encompassing chaos — a subset of complexity), a nascent domain, although, it possesses a historical root. Some fundamental properties of chaos/ complexity (including complexity mindset, nonlinearity, interconnectedness, interdependency, far-from-equilibrium, butterfly effect, determinism/in-determinism, unpredictability, bifurcation, deterministic chaotic dynamic, complex dynamic, complex adaptive dynamic, dissipation, basin of attraction, attractor, chaotic attractor, strange attractor, phase space, rugged landscape, red queen race, holism, self-organization, self-transcending constructions, scale invariance, historical dependency, constructionist hypothesis and emergence), and its development are briefly examined. In particular, the similarities (sensitive dependence on initial conditions, unpredictability) and differences between deterministic chaotic systems (DCS) and complex adaptive systems (CAS) are analyzed. The edge of emergence (2nd critical value, a new concept) is also conceived to provide a more comprehensive explanation of the complex adaptive dynamic (CAD) and emergence. Subsequently, a simplified system spectrum is introduced to illustrate the attributes, and summarize the relationships of the various categories of common systems.

Next, the recognition that human organizations are nonlinear living systems (high finite dimensionality CAS) with adaptive and thinking agents is examined. This new comprehension indicates that a re-calibration in thinking is essential. In the human world, high levels of human intelligence/consciousness (the latent impetus that is fundamentally stability-centric) drives a redefined human adaptive and evolution dynamic encompassing better potentials of self-organization or self-transcending constructions, autocatalysis, circular causation, localized spaces/networks, hysteresis, futuristic, and emergent of new order (involving a multi-layer structure and dynamic) — vividly indicating that intelligence/consciousness-centric is extremely vital. Simultaneously, complexity associated properties/characteristics in human organizations must be better scrutinized and exploited — that is, establishing appropriate complexity-intelligence linkages is a significant necessity. In this respect, nurturing of the intelligence mindset and developing the associated paradigmatic shift is inevitable.

A distinct attempt (the basic strategic approach) of the new intelligence mindset is to organize around human intrinsic intelligence — intense intelligence-intelligence linkages that exploits human intelligence/consciousness sources individually and collectively by focusing on intelligence/consciousness-centricity, complexity-centricity, network-centricity, complexity-intelligence linkages, collective intelligence, org-consciousness, complex networks, spaces of complexity (better risk management <=> new opportunities <=> higher sustainability) and prepares for punctuation points (better crisis management <=> collectively more intelligent <=> higher resilience/sustainability) concurrently — illustrating the significance of self-organizing capability and emergence-intelligence capacity. The conceptual development introduced will serve as the basic foundation of the intelligent organization (IO) theory.

Key Words: Chaos, complexity, ordered systems (OS), disordered systems (DS), complexity theory, degrees of freedom, dimensionality, deterministic, in-deterministic, unpredictability, stability-centric, logistic map, bifurcation, phase transition, non-periodic state, sensitive dependence on initial conditions, butterfly effect, strange attractor, complex adaptive systems (CAS), relativistic determinism, deterministic chaotic systems (DCS), complex systems (CS), self-organizing criticality, heterogeneous agent, self-organization, edge of chaos, far-from-equilibrium, dissipative structure theory, edge of order, edge of emergence, econophysics, relativistic complexity, power law, PL phenomenon,

Pareto distribution, interdependency, scale-free theory, scale invariance, intrinsic intelligence, self-powered, intrinsic leadership, collectiveness capacity, adaptive capacity, collective intelligence, orgmindfulness, mindful culture, complexity-intelligence linkage, complexity-centric, intelligence-intelligence linkage, intelligent biotic macro-structure, intelligent person, deliberate strategy, emergent strategy, space of relativistic order, relativistic static equilibrium, intelligence governance strategy, intelligence leadership strategy, mental capacity, complexity mindset, systems thinking, Cartesian belief, Laplace belief, holism, evolution/biotic thinking, cybernetics/connectionist thinking, law of requisite variety, Poincare–Bendixson theorem, phase space, nonlinearity, discrete time, continuous time, bifurcation theory, bifurcation point, bifurcation diagram, bifurcation parameter, Lorenz attractor, phase diagram, phase space trajectory, scalability, fractal geometry, self-similarity, complex adaptive dynamics (CAD), localized order, space of order, consciousness, law of complexity/consciousness, law of complexity/intelligence, law of consciousness/intelligence, connectivity, dissipation, adaptive, emergence, space of in-deterministic chaos, surface pattern, autopoiesis, self-transcending constructions, self-organizing capacity, emergence-intelligence capacity, feedback, hypercycles, circulation coupling, connectionist hypothesis, broken symmetry, red queen race, systems spectrum, intelligent human organization, in-deterministic chaotic systems (ICS), ontological reductionism, network-centric, network theory, graph theory, small world theory, complex adaptive network, self-organizing communications, uncertainty, unknown unknowns, global optimality, stasis, punctuation point, self-centricity, stability-centricity, principle of locality, behavioral schema, exaptation, synergetic, intelligence/consciousness-centricity, physical stability, biological stability, mental stability, awareness, mindfulness, 'feeling' system, intelligence advantage, intelligence mindset, intelligence paradigm, relational capacity, unifying capacity and intelligent organization (IO) theory.

2.1 Introduction: The World of Complexity

2.1.1 *Some historical aspects of chaos*

The study of **chaos/complexity** both in the natural sciences and its extension to humanities (social, economic, political, military, and environment) is a relatively new domain. Traditional or exact natural sciences focus on linear and orderly characteristics (for instance, classical mechanics — **ordered systems (OS)** or infinite random systems (for instance, statistical mechanics — **highly disordered systems (DS)** that can be analyzed with high precision. The domain of chaos/complexity concentrates on the range of systems inbetween the two extreme ends (mainly nonlinear dynamical systems — see **systems spectrum** below), that is, venturing from low (more closely associated with deterministic chaos) to high (more closely associated with complexity) finite dimensionality (high but still finite **dimensionality/degrees of freedom** — every new degree of freedom requires an additional dimension in the **phase space**), and its new unfamiliar nonlinear characteristics and properties. The latter include **deterministic** (can be accurately measured or computed — a deterministic system can be periodic and non-periodic), and **in-deterministic** relations and behavior, and **unpredictability**. [Thus, chaos eliminates the Laplace brief of deterministic predictability (determinism ≠ predictability) — see Appendix 7.]

Historically, an early significant discovery associated with chaos/complexity theory is the study on chaotic motion (**simplicity to chaotic**) of three-body systems by **Henri Poincare** (1854–1912, coined the term, **bifurcation**, in 1885) — leading to the discovery of the existence of **non-periodic (aperiodic) state**, while **Aleksandr Lyapunov** (1857–1918), is known for his development of the **stability theory** of dynamical systems (see Appendices 3 and 4). For the former observation, Newtonian mechanic can only prove that the orbit of a planet (moon) is elliptical if it is under the influence of only another planet (Earth). If the influence of another planet (Sun) is present (three-body system), the prescription of the orbit is just an approximation (the gravitational force is nonlinear, $G \, \alpha 1/r^2$) — thus, rendering long-range precise/accurate prediction of the orbit of the moon impossible. Subsequently, the intensive studies on the new domain re-emerged in the early 1960s focusing on **chaos**, involving rather simple mathematical nonlinear equations or models that manifest deterministic but unpredictable characteristics (for instance, the popular **logistic map**, a simple nonlinear discrete-time difference equation with dimension one — see Appendix 3).

Over the next two decades, there were several pioneer researchers that had contributed significantly to the development of this domain, including **Edward Lorenz** (1903–1987, Lorenz attractor, **sensitive dependence on initial conditions, butterfly effect**), **Benoit Mandelbrot** (1924–2010, fractal geometry, Mandelbrot set), **Stephen Smale** (1930–present, nonlinear oscillators, topological transformation) and some others in the 1960s; and **David Ruelle** (1935–present, **strange attractor**), **Floris Takens** (1940–2010, strange attractor), **Mitchell Feigenhaum** (1944–present, bifurcation, Feigenhaum constant, universality), **Tien-Yien Li** (1945–present, chaos), **James Yorke** (1941–present, chaos), and **Robert May** (1936–present, logistic map) in the 1970s (see Appendix 4). In particular, Lorenz's confirmation of sensitive dependence on initial conditions, and the first 'physical' observation of the (three-dimensional) strange attractor provided a significant foundation for the emergent and proliferation of the complexity theory (encompassing deterministic chaos).

Primarily, both **deterministic chaotic systems (DCS)** and **complex adaptive systems (CAS)** are nonlinear dynamical systems. But it is important to note the differences and similarities (and focuses) between chaos and complexity (studies) — will be discussed later in this chapter. In the 1970s to 1980s, as a re-emerge new nascent discipline, many research studies intertwined the two categories of systems, and their boundaries were not well defined. However, for researchers and practitioners that are focusing on human organizations/systems recognizing their similarities and differences is highly significant and critical as all human organisations are high finite dimensionality nonlinear CAS with in-deterministic (relativistic determinism) characteristics and unpredictable behaviour (encompassing unknown unknowns — in-complete phase space), and not low-dimensional chaotic systems (see human organization, intelligent organization, and dimensionality in Appendix 7). Fundamentally, a **complex system (CS)** encompasses both coherency and turbulence (co-existence of order and complexity) concurrently — hence, in this case, the exploitation of order or **relativistic order** is still vital and beneficial (see **relativistic complexity** in Appendix 7).

2.1.2 *Some historical aspects of complexity*

During the 1980–2010s, the focus of researchers extended/shifted to **complexity**, in particular, after the establishment of the Santa Fe

Institute in 1984 [the study of CS, and CAS — **system dynamics vary from complexity to simplicity**] by scientists mainly from the Los Alamos National Laboratory. Currently, complexity theory is a domain that encompasses both complexity and chaos (as well as networks), and its influence on research institutions and all categories of human organizations is intensifying (complex originates from a Latin word that means 'intertwined' — indicating the significance of holism, and the failure of reductionism).

Originally, there were several clusters of researchers that were contributing to the development of this interesting domain (see Appendix 3). The 'American Complexity School' concentrated on **how complexity is created (self-organizing criticality)**, and the **emergent of order** in a disorganized system (encompassing heterogeneous agents, agents interaction, co-evolution, inter-system process, interdependency, agent-based modeling, self-organization, and the **edge of chaos (old)** — **second critical value** — see Appendix 7 for new explanation. The pioneer researchers, include **Stuart Kauffmann** (self-organization, **order for free, rugged landscape**), **Per Bak, Chao Tang and Kurt Wiesenfeld (self-organized criticality — SOC), Philip Anderson** (1923–present, Nobel Prize in Physics, 1972, **constructionist hypothesis**), and several others (see Appendix 4).

The other cluster was the '**European Complexity School**' that focused on the emergent behavior (dynamics that initiate and sustain order creation) in far-from-equilibrium systems. The environmentally imposed **adaptive tensions** due to **energy differentials** drive the system dynamics. A highly prominent researcher in this cluster was **Ilya Prigogine** (1917–2003, Nobel Prize in Chemistry, 1977). His main contribution is the **dissipative structures theory** (concentrated on the **edge of order — first critical value** — systems that decrease **thermodynamical entropy**, and the emergent of new **intra-system order**). Recently, the 2013 Nobel Prize in Chemistry was awarded to **Martin Karplus** (1930–present), **Michael Levitt** (1947–present), and **Arieh Warshel** (1940–present) for their contributions in multi-scale models for complex chemical systems.

In humanities, **Joseph Schumpeter** (1883–1950), an economist, developed **evolutionary economics, theory of economic development**, and popularized the term **'creative destruction'** which is closely associated with self-organization (endogenous) and emergence (emergent of new order); and **Friedrich Hayek** (1899–1992, Nobel Prize in Economics, 1974), another economist contributed to the concept on **spontaneous order** in economics — self-organization is due to human action and not human design. In addition, **Niklas Luhmann** (1927–1998), a sociologist, and a significant contributor to human system theory focused on **self-organizing communications** — a communication process that generates more communications spontaneously. He also conceived the **social spontaneous order theory**.

In addition, there are two other interesting developments during this period namely, **econophysics**, and the **intelligent organization theory (relativistic complexity)**. The econophysics (coined by **Harry Eugene Stanley**, 1941–present) approach (a **scale-free theory**) focuses on the use of **power laws (PL)** to explain the unrestricted self-organizing behavior in economics and human systems (physics, economics) using PL phenomena/effects, and PL theory. This theory was also exploited by **Doyne Farmer** (1941–present) in the domain of finance. **PL phenomena** and **Pareto distribution** are normally due to interdependency of components/agents, and they are scale-free (**scale invariance**). **A scale-free theory explains the emergent organizing dynamic of a multiple levels system using a single rule/function** (see scalability, and PL phenomena in Appendix 7) — contradicts the **constructionist hypothesis**.

Finally, the **intelligent organization theory** (including **relativistic complexity** in intelligent human organizations/systems, introduced in 1998) focuses on the **intrinsic intelligence and consciousness** of the individuals (**self-powered** human agents — intelligent persons naturally endowed with **intrinsic leadership** capability — high **collectiveness capacity** and **adaptive capacity — 'everybody is in charge'**), and the **collective intelligence** and **org-consciousness** (**orgmindfulness** and **mindful culture**) of organizations with respect to **intelligence-intelligence linkages** — high **intelligence/consciousness-centricity** and **network-centricity**. Concurrently, the theory also focuses on **complexity-intelligence linkages** — high **complexity-centricity** (exploiting the co-existence of order and complexity, and certain spaces of complexity, and making preparation for punctuation points). The three linkages are closely associated with autopoiesis, self-organizing communications, truthful engagement, self-organization/self-transcending constructions, and innovative emergent of order (high **self-organizing capacity** and **emergence-intelligence capacity**). The new **intelligence mindset** exploits characteristics, concepts, and tools such as **organizing around intelligence, intelligent biotic macro-structure, intelligent person** (model), orgmindfulness (core of supportive culture), mindful culture, third-order stability (encompassing physical stability, biological stability, and mental stability), network-centricity, co-evolution (nested/composite systems), no global optimality, **integrated deliberate and emergent strategy, space of relativistic order, relativistic static equilibrium, intelligence governance strategy**, and **intelligence leadership strategy**. Concurrently, there is also a significant focus on capacity nurturing. As human agents possess an intense mental dimension (high **mental capacity**) which is strongly self-centric (versus org-centric) and stability-centric, complexity in the human world becomes **relativistic — 'complexity is in the mind of the beholder'.**

Notes: **Two important primary dynamics observed:**

- Deterministic chaotic dynamic develops from simplicity to chaotic through constant bifurcation or phase transition (deterministic but unpredictable).
- Complex (adaptive) dynamic develops from complexity to simplicity through self-organization/self-transcending constructions, autocatalysis, feedback, and emergent of new order (in-deterministic and unpredictable).

Gradually, the details of the intelligent organization theory will be developed and analyzed more comprehensively in this book.

2.1.3 *The complexity mindset*

With the above introduction (and those in Chapter 1), the constraints and ambiguities of the Newtonian mindset are apparent (although, it has served humanity well in some aspects). Thus, to better comprehend, accommodate, explore, and exploit complexity a shift from the Newtonian mindset to the **complexity mindset** is a compelling and inevitable trans-formation. The fragilities, incoherency, and anomalies of our current thinking are encountering high volatility. Thus, nurturing the complexity mindset (to a great extent defined the boundaries of complexity theory) is a new necessity. Originally, this mindset encompasses three components and a fourth component has been included when analyzing human CAS. The four components are as follows:

- Systems thinking
- Evolution/Biotic thinking
- Cybernetics/Connectionist thinking
- Network thinking

a. Systems Thinking

Systems thinking originates from the development of the General Systems Theory (GST) by **Ludwig von Bertalanffy** (1901–1972) in the 1940s that concentrates on common properties (**holistic approach** — opposite from the **reductionist thinking** of **fundamentalism**, and the **Cartesian belief**) in all categories of systems, including abstract/conceptual systems. During that period, system thinking and systems theory have been extensively studied in sociology — action theory by **Talcott Parsons** (1902–1979), and social systems theory by **Niklas Luhmann** (1927–1998). A key characteristic of systems theory is feedback (see Appendix 7) — self-regulating systems. The term **holism** was coined by **Jan Smuts** (1870–1950) in 1926. The holism thinking believes that the components of the system can best be understood in the context of relationships with each other and with the system, rather than in isolation due to high inter-connectedness and interdependency (opposes hierarchical decomposition). Reductionism that works for simple linear systems does not work for nonlinear CS and CAS. Holism thinking leads to systems thinking, and the approach is beneficial and much exploited in complexity theory. A key property of GST is the 'whole' can be more than the sum of the parts [(synergetic effect — **synergetics**, introduced by **Hermann Haken** (1927–present), in 1978 using the laser theory].

b. Evolution/Biotic Thinking

The **evolution/biotic thinking** (from simplicity to complexity — **bio-complexity** — from molecules to cells to organisms to species — diversification) focuses on the characteristics and dynamics of the **Evolution Theory (Charles Robert Darwin**, 1809–1882, natural selection and blind variation, 'On the Origin of Species' in 1859), including evolution and co-evolution, and ecosystems/Gaia [**James Lovelock** (1919–present), in 1988] — in particular, on autopoietic systems (autopoiesis, self-organization, and emergence) proposed by **Humberto Maturana** (1928–present) and **Francisco Varela** (1946–2001), in 1972. These living systems are self-producing, self-maintaining, adaptive, and changing behavior over time (innovative and sustainable). (The evolution theory believes that organisms that reproduce quickly and in large numbers possess an evolutionary advantage. The generation of CAS have been confirmed as a natural part of evolution by some artificial life researchers.) In addition, their subsystems interactions can be complex, and the control is concurrently distributed and centralized (that is, neither totally orderly nor random). Such systems defy the second law of thermodynamics (see Appendix 7). However, to a great extent, human organizations are recognized as more **symbiotic (Lynn Margulis**, 1938–2911, theory of symbiotic relations) than solely autopoietic (see **symbiosis** in Appendix 7).

c. Cybernetics/Connectionist Thinking

Next, the cybernetics/connectionists thinking (originates from **Norbert Wiener** (1894–1964), and **Ross Ashby** (1903–1972) — **Ashby's law of requisite variety**, 1956 — (see Appendix 7) focuses on the 'right' connectivity, communications, feedback, and circular causation (**Ashby**, 1956; **Wiener**, 1948). In general, the processes of self-organization/self-transcending constructions, and emergence are highly correlated to connectivity — varying from a network to **complex networks** to new organizational structure/order (see S(1)-S(4) in Appendix 7). In addition, in cybernetics, knowledge is perceived as intrinsically subjective — that is dependent on the agents exploiting it. **With the Newtonian mindset, subjectivity and uncertainty are negative factors of the**

absolute mechanism. However, they are positive factors associated with adaptation, creativity, and evolution in complexity studies.

d. Network Thinking

The network thinking is a newer addition to the complexity mindset. Human organizations are embedded with network of networks. Basic network concepts originate from **graph theory**, a subset of discrete mathematics. The latter was formalized as a domain when a related paper was published by **Leonhard Euler** (1707–1783), in 1736. The paper focuses on the study of graphs as mathematical structures with **nodes (vertices)** and **links (edges).** Subsequently, the foundation of **network theory** is derived from graph theory — initiated later by **Paul Erdos** (1913–1996) and **Alfred Renyi** (1921–1970). They focused mainly on random networks. Besides **randomness** (hypothetical, evenly distributed, static, no growth or preferential attachment characteristic — for instance, a bell-curve), networks can be **scale free** (**'real world' networks**, exhibit growth and preferential attachment characteristics, large number of nodes and links) — see scale free network, small world network in Appendix 7. Currently, network applications ('real world' networks) have spread to other human domains, including sociology (**social networks**), biology (**molecular networks**), economics (**market internal relations networks**), and computer science (**artificial neural networks**). In human CAS, networks (**complex adaptive networks**) are inherent components. Thus, focusing on the nodes and links of the structure is crucial. In the human context, links can be relational (encompassing relational friction in the human dynamics), intangible, and nonlinear (see complex network, and complex adaptive network in Appendix 7).

2.1.4 *Boundaries of complexity theory*

As complexity theory (science of complexity) is a fairly new emerging domain with rather diversified research frontiers, different researchers have slightly dissimilar explanations/definitions for some terminologies, including the boundaries of the study itself. Therefore, to avoid ambiguity a stand has been adopted in the conceptualization of the intelligent organization theory. In this analysis, the complexity theory is summarized or briefly defined as follows:

Complexity Theory (I)

This domain is the study of nonlinear dynamical systems (discrete-time and continuous-time) of low (deterministic) to finite high (in-deterministic due to in-complete variables) dimensionality that are sensitive dependence on initial conditions (butterfly effect), unpredictable, and possesses strange attractors.

With the above definition, complexity theory involves the study of three types of systems (that possess the characteristics/properties stipulated above) spreading into numerous disciplines in the natural sciences and humanities. Over time, many of the complexity studies executed are highly interdisciplinary (across and including the biological, chemical, physical, social, economic, political, and anthropological domains). The categories of system involved are as follows:

- DCS
- CS
- CAS

Fundamentally, a key commonality (two properties) among the three categories of systems is **nonlinearity** and **sensitive dependence on initial conditions (butterfly effect)**, that is, a small change in initial inputs could lead to a totally unpredictable output — rendering them longer-term **unpredictable** (limited predictability), and the emergence of **strange attractor**. Lorenz (in 1963) was the first to 'observe' this interesting property (butterfly effect) in a physical system during his weather forecasting computation, which renders weather forecasting beyond a few days/weeks meaningless. The confirmation of the presence of unpredictability changes the humanity mindset (sensitive dependence on initial conditions <=> butterfly effect <=> unpredictability). The dominance of the Newtonian mindset on linearity, high precision, determinism, and predictability in 'mechanical' systems do not necessarily apply to human systems/organizations at all time. [However, it is important to note that in CS coherence and turbulence (order and complexity) co-exist — for instance, the great red spot (**self-organizing system**) of Jupiter].

A new set of attributes emerges. The additional key characteristics and properties of the three categories of systems (DCS, CS, and CAS) and their dynamics will be discussed below.

2.2 Basic Chaos Theory and DCS

2.2.1 *Key properties and definitions*

The word **chaos** with its current interpretation was coined as a mathematical term by **Tien-Yien Li** (1945–present) and **James A. Yorke** (1941–present) in 1975, in their paper, 'Period Three Implies Chaos'. Thus, chaos is a mathematical theory that deals with **nonlinearity** and **deterministic chaos** (rather different from the general usage of the word). In this case, **chaos theory** is the popular name for the study of **nonlinear dynamical systems (discrete-time and continuous-time) with relatively low finite dimensionality (DCS)**, and how their low finite dimensionality creates deterministic chaos through **bifurcation** (a small change in the bifurcation parameter causes a sudden leap/change in the system behavior resulting in unpredictability — see bifurcation in Appendix 7), and phase transition. (A deterministic system has no randomness. A random or stochastic process is probabilistic.) The earlier studies focused mainly on low dimensionality discrete-time DCS (**mathematical chaos**) as high dimensionality chaotic systems are in-deterministic (**in-deterministic chaotic systems (ICS) — catastrophe theory** — see Appendix 7).

Most of the pioneers of chaos (during the 1960s and 1970s) were physicists and mathematicians who analyzed the numerous aspects (properties, characteristics, structures, and possesses) of many simple nonlinear dynamical systems/ conceptual models using mathematical models (see Appendix 3). Thus, chaos theory concentrates on DCS with low finite dimensionality, that is, they do not involve many variables — some of which are nonlinear (at least one nonlinear variable or parameter) [for instance, the **logistic map** is a single variable equation with one parameter, $x_{n+1} = x_n r (1 - x_n)$].

Physical systems and mathematical/conceptual models that are popular DSC, include Lorenz weather system, rolling fluid, convection system, the logistic map, Henon map, double rod pendulum, Rossler system, Lorenz waterwheel, and van de Pol electrical oscillator that could be modelled with one or a set of difference equations or differential equations with a few variables, and their chaotic behavior could be easily observed (bifurcation — from simplicity to chaotic, shown in a **bifurcation diagram**, and the appearances of strange attractors — a large set of non-periodic states confined within a finite space, can be better observed in a **phase diagram**). Discrete-time DCS can be modelled with **difference equations** (equations with **recurrence relations**, for example, logistic map) and undergo bifurcation, while continuous-time chaotic systems (for example, Lorenz weather system) can be modelled with a set of **differential equations**, and undergo phase transition (there are different types of differential equations used depending on the details behavior of the systems).

It is important to note that Edward Lorenz through his weather system, and convection system initiated the re-emergent of chaos, and provided a vital portion of its conceptual foundation. The weather system is nonlinear partly due to energy inflow from the sun and energy dissipated outside the earth atmosphere, and the frictional effect of the air and water movement. Concurrently, a second vital chaos contribution comes from the study of the logistic map, a mathematical model, with significant outputs from Robert May, Mitchell Feigenbaum, and Albert Libchaber (see Appendix 3).

With the above illustrations, chaos theory (as a subset of complexity theory) could be defined briefly as follows:

Chaos Theory

This domain is the study of low finite dimensionality (deterministic) nonlinear dynamical systems (discrete-time and continuous-time) that are sensitive dependence on initial conditions (butterfly effect), undergo bifurcation or phase transition, unpredictable, and possess strange attractors — encompassing a simplicity to chaotic dynamic.

For discrete-time systems the chaotic behavior arises from one dimensionality, while for continuous-time systems the chaotic behavior emerges from dimension three and above — (see **Poincare–Bendixson theorem** in Appendix 7). In addition, the deterministic (involving a few known variables) nature of chaotic systems does not ensure that their output/behavior is predictable (**determinism ≠ predictability**). While some DCS such as the logistic map can be chaotic everywhere, most other DCS their chaotic behavior is confined to a subset in the phase space.

With this understanding, DCS could be defined briefly as follows:

Deterministic Chaotic Systems (DCS)

DCS (discrete-time or continuous-time) are nonlinear dynamical systems with low finite dimensionality, sensitive dependence on initial conditions (butterfly effect), undergo bifurcation (sudden leaps — splits into two paths) or phase transition, deterministic but unpredictable, and possess strange attractors.

In this respect, **a deterministic chaotic dynamic can evolve from a few intensely coupled variables interacting in a nonlinear manner (with nonlinear relationships).** In general, **chaos theory focuses on how the simplicity of low-dimensional deterministic system creates a chaotic dynamic.** The discrete-time logistic map moves from simplicity into deep chaos after the fourth bifurcations (see logistic map in Appendix 1). The outputs can be accurately computed but certain values can be surprising. In this respect, **chaos eliminates deterministic predictability**, and chaotic dynamic could be defined as follows:

Deterministic Chaotic Dynamic (DCD)

This dynamic (deterministic but unpredictable) evolves from simplicity (in 'equilibrium') to deterministic chaotic through frequent bifurcation or phase transition (the output can be computed with accuracy but the value of the output can be surprising).

2.2.2 *Analyzing some additional properties of DCS*

In the natural sciences, the study of mathematical chaos (deterministic nonlinear models) identified bifurcation, butterfly effect, strange attractors, and scale invariance as some primary properties of chaotic systems. However, it is important to note that a critical characteristic needed for chaotic behavior to exist/appear is nonlinearity. (Note that finite dimension linear systems are never chaotic.)

a. Nonlinearity

Linearity is a proportional relationship — mathematically, it is a straight line (in dimension two). Thus, one extreme interpretation is that nonlinearity indicates a shift from the straight line, for instance, an exponential function. However, the nonlinearity characteristic in nonlinear dynamical systems can be more sophisticated than that. The relationships among variables may change over time. An example of nonlinear variables with varying relationship is the change of speed and friction relationship (for instance, of a car). In this case, nonlinearity could manifest to the extent that as the values of the variables change their relationship also changes in an in-deterministic manner — resulting in unpredictability. Thus, **there exists a direct link between nonlinearity and unpredictability**.

b. Bifurcation and Bifurcation Diagram

DCS (discrete-time and continuous-time) evolve through **bifurcation** and **phase transition** (respectively). Bifurcation means splitting into two. **Bifurcation theory** (a subset of mathematics) is the study of bifurcation in nonlinear dynamical systems. The term bifurcation was coined by **Henri Poincare**, and the process was more deeply analyzed and confirmed by **Mitchell Feigenbaum** in 1978 (mathematically), and **Albert Libchaber** in 1979 (empirically). They focused on the common discrete-time chaotic model the logistic map, a one-dimensional system. Through bifurcation the attractor of the model splits into 2, then, 4, 8, 16, 32, 64, and quickly to infinity — the process accelerates swiftly with time.

The simple illustration commonly used to capture bifurcation is the **bifurcation diagram**. The x-axis of the diagram is the **bifurcation parameter**. At a bifurcation point the developmental path of the logistic map splits into two different paths. The new path develops 'suddenly', and at the nexus of each path is another **bifurcation point**. In the process, the numbers of path increases rapidly with further bifurcations — **cascading effect**. The path inbetween two bifurcation points is a **period of stability**. In general, the period of stability becomes shorter and shorter as the system evolves through the process of bifurcation (Feigenbaum constant ≈ 4.66). In addition, the outcome for selecting any one path will be very different. For the logistic map, the system moves into deep chaos at the 4th bifurcation point. On the other hand, phase transition, an 'older' characteristic common in the natural sciences (see Appendix 7) is observed in continuous-time DCS (see Appendix 1).

c. Attractor

Attractor is a set of states (subset) in the **phase space** of dynamical systems. In DCS/CS/CAS, the four attractors are as follows:

- Point (fixed) attractor — 1 state.
- Periodic (cyclic) attractor — 2 states or more (finite).
- Strange (non-periodic) attractor — a large number of states within a confine space.
- Chaotic (in-deterministic) attractor — a large number of random states with no define boundaries.

In linear physical systems (dimension three or less), the point attractor (one state) and periodic attractor (a few states) are very common. **A strange attractor only exits in nonlinear systems.** A common example of a strange attractor is the **Lorenz attractor** — its **phase diagram** (a large number of states) is a deep spiral (**phase space trajectory**) that never intersects (confined in a finite three-dimensional space — Edward Lorenz, 1963, see Appendix 1). In a human society, sociality is a biological attractor. In mathematics, the term attractor was coined by David Ruelle and Floris Takens, in 1971. In finite dimensionality dynamical systems, **the evolving variables of an attractor are represented by an n-dimensional vector** — attractor in an n-dimensional space; and when $n > 3$ it is difficult to perceive an attractor mentally (in physical systems, an attractor commonly has only a two to three positional coordinates).

Attractors are not equal in the **rugged landscape**. In DCS, each attractor has a **basin of attraction**. The basin is the region 'surrounding' an attractor where by all trajectories will end up in it (see basin of attraction in Appendix 7). The basins of the respective attractors are close together. For discrete-time DCS, a small fluctuation can cause the system to move from one basin to another.

d. Strange Attractor

This is the third category of attractor (non-periodic) out of the four types of attractors that exist in nonlinear dynamical systems. The first strange attractor of a physical system was 'observed' by Edward Lorenz from his weather prediction system in 1963. The new attractor reveals that there is a link between non-periodicity (which is 'stable') and unpredictability. It possesses some kind of patterned order and boundary, and when represented by a three dimensional phase diagram it appears as an infinite line that never passes through the same point twice but continues indefinitely within a bounded space. It also possesses a **fractal structure (scale invariance). A strange attractor is given the name 'strange' because it possesses a non-integer dimension.** Other common (mathematical) strange attractors include the Henon attractor, Rossler attractor, and Chua (double-scroll) strange attractor (see Appendix 3).

e. Phase Space and Phase Diagram

The phase space concept was first introduced by **Willard Gibbs** (1839–1903) in 1901. It is the space that represents **the set of all possible states of a system** with each possible state of the system corresponding to one unique point in the phase space. Thus, **an attractor is a subset of the phase space**. A phase diagram of a strange attractor is a plot of position and momentum variables with respect to time. The path of the Lorenz attractor commonly observed in its phase diagram is the phase space trajectory. The phase diagram reveals the unique properties of strange attractors more explicitly.

f. Scale Invariance

The concept of **scalability** appears from **Benoit Mandelbrot** (1924–2010) study on **fractal geometry** in 1963. Scale invariance indicates that the phenomenon is **scale independent, scale-free, or self-similarity** (scale invariance is a subset of self-similarity) — see self-similarity and scale invariance in Appendix 7. Scale free dynamic or scale invariant behavior can cascade across scales — from local to regional to global, and the same law holds truth for all scales — its contradicts the **constructionist hypothesis** (see constructionist hypothesis in Appendix 7). Strange attractors are scale invariance. Such systems/phenomena can be Pareto distributed, that is, they possess infinite variance, unstable means, and unstable confidence intervals. Power law phenomena are a subset of nonlinear phenomena (see power law, and power law phenomena in Appendix 7).

2.2.3 *Summary of key properties and characteristics of DCS*

- Deterministic — low finite dimensionality — all variables, parameters, and path of development (equations, mathematical model) are known.
- Discrete-time or continuous-time nonlinear dynamical systems.
- Nonlinearity — contain nonlinear variables, parameters, and/or changing relationships.
- Discrete-time DCS possess chaotic behavior from dimension one onwards.
- Continuous-time DCS possess chaotic behavior from dimension three onwards.
- Sensitive dependence on initial conditions — butterfly effect — unpredictability.
- DCS dynamic varies from simplicity to chaotic.
- Discrete-time DCS undergo bifurcation (discrete, sudden) constantly (cascading).
- Continuous-time DCS undergo phase transition (more gradual, strange attractor).
- Could possess four types of attractor — point, periodic, non-periodic (strange attractor), and in-deterministic chaotic.

- Scale invariance.
- Independent of their history.
- Could disintegrate.

Briefly, the most significant discoveries in the study of chaos are low dimensionality nonlinear DCS are highly sensitive dependence on initial conditions (unpredictable, butterfly effect), bifurcate or undergo phase transition, and possess strange attractors which are non-periodic states that are 'stable' (confirmed within a limited space). Their dynamics vary from simplicity to chaotic.

2.3 Basic Complex Theory and CAS

In the 1980s, the focus on chaos was expanded/redirected to **complexity theory**, which concentrates on **complexity, CS, complex dynamics (CD), CAS**, and **CAD — both CD and CAD vary from complexity to simplicity** (a continuously changing dynamic through **self-organization/ self-transcending constructions** — usually exists in high dimensionality systems, that eventually leads to the **emergent of new order**). An example of a CAS is the food chain (herbivores, carnivores, omnivores, parasites), a highly complex (intertwined) network of interdependent agents — however, there are predators and preys patterns (that is, in CAS agents are living and adaptive, and surface patterns exit — emerging from local interactions with the formation of **local spaces/networks**, and affecting the global dynamic eventually).

The shift expanded with the establishment of the Santa Fe Institute (SFI) in the US, in 1984. The term CAS was first used by the pioneers at the Santa Fe Institute in the early 1990s to indicate CS that are adaptive (living systems). SFI was founded by scientists mainly from the Los Alamos National Laboratory, including **George Cowan** (1920–2012), **Murray Gell-Mann** (1927–present), and **Doyne Farmer** (1952–present). Subsequently, many other prominent researchers from diversified disciplines (natural sciences, computer science, economic, sociology, anthropology, archaeology, and others), including **Norman Packard** (1954–present, physicist), **John Holland** (1929–2015, computer scientist), **Kenneth Arrow** (1921–present, economist), **Chris Langton** (1948–present, artificial life), **Jeffery Dean** (archaeologist), and **Brian**

Arthur (1948–present, economist) were also attracted to institute — see Appendix 4.

(As indicated earlier, complexity came from a Latin word that means 'intertwined' — thus, CS/CAS cannot be analyzed with the reductionist approach — due to the **Humpty Dumpty effect** — a term used by **Stuart Kauffman** (1939–present). In particular, CS are usually physical, chemical, or mathematical/conceptual nonlinear dynamical systems, while CAS are usually biological/living systems, including human organizations.)

2.3.1 *Key properties and definitions*

A primary characteristic of CS/CAS is the continuous **co-existence of order and complexity**. The dynamic involving fluctuating order and complexity [**stasis** and **punctuation point** — **Stephen Gould** (1941–2002) and **Niles Eldredge** (1943–present), in 1972, proposed the **punctuated equilibrium theory**] is intriguing — also associated with sudden and unexpected rapid changes. In general, it is accepted that the Universe as a whole is expanding, and hence **entropy** and disorder are increasing at all moments in time. This phenomenon is captured in the big bang theory, and the second law of thermodynamics. However, in the midst of high complexity, countless **centers of localized order (spaces of order)** emerge, each serving as a **local center for structure and order** of different kinds to be created and enforced. Against main stream expansion, the atomic (physical matter) world emerges first (proto-intelligence, physical self-organization). Lives and living systems of various forms and levels such as unicellar organisms, higher levels organisms, different species, human beings, ecosystems and human organizations, are subsequent products of this inwards focusing dynamic (**extropy**) — biological world/Gaia. In universal expansion, dynamic equilibrium is achieved at maximum entropy, while in the centers of localized order, dynamic equilibrium (relativistic static equilibrium) is achieved at lowest entropy (see extropy and dissipation in Appendix 7).

All the CS with life are CAS — complex, evolutionary, biological, and adaptive in nature. Another key property of CAS is that **the agents are also living organisms/beings**. The living systems learn, adapt, and evolve continuously in the process. Thus, all CAS are constantly adapting and seeking new **dynamical equilibrium**. (In CAS, there is no absolute

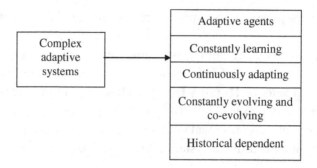

Figure 2.1   Some basic characteristics/abilities of CAS.

static equilibrium.) Some additional basic abilities and characteristics of CAS (as compared to CS) are captured in Figure 2.1. Thus, the study of CAS focuses on the relationships and interactions of the agents that give rise to the collective behavior of the systems, and how the systems establish relationships and interact with the environment.

Apparently, these systems are embedded with different levels of **intelligence** and **consciousness**. The **emergence dynamic** of evolution sustains and prolongs the existence of such systems. (Some common examples of CAS include ant colonies, human thinking systems, human organizations, economies, stock markets, ecosystems, regional organizations, and cyberspace.) Systems that fail to maintain their adaptive dynamics or abilities dissolve into the mainstream expansion and vanish. Such appearing and disappearing acts are taking place perpetually on this planet, as well as in the Universe. (Thus, everything that is composed will decomposed eventually, and spread into main stream expansion.)

In this respect, complexity theory could also be briefly stated as follows:

Complexity Theory (II)

It focuses on the analysis of how new (localized) order arises spontaneously in the physical and biological worlds, that is, continuously reducing complexity and entropy through the process of emergence (involving agent–agent interaction, autocatalysis, dissipation, feedback, circular causation, homeostasis, self-organizations, far-from-equilibrium, and self-transcending constructions) — extropy.

And the definitions of CS, CAS, CD, and CAD are as follows:

Complex Systems (CS)

They are nonlinear dynamical systems with high finite dimensionality (in-deterministic), sensitive dependence on initial conditions (butterfly effect), unpredictable, autocatalysis, circular causation, dissipation, self-organization, emergence, and strange attractor characteristics/ properties.

Complex Dynamic (CD)

This dynamic evolves from complexity to simplicity (new order) through continuous phase transitions at criticality (crossing the edge of order, and edge of emergence) involving agent–agent interaction, autopoiesis, dissipation, autocatalysis, circular causation, self-organization/self-transcending constructions, and emergence.

Complex Adaptive Systems (CAS)

CAS are 'living' complex systems with adaptive agents that possess certain level of intelligence and consciousness that enables the systems to learn, respond, communicate, adapt, evolve and co-evolve continuously. They encompass homeostasis, possess high adaptive capacity, and thus are more resilience to perturbation. They are also self-similar, far-from-equilibrium, and historical dependent.

Complex Adaptive Dynamic (CAD)

This (spontaneous) dynamic evolves from complexity to simplicity (new order) through continuous interactions among (living) agents involving autopoiesis, interdependency, dissipation, adaptation, autocatalysis, feedback, circular causation, symbiosis, self-organization/ self-transcending constructions, and emergence (crossing the edge of order, and edge of emergence). The local interacting activities of the agents will lead to a global dynamic.

A central axiom of the complexity theory is the inseparability of order and complexity, that is, the Universe and all its subsystems are intrinsically complex and orderly at the same time. In addition, from the human perspective, the Universe is a tapestry of thought (a visual and mental perception, cognition) produced by the abilities and constraints of the human thinking systems and its sensory systems (see **law of complexity/ consciousness, law of complexity/ intelligence, and law of consciousness/intelligence** in Appendix 7). This realization indicates that the whole of humankind, including its systems and environment, is merely a creation of human intelligence and consciousness (also supported/restricted by **Heisenberg's Uncertainty Principle**, $\Delta x \Delta y \approx \hbar$ — see Appendix 7).

The five core properties of this Universe and its microcosms proposed by some earlier chaos/complexity researchers are namely **consciousness, complexity, connectivity, dissipation**, and **emergence** (see Figure 2.2). This set of properties identified a significant anomaly, established a new mindset, and provided a redefined foundation for better comprehension of humanity, human organizations and their dynamics, as well as their changing external environment. In particular, the property of **consciousness** (a shift from a machine world to a living world mindset) indicates the significance and presence of the minds (thinking systems) in this Universe — **awakening to a cosmic mind**, and the criticality of **intelligence/consciousness-centricity** in human organizations.

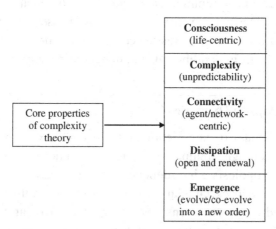

Figure 2.2 The (original) five core properties of CAS.

Apparently, the presence of self-organizing capability and emergence is the main focus of complexity theory — the emergent of **macro-properties** from **micro-properties** (**ontological reductionism** — see Appendix 7), and ultimately the emergent of new order. The latter is the most critical component in the continuous process of CAD. In this respect, some researchers defined complexity theory simply as a study of emergent of order. Emergence is a key focus of complexity studies because through emergence a new order with higher robustness (structures and possesses), and a complete new set of characteristics/laws may surface — **constructionist hypothesis**.

2.3.2 *Analyzing some additional properties of CS/CAS*

a. In-determinism and Unpredictability

Similar to DCS, CS and CAS are also sensitive dependence on initial conditions — butterfly effect — unpredictable. As stated above a small variation in initial conditions in nonlinear dynamical systems can lead to a totally unpredictable output. Apparently, recognizing and exploiting the butterfly effect is extremely crucial and beneficial when analyzing CS/CAS, especially when managing human CAS (tipping point, space of complexity, punctuation point — see Appendix 7).

Besides sensitive dependence on initial conditions there are additional constraints that increase unpredictability in CS/CAS. CS/CAS are high finite dimensionality nonlinear dynamical systems, very often with unknown unknowns and/or not precise variables — thus, rendering them in-deterministic. Therefore, their present state cannot be measured with absolute precision. In addition, their evolution trajectory may not be described or determined accurately due to unknown or changing relationships (nonlinearity). This combination of characteristics exists frequently in human organizations too (can be both in-deterministic and unpredictable). As the systems are sensitive dependence on initial conditions, and yet the present state and developmental path cannot be accurately and completely defined, exact solutions in the form that are commonly understood (the Newtonian paradigm and the machine-like approach) do not exist. Consequently, it has a critical impact on future strategy, prediction, and forecasting — a common underperformance in human organizations today (see futurology in Appendix 7). This is a significant observation and reality that leaders and managers of all categories of human organizations must comprehend and learn to handle.

b. Adaptive and Dissipative

CS/CAS are constantly changing in space-time, and CAS are **adaptive**, that is, they are living systems that continuously consume new information and react on it, if necessary. Thus, CAS consume information, learn, adapt, and evolve, and swift adaptation (associated with **intelligence** and **consciousness**) is a significant property of evolution. In addition, CS/CAS are more sustainable if they are **dissipative** as well — for instance, the rising of energy tension that speed up dissipation — to release excess/redundant energy in the system [also occurs in physical (non-living) systems (see Prigogine's **dissipative structures** theory in Appendix 7)]. Dissipation in open systems opposes the second law of thermodynamics, and gives rise to localized order (see extropy in Appendix 7) — the reverse of universal expansion. In general, all living systems (with living agents) are open, adaptive and dissipative, and in particular, human systems (human beings, corporations, nations) are dissipative with respect to many entities (inputs and outputs).

In CS/CAS their agents' interactions are usually localized and recurrence (**localized order**) initially. However, for better sustainability interacting agents (**self-centric** and **org-centric**) and their CAS co-evolve (**symbiosis**), while the CAS also co-evolve with their environment — multi-levels. The latter is usually a composite CAS with respect to the original system/agent (CAS and composite CAS). For instance, an ecosystem and a pack of wolves, an economy and its businesses, and a nation and its education institutions/schools demonstrate such a relationship. Thus, due to intense interconnectedness and high interdependency, co-evolution through self-organization or self-transcending constructions can be activated at multi-levels (nested).

c. Autopoiesis, Self-Organization and Self-Transcending Constructions

A CAS comprises a group of nonlinear dynamically interactive and changing **heterogeneous** agents that are **autonomous** and **autopoietic** (the term

autopoiesis was proposed by **Humberto Maturana** and **Francisco Varela** in 1972) — associated with self-centricity and stability-centricity; a self-maintaining and self-reproduction process. The system itself is open and in perpetual motion. Even the set of rules governing its dynamic is evolving. New information modifies the dynamic of the system as it tries to adapt by **self-organizing** [the term was first used by **Ross Ashby** (1903–1972) in 1947, and popularized by **Stuart Kauffman** in 1971 — **order for free**], and co-evolving. In 1966, **Per Bak** (1948–2002) introduced the term **self-organizing criticality (SOC)** where **phase transition** occurs (spontaneous emergence of global 'structure' out of local interactions). In addition, self-organization in human organizations possesses heterogeneous **frictional effect**, that is, its dynamic is not evenly distributed.

In this respect, the more constructive organizing dynamic (**self-transcending constructions**) in some CAS (in particular, human organizations) is usually subtly or subconsciously orchestrated by some latent impetus/forces (**order not totally for free**) — a concept introduced by **Jeffrey Goldstein**. (In intelligent human organizations, this latent impetus is the **intelligence/consciousness** of the interacting agents and/or the **collective intelligence/org-consciousness** of the organization — including **latent intelligence** and **latent leadership**) Overall, the ability of the system to anticipate, respond to, and influence the change in environmental conditions is vital — the sensory ability. A primary goal of all CAS is the successful emergent of new order (see Appendix 7 for a more detailed explanation of autopoiesis, self-organization, self-transcending constructions, synergetic, emergence, and edge of emergence).

d. Rugged/Fitness Landscape

Very often, the environment a CAS exists in is a changing rugged landscape. The latter is a surface/space (terrain of adaptation) with many peaks and valleys/troughs, where the fittest has the highest peak, and the steepest slope indicates the 'highest' selection pressure. Whenever a system moves up a slope towards a peak, self-organization is taking place. The landscape changes over time with the changing environment (forming a fluctuating three-dimensional space). In this case, a peak can become a trough, and to move from one peak to another higher peak, a downward journey into a valley (local minima) first is inevitable — (for instance, in some biological cases, **natural selection** alone is not good enough to move a species from one peak to another, the **genetic system** has to be involved — nonlinearity). This concept was further exploited by **Stuart Kauffman** (1939–present) in his NK model — a mathematical model with two variables N and K (see *NK* model in Appendix 7).

e. Autocatalysis, Circular Causation and Feedback

CAD are **autocatalytic** — a process that creates itself by catalytic action. **Positive feedback** create/support autocatalysis and **hypercycles** [proposed by **Manfred Eigen** (1927–present) in the 1970s]. Feedback is a linkage from the output of a system back to its input. Feedback (**circulation coupling**) can be negative (convergent) or positive (divergent). The terms 'negative' and 'positive' refer to the directions of change (mathematical) rather than the desired change. CS/CAS possess both types of feedbacks.

Feedback in human organizations was first recognized by **Norbert Wiener** (1894–1964), in 1948, and is broadly used in cybernetics. In cybernetics, excessive number of positive feedbacks amplifies processes, increases the complexity and instability of the system, leading to exponential growth, unpredictability, and the butterfly effect. On the other hand, negative feedback stabilizes the system through convergent (see Appendix 7 for details on autocatalysis, autocatalytic set, and feedback). However, positive feedback was only better comprehend in the 1990s when **Fritjof Capra** (1939–present) in 1996 pointed out that such feedback can be a source of new order and complexity in dissipative structures.

f. Constructionist Hypothesis

This important hypothesis (More Is Different, Science, 1972 — **broken symmetry** and the nature of the hierarchical structure of science) was observed by **Philip Warren Anderson** (1923–present, Nobel Prize in Physics, 1972) is a significant basic characteristic of emergence and CAS. It indicates that although it is possible to reduce nature (CS/CAS) to simple fundamental laws, this does not entail a similar ability to re-construct the Universe using the same set of simple laws. The reason being that **at each new level of complexity, new properties/attributes and laws not**

present in the lower stages appear. In this case, each new level of complexity exhibits the presence of new structures and properties that transcend lower level of characteristics and dynamics — that is, emergence is associated with new sophistication, property, robust structure, and order. For instance, between molecules and cells, a new attribute, life, emerges. Thus, it contradicts the Cartesian belief.

g. Red Queen Race/Hypothesis

Finally, CAS (as well as their interacting agents) can be locked/trapped in a **red queen race** (first used by **Leigh Van Valen** (1935–2010) in this context/manner, in 1973). In such a situation, a competitive advantage can only be sustained for a very short period. Thus, a niche created does not last long. In the red queen race, the winners are the faster runners. The winning positions must be renewed at all times–as a niche created is not quite sustainable. Thus, in such an environment, the approach to survival is to develop continuous temporary advantages. As there is also no known/ultimate destination, being trapped in such a situation does not appear to be too pleasant or comfortable. This situation synchronizes well with reality as for many people the human life journey is itself a red queen race. (A simpler explanation of this term is no matter how long a person runs s/he is always at the same spot — no niche gain.)

2.3.3. *Summary of key properties and characteristics of CS/CAS*

- In-deterministic (uncertainty) — low to high finite dimensionality with in-precise known and unknown variables — thus, path, equations, and mathematical model may be known but incomplete, or unknown.
- CS/CAS are continuous-time, that is, they are open systems in perpetual motion.
- Nonlinearity — contain nonlinear variables (and parameters) with changing relationships.
- Sensitive dependence on initial conditions — butterfly effect — unpredictability (complexity <=> unpredictability).
- Order and complexity co-exist, and fluctuate continuously — varying complexity density.

- Dynamic varies from complexity to simplicity — from localized to globalized — emergent of new order.
- Agents may not know that a localized action will lead to a certain global dynamic.
- Possess four types of attractor — point, periodic, non-periodic (strange attractor), and in-deterministic chaotic.
- Autocatalytic and circulation coupling/feedback.
- Self-organizing — spontaneous — order for free.
- Reductionist strategy fails; must focus on holism.
- Constructionist strategy can be adopted.
- Interconnectedness, engagement, and self-organizing communications.
- Interdependency.
- Far-from-equilibrium.
- Autopoiesis — self-centric, and stability-centric.
- Symbiosis — network-centric, org-centric.
- Self-transcending constructions — facilitated by internal latent impetus or driving force — order not totally for free.
- Emergence.
- Dependent on their history — hysteresis (time-based dependency).
- CAS (only) — living agents, learn, communicate, information processing, adaptive, behavioral schema, self-organizing, evolve, co-evolve, emergence.
- Could disintegrate.

2.3.4 *The new edge of emergence*

Macroscopically, emergence appears to be both divergent and convergent. The dynamic of emergence could be better comprehended by analyzing more deeply the **edge of order**, and the new **edge of emergence (conceptualized by TY Liang** in 2013, 'Edge of emergence, relativistic complexity and the new leadership'). Subsequently, any systems that fail to re-emerge with self-organization and/or self-transcending constructions will move across the **edge of chaos (new)** into the **space of in-deterministic chaos (a space with no potential surface pattern)** and disintegrate. All these edges (see Appendix 7) are critical boundaries (phase transition) that CAS will encounter during their existence.

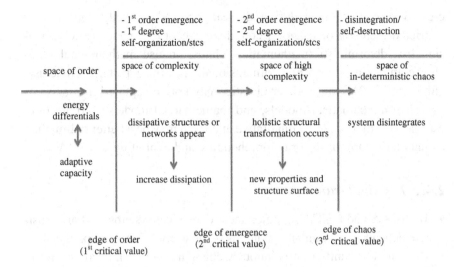

Figure 2.3   A micro interpretation of emergence with three transition boundaries/edges.

Briefly, the general emergent process is summarized as follows (also see the illustration in Figure 2.3):

- **Edge of order (1st critical value):** before — space of order; after — space of complexity => intra-system (local space/network) order [1st degree self-organization/self-transcending constructions, 1st order emergence]
- **Edge of emergence (2nd critical value):** before — space of complexity; after — presence of surface pattern => global or inter-system order => emergence of new order [2nd degree self-organization/self-transcending constructions, 2nd order emergence]
- **Edge of chaos (new — 3rd critical value):** before — space of high complexity; after — space of in-deterministic chaos => towards disintegration/self-destruction

2.4 Main Similarities and Differences between Chaos and Complexity

It is important to recognize the main similarities and differences between chaos (DCS) and complexity (CS/CAS) as the two terminologies have created some confusion during the early period of study due to their restricted meaning or usage in complexity theory — chaos (low dimensionality, deterministic/mathematical chaos, precise mathematical models), complexity (finite high dimensionality, surface pattern still exists although CS/CAS are in-deterministic, may not be captured in precise or complete mathematical models, and mathematical models used are only estimation). In this case, a qualitative approach may be a better option than a quantitative approach for comprehending and exploiting CAS/CAD.

2.4.1 *Key similarities*

- Both DCS and CS/CAS are nonlinear dynamical systems, and are sensitive dependence on initial conditions — butterfly effect — unpredictable.
- Both are constantly or continuously changing — no static equilibrium.
- Both possess the same four types of attractor namely, point, periodic, non-periodic (strange attractor), and in-deterministic chaotic.
- Both could disintegrate (when the dynamic becomes in-deterministic chaotic).

2.4.2 *Key differences*

- DCS are low finite dimensionality and deterministic (mathematical chaotic models) but unpredictable (determinism ≠ predictability).
- The starting point of chaotic dynamic is simplicity (due to small number of variables involved) to chaotic (due to bifurcation or phase transition).
- Thus, it is easier to conceive mathematical models for DCS and work on them.
- CS/CAS have high finite dimensionality, 'relativistic deterministic' or in-deterministic, and unpredictable (in-determinism = unpredictability).
- Agents in CS/CAS are highly interconnected and interdependent.
- Agents in CAS are living and adaptive, and local spaces/networks also exist (the relationship parameter can be highly nonlinear).
- The starting focal point of CAD is complexity and nonlinearity (due to the large number of agents/variables involved, as well as their changing relationships) to simplicity (emergence of new order) — involving autocatalysis, circular causation, self-organization/self-transcending constructions (stasis and punctuation point).

- CAD develops locally (local interactions of agents and the formation of local spaces/networks) to globally with autocatalysis, circular causation, self-organization/self-transcending constructions, and emergence.
- The study of CS/CAS usually adopts a qualitative (not determining precise solutions which may be difficult or impossible to achieve) longer term approach — focus on whether the system will settle into a particular state in the attractor after some changes.
- Thus, the mathematical model and algorithmic (step-wise) approach used to study CS/CAS (especially, for in-deterministic human organizations commonly with in-complete variables and/or unknown unknowns — in-complete phase space) is only an estimation (although, there are mathematical modelling exploited in complexity studies in human organizations/systems).
- DCS are independent of their history, while CAS are dependent of their history (hysteresis) — the present behavior of a CAS can be partially dependent on its past.
- Thus, CAS are not ordinary multi-agent systems (MAS). The agents and networks are adaptive, communicating, exchanging information, and changing.

2.5 Wider Classifications of Systems

2.5.1 *Types of systems*

Moving beyond complexity theory, the common categories of systems and their characteristics encountered are as follows:

a. **Ordered Systems — OS** (Newtonian theory, usually closed systems, static equilibrium, orderly, linear, fundamentalism, reductionist hypothesis, predictable, fixed point, and periodic point.)

b. **Deterministic Chaotic Systems — DCS** (Chaos theory, closed or open systems, low dimensionality, nonlinear, deterministic, butterfly effect, unpredictable, bifurcation, phase transition, and strange attractor.)

c. **Complex Systems — CS** [Complexity theory, open non-living systems, high finite dimensionality, nonlinear, in-deterministic (mathematically), far-from-equilibrium, dissipative, continuous change, interconnectivity, interdependency, stasis and punctuation, butterfly effect, unpredictable, autocatalytic, self-organizing, symmetry breaking, emergence, and strange attractor.]

d. Complex Adaptive Systems — CAS [Complexity theory, open living systems, high finite dimensionality, nonlinear, in-deterministic (mathematically), far-from-equilibrium, dissipative, continuous change, interconnectivity, interdependency, adaptive, stasis and punctuation, butterfly effect, unpredictable, autopoietic, autocatalytic, circular causation, self-organizing, self-transcending constructions, constructionist hypothesis, symmetry breaking, emergence, and strange attractor.]

e. Intelligent Human Organizations/Systems — *i*CAS [Intelligent Organization theory, complexity theory, open systems, high finite dimensionality, order and complexity co-exist, nonlinear, interconnectivity, engagement, autonomous, interdependency, dissipative, far-from-equilibrium, relativistic deterministic and/or in-deterministic (mathematically), butterfly effect, uncertainty, unpredictable, anticipatory, red queen race, basin of attraction, attractor, intelligence/consciousness-centric, continuous change, complexity-centric, learning, information processing, knowledge accumulation, adaptive, integrated deliberate and emergent strategy, smarter evolver, emergent strategist, self-organizing, self-transcending constructions, emergence, constructionist hypothesis, symmetry breaking, hysteresis, relativistic complexity, relativistic static equilibrium, space of relativistic order, emergence, extropy, network-centric, and 'equilibrium' at minimum entropy.]

f. Highly Disordered Systems — HDS (Statistical mechanics, usually closed systems, infinite randomness/dimensionality, stochastic, and equilibrium at maximum entropy.)

g. In-deterministic Chaotic Systems — ICS [Nonlinear in-deterministic dynamical systems (high dimensionality chaotic systems); these are also systems that after crossing the redefined edge of chaos (new — 3rd critical value) fail to self-organize and emerge, and have moved into the space of in-deterministic chaos — they will eventually disintegrate due to high in-determinism and turbulence.]

2.5.2 *The systems spectrum*

The above categories of systems could be captured in a spectrum (see Figure 2.4). The systems spectrum provides a clearer illustration on the spread (diversification) and relationships of the different systems with respect to dimensionality. The two extreme ends of the spectrum are OS (very low dimensionality) to HDS (infinite dimensionality). Systems in between are DCS, CS, CAS, and human organizations. During the life span of these systems when emergent of new order fail, the systems move into a space of in-deterministic chaos and disintegrate.

It is also interesting to note that nonlinear dynamical systems with the highest complexity are approximately in the middle of the spectrum (at high finite randomness and not at infinite randomness), including human organizations (see Figure 2.5) — also simply indicating that complexity is a state inbetween order and high disorder. HDS are not complex because they move into static equilibrium at maximum entropy (towards 'simplicity') — see the second law of thermodynamics in Appendix 7.

2.6 Human Organizations are Intrinsic CAS

2.6.1 *Basic thinking and conceptual foundation*

The study of chaos attracted numerous pioneer researchers because of the interesting observation that simple low dimensionality (mathematical) dynamical systems do not necessarily possess only 'simple' characteristics/

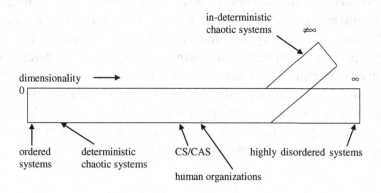

Figure 2.4 A simple illustration of the systems spectrum.

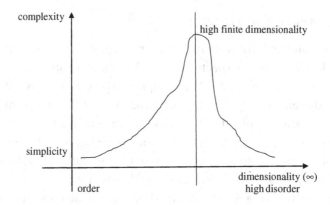

Figure 2.5   An 'approximate' relationship between complexity and system dimensionality.

dynamics — leading to the emergent of the **science of deterministic/ mathematical chaos**. However, human organizations are not DCS. **Human organizations are high finite dimensionality nonlinear dynamical systems (CAS) with in-complete phase space**. In addition, human organizations are open, adaptive, and dissipative living systems (with living interacting and adaptive agents embedding a changing behavioral schemata). Thus, **all human organizations are intrinsically continuous-time CAS that are trapped in the stasis and punctuation point cycle.** In this respect, complexity is an inherent attribute or essence of humanity — as the evolution-time path progresses, complexity density escalates.

In particular, for a large human organization, its dimensionality is greatly elevated by the presence and characteristics of every interacting agent (**micro-variables**) — which added on to the huge numbers of **macro-variables** that are already affecting the system (see **ontological reductionism** at 2.6.3e). This situation is similar to Lorenz weather prediction system. A system that is conceived with macro-variables such as pressure, temperature, and wind direction is very different from one that is determined by the properties of the atoms and molecules that are involved in the atmospheric system. The micro-variables elevate its complexity further due to the presence of unknown dimensionalities and relationships. Hence, such a system is difficult or cannot be conceived as a mathematical model with absolute precision because of the presence of unknown variables and links (see satisficing principle in Appendix 7).

Human organizations encounter a similar problem due to the large numbers of interacting agents and variables involved, as not all are 'known' — **uncertainty. Uncertainties are also defined as 'unknown unknowns'**. With uncertainties and/or undefined/known unknowns (risks), the **phase space** is in-complete. In addition, their micro-variables and relationships (especially, the mental states and behavioral schemata of agents) are not totally explicit, and/or information of known variables may not be complete. In this case, the output of the 'conceived system' is even more in-deterministic and unpredictable — as well as there is no **global optimality** (see global optimality in Appendix 7). Thus, creating a mathematical model of a human organization/system is not always feasible or beneficial (Laplace belief is not applicable). The underperformance of such a model is apparent. It is at best just an estimation of the 'actual' system due to uncertain dimensionalities. Consequently, with the right focus, the qualitative approach may be more appropriate. In addition, as linearity and order are not the only characteristics of human organizations the idea of fundamentalism and hierarchical decomposition cannot be practiced (failure of the Cartesian belief) — see Laplace belief, and Cartesian belief in Appendix 7.

2.6.2. *Key properties and definition*

In general, all human organizations are inherently nonlinear dynamical systems (changing continuously with time), and in particular, highly sophisticated intrinsic CAS (learn, adapt, dissipate, and emerge) with human beings (intense nonlinear intelligence and consciousness) as interacting agents (who themselves are also CAS — presence of nested/composite structure in organizations) => **human complexity theory is also a theory of change**. Consequently, throughout our existence, all human organizations (nations, civilizations, communities, economies, corporations, education institutions) fluctuate continuously between **stasis** and **punctuation point** — also constantly avoiding in-deterministic chaos (catastrophe, destruction) whenever possible. The macro-variables of the system and the micro-variables arising from the interacting agents render the dimensionality of the organization/system very high, and most of the time cannot be completely identified (although, not into total randomness — not highly disordered systems).

The primary macro-dynamic of all human organizations (social, economic, political, environmental) involves the co-existence of order and complexity that vary continuously in space–time. It also indicates that order **(relativistic order)** can be reinforced by comprehending and exploiting the (potential) latent structure surface of complexity. In this respect, order is still of fundamental importance in the new context — re-emphasizing the fact that complexity theory is the study of emergent of new order. Order (relativistic) provides the core stability for survival, existence, resilience, and sustainability. This observation provides a key starting point for exploiting complexity theory in human organizations. **Every human interacting agent and human organization focuses on self-centricity and stability-centricity — localized order is significant.** Thus, certain types of order must be further strengthened and enlarged to prolong the existence and sustainability of both the agents and their systems. **This desire for continual existence can best be achieved by tapping into the potential opportunities embedded in unexplored spaces of complexity.** Thus, a definition of human organizations/systems is as follows:

Human Organizations as unique CAS

Human organizations are intrinsic high finite dimensionality (continuous-time, composite) CAS (possessing properties/characteristics of other CAS, and more — self-organizing communications, exchanging information, mental space) with a large number of human interacting agents and other variables, and changing relationships (some of which are unknown unknowns — uncertainties, and some known variables but cannot be measured accurately/precisely), that is, they are in-deterministic and unpredictable (thus, human organizations possess an in-complete phase space). They are driven by CAD (complex to simplistic and emergent of new order with elevated robustness) involving interactions of agents, networks, and the entire organization (symbiosis, ambidexterity).

Hence, in summary, all categories of human organizations are in-deterministic (and/or relativistic deterministic) high finite dimensionality CAS because of the following reasons:

- In-complete variables set — uncertainty — presence of unknown unknowns.
- Inaccuracy of known variables — certain known variables/inputs that cannot be measured/computed precisely.
- Latent/undefined/varying relationships — certain relationships (nonlinear links) among agents and variables are not totally explicit, and therefore cannot be captured (by mathematical equations/model) com-pletely — presence of a highly **nonlinear relationship parameter**.
- In this case, human organizations are not DCS with low dimensionality that can be represented by a simple mathematical model.
- All human organizations (corporations, education institutions, com-munities, economies, cities, stock markets, political systems, nations, civilizations, regional institutions) are high finite dimensionality non-linear continuous-time CAS with an incomplete phase space.
- Thus, human organizations can be better analyzed qualitatively — focusing on longer-term development and solutions (smarter evolver) with a strong intelligence/consciousness-centricity, complexity-centricity, and network-centricity strategic approach (including futuristic).

In this respect, due to the 'outdated' Newtonian mindset, and the sig-nificant presence of intense complexity (including continuous and rapid changes) and its associated attributes [sensitive dependence on initial conditions (butterfly effect), unpredictability, and in-determinism (high finite dimensionality that cannot be completely captured)], a paradigmatic shift in thinking, leadership, governance, strategy, management, and prac-tices is a compelling need in all human organizations — to minimize constraints, incoherency, distortions, deficiencies, and dysfunctions.

2.6.3 *Analyzing some additional properties of human CAS*

There are several significant and dissimilar properties/characteristics of human organizations (greatly differentiating them from other CAS) that

require further illustrations, including the uniqueness of human interacting agents:

a. Human Interacting Agent

Agents are the elementary entities/components of CAS. In human organizations, the interacting agents are human beings each embedded with an
intense intelligence/consciousness source (**human thinking systems**).
The characteristics of the agents are vital to the system. Human interacting agents are autopoietic, autonomous, heterogeneous, adaptive, interconnected, interdependent, and anticipatory. Thus, every human agent is
self-centric, **stability-centric**, and embedded with a set of changing
behavioral schemata. Their interactions are initially localized (**principle
of locality**) but can lead to the emergent of global dynamic encompassing
self-organization/self-transcending constructions, and eventually emergence (**adaptive capacity**). The significant characteristic unique to human
interacting agents is their intense intelligence and consciousness — high
awareness and **mindfulness** (they are intense nonlinear intelligence
sources that surpass that of all other living interacting agents), allowing
them to exploit intense intelligence/consciousness-centricity (an inherent
strengths of human organizations) in multiple perspectives — (see intelligent person, human agent, and human thinking systems in Appendix 7).

b. Behavioral Schemata

The set of behavioral schemata embedded in the human thinking systems
(brain and mind combined) decides how the agent will behave — act and
react. In general, the initial interaction is localized — confined within a
local space or **network**, and towards 'equilibrium' at lower entropy. In
this respect, the local context is vital to the agent. Gradually, the influence
may become more global (may not be the intention of the agent). The
behavioral schemata of human agents are always changing through **continuous learning** and cognition with time (adaptive — to reduce potential
negative effects, and elevate stability). Thus, the set of behavioral schemata of a human agent is closely associated with their **intrinsic intelligence** and **consciousness (awareness, mindfulness)**, and the **collective
intelligence** and **org-consciousness (org-awareness, orgmindfulness)**

of the system (including knowledge structure and experiences, thus, rendering **intelligence/consciousness-centricity** highly significant). Concurrently, it greatly affects the dynamics of autopoiesis, dissipation, self-organization/self-transcending constructions, and emergence. In addition, due to the intense **mental capacity** of human agents their behavioral schemata can be highly '**language dependent**' (see Chapters 4–6), **nonlinear,** and **relativistic** (see relativistic complexity Appendix 7). The set of behavioral schemata of a human organization is the 'selective' summation of the behavioral schemata of all the interacting agents with coherency and **synergetic effect** (introduced by **Hermann Haken,** 1927–present) — that is, often transforming incoherency to coherency — **collectiveness capacity,** and the output of the organization is more than the sum of the individual agent output (see synergetics and collectiveness capacity in Appendix 7).

c. Adaptive Capacity

Adaptive capacity includes the ability of a CAS to learn, store knowledge and experience; the flexible problem-solving and decision-making characteristics; and the power structure that is responsive to the (changing) needs of the interacting agents. This recognition is crucial to the leadership, governance, strategy, management, and sustainability in intelligent organizations (also linked to **intelligence/consciousness management, and complexity management** — see Chapters 4 and 6). The adaptive capacity of a human organization depends on its structure (**structural capacity**) and **mental capacity** as well. In this respect, an intelligent biotic macro-structure that resembles a highly intelligent biological being (rather than a machine) will enhance the adaptive capacity of human organizations — better structural and dynamic coherency. In addition, it is also important to note that characteristics such as nonlinearity, innovativeness, and **exaptation** (see Appendix 7) also linked to adaptive capacity.

d. Space of Complexity and Complexity-Centricity

As stipulated earlier, human organizations encompass both spaces of order and spaces of complexity concurrently. In intelligent organizations, not all spaces of complexity (no suddenness or surprises) are punctuation points (for instance the Chernobyl disaster in 1986). With globalization and urbanization, the complexity density of humanity is continuously elevating. A cosmopolitan city (a newer emergent order) is much more complex (relativistic order) compared to a simple village. In general, an intelligent human organization (corporation, education institution, city, community, and nation) must possess the ability to exploit certain spaces of complexity to reinforce new order (higher robustness) with the aim of sustaining and prolonging their existence. This is also a learning, adaptation, and dissipation process that supports the system achieves its goal at a higher level. Thus, **certain spaces of complexity are embedded with new opportunities (surface pattern exists),** and exploring and exploiting them must be an entrenched activity in all intelligent organizations. In this respect, for any human organizations, the **integrated deliberate and emergent strategy** approach will enable the systems to switch between the two types of spaces appropriately (see **deliberate-emergent auto-switch** in Appendix 7). If the intelligence of the agents/systems is sufficiently high, spaces of complexity may appear as **spaces of relativistic order** (see 2.6.3f below). In this case, the unexplored spaces of relative order that are embedded with new opportunities could be better exploited with innovation and creativity to enhance competitive advantage — (see **intelligence advantage** in Appendix 7).

e. Ontological Reductionism

As indicated above, the analysis of human organizations encounters problems linked with ontological reductionism due to presence of **macro-variables** and **micro-variables**. This concept is associated with the idea that entities, properties, or processes at one level are typically a manifestation (summation) of entities, properties or processes that occur at a lower level, that is, macro-properties are simply identified with the micro-properties — for example, heat and molecular energy (see **scale invariance** in Appendix 7). In the human world, the behavior of a 'market' is the coherent dynamic of all its interacting agents. However, the conceptual model of a 'market' using macro-variables does not or may not be able to include all the micro-variables involved in totality. Hence, due the high dimensionality of human organizations, conceiving mathematical models of any human systems/ organizations is therefore at best an estimation of the 'actual' system.

f. Relativism and the Intense Mental Dimension

Both human agents and human organizations are highly **stability-centric** and **intelligence/consciousness-centric** — resulting in a three-dimensional phenomenon on self-stability encompassing **physical stability, biological stability,** and **mental stability (third-order stability).** In this respect, **relativistic complexity theory** (*i*CAS <=> *r*CAS, and *i*CAD <=> *r*CAD) is part of the **intelligent organization theory** — emerges due to the intense mental dimension of the human thinking systems. The latter characteristic (mental dimension) arises because of the high intensity and nonlinearity of human intelligence, consciousness, and accumulated knowledge, and its usage. Thus, it is associated with the awareness, mindfulness, orgmindfulness, knowledge structures, **subjectivity,** innovativeness, and behavioral schemata of the interacting agents (see intelligent person in Appendix 7), and the collective intelligence and organizational consciousness of the system.

In this case, the level of complexity in a **space of complexity** (including **punctuation point**) may 'become' relativistic (**space of relativistic order**) depending on the state of the intense intelligence source involved — also linked to higher level **intelligence advantage.** Similarly, dynamic equilibrium is perceived or appeared as **relativistic static equilibrium.** In this respect, complexity in the human world (individuals and organizations) is not exactly the same as the physical world or even the basic life-intelligence biological world, as certain spaces of complexity are spaces for deeper contemplation, exploration and exploitation. (Relativistic complexity will be further discussed in Chapter 9.)

g. Network-Centricity

Human agents usually interact with their 'neighboring' agents forming a network/cluster — a local space of interactions (see principle of locality in Appendix 7). Thus, networks, both formal and informal, are parts of the human organizational structure. The foundation for **(random) network theory** (initiated by **Paul Erdos,** 1913–1996) is derived from **graph theory** (initiated by **Leonhard Euler** (1707–1783), subsequently with applications (**'real world' networks**) in numerous domains including sociology (**social networks**), biology (**molecular networks**), economics (**market internal relations networks**), and computer science (**artificial**

neural networks) — see network theory Appendix 7. A graph is a mathematical structure with **vertices (nodes)** and **edges (links)**. A subset of network theory focuses on **link analysis** which explores the relationships (for instance, **a set of dyadic ties** in a social network) of the nodes. In human networks/organizations (**complex adaptive networks**), the links are or can be relational and intangible.

Currently, network theory is also regarded and analyzed as a subset of complexity theory. In this respect, nodes in networks are the equivalent of human agents in CAS where information is consumed (internalized), created (externalized), and/or transmitted — significantly associated with interconnectivity, engagement, self-organizing communications, self-organization or self-transcending constructions. In addition, the small world theory, a subset of network theory focuses on small world networks in the 'real world'. Erdos found that even for a large network (with a large number of nodes), a small percentage of randomly selected links will be sufficient or good enough to generate the characteristics/impact of the entire network — a small world effect/phenomenon. ('Real world' networks include small world networks and scale free networks — see Appendix 7 and Chapter 10). Complex networks are part of the meso-structure of human organizations (see Chapter 4).

h. Self-organization and Self-transcending Constructions

In general, human organizations are **self-organizing systems** driven by the intelligence/consciousness of the agents, and the collective intelligence/org-consciousness of the local spaces/ networks and organization that can be constructive (emergent of new order) or destructive (disintegration). Very often, in human organizations frictional effects are also present during self-organizations, and these effects are not homogenous. (To avoid contradicting the 'order for free' concept, **self-transcending constructions** is a more appropriate term as there is a **latent impetus** involved.)

Self-transcending constructions ('self-organization' driven by a latent impetus — the intelligence of agents and collective intelligence of systems) is a vital dynamic in human organizations. Conceptually, it enhances **self-stability** at all levels (agent, network, global) of the organization. The rate and quality of the self-organizing possesses are also closely associated with the characteristics of their leadership and governance system. Thus, the quality of human dynamic is closely related to its collectiveness capacity and self-organization/self-transcending constructions capability (nurturing **self-organizing capacity**, and **emergence-intelligence capacity** — see Appendix 7). Highly intelligent organizations adopt the **intelligence leadership** strategy that focus deeply on the orchestration of constructive self-organization — also related to the presence of a **latent leader** that concentrates on lateral/collective participation, that is, exploiting the **intrinsic leadership** of as many human agents (**self-powered capability**) as possible.

Notes: Intelligent human organisations are both iCAS and rCAS:

- iCAS — intelligent complex adaptive systems
- rCAS — relativistic complex adaptive systems
- iCAS <=> rCAS — highly intelligent CAS are also relativistic
- iCAD — intelligent complex adaptive dynamics
- rCAD — relativistic complex adaptive dynamics
- iCAD <=> rCAD — highly intelligent CAD is also relativistic

2.7 Conclusion

This chapter introduced the fundamental concepts of (mathematical) chaos (DCS, chaotic dynamic), and complexity (CS, CD, CAS, CAD), and their properties/characteristics (see Appendices 1 to 3). The discussion also vividly reviews that the entire humanity and all its organizations (including economic, social, political, military, education, and environmental perspectives) are inherently complex adaptive. They process information, learn, adapt, create knowledge structure, interconnect, communicate, accumulate experiences; and possess dissipative, autocatalytic, feedback, network-centric, self-organization/self-transcending constructions, and emergence capabilities. In addition, the various perspectives mentioned are also intertwined in a complicated manner that further elevates complexity in the current human world significantly. Thus, comprehending the entire set of complexity properties, and being able to exploit them is highly beneficial. Apparently, complexity theory is a domain that deserves deeper contemplation and scrutiny. The intelligent organization theory is an attempt to exploit complexity theory in humanity (co-existence of order and complexity, self-organizing capability, relativistic complexity), its organizations and dynamics, so that better coherency, and synergy, and a higher order of existence can be achieved.

First, **the intelligent organization theory emphasizes that the inherent strengths of all intelligent human organizations is the intense intelligence and consciousness of the interacting agents** — the highest intelligence/consciousness sources on this planet, confirming that a paradigmatic shift towards intelligence/consciousness-centricity is of utmost important, and extremely vital (that is, focusing on the criticality of primary human capability, and its links to the longevity of the organization).

Next, **the constraints of human organizations include the fact that they are intrinsic complex adaptive systems (high finite dimensionality) that possess a very large numbers of variables or inputs — and not all are well-defined or known** (not fully deterministic, in-complete phase space). This situation reduces the accuracy of analyzing human organizations (especially, mathematically). Formulating a mathematical model of a human system/organization (for instance, a financial market, a social community) is at best an approximation — an estimated model with estimated outputs (contradicts the Laplace belief). In addition, the sensitive dependence on initial conditions characteristic of human organizations further elevated their unpredictability. In this respect, **there are only best possible (satisficing) solutions and no global optimality in human organizational dynamics, as their phase spaces are never completely known.** This recognition serves as another starting point for the development of a new mindset and thinking.

Finally, the interacting agents in human organizations are intrinsically biological/social/economic/political CAS, each embedded with a set of behavioral schemata (relativistic, construal, and cognitive) that is constantly changing. Apparently, complexity in the human world is fairly intense and nonlinear, and to a great extent different from other biological or physical systems. Identifying these differences and constraints (the new insights) is beneficial to the existing leadership, governance, management, strategic thinking, risks management, and crisis management, as they redefined human org-consciousness. Thus, the intelligent organization theory (encompassing relativistic complexity — see Chapters 9 and 10) that focuses on intelligence/consciousness-centricity, intelligence-intelligence linkages, organizing around intelligence, collective intelligence, org-consciousness, structural capacity, collectiveness capacity, adaptive capacity, complexity-centricity, complexity-intelligence linkages, network-centricity, complex networks, self-organizing capacity, emergence-intelligence capacity, **relational capacity**, **unifying capacity**, and **'feeling' system** provides a more 'realistic' approach that can handle the incoherent current situation better (see Figure 2.6). Apparently, the intelligence mindset and intelligence paradigm are new critical foundation pillars of the human world (further analyzed in Chapter 3).

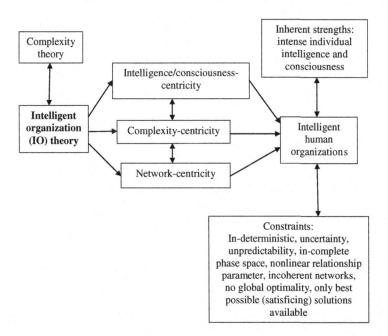

Figure 2.6   The three centricities, strengths of human agents, and constraints of human organizations constitute a fundamental strategic pillar (the basic inherent foundation) of the intelligent organization (IO) theory.

Mindfulness is considered as the strongest strand for it plays an important role in the acquisition of both calm and insight. Mindfulness is awareness (of the mind); it is a certain function of the mind and, therefore, is a mental factor. Without this all-important factor of mindfulness one cannot cognize sense objects, one cannot be fully aware of one's behavior.

Piyadassi Thera, *The Buddha's Ancient Path*

Chapter 3

The Intelligence Mindset and Intelligence Paradigm

"The more intense the intelligence/consciousness sources the more
difficult it is to establish effective linkages and nurture collective
intelligence"

"Mindfulness (core of self-awareness) is the unique attribute of deeper
human consciousness"

Summary

In this chapter, an introductory analysis of human intelligence and consciousness is executed to establish a conceptual foundation for the intelligent organization theory. Fundamentally, the new intelligence mindset
and thinking, and intelligence paradigm focus on high intelligence/
consciousness-centricity. It concentrates on human intrinsic intelligence/
consciousness sources (its intense intelligence and consciousness —
awareness and mindfulness), and stipulates that organizing around intelligence (a strategic component of the complexity-intelligence strategy)
is the new strategic direction to be adopted by all human organizations
in the present knowledge-intensive, fast changing, and not always predictable environment (limited predictability). In addition, the characteristics and variation in capabilities of intelligence and consciousness are
further scrutinized using an intelligence spectrum (compared to other
biological intelligence sources on this planet — encompassing proto-
intelligence, basic life-intelligence, basic human intelligence and
advanced human intelligence). In the intelligent organization theory, consciousness (awareness, mindfulness) only exists in the living/biological
world, and mindfulness is confined to humanity.

Subsequently, intelligence/consciousness management and its associated dynamics that are critical activities of intelligent human organization (*i*CAS) are more deeply examined with respect to complexity-centricity (encompassing attributes such as stability-centricity, autopoiesis, symbiosis, self-centric, network-centric, org-centric, independency, interdependency, intelligence-intelligence linkage, engagement, self-organization/self-transcending constructions, local space, complex networks, constructionist hypothesis and emergence). Concurrently, the urgency and impact for nurturing the new intelligence mindset and intelligence paradigm is also discussed. In a situation with escalating complexity density, this paradigmatic shift in mindset and thinking in leadership, governance and management of human organizations is highly significant for higher functionality and coherency — to all human interacting agents (both leaders and followers), as well as the organizations themselves.

Another component of the complexity-intelligence strategy examined is the nurturing of an intelligent biotic and complex adaptive macro-structure that will serve all human organizations better (towards higher coherency, synergy and structural capacity). The analysis clearly indicates the necessity of systemic transformation or structural reform that is more coherent with intelligence/consciousness, and information processing and knowledge acquisition capability. In this case, a greater operational/practical utility and higher structural capacity can be achieved with the presence of the intelligent biotic macro-structure and agent-agent/system micro-structure (principle of locality) that concurrently supports the intelligent complex adaptive dynamic (*i*CAD) better — a finer synchrony between structure and dynamic — higher intelligence advantage.

Keywords: Intelligence mindset, intelligence paradigm, raplexity, complex adaptive systems, intelligence/consciousness-centric, intelligence, consciousness, self-centric, self-powered, interconnectedness, independency, interdependency, intelligence-intelligence linkage, collective intelligence, org-consciousness, org-centric, complexity, human thinking systems, principle of locality, Abilene paradox, defensive routine, coherency, synergetic, punctuation point, entropy, extropy, space-time compression, connectivity, engagement, unpredictability, autopoiesis, symbiosis, fundamentalism, cascading behavior, self-organizing communications, butterfly effect, complexity-intelligence-centric, static equilibrium, rugged landscape, red queen race, self-organization, self-transcending constructions, network, holism, global dysfunction, social conformity, emergence, entropy, extropy, complexity-intelligence strategy, awareness, mindfulness, proto-intelligence, intelligence spectrum, stability-centric, constructionist hypothesis, broken symmetry, 1st order consciousness, 1st edge of consciousness, basic life-intelligence, 2nd order consciousness, 2nd edge of consciousness, basic human intelligence, latent impetus, character set, nonlinearity, orgmindfulness, org-awareness, mindful culture, mental cohesion, advanced human intelligence, swarm intelligence, intelligent complex adaptive systems (*i*CAS), complexity-centric, complexity-intelligence linkage, behavioral schemata, latent intelligence, self-powered governance, network-centric, network theory, complex network, small world network, integrated deliberate and emergent strategy, intelligent complex adaptive dynamic (*i*CAD), orgmind, intelligent biotic macro-structure, space of complexity, organizing around intelligence, mental cohesion, intelligence/consciousness management, complexity management, structural capacity, adaptive capacity, collectiveness capacity, self-organizing capacity, emergence-intelligence capacity, unifying capacity, metal cohesion, intelligence advantage, relativistic complexity and intelligent organization theory.

3.1 Introduction: The World of Life

3.1.1 *Towards unprecedented 'raplexity'*

Nature is inherently complex. Similarly, humanity (Gaia, ecosystems, human organizations) is inherently complex. Over the past three decades, new developments and challenges (partially indicated in Chapter 1) have been substantially affecting existing thinking and theories, as well as present human living conditions — in particular, the human mental space. The '**raplexity**' of change cannot be fully comprehended or managed with the present knowledge, governance, leadership, and strategies (see raplexity in Appendix 7). Vividly, the **Newtonian mindset** (orderly, linearity, determinism, equilibrium, fundamentalism, hierarchical leadership and governance, control, and high predictability) is manifesting its constraints and vulnerability more frequently and prominently. In the human world, equilibrium does not lead to optimality. Fundamentally, human beings are not machine parts, and human organizations possess characteristics beyond that of a piece of machinery (hierarchical structure, reductionist hypothesis). They are embedded with intelligence/consciousness sources.

Thus, a deeper analysis and comprehension on the changing dynamics of human organizations and their interacting agents is essential to justify a change in the undermining mindset. To begin with, human systems/organizations (a collection of interacting human minds) are living systems, and more specifically they are intrinsic **complex adaptive systems** embedded with collective intelligence rather than mechanical systems. Overall, in the world of life the dynamic involved is complex adaptive (nonlinear, butterfly effect, unpredictable). Complexity has always been around. This characteristic is a natural component of this Universe including our biosphere since the beginning. In this respect, re-establishing the 'right' or better conceptual foundation with a new mindset is essential. In this respect, the significance of **intelligence/consciousness-centricity** and **complexity-centricity** in human organizations is highly apparent, and its benefit is a new criticality.

3.1.2 *Current and emerging constraints and distortions*

A deeper analysis and comprehension of the current distortions, deficiencies, and constraints in human organizations that lead to their overall incoherency are essential. Certain attributes/factors and interactive discrepancies are as follows:

- The intelligence, consciousness, and knowledge structures of individual **human thinking systems** have been continuously and rapidly elevated through better education and knowledge acquisition — a worldwide phenomenon — resulting in more knowledge-intensive and nonlinear activities, a more diversified social commitment, and redefined values, norms, and expectations.
- Information, a vital input to all human thinking systems, once travels at the speed of horses/planes now travels at the speed of light (information communication technological advancement — internet, wireless/mobile phone, and social media). This development greatly enhancing human mental connectivity, communications, information acquisition, and also resulting in excessive information 'flooding' — (intense *i*-**empowerment/e-empowerment**, and intense **self-organizing communications**).

Social media or wireless technologies usage have gone beyond disseminating information and enhancement of transaction to the establishment of new relationships and viability of human organizations. A significant percentage of human beings interact more frequently through media connection than direct interaction. Information processing capacity is power, and a wisp of information could move the system towards a **tipping point** or **punctuation point** suddenly (for instance, impact of a new technological output — can be constructive or destructive). In particular, the e-landscape, a creation of global human collective intelligence is an extension of the abstract/intangible and nonlinear mental world. In this respect, the boundaries of **human interdependency** have expanded, and an intense virtual dimension has emerged in the human world. Thus, the intrinsic rules governing human interaction dynamics have been transformed due to escalated **cascading behaviors**.

- Human beings can now travel faster than sound (greatly enhancing physical connectivity; air travel), and more frequently (due to a more affluent global population) — both the **physical and human mental world have 'shrunk'**, and the interdependency of agents has been elevated. In this case, stability at all levels (agents/networks/organizations) has been redefined, and it is changing at all time.

- In addition, the entire humanity is also more closely and intensely interconnected due to **globalization** and **urbanization** — deceasing local, geographical, and national cultural boundaries (resulting in multi-cultural intensity and greater diversification in general). It physical and mental dynamics and impacts tantamount to a **'space-time compression'** — the human world has shrunk further, processes are accelerating, complexity density is escalating, and consensus becomes more nonlinear. Many people are becoming 'global citizens' (transnational migrants). Concurrently, some business (multi-national corporations), social/political (escalating migration), and environmental (integrated effort and/or condemnation) associated agents are attempting to enforce global coherent and synergetic thinking and activities — towards a **global mindset** (see Appendix 7).

In this context, competitions are no more localized for both individuals and organizations. Instead, worldwide competitions and impacts are becoming more common — for instance, in the business world and tertiary institutions, a competitor is no more another agent/organization/institution in the same economy or country. Instead, it could be located in any other economies or countries revealing broader and more intense competition. In addition, for complex adaptive systems, it is significant to note that a local activity can develop into a global phenomenon — see **principle of locality** in Appendix 7).

- **Leadership** characteristics that were once effective for the older generations (aristocratic, hierarchical, bureaucratic) are losing their functionality (even for transformational leadership introduced around 1990 — empowerment). The leadership, governance, and management thinking and practices in most present human organizations that are still highly hierarchical and machine-like is a great restraint by conventional inhibitions (design paradigm, command and control, empowerment) — see **Abilene paradox** and **defensive routine** in Appendix 7.

  Possesses and activities of the hierarchical/bureaucratic mindset contradict the expectation of highly educated interacting agents (possessing a different set of behavioral schemata), and does not synchronize with the changing values — thus, resulting in emergent of more networks (local optimality, local spaces, formal or informal, constructive or destructive), frequent crises, and high incoherency (social, political, economic, and environmental mismatch). Consequently, a more intense intelligence-intelligence linkage is essential. And establishing new a foundation and normative knowledge in the domain of leadership, governance, and management is inevitable (for higher collectiveness capacity, adaptive capacity, self-organizing capacity, and emergence-intelligence capacity — see Chapters 9 and 10).

- Concurrently, more **spaces of complexity** (economic, social, political, education, military, physical/environmental spaces — better risk management, may be potential opportunities) and unfamiliar punctuations points (better crisis management needed) are surfacing more frequently, rendering the humanity dynamics rather difficult to comprehend and manage — resulting in more unpredictability or failures in forecasting. In this case, a paradigmatic shift is crucial. Inevitably, the shift has to be **complexity-intelligence-centric.**

- Apparently, being trapped in the stasis and punctuated equilibrium cycle, there is no **static equilibrium** in the human world — that is, no spaces of absolute order; nothing remains status quo. It is even more so in the present context that is dominated by elevating complexity density. Thus, it is significant to recognize that human organizations are complex dynamical systems that are nonlinear, continuously changing, learning, and adaptive. In the continuously changing environment, all agents and organizations are also innately trapped in the **rugged landscape** and **red queen race** (see Appendix 7).

- Finally, in all human perspectives the spontaneous formation of diversified informal **networks** (localized connectivity) has expedited to the extent that human organizations are also perceived as **network organizations.** These networks (**engagement, local optimality, global dysfunction**) may contradict the formal structure, leadership, and governance [see S(1)–S(4), and network theory in Appendix 7]. There is an apparent increase in localized **self-organizing** and **self-transcending constructions** capabilities that may be incoherent with the global dynamic — resulting in lower collectiveness capacity.

Thus, the greater needs for higher interdependency and **holism** have to be accelerated. A **global emergent** dynamic that is unconsciously or sub-consciously (spontaneously) driven by a more collective latent impetus is essential. Overall, a greater focus on the holistic organizational complexity and dynamic is vital (by elevating org-mindfulness). Apparently, a paradigmatic shift is greatly needed to replace the current underperforming mindset (including lack of information sharing from the leadership) for greater social conformity, organizational competitiveness, resilience, and sustainability. Hence, nurturing the intelligence mindset and intelligence paradigm is strategic.

3.1.3 *Necessity for nurturing intelligent human organizations*

In the physical matter world that is dominated by rigid structure (atoms/molecules/crystals — low dimensionality), and **entropy**/change (gases, infinite randomness, towards maximum entropy — infinite dimensionality), order exists due to the presence of some forms/levels of intelligence. Proto-intelligence establishes the physical structure, while other intelligence sources provide the ability to reverse disorder (**extropy**). Therefore, in the 'raplexity' context, human beings and hence human thinking systems (intelligence/consciousness sources) must be valued as the primary and most important components/entities/assets in all human organizations/systems, irrespective of their primary function or objective (social, economic, education, military, medical, political or spiritual). Similarly, these intrinsic intense intelligence/consciousness sources are also the primary focus of the intelligent organization theory. (Intelligence/human being is an asset and not just an economic resource.) The shift towards intense intelligence/consciousness-centricity elevates both strategic and tactical agility (although some human organizations are inherently intelligence but for most organizations their collective intelligence can be much further enhanced).

Fundamentally, it has been revealed that some of the new critical changes and daunting problems that surpassed traditional understanding are innately linked to lack of intelligence/consciousness-centricity (intelligence, consciousness, self-powered agents, interconnectedness, interdependency, intelligence-intelligence linkage, collective intelligence, organizational consciousness, intelligence/ consciousness management), complexity-centricity (complexity-intelligence linkage, and complexity management), and network-centricity (network management, complex networks, complex adaptive networks, and small world networks) — a new critical necessity. Intelligent human organizations should be constantly adapting and seeking new dynamical equilibrium (relativistic complexity, self-organizing capability, emergent of new order). Concurrently, certain key organizational characteristics/norms, including social consensus and causality must be recognized, better comprehended, enhanced, and allocated transformational efforts.

In this respect, **a human organization is primarily a collection of intense intelligence/consciousness sources** (this should be the key perception of all human organizations today) that are put together to achieve certain organizational goals. The complexity-intelligence strategy introduced in the intelligent organization theory focuses on how this collection of interacting intense intelligence/consciousness sources can be better interconnected, engaged, and integrated (coherent and synergetic) to exploit continuous changes, increasing complexity (certain spaces of complexity), and complex networks so that the organization is always competitive and sustainable. An intense divergent and convergent, and adaptive mental and operational dynamic is critical. Overall, rationalizing interactions that also encompasses unity (unifying capacity) through diversification is vital (mental cohesion) — see mental cohesion in Appendix 7.

Summary: The fresh focal centers and their entities:

- Human thinking systems (the brain and mind combined) => individual intrinsic intelligence, and consciousness (awareness, self-awareness, mindfulness) — every intense intelligence/consciousness source must be well-engaged and exploited
- Orgmind => collective intelligence, and org-consciousness (org-awareness, orgmindfulness) — all intelligence consciousness sources (if necessary) must be well-interconnected, integrated, and collectively exploited
- Complexity => spaces of complexity, dynamical equilibrium, punctuation point — the co-existence of order and complexity, certain spaces of complexity must be effective exploited
- Network => complex network, network of networks, small world network, complex adaptive network — all networks (formal and informal) must be well-integrated and exploited

The above analysis reveals the agent-agent/system micro-structure and its dynamics of human organizations. This model is briefly captured as follows: (It will be further discussed in Chapter 7.)

> **Agent-Agent/System Micro-Structure of Intelligent Human Organizations**
>
> In the intelligent organization theory, all human organizations are perceived primarily as a collection of interacting intrinsic intense intelligence/consciousness sources (human thinking systems => human interacting agents, the basic entities), irrespective of the functions and goals of the systems. Thus, human agents must be valued as vital organizational assets, and the details associated with their interconnectivity, communications, engagement, conformity, and exploitation must be well-managed (the micro-dynamic). Vividly, human intelligence/ consciousness sources are different from other natural/biological intelligence resources because of their consciousness intensity (possessing mindfulness capability). Concurrently, the collective intelligence of the organization is a significant latent impetus (for more effective self-transcending constructions) that can best be nurtured with orgmindfulness (the presence of a mindful culture — core of the supportive culture, and high intelligence-intelligence linkages are essential).

3.2 The Intelligence Spectrum and Consciousness

3.2.1 *The intelligence spectrum*

Vividly, intelligence is the most significant entity (asset) in the intelligent organization theory — **intelligence is the first inherent strengths of a human interacting agent**. On this planet, intelligence exists as a spectrum (perceives as a spectrum of phenomena associated with **stability-centricity**) — restricted by the two limits, varying from **proto-intelligence** to **human global collective intelligence** (the latter should be the upper limit but is currently at a very low level), the two extreme ends of the **intelligence spectrum** (see Figure 3.1). All other biological intelligence sources are engulfed in between. Concurrently, very different forms of **consciousness** emerge with respect to the level of

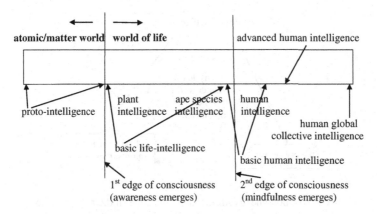

Figure 3.1 A simple illustration of the intelligence spectrum — from proto-intelligence to human global collective intelligence.

intelligence. Consciousness is confined only to the living world, and human consciousness is significantly different from all other levels of consciousness, in particular, due to the presence of **mindfulness**. The intelligence spectrum to be introduced is a simplified illustration that can support better subsequent analysis (see Figure 3.1).

In the atomic world, the proto-intelligence of atoms and molecules enhances their stability (a natural dynamic without external forces) — leading to the formation of the physical/matter world in this Universe (a phenomenon that defies universal expansion). Thus, intelligence is fundamentally stability-centric — and proto-intelligence is responsible for spontaneous 'ordering' of atoms and molecules. Atoms that are stable do not react, and other atoms react because they are not stable (see intelligence spectrum, stability-centric, **constructionist hypothesis**, and **broken symmetry** in Appendix 7). In this case, the intelligence and stability-centric relationship spontaneously enhances the formation of higher level physical structure (see Figure 3.2) — enforcing deeper structural stability. In this respect, the Universe is intrinsically embedded with intelligence (and consciousness) that led to the spontaneous formation of the physical world, and subsequently the living world.

These intelligence-driven processes progress up the matter, structural, and biological hierarchies, and eventually, consciousness emerges when

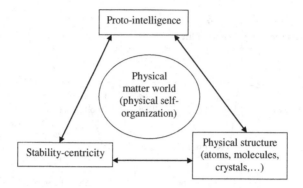

Figure 3.2 Spontaneous formation of structure in the matter world.

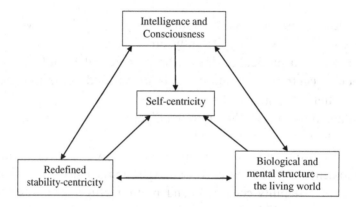

Figure 3.3 Emergent of conscious self-centricity in the living world.

moving across the boundary between the non-living and living worlds — **1st order consciousness** emerges starting with the mental function of **awareness**. Thus, awareness (externally focus) emerges from **basic life-intelligence** when crossing the **1st edge of consciousness** (see Figure 3.1). Trees and amoeba exist at the boundary of this space. Subsequently, varying degrees of **self-awareness** (internally focus) emerges too. In the world of life, a **2nd edge of consciousness** exists. Consciousness when crosses the 2nd edge, a second mental function, **mindfulness** (internally mind focus) surfaces — **2nd order consciousness** that emerges from **basic human intelligence**. To date, it appears that the function of **mindfulness is confined or apparent only in the human world**.

3.2.2 *Correlation between intelligence and consciousness*

Some details of the above spectrum and the correlation of intelligence and consciousness are summarized as follows:

- The width of the spectrum varies from proto-intelligence (at atomic level) to human global collective intelligence (the optimal intelligence state on this planet).
- The **1st edge of consciousness** is the boundary between the non-living and living world. (In the intelligent organization theory, it is believed that consciousness emerges from basic life-intelligence — that is, consciousness is confined only in the living world.) At this edge, low level awareness (basic reflexive abilities) similar to that of amoeba and plant emerges — **basic life-intelligence <=> 1st order consciousness <=> awareness**).
- Subsequently, with the formation of more sophisticated neural networks (especially with the development of the brain — see Appendix 5) in certain animal species, higher level intelligence, awareness (the ability of recognizing and responding to the changing environment, and the formation of colony or group), and self-awareness (recognizing the 'self') emerges.
- The **2nd edge of consciousness** is the boundary between humanity and all other animal species (due to the development of the fairly well-developed cerebral cortex in human beings — see Appendix 5). Upon crossing this edge, basic human intelligence enhances — encompassing the ability of creating of a **character set** — distinctly beyond the intelligence of all other animal species (see character set in Appendix 7 and Chapter 5). Concurrently, the emergent of the mental function of **mindfulness** (I exist) also becomes prominent [**basic human intelligence (higher nonlinearity and creativeness) => 2nd order consciousness => awareness, self-awareness, and mindfulness** (human beings were able to meditate even before the creation of a written language)].

- In the intelligent organization theory, it is specified and emphasized that **human intelligence is different from that of all other animal species because of its ability to create the character set.** In addition, **human consciousness is different from the consciousness of all other animal species because of the prominent presence of mindfulness** — the ability to observe and control the mental state of the thinking systems — linked to the α-state.

- It is highly significant to recognize that the human thinking systems are emotional systems that can be logical (see Chapter 5). Thus, human intelligence is a nonlinear entity in the dynamics of human organizations. Consequently, **human relationship is a highly nonlinear variable/parameter** (in this respect, human organizations are inherently nonlinear systems).

- Thus, mindfulness at both agent level (autopoiesis, self-centric, self-organizations, self-transcending constructions, and intelligent person), and orgmindfulness at organizational level (org-centric, mindful culture) must be better exploited by competitive organizations — for nurturing a higher level collective intelligence and collectiveness capacity (through better interconnectedness, communications, and engagement). Thus, balancing internal focus (orgmindfulness, local talents, employees) and external focus (foreign talents, customers) is a key necessity of the intelligent organization theory.

- The capability of the mindfulness of agents and the orgmindfulness of the system is substantially enhanced with **advanced human intelligence** that encompasses the characteristics of better interconnectivity, mass communications (self-organizing communications), utilizing a 'common' language, abstract concepts creation, exploiting unique nonlinear strategies, activating self-transcending constructions, and co-evolution — also associated with self-organizing capacity, emergence-intelligence capacity, and unifying capacity of the organization.

3.2.3 *Additional comprehension and perception of intelligence*

Thus, in the world of life, a spread of intelligence and consciousness exists, and that redefined system structure and dynamic, leading to competition (survival or elimination), evolution, and biological emergence. In general, lower level intelligence (basic life-intelligence) appears to be more linear and exhibits orderly behavior — hence, more predictable (due to its own capability and constraint). This portion of the spectrum (although, there is diversification) includes the intelligence of cells, organisms, plants, and certain species of insects/animals. Some insects can only survive in colony with a noticeable level of **swarm intelligence** — created from a group of basic life-intelligence sources (see swarm intelligence and collective intelligence in Appendix 7). However, they cannot survive for long once they venture out of the group. (Note that the gap between lower basic life-intelligence and collective basic life-intelligence (for instance, the intelligence of an ant versus the swarm intelligence of an ant colony) is relatively large. It also appears that the 'formation' of swarm intelligence is fairly linear and orderly.) Thus, in general, intrinsic basic life-intelligence can be defined as follows:

Basic Life-Intelligence

It can be perceived as a unique energy (a latent impetus) that emerges from biological organisms/species, in particular, those with a brain (at least containing a small collection of neurons) that allows them to evolve more sustainably through better awareness (basic consciousness) with enhanced survival and sensory ability/capability.

Apparently, the levels of intelligence of all other animal species are relatively low compared to human intelligence (**basic human intelligence — includes the abilities to create character sets and the emergent of mindfulness, and advanced human intelligence is able to conceive abstract concepts and engage in sophisticated mass communications with an integrated verbal and written language, as well as exploiting diversified technologies** that vividly distinguishes between human intelligence and all other animals intelligence). Thus, the human thinking systems (brains + minds) are the most intense intrinsic intelligence and consciousness (awareness, self-awareness, mindfulness) sources that have emerged on this planet (see Figure 3.4 and Chapters 4 to 6). In this respect, human intelligence can be perceived as follows:

Human Intelligence (I)

It is a unique energy/entity (an intense nonlinear latent impetus) that emerges from the human thinking systems (comprising basic human intelligence and advanced human intelligence). It possesses information processing, knowledge accumulation, learning, adaptation, and sophisticated decision-making capabilities. It is also the only type of intelligence that creates character sets and languages on this planet, and advanced human intelligence is capable of creating abstract conceptual knowledge and exploiting technologies. Overall, it is also responsible for nurturing a huge mental capacity, and intense consciousness (awareness, self-awareness, and mindfulness) in human agents (that is absent in other species).

Currently, in many human organizations not all the intelligence/consciousness sources are well-connected and/or activated near optimality — their **collective intelligence** capacity is poorly developed or under-utilized. For instance, business organizations are very much externally focused (**org-awareness** — customers, regulations), and have weaker emphasis on internal connectivity (**orgmindfulness** — employees, stakeholders). Thus, the current exploitation of awareness and mindfulness in human organizations is not balanced, and this resulted in leadership, governance, and management deficiencies/issues (see organizational justice and dialogue in Appendix 7). A common basic distortion manifested is **only if we know what we know**.

3.2.4 *Definition of consciousness and mindfulness*

The intelligent organization theory stipulated that consciousness exists only in the world of life — **consciousness is the second inherent strengths of a human interacting agent.** Human consciousness possesses two mental functions namely, awareness and self-awareness (with **mindfulness** at its core). Apparently, consciousness is the latent attributes

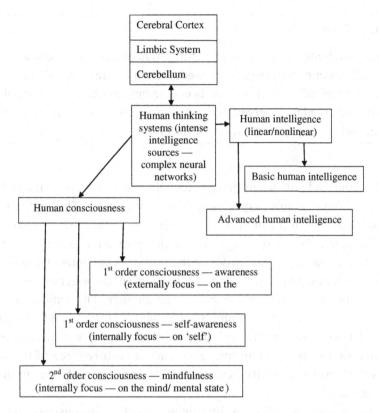

Figure 3.4 Human thinking systems: Sources of human intelligence and consciousness.

that clearly differentiates biological systems from physical/mechanical systems. (A mechanical system can be intelligent — artificial intelligence, but is not conscious.) Similarly, mindfulness is the unique mental ability that differentiates the human race from all other animal species. Thus, human consciousness and mindfulness can be defined as follows:

Human Consciousness (I)

It is the ability to recognize and observe the presence of changes in the environment and the mind (self). It possesses two mental functions, namely awareness (1st order consciousness — externally focus) and mindfulness (2nd order consciousness — internally focus — the latter only exists in human thinking. systems).

> **Mindfulness**
>
> It is an internally focusing mental ability/function of human consciousness (2nd order consciousness) created by human intense intelligence. It is the core of self-awareness, and is unique only to humanity. It enables the human mind to observe (and also control) its own (internal) mental state, and enhances the presence of the 'I'.

No other animal species have been able to activate mindfulness (for instance, no other animal species are able to meditate). This ability (can best be activated in the human mind when it is in the α-state) also enables the human mind to recognize that thoughts are quantized, that is, they exist as packages and only one thought package enters the mind at a time. Besides, two consequent packages that are entering in series may not be interlinked or related to one another. This unique ability confined to human beings alone must be better nurtured and exploited in human organizations through **orgmindfulness** (intense intelligence-intelligence linkages) by nurturing a **mindful culture** (core of the supportive culture) leading to the emergent of the **orgmind** (see orgmind in Appendix 7).

The deeper analysis on intelligence and consciousness clearly indicates that a new mindset that is beyond the Newtonian mindset and complexity mindset is essential for the continual existence of humanity in the current environment. Fundamentally, the recognition that human organizations are living intelligent systems (**intelligent complex adaptive systems — *i*CAS**) and not mechanistic systems enhances the significance and roles of intelligence/consciousness-centricity. In this respect, the emerging mindset is the **intelligence mindset**. Consequently, intense human intelligence and consciousness (awareness and mindfulness) which are the key assets of all human organizations (orgmindfulness, mindful culture) and their interacting agents must be the key focal points — the most valuable intangible assets (see Table 3.1). Thus, an **intelligence paradigm**, that concentrates on nurturing and exploiting an intelligence/consciousness-centric path and direction leading to

Table: 3.1   Some basic functions/characteristics initiated by human intelligence.

Some functions/characteristics that are initiated by human intelligence:

- Consciousness (awareness, mindfulness)
- Information processing
- Information decoding
- Creating/exploiting character set and language
- Learning (individual and group)
- Knowledge acquisition and accumulation
- Thinking, perception, and reasoning
- Problem solving and decision making
- Adaptation
- Autopoiesis and symbiosis (enhancing self-stability)
- Self-transcending constructions (enhancing self-stability, formation of localized space/ network)
- Evolving and co-evolving
- Emergence

achieving an **intelligence advantage** is crucial — the new sustainable competitive advantage.

3.3   The Emerging Intelligence Mindset

3.3.1   *The intelligence mindset and its key thinking*

Apparently, the above transformations in thinking are challenging, inevitable, and critical to all human organizations that are involved in the next round of competitions and existence. The rapidly changing and highly complex multi-levels/dimensions situations can only be better managed if human organizations are **organized around intelligence**, rather than around processes or functions. This new intelligence mindset is a necessity as the competitiveness and sustainability of humanity and its organizations is highly dependent on their levels of collective intelligence (intelligence-intelligence linkages) and **complexity-intelligence linkages**. Hence, managing and exploiting complexity and emergence in the human world is part of its complex adaptive dynamics. In this respect,

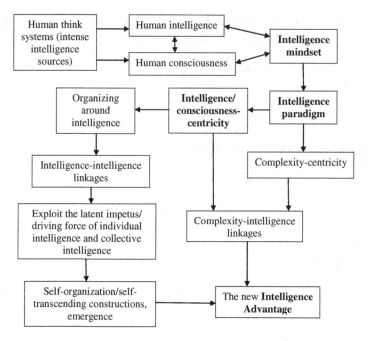

Figure 3.5 The intelligence mindset, intelligence paradigm, and the intelligence advantage.

nurturing an intelligence paradigm is critical, and a key reassurance to all human future endeavors. The new niche that maintains resilience and sustainability in the new competition is the **intelligence advantage** (see Figure 3.5).

Overall, the intelligence mindset subtly encompasses (a unique integration) part of the Newtonian mindset (orderly, linearity, determinism, predictability) and complexity mindset (complexity, nonlinearity, connectivity, interdependency, in-deterministic, unpredictability, autopoiesis, autocatalysis, self-organization, self-transcending constructions, constructionist hypothesis, emergent of consciousness, emergent of order), plus a special focus on all levels of intelligence (individual intrinsic intelligence, collective intelligence, latent intelligence). Hence, focusing on intelligence/consciousness-centricity, and exploring and exploiting intelligence-intelligence linkages, complexity-intelligence linkages, self-organizing networks, intelligence leadership, intelligence governance, and 'constructionist emergent of new order' are parts of the new thinking and strategy. Obviously, the current entrenched thinking confined to order and linearity alone is insufficient. The intelligence mindset can be summarized as follows:

The Intelligence Mindset

This new mindset primarily focuses on intelligence/consciousness-centricity (encompassing intelligence, awareness, mindfulness, collective intelligence, orgmindfulness, and org-awareness). It also encompasses the complexity mindset, and part of the Newtonian mindset — overall, emphasizing the presence, significance, and exploitation of intelligence and collective intelligence, co-existence of order and complexity, linearity and nonlinearity, intelligence-intelligence linkages, complexity-intelligence linkages, spaces of complexity, complex networks, and the constructionist emergent of new order (establishing the complexity-intelligence strategy).

3.3.2 *The intelligence paradigm and its new direction*

In this respect, a totally redefined paradigm is essential to understand, exploit, and survive in the new context — the intelligence paradigm. The new paradigm primarily focuses on engaging and optimal usage of intrinsic individual intelligence (intelligence-intelligence linkages), extracting/mining latent intelligence, orchestrating the right set of behavioral schemata, and nurturing collective intelligence (**collectiveness capacity**, **adaptive capacity**), reaping the best possible rewards from certain spaces of complexity (whenever possible, complexity-centric, complexity-intelligence linkages, elevating innovation and creativity), to achieve the organizational goals (stability-centricity).

Overall, the intelligence paradigm adopts and exploits the **complexity-intelligence strategy** that possesses several sub-components (including **organizing around intelligence**, and the **integrated deliberate and emergent strategy**) to nurture highly competitive intelligent organizations (*i*CAS) driven by highly *i*CAD — the latter will be further elaborated in later chapters.

In this respect, the intelligence paradigm is defined briefly as follows:

The Intelligence Paradigm

This new paradigm indicates the significance and direction of a highly intelligence/consciousness-centric path. Primarily, it focuses on organizing around intelligence (optimizing individual intrinsic intelligence, awareness, mindfulness, orgmindfulness, mindful culture, and nurturing collective intelligence and org-consciousness) — higher collective capacity and adaptive capacity. In addition, the new path is also complexity-centric, exploiting the co-existence of order and complexity (exploiting certain spaces of complexity, and making preparation for punctuation points). Overall, the holistic complexity-intelligence strategy adopted focuses on nurturing competitive *i*CAS (highly intelligent complex adaptive systems) that are driven by *i*CAD (highly *i*CAD) — higher self-organizing capacity, emergence-intelligence capacity, and unifying capacity.

3.3.3 *Integrating awareness and mindfulness: Nurturing orgmindfulness*

Apparently, the intelligence paradigm also places significant emphasis on the uniqueness and intensity of human consciousness. Associated with the above perception and discussion, the current humanity (especially, the generations Y and Z — employers and employees; teachers and students, leaders and non-actors) will have to better exploit the latent dimension of consciousness and its abilities.

The higher level of human awareness, self-awareness and **mindfulness** (the **core of self-awareness**) that emerge from human intelligence and consciousness (due to the better developed cerebral cortex in the human thinking systems — see Figure 3.4) can be better optimized (individually and collectively) with the following comprehension and approaches:

a. The human agents and their organizations that were once linear, orderly structured (at least perceived to be so), hierarchical, and deterministic have become more nonlinear, complex, and unpredictable due to 'raplexity', including changes in values and norms.
b. Human organizations that were once machine-like (mechanistic structure and predictable dynamic) have to be more mind-centric (intelligence/consciousness-centric).
c. The connectivity, engagement, interdependency among individuals, individuals and human organizations, as well as human organizations and their environment (the entire integration of Gaia) has increased substantially, leading to elevated uncertainty and fragility.
d. The two mental functions of awareness and mindfulness that emerge from human consciousness have a key role in the above changes, and they are equally significant. Although, to date the second function (orgmindfulness) has always been neglected in many human organizations. (The right hemisphere of the human brain is believed to be better at achieving mindfulness — see Appendix 5).
e. Thus, orgmindfulness (organization focusing internally on the mental states of the interacting agents) and the nurturing of a mindful culture is a vital possess for elevating the collective intelligence of the organization (see mental cohesion in Appendix 7). Collective intelligence is the key critical entity that latently orchestrates self-organization/self-transcending constructions, and is highly beneficial in the new competition — **collective intelligence is also the key primary strengths of any human organizations**.
f. Finally, the intense human intelligence/consciousness sources and other intangible assets, such as intellectual property (innovative knowledge, and mental capitals that are embedded in human thinking systems) are becoming much more valuable than traditional economic resources. Thus, being highly intelligence/consciousness-centric is a critical path.

***Summary*:** Localized versus global dynamics:

- (Awareness/self-awareness/mindfulness <=> orgmindfulness/ org-awareness) => autopoiesis versus symbiosis <=> independency versus interdependency <=> self-organization/self-transcending constructions (agents versus networks versus organization) <=> constructionist emergent of new order

3.3.4 *Some critical aspects of the new paradigmatic shift*

The intelligence paradigm perceived intelligence and consciousness as the most critical assets or entities. The fresh intelligence/consciousness-centric thinking indicates a fresh direction for individuals to lead, organize, strategize, manage, and survive more comfortably in the current and emerging environment. The critical aspects of the paradigmatic shift encompass the following recognitions:

a. Human organizations and its human thinking systems are intrinsic complex adaptive systems (living systems), and therefore the current hierarchical (control-oriented) leadership, governance, and management philosophy and practices must be transformed (beyond the contemporary stakeholder theory and hierarchical empowerment) to accommodate nonlinearity, complexity, learning, adaptation, intrinsic leadership, network-centric dynamic, self-powered self-organization, innovation and creativity, and other intelligence/consciousness-centric characteristics — overall, towards greater collectivity and a more **lateral and collective leadership** is essential (see Chapters 9 and10).

b. The mental state of the interacting agents in the organization must be allocated top priority (orgmindfulness). An effective relationship among the interacting agents (consensus, organizational justice) must be carefully cultivated, and constantly reinforced with by intelligence/ consciousness-centric thinking — that is, enhancing intelligence-intelligence linkages at all time, and balancing org-awareness and orgmindfulness is significant. (Currently, human beings have been handled as machine parts due to industrialization mindset.)

c. Human organizations must be nurtured and managed as highly intelligent biological beings (**intelligence/consciousness management** — see

Section 3.4), as intelligent human organizations must process high **collective intelligence** and **org-consciousness**, and behave like intelligent corporation beings.

d. In this respect, human organizations must be organized around intelligence — nurturing an intense collective intelligence source (**org-mind**) with optimal consciousness that is also supported by an equivalent of the central nervous system (a holistic intelligent biotic macro-structure) — achieving systemic transformation, and resulting in better structural and dynamic coherency.

e. New opportunities embedded in certain **spaces of high complexity** must be carefully explored and effectively exploited (changing uncertainties to new opportunities and niches — also towards better **risk management**) whenever possible. Concurrently, making preparation for the sudden appearance of **punctuation points** must be initiated (an **emergent strategist** and a redefined **futurist** — also towards better **crisis management** — see emergent strategy, futurology, and relativistic complexity in Appendix 7). The new advantage is the **intelligence advantage**.

3.4 Two Key Aspects of Intelligence/ Consciousness-Centricity

The above conceptualization has vividly indicated the significance and value of human intelligence/consciousness sources, and the intelligence and consciousness of every interacting agent has to be carefully or subtly activated, connected, and optimized. In this respect, the two key new crucial aspects are better **intelligence/consciousness management,** and nurturing an **intelligent biotic macro-structure** (systemic transformation).

3.4.1 *The necessity of intelligence/consciousness management*

The central theme of the intelligence paradigm indicates that the individual mind and intense human intelligence/consciousness (mindset and thinking) must be the center of concern, analysis, experimentation, and careful exploitation. Thus, effective intelligence/consciousness management is a significant activity and foundation of the intelligent organization

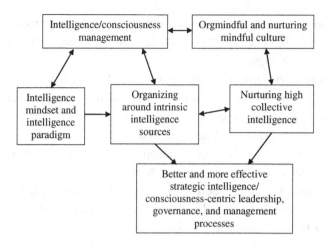

Figure 3.6 The primary focus of intelligence/consciousness management.

theory. This fresh nonlinear strategic thinking and new recognition clearly points towards the emergent of new intelligence/consciousness-centric approaches (illustrated in Figure 3.6).

The new priority for leading and managing human organizations is the better and more subtle management of the human thinking systems and their nonlinear behavior. The intrinsic intelligence, consciousness, and knowledge structures in the individual minds must be more optimally utilized by all farsighted organizations. Concurrently, their interconnectivity and engagement (effective intelligence-intelligence linkages) with the organization must be better comprehended and more efficiently utilized. Inevitably, intelligence/consciousness management is a new critical possess in human assets/resources management (human beings are more an asset rather than resource). This approach initiates the beginning of nurturing a mindful culture (core of a supportive culture) through orgmindfulness that focuses on the mental state of every human interacting agent, attempting to achieve higher mental cohesion. This approach will help to elevate the collective intelligence and collectiveness capacity of the organization, and will improve the overall organizational governance, strategic leadership, and management processes. (More details on intelligence/consciousness management will be introduced in subsequent chapters.)

3.4.2 *Systemic transformation: Towards an inherent intelligent biotic macro-structure*

The nurturing and subtle reforming (systemic transformation) of an **intelligent biotic macro-structure** (a macro structural framework similar to a highly intelligent biological entity with higher **structural capacity**) is another necessity in the new paradigm (better structural and dynamical coherency). Its presence also better facilitates intelligence/consciousness management (enhances information processing capacity, and towards a better global/holistic integration) — (see structural capacity in Appendix 7). The presence of the orgmind — the equivalent of a highly developed mind of a highly intelligent biological being (in particular, that of a human being) is an important component of an intelligent human organization (*i*CAS). It is a significant fraction of the source of collective intelligence (a vital latent impetus) that must be nurtured by the right interconnectivity, engagement, orgmindfulness, and a mindful culture.

In this respect, an **orgmind** (core of the intangible structure) and its collective intelligence and org-consciousness has to be nurtured in all intelligent human organizations to ensure better competitiveness and sustainability. It is from the orgmind and the **intangible deep structure** that the **physical structure** of the organization evolves (see Figure 3.7) — that is, it has a three-layer structure. Thus, in the new situation, leaders and managers of human organizations must examine and search beyond the physical structure. They must immerse themselves into the orgmind and intangible structure and their dynamics to better observe, understand, and exploit the mysterious power of intrinsic intelligence/ consciousness and collective intelligence/org-consciousness. The new macro-structure, an intelligent biotic complex adaptive structure, is more biological, and adaptive in nature.

As the new paradigm focuses on elevating collective intelligence by enhancing the quality of interconnectivity and engagement, and exploiting the bio-logic aspect of human organizations through orgmindfulness, inherently, group features such as organizational learning, corporate knowledge structure, adaptation, and emergence are highly significant and integrated characteristics. In this respect, an effective human organization

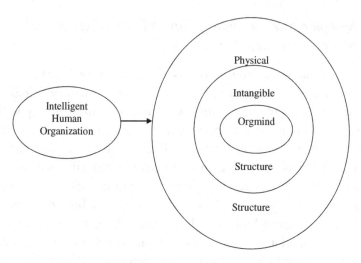

Figure 3.7 The simplified basic intelligent biotic macro-structure of an intelligent human organization with better complex adaptive ability.

in the new intelligence era has to be an intelligent complex adaptive system that can evolve, compete, and emerge successfully in a fast changing, complex, and nonlinear environment similar to any intelligent biological organisms competing in an eco-system with a biotic macro-structure. (Further illustrations on the intelligent biotic macro-structure model will be done in Chapters 4 and 6.)

3.5 Conclusion

This chapter establishes the basic conceptual foundation of intelligence and consciousness, and introduces a set of new attributes (establishing a foundation for further conceptual and applications analysis in subsequent chapters). It also illustrates that a paradigmatic shift in mindset is inevitable, and the new development has to be supported by redefined theory for strategic thinking, leadership, governance, management, and operations. The new theory introduced in this book embraces intelligence and consciousness as significant elementary entities in all human domains/ perspectives (social, economic, political and many other perspectives), activities, and their dynamics. Thus, a basic foundation of this theory (intelligent organization theory) focuses on the primary inherent strengths of human agents that is their intense and nonlinear intelligence and high level of consciousness (awareness and mindfulness). Apparently, intelligence and consciousness are the key attributes that have led humanity to its present stage of development.

In this respect, it is significant for all individuals who wish to be an effective member of the current/new global society and its organizations to comprehend and exploit such a theory. Fundamentally, this theory provides a more holistic, complete, and realistic view of human agents (human thinking systems) and their organizations, as well as their interactive dynamics. The basic path includes organizing around intelligence, better intelligence/consciousness management, and nurturing an organizational structure that resembles highly intelligent biological beings (intelligent biotic macro-structure). The basic goals are to achieve better integration, coherency, and synergy, so that the organization is more competitiveness, resilience and sustainability.

Therefore, leaders of human organizations, whether they are top business executives, political leaders, or key social/welfare/education administrators must nurture the intelligence mindset and exploit the intelligence paradigm to remain relevant and credible in the more complex and unpredictable future. The integrated intelligence/consciousness-centricity, complexity-centricity, and network-centricity is a new thinking or phenomenon that must be exploited with intense intelligence and consciousness (individually and collectively) — achieving a new niche known as intelligence advantage. A summary of the basic coverage on the intelligence mindset and intelligence paradigm is illustrated in Figure 3.8.

Summary: The new intelligence mindset, thinking, paths, directions, and certain key attributes involved.

* Intelligence mindset => intelligence paradigm => intelligence/consciousness-centricity => complexity-intelligence strategy => intelligence/consciousness management => organizing around intelligence => intelligence-intelligence linkage => orgmindfulness /mindful culture => orgmind => agent-agent/system micro-structure => interconnectivity/self-organizing communications/ engagement =>

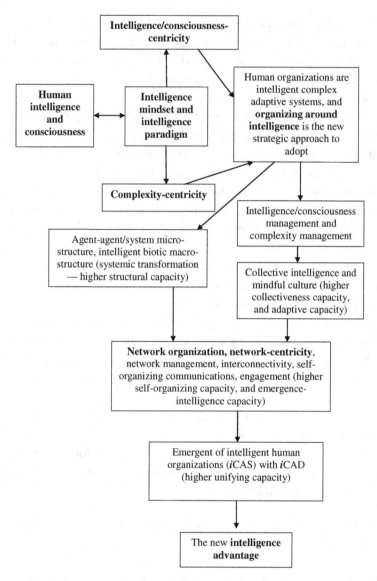

Figure 3.8 The intelligence mindset, paradigm, and structural and dynamical reforms in intelligent human organizations.

collective intelligence and collectiveness capacity => intelligent biotic macro-structure => better structural and dynamic coherency (structural capacity and adaptive capacity) => complexity-intelligence linkage => complexity-centricity => complexity management <=> complexity-intelligence linkage => co-existence order and complexity => spaces of complexity and punctuation points => => network-centricity => network management => small world networks => complex adaptive networks => self-organization/self-transcending constructions => self-organizing capacity and emergence-intelligence capacity => emergence => coherency and synergetic => *i*CAD and intelligent human organization (*i*CAS) => unifying capacity => mental cohesion => intelligence advantage

Aggregation of complex adaptive systems into a composite complex adaptive system is an effective way to open up new level of organization. The composite system then consists of adaptive agents constructing schemata to account for and deal with one another's behavior.

Murray Gell-Mann, *The Quark and the Jaguar*

Chapter 4

Multi-Layer Structure/Dynamic and Structural Capacity of Human Organizations

"The challenge is in the achieving and not the achievement"

"In complexity theory, the process of 'becoming' is more significant and domineering than the state of 'being'"

Summary

The inherent micro-structure (agent-agent/system) of human organizations has been introduced in Chapters 2 and 3. Fundamentally, human organizations are composite complex adaptive systems with human beings as interacting agents (each an intrinsic complex adaptive system). This chapter further analyzes the basic conceptual foundation of the multi-layer structure, including advantages of the intelligent biotic macro-structure (with inherent features similar to that of an intelligent biological being — a structural reform), and its unique and more integrative complex adaptive dynamic in intelligent human organizations (towards iCAD). The necessity of nurturing an intelligent biotic macro-structure with vital characteristics that better synchronize and enhance sophisticated information/knowledge-related activities is highly beneficial — achieving a higher structural capacity. Thus, the attributes, functions and higher structural capacity of the more intelligent biotic macro-structure can reinforced the competitiveness of any categories of human organizations extensively.

In this respect, connecting and engaging of intelligence/consciousness sources (individual and collective), organizing around intelligence, intelligence/consciousness management, and the intelligent biotic macro-structure are mutually enhancing (towards higher coherency). Apparently, being intelligence/consciousness-centric is a beneficial and critical activator (strategic foundation) of the intelligence paradigmatic shift. In the present context, the roles and integration of intelligence, information and knowledge, as well as nurturing a 'common' language and elevating coherency in human organizations (with respect to the macro-structure and micro-structure, as well as their higher collectiveness — collectiveness capacity) must be more deeply scrutinized and utilized. The presence and significance of the individual intelligence enhancer encompassing three entities namely, intelligence, knowledge, and theory in the human thinking systems, and the necessity of nurturing a similar and effective intelligence enhancer at organizational level are analyzed. Subsequently, the supporting roles and contributions of artificial intelligence systems are also examined.

In between the macro-structure and micro-structure are two meso-structures. In the intelligent organization theory, the complexity meso-structure encompasses spaces of complexity and punctuation points. In this respect, complexity is a highly significant focal point, and the exploitation of co-existence of order and complexity is a new necessity (complexity-centricity). Next, the network meso-structure encompassing complex network (network of networks) is also an inherent structure and dynamic in all human organizations. This meso-structure is briefly introduced, and will be more deeply analyzed with respect to governance (network-centricity, network governance).

Hence, it is crucial to lead and manage human organizations with a strategic approach that integrates the above multi-layer structure/dynamic at all time so that a higher structural capacity, collectiveness capacity, adaptive capacity, self-organizing capacity, and emergence-intelligence capacity can be nurtured. In the current highly competitive context, possessing these positive capabilities to elevate coherency and synergetic characteristics (including social consensus and the construal aspect) and dynamic is also highly crucial — a key focus of the complexity-intelligence strategy (towards achieving higher organizational mental cohesion). Hence, the significance and impact of nurturing intelligent human organizations with the complexity-intelligence-centric and network-centric approach that leads to the emergent of smarter evolvers and emergent strategists must be better understood and adopted. (The conceptual foundation on structural-dynamic coherency and synergy in intelligent human organizations developed in this chapter will be more deeply reviewed and exploited in later chapters.)

Keywords: Intelligent organization theory, organizing around intelligence, intelligence/consciousness sources, intelligence/consciousness management, intelligence capacity, agent-agent/system micro-structure, intelligent biotic macro-structure, human thinking system, consciousness, mindfulness, mindful culture, information, language, space of order, space of complexity, co-existence of order and complexity, butterfly effect, principle of locality, reductionism, nonlinearity, unpredictability, deliberate strategy, emergent strategy, smarter evolver, human intelligence, local space, complex network, physical symbol system, internalization, mental function, behavioral schemata, feedback loop, rugged landscape, self-organizing communications, autocatalysis, cascading effect, proto-intelligence, intense intelligence source, orgmind, intelligence web, environment scanning and responding component, physical structure, engagement, theory, analytical lens, mental compass, knowledge structure, deterministic chaos, org-neuron, natural node, artificial node, remote sensory node, composite complex adaptive systems, 'common' language, dialogue, collective intelligence, swarm intelligence, artificial intelligence systems, individual intelligence enhancer, organizational intelligence enhancer, theory/philosophy, knowledge structure, orgmindfulness, thought technology, dialogue, emergent strategist, complexity meso-structure, network meso-structure, complexity management, network management, Cambrian explosion, natural selection, exaptation, principle of locality, coherency, synergetics, mental cohesion, latent leadership, self-organizing governance, futurology, uncertainty, intelligent corporate being, structural capacity, adaptive capacity, collectiveness capacity, economic capacity, relational capacity, self-organizing capacity, emergence-intelligence capacity, intelligence advantage, complexity-intelligence strategy, Newtonian mindset and intelligence mindset.

4.1 Introduction: The World of Intelligent Structure

In both the physical matter world and the biological world, intelligence, stability, and structure are inherently inter-related. A structure with better structural capacity is more stable, and it is established with its associated intelligence. In the physical world, many fascinating structures have been observed. In the living world, some structures are fairly abstract — including presence of synergetic effects and new attributes (constructionist). The latter impact is even more apparent in the human world, including the emergent of mindfulness in human beings.

4.1.1 *The multi-layer structure of intelligent human organizations*

Fundamentally, human organizations are **composite complex adaptive systems** with human beings (each a complex adaptive systems) as basic entities/agents — the **agent-agent/system micro-structure** model. The interactive dynamic is complex and adaptive, but can be highly **sensitive dependence on initial conditions (butterfly effect)**, as a small local event can be amplified into system/global change. At the macro level, many human organizations are structured based on functions and processes — the Newtonian-oriented and machine-like structure (reductionism, orderly, control, determinism, predictable). With this approach, it is the physical structure of the organization that determines its dynamics and the intangible structure (a source of the current constraint, controversy, and incoherency). Thus, nurturing a more constructive and coherent **intelligent biotic macro-structure** (with natural and artificial nodes) is essential.

In the intelligent organization theory, an ideal macro-structure is one that is similar to an intelligent biological being. The presence of an **orgmind** is crucial — the vital source of collective intelligence and org-consciousness. Thus, a deeper analysis on the roles and significance, and the details of nurturing an intelligent-centric biotic macro-structure are highly beneficial — a fundamental structure that focuses on intelligence, enhances engagement and communications, facilitates better information processing and knowledge acquisition/accumulation/exploitation, and higher coherency. Basically, the macro-structure must encompass the three-layer inherent structure namely, the orgmind, **intangible structure**, and **physical structure**.

In addition, two **meso-structures** involving integrated spaces of order and spaces of complexity, and complex networks (network of networks) are also inherent parts of human organizations. They are not well-understood and causing incoherency, Thus, the meso-structures must be better integrated and exploited. In this case, it is recognized that human

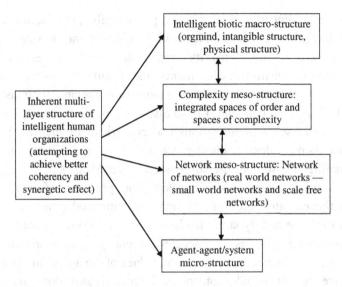

Figure 4.1 The multi-level structure of intelligent human organizations.

organizations inherently possess a multi-layer structure namely, agent-agent/system micro-structure, intelligent biotic macro-structure, complexity meso-structure, and network meso-structure (see Figure 4.1) that must be better comprehended, explored, and exploited concurrently (holistically) with higher synergy. Thus, in reality, most competitive human organizations encompass a large numbers of parts (agents, local spaces/networks, and network of networks) resulting in a complex environment that required redefined leadership, governance, and management. The latter must be intelligence/consciousness-centric (intelligence-intelligence linkages), complexity-centric (complexity-intelligence linkages), and network-centric (unifying).

4.1.2 *Criticality for a more adaptive structure and dynamic*

Vividly, a current weak alignment is that the existing structure and dynamics (based on the thinking and concepts of the design paradigm — hierarchical, functionality, machine-like, high linearity, command and control, forecasting) of most human organizations are 'artificially' created or enforced. This is due to tremendous influences and inputs from the **exact**

sciences (order, linearity, determinism, predictability, precise mathematical modeling). In general, the **Newtonian mindset** and its linear-centric paradigm have served humanity 'reasonably well' to certain extent (despite certain constraints, discontents, and disputes). However, in some cases, extreme practices, for instance managing human agents as slaves (agents with no independency) have also been unethically implemented (still present in some organizations and countries). In such an environment, there is no collective intelligence in the system — in fact, the individual intelligence sources are suppressed or deactivated.

Within the traditional environment, the presence of incoherency between the existing 'enforced' formal structure and dynamic and the inherent structure and dynamic leads to the result of low social conformity, as well as other issues. The accelerated changing environment of the systems, and modified expectations and values of the agents are perceived as negative factors. In addition, many human organizations are merely focusing on global/organizational interests and objectives (short-term goals), and minimal emphasis or concern is placed on the interacting agents (employees, citizens), or in general human existence (a longer-term perspective). Therefore, a key crucial weakness for collective survival in the present organizations and their environment is as follows:

A Key Fundamental Problem:

There is insufficient focus on the human intelligence/consciousness sources and expectations/values/state of the human agents that form the organization; and there is a significant deficiency in complexity comprehension, management, and innovative exploitation.

The intelligent organization theory supported by complexity theory is a domain that better unite the humanities (sociology, economics, political science — any domains involving human interactions) and the 'newer' sciences — that provides a conceptual foundation to better manage the above problems (through effective integration of **intelligence/consciousness sources,** and exploiting the **co-existence of order and complexity**). In general, the theory offers a more logical and 'realistic' explanation, balancing, decision making, and action for human organizations (org-centricity, competitiveness, resilience, sustainability), as well as their agents (self-centricity, stability-centricity), in aspects that are ambiguous with the traditional theories and the human organizational operating environment. In particular, the intelligent organization theory is totally anthropo-centric — dealing only with systems/organizations with human beings as agents (especially, focusing on the attributes that are unique to humanity).

As indicated in the earlier, the theory emphasizes that human organizations are a collection of interacting human agents (micro-structure — agent-agent/system interacting structure), and are inherently complex adaptive systems. In many present cases, the irony is that the complex adaptive characteristic is suppressed leading to increase in internal dysfunctional issues. To begin with, the human **mind (human thinking systems)** and the 'formation' (nurturing) of the orgmind should be the 'epicenter' of all human setups. Human thinking systems are intrinsic complex adaptive systems, and all human organizations and their orgmind are composite complex adaptive systems. With this thinking, elevating **adaptive capacity** is vital, and the first focal point is as follows:

Focus 1:

The first primary paradigmatic shift initiated by the intelligent organization theory is concentrating on emphasizing, nurturing, and implementing intelligence/consciousness-centricity.

Next, the basic entities (interacting agents) of these organizations, human beings (human thinking systems — each embedding a changing **behavioral schemata**), interact with one another to form **local spaces** (**networks** — formal and informal), and **feedback loops** (local and global, negative or positive — see feedback and circular causation in Appendix 7), that influence the entire organization, as well as the environmental composite system — for instance, an economy is the ecological system of business organizations. In this situation, any one agent/organization can have a direct or indirect influence on another agent/organization — that is, possesses the ability to change the **rugged landscape**. Thus, the overall commitment and coherency of integrating agents and networks is crucial, and its constructiveness is closely linked to the leadership, governance, and management of the organization (see Chapters 9 and 10).

For instance, the influence from a message communicated between agents is under-reacted or over-reacted upon (see autocatalysis, cascading effect, and self-organizing communications in Appendix 7). Thus, human group behavior is not simply the sum of the individual behavior (synergetic). Hence, the dynamic and the outcomes of human (organizational) interactions include a highly complex nonlinear dimension. In this case, a network/cluster behavior and the organizational collective behavior may not be coherent. Thus, the ability to manage the multi-level structure and dynamic well is critical — collectiveness capacity. Therefore, possessing the next focal point is crucial:

Focus 2:

The paradigmatic shift must also focus on emphasizing, nurturing, implementing, and exploiting network-centricity and complexity-centricity concurrently — fundamentally encompassing the integrated exploitation of the inherent co-existence of order and complexity, and inter connectivity and interdependency.

Inevitably, in the consolidating knowledge-intensive environment, human organizations must behave and evolve (and manage) as **intelligent organizational beings**. (There is a high positive correlation between higher intelligence and intense knowledge usage.) Similar to highly intelligent biological entities, human organizations must also embrace the abilities of learning, adapting, evolving, and competing. The intrinsic impetus driving the above dynamic is intelligence/consciousness (individual and collective). In this aspect, the unique human intelligence is manifested as sophisticated information processing and communicating abilities, and knowledge acquisition capacity — highly intensified by the presence of a written language, and the rapid development of digital/wireless media technology. Consequently, a deeper understanding of intelligence/consciousness sources, intelligence-intelligence linkages, data collection, information processing and communications, and formation of knowledge structure is a key to understanding the nurturing of an orgmind. In this respect, the presence of an intelligent biotic macro-structure is beneficial, and comprehending how it assists in elevating **structural capacity** is vital. Thus, the third essential focal point is as follows:

Focus 3:

In the present context, **organizing around intelligence** for the better nurturing of an intelligent biotic macro-structure (higher structural capacity and adaptive capacity, and structural-dynamic coherency) with quality interconnectivity, information processing, learning, and knowledge acquisition capabilities; structuring and exploitation abilities [encompassing an orgmind (an intense collective intelligence source), a well-interconnected intelligence web (equivalent to the central nervous system), and an environmental scanning and responding component (equivalent of the sensory system)], with an underlying structure comparable to the biological neural networks supporting its strategic activities, is the third focal point.

4.1.3 *Different levels of organizational intelligence*

Historically, human organizations/systems (civilizations, empires, nations, tribal villages, businesses) with varying collective intelligence had existed. An observation of current human organizations also reveals that there is a significant diversification in the collective intelligence of the organizations. A beneficial guide is to categorize human organizations based on their collective intelligence that reveals the niches and competitive abilities of these organizations with respect to the rapid changing environment or rugged landscape. Although intelligence is manifested as a continuous spectrum in nature, and intangible, constructing a simple and discrete conceptual structure containing different collective intelligence levels provides a model that renders the objective for analysis and nurturing intelligent human systems more comprehensible. In this chapter, a four-level structure/model is conceived, with each level defined by certain unique characteristics is as follows:

a. Level 0 — Organizational Intelligence: Slavery

A human organization at this level/band literally has no collective intelligence (extreme dictatorship). To a great extent, a business organization operating at this level is only capable of economic production and nothing beyond. It has no intelligence changing or enhancing capability and no environment scanning and responding component. It is a non-thinking, purely mechanistic system. It behaves like a pathetic group of slaves (for instance, in ancient Egypt or even illegal factories in certain countries) where agents' intelligence is totally controlled and suppressed. As far as the human intelligence domain is concerned, the system is dumb (inhumane). A mechanical machine exists at an extreme end of this state.

b. Level I — Organizational Intelligence: Instinctive

Besides focusing on its primary functions, for instance, economic production, a system in this case is capable of sensing simple changes in the environment (low awareness exists), such as changes in demand, and responds by varying the quantity of its output — manifesting minimal biological characteristics. The behavior of such a system is instinctive. Its level of intelligence is low (within basic life-intelligence band). Some business organizations, at the moment, exist in this state, similar to plants (that turn according to the direction of the light rays) in an ecological system. Historically, colonies were governed/'constructed' intentionally (biologically) in this manner too — no innovation is required as it is perceived as contradicting or destructive (for instance, colonists are educated 'just enough' to perform their role). Consequently, there is not much 'mobility' in this state.

c. Level II — Organizational Intelligence: Survival Seeking and Adaptive

A system can be classified in this category if an attempt has been made to improve its environment scanning and responding component (higher awareness). Such a system is also aware of the significance of having a well-established intelligence web. It is better informed, increasingly reactive to changes, and possesses assimilated learning and adaptive capabilities. In this case, the presence of collective intelligence is 'observed'. It is a mobile and competitive intelligent being. Such a system can diversify, 'migrate' and have 'offspring' (subsidiary). However, its thinking system (organizational neural networks) is not fully developed or well-integrated. Many current human organizations exist in this state, including developed and certain developing countries.

d. Level III — Organizational Intelligence: Highly Intelligent and Innovative

In addition to features specified in level II, a human organization in this category possesses multi-layer structure, including an intelligent biotic macro-structure (similar to an intelligent biological being and beyond) encompassing sophisticated networks, and driven by an intelligent complex adaptive dynamic (*i*CAD). It is highly reactive, as well as proactive to the changing environment. In addition, it is intelligent enough to influence the environment to enhance its competitiveness and existence. Whenever possible and necessary, this option is exercised. Thus, existing in this state, the system possesses its own orgmind with intense collective intelligence, well-established intelligence web and networks integration, and behaves as a highly intelligent biological being (encompassing effective and adaptive leadership, governance, strategy, and management). Thus, the presence of high organizational awareness and orgmindfulness is highly visible — presence of stability-centricity at all levels. The organization is also continuously learning, adapting, and highly innovative. This is the 'conceptual ideal state' (a 'dynamical' ideal intelligent human organization model) that the intelligent organization theory focuses on when exploiting the complexity-intelligence strategy. However, this 'conceptual ideal state' is also constantly changing (upgrading — new emergent of order)

Hence, the intelligent organization theory concentrates on nurturing level III organizations — encompassing and optimizing the characteristics/properties of the elementary entities/agents, and the structure, characteristics, and dynamics (including leadership, governance, strategy, and management) of the system. A balanced inward and outward (ambidexterity) focusing strategic approach is a key necessity — that is, both the interest of the agents and the organization must be well-managed. However, this approach is not possible without the recognition, exploration, and exploitation of raplexity, and intense practices of **intelligence/consciousness management** (in particular, organizing around intelligence), **complexity management** (adopting an integrated deliberate and emergent approach), and **network management (lateral/collective leadership, self-organizing governance**, unifying capability, and holistic coherency). Concurrently, nurturing and exploiting the multi-layer structure and its unifying dynamics provides the initial foundation for nurturing the new **intelligence advantage** — 'something that is inherent but has not been noticed or explicitly exploited'.

4.2 Conceptual Foundation of the Intelligent Biotic Macro-Structure Model

4.2.1 *Human intelligence, consciousness and their critical traits*

Intelligence is the primary entity that enables a biological being to enhance its adaptive capacity, to compete for survival, to undergo evolution, and to save itself and its species from extinction. Thus, the presence of intelligence allows the organism/species to interact more constructively with its environment, and to make adjustments to itself — awareness and self-awareness. The act of adaptation, evolution, and emergence is a key to survival in nature. Consequently, the same basic principles will also ensure that human organizations (composite complex adaptive systems) survive and compete better in the knowledge-based economy. On a broader perspective, humanity must be constantly reflected upon and exploited all the five core properties of complexity theory namely, consciousness, complexity, connectivity, dissipation, and emergence, whenever necessary. This set of five properties is the fundamental stratum of the new complexity thinking, as well as the intelligence paradigm.

So, what is intelligence? Basically, intelligence is a mental ability (an intrinsic latent impetus); at a higher level it is the power of perceiving, learning, comprehending, exploring, and strategizing — and even 'creating' (the creation of sophisticated equipment/technology and the character set — unique to humanity). Subsequently, decision making and action will be activated, if necessary. Such a definition of intelligence is closely associated with stability-centricity. It may be interesting to determine at what level of intelligence human consciousness emerges. This is a puzzle of the mind that the mind itself cannot resolve explicitly. It is a mystery that has pre-occupied some of the best minds for centuries. A school of thought believes that this mystery can never be resolved because it is beyond the capability of a physical network (neural network) that possesses the order of billions of neurons. It is a structural constraint. Perhaps, a multi-trillion neural network is required to unveil the secret more accurately. However, the intelligent organization theory 'assumes' that consciousness is only associated with life — the living world, starting with basic life-intelligence. And human consciousness is different from other highly developed biological species because of the presence of **mindfulness** — the 2nd order consciousness (see Chapter 3).

Thus, in the intelligent organization theory, intelligence is conceptually perceived as an intangible entity similar to energy in the sciences and technologies. It emerges intrinsically from biological structures or neural networks that contain neurons. Intelligence is invisible, intangible, and at the moment its capacity is not easily quantifiable. But its presence can be felt. Hence, its status is similar to energy a century ago. It is the existence of intelligence as an entity that enables intelligent traits to be manifested. It is the presence of this intangible entity (in particular, advanced human intelligence) that allows intelligent mental abilities such as information processing, knowledge acquisition and structuring, perception, and decision making to be manifested or executed. The **economic capability** of a human being is also fueled by the same entity — there is no other species that have to work throughout their life to accumulate wealth for survival (weakness of being too intelligence?). In this respect, intelligence and all intelligence/consciousness sources in human organizations must be carefully managed (that is, well-strategized intelligence/consciousness management is critical). The existence and emergence of these fundamental entities from both agents and organizations is stated as the first few axioms of the theory.

Axiom I — Individual intelligence

There exists an intangible entity known as intelligence in all human beings (intense intelligence sources) that provides the fundamental driving force for all their cognition/mental functions, and other associated activities.

Axiom Ia — Collective intelligence

There exists an intangible entity known as collective intelligence (could be nurtured from a 'collection' of human agents — involving interconnectivity, communications, engagement, networking, interdependency, coherency, synergy) in intelligent human organizations that provides the fundamental driving force (latent impetus — self-organization/ self-transcending constructions) for all their cognition/mental functions, and other associated activities (leadership, governance, strategy, and management).

Axiom II — Individual consciousness

There exists an intangible entity known as consciousness [awareness (internally focus), and mindfulness (externally focus)] in all human beings that elevates recognition of environmental changes, and also facilitate the observation of mental states of the human thinking systems — self (including 2nd order consciousness — unique to humanity).

Axiom IIa — Org-consciousness

There exists an intangible entity known as org-consciousness [org-awareness (externally focus — present in most competitive organizations), and orgmindfulness (internally focus — minimal or absent in most current human organizations)] in intelligent human organizations that elevates and redefines the intensity and quality of collective intelligence (different from swarm intelligence) — in particular, due to the presence of orgmindfulness (2nd order consciousness) leading to better organizational mental cohesion.

4.2.2 *Nurturing the org-brain/orgmind and intelligence web*

Vividly, there exists a close relationship between intelligence and consciousness. However, the exact formula of the relationship is unknown (see 'physics and consciousness' in Appendix 5). As higher levels consciousness is associated with higher levels intelligence, the intense intelligence sources in a human organization are highly significant, and must be utilized coherently (intense intelligence-intelligence linkages). A well-integrated intense intelligence sources (intangible connectivity) is needed to generate higher levels collective intelligence and organizational consciousness (significance of **orgmindfulness** and the **mindful culture**). Inevitably, a dense and well-connected 'organizational neural network' with an enormous number of '**org-neurons**' (human thinking systems are organizational neurons) must be nurtured to better explore and exploit complex phenomena.

In this respect, the org-brain (a self-organizing and integrated collective intelligence source, although, not physically connected) must be able to 'project' an effective orgmind (with appropriate interconnectivity, engagement, and quality) which is reflected by the intensity of its collective intelligence. Thus, it greatly depends on the quality coherency of the 'org-neural network'. The above recognition leads to the first postulation of the intelligent biotic macro-structure — the presence of the org-brain, leading to the emergent of the orgmind.

Postulate I

A necessary condition for higher levels collective intelligence and organizational consciousness (org-awareness and orgmindfulness) to exist (in an organization) is a sufficiently intense collective intelligence source must be nurtured — the presence of the org-brain and an orgmind.

The absence of the intense source indicates the absence of human-level or 2nd order consciousness (in particular, the absence of mindfulness). A feeble source is not able to generate the same level of consciousness. Lower level consciousness, mainly raw sensations or qualia are not very useful by themselves (with respect to human learning, economic, social, adaptive, and creative activities). In this respect, a colony of ants is only an intelligence web, and its activities can never flourish beyond its present status, unless an intense (collective) intelligence source emerges — thus, a significant difference between swarm intelligence and human collective intelligence exists. The weakly ('bio-chemical') connected network (without the presence of a language) of an ant nest is not sufficiently intense.

The structure is inherent, hierarchical and rigid, and there is no social mobility. In this respect, the 'entity' that connects the web also determines its level of collective intelligence. This recognition is stipulated as the second postulate.

Postulate II

The presence of an intelligence web is a necessary but not a sufficient condition for generating higher levels mental activities, and second-order consciousness. However, its presence is significant for a more holistic connectivity and engagement of the organization if the (collective) intense source is already present.

In this respect, the presence of an intelligence web in a living organism is significant because it is this internal network (comparable to the **central nervous system**) which allows intelligence (intelligent signals) to be transmitted from the intense intelligence source to the other parts of the organism, and vice versa. Such a web is also an internal information action and reaction system. It forms a vital communication structure within all intelligent beings. In this case, local spaces or networks (complex networks) in human organizations can be perceived as vital organs in a biological structure (see complex networks in Appendix 7).

Similar to the org-brain, the tangible components of the intelligent web form a complex network that supports the communications of information, engagement, decisions, and other intelligent-related entities. Basically, a network comprises intelligent nodes and connections (links) that can be both natural (human thinking systems) and constructed (artificial nodes) — see network theory in Appendix 7. Therefore, the intelligent web can be expanded artificially. In human organizations, knowledge bases and other artificial intelligent systems are also part of this web. The manner in which the natural nodes communicate among themselves, the types of information that flow between any two nodes, the effectiveness and efficiency of the network, and ultimately the level of intelligence of the web, are some major concerns when nurturing this internal web structure — the level of quality, and extent of coherency and synergy is critical.

In the current context, the interactive dynamic of intelligence web and orgmind in many human organizations (including nations and corporations) are increasingly manifesting different micro-level activities. This emerging phenomenon is escalating incoherency within the organizational structure. Thus, there is an elevating need to redefine the current leadership and governance of the organizations (see Chapters 9 and 10).

4.2.3 *Presence and roles of the environment scanning and responding subsystem*

A significant extension of the micro-structure is the presence of an **environment scanning and responding component/subsystem** (sensory subsystem) — providing external connectivity and increasing the org-awareness of the organization (the presence of sensory nodes is vital). Any intelligent system that scans, learns, adapts, and evolves must possess such a component — in particular, the visual and audio capabilities. The awareness of the environment is vital for better sustainability. Otherwise, it is literally 'dead', and its consciousness does not exist — no or low awareness, such as an amoeba. At the extreme, it is then no different from a crystal or a snowflake that contains only proto-intelligence. This requirement indicates that a system is highly intelligent only if it is open and continuously interacting with its environment — links to the futuristic attribute. Although, it has been stated earlier that highly intelligent beings must highly internal focus — do lots of internal searches (mindful/orgmindful).

The environment scanning and responding component of the biotic macro-structure must possess certain characteristics before it can be regarded as functioning intelligently. Some of the basic essential features include the following abilities:

a. To scan and detect environmental signals coming from environmental targets — also performing the data collection function of an early warning system.
b. To process the environmental signals locally or to transmit them to the (collective) intense intelligence source for processing and decision

making — that is, it must be well-integrated with the org-brain and intelligence web.

c. To respond well to the environmental signals — highly reactive and intelligent.

d. To introduce changes, and thus have the ability to influence the environmental targets — proactive.

e. Conceptually (in general), this subsystem must possess the ability of recognizing changes in the rugged landscape, and also assist the organization to introduce changes to the external landscape.

With respect to a business organization, some environmental targets are its customers, suppliers, competitors, and related government institutions. The environmental functions are to detect, evaluate, respond, and change. And the target functions include sensing, influencing, buying, selling, competing, strategizing, and entering into an alliance with another organization.

Thus, the third postulate of the model that captures the existence of the environment interacting component as an important subsystem of an intelligent organization is listed below:

Postulate III

The presence of an environment scanning and responding component is a necessary and critical requirement for the continuous survival and evolution of an intelligent human organization (especially, in a fast changing environment) — thus, it is associated with its levels of organizational consciousness, and determines its competitive advantage (first mover advantage, intelligence advantage), and its sustainability in the ecological system (economy, humanity, Gaia).

4.2.4 *Emergence of the basic intelligent physical macro-structure*

The dynamic involved in the nurturing of the intelligent biotic macro-structure discussed above can be highly complex and time consuming.

It involves continuous intangible–tangible interactions, and an emergent from the intangible to the tangible. It will also involve unique leadership abilities and governance characteristics that encompass different capacities to handle individuals, networks, and organizational differences. In particular, it is beneficial to possess a well-developed physical structure — emerging from the intangible structure with higher coherency. Consequently, it is significant that an intelligent human organization must possess the following three physical sub-features at all time (see Figure 4.2):

a. An intense collective intelligence source (org-brain) — a dense and well-connected human neural network, with each individual intrinsic intense intelligence source acting as an organizational neuron (decision-making node) that is well-integrated in certain respect.

b. An intelligence web that spreads and permeates the entire organization (equivalent to the central nervous system with information processing nodes) — a relatively less tense human neural complex network, that is, encompassing network of networks (formal and informal) — similar to the central nervous system and biological organ networks.

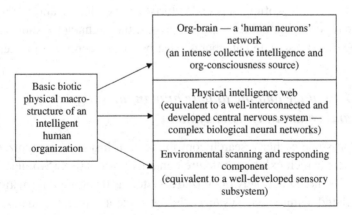

Figure 4.2   Components of the basic physical biotic macro-structure of an intelligent human organization for better intelligence and information exploitation.

c. An environment scanning and responding component encompassing organizational neurons with specialized ability (equivalent to a well-developed sensory subsystem with sophisticated input and output abilities — including visual, audio, and information processing capabilities).

4.3 Conceptual Foundation of the Intelligent Organization Dynamics

Concurrent to the presence of an intelligent macro-structure (intangible and tangible/physical), the dynamic of an intelligent organization must also manifest intense intelligence/consciousness-centricity (high collective intelligence and org-consciousness) in order to achieve better coherency and the synergetic effect. It is interesting to recognize some exceptional special abilities that contribute to the uniqueness of intelligent complex adaptive human dynamics — in particular, mindfulness, orgmindfulness, mindful culture, and 'feeling' system that can elevate human social conformity and mental cohesion. These special abilities that are confined to humanity alone enable human beings to emerge as the most prominent and dominant species on this planet — also note the concept of Malthusian catastrophe (**Thomas Malthus**, 1766–1834) — see Appendix 7. Very often, the characteristics mentioned above must be more 'cautiously' or subtly exploited. Thus, these characteristics, as well as some other associated attributes must be more deeply comprehended.

4.3.1 *Language and the unique human thinking and communications dynamic*

Based on some earlier research contributions, it has been recognized that any system which exhibits structure contains information (**Stonier**, 1990, 1992). The more intricately organized a system is the more information has accumulated within that system. This statement stipulates that a more 'organized' system contains more structured information or knowledge (a set of accumulated information with established relationships), and hence is embedded with a higher level of intelligence, and is generally more robust. As indicated in earlier chapters, a piece of crystal contains proto-intelligence but it is non-living. An ant colony is an intelligence web, and an ant cannot survive on its own — that is, its agents are not sufficiently intelligent for self-independency. However, a human being that possesses an intense intelligence source (complex neural networks) has the capability of creating high consciousness. Hence, the human mental space is unique, complex, and abstract. Very often, it is supported by cognition that has better capability of individual learning, adaptation, and survival.

Information is derived from data. Under any circumstances, data are useful only with respect to a context (as well as the presence of a user/decoder), that is, data must be transformed into useful information (with attached value) when the necessity for consumption arises (even if it is a one-to-one transformation). The ways in which a set of information is structured, communicated, and utilized further determine its usefulness. Besides, certain relationships must be established between a new set of information and an existing knowledge structure. When a set of information is consumed, the knowledge structure is altered, and **internalization** is said to have taken place in the human thinking system. In the human world, data (see **character set** in Appendix 7 and Chapter 5 that greatly redefined data) and information are entities emerging from a **physical symbol system**, and they collectively form a language.

Underlying and quietly forging the unique thinking processes of a human being is the presence of such a language. Without the existence of a language (especially the written form), human thinking activities would be simplistic, and human civilizations would not have flourished to their present level of sophistication. It is been stated by **Albert Einstein** (1879–1955) that 'without language our mental capacities would be poor indeed, comparable to those of the higher animals' (**Einstein**, 1954, p. 13). The processing of pictorial signals and audio/sound signals would not have the same level of conceptualization, dynamism, connectivity, and depth as manipulating a physical symbol system — a complex written language. Even a verbal language is simplistic, and communications of knowledge from one generation to another may not be complete or permanent. In addition, there is an association between the density of neurons present within an intelligence source, and its ability to manipulate and to create abstract concepts and intelligence/complexity strategy (the level of development of the cerebral cortex, a significant threshold — see Appendix 5). Therefore, another definition of intelligence is as follows:

Unique Intense Human Intelligence (II)

Human intelligence that emerges with the more advanced development of the cerebral cortex possesses the ability to conceptualize a physical symbol set that leads to the emergence of a sophisticated written language. The presence of such a language facilitates abstract perception and conceptualization, more in-depth engagement (especially, mental) and communications, and the storage of knowledge externally. This ability is unique to humanity. (No other species has ever created a physical symbol set.) It is the crossing of this threshold (a significant phase change) that enables human beings to exist in its present state (from jungle to cosmopolitan city with an intense exploitation of technologies) on this planet.

Apparently, the development of a language is a sophisticated process. During initial usage, a piece of information is simply expressed as a linear combination of some characters from a physical symbol system (the latter is continuously expanding). Capturing an event is slightly more complex. However, visualizing and communicating an abstract concept is a highly nonlinear and complex process. If the language used to transmit the concept is linear, some richness in ideas may be lost during communications. 'A language rooted in a linear, mechanistic view of the Universe creates different actions and opportunities from a language that emerges from a complex intelligent view of the Universe' (**Michael McMaster**, 1996, p. 32). In fact, the relationships among information, knowledge, concept, and the language used to create and communicate them are intriguing, if not mystical. Very often, masters speak differently from others in their discipline. When people attain a certain level of mastery, it is not merely their words that are different, but also the abstract meaning of their words, and their understanding of their existence that contributes the depth of the conceptual world. For instance, a single word or a short collection of words (a brief statement) can convey a very deep thought or 'latent' meaning. This ability confirms the high nonlinearity of human intelligence/

consciousness, and the unique relationship between (abstract) knowledge and a ('deep') language.

In a human organization, language is also the medium that helps to facilitate the connectivity and dynamic of the intangible component of the intelligent structure. It penetrates and flows through the web, and binds the organization. The 'automatic'/spontaneous behavior and thinking of a human organization is made possible by the presence of a **'common' language** — when words also manifest 'feeling'. Thus, the dynamic of the system can also be enhanced by the ways the language is used. A change in the ways of speaking and thinking will obviously change its coherency, consensus, and competitiveness. A change in the language of interpretation will generate new information from existing data. The new information generated may be crucial. Concurrently, communications and engagement (abstract and intangible) supported by a common language, a unique critical activity in all human-related setups, will lead to the 'formation' of formal and informal self-organizing networks with different characteristics — the emergent of a network meso-structure.

Therefore, an intelligent human organization must create a conscientious effort to ensure that its level of interpretation in using language is more advanced and sophisticated than that of its rivals — leading to better mental cohesion. The exact communications and engagement between any two agents in the organization, the meaning of the language used, the more subtle interpretation of the language used, must be areas for repetitive scrutiny. In this respect, the long-neglected role of language operating in the deep conceptual/intangible structure of human organizations must be constantly re-examined. This **'binding medium'** must be better understood, and constantly and meticulously exploited (in particular, with the introduction of the social/wireless media technology the boundaries and complexity of human connectivity has been transformed).

In this respect, the capability to nurture a 'common' language is extremely vital to the leadership (lateral/collective, consultative) and governance (e-governance/*i*-governance) of the organization as it facilitates better self-organizing communications, the formation of constructive networks, and achieving higher collectiveness capacity (see Chapters 9 and 10). Thus, the coherency of the system structure and dynamic is highly dependent on the mental functions of orgmindfulness that greatly enhanced

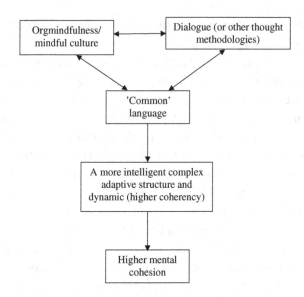

Figure 4.3   The significance and function of a 'common' language.

a 'common' language ('common' language <=> orgmindfulness <=> mindful culture <=> dialogue <=> intelligence-intelligence linkage <=> coherency) in the organization (see Figure 4.3, see dialogue in Appendix 7, and Chapters 7 and 8). The above analysis leads to the proposal of the fourth postulate.

Postulate IV

The survival of an intelligent human system is highly dependent on the org-awareness, orgmindfulness, connectivity, engagement, self-organizing communications, and coherency of the orgmind, intangible deep structure, and external scanning and responding dynamics. An ideal/optimal physical macro-structure can only emerge from a highly intelligent intangible structure and its dynamics. Thus, the intelligent physical structure cannot be enforced and sustained artificially without a highly intelligent intangible structure (dynamic) as its foundation.

4.3.2 *Significance and roles of theory and knowledge structure*

Within a certain domain, evolving from the physical to the conceptual utilization of a physical symbol system, abstract concepts or a **theory** arises. There is a close inter-relationship among intelligence, knowledge, and theory. Partially, a theory is a set of statements which allows an intelligent human agent better self-examination. Frequently, it is a reference source for internal searching. In addition, a theory also serves as an **analytical lens** that enables the intelligent system to examine its environment, and some events happening in it. Without a theory, there is no proper basis or path for analysis and explanations. A thought that emerges without a foundation may not be very valuable. Therefore, a theory is an **intelligence enabler**.

A theory is not and cannot be stagnant. Very often a theory has a 'life-cycle'. It emerges and evolves with time (and may become obsolete). In many instances, it has never been fully explicit or understood, even if its fundamentals may be well-established and widely practiced by the community/organization that adopts it. However, to understand the logic of a theory, and to use it consciously as an analytical lens and/or compass is a mindset that is critically needed to enhance intelligence. In this respect, a theory is also a **mental compass** indicating the direction and path (may be a paradigmatic shift) to steer. A highly developed group of human beings (scientific/social community, business organization, market) possess and exploit many theories concurrently.

In particular, new theory drives leadership. Fundamentally, leadership is meaningless (or nothing is new) without a new theory to support and explain its defined or redefined mission. When a person with a new mindset leads, the theory helps to consolidate his/her leadership by indicating the intention, direction, path, and destination more vividly (futuristic but bearing in mind the presence of unknowns) — (see **futurology** and **uncertainty** in Appendix 7). Meanwhile, a theory also helps to ensure that an intention and its actions must be coherent, and such a match is vital for any human organization to develop and/or compete successfully.

Beyond specialist communities, a theory is not necessarily an integration of abstract concepts — it is not always a 'theory of relativity'. In reality, an operational theory can be fairly simple. At times, some people utilize theories without realizing their existence and importance. Such theories are subconsciously nurtured or embedded in the mind, 'automatically' utilized, and thus can be relatively simple. However, under certain conditions, it is much more beneficial if a theory is well-understood, made explicit, and be fully supported by the entire society/organization that exploit it. In this case, its presence must be made known and accepted before the theory can be more extensively exploited. The existence of theory in intelligent systems is stated as the next axiom.

Axiom III — Individual theory

There exist one or more theories in all intelligent human agents that serve as their compass, analytical lens, and thinking foundation.

Axiom IIIa — Corporate theory/philosophy

There exist one or more theories (evolving into a corporate philosophy) in all intelligent human organizations that serve as their compass, analytical lens, and thinking foundation.

In the human world, knowledge acquisition and accumulation is associated with learning, adaptation, and self-enhancement. It is through a theory that information is better consumed, and added on to a **knowledge structure**. A knowledge structure is a large-scale accumulation of related pieces (with well-determined or well-defined relationships) of information over a long period of time. When a subsequent piece of information is consumed by a thinking system, it alters the knowledge structure in the thinking system. In addition, its value is defines by the knowledge structure that exploits it. Thus, the consequence of a decision-making process is influenced by state of the existing internalized knowledge structures (construal and relativistic). Therefore, the presence of quality knowledge structures in intelligent systems (individual and organizational) is essential and crucial. In this respect, a knowledge structure is another intelligence enabler. The next axiom on knowledge structure is stated below.

Axiom IV — Individual knowledge structure

There exist one or more internalized knowledge structures in all intelligent human agents (embedded in the human thinking systems) that are the reference sources for intelligent activities and actions.

Axiom IVa — Corporate knowledge structure and repository

There exist one or more internalized knowledge structures and externalized repositories (part of the org-brain/orgmind) in all intelligent human organizations that are the reference sources for intelligent activities and actions.

4.3.3 *Necessity and roles of the intelligence enhancer*

In this respect, intelligence/consciousness, knowledge structures, and theories are constantly enriching each other in all intelligent systems (human beings, human networks, and human organizations). These three entities form an intelligent enabler triad. This triad is the **intelligence enhancer** embraced by the mind and orgmind. The presence of such an enhancer in human thinking systems is vital as it also helps to exploit latent intelligence as well. (Most or all intrinsic intelligence sources do not exploit their **intelligence capacity** optimally.) Thus, the enhancer is the most significant dynamo that drives complex thinking in a human being. Its quality can be substantially improved with the presence of a written language. The dynamic of the intelligence enhancer is illustrated in Figure 4.4.

Similarly, an intelligent human organization must also possess an organizational intelligence enhancer (see Figure 4.5 and Chapter 8). Its ability to nurture and integrate the three components is more complex but crucial — greatly depending on its ability to establish and exploit a 'common' language. The presence of a 'common' language better facilitates the interaction among the three entities in the enhancer, and also

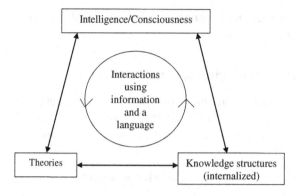

Figure 4.4   The intelligence enhancer of human thinking systems.

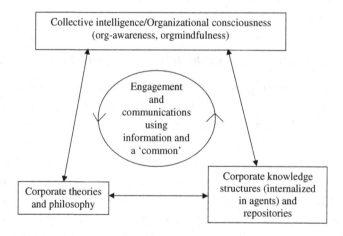

Figure 4.5   The corporate intelligence enhancer of human organizations.

among the interacting agents in the organization. A language is 'common' when it is acceptable by all agents or at least the majority with mutually acceptable resolution (with a deeper meaning and a 'latent' component). The functions of this enhancer will be further analyzed in subsequent chapters — associated with leadership, governance, corporate culture, and management.

Overall, the above analysis revealed the roles and necessity of the intelligent biotic macro-structure of intelligent human organizations. The presence of an appropriate macro-structure elevates the coherency of the dynamic of the organization more swiftly. In this respect, the fundamental intelligent biotic macro-structure and dynamic of an intelligent human organization is captured in the next postulate:

Postulate V

In general, an intelligent human organization must possess an intelligent biotic and adaptive physical macro-structure (org-brain, physical intelligence web, physical sensory sub-system), an intelligent intangible structure (orgmind — org-awareness, orgmindfulness; intangible intelligence web — intangible complex network, informal networks); and an intangible sensory web; and an intelligent dynamic (organizing around intelligence; presence of a 'common' language, self-organizing dynamic, network integration, self-organizing governance, intelligence leadership, and a holistic complex adaptive dynamic). In particular, the presence of a comprehensive and effective organizational intelligence enhancer in a human organization is crucial.

4.4 Artificial Intelligence Networks and the Intelligent Biotic Macro-Structure

4.4.1 *Significance and roles of artificial intelligence nodes*

In the present context, where speed of information transfer and information processing capacity escalates power, the quantity and quality (due to certain natural constraints) of intrinsic intelligence sources/nodes in an organization is usually not sufficient. Artificial nodes are always included to substantiate the natural nodes and the intelligence enhancer of the entire system. Artificial networks (including artificial neural networks, e-landscapes, remote sensing/sensory devices, and social media/wireless connectivity) have substantially redefined and accelerated the speed and intensity of human communications and engagement. Vividly, appropriate intense connectivity, swift communications, faster computing speed, larger information/knowledge storages, and new artificial nodes are current characteristics and dynamics in all competitive human organizations (social, economic, education, military, political, and regional). The increasing dominance and substantive use of artificial intelligence networks has further differentiated the human world from that of other biological species — as the latter has no artificial component.

It has been noted in Chapter 1 that besides the awakening to intelligence, consciousness, complexity, and nonlinearity, there are several other significant changes that have also altered the environment in which human agents and organizations learn, operate, co-operate, and compete. In particular, the emergence and strengthening of an integrated global economy that leads to the diminishing geographical and economics boundaries can be better managed with technological exploitation. Consequently, a way to evaluate and compete with competitors is through the use of better quality information and swift communications, and the consequence of this transformation is that an organization does not only compete with its local competitors only but also with those in other parts of the world.

The next change is that human beings (intrinsic intelligence nodes) are not always learning directly from other human beings. Instead, it is now rather common that the intrinsic nodes are learning from artificial knowledge nodes, although, the external knowledge sources are created by (some other) human beings. As a result, the learning rate of both agents and organizations has accelerated tremendously. Apparently, the above developments also indicate that new opportunities can be created through effective use of information/knowledge and its networks, elevating the collectiveness capacity and adaptive capacity of the organization. This emphasis is highly significant to the structure and dynamics of intelligent organizations (structural capacity). Basically, all intelligent human organizations also require a higher quality 'organizational nervous system', and environmental scanning and responding subsystem that can be enhanced artificially.

With the emergence of the new global knowledge/intelligence-centric society, the needs for a transformation in leadership, governance, and management philosophy, strategies, organizational structure, and planning and operation is crucial. As every new generation of human beings are carrying more sophisticated knowledge structures, and different thinking, values, and expectations, certain associated changes are inevitable. Overall, much emphasis has shifted from the tangible to the intangible.

For instance, businesses will be producing more and more intangible products (knowledge associated services). In fact, the fast developing businesses are those that offer knowledge-based services such as consultancy (expertise of experts), and research and development (for instance, information/knowledge technology, biotechnology, aero-space technology, and quantum technology). Even for those who are producing physical products, information is assuming a more crucial role. In addition, the power of an army now depends more on technology and intelligence strategy rather than the physical capability of its troops. Hence, the trend clearly confirmed that using intelligent equipments and artificial intelligent nodes/networks will be a significant part of human existence.

Vividly, intelligent biotic macro-structure of the organization is highly dependent on artificial intelligence networks. The artificial networks form a significant proportion of the physical structure of an intelligent human organization (as shown in Figure 4.6) that assists in elevating the collective intelligence of the system (encompassing natural nodes, artificial nodes, and **remote sensory nodes**). Therefore, focusing on the nodes'

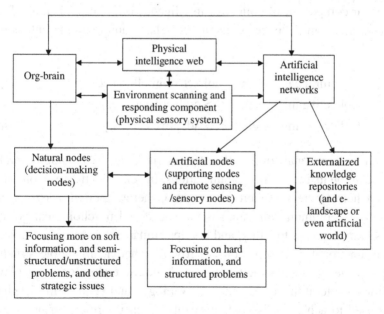

Figure 4.6 The integrated (intrinsic and artificial) physical macro-structure of an intelligent human organization.

characteristics, including natural nodes (decision-making nodes, strategy supporting nodes, information processing nodes, sensory nodes), and artificial nodes (artificial information processing nodes, knowledge accumulation nodes, and artificial remote sensory nodes) is vital — see network theory in Appendix 7.

4.4.2 *Towards a higher structural capacity*

As illustrated earlier, an intelligent human organization possesses both a physical structure, as well as an intangible deep structure. Embedded in the core of the deep structure of an organization is its orgmind — its source of collective intelligence and org-consciousness. The level of individual consciousness (collectively) determines the level of org-awareness and orgmindfulness. The latter through an orgmindful culture, in turn, is responsible for nurturing the collective intelligence, and enhancing the connectivity and coherency of the system. It is only when an organization is highly orgmindful that innovative and creative ideas will emerge from its interacting agents. Thus, a high level of orgmindfulness enhances the nonlinear component of collective intelligence of the organization. Thus, in general, a significant relationship (correlated and mutually enhancing) is as follows:

$$\text{Structural capacity} <=> \text{collective intelligence} \qquad (4.1)$$

$$\text{Collective intelligence} <=> \text{collectiveness capacity} \qquad (4.2)$$

$$\text{Collective intelligence} <=> \text{adaptive capacity} \qquad (4.3)$$

In the operational context, the connectivity of an organization is highly dependent on its mode of communications. In general, effective communications help to create coherent thought. Coherent thought (better facilitated by a 'common' language) is the social and psychological gel that binds human beings together, and it helps human organizations to achieve social/functional cohesion more swiftly. A coherent intangible structure supports the physical structure better. **Thought technology** can play a significant role in this engagement — **dialogue** and **visual thinking** have been used to achieve this goal. In reality, often informal self-organizing networks that may or may not be coherent with the organizational structure also emerge (see principle of locality in Appendix 7). Thus, another important relationship is as follows:

Coherent thoughts <=> 'common' language   (4.4)

Ideally, the information processing and knowledge creation capabilities of the organizations and the overall organizational structure capacity must be mutually enhancing (intense intelligence/consciousness-centricity <=> intelligent biotic macro-structure). Hence, the information networks (natural and artificial) must enhance the nervous system and the org-brain of the intelligent organization, irrespective of its primary function. Apparently, the quality of interconnectivity and capability of the natural and artificial networks determine the success in structuring and nurturing intelligent organizations — high structural capacity is a vital attribute.

4.4.3 *Integrated natural and artificial physical macro-structure: A summary*

The intelligent organization theory indicates that the ideal physical structure of intelligent organizations must emerge from the deep structure. The associate dynamic is continuously changing or updating. Hence, the details of the physical structure are also constantly modified. As mentioned earlier, the basic physical structure of an intelligent organization possesses three features, namely, an intense intelligence source, an intelligence web, and an environment scanning and responding component (an intelligence/consciousness-centric structure that enables a human organization to correlate better with an intense information/knowledge-centric environment). This basic physical structure when enhanced by artificial systems introduced additional important characteristics and capabilities to the three components, and they are summarized below:

a. The existence of an intense intelligence/consciousness source is vital to all higher levels intelligent organisms. In human organizations this intelligence source/consciousness is the org-brain of the system. The org-brain is at least a ('partial') collection of brains of the interacting agents (each functioning as an organizational neuron) — not all the organizational neurons are in the org-brain. The absence of such a collective source indicates the absence of leadership nodes, and collective intelligence in that organization. The mental capacity of the org-brain can be elevated through better utilization of artificial nodes (no consciousness, and not part of the org-brain) that support the natural nodes. The ultimate capacity and effectiveness of the org-brain and orgmind depends on orgmindfulness and the presence of a mindful culture.

b. The intelligence web (a more 'sparsely connection' of organizational neurons) that spreads and permeates the entire system provides the organizational interconnectivity. This web intertwines and supports all the organizational functions and activities. Through this web information and decision are communicated, and localized knowledge structures are created and stored. This is the 'nervous network' of intelligent organizations. The general usage of information and communications technology that greatly increases the quantity and quality of supporting nodes is vital in this component. In the present context, the characteristics and dynamic of the physical intelligence web has also been greatly enhanced by the e-landscape, and social media/ wireless technology.

c. A highly intelligent human organization must also be continuously responsive to its environment. It must act, and react better and more swiftly than any intelligent biological entities or competitors. Therefore, the sensing, scanning, and responding capabilities of the environmental component are important assets of human organizations as well. The ability to scan and detect environmental signals coming from environmental targets, the ability to respond to such signals swiftly, and the ability to influence the environmental targets are vital features of intelligent human organizations. In such organizations, their competitive intelligence activities are substantially enhanced using artificial systems — in particular, with early warning systems — also associated with remote scanning and futuristic capabilities.

Therefore, at the physical level, the intelligence web, and the environmental scanning and responding component can be greatly enhanced by utilizing appropriate well-integrated artificial intelligence networks. [The number of information processing nodes in the physical structure an organization can be substantially increased with the connection of artificial nodes (supporting nodes) — enhancing the performance of the decision-making nodes.] And the effectiveness of the latter is also closely correlated with the collective intelligence of the organization (artificial nodes can be intelligent but not conscious). Therefore, the ability for designing an effective holistic artificial intelligence network, and integrating it with the natural intelligence network constructively, so that the overall information network structure is congruous in the organization, is crucial. This necessity is stated in the next postulate.

Postulate VI

In general, an intelligent human organization (a complex network of natural nodes) also possesses a substantial and complex artificial intelligence network (artificial intelligence nodes, and remote sensory nodes) for better connectivity, communication and engagement, higher structural capacity, and more intense collective intelligence. The artificial intelligence network (subsystem) encompasses supporting nodes (with faster computing ability but not decision making ability), and extensive knowledge storage (external repository), that also accelerates individual and integrated organizational learning. In addition, its presence redefined the ways the intrinsic nodes/agents are interconnected, elevates organizational awareness and orgmindfulness, and how strategies are exploited.

4.5 An Introduction to the Two Meso-Structures

Besides the agent-agent/system micro-structure and the intelligent biotic macro-structure, intelligent human organizations are also embedded with two meso-structures (see Figure 4.1). The micro-structure and two meso-structures are continuously changing guided by the boundaries of the biotic macro-structure, and vice versa. However, there are also two meso-layers that must be exploited concurrently to achieve better coherency that elevates the competitiveness, resilience, and sustainability the organization.

4.5.1 *Complexity meso-structure*

Designing around intelligence is a creation of nature. It is an inherent feature of the Universe, and all its microcosms that exhibit stability (the physical matter world is stable due to proto-intelligence-centric, while the living world is intelligence/consciousness-centric — varying from physical self-organization to biological self-organization). In the sea of complex expansion, infinite numbers of 'bubbles of order' proliferate (integration of order and complexity). The centers of these bubbles are the 'local order centers' (**space of order**). A space of order is a region of established structure and stability, where activities constantly reduce entropy, and relationships are linear. Every source of intelligence present in this world manifests this desire and ability. Similarly, every human being, an intense source of intelligence/consciousness, establishes such a space as well (autopoietic, self-centric, and stability-centric). The characteristics of such a space are significant to the entire humanity, as their predictability provides confidence, comfort, and certainty.

However, in a space of order, intelligence is not optimized — especially in the human world. Information use is rigid and information redundancy is not acceptable or carefully avoided. Its dynamic is linear and usually simplistic. 'Undesired' activities are prevented. Consequently, risk taking is minimized, and creativity and innovation are unconsciously suppressed (for many agents). For a human organization to prolong its existence, its spaces of order have to be constantly strengthened and enhanced. However, this can only be achieved effectively when **spaces of complexity** are exploited as well. Thus, venturing beyond order into the unfamiliar territories of complexity (**complexity meso-structure**) is the best option to explore and discover new opportunities and achieve new goals — higher **exploratory capacity**.

Quite often, just 'beyond' a space of order is a space of complexity. This 'mysterious' space can be embedded with new unexplored opportunities. The main attributes guiding activities in the space of complexity are high level intelligence, intense information processing and knowledge exploitation, and to a great extent innovation and creativity (see relativistic complexity in Appendix 7). The characteristics of the space of complexity are nonlinear, and the butterfly effect can manifest itself. Thus, the returns for venturing into such spaces can be enormous, if managed appropriately (risk management). Nature frequently exploits this dynamism of complexity with nonlinearity to support its evolutionary dynamics — changes and unexpected changes (see Cambrian explosion, natural selection, and exaptation in Appendix 7). Thus, these spaces allow dynamics that contradict the exact sciences to exist. For instance, matter can exist in a state inbetween solid and liquid in such a space (time-functionality/adaptive dependent).

Currently, most human organizations either have not realized the existence of spaces of complexity or have avoided these uncertain spaces. Operating within spaces of order has always been the norm (Newtonian boundaries). However, in the present rapidly changing world, confining organizational activities within spaces of order can only sustain survival for a limited period of time. The structure of the spaces of order of a mechanistic setup (by themselves) is unnatural, as it does not take on a form congruous with biological systems that inherently support their own growth and survival by reaping benefits from spaces of complexity. Therefore, the common existing practice of fitting human beings into a machine setup is not a natural/inherent thinking and process.

Apparently, nurturing an intelligent biotic macro-structure and recognizing the four-layer structure of human organizations is advantageous and significant. It allows the organization to better exploit both spaces of order and spaces of complexity — comprehending and exploiting the co-existence order and complexity through an integrated deliberate and emergent strategy (see Chapter 6). Inherently, the complex adaptive dynamic encompasses stasis and punctuation points. Niches cannot be easily found in territories that are commonly understood (spaces of order). Thus, some spaces of complexity are unexplored goldmines. Anyone (agents or organizations) that is able to recognize new order and structure in complexity spaces acquires an intelligence advantage.

4.5.2 *Network meso-structure*

Human organizations have been perceived as **network organizations**. A well-networked organization is more adaptive to changes. In the intelligent organization theory, human organizations embed a **network meso-structure**. A network is a connection (links) of nodes (see network theory in Appendix 7). In human organizations, the nodes can be natural (human agents) and artificial (artificial intelligence sources), and the links are relational-centric. Every node is subjected to constraints and enablers. In this respect, a human network is a complex adaptive cluster that embeds a relationship web, and is engaged in certain activities with a self-organizing and far-from-equilibrium dynamic. Hence, very often localized spaces (just beyond an agent) in human organizations are networks (complex network — network of networks; real world networks — small world networks, scale free networks), and to certain extent their roles can be perceived as equivalent to biological organs that must be well-connected ('unified') to the entire system. In reality, in human organizations these networks can be informal or even not supportive of the existing structure and dynamic — that is, 'cancerous' to a certain extent. Common human networks include social networks, policy networks, and leader networks. In this respect, the network-centric mindset of the leadership and the governance structure are vital for ensuring the coherency of the entire organization (see intelligence leadership, self-organizing governance, and network management in Appendix 7; and see Chapters 9 and 10).

4.6 Further Analysis on Organizational Coherency

4.6.1 *Summary of the multi-layer structure and dynamic*

The outcome of the above analysis on the four inherent layers of the human organizational structure is summarized as follows (also see Figure 4.7):

- **Agent-agent/system micro-structure**: It is a collection of coherent and incoherent human agents [with a large numbers of interacting agent (agent-agent/system), each embedded with an intrinsic

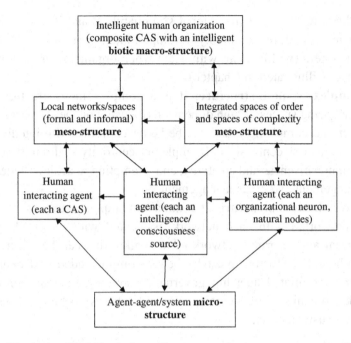

Figure 4.7 A simplified illustration of human organization as a composite CAS with multi-layer structure and dynamics.

intense intelligence/consciousness source, and a changing behavioral schema — the key asset of all human organizations] with characteristics including self-centricity, stability-centricity, independency, interdependency, interconnectivity, communications, engagement and principle of locality, facilitating the formation (self-organization/self-transcending constructions) of local spaces (networks), self-enrichment processes and global forces — will be analyzed more in-depth in Chapter 7.

• **Intelligent biotic and adaptive macro-structure**: It is an intelligence/consciousness-centric macro-structure (with an orgmind, intangible structure, and physical structure) that attempts to optimize the contribution of the intrinsic intelligence/consciousness sources through appropriate intelligence-intelligence linkages, and elevating information processing and knowledge accumulation/utilization abilities to achieve better global sustainability; and it resembles the inherent structure of a highly developed intelligent biological organism/system (will be dealt with again when organizing around intelligence is illustrated in Chapter 6).

- **Complexity meso-structure**: It is a complex meso-structure with overlapping spaces of high dimension (focusing on the co-existence of order and complexity), and can be better exploited with intelligence/ consciousness-centricity and complexity-centricity — through enhancing innovativeness and creativity, and attempting to achieve better risk management and crisis management.
- **Network meso-structure**: It contains a complex networks (network of networks) with each network associated with localized spaces (formal and informal network of networks) that can be coherent or incoherent. Networks must be better comprehended and exploited with appropriate leadership, governance, strategy, and management in order to achieve holistic coherency and synergy — higher organizational sustainability.

4.6.2 *The significance of higher organizational coherency and synergy*

The intelligent organization theory stipulates that human organizations designed around intelligence (agent-agent/system micro-structure with appropriate intelligence-intelligence linkages) are more coherent, adaptive, and competitive. Coherency is a significant attribute of an intelligent human organization. Human beings each carrying an intense intelligence/ consciousness source are interacting to form local spaces (networks) that may have a global impact. As indicated earlier, their connectivity is determined by their mental space and mode of communications. In this respect, coherent thought is the social and psychological gel (feeling system, social consensus, relational capacity, coherency, mental cohesion and stability) that binds human agents together, and it helps human organizations to achieve more extensive cohesion. This relationship is summarized as follows:

$$\text{Coherent thoughts} <=> \text{mental cohesion} \tag{4.5}$$

Coherent thoughts can be better achieve with the presence of a 'common' language ['relationship/equation' (4.4)]. The latter facilitates engagement and the flow of information, and binds the interacting agents more smoothly. Language also allows for more abstract and intense interaction. Very often, concepts (creating deeper thoughts) can only be successfully explained using a more 'developed' language. In addition, language also enhances the linguistic act of interpretation. Therefore, language is a major concern when nurturing the intangible structure, and when extending the boundaries of complexity exploitation. Without a highly developed 'common' language, the organizational intelligence enhancer cannot function at a high level of effectiveness — or achieving a new level of coherency and sustainability. Thus, a 'common' language and collective intelligence are also closely associated.

$$\text{Common language} <=> \text{mental cohesion} \qquad (4.6)$$

Mental cohesion is beyond 'traditional' coherency. For instance, agreeing to disagree encompasses both coherency and diversifications. In this respect, there is mental cohesion, although, the system may not be fully coherent. In addition, beyond coherency is the synergy (see constructionist hypothesis and synergetics in Appendix 7). Synergetic effects are valuable if the new surfacing attributes are constructive to the organizations. In this respect, the new attributes are also associated with innovativeness and creativeness. Thus, in this case, synergy can be summarized as follows:

- Synergetic effect => from incoherency to coherency
- Synergetic effect => the system effect is greater than the sum of the effects from the components/parts

Apparently, human organizations must ensure that their strategies and actions are only confined within spaces of order. Intelligent human systems must exploit their inherent multi-layer structure collectively, and must venture into newly comprehended territories (spaces of complexity) to reap the latent benefits. In general, structural fluidity, information redundancy, knowledge enhancement, and nonlinear use of intelligence and consciousness are some of the main attributes that must be better exploited. These characteristics have been manifested as some key life-supporting features of biological evolutionary systems. Therefore, the intelligent biotic macro-structure, and the integrated deliberate and emergent strategy two key components of the complexity-intelligence strategy (with several sub-strategies, models, and frameworks), have to be innovatively adopted (see Chapter 6).

4.7 Conclusion

For better omniscient understanding, it may be beneficial to briefly recollect the multi-layer structural foundation of the intelligent organization theory, and how the structural capacity of the organization can be elevated before concluding this chapter. The most basic concepts that have been discussed are as follows:

a. Intelligent human organizations are 'living' intelligent beings.
b. At the microscopic level, a human organization is a composite complex adaptive system with a collection of human agents (the elementary entities, each a complex adaptive system).
c. They are organizational/corporate beings (intelligent/'biological' and 'living' rather than mechanical and reductionist) encompassing an orgmind, collective intelligence, and well-integrated information/knowledge networks.
d. Their level of collective intelligence can be elevated through better intelligence/consciousness management (through a 'common' language, truthful engagement, orgmindfulness, mindful culture, intelligence-intelligence linkage, social consensus) of their internal intelligence sources (natural and artificial), and proper design.
e. Their physical biotic macro-structure can be enhanced with the proper integration of artificial intelligence networks introducing artificial nodes (including remote sensory nodes).
f. The more intelligent the organization the more adaptive, competitive, innovative, and sustainable it is (high adaptive capacity, and collectiveness capacity).
g. Such a new competitive advantage achieved is the fundamental intelligence advantage.

Therefore, there exists a critical relationship between intelligence and human organizations that is similar to the relationship between intelligence and biological organisms. The characteristics and requirements of this vital connection can be better captured in the inherent intelligent biotic macro-structure. The critical points are summarized below:

a.   The presence of an intense collective intelligence source is vital; otherwise, the activities of the human organization will have no proper co-ordination and direction — due to leadership deficiency, and governance failure.

b.   The existence of an efficient environment scanning and responding component is essential because such a component not only enables organizations to interact with their environment, but also enables organizations to elevate their collective intelligence. It also serves as the key early warning component through sensory nodes and remote sensory nodes — a higher level of org-awareness.

c.   The spread and integration of the intelligence web supporting the entire set of functions of connecting/engaging the components specified in (a) and (b) is a necessary but not sufficient condition for nurturing high collective intelligence. However, the absence of the web indicates that the organization is paralyzed.

d.   Overall, the flexible physical biotic macro-structure must be supported by a highly intelligent deep intangible structure. In addition, an intelligent and coherent orgmind (balancing org-awareness and org-mindfulness) is the fundamental intelligent stratum of all intelligent organizations (overall, a higher structural capacity).

In particular, it is also crucial to recognize that the collective intelligence in human organizations can be elevated through a more effective design and nurturing approach — organizing around intelligence. Some benefits derived from this strategic path, and the exploitation of the multi-layer structure is as follows:

a.   Organizing around intelligence/consciousness focuses on the intelligence-intelligence linkages that help to elevate the collective intelligence through orgmindfulness — the presence of a mindful culture.

b. This new intelligence/consciousness-centric approach allows human organizations to settle more spontaneously into a competitive state that is closer to an inherent intelligent biotic macro-structure of nature.

c. Human organizations with an intelligent biotic macro-structure are more coherent with learning, adaptation, and information/knowledge-related functions, and therefore they survive better in the knowledge/intelligence-intensive environment.

d. Intelligent human organizations are more adaptive to both linear and orderly changes, as well as nonlinear and complex changes by adopting an integrated deliberate and emergent strategy. In this respect, intelligent human organizations are smarter evolvers and emergent strategists.

e. In addition, the better management of the complex networks meso-structure also elevates the collective intelligence, innovation, competitiveness, resilience, and sustainability of the organization.

Finally, the basic structural and dynamical foundation illustrated in this chapter will better support more conceptual and operational aspects of the intelligent organization theory that are to be further developed in subsequent chapters (see Chapters 6 to 10). Fundamentally, intelligent human organizations must possess an intelligent biotic macro-structure and agent-agent micro-structure with well-interconnected intelligence/consciousness sources that can adapt best in a highly complex and changing environment. Concurrently, comprehending certain details of the agent-agent/system micro-structure and the two meso-structures, and their dynamics, coupled with better supportive governance, leadership, and management, including ensuring stability at all levels (agents/networks/organization) is a strategic path towards achieving higher coherency, and reaping new synergetic effects. In addition, it is vital to continuously remember that the intelligence mindset also indicates that that change and uncertainty are key attributes in the current context (not always negative).

Without language our mental capacities would be poor indeed, comparable to those of the higher animals; we have, therefore, to admit that we owe our principal advantage over the beasts to the fact of living in human society.

Albert Einstein, *Ideas and Opinions*

Chapter 5

Human Thinking Systems
and the General Information Theory

"The physical biotic brains and the projected latent abstract
minds of human interacting agents are the most vital assets
of all human organizations"

Summary

This chapter focuses on establishing the conceptual foundation of the
macroscopic perspective (structure and processes) of human thinking
systems — the conceptualization of the general information theory
(a component of the complexity-intelligence strategy). In this analysis,
the human thinking system is perceived to be comprised of two components namely, the energy–matter subsystem (the natural component),
and the physical symbol subsystem (an artificial component unique to
humanity). The general procedure in which the human mind handles and
exploits one or more physical symbol systems (symbols manipulation)
is analyzed. The conceptual development encompassing the creation of
the character set, capturing and transformation of data and information,
acquisition of knowledge and emergent of wisdom (the four external
entities), and the significance of a written language, as well as the additional associated functions are investigated.

The unique ability of creating a character set is confined to humanity
indicating that human thinking systems are the most intense intelligence
sources on this planet. The intrinsic and interactive properties of the character set and the language depict the characteristics and sophistication/
complexity of the physical symbol system. Besides interacting among
themselves (data, information, knowledge and wisdom), these external

entities also interact with the natural entities, the information-coded energy quanta, according to certain rules and principles. Subsequently, the energy quanta interact with the information-coded matter structure (the brain's complex neural network). This unique ability (the presence of a written language) allows knowledge to be stored externally, and abstract concepts (including theory) and complex strategizing to emerge for the first time in the human world. In this respect, in the intense human intelligence source (individual or collective), information and knowledge exists in physical, energy and matter forms, and they are inter-convertible (internalization and externalization). The interactions among the six entities and the conversion from one form to another vividly review the presence of the uniqueness of the human thinking system, as well as the orgmind — greatly redefining the interactions and dynamic in the humanity and its organizations.

Subsequently, the boundaries and objectives of human thinking systems as information processing systems, and the necessity of artificial information systems are conceived as four postulates. In the intelligent organization theory, a deeper comprehension of the human thinking systems (complex adaptive systems) is vital, as they are the vital assets closely associated with the nurturing of highly intelligent human organizations (*i*CAS), including the coherency and contributions of a multi-layer intelligent structure (intelligent biotic macro-structure and agent-agent/system micro-structure). In this respect, the cognitive perspective must be better comprehended and utilized.

Keywords: Human thinking system, intelligence, consciousness, energy–matter subsystem, physical symbol subsystem, biological neural network, information decoder, intelligence spectrum, proto-intelligence, basic life-intelligence, matter structure, physical entity set, data, information, knowledge, wisdom, language, neuron, neurotransmitter, neural network, information-processing perspective, information consumption, general information theory, intelligent organization theory, complexity-intelligence strategy, character set, artifact, basic entity, intelligence space, basic human intelligence, advanced human intelligence, symbol creation function, basic entity coding/capturing function, basic entity transformation function, perception function, decision-making function, cognitive perspective, concept, cognitive structure, cognitive intelligence/functions space, cognitive space, knowledge structure, information-coded energy quantum, internalization function, externalization function, energy–matter interaction, matter–matter interaction, energy–matter function space, feeling system, artificial supporting node, intrinsic decision-making node, and four postulates of the general information theory.

5.1 Introduction: The World of Neural Networks

5.1.1 *Human thinking systems: Biological neural networks and beyond*

The human thinking system in which the human mind and brain reside ranks among the most exciting research domains of the entire last century, and it will continue to attract the same level of interest over the next few decades. It has been mentioned that "the nature of the mind, ..., how a biological organ like the human brain can be an organ of thought, ..., how biological organs like neurons which carry on chemical and electrical processes can support our thinking,..., and the processes of thinking at the level of symbols — the kind of symbolic processes that are going on when a human being thinks," are some aspects of this fascinating discipline that have captivated both information scientists and neuroscientists alike [**Simon**, 1989, p. 1 (**Herbert Simon**,)]. This group must be extended to include all individuals that lead and manage or have interest in human organizations.

At the moment, the microscopic principles and dynamics of the human brain (the biological organ that is engulfed in the cranial space) at the neuronal or atomic level are still far from being fully understood. However, since **Santiago Ramon Cajal** (1852–1934) confirmed that the brain is made up of a large number of discrete units using Golgi's method (**Camillo Golgi**, 1843–1926) of staining **neurons** with silver salts [using silver nitrate and potassium dichromate to fix silver chromate to the neurolemma, the neuron membrane — creating a picture of black neurons (**biological neural networks**) with a yellow background] about a 150 years ago (in 1873), the neuron doctrine (neural network) has been further examined by numerous researchers rigorously (see Appendix 5). Today, the brain is known to contain between 10 billion and a trillion neurons encompassing about 100 trillion synapses, forming an extremely complex three-dimensional maze of neuronal circuitry.

A neuron (a term coined by **Heinrich Wilhelm Gottfried von Waldeyer-Hartz** (1836–1921) to differentiate it from other cells) is a nerve cell that is excitable electrically (presence of energy differential) and transmits neurotransmitters (see Appendix 5). They are the key components of the human brain and spinal cord. The neuronal codes travel as electrical (energy) codes in the axon and biochemical (matter) codes in the neurotransmission at the synaptic gaps (to the dendrites on other neurons). Overall, the brain (an electrochemical system with formation processing and storage capacity — see Figure 5.1) generates a global neural pattern based on massive interactions at the level of the synapse.

The mechanism at the neural level that enables the brain to generate neural patterns remains a mystery in neuroscience even though over the last two decades new technologies (functional neuroimaging) have greatly enhanced the research activities in this area (including biological cybernetics). However, the discovery of the first **neurotransmitter** in 1973 was a significant advancement. It signified that neural codes are decipherable at the atomic level. Neuroscientists estimated that there are as many as 300 neurotransmitters (more than 100 have been identified). Although this number is large, the existence of order that holds the key to unfolding the neural code must be present.

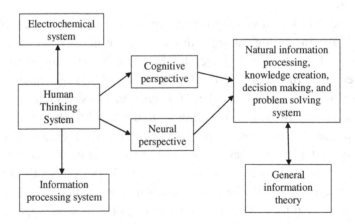

Figure 5.1 The primary functions of the human thinking system captured as the general information theory.

The creation and operation of the abstract mind form by these neural dynamics is equally if not more mysterious. The cognitive or neuropsychological dimension of the mind will always remain a significant component of human behavioral analysis even after the neural mechanism of the brain is fully established. In fact, determining the relationships between the neural activities of the brain, and the behavioral functions of the mind will always remain a key research domain. Perhaps a better understanding of this unique system and its dynamic could be obtained eventually using some fundamental principles/concepts from the science of complexity.

5.1.2 *The information-processing perspective*

Cognitive science has always emphasized that human beings are information processors. And information processing appears to be an important connection between the function of a human thinking system and its behavior. Basically, cognitive science perceives a human thinking system as having components such as sensory memory, short-term memory, and long-term memory. Such a setup is an information-processing-related structure with capabilities to explain operations of different complexities including **information processing, information consumption**, information/knowledge storage, concept-attainment, reasoning, decision making, as well as information/knowledge creation. Information, similar to physical matter and energy, is a basic entity/property of this Universe.

The above basic foundation is further supported by the presence of consciousness, and the belief that our conscious conception of self is largely derived and/or enhanced by our ability to acquire and use at least one natural language or a symbol system — the deeper mental ability that focuses inward. The creation of an artificial physical symbol subsystem by the human mind leads to the extension of the natural system. The evolutionary development of the symbol subsystem is a fairly recent phenomenon in the context of evolution theory. The creation of logograms by the Sumerians took place around 3000 B.C. (a logogram is a morpheme or word — the smallest unit of a language with meaning rather than a sound).

By 800 B.C. a complete alphabet system was finally used by the Greeks. Similarly, the Chinese characters (including pictograms, ideograms, and other forms), and Egyptian hieroglyphs were conceived many thousands of years back. The evolution of the above developments (the establishment of a sophisticated written language) has altered human-thinking capabilities significantly — with characteristics that cannot be duplicated by any other biological species.

Similarly, the substantive claim by neuroscience that the human brain is an information-processing machine is another strong impetus for this analysis. Almost every major development in neuroscience from the 1960s to the present has served to reinforce this claim. The assumption now is that the brains and hence human thinking systems, from both the neural and cognitive perspectives, are at least information processing systems (see Figure 5.1). The convergence of all brain–mind-related studies towards information-processing activities indicates and supports the necessity of establishing the **general information theory**.

5.2 Introduction to the General Information Theory

5.2.1 *The two subsystems of the human thinking systems*

Conceptualizing the general information theory is a challenging task (see Appendix 7). It is a theory that explains the macroscopic dynamic of the **human thinking systems** that are composed of two subsystems namely, the **physical symbol subsystem** (artificial subsystem) and the **energy–matter subsystem** (natural subsystem). A human thinking system is also inherently a highly abstract system that originates from the brain (a biological organ) with dynamic that projects an intangible system, the mind (see Figure 5.2). Since a human thinking system encompasses both a natural component, as well as an artificial component, among others things, the theory must be able to account for the interactions between the artificial and the natural (entities). The interactions include transformations of human-created entities into naturally occurring entities and vice-versa. Therefore, the general information theory to be introduced must engulf a theory of artifacts that is immersed in a theory of energy and matter.

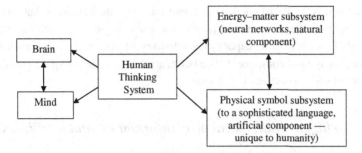

Figure 5.2 The two components of human thinking systems.

In this respect, a human thinking system is an open system that interacts with its environment via a physical symbol subsystem. Therefore, it fundamentally possesses physical symbol creation, manipulation, and processing capabilities. It must also be able to convert physical symbols into information-coded energy quanta in the energy–matter subsystem and vice versa. Subsequently, the energy quanta interact with the information-coded matter structure in the brain. Thus, it may be appropriate to define a human thinking system with respect to the knowledge already conceptualized as follows:

Definition I

A human thinking system encompasses at least an energy–matter subsystem and a physical symbol subsystem. The former is the natural component that resides in the brain, while the latter is a human-created component that is an extension created by the human mind. The functional capabilities of the human thinking systems include a physical symbol perspective (emerging from a character set to an abstract language), a cognitive perspective, an energy–matter perspective, and an underlying subatomic neuronal/ neural dimension.

With respect to the above definition, the human mind is also given a definition that reflects its boundaries and capabilities as follows:

Definition II

The human mind is an abstract intangible space projected by the brain's intelligence consciousness and activities. It is an intangible complex adaptive system sustained by the neuronal and underlying subatomic functions of the brain matter (an electrochemical system), as well as the symbol manipulation capabilities/activities of the artificially created physical symbol component. The boundaries of this mental space evolve continuously (redefined) with time.

5.2.2 *Intelligent matter structure, information and intelligence*

Matter structure is coded with some form of information. In particular, 'biological matter' such as DNA and brain matter exhibit certain levels of intelligence capability. In this situation, a higher level of intelligence emerges when information-coded energy quanta interact with information-coded matter packages, and when the latter interact among each other. These unique activities occur only when an appropriate decoder (**information decoder**) is present. In this respect, there is a correlation between the level of intelligence, and the quantity and density of such matter present. The level of intelligence in turn determines the complexity of the information processing ability of such systems. Thus, intelligence and information processing abilities appear to be very closely coupled and mutually enhancing.

Natural information existing in energy–matter form is an extremely powerful latent force that determines how nature evolves, and how the entire Universe behaves. Thus, the Universe is not dumb. The presence of intelligence gives rise to consciousness (the first core property of complexity theory). It has intelligent matter that carries its 'secret' codes. An intelligent matter system with encoded information responds to the changing environment. On the other hand, the information that exists in physical symbol form is usually created by human beings. This form of information not only enables human beings to interact with each other more meaningfully; it also enables humanity to understand nature in a totally different dimension, a new dimension which other living organisms have never experienced.

It may be important to mention again the existence of the intelligence spectrum, and to note the difference between **proto-intelligence**, and **basic life-intelligence, basic human intelligence,** and **advanced human intelligence** (discussed in earlier chapters). Examples of proto-intelligence are associated with structures embedded in atoms, molecules, and crystals. These are non-living systems carrying coded information. However, living biological systems exhibit the capacity to learn and adapt. The highest extreme end of the intelligence spectrum encompasses intelligent systems that can manipulate symbols and possess a pivotal structure known as the human thinking systems (mind) — the advance intelligence of human beings, and especially, the collective intelligence of the entire humanity/Gaia.

5.2.3 *The general dynamic of the human thinking systems*

Intelligent energy–matter systems with encoded information respond to the changing environment. They may have complex internal activities including duplicating (reproduction) capability. The human thinking systems are prominent examples of such intelligent energy–matter systems — they are electrochemically sensitive. The global characteristic of the human thinking systems is captured in the following general interaction equation as follows:

$$\text{environment} \leftrightarrow \text{artifact} \leftrightarrow \text{energy} \leftrightarrow \text{matter} \qquad (5.1)$$

This equation provides an overview of the macroscopic phenomena (could be symbolic, imagery or acoustic processes) occurring in the human mind. It also indicates that such a system has a natural component (energy–matter) and a human-created (artifact) component, and that it is an open system.

The boundaries of the physical symbol subsystem are defined by the entities of the human-created basic **character set**, and **physical entity set**, with four entities namely, **data, information, knowledge** and **wisdom**. These sets of entities are externalized entities, and each of them can be a set. In addition, the boundaries of the energy–matter subsystem are defined by the natural basic entity set, containing a set of information-coded energy quanta, and a set of neural matter packages that collectively form the information-coded matter structure. Therefore, the four human-created basic physical entity set and two natural basic entity set define the operational boundaries of the human thinking systems.

Besides the natural and artificial entities, another important aspect of the human thinking system is the presence of the **intelligence space**. The human thinking systems include a fairly advanced intelligence space can be divided into four sets of functions. The first set enables the physical symbol subsystem to evolve and interact with the environment. It encompasses capabilities such as primitive **character set creation** and **event capturing**. The second set of functions facilitates basic entity and basic entity interactions. Therefore, it includes activities such as basic entity transformation and manipulation, that is, data processing, information processing, and knowledge accumulation (creation of knowledge structure).

The next set of functions connects the physical symbol subsystem and the energy–matter subsystem. It transforms a human-created entity into an information-coded energy quantum and vice-versa, which includes the abstract perception or concept-attainment capability. Finally, the last set of functions facilitates energy–matter and matter–matter interactions. The cognitive interpretation of such interactions includes reasoning and decision making. The neural equivalences are the information-coded energy quanta manifested as electrical signals and the information-embedded matter packages transmitted as chemical signals (neurotransmitters) — see Appendix 5. The interaction between the intelligence space and the physical entity set of the human thinking system are illustrated in Figure 5.3.

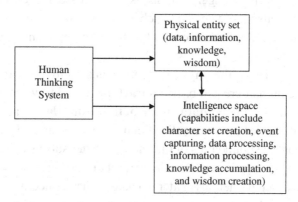

Figure 5.3   Interaction between the intelligence space and the physical entities set in the human thinking system.

5.3 The Physical Symbol Subsystem

5.3.1 *Basic human intelligence and the character set*

Symbols lie at the root of advance intelligent action, and the symbols can be physical or non-physical. A requirement of intelligence, at a basic human level, is that such a system must have the ability to store and manipulate symbols. The characteristics of the physical symbol subsystem are defined by the equation:

$$\text{environment} \leftrightarrow \text{artifact} \tag{5.2}$$

or

$$\text{environment} \leftrightarrow \text{basic entity} \tag{5.3}$$

which is fundamentally a data creation and capturing phenomenon, and the equation:

$$\text{artifact} \leftrightarrow \text{artifact} \tag{5.4}$$

or

$$\text{basic entity} \leftrightarrow \text{basic entity} \tag{5.5}$$

that embodies the information processing and knowledge structuring processes (the first two sets of functions).

The creation of a character set and physical symbols by a certain community of human beings constitutes the birth of basic human intelligence (basic human intelligence <=> the intelligence with symbols creation and manipulation capabilities). It may not be too extreme to equate the above emergence to the beginning of human civilization. The discovery of this ability also distinguishes basic human intelligent action itself from instinctive (animal intelligence — basic life-intelligence) action. This unique human intelligence trait separates humankind from the other species.

The creation of a symbol set by a particular human civilization is a fascinating phenomenon. It marks the crossing of an 'intelligence threshold'. The character set containing primitive elements is created by the interactions between the thinking systems and their environment. This event is extremely significant for all human thinking systems as its discovery signifies the extension of the natural component of the thinking system to include an artificial component, the physical symbol subsystem. The artificial component in turn facilitates the evolution of the natural component to achieve a more sophisticated level of thinking activity. This evolution has been slow, gradual and ongoing for the past few thousand years. The character set also enabled a community to store knowledge externally in written form for the first time (see Figure 5.4).

The creation of a symbol set is only made possible by the emergence of the unique function to create it. Thus, there exists a **symbol creation function** that can create a primitive symbol or character set when a human thinking system interacts with its environment. The character set contains all the symbols that are created for the use of a particular community (constantly changing and upgrading). In a community that uses the English language, the **character set** (C) can be represented as follows:

$$C = \{a,b,c,..., A,B,C,...,1,2,3,...,+,-,...\} \tag{5.6}$$

The character set together with the **physical entity/symbol set** (PE) form the basic foundation that leads to the emergent of a language (see Figure 5.4).

$$PE = \{data, information, knowledge, wisdom\} \tag{5.6a}$$

Each entity is itself a (set of) morpheme or word (and their combination) — data and information.

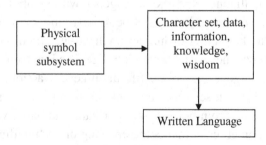

Figure 5.4 Creation of a written language from the character set and physical entity set of a physical symbol system.

5.3.2 *Basic entity capturing and processing*

The creation of a character set leads to the emergence of a written language that facilitates event capturing and basic entity processing. The occurrence of this event is incremental, and it is made possible by the existence of certain favosrable conditions — illustrated as axioms I to III below.

Axiom I

There exists at least one natural language that is not a null set and it has a character set with a large number of primitive elements.

Axiom II

There exists a **coding function** that can code/capture an event into a data element or data set.

Axiom III

There exist **higher-order basic entity transformation functions** that transform the basic entities for (subsequent) better problem solving and decision making, as well as knowledge accumulation.

When an event occurs, the coding function is activated and captures the occurrence of an event using the character set. The data set created contains the raw facts of the event. Very often, at a more complex stage, the coding process must observe a set of grammatical, semantic, and computational rules.

Subsequently, additional transformations (**basic entity transformation functions**) are required before the basic entity is useful. Thus, the data set has to be processed to generate a useful or valuable set of information that is relevant to a particular situation (problem solving). The information is matched against a knowledge structure in the human thinking system. The **knowledge accumulation process** is perceived as a large-scale selective combination or union of related pieces of information. A **knowledge structure** contains chunks of information with established relationships. The value of later pieces of information will be determined by the quality of the knowledge structure.

5.3.3 *The cognitive perspective*

Cognitive science is an interdisciplinary domain that focuses on the mind and its processes. The psychological and neuropsychological characteristics of a human thinking system observed at the macroscopic level form the cognitive dimension. Cognition is the mental abilities and processes of the human thinking systems encompassing attention, memory, comprehension, reasoning, evaluation, problem solving, and decision making (very often, involving a language). The cognitive phenomena associated with information processing and consciousness is studied at the brain code level (neural substrates) in neuropsychology (cognitive neuroscience). It is at this level that a relationship between human thinking (neural processes) and behavior (psychological processes) can be established.

From this perspective, perception signals are interpreted as concepts. A **concept** is a basic cognitive entity of the mind. And concepts interact with the **cognitive structure** during thinking processes, and there is a possibility of re-organizing it. Therefore, a concept is a basic cognitive entity of a human thinking system, and it contains one or more pieces of related information that have been understood.

Therefore, a concept is formed when a piece or a body of information is integrated and comprehended. At the least, its structure and content must have been recognized. The requirement is that a concept must be meaningful, and that it can be integrated into the cognitive structure (encompassing a **cognitive intelligence/functions set**, and a **cognitive space** — a space of memories, thoughts, and ideas) — see Figure 5.5. The level of sophistication of the concept-attainment process is determined by the **cognitive intelligence** present. The cognitive intelligence (including reading, comprehending, writing, logic, reasoning, and analyzing — the

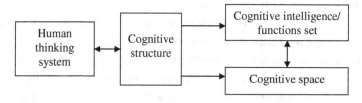

Figure 5.5   Cognitive perspective of the human thinking system.

intellectual abilities) of the human thinking systems is more complex than basic human intelligence. This higher form of intelligence is denoted as advance human intelligence in this theory.

5.3.4 *Advanced human intelligence and the abstract mental space*

The **advanced human intelligence** of the human thinking system is expressed differently from basic human intelligence. It is manifested in the 'concept-attainment' dimension (more deeply associated with the exploitation of a sophisticated language, and beyond — will be dealt with in more details later chapters). Basically, its presence is manifested as a perception function and a decision-making function. The combinations of these two functions form a reasoning process. The existence of the two functions is vital to the evolution of advanced human intelligence.

Axiom IV

There exists a perception function that maps related, human-created basic entities into a concept or a set of concepts.

Axiom V

There exists a decision function that acts on concepts or perception signals to create a decision choice (decision making) and an action (problem solving).

In this respect, a concept is a perception signal capturing an information state in the mind (neural code). The signal can be absorbed into the cognitive structure if it is consumed. The ability of a thinking system to handle and consume concepts is associated with the presence and quality of an advanced intelligence source.

A cognitive structure processes an intelligence source embedded within it. It is important to distinguish between the two components of a cognitive structure: the basic store of internalized information/knowledge, and intelligence as the means for its internal processing. In this model, the basic store of internalized knowledge is the cognitive space, and intelligence is the set of cognitive functions.

Information and the other basic entities are external entities with respect to the cognitive structure. A piece of information can be scanned by the mind but it is only integrated into the knowledge structure after it has been consumed or internalized, that is, after a relationship with a particular knowledge structure/space is established. In this sense, a knowledge space is internalized within the cognitive structure, while a knowledge entity is an external entity (in a repository). As a particular knowledge space grows, the cognitive structure as a whole is enhanced.

Thus, there exists an **internalization or consumption function** that enables concepts to be integrated into the cognitive structure. The internalization function enables a concept to be consumed by the cognitive structure once the relationship between the concept and an internalized knowledge space is established. The various functions are summarized in Figures 5.6 and 5.7.

In the general information theory, a human thinking system is perceived to have a cognitive structure comprising a cognitive space and a set of cognitive intelligence/functions (see Figure 5.5). The cognitive space is a store containing the various internalized knowledge spaces/structures. The union between the various knowledge spaces forms the cognitive space, and each knowledge space is therefore a subset of the cognitive space.

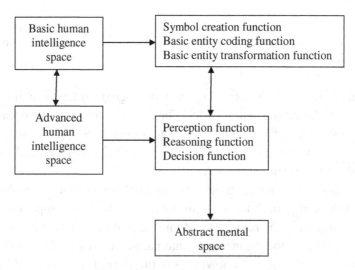

Figure 5.6   Intelligence functions of the human thinking system.

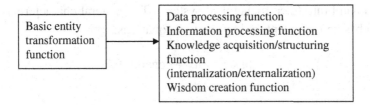

Figure 5.7   Sub-functions of basic entity transformation function.

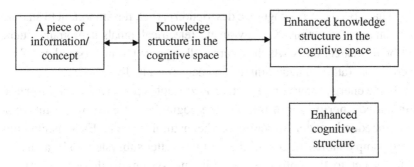

Figure 5.8   Internalization of a piece of information/concept.

Thus, internalization occurs when a concept or a set of concepts is consumed and absorbed into the cognitive space. When a concept is absorbed into a particular knowledge space, some restructuring takes place in that space. Therefore, understanding a concept, establishing the relationship between the concept and the knowledge space concerned, and finally identifying a proper fit between the two units, leads to the internalization of the concept. Thus, absorption and restructuring are necessary conditions for internalization to occur. In this regard, an internalized knowledge space can be perceived as a large collection of concepts arranged in a certain meaningful structure (see Figure 5.8).

5.4 The Energy–Matter Subsystem

5.4.1 *Basic entity–energy quantum interaction*

In the general information theory, the other subsystem of the human thinking systems is the **energy–matter subsystem**. The latter resides within the human brain (electrochemical system). The general characteristics of this subsystem are captured by the two equations:

$$\text{basic entity} \leftrightarrow \text{energy} \tag{5.7}$$

and

$$\text{energy} \leftrightarrow \text{matter} \tag{5.8}$$

which have been given a cognitive description earlier. It is important to analyze the brain's operations on the energy–matter (electrical signals, neurotransmitters, and brain matter) basis which in turn will support the understanding of the microscopic (atomic) neural dimension better eventually.

In the energy–matter perspective, a concept is perceived as an **information-coded energy quantum**, and the cognitive structure is the information-embedded matter structure of the natural system. Establishing this relationship enables the role of the energy–matter subsystem to be analyzed with respect to the entire human thinking system in the energy–matter dimension.

When one or more pieces of information are assimilated by the natural component of a human thinking system, this is done by the perception function. Therefore, the perception function is also the artifact-energy conversion function, which transforms one or more pieces of information into one or more packages of information-coded energy quanta. As an energy quantum in which information codes are embedded is a concept, the latter can be redefined in the new context as one or more related information-coded energy quanta. Thus, the artifact-energy conversion function or perception function possesses a cognitive perspective. Therefore, a perception function is one that has the ability to convert one or more human-created basic entities into a concept, and transforms it into an information-coded energy quantum.

5.4.2 *Energy quantum–matter structure interaction: Internalization*

The information-coded energy quanta created during the interactions of the two subsystems are scanned with respect to an appropriate matter knowledge structure. No consumption occurs if an energy quantum is merely scanned and rejected. Consumption of an energy quantum only happens if that quantum causes a re-organization in the matter structure. In such a case, internalization is said to have occurred. Therefore, the **internalization function** is an **energy–matter interaction** function that facilitates the knowledge restructuring process.

The matter structure is perceived as a discrete structure comprising a large number of information coded matter packages or brain matter with certain established relationships. A different perception of the internalization function must now be re-established. It is perceived as the function that enables an energy quantum to be consumed by the matter structure, and in the process enhances the thinking structure itself.

5.4.3 *Matter structure–energy quantum interaction: Externalization*

There also exists a function that enables the information-coded matter to create and emit energy quanta. This function is represented as an **externalization function** that acts on the matter package involved in the emission process. In the event, the matter structure creates an energy quantum when responding to the consumption of another energy quantum. Thus, there exists an externalization function that enables the matter structure to create and emit one or more energy quanta when the latter consumes an energy quantum.

It must be noted that the internalization and externalization functions are not mathematically inverse functions. Besides, the matter structure remains intact or unaltered after externalization. The process appears to be more a duplication function where the information quantum created is identical to the portion of the matter structure concerned. Externalization is important as it enables the internal content (tacit) of a thinking system to be made known to the environment or other intelligence sources (explicit), and yet the contents in the source remain unaltered (see Appendix 6).

5.4.4 *Energy quantum–basic entity interaction*

After externalization, the energy quanta created interact with the physical symbol subsystem. The energy quanta are converted into combinations of physical entities for communication or other external manipulations. This process is executed by the **energy-to-artifact conversion function**. Its operation is the reverse of the perception function. Thus, there exists an energy-to-artifact conversion function that enables an information-coded energy quantum to be converted into one or more human-created basic entities. Again, the two functions may not be exact inverse functions.

5.4.5 *Matter–matter interaction*

As mentioned earlier, the matter structure is a discrete structure containing an infinitely large number of information-coded matter packages and processors. The different information-coded matter packages and processors interact among themselves internally within the structure. This activity is **matter–matter interaction**. It is facilitated by an intermediary matter package, a neurotransmitter. The process also leads to re-organization and enhancement of the matter structure as a whole.

Therefore, there exists a matter–matter interaction function, which can enhance the matter knowledge structure. Such interaction occurs when reasoning and decision-making processes take place in the human mind. Thus, there also exists a matter–matter interaction function that enables information coded matter packages to interact among themselves, and in the event enhances the intelligence space. In this respect, matter–matter interaction and mindfulness may have an interesting relationship.

5.4.6 *Wisdom creation*

Wisdom creation is a special form of energy–matter and matter–matter interactions. It is perceived as the creation of matter packages with a new set of information codes (unknown to the community using the knowledge). It is an intense self-enhancement process that is taking place within the matter structure — facilitated by a high level intelligence space. It is an internal process, and usually it can be activated only if that particular human thinking system has been consistently consuming energy quanta in a certain knowledge domain or interrelated areas — an expertise or master. Concurrently, rigorous analysis and re-structuring of the matter structure must have taken place in that knowledge domain concern too.

The creation of a new information state (new knowledge creation) can only emerge in a mind that has made preparation for it — presence of a consciously and/or sub-consciously prepared mind. A reasonable knowledge space must have evolved before wisdom creation can occur. Even though 'wisdom' has been defined as a body of new information, very often, it also encompasses the capability of an expert (specialist, master, a person that has been in a domain for a considerable period of time) to conceive the new information as well. The consequence may amount to a discovery, an invention, or an innovative and creative contribution. Thus, the creation of wisdom is highly nonlinear. It is not merely a linear extension of the existing knowledge matter structure. Thus, this function is closely associated with complexity and nonlinearity, and intense intelligence (see Figure 5.9).

5.4.7 *Energy–matter function space*

The **energy–matter function space** is also an abstract space that stores the intelligence of the human thinking systems. The intelligence space is located within the discrete neural structure of the energy–matter subsystem.

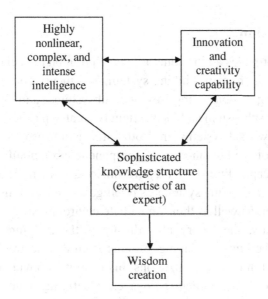

Figure 5.9 Some characteristics of innovation and creativity functions.

It is the intrinsic dynamo of the human mind. The intelligence space is perceived to give rise to all the mental functions discussed earlier in this chapter. When activated, the intelligence generation function generates packages of intelligence (energy) during neuronal activities. In this respect, intelligence is quantized and very likely, consciousness is also quantized. It is the large quantity of intelligence packages emitted at one point in time that makes intelligence appear to be a continuum. Thus, there also exists an elementary intelligence function that manipulates the intelligence space.

In this respect, the human thinking system is a highly concentrated source of intelligence. It is the most intense source of intelligence on Earth. However, the Universe as a whole embodies infinite sources of intelligence, in particular, at the proto-intelligence level. In general, all intelligent systems, natural and artificial, living and non-living, contain some degrees of structured information and intelligence (there may be other intense intelligence sources that are not known to us, including those in the dark energy and matter world). In some sense, intelligence is the ability or power to decode and process data embedded in the Universe. It is a mysterious energy created by nature to decode itself. The degree of decoding depends on the 'intelligence' of the decoder.

5.5 Conclusion

This chapter provides an introductory description on the general information theory of the human thinking system. The theory conceived that the human thinking system comprises two subsystems, namely the natural energy–matter subsystem and the artificially created physical symbol subsystem. The two subsystems are both information processing systems. The presence of the human-created component substantially extends and enhances the capabilities of the entire thinking system. The theory also perceives human thinking systems as intelligent open systems that interact with each other, as well as their immediate environment.

Concurrently, the theory also illustrates the structure and macrodynamics of the human thinking systems from the electrochemical perspective. For all human organizations this is a vital domain as their basic interacting agents are human beings each carrying a human thinking system. The latter are the most intense intelligence sources on this planet, and they are complex adaptive systems that can be nonlinear (emotional, innovative and creative). In the intelligent organization theory, human intelligence is the most valuable asset of human organizations, and must be well-managed and integrated, as the agent-agent/system interaction form the holistic micro-structure. In this respect, it is vital to better comprehend the dynamic of these intelligence sources for higher individual optimization and collective nurturing.

In this respect, the conceptualization vividly indicates that possessing information without a language (for instance, in the world of an insect colony), especially a written language is very different from one with a sophisticated language (confined only to human communities). Apparently, symbolic processes are much more superior compared to imagery processes or acoustic processes. In this respect, nurturing a 'common language' vital for better communication and self-organization is a key role of an intelligence leader (see Chapters 9 and 10). Self-organizing communications is significantly elevated with the presence of such a (written) language (and the exploitation of information/communication/social media). Therefore, human collective intelligence is different from swarm collective in many aspects.

Apparently, with a better comprehension of the human thinking systems (as the natural information processing and knowledge creation system, and the key decision-making nodes in any information networks) on a macroscopic perspective, the complexity aspect of the interactive dynamics of human organizations (with the human thinking systems as their interacting agents), encompassing autopoiesis, symbiosis, interconnectivity, self-organizing communications, adaptation, symbiosis, self-organization/self-transcending constructions, interdependency, attractor, evolution, co-evolution, and emergence of the characteristics/properties of composite complex adaptive systems must be examined more in-depth and better integrated, is highly critical. Particularly, the relational aspect (highly nonlinear relational parameter) that could be better achieved with the presence of a 'common' language that nurtures deeper mental coherency (feeling system) will also be analyzed over the subsequent chapters (see network management and network theory in Appendix 7).

At the moment, the above conceptualization only provides a funda-mental conceptual structure that can explain the macroscopic dynamics of the human thinking systems. Besides the macroscopic dynamics, human thinking systems also possess a neuronal and subatomic dimension (neural networks), as well as a complex adaptive perspective. Ideally, the general information theory conceived to explain the human mind must take care of all these perspectives eventually. When that is achieved, the mysterious phenomena that enable the material brain to give rise to a non-material abstract mind including, the behavioral/cognitive dimension will be more fully understood.

Finally, the general information theory is summarized with its four postulates that define the boundary of the theory, stipulate the basic objective of information processing, and explain the purpose of creating and integrating artificial information systems (see Chapters 4 and 6) into human information processing networks. The four postulates are as follows:

Postulate I: Law of Boundary

Data, information, knowledge, and wisdom are the human-created basic entities, and information-coded energy quanta, as well as information-coded matter packages are the natural entities that define the boundaries of the general information theory.

Postulate II: First Law of Interaction

The basic objective of all human-created entity interactions is to transform a physical entity with higher entropy to one with lower entropy so that the knowledge creation/accumulation (establishing relationships), conceptualization, reasoning, and decision-making processes can be enhanced.

Postulate III: Second Law of Interaction

The basic objective of energy–matter and matter–matter interactions (within the complex neural network) is to enhance the matter knowledge structure of a human thinking system so that it can function more effectively. In this respect, both the information-coded matter subspace and the intelligence subspace are enriched in the process (higher capacity).

Postulate IV: Law of Artificial Systems

The primary objectives of all constructed basic entity systems (including, computerized information systems) are to achieve the first law of interaction more effectively using artificial means (presence of artificial supporting nodes), and to support the second law of interaction by complementing the shortcomings of the natural component (human thinking systems — decision-making nodes).

Specialized Topics of the IO Theory

Without the randomness of chaos (complexity), the rich variety and diversity of evolution would be stifled and throttled. Chaos (complexity) is the rich soil from which creativity is born.

Uri Merry, *Coping with Uncertainty*

Chapter 6

Fundamentals
of the Complexity-Intelligence Strategy

"The instinct of greater human group survival is a powerful collective
force that arises from mindfulness and orgmindfulness"

"The longevity of humanity is greatly dependent on the success of
preparing for unpredictability"

Summary

The five earlier chapters introduced the basic foundation (co-existence of
order and complexity, sensitive dependence on initial conditions, complexity <=> presence of in-determinism and unpredictability, necessities
to change, the intelligence paradigmatic shift, structural reform, complex
adaptive systems and dynamic, and some other fundamental and critical
properties/characteristics involved) of the complexity theory and intelligent organization (IO) theory. This chapter introduces the global/holistic
complexity-intelligence strategy (with two macro-paths) of the IO theory
(although, some sub-strategies/models have been mentioned or partially
analyzed in earlier chapters). The new strategy attempts to provide more
comprehensive linkages and coverage on some specialized aspects indicating that human organizations must be led and managed differently in
the current context because of high complexity density. In this chapter,
three sub-strategies of the holistic complexity-intelligence strategy that
is vital for nurturing highly intelligent human organizations (iCAS) are
examined. They are namely, organizing around intelligence, nurturing
an intelligent biotic macro-structure, and the integrated deliberate and
emergent strategy.

The intelligence/conscious-centricity aspect begins with a deeper analysis on human level intelligence and consciousness, complexity, collective intelligence, org-consciousness and their associated dynamics relative to that of some other biological species (swarm intelligence), as well as other physical complex adaptive systems (CAS) characteristics. It has been observed that human interconnectivity, interdependency, self-organizing communications, truthful engagement, complex networks, collective intelligence, orgmindfulness, orgmind, and emergence can be significantly dissimilar. The four different perspectives of organizing around intelligence are examined.

Next, the intelligent biotic macro-structure (introduced earlier in Chapters 3 to 4) that resembles a highly intelligent biological being, and is more effective at exploiting information processing and knowledge accumulation, and a smarter evolver are more deeply scrutinized. There exists a high synchrony between organizing around intelligence and the presence of a biotic macro-structure. Thus, the advantages and significance for intelligent human organizations to possess such an inherent biotic macro-structure to better exploit certain biological and complexity associated characteristics and dynamics (including intelligence-intelligence linkage, complexity-centricity, complexity-intelligence linkage, more efficient natural decision-making node, information processing capability, learning and adaptation, knowledge acquisition and creation, organizational neural network, artificial node, and structural and dynamical coherency) to compete more effectively and efficiently in the current 'raplexity' context is also illustrated. In addition, the uniqueness and roles of artificial information systems (artificial nodes) is further examined.

Finally, the integrated deliberate and emergent strategy is scrutinized with respect to its significant association with the co-existence of order (deliberate planning, determinism, completeness and predictability) and complexity (continuous nurturing processes, in-determinism, unpredictability, unknown unknowns, risk management, new opportunity, crisis management, self-transcending constructions, futuristic and emergence) — in particular, highlighting the criticality of the deliberate and emergent auto-switch (better ambidexterity). Currently, the holistic integrated smarter evolver and emergent strategist approach is absent in most human organizations.

Keywords: Intrinsic intelligence, consciousness, complexity, dimensionality, intelligence/consciousness-centricity, structural and dynamic coherency, intelligent biotic structure, organizing around intelligence, integrated deliberate and emergent strategy, complexity-intelligence strategy, awareness, mindfulness, orgmindfulness, mental cohesion, self-powered capacity, intrinsic leadership capacity, concentrated calmness, structural capacity, adaptive capacity, collectiveness capacity, collective intelligence, org-consciousness, mindful culture, punctuation point, tipping point, physical symbol set, basic life-intelligence, 2nd order human consciousness, α-state, intelligent complex adaptive systems (*i*CAS), orgmind, connectivity, engagement, interdependency, intelligence-intelligence linkage, intelligence advantage, space of order, space of complexity, risks management, ambidextrousness, sustainability, nonlinear intelligence, complexity-intelligence linkage, complexity-intelligence centricity, butterfly effect, intelligent organization (IO), emergence, constructionist hypothesis, rugged landscape, intelligent complex adaptive dynamic (*i*CAD), in-deterministic chaos, relativistic complexity, uncertainty, ontological reduction, phase space, deliberate-emergent auto-switch, dissipative, autopoiesis, symbiosis, self-organization, self-transcending constructions, autocatalysis, intelligence mindset, intelligence paradigm, decision-making node, secondary/supporting node, evolve, co-evolve, far-from-equilibrium, red queen race, latent intelligence, intelligence era, thought technology, human thinking systems, interacting agent, behavioral schemata, bio-diversification, coherency, synergetic, organization brain, organizational neural network, intelligent biotic macro-structure, morphogenesis, structural capacity, dynamical equilibrium, humanizing organization, organizational central nervous system, intrinsic leadership, self-powered, phobic mindset, Abilene paradox, intangible structure, physical structure, external information, internal information, learning, adaptation, intelligence/consciousness management, organizational justice, mental cohesion, constructionist hypothesis, complexity management, crisis management, intelligence leadership, punctuated equilibrium, ambidexterity, smarter evolver, emergent strategist, self-organizing capacity, emergence-intelligence capacity, unifying capacity, leadership capacity, governance capacity, futuristic, network-centric, graph theory, network theory, small world theory, complex networks and complex adaptive networks.

6.1 Introduction: The World of Intelligence-Complexity

6.1.1 *Fundamentals of the intelligent organization (IO) theory*

Human organizations, especially large organizations such as corporations and nations are inherently multi-layer including agents, local spaces/networks, network of networks, the global system, and its environment (may be the composite system). Uncertainty and change are always present — with more spaces of complexity emerging, including technospheres (the unique creation of humanity). In this respect, ensuring time-dependent stability at all levels is highly significant. In general, better 'rationalization' of the behavioral schemata of the agents and their interactions is beneficial as human organizations are **self-organizing systems** (of voluntary collaboration — elevating the constructive **self-organizing capability**). The construal, emotional, and nonlinearity attributes of these agents are also vital aspects. The presence of hierarchical dysfunction in most current organizations is apparent. In addition, it is beneficial to look forward (foresight, scenario planning, **futuristic**) and backward (hindsight, **hysteresis**) with better **ambidextrousness** for higher effectiveness and efficiency.

The situational characteristics vividly indicate the significance and benefits of **intelligence/consciousness-centricity**. The latter coupled with **complexity-centricity** and **network-centricity** forms a key foundation of the IO theory (see Chapter 2). In addition, **stability-centricity** at different levels, including the agents, networks, and global/organizational must be achieved concurrently — vital to coherency, mental cohesion, and synergy. In this respect, the primary focal points are the intelligence/consciousness sources in the systems/organizations, and how they can be 'optimized' involving effective exploitation of intelligence-intelligence linkages and complexity-intelligence linkages, including constantly exploiting the co-existence of order and complexity. Holistically, the mindset, thinking, and strategies also concentrate on elevating collective intelligence, org-consciousness, structural capacity, adaptive capacity, collectiveness capacity, self-organizing capacity, emergence-intelligence capacity, and unifying capacity.

6.1.2 *The two macro-paths of the complexity-intelligence strategy*

The holistic strategy of the **IO theory** is the **complexity-intelligence strategy** that adopts two macroscopic strategic paths. They are namely (path 1) the **three-centricity approach** (integrating intelligence/ consciousness management, complexity management, and network management), and (path 2) the **integrated deliberate and emergent approach** (exploring and exploiting the co-existence of order and complexity). Concurrently, they define the general boundaries of the theory. Path 1 of the complexity-intelligence strategy encompasses numerous microscopic sub-strategies/models/frameworks (see Figures 6.1 and 6.2, and Section 6.4).

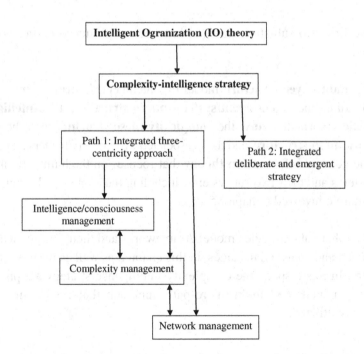

Figure 6.1   The two macroscopic paths of the complexity-intelligent strategy.

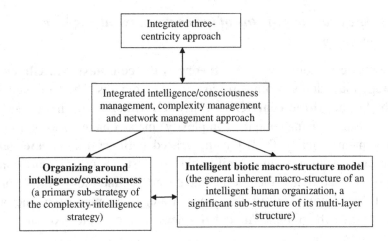

Figure 6.2 Organizing around intelligence/consciousness and the intelligent biotic macro-structure are highly interdependent.

The first two sub-strategies that have been introduced earlier are as follows:

- The **multi-layer structure** model of (intelligent) human organization, including the **agent-agent/system micro-structure**, the **intelligent biotic macro-structure**, the **complexity meso-structure**, and the **network meso-structure**, and their associated dynamics (Chapters 3 and 4).
- The **general information theory** that focuses on the human thinking systems and their two subsystems, including the entities and functions/dynamic involved (Chapter 5).

The other sub-strategies/models/frameworks and their focuses will be introduced and analyzed in stages, in this chapter, as well as in subsequent chapters. In this respect, the complexity-intelligence strategy adopts and exploits an integrated multi-micro-path approach that can or must be selectively utilized.

6.1.3 *The three sub-strategies/models to be analyzed*

The key entities of the **IO theory** are human **intrinsic intelligence**, **consciousness (awareness, mindfulness), collective intelligence,**

org-consciousness (org-awareness, orgmindfulness), complexity, and **network**. This chapter will begin with a deeper analysis on the signifi-cance, characteristics, and roles of intelligence and consciousness as the basic latent entities and impetus that drive human complex nonlinear dynamics, as well as the thinking and processes of **organizing around intelligence** and its synchrony with the **inherent biotic macro-structure model** — a primary component of **intelligence/consciousness manage-ment**. Subsequently, the **integrated deliberate and emergent strategy** will also be introduced.

The boundaries of the three components are briefly as follows:

- **Organizing around intelligence/consciousness** (the key aspect of intel-ligence/consciousness-centricity, and a sub-component of intelligence/consciousness management) — focusing on intrinsic intelligence sources (individual intelligence, awareness, mindfulness) — nurturing and exploit-ing collective intelligence, and org-consciousness (org-awareness, org-mindfulness, mindful culture, intelligence-intelligence linkages, collectiveness capacity, adaptive capacity, voluntary collaboration, unify-ing capacity, coherency, mental cohesion) in human organizations — thus, establishing the key intelligence/consciousness foundation.
- **Intelligent inherent biotic macro-structure model** (another sub-component of intelligence/consciousness management — introduced earlier as a sub-structure of the **multi-layer structure model** will be further analyzed in this chapter) — a systemic transformation that is vital to ensure better structural and dynamic coherency (ideally, also synergetic) — focusing on the fact that human organizations are com-plex biological systems embedded with collective intelligence and org-consciousness that learn, adapt, compete, evolve, and co-evolve (higher structural capacity and adaptive capacity). Thus, the model provides a better structure for achieving higher integrated intelligence/consciousness, engagement, information processing, and knowledge accumulation/exploitation as an organizational foundation.
- **Integrated deliberate and emergent strategy** — a more holistic (complexity-intelligence-centric) exploitation of co-existence of order and complexity, and preparation for unpredictability — a significant component of the intelligent complex adaptive dynamic (*i*CAD) that managed the variation of complexity density better — that is, better

preparation and management of tipping points, spaces of complexity, and punctuation points. Thus, this strategic approach provides a more complete broad-based exploitation of determinism, predictability/ unpredictability, and in-determinism with better ambidexterity, and achieving higher self-organizing capacity, emergence-intelligence capacity, unifying capacity, **futuristic capacity**, innovativeness, resilience, and sustainability.

6.2 Deeper Analysis of Human Intelligence, Consciousness and Complexity

6.2.1 *Better integration and utilization of human intelligence and consciousness*

The pivotal development in the final stage of brain evolution is confined to the Homo sapiens that emerge around 250,000 years ago (see Appendix 5). The better developed cerebral cortex (a complex neural network) is the most intense intelligence/consciousness source on this planet. In the earlier chapters, human intelligence and consciousness have been introduced, and they are significantly different from that of all other living species, including other members of the primate family. Consequently, human intense intelligence and deep consciousness (awareness, mindfulness) is the **inherent strengths** of all human agents, and if integrated appropriately the collective intelligence and organizational consciousness (orgawareness, orgmindfulness) is also the inherent strengths of intelligent human organizations.

The intensity of human intelligence, the diversification and uniqueness of human consciousness, and their differences from other species is enormous. The consequence is the emergent of the following abilities/ functions:

a. The human brain is the most intense intrinsic intelligence/consciousness source known in this biosphere. Human intelligence after the development of the cerebral cortex has enabled human beings to see seven colors, visualize a three-dimensional space, activate bipedal locomotion, and in particular, conceptualize a **physical symbol set**, intensively exploit written language (see Chapter 5), and strategize, plan, and forecast. A summary of human level intelligence is as follows:

Human Level Intelligence (III)

In the IO theory, human intelligence is divided into two components namely, basic human intelligence (encompasses the abilities of basic life-intelligence and beyond — bounded by the upper limit of creating the character set and physical symbol subsystem), and advanced human intelligence (encompassing the abilities to mass communicate, strategize and plan, create abstract concepts, innovativeness and creativity, and other nonlinear thinking capabilities — through effective exploitation of a (at least) sophisticated language, and a range of technologies.)

---

b.   Similarly, from this intense intelligence source **2ⁿᵈ order human consciousness** emerges which encompasses the unique function of **mindfulness**. With this level of consciousness, human beings are able to observe (and control) the mental state of their own mind. This function is highly significant because potential detrimental actions can be prevented before they are activated (again unique to humanity). A summary of human consciousness is as follows:

Human Level Consciousness (II)

Human consciousness activates two mental functions namely, awareness (externally focus) and self-awareness (internally focus). At the core of human self-awareness is mindfulness. Mindfulness is unique to human level consciousness, and therefore is confined to humanity alone. Every individual human being can be mindful (associated with α-state and lower frequency). This is the special mental function that human organizations must learn to nurture (orgmindfulness, mindful culture) and exploit, as it is vital for cultivating collective intelligence, org-consciousness and beyond.

The above two recognitions are highly significant and must be effectively utilized when nurturing highly intelligent human organizations (**highly intelligent complex adaptive systems, *i*CAS**). They redefined the evolution dynamics, structural efficiency, complexity (relativistic) and nonlinearity, and the unique competitiveness of humanity. Hence, highly intelligent human organizations must possess intense **collective intelligence** (which signifies the presence of an **orgmind**), and orgmindfulness (the organizational level equivalent of individual mindfulness). In the IO theory, orgmindfulness is defined as follows:

Orgmindfulness

Orgmindfulness is the mental function that observes the mental states of all the interacting agents in an organization to ensure more effective utilization of every intrinsic intelligence sources, through better interconnectivity, self-organizing communications, and engagement — concentrating on enhancing intelligence-intelligence linkages, collective intelligence, coherency, and mental cohesion. The processes involved can more effectively get facilitated by the presence of a language.

Thus, among others, some of the key thinking and functions that an intelligent human organization must encompass are as follows:

- Optimizing individual intelligence and consciousness.
- Balancing between external focus (awareness) and internal focus (mindfulness, orgmindfulness).
- Enhancing intelligence-intelligence linkages.
- Focusing on intelligence/consciousness management.
- Nurturing high collective intelligence and org-consciousness.
- Orchestrating self-organization/self-transcending constructions.
- Orchestrating the emergent of new order.
- Creating a new intelligence advantage.

Consequently, the primary goal of all intelligent human organizations is to achieve a new competitive niche/advantage (intelligence advantage), and a constantly increasing level of stability (resilience and sustainability), a new order, with capacities that can be elevated with the above functions.

6.2.2 Complexity-intelligence linkage: Exploiting certain spaces of complexity

Concurrently, the intelligence advantage is also closely associated with the better exploitation of complexity. Human organizations possess a large collection of **spaces of order** and **spaces of complexity** (see Figure 6.3). A space of order is linear, and its events are more easily understood. This space provides predictability, comfort, and confidence that most human beings would like to be associated with (traditionally). However, depending or operating solely in a space of this nature (no change, static equilibrium) can only sustain survival for a limited period of time ('do not rock the boat' mentality) — eventually, the organization will self-destruct. Niches cannot be easily found in a territory that is commonly understood. To increase competitiveness and achieve higher sustainability, human organizations will have to endeavor beyond order, and navigate more frequently into spaces of complexity (new and

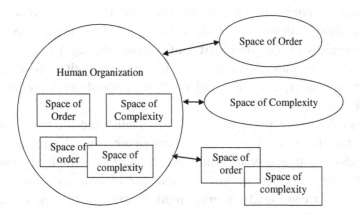

Figure 6.3 A large number of spaces of order and spaces of complexity (internal and external) co-exist in a human organization both internally and externally — a simplified illustration.

unexplored territories, risks management) [according to the IO theory, some spaces of complexity are assumed to present in the organization and its environment at all times, while **punctuation points** (including natural disasters and political disasters) refer to intense spaces of complexity that appear suddenly — see punctuation point in Appendix 7]. Hence, in the present context, these spaces are always surfacing (expectedly or unexpectedly), and these happenings may lead to discomfort or even elimination.

Some spaces of order and spaces of complexity possess 'rather well-defined' boundaries but under other circumstances the two set of spaces can be intertwined in a very complicated manner, and very often 'sophisticated' nonlinear intelligence (innovativeness) is required to identify their boundaries. Hence, conscientious effort must be invested to identify their certain boundaries, and spaces of complexity.

In this respect, spaces of complexity are 'new territories' [mentally and/or physically (for instance, technology R&D spaces)], and not all spaces of complexity are punctuation points (for instance, global financial crisis, social/political crisis, and tsunami) [the **punctuated equilibrium theory** was proposed by **Stephen Gould** (1941–2002) and **Nile Eidredge** (1942–present), in 1972]. Therefore, certain spaces of complexity are significant unexplored 'goldmines'. Exploring, comprehending, and exploiting these new territories requires a new mindset, nonlinear thinking, intense intelligence, and risk-taking. Innovation and creativity (usually associated with — and also greatly dependent on the success of the **complexity-intelligence linkage**) can be better nurtured and employed to explore spaces of complexity where activities are nonlinear, complex, and not fully understood — relativistic complexity.

Basically, the concept of complexity-intelligence linkage is to tap into and exploit innovation and creativity (intense intelligence and consciousness) so that new deterministic disorder or complexity can be exploited to further strengthen the structure of order (relativistic) — towards better **complexity management**. Because of their nonlinearity, many complexity spaces may contain an enormous amount of unpredictable outputs awaiting a more prepared, curious, and risk-taking mind and/

or orgmind. Any individual or organization that is able to discern some surface patterns/structures in such a space early acquires an intelligence advantage (closely associated with effective usage of intense individual intelligence and/or extensive collective intelligence) — very likely activating the butterfly effect. As the benefits derived from understanding and exploiting the new spaces of complexity (some spread over several perspectives including social, education, economic, and political) can be enormous, competitive human organizations should continuously channel resources into such spaces to sustain or elevate their competitiveness. Apparently, moving towards complexity-intelligence-centricity is inevitable.

Usually recognizing and comprehending certain potential surface patterns a space of complexity requires new knowledge that leads to the emergent of new order — the primary characteristic of emergence. In the process, through deeper comprehension of new opportunities, the competitiveness and sustainability of the organization are broadened. Subsequently, the organization can then move on to explore other complexity spaces. This dynamic is continuous as the rugged landscape keep changing — spaces of complexity with niches will also change. This cyclical process continually elevates the adaptability, and ensures the existence (survival) of the organization. It is part of the *i*CAD. It is an evolutionary dynamic that can best be sustained by the intense human intelligence/consciousness of the interacting agents, and the high level of collective intelligence/org-consciousness of the organization.

Note: Some Common Spaces of Complexity (that are not Punctuation Points):

- Diversified multi-generation human assets space of complexity (will be dealt with later).
- Uneven wealth distribution space of complexity (in a nation or the entire humanity).
- Bio-technology R&D space of complexity.
- ICT R&D space of complexity.
- Medical-engineering R&D space of complexity.

Based on the above discussion a space of complexity and punctuation point can be briefly defined as follows:

Space of Complexity

A 'single' space of complexity (confined to one perspective) exists prominently in human organizations. It possesses a nonlinear and continuously changing dynamic that may manifest a surface pattern, although, the detail situation of the interacting agents/entities may not be apparent. In general, it could be a space of opportunity embedded with 'gold nuggets', if constructively exploited (involving risk management) with intense intelligence/consciousness.

Punctuation Point

A punctuation point is a space of high complexity (with unknowns) that appears suddenly in human organizations (part of the stasis and punctuated equilibrium cycle). Its dynamic is highly complex, nonlinear, in-deterministic, and unpredictable. Consequently, there is a probability that the organization will drift into a space of in-deterministic chaos, and self-destruct if the situation is not appropriately managed (especially due to lack of collective intelligence). With better crisis preparation the negative outcome of a punctuation point can be diminished or eliminated.

6.3 Fundamental Properties and Focuses of the IO Theory

6.3.1 *Some key properties and definition of IO*

The above analysis has identified some key basic entities/properties of intelligent human organizations. Briefly, these attributes and associated functions are listed as follows:

- **Human intelligence** — basic human intelligence (linear, orderly, self-organizing capability, character set creation), advanced human intelligence (nonlinear thinking, sophisticated written language, mass communication, information processing capacity, plan/strategize and design, abstract concept, cognitive, innovative and creative), self-powered agent, intrinsic leadership, intelligent person.

- **Collective intelligence** — nurture through effective **intelligence-intelligence linkages**, better interconnectivity, mindful culture, truthful engagement, interdependency versus dependency, self-organizing communications, intelligence/consciousness management — presence of the orgmind.

- **Human consciousness** — awareness (external focusing), self-awareness (internal focusing), and mindfulness (internal focusing, core of self-awareness).

- **Organizational consciousness** — org-awareness (external focusing, present in most competitive business organizations), orgmindfulness (internal focusing, mindful culture, lacking in most human organizations today).

- **Complexity** — presence of a complexity meso-structure — spaces of complexity (surface patterns may still exist, risk management), spaces of relativistic order (surface patterns are subjective), punctuation points (sudden, unexpected, crisis management), and spaces of in-deterministic chaos (no surface pattern, self-destruction), and relativistic complexity.

- **Complexity-intelligence linkage** — another key linkage for higher adaptive capacity, coherency, intelligence advantage, resilience, and sustainability — achieve through the mindset that intense intelligence/consciousness sources have to be better optimize to exploit complexity more effectively — integrating intelligence/consciousness management and complexity management.

- **Network** — presence of a network meso-structure (composite entity) — complex networks (network of networks), small-world networks — requires better self-organizing communications, intelligence governance, self-organizing governance, intelligence leadership, lateral/collective leadership, coherency — network management (see Chapter 10).

In general, the IO theory (encompassing complexity theory and **relativistic complexity**) works on the basis that **human organizations are high finite dimension nonlinear complex adaptive systems** (CAS) (not deterministic chaotic systems) involving a large collection of human agents (intelligence/consciousness sources) and variables (some of this variables are unknown unknowns — **uncertainty, and in-complete phase space**), and may involves nonlinear and/or unknown relationships — relational friction (see **ontological reductionism** in Appendix 7). In this respect, complexity in human organizations encompass both indeterminism and unpredictability (sensitive dependence on initial conditions), and has to be analyzed qualitatively (long-term solutions) and not quantitatively (no precise solution) as conceiving a mathematical model is difficult or impossible/incomplete (that is, at best an approximation can be conceived).

The primary aim of the IO theory is to nurture highly intelligent human organizations (*i*CAS) driven by an *i*CAD — enhancing unifying capacity through voluntary collaboration (self-organizing capability). Such organizations possess high collective intelligence (the presence of an orgmind becomes apparent) derived from the effective integration of intrinsic individual intelligence/consciousness of the interacting agents through constructive intelligence-intelligence linkages — involving orgmindfulness and mindful culture (presence of high org-consciousness).

Therefore, cultivating a highly *i*CAD is a crucial responsibility of leaders and managers (ideally, all actors). Fundamentally, the *i*CAD possesses several key activities as follows:

- Focusing on all intense intrinsic intelligence sources.
- Optimizing individual intelligence and consciousness through intense orgmindfulness, effective intelligence-intelligence linkages, and holistic intelligence/consciousness management.
- Nurturing high collective intelligence through effective interconnectivity, self-organizing communications, truthful engagement, intense orgmindfulness, and the presence of a mindful culture (elevating structural capacity, adaptive capacity, collectiveness capacity, and self-organizing capacity).
- Establishing extensive complexity-intelligence linkages, and constantly exploiting certain spaces of complexity (**complexity management** — better risk management).
- Optimizing both order and complexity by mapping and exploiting a deliberate strategy and nurturing an emergent strategy concurrently,

that possesses a deliberate-emergent auto-switch — **smarter evolver** and **emergent strategist.**

- Optimizing networks (formal and informal) that have manifested through self-organization for better coherency and synergy of the entire system (exploit the constructionist effect, if possible).
- Nurturing higher self-organizing capacity and emergence-intelligence capacity — better preparation for the sudden appearance of punctuation points (totally unexpected) for higher resilience and sustainability (a even more abstract aspect of complexity management — better crisis management).

With the above fundamental recognitions and conceptual foundation intelligent human organizations can be defined briefly as follows:

Intelligent Human Organization (I)

Intelligent human organizations (IO) are highly intelligent complex adaptive systems possessing individual intrinsic intelligence (intelligent interacting agents) and organizational collective intelligence (presence of an orgmind). They are driven by a highly intelligent complex adaptive dynamic that exploits individual intelligence, consciousness (awareness, mindfulness), collective intelligence, and org-onsciousness (org-awareness, orgmindfulness) — high intelligence/consciousness-centricity. In this respect, ideally their structure should include a biotic macro-structure similar to a highly developed biological organism for better synchrony. Concurrently, they are constantly exploiting certain spaces of complexity (through effective complexity-intelligence linkages) to enhance their competitiveness, resilience, and sustainability — intense complexity-centricity. Thus, IOs constantly focus on creating a new niche known as intelligence advantage.

6.3.2 *Core properties and primary focuses*

a. Core Properties of the IO Theory

In addition to the five core properties of CAS/dynamic, the IO theory also concentrates closely on intelligence/consciousness, relativistic complexity, stability, and new order.

The 10 core entities/properties of the IO theory are as follows:

- Intelligence (intelligence-centric).
- Consciousness (advanced life-centric).
- Complexity (complexity-centric, risk-centric, unpredictability).
- Dissipative (self-renewal).
- Connectivity (agent-centric, network-centric, org-centric).
- Engagement (agent-centric, network-centric, org-centric).
- Punctuation point (complexity-centric, crisis-centric).
- Relativistic complexity (mental-centric, risk-centric, innovation and creativity).
- Emergence (autopoiesis, self-organizing/self-transcending constructions, autocatalysis, symbiosis, self-organizing capacity, emergence-intelligence capacity).
- New Order (emergence-centric, stability-centric, resilience/sustainability-centric).

b. Primary Focuses of the IO Theory

Briefly, the primary focuses and directional paths of the IO theory are high intelligence/consciousness-centricity, complexity-centricity, network-centricity, and their integration and linkages. The various components (thinking, entities, characteristics, and micro-paths) involved are more comprehensively listed below:

- Intelligence mindset and intelligence paradigm (a new thinking and paradigmatic shift).
- Human thinking systems (human agents, intense intelligence sources, nonlinear, emotional, behavioral schemata, mental space, new organizational assets, and decision-making nodes).
- Intelligence/consciousness management (intelligence-intelligence linkage, higher collectiveness capacity, and higher adaptive capacity).
- Mindfulness (intelligence-consciousness linkage).
- Orgmindfulness (individual intelligence sources, intelligence-intelligence linkages, and orgmind).

- Nurturing collective intelligence (orgmindfulness, mindful culture, and enhancing collectiveness capacity).
- Autopoiesis, self-organization/self-transcending construction, symbiosis, autocatalysis/circulation coupling (self-powered and subtly driven by latent impetus, and higher self-organizing capacity).
- Redefinition of organizational mindset, and leadership, governance, management thinking and processes (focuses on intelligence/consciousness-centricity, relational capacity, voluntary collaboration, coherency, synergetic effect, and organizational mental cohesion).
- Complexity management (complexity-intelligence linkages, exploiting spaces of complexity, and preparing for punctuation points).
- Co-existence of order and complexity (concurrent exploitation — integrated deliberate and emergent strategy).
- Holism, interdependency, constructionist hypothesis, hysteresis, futuristic.
- Complexity-intelligence strategy (numerous sub-strategies and components, including organizing around intelligence, multi-layer structure, integrated deliberate and emergent strategy, general information, theory, intelligent person model, intergarted 3C-OK framework, relativistic complexity, intelligence leadership theory, and intelligence governance theory).
- Emergence and new order (high collective intelligence and emergence-intelligence capacity).
- Intelligence advantage (a new niche).
- Resilience and sustainability (longevity).

The above core properties and key focuses of the IO theory approximately define its boundaries, the basic entities involved, properties/characteristics, and short-term goals, as well as longer-term objectives. In particular, the significance of the latter (longer-term objectives) must be recognized and allocated with resources, as some spaces of complexity and their dynamics may be latent (not apparent but constantly evolving) and possess critical future impact (futuristic). In particular, the objectives and goals of the organization must be in synchrony with stability-centricity at all levels — agents, networks, and organizations. In-between focusing on nurturing, enhancing, and integrating certain critical capacities are equally significant. Some of these capacities (will be analyzed subsequently) are as follows:

- Self-powered capacity (agents)
- Intrinsic leadership capacity (agents)
- Structural capacity
- Collectiveness capacity
- Adaptive capacity
- Relational capacity
- Self-organizing capacity
- Emergence-intelligence capacity
- Leadership capacity
- Governance capacity
- Unifying capacity

6.4 Boundaries of the Complexity-Intelligence Strategy

6.4.1 *The two macro-paths and their sub-strategies/models/ frameworks*

The complexity-intelligence strategy is the global/holistic strategy of the IO theory. (Its boundaries have been introduced at the beginning of this chapter, and a more comprehensive illustration will be done in this section.) There are two macroscopic paths (with a fair amount of overlapping), and the first path encompasses a spread of sub-strategies, models, and frameworks as follows:

Path 1: Three-Centricity Approach

- Integrated intelligence/consciousness management, complexity management and network management macro-path.

The Sub-Strategies/Models/Frameworks of Path 1

- **Organizing around intelligence/consciousness:** Intelligence/consciousness-centricity, human intelligence/consciousness sources, unique human consciousness (mindfulness), intelligence-intelligence linkage, collective intelligence, org-consciousness, orgmindfulness, mindful culture, adaptive capacity, relational parameter, nonlinearity, collectiveness capacity, nurturing an intelligent human organization, and intelligence advantage (mentioned earlier in Chapters 1and 4, and will be further analyzed in this chapter).

- **Multi-layer structure model:** (Chapter 4) encompassing the **intelligent biotic and complex adaptive macro-structure** model [better structural and dynamic coherency (partially illustrated in Chapters 3, its conceptual foundation was established in Chapter 4, will further analyzed in this chapter)]; **agent-agent/system micro-structure** model [inherent structure and dynamic of CAS (mentioned in Chapters 3 and 4), and will be further analyzed in Chapters 7 and 8], the two meso-structure models [**complexity meso-structure** and **network meso-structure**, (Chapters 4 and 10)]; and **artificial systems** and artificial nodes, higher structural capacity, and coherency and synergetic.
- **General information theory**: Human thinking systems, energy-matter subsystem, physical symbol subsystem, unique human intelligence, entity creation and transformation functions, internalized knowledge structure and external knowledge repository, and the emergent of a sophisticated language (Chapter 5).
- **Intelligent person model**: Self-powered agents, intrinsic leadership, information decoder, mindful, orgmindful, rugged landscape, recognizing constraints of human CAS, smarter evolver, and emergent strategist (Chapter 7).
- **Integrated 3C-OK framework**: Collective intelligence, connectivity, culture, organizational learning, knowledge management, interdependency, mindful culture, collectiveness capacity, unique human integrated/collective intelligence/consciousness dynamic, 3C-OK is the basic foundation of *i*CAD, and the latter is different from normal CAD (Chapter 8).
- **Intelligence leadership theory/strategy**: Everybody is in charge, self-powered, intrinsic leadership, lateral/collective leadership, learning leadership, unifying leadership, adaptive leadership, latent leadership, leadership consultative leadership, intelligent person characteristics,

calmness, low key, soft voice, relational parameter, voluntary collaboration, coherency, and 'feeling' system (Chapter 9).

- **Relativistic complexity theory**: Complexity is in the mind of the beholder, complexity-centricity, human intelligence/consciousness intensity, space of relativistic order, relativistic static equilibrium, complexity density versus intelligence intensity, innovation and creativity, and higher intelligence advantage (Chapter 10).
- **Intelligence governance theory/strategy**: Self-organizing governance, adaptive governance, e-governance, collectivity, relational parameter, governance capacity, network-centricity, network management, unifying capacity, relational parameter, hysteresis, synergetic dynamic, mental cohesion, and 'feeling' system (Chapter 10).

Path 2: Integrated Deliberate/Emergent Approach

- **Integrated deliberate and emergent strategy:** Better exploitation of the co-existence of order and complexity (ambidexterity, predictability may be probabilistic), a deliberate-emergent auto-switch, adaptive capacity, and nurturing higher self-organizing capacity and emergence-intelligence capacity (Chapter 6)

6.4.2 *Analyzing two sub-strategies/models of the three-centricity approach*

Two components of macro-path 1 [focusing on organizing around intelligence/consciousness (four different perspectives), and the intelligent biotic macro-structure (artificial networks), as well as intelligence/consciousness management and complexity management] will be more comprehensively analyzed in this chapter — see Figure 6.2.

6.5 Organizing Around Intelligence/Consciousness

The strategic path of **organizing around intelligence** (a foundation pillar of the IO theory) concentrates on four intelligence/consciousness-centric and complexity-centric perspectives that can be better support by an

intelligent macro-biotic structure and vice versus. The four perspectives are as follows:

- Organizing around intelligence/consciousness sources (the mind and orgmind — decision-making nodes, intense intelligence/consciousness-centricity).
- Organizing around information processing and knowledge acquisition and accumulation related activities/capabilities (including artificial networks — secondary/supporting nodes).
- Organizing and focusing on constructive evolution capabilities (learning, adaptation, self-organizing communications, engagement, autopoiesis, symbiosis, voluntary collaboration, risk-taking, evolve, co-evolve, and emergence).
- Organizing and focusing on capabilities to better comprehend and exploit complexity associated characteristics/properties, such as non-linearity, indeterminism, interconnectivity, engagement, interdependency, far-from-equilibrium, butterfly effect, unpredictability, rugged/fitness landscape, self-organization, self-transcending constructions, red queen race, and emergence

6.5.1 *The first perspective of organizing around intense intelligence sources*

The primary focal centers of the IO theory are the **minds** and **orgmind** (the first perspective of organizing around intelligence) in the organization/system as they are the origins of thoughts and actions. A thought originates in the mind, while an action is initiated by a thought. When there is no thought, there is no action. Thus, a more mindful mind is perceived to exercise a better course of action, and hence is more intelligent and conscious (manifestation of **latent intelligence**). On the same note, the best means to enhance the collective intelligence of organization is to concentrate on **quality interconnectivity** and **truthful engagement** of the intrinsic intelligence sources (intense intelligence-intelligence linkages). As indicated earlier, human organizations can elevate their collective intelligence through better orgmindfulness by focusing on connecting or changing the thoughts of the individual minds subtly. Therefore, an **orgmindful organization** is one that is highly concern with the state of the mind of its interacting agents — reflecting the presence of a **mindful culture**.

Human thinking systems are intrinsically nonlinear complex adaptive systems, and they are the basic elements (organizational neural nodes) that form an org-brain. Thus, **an org-brain could be perceived as an organizational neural network with each individual human thinking system functioning as an organizational neuron**. In the new perspective, an organization as a unique single 'living' entity is perceived to behave as an evolving **intelligent organizational being** driven by its own collective intelligence and org-consciousness that originates from its orgmind/org-brain. Similar to biological entities, organizations with an orgmind are able to learn, adapt, compete, evolve, and sustain with time. As mentioned, the intrinsic energy (latent impetus) that drives the above development is primarily human intelligence/consciousness. Inevitably, intense intelligence from sources with the right mindset are required to facilitate the new leadership, governance, and management dynamics — intelligent person, intelligence leadership, and intelligence governance (see Chapters 7 to 10).

Apparently, as the human world drifts into the **intelligence era**, organizations must first discern the primary importance of intelligence/consciousness, and the existence of an orgmind (its boundaries may be situation dependent) in their setup (a new systemic transformation). Hence, an intelligent human organization must nurture an intelligent biotic macro-structure that orchestrates a dynamic that allows its own orgmind and collective intelligence to emerge. In addition, it should possess a dynamic that continually internalizes and accumulates knowledge, and allows its corporate theories and philosophy to evolve with time. In the process, the orgmind will then be expanded and further consolidated. In this respect, an orgmind is somewhat different from a human mind. The former can be significantly enlarged, and its collective intelligence can be elevated substantially with orgmindfulness and other appropriate activities.

It is significant to note that the ratio of the collective intelligence of most current human organization with respect to its average individual agent intelligence is very much lower than that of swarm intelligence with respect to its average individual agent intelligence (ant or bee). Apparently, human agents being much more intelligent and autonomous are more difficult to connect. Most human agents will still survive (high independency) after leaving an organization, while a bee (low independency, high interdependency) that is lost does not survive for long. These inherent characteristics render a human agent much more complex, nonlinear, and unpredictable. In this respect, better connectivity and truthful engagement are vital. However, interconnectivity and engagement in a human organization does not simply imply uniformity and homogeneity alone due to the complex mental space. A secret embedded here may be unity through diversity that is, establishing connectivity by accommodating diversification (an integration of multi-layer differences, diversification, and commonalities) with 'unpredictable' global functional coherency — organizational mental cohesion.

Overall, to enhance connectivity, communications, and engagement, a new technology (**thought technology**) can be exploited. This technology focuses on the nurturing broader and deeper understanding and acceptance (higher mutual trust and respect) of the interacting agents, and the intangible aspect of the organization. Thus, although putting in place an effective physical structure is important, the underlying dynamic in the deep structure that makes the tangible structure work coherently is even more significant. In an ideal situation, the deep structure should provide the foundation for an intelligent and flexible surface structure to be established. The process is usually continuously, and re-modification is always taking place.

Primarily, orchestrating organizational growth and ensuring the coherency of the intangible structure originates from the orgmind. At the moment, few organizations actually place sufficient attention on the existence of the orgmind and the intangible structure. Those that have artificially erected their physical structure (with machine-like features, bureaucratic mindset) should recognize that their structural components are not well-synchronized. An artificially enforced structure can never come close to expected performance if the intangible structure is weak and divided. Therefore, a deeper understanding of the interconnectivity and engagement of the intrinsic intelligence sources, and that collective intelligence, org-consciousness (org-awareness, orgmindfulness), and corporate knowledge management

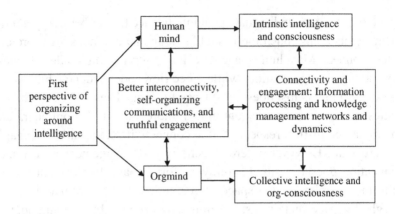

Figure 6.4   Illustrating the first perspective of organizing around intelligence.

are vital entities of human organizations is the key necessity. The above discussion is summarized in Figure 6.4.

6.5.2 *Intelligent human interacting agents*

Human beings are **self-powered** heterogeneous interacting agents that constitute all human organizations. Each of these agents is embedded with an intense intrinsic intelligence/consciousness source. They could behave and interact nonlinearly (presence of emotions, and high perception ability) — each carrying a set of constantly changing **behavioral schemata**. When they form a human organization, they do so with a specific mission/ purpose in mind, such as economic production or provision of certain services — fundamentally, for the purpose of self-centricity and stability-centricity. Concurrently, they will contribute to the org-consciousness and collective intelligence if the environment is 'acceptable'. Irrespective of its mission, a human organization is an **open system** (dissipative) because all human systems interact with the environment, including the fact that agents (employees, citizens) can enter and leave the system/organization.

Thus, each human thinking system must be managed professionally and cautiously/subtly (especially, for a well-educated/informed person and a smart evolver — will be dealt with later). In this respect, the state of every mind is a vital factor that can decide whether the organization will succeed or disintegrate. However, in general, the exact patterns of adaptation, evolution, and survival of the individuals in human organizations may not be predictable in advance (relational, butterfly effect). Those that do not or cannot adapt to the group dynamic will leave (some agents may be destructive). And those that can adapt evolve with the system — co-evolution. Several evolutionary activities such as autopoiesis, autocatalysis, symbiosis, circular causation, dissipation, self-organization/self-transcending constructions, bio-diversification, emergence, and co-evolution can be unfolding concurrently. Overall, the whole phenomenon is complex adaptive with a surface pattern (but the stability the agents are not ensured — a significant difference between CAD and *i*CAD).

In this context, an important focal point of the new intelligence mind-set is to nurture *i*CAD, and ensure the stability of all agents. This process needs a better understanding of the human thinking systems. The dynamic of the mind can be highly sensitive to initial conditions. A significant factor is getting the individual mind to be mindful first. To be mindful is to be more aware of the mind itself, its internal state. It is a deep **self-observation** and **self-reflection** functions. The intention is to ensure that the mind is in better control of its (own) thoughts, decisions and actions — usually associated with calmness, and the α-state. Over all, the higher the level of mindfulness of the mind, the greater is its ability to manage itself and solve problems constructively (also better symbiosis). In practice, nurturing this process is by no means a simple task as the human thinking system is an emotional system that can be logical (see Appendix 5).

A high level of mindfulness can only be attained through conscientious effort over time. To enhance his/her mental state the individuals must first be aware of their thoughts. Thus, the mind must continuously and perpetually search itself. Observing their thoughts increases mindfulness. As a thought begins in the mind, it is at the source, the mind, that it must be checked. The persistent practice of watching helps to avoid interferences by revealing the errors in thoughts at an early stage. In this way, inappropriate actions can be avoided. It must also continuously build up a set of theories that facilitates more coherent thoughts (that enhance confidence and self-stability). Concurrently, the same process also helps to identify new opportunities (including, 'observing' certain spaces of complexity for better exploitation). There is no shortcut to this endeavor.

Concentration is a vital attribute required to achieve a well-focused mind, and **concentrated calmness** and clarity are needed to promote better understanding and decision making. Calmness is a new critical characteristic associated with the intelligence leadership (see Chapter 9). Overall, the individuals must mind the mind, and not allow it to drift in the wrong (not acceptable) direction. This is the basic criterion that must be achieved in mind cultivation. The entire process is smooth and soothing only if there is a high level of mindfulness. The decision and action that emerge from such a mental state is substantially different — towards a **smarter evolver**, and an **intelligence person** — see Appendix 7. The primary entities that determine the characteristics of human agents are shown in Figure 6.5. The summary of a human interacting agent is listed below:

Human Interacting Agent (I)

In the IO theory, human interacting agents are primarily perceived as intense intrinsic intelligence/consciousness sources — the key vital assets. Each of these agents is embedded with a set of complex and constantly changing behavioral schemata (with high perception capability). They are inherently emotional (amygdala) but can be logical (frontal cortex). Thus, human interacting agents (human thinking systems) are complex adaptive systems, and their complex adaptive dynamics and characteristics encompasses autopoiesis, self-centricity, stability-centricity, self-powered capability, intrinsic leadership, nonlinearity, localized space/network, symbiosis, autocatalysis, unpredictability, self-organization/self-transcending constructions, butterfly effect, and emergence.

6.5.3 *Orgmind and orgmindfulness*

In a human organization, the orgmind embraces the minds of some or all its agents — can be structure and situation dependent. An effective orgmind needs members of the organization to voluntarily connect their minds (intense intelligence-intelligence linkages, the core of an integrated

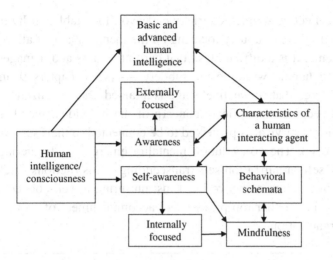

Figure 6.5 The primary entities that determine the basic behavior of human agents.

network of minds) through appropriate engagement (self-organizing communications) to form the pivotal portion of the organizational structure. They must be bounded due to their own volition. There must be no coercing. Orgmindfulness has been mentioned earlier as a key characteristic/ dynamic required. The presence of the orgmindfulness dynamic leads to the nurturing of a mindful culture. Intangibly, it may appear to be the fusion of the individual minds into the orgmind (conceptually perceived to be so). Physically, it is a high/'right' interconnectivity of the human thinking systems with each human thinking system behaving like an **'organizational neuron'**. (A well-structured org-brain is a well-integrated 'organizational neural network'.) In addition, it is not always possible to identify its boundaries as the latter may vary with time, as well as the situation or problem encountered.

It is apparent that the state of the individual minds will have a profound effect on the orgmind, and the mental state of the orgmind is not a simple linear combination of the individual minds. Certain **coherency** and **synergetic effects** can only be achieved if the individual minds are connected in the right manner — for instance, with deeper truthful engagement. Therefore, the integration of all the intrinsic intelligence sources into one collective source is a tricky endeavor. Inevitably, an IO must be orgmindful — continuously focusing on the mental states of all the interacting agents. It is a difficult task that current leaders and managers have to learn to handle with greater subtlety — (see Chapters 9 and 10). However, once that 'collective' stage is attained, the organization's concern will become a significant concern of the individual members. The organization's survival is perceived to be connected to their survival (better symbiosis). The co-evolution mentality emerges — triggering more effective self-organization/self-transcending constructions including, effective integration of networks. Thus, nurturing a well-connected orgmind must be another top priority and accomplishment of an intelligent human organization.

Orgmind

The orgmind is a collection (unique integration) of some (key agents) or all (everybody is in charge) the minds that form the system/organization — an intense organizational neural network (org-brain). It is an intangible organizational structure (core of the intelligent biotic macro-structure) where collective intelligence and org-consciousness emerges. Each human thinking system assumes the role of an 'organizational neuron' in this abstract, complex, and changing network. Hence, its level of collective intelligence is highly dependent on the quality of its interconnectivity, relationships, and engagement of the individual minds. In this respect, orgmindfulness is a critical organizational mental function.

Once an orgmind is established, orgmindfulness must be further enhanced (vice versus). It can be achieved in the same manner as nurturing individual mindfulness, although the task involved here is more delicate. Vividly, a mindful culture (core of the supportive culture) must be present/cultivated. The attributes of a well-focused, clear, calm, and well-controlled orgmind also apply to organizations. A drifting and disconnected orgmind is disastrous. Hence, an organization that aims to exploit the intelligence paradigm must attain a high level of orgmindfulness, and

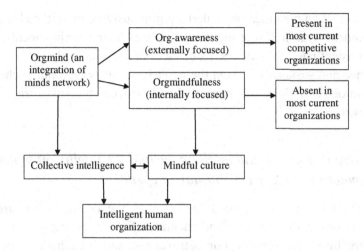

Figure 6.6   The crucial key characteristics/functions of the orgmind of intelligent human organizations.

nurture a mindful culture and an orgmind. It is only when the orgmind is highly orgmindful is the organization ready to adopt other intelligence/consciousness-centric re-structuring and strategies (see Figure 6.6).

If a mind exists within the 'body', logically it ought to thoroughly comprehend the internal environment of its body first. Very often, human beings tend to be more attracted by external events (awareness >> mindfulness). Many organizations are observed to have the same traits (org-awareness >> orgmindfulness). Focusing internally, in particular, on the mental space and intangible dynamic of its agents is an important aspect that is always neglected. It must be emphasized that a human organization must direct its attention internally first if it is to achieve a high level of collective intelligence. This is the basic mission of orgmindfulness. By constantly and conscientiously checking and changing the mental state of the interacting agents, the organization is in a better position to elevate its competitiveness as an integrated entity.

In this respect, the primary reason for the failure of many past organizations is the absence of an effective orgmind. In other cases, it is the deterioration of the orgmind that causes the collapse of the organizations. Very often, failed businesses are not directly eliminated by other businesses. If an organization is alert, continuously aware of the changing environment, orgmindful of the mental state of its interacting agents, and does constant internal searches, its chances of survival is higher — better resilience and sustainability. On the other hand, if its orgmind is chaotic or brain-dead, it does not have to be destroyed by others; rather, it self-destructs.

6.5.4 *Organizing around intelligence and the intelligent biotic macro-structure are mutually dependent*

Conceptually, the critical need to focus on the detailed structure of organizations is due to one fundamental belief — the capacity of the structure limits the growth, competitiveness, and sustainability of the systems. Thus, the **structural capacity** and dynamics of organizations determine their potential for successful competition and evolution (note structural and dynamic coherency). As indicated above, organizing around intelligence leads to the enhancement of the interconnectivity of the human thinking systems, and the emergent of the intangible intelligent biotic macro-structure (orgmind, intangible structure, and physical structure). The level of collective intelligence and org-consciousness of the orgmind that is responsible for the overall performance of the organization is highly dependent on intelligence-intelligence linkages (an intense organizational neural network). In addition, it is significant to note that consciousness and mental interconnectivity among human agents are two mutually enforcing properties. It is only when an organization is highly conscious of its existence, the mental state and activities of its agents, and possessing an 'effectively' connected structure, that collective learning, adaptation, and co-evolution can emerge successfully. Thus, the presence of an intelligent biotic macro-structure will better integrate and utilize intelligence/consciousness sources, and will lead to a tremendous improvement in decision-making, competitiveness, and sustainability — see Figure 6.7. Concurrently, the presence of an *i*CAD is crucial — see 3C-OK framework in Chapter 8. (A well-integrated 3C-OK dynamic is a key foundation of *i*CAD of intelligent human organizations.)

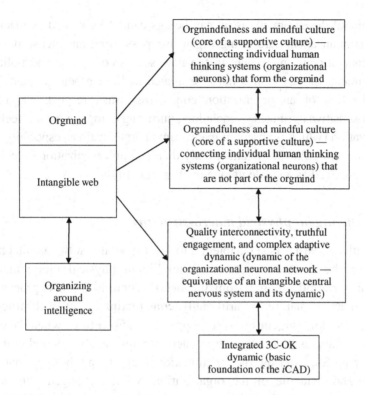

Figure 6.7 Organizing around intelligence and the intelligent biotic macro-structure are mutually enhancing.

In particular, the relational friction (nonlinear relational parameter) is a critical characteristic of all human organizations. The increase in the quality of relationships among all the interacting agents (organizational neurons) in the organization must be faster than the increase in complexity (see **relativistic complexity** in Appendix 7). A special focus on the relational parameter (high **relational capacity**) is the concept of '**humanizing organizations**', including **organizational justice** (see Appendix 7). This development is by no means a coincidence. It is associated with the change in mindset, from the Newtonian machine world to the current complex and nonlinear living world — complexity/intelligence mindset. In an environment that strongly enforces intelligence/consciousness-centricity, humanizing of organizations is a parallel development, as human beings cannot be treated as machine parts. Human agents are living organisms possessing an intense mental/ emotional dimension. Hence, in the new socio-economical and political environment, human beings must be treated as human beings again. The humanization of an organization emphasizes trust, respect, and other human-sensitive attributes — including, nurturing compassion and 'feeling' organization (which is absent in many human organizations, especially corporations and political systems). Only then can an organization be collectively perceived as a single unique intelligent entity.

6.5.5 *Intelligent physical macro-structure*

As stipulated earlier (see Chapters 2 to 4), it is vital that the architectural setup of the surface structure (an intelligent physical biotic macro-structure) should emerge from the deep structure. Such a process is evolutionary in nature — artificially constructing a physical structure contradicts **morphogenesis** — see Appendix 7. Over time, when the deep structure changes gradually, the surface structure is also altered, but not vice-versa. So, altering the organizational chart and hoping that the culture and dynamic of the organization will be changed will never materialize — contradicts the bureaucratic mindset and hierarchical leadership thinking (see intrinsic leadership and self-powered in Appendix 7). In particular, such a dynamic is not sustainable with highly intelligent agents. Thus, time and effort must be invested into nurturing the intangible structure. It is only when the deep structure supports the surface structure it helps to create, that an organization becomes more nimble, flexible, collaborative, learn, adaptive, competitive, and collectively intelligent.

However, the physical structure itself is also an extremely significant component. This is the structure that the agents are constantly in contact (associated) with during their daily operations. In general, the physical structure of an IO possesses three features, namely, an organization brain (a collection of human brains), an environment scanning and responding component (natural and artificial), and a physical intelligence web (a collection of human brains that are not part of the organization brain, and artificial nodes). The existence of an intense collective intelligence source (presence of the org-brain) is the pivotal factor that distinguishes higher levels intelligent human systems from others. The absence of such an organizational neural network indicates the absence of effective integration, as well as leadership nodes. Apparently, an organization cannot compete beyond a certain limit without proper co-ordination, integration, consensus, and direction, and this role is initiated and performed by the intense collective intelligence source.

Briefly, the physical intelligence web that spreads and permeates the entire system has its own significance and value. For highly developed biological organisms, this web is the nervous system that spreads from the brain to all parts of the body — provides the global connectivity, communications, engagement, and integration. For instance, in business organizations, this web must spread from the intense collective intelligence source, and intertwine with and support the economic production system. In all human organizations, the relationship between the physical intelligence web and the org-brain is delicate. In many instances, the demarcation between them may not be clear. In addition, extra precautions (better ambidexterity) are necessary to balance the roles of the two components; otherwise, certain evolutionary characteristics, and innovation and creativity may be suppressed.

In addition, a highly intelligent system has to be responsive to its changing environment. It must act, react, and think like an intelligent biological entity. Therefore, the scanning and responding capability of the environmental component is an important asset. The ability to scan and detect environmental signals coming from environmental targets, the ability to respond swiftly to such signals, and the ability to influence the environmental targets are significant features of this component. This environmental component is highly important to **competitive intelligence** activities most businesses and nations. Thus, the presence of a comprehensive physical sensory system is vital. Therefore, the overall **scanning and responding capability** of the sensory component is an important asset — see Figure 4.6.

6.5.6 *Artificial networks and connectivity: Intrinsic and artificial nodes*

As mentioned, quality connectivity in an organization is a key factor for successful emergence. In general, human interacting agents will express

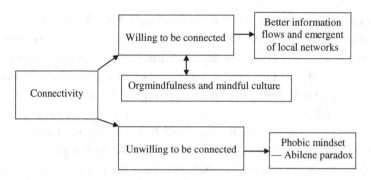

Figure 6.8   Positive and negative connectivity possibility.

willingness or unwillingness to be connected depending on their mental state. If the option is willingness, then higher quality connectivity can be achieved by better information flows and truthful engagement (see Figure 6.8 and Appendix 7). Otherwise, the connectivity, communications, relationship, and engagement among the interacting agents will be extremely low and/or negative (see **phobic mindset**, and **Abilene paradox** in Appendix 7). In this respect, the connectivity of the physical structure is always an important area of concern. The networks, and the integration of agents/systems, in particular, the intelligent information systems network and the economic production system, are important components of the physical structure in business corporations.

In many human organizations (business corporations, military units, nations), a sizable capabilities of the physical structure comprises integrated information processing and communications. Intelligent information system networks enhance the connectivity of an organization through better communications (including media/wireless technology), and faster processing of information. This feature is particularly significant in a knowledge-intensive environment. In this respect, **artificial intelligent information processing networks** support the organization nervous and sensory systems of an IO. Thus, highly intelligent artificially created information systems also serve as artificial information processing nodes in intelligent organizations (see Figure 6.9 — a significant component of the physical intelligent biotic macro-structure). (In fact,

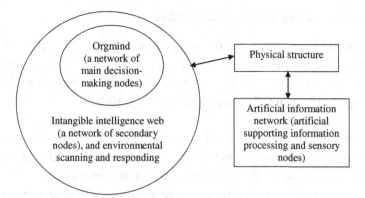

Figure 6.9 An effective intelligent physical macro-structure supported by an effective artificial information network.

intensive use of ICT has gone beyond information dissemination and transaction enhancement to relationships development. This dynamic has establishes new informational linkages that redefined the human socio-economical dimension.)

Thus, in intelligent human organizations, the core of the entire information systems network is the set of human minds, the natural thinking systems (a collection of natural decision-making nodes — the org-brain), which provide the decision making and leadership roles of the organizations. Thus, this set of natural thinking systems is the major component of the collective intelligence source that assumes and performs the leadership and decision-making functions. A well-connected and coherent intense source forms the vital center from which the orgmind emerges. It is linked to all other parts of the organization by the physical intelligence web and sensory subsystem. Within the web, there are other secondary 'decision-making' nodes that may possess specialization capabilities, some of which are artificial nodes (artificial information processing systems and knowledge repositories) and sensory nodes (early warning systems and remote sensory devices). Overall the last few decades, an increasingly important component of the nervous system is the e-landscape, and the fast developing *i*-space (media/wireless) — rendering the situation even more complex.

6.5.7 *Summary of the first perspective*

The synopsis of the basic briefs and approach of the first perspective of organizing around intelligence is re-captured below. It is envisaged that the following suppositions are vital to the success of implementation of other aspects of the intelligence paradigmatic shift:

a. A structure designed around intrinsic intelligence sources (human thinking systems) is the best option to create a more intelligent human organization that is also a smarter evolver and emergent strategist — optimizing the contributions of every intrinsic intelligence source (intelligence/consciousness-centricity).

b. The intelligence/consciousness-centric approach optimizes the structural capacity of the entire macro-structure by improving the connectivity, and engagement of the intangible structure (in particular, the orgmind). A well-connected intangible deep structure (including the effective dynamic) supports a more effective physical structure. It is important to note that the effectiveness of organizations is bounded by their overall structure — structural coherency and higher structural capacity.

c. An intelligence/consciousness-centric design (with an intense intelligence mindset — orgmindfulness) helps to 'humanize' organizations (intelligence-intelligence linkages, coherency, synergy, 'feeling' system, and mental cohesion), and to elevate collective intelligence and organizational consciousness (higher collectiveness capacity).

d. An intelligence/consciousness-centric design elevates the adaptive, learning, and evolving mindset (higher adaptive capacity).

e. An intelligence/consciousness-centric design places more attention on the spaces of complexity (complexity-intelligence-centricity), and therefore encourages more innovative and creative endeavors, and ensures better risks management (investing sufficient resources in the certain spaces of complexity is a new niche).

f. An intelligence/consciousness-centric design stimulates more effective self-organization/self-transcending constructions, and the emergent of new order — including preparation for punctuation points (better crisis management). Self-organization/self-transcending constructions, connectivity, engagement, dissipation, autocatalysis, emergence, co-evolution, and collective intelligence (better orchestration of the latent impetus) are closely associated attributes (higher self-organizing capacity and emergence-intelligence capacity).

g. An intelligence/consciousness-centric design supports co-evolution with the composite system (interdependency, symbiosis, agent/network/organization centricity, and unifying capacity). This dynamic creates better sustainability through the new intelligence advantage.

This set of conceptual foundation is vital for putting an intelligent human organization in its appropriate status, and heightened its functionality. They form the first set of primary initiators that can effectively make a human organization more intelligent.

6.6 The Three Other Perspectives of Organizing Around Intelligence

In addition, the concept for organizing around intelligence also encompasses three other secondary/associated perspectives (certain amount of overlapping with the first perspective). The second perspective involves **organizing around knowledge and information-related activities**. Natural organisms, especially the more sophisticated and intelligent species are inherently structured in this manner — species with a better developed brain (large memory storage), and well-integrated nervous system. The information-related activities are responsible for the information processing, knowledge acquisition and structuring, thinking, and decision-making capabilities of these natural intelligent systems, including human beings. For human organizations, this approach engulfs the following functions:

a. Scanning the environment for relevant **external information**.
b. Creating useful **internal information** from thought processes.
c. Distributing information to all parts of the system/organization.
d. Consuming information to update the knowledge structures.
e. Consuming information to improve decision making.

f.   Creating new knowledge structures.

g.   Advancing to a higher stage of discernment and existence by means of an enhanced written language — including the creation of external knowledge depositories.

The third perspective of organizing around intelligence involves a more in-depth focus on **organizing around evolution and adaptive dynamic (learning, adaptation, and emergence)**. Successful evolution means that the organism possesses high awareness, and continuously adapts itself to the changing environment so that it remains alive and competitive (adaptive capacity). Thus, a living system continuously consumes information, learns, adapts, and attempts to evolve successfully. The ability to perform this series of functions prolongs the existence of that entity/ system. Thus, human organizations must also internalize the following abilities.

a.   Human organizations must learn, adapt, compete, survive, and evolve like any intelligent beings.

b.   Intelligent human organizations must learn and relearn faster than their competitors.

c.   Intelligent human organizations must continuously learn correlatively with the changing situation and environment to further enhance their adaptive capacity and competitiveness, and elevate their sustainability.

d.   Intelligent human organizations must continuously enhance their interconnectivity and learn as an integrated whole — ensuring all levels of learning (see organizational learning in Appendix 7).

e.   Intelligent human organizations must learn to achieve a high level of orgmindfulness, and nurture a mindful culture (core of the supportive culture, higher collectiveness capacity) to drive all the above factors (enhancing the first perspective).

The fourth perspective involves the better exploitation of complexity properties (complexity-intelligence-centricity) such as complexity, nonlinearity, far-from-equilibrium, interconnectivity, interdependency, sensitive dependence on initial conditions, rugged landscape, smarter evolver, emergent strategist, self-organization, self-transcending constructions, autocatalysis, and red queen race where appropriate — that is, focusing on **complexity-intelligence linkages** and their usage. These are natural nonlinear phenomena that have stimulated and sustained the existence of different forms of life and their environment on this planet. In this respect, these are also the niches that should be exploited by intelligent human organizations, if the latter wish to reap the astronomical returns of nonlinearity through the butterfly effect. Intelligent human organizations must be aware and ready to exploit these opportunities.

6.7 Key 'Entity' Management that Nurtures *i*CAD

Nurturing the *i*CAD of an intelligent human organization (*i*CAS) depends on its coherency with the complexity-intelligence strategy. As indicated earlier, its basic possesses must first encompass the three-centricity substrategies (path 1), and the integrated deliberate and emergent dynamics (path 2). In the first path, certain key 'entities' must be better managed for establishing a more robust organizational foundation. The new dynamic encompasses intelligence/consciousness management, complexity management, and network management. These three entity management processes must be more deeply scrutinized for better exploitation. The basic focal points of each of the management approach, and the integrated deliberate and emergent strategy are as follows:

- **Intelligence/Consciousness Management:** 'Caring' and exploiting all intrinsic intelligence/consciousness sources, and nurturing collective intelligence and org-consciousness (orgmind) — focusing on intelligence/consciousness-centricity, intelligence-intelligence linkage, self-powered agent, interconnectivity, truthful engagement, self-organizing communications, mindfulness, orgmindfulness, autopoiesis, symbiosis, and achieving higher collectiveness capacity.
- **Complexity Management:** Exploring and exploiting certain spaces of complexity, and preparing for punctuation points — focusing on complexity-centricity, complexity-intelligence linkage, butterfly effect (may be enormous returns), unexplored territories/spaces, innovation and creativity, risk management, crisis management,

self-organizing complexity, emergence-intelligence capacity, and achieving higher resilience and sustainability.

- **Network Management:** Exploring and integrating networks (both formal and informal) — focusing on nurturing collective intelligence, natural nodes, artificial nodes, local versus global dynamics, dissipative structure, higher coherency and synergy in governance, leadership and objectives, and unifying capacity.

- **Co-exploitation of Order and Complexity with Intense Intelligence/Consciousness:** Mapping and exploiting a deliberate strategy and nurturing an emergent strategy concurrently (with an effective deliberate-emergent auto-switch) — focusing on varying complexity density, better ambidexterity, smarter evolver, emergent strategist (see intelligent person in Appendix 7), and sustaining an intelligence advantage.

6.7.1 *Introduction to intelligence/consciousness management*

Intelligence/consciousness management that has been introduced in Chapter 3 is a primary and critical activity in intelligent human organization that deeply concentrates on intelligence/consciousness-centricity. It focuses on the intelligence and consciousness of all the intrinsic intelligence sources — human thinking systems — human interacting agents. Besides the knowledge and skills possess by the interacting agents, their mental state is also highly significant. Thus, focusing on the mental state of every agent is a key necessity for better intelligence-intelligence linkage — orgmindfulness. It is closely associated with the quality of interconnectivity, relationship, engagement, and contribution of the agents. Thus, it also determines the 'level of intelligence and consciousness' that each agent is 'committed' to the organization — a significant process for nurturing collective intelligence and organizational consciousness. In addition, intelligence/consciousness management also redefines the governance system, and leadership characteristics that elevate the nurturing of a 'feeling' organization (see Chapters 10 and 11).

Collective intelligence arises from the coherent and synergetic integration of the individual intrinsic intelligence from all (if necessary) interacting agents that form the organization — better mental cohesion (see more on agent-agent/system micro-structure and dynamics in Chapter 7).

It is present and observable in all biological organisms/species that exist in a group (an ant colony, a pack of wolves, and in particular, a human community). However, there is a significant different between human collective intelligence and swarm intelligence. Human agents are embedded with an intrinsic intense intelligence source, and they are highly autopoietic, stability-centric, and self-centric (see Abilene paradox, phobic mindset, defensive routine, and dialogue in Appendix 7). To connect them effectively requires certain subtlety and understanding. In mentioned earlier, the direct intelligence-intelligence linkages help to nurture a sophisticated and intelligent mental space known as the orgmind. When the nurturing process exceeds a certain threshold it becomes emergent in nature, and the collective intelligence that emerges possesses new characteristics and abilities (nonlinearity, synergetic, and constructionist hypothesis). A collective intelligence with higher level capacity enables the organization to self-organize or self-transcending construct (with latent impetus) more effectively — that is towards a highly intelligent human organization (*i*CAS) with greater self-organizing capacity and emergence-intelligence capacity.

6.7.2 *Introduction to complexity management*

Another critical capability associated with the *i*CAD is better complexity management. The recognition that human organizations are intrinsic complex adaptive systems further enforces that complexity theory is a nascent domain that must be more deeply comprehended and effectively utilized in all aspects of organizational thinking, strategy, leadership, governance, and management. This is a fresh beginning towards higher complexity-centricity. In complex adaptive systems **order and complexity co-exist** (will be further discussed with integrated deliberate and emergent strategy), and **spaces of complexity** are the most critical territories that must be better understood, explored, and exploited for elevating competitive advantage. However, many spaces of high complexity have always been avoided by human organizations because of the higher risk involved due to unknown unknowns, that it is foreign and not comprehensible (Newtonian mindset). In the current context, such a space (for instance, technological R&D spaces) may be embedded with new potentials and 'gold nuggets' and can be creatively or innovatively identified and exploited. Thus, an IO must be **complexity-centric**.

In reality, all human organizations have encountered spaces of high complexity and punctuation points (for instance, a global financial crisis, the environment/state just before the disintegration of USSR, or the situation caused by a tsunami in Acheh and Bangladesh). When USSR disintegrates, it had moved into the fourth state (in-deterministic chaotic state), and had gone beyond the edge of chaos (new — 3rd critical value) — into a space of in-deterministic chaos [see edge of order, edge of chaos (old and new), edge of emergence, and punctuation point in Appendix 7]. They had not been able to observe or manage the surface pattern/structure when they were 'trapped' in that punctuation point. They did not possess a sufficient level of collective intelligence that could overcome the presence of high incoherency, as they did not possess the self-organizing capability needed to strengthen the organization with a more robust structure — emergent of new order. Hence, the system self-destructed.

Therefore, recognizing and exploiting the presence of spaces of high complexity, and making preparation for punctuated points is extremely significant. All human organizations are marked by stasis, a stable pattern of activity lasting for a period of time, and disrupted by short periods of sudden rapid changes — punctuation points (crisis management). Punctuated equilibrium makes it difficult for a system with low adaptive capacity and collectiveness capacity to survive for long. Such a system tends to be complacent during a period of calm (low collective intelligence and org-consciousness), and cannot adjust fast enough when the situation turns complex. A highly adaptive system, on the other hand, is always dynamic, innovative, reactive, and even proactive — constantly making preparation for new and unexpected complexity. In this respect, a smart evolver is also an emergent strategist. Apparently, as human organizations evolve they drift into spaces of high complexity constantly. Those organizations that managed to reap some benefits from such a space move into a new state with more robustness, 'greater order', and higher stability. This fluctuating dynamic is continuous and a part of the complex-adaptive scene.

In this respect, being complexity-centric is critical. Primarily, human agents must be nurtured to venture into unexplored, nonlinear, complex and also 'rich' territory with a high quality knowledge structure and calmness (see intelligence leadership in Appendix 7). The organizational culture must also be supportive to such new endeavors. As the new approach and journey can be haphazard and risk-taking, therefore, failure must be accepted with a more positive mindset. It must be taken as a learning process. The key incentive for venturing into and exploiting unexplored territories is that the rewards may be enormous returns from a small investment (when the butterfly effect is activated), if the endeavor is successful. In the process, the organization also achieved the first mover advantage, intelligence advantage, and greater resilience and sustainability.

Summary: A brief explanation of risk management and crisis management:

- Better exploitation of individual intelligence and/or collective intelligence to explore certain spaces of complexity innovatively and/or creatively is associated with better risk management.
- Better preparation for sudden surfacing of (unknown) punctuation points by nurturing more intense collective intelligence and org-consciousness, as well as the emergent strategy (with self-powered agents) is better crisis management.

[Network management will be analyzed in Chapters 9 and 10 (also see network theory in Appendix 7), while the concurrent exploitation of order and complexity will be discussed below.]

6.8 Introduction to the Integrated Deliberate and Emergent Strategy

6.8.1 *Structural, thinking and dynamical disparities*

The co-existence of order and complexity is apparent in all human organizations, irrespective of their primary functions (economic, social, environmental, political, education, military), and must be effectively exploited. The presence of order (high inertia of status quo) in the human world has been perceived and enforced by the strong human mental capacity of the human thinking systems. In some respect, it is beyond Newtonian mechanics, although the mindset adopted is the Newtonian mindset that concentrates on order, linearity, and prediction/forecasting — **the presence of a relativistic dimension**. The values of such a **deliberate strategy** mapped and exploited are evaluated based on the accuracy of the prediction (forecasting, futuristic) and the actual occurrence of the event. In general, despite certain drawbacks, this deliberate approach has served humanity well since its introduction. It has provided a comfort space (mentally and physically), and has led humanity to its present state of advancement.

However, currently (over the last few decades) the development in the human world is accelerating beyond traditional 'enforced order'. Both the rate of change and the frequency of unpredictability of future events (especially, punctuation points — for instance, world financial crisis, nuclear disaster, political disaster, military/armed activity, and environmental disorder) have elevated both human physical and mental stress level tremendously. Human systems that could be perceived as relatively closed (even for nations, for instance, China and Myanmar for a certain period of time in history were 'closed') are now more open due to globalization — resulting in greater interconnectivity, engagement, and interdependency. In general, there is an escalated and faster inflow and outflow of human assets, materials, information, knowledge, and technologies in all human organizations, including countries. The presence and impact of complexity (more spaces of complexity) cannot be managed or contained with the Newtonian mindset alone. The whole development clearly revealed the 'unpreparedness' and incoherency (structural, thinking and perception, dynamic) in many human organizations. With this disparity, adopting an emergent approach is crucial. In particular, human organizations have to be recognized, explored, managed, and exploited as high finite dimensionality (continuous-time) nonlinear open dynamical systems with in-complete phase space (adding on to its level of complexity).

Consequently, the adaptive capacity of human beings and human organizations are beyond the standard biological adaptive capacity of other animal species and organisms due to the intense mental capacity of the agents. The highly abstract and nonlinear mental dimension (partly due to the characteristics of human thinking systems — emotional — not always logical and could be highly nonlinear) orchestrated a nonlinear complex adaptive dynamics that is unique to humanity — with intense awareness and mindfulness, and at times unpredictable actions emerge. Thus, in the IO theory, the new **intelligence mindset** encompasses certain aspects of the Newtonian mindset, as well as the complexity mindset and beyond. Quality complexity-intelligence linkages and intelligence-intelligence linkages in human complex adaptive systems are highly crucial, and must be constantly nurtured, monitored and exploited. As indicated above the first new strategic path is organizing around intelligence, and new niche is intelligence advantage. The next strategic path is an integrated deliberate and emergent approach. The entire process points towards the necessity of nurturing of various capacities (including adaptive, collectiveness, self-organizing, and emergence-intelligence capacities) that could facilitate an effective **emergent strategy** — especially, through the surfacing of collective intelligence, and self-powered agents.

Understanding these new properties and dynamics is significantly valuable to leaders and managers, as well as any other human interacting agents/actors. Fundamentally, nurturing highly intelligent human organizations (*i*CAS) requires an integrated deliberate and emergent approach as one of the key foundation. During stasis the deliberate path is still valuable. Adaptive management and the presence of monitoring, responding, and predicting activities remain useful (although, more relativistic). However, the emergent path has to be nurtured and monitored with a deeper focus on intrinsic intelligence, collective intelligence, orgmindfulness, and mindful culture. The adapted path must elevate the efficiency of constructive self-organization/self-transcending constructions, and emergent of new order. Thus, the second path has to be continuously enhanced at all time as the next punctuation point is sudden, unknown, and unpredictable.

6.8.2 *Integrated exploitation of order and complexity*

Under the existing 'raplexity' circumstances, human organizations appear to be encompassing infinitely large number of points of crisis, each of them with the ability to magnify small changes (butterfly effect). Therefore, these negative critical points can create high instability. The whole situation appears to be highly complex. At first sight (in the 1960s and 1970s), the sensitive dependence on initial conditions and unpredictability observed seem to render strategic planning, and long-term forecasting of human organizations totally meaningless. Nothing effective can be organized or accomplished in such a complex situation — even with longer-term planning. Fundamentally, order is absolutely associated with self-destruction. However, it is not totally true — see relativistic complexity in Chapters 9 and 10.

Thus, the integrated deliberate and emergent strategy is a significant and beneficial approach for handling varying order and complexity. As indicated, it provides a vital link to the intelligence mindset — to optimize both order and complexity. Thus, the intelligence mindset still supports deliberate strategic mapping (with redefined thinking of the Newtonian mindset, and the presence and significance of order — encompassing relativistic complexity and futurology). Fundamentally, the deliberate strategy commonly adopted today is useful only when the situation is stable (relativistic) indicating the presence of predictable — stasis, spaces of order, and spaces of relativistic order. However, when the environment becomes highly complex and the future cannot be well-predicted, an emergent strategy is more viable. Thus, the additional focus is on nurturing the emergent strategy — a new component that is absent in most human organizations currently. Hence, possessing a well-integrated deliberate and emergent strategy is critical in the new emerging context.

In a constantly fluctuating environment, the deliberate (associated with order, linearity, and predictability) and emergent (associated with complexity, nonlinearity, unpredictability, higher collective intelligence, and org-consciousness) paths of an organization may be intertwined in an unknown manner. In this case, the two alternating strategic paths of development should co-exist at all time in intelligent human organizations

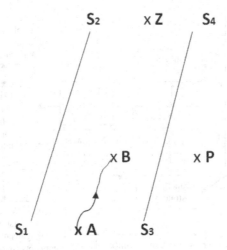

Figure 6.10 A simplistic illustration of strategic path, operational path and punctuation point.

irrespective of its current situation. The deliberate path should be mapped and well-exploited during (relativistic) order/stasis, and the emergent path should be nurtured (futuristic, hysteresis) for exploiting certain spaces of complexity and making preparation for punctuation point simultaneously (see Figure 6.10 — traditionally, AB is the operational path, $S_1S_2S_3S_4$ is the strategic path, and P is a punctuation point). In this case, the scan-respond-evolve cycle will have to be exploited frequently or even continuously — a self-oscillating dynamic that is supported by the high collective intelligence and org-consciousness of the system. Concurrently, some forms of scenario planning may be beneficial. Very often, due to varying complexity density, the presence of the **deliberate-emergent auto-switch** is crucial.

In general, this new integrated approach is a new redefined thinking of strategic governance, leadership, and management (see Figure 6.11). It must be emphasized again that recognizing the presence and making preparation for punctuated equilibrium is a new awareness that current political/corporate leaders, social scientists, economists, and political leaders must acquire. Punctuated equilibrium makes it difficult for a

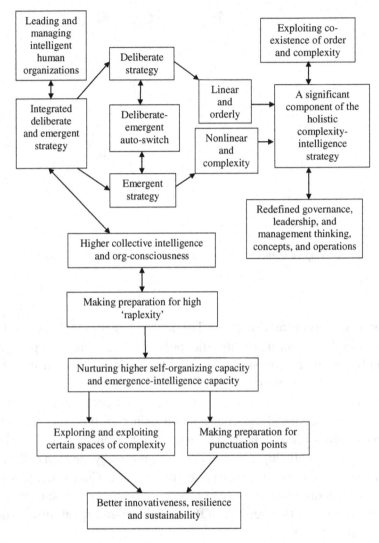

Figure 6.11 The integrated deliberate and emergent strategy: A new holistic and strategic approach for leading and managing human complex adaptive systems.

system that is not adaptive to survive for long. Such a system that tends to be complacent during a period of 'calm' cannot adjust when the situation turns turbulence (highly complex, incoherent, and destructive) suddenly. On the other hand, a highly adaptive system that is always learning, nimble, active and proactive, and innovative and creative possesses an intelligence advantage. Thus, the emergent strategy has to be nurtured continuously over time, and its success is closely linked with the level of collective intelligence and org-consciousness of the system. In this respect, a smart evolver must also be an emergent strategist. A deeper

Table 6.1   Some differences between deliberate strategy and emergent strategy.

Deliberate Strategy (Effective in a space of order)	Emergent Strategy (Needed in a space of complexity)
Presence of planned intention (strategy and plan mapping activities exist).	Absence of direct planned intention (nurturing collective intelligence with more intense orgmindfulness).
Destination and environment are highly predictable (deterministic).	Destination and environment cannot be predicted (in-deterministic, unpredictability), in particular, punctuation points.
Paths of advancement (primary and secondary) are charted.	Path of advancement 'cultivated', and strategy emerges when needed (self-powered agents, intelligence leadership, and lateral leadership): (1) risk management — exploiting certain spaces of complexity; (2) crisis management — preparing for sudden surfacing of punctuation points.
An action plan exists.	An action 'plan' emerges through self-organization/ self-transcending constructions.
The plan is usually centrally formulated (should be more lateral in the present context).	Formulation requires broad consensus, depends on collective intelligence, mindful culture (lateral/ collective leadership, network integration, actors/ non-actors).
The action is implemented with high precision according to the plan when forecasting is accurate.	Implementation by subtle orchestration (orgmindfulness, mindful culture, latent leadership, self-organizing governance, and high adaptive, collectiveness, self-organizing, and emergence-intelligence capacities), and requires a higher degree of tolerance for risks and mistakes — at punctuation points the collective intelligence serves as the latent impetus for self-transcending constructions — self-powered agents — everybody is in charge.

analysis of this integrated strategy will be done in Chapters 9 and 10. For simplicity, some differences of the two strategies are summarized in Table 6.1.

6.9. Emergence and Edge of Emergence

6.9.1 *Deeper analysis of emergence*

Emergence is the primary focus of a large percentage of complexity researchers. Many researchers perceived complexity theory as the study of emergent of new order. The term (in the modern sense) was first introduced by psychologist **George Henry Lewes** (1817–1878), in 1875. It is the creation of a new global properties, structure, organization, and behavior (a transformation process driven by self-organization) by interacting agents due to some local rules, although the exact patterns that emerge cannot be predicted in advance. The reason being that emergence always leads to unexpected and unpredictable outcome which is totally different from the old properties, structure, organization, and environmental forces (constructionist hypothesis). In addition, in human organization, the agents involved are intrinsically subjective and uncertain about the consequences of their actions 'globally' (high local awareness but little 'global' awareness). They can self-organize into a new local adaptive emergent system (network) when the necessity arises — not knowing its impact on the organization.

To date, emergence is not a fully understood process/dynamic. Prigogine's dissipative structures theory indicates that emergence is driven by adaptive tension caused by energy differentials, leading to intra-system order (see Chapter 2). The American school approach focuses on inter-system order, co-evolution, edge of chaos, and their association with emergent of new order. And the constructionist hypothesis approach considers symmetry breaking, and localization as emergence. In addition, "... emergence offers itself as a way to rethink organizational adaptability, particularly when emergence is understood as incorporating 'self-organizational logic' but also utilizing various constructional and constraining operations as proposed in the model of self-transcending constructions"

(Goldstein, 2011) — will be discussed more in-depth later. In general, it is a divergent-convergent phenomenon with 'conflicting' impetus, and disorganized fluctuations that lead to the creation of a more robust complex structure with new properties and laws.

6.9.2 *Edge of emergence the 2nd critical value*

A better understanding of emergence at the macroscopic level could be achieved by re-examining the position/location of the edge of chaos (see Chapter 2). Prigogine's dissipative structures theory indicates that dramatic phase transition occurs at the **edge of order**, the first critical value. When external energy drives a system across the edge of order, dissipative structures appear. In this respect, the edge of order is a transition boundary. Dissipative structures are emergent self-organized structures that accelerate dissipation imposed by energy differentials (adaptive tension) through the creation of new intra-system order. In the IO theory, when human organizations move across the edge of order (into the space of relativistic order — to be discussed later), first degree self-organization/self-transcending constructions occurs. The human agents 'automatically' (led by their respective individual intrinsic intelligence — self-powered agents) self-organize forming organizing groups, local space, or networks — the equivalence of dissipative structures — see self-organizing capacity in Appendix 7.

In the earlier American school thinking, the **edge of chaos**, the second critical value, is a state of bounded instability and high complexity in CS/CAS. It has also been perceived as the upper bound of criticality, a 'region of emergence'. Thus, it is a space of high complexity where emergent of order is still possible. A CAS existing in this space possesses the highest level of fitness and adaptability. The edge of chaos was a key focal area of Santa Fe Institute during its earlier days. In this respect, there appears to be a contradiction in the explanation of the two 'edges'. The edge of order is a 'transition boundary', while the edge of chaos is more a 'space' than an 'edge'.

244 Complexity Intelligence Strategy

A closer analysis of emergence showed that the edge of chaos should be shifted to the third critical value. The second critical value should be redefined as the **edge of emergence** (see Chapter 2). This allows the macro-dynamic of emergence to be better comprehended. Upon crossing the edge of order (first critical value), first degree self-organization or self-transcending constructions occurs leading to intra-system emergence (first degree emergence) — see self-organizing capacity in Appendix 7. Similarly, after crossing the new edge of emergence (second critical value), second degree self-organization or self-transcending constructions occurs leading to inter-system emergence (second degree emergence — organizational emergence) — see emergence-intelligence capacity in Appendix 7. Thus, the edge of chaos has been redefined as the edge of emergence. Similar to the edge of order, it is a boundary/edge and not a space or a 'region' — located just before the system moves into an in-deterministic chaotic state.

In the new understanding, the edge of chaos, now assumes the third critical value is also an edge. Upon crossing this transition boundary the system moves into in-deterministic chaos/complexity (beyond deterministic chaos and mathematical chaos, into infinite degrees of freedom), and the system will disintegrate eventually. This recognition and conception provides a clearer explanation on the macro-dynamic of emergence encompassing self-organization, self-transcending constructions, emergent of new order, and self-destruction at different levels.

6.10 Conclusion

This chapter introduces the global/holistic complexity-intelligence strategy of the IO theory that focuses on the new paradigmatic path of high intelligence/consciousness-centricity, complexity-centricity, and network-centricity, and the co-existence of order and complexity. Intelligent human organizations must attempt to optimize intelligence and consciousness in the organization to the maximum possibility, both individually and collectively (intelligence-intelligence linkage, collectiveness capacity, adaptive capacity, unifying capacity, and intelligence/consciousness management). Concurrently, these organizations must also recognize the significance, potential, and contributions of being complexity-centric (complexity-intelligence linkage, self-organizing capacity, emergence-intelligence capacity, and complexity management). At the moment, the co-existence of order and complexity (in multi-dimensional spaces — social, economic, political, education, military), and the presence of certain spaces of complexity that provide new opportunities are not fully comprehended or exploited by most organizations. Any human organizations that manage to create a new niche with the above thinking, strategic approach, and operation will achieve an intelligence advantage that is more sustainable. (The network-centric aspect will be discussed in Chapters 9 and 10, also see graph theory, network theory, small world theory, complex networks, and complex adaptive networks in Appendix 7).

The above recognition clearly endorsed that the machine-like structure (still existing in many human organizations) that is derived from the Newtonian mindset (order, linear, predictable, forecasting), and supported the industrial era (design paradigm, bureaucratic mindset, hierarchy and control) for the past few hundred years is manifesting greater constraints, incoherency, and irrelevance in the current rapidly changing context. Meanwhile, a more natural biotic structure and an intelligence driven complex adaptive dynamic that emerges from the intelligence mindset provides a more comprehensive paradigmatic shift. In this respect, the fundamental principle to exploit is nurturing intelligent human organizations (*i*CAS) that are driven by an *i*CAD — thus, organizing around intelligence/consciousness sources is critical. In addition, an intelligent biotic macro-structure that inherently supports *i*CAD is beneficial. Another component of the complexity-intelligence strategy, the integrated deliberate and emergent strategy that focuses on exploiting both order and complexity more effectively is also a key necessity. This strategy emphasizes that order must be well-exploited (deterministic, predictability, futuristic), certain spaces of complexity are potentially goldmines, and making effective preparations for punctuation points is critical.

Complexity Intelligence Strategy

Finally, the 'definition' of an intelligent human organization as perceived in the IO theory is re-summarized as follows:

Intelligent Human Organization (II)

It is a human organization with an extensive 'organizational neural network' that focuses on the intelligence and consciousness (mental state) of all its interacting agents (organizational neurons) — high orgmindfulness. Thus, it must encompass high collective intelligence, org-consciousness, and knowledge-centricity, as well as possesses an intelligent biotic macro-structure, including an orgmind, an intangible structure, and a physical structure (org-brain, intelligence web, and environmental scanning and responding component). It is also an autonomous, nimble, and anticipatory system driven by a continuously changing complex and adaptive dynamic that exploits intelligence/consciousness management, complexity management, network management, self-powered agents, autocatalysis, circular causation, dissipation, self-transcending constructions, intelligence governance, intelligence leadership, hysteresis, and emergence. In this respect, a highly intelligent human organization (*i*CAS) is also a smarter evolver and emergent strategist (futuristic) with high structural capacity, adaptive capacity, collectiveness capacity, self-organizing capacity, emergence-intelligence capacity, and unifying capacity, ensuring that its agents and the organization co-evolve concurrently.

The complexity-intelligence strategy facilitates the unprecedented shift from hierarchical empowerment to exploiting the inherent self-powered self-organizing capability of all human agents.

It is argued that replicators evolving through natural selection on the basis of fitness are intrinsically selfish. Though the synergy resulting from cooperation is generally advantageous, selfish or subsystem optimization precludes the reaching of globally optimal cooperative arrangement.

Francis Heylighen,
Evolution, Selfishness and Cooperation

Our world is unable to deal the multiplicity of unintended consequences of its own earlier actions that are currently emerging.

Sander Van Der Leeuw

Chapter 7

Human Agent-Agent/System Micro-Structure
and Dynamic, and the Intelligent Person Model

"Change is the only attribute that does not change"

Summary

In this chapter, basic life-intelligence, and the evolution and co-evolution dynamics of eco-systems are further examined and compared to certain processes in human organizations. A special reference on human thinking systems as intelligence/consciousness sources, information decoders, information processors and complex adaptive systems (CAS) is re-emphasized. In addition, the significance of connectivity, communications, engagement, and orgmindfulness is analyzed with respect to the Abilene paradox, defensive routines and dialogue, as well as the human agent-agent/system micro-structure and micro-dynamic. The individual local self-centric (local self-enrichment processes) and the global org-centric (global forces) evolutionary dynamics of intelligent human organizations (no global optimality) and their interacting agents (no optimal rationality) are investigated more explicitly with the exploitation of the certain complexity properties. It is observed that local order (stability of agents and networks/subsystem) is highly critical in human dynamic. It is beneficial to recognize that the intelligent complex adaptive dynamic (iCAD) driving an intelligent human organization (iCAS) is not similar to complex adaptive dynamic (CAD) in totality. This recognition provides a significant foundation and better understanding of the intelligent human organizational micro-structure and dynamic.

Essentially, there is a vital need for the transformed mindset, thinking, values, and expectations of human agents (leaders, actors,

249

and non-actors) to be better synchronized. The intelligent person model (an ideal set of attributes) is introduced to substantiate the criticality of new vital characteristics of the human interacting agents in intelligent human organizations. Primarily, intelligent persons (a new category of agents, in particular, intelligence leaders and synergists) are concurrently intelligence/consciousness-centric, complexity-centric and network-centric. The new set of attributes includes high self-powered, intrinsic leadership, information decoding, smarter evolver, emergent strategist, and futurist capabilities. For instance, such a person is in a better position to function as a smarter evolver and emergent strategist that helps to bind a group (network, community, corporation, nation) of human thinking systems more optimally by elevating the quality of collective intelligence in the organization through better mindfulness, orgmindfulness, symbiosis, self-transcending constructions, co-evolution; deeper recognition of the characteristics of the rugged landscape and red queen race; innovative exploitation of relativistic complexity, and possessing futuristic thinking. Apparently, the presence of intelligent persons/agents will lead to a redefinition in leadership and governance strategy.

Keywords: Intelligence evolution dynamic, self-centric, local order, stability-centric, org-centric, intelligent organization, interacting agent, human thinking system, basic life intelligence, self-powered, basic human intelligence, advanced human intelligence, Cambrian explosion, order for free, rationality, smarter evolver, adaptive capacity, relational capacity, collectiveness capacity, organizational thinking system, collective intelligence, mindfulness, orgmindfulness, co-evolution, butterfly effect, self-organization, criticality, local activity center, space of order, space of complexity, punctuation point, nonlinear activity, basin of attraction, attractor, information decoder, strategic planning, competitive advantage, structuring organization, organizational/societal DNA, omega point, noosphere, autopoiesis, Abilene paradox, thought technology, dialogue, defensive routine, organizational relational parameter, self-enrichment process, principle of locality, intelligence advantage, first mover advantage, bounded rationality, intelligence enhancing function, economic man, administrative man, satisficing principle, intelligent person, constructive global forces, orgmindfulness, mindful culture, organizational justice, feeling system, relational capacity, mental cohesion, emergent strategist, rugged landscape, integrated deliberate and emergent strategy, ambidextrous, self-organizing capacity, emergence-intelligence capacity, relativistic complexity, intelligence leadership and intelligence governance.

7.1 Introduction: The World of Complex Adaptive Dynamic

7.1.1 *Evolution, the basic life intelligence and beyond*

The Darwinian theory (**Charles Darwin**, 1809–1882 and **Alfred Wallace**, 1823–1913) based on natural selection suggests that evolution is a slow and gradual process, adopting a tactician approach, including **phyletic gradualism** (see phyletic gradualism, and natural selection in Appendix 7). The theory also encompasses the concept of survival of the fittest (from physical fitness to biological fitness, to mental fitness). In this situation, any structures that exist in 'physical form' possess proto-intelligence, and in 'biological form' possess basic life-intelligence that is closely correlated with successful evolution. For instance, from an amoeba to a colony of ants, to a pack of wolves, to the ape family, different levels of life-intelligence abilities have been manifested. The key factor that is responsible for the dissimilarities among the different species is the presence of different density of neurons in their intelligence networks — that is, the presence of the unique organ, the brain.

In the intelligent organization theory, the evolution process is differentiated into three stages with respect to different levels of life-intelligence, namely as follows (see Figure 7.1):

- **Basic life intelligence** evolution dynamic (starting from unicellular organisms to the ape family — from those without a neuron to a small collection of neurons, to the emergent of the cerebral cortex (complex neural networks) that supports new physical and biological functions, including bipedal locomotion, and three dimensional vision — but without the ability to create a character set, and no mindfulness).
- **Basic human intelligence** evolution dynamic (presence of a more prominent cerebral cortex, encompassing the basic human instincts

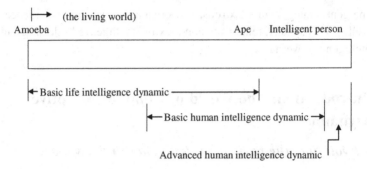

Figure 7.1 A simplified evolution dynamic spectrum with respect to intelligence/species.

and capabilities, higher consciousness that redefined social interactions, including mindfulness and the creation of the character set).

- **Advanced human intelligence** evolution dynamic [presence of intense neural networks (especially, the frontal cortex), highly dependent on mental fitness, leading to the development of an enormous intangible and abstract conceptual space — encompassing the capabilities to conceptualize a sophisticated written language, and abstract/innovative concepts/knowledge, including technological developments and exploitation that are beyond the capabilities of all other biological species, and in particular, a more intense presence of mindfulness — leading towards an intelligent person characteristics (see Section 7.5 and Appendix 7), with ability to strategize an integrated deliberate and emergent approach].

7.1.2 *Evolution, complexity and punctuation point*

Ironically, the model of **Cambrian period** proposed by **Adam Sedgwick** (1875–1873, the academic advisor of Charles Darwin) indicated that the claims of Darwin and Wallace may not have been totally right. The observation of sudden increase and the richness of life forms existing on the Earth during the Cambrian era/period suggested that there is a contradiction on slow and gradual changes — beyond linearity and predictability. This event, termed the **Cambrian explosion**, manifesting nonlinearity, complexity, and unpredictability took place very swiftly about 600 million years ago, after 3 billion years of biological silence (punctuation point). Thus, evolution does not appear to be entirely a gradual process. Current interest on the Cambrian explosion is influenced by the studies of **Harry Whittington** (1916–2010), and the introduction of the **punctuated equilibrium theory** by **Stephen Gould** (1941–2002) and **Niles Elderedge** (1943–present) — (see Cambrian explosion in Appendix 7).

Another important associated discovery is the property of spontaneous order or '**order for free**' (introduced by **Stuart Kauffmann**, 1939–present). Stuart suggested that this property indicates that **self-organization** is an intrinsic characteristic of complex genetic systems, and probably of all complex adaptive systems (CAS). Basically, there is no need for any forces to execute or influence an evolution process. Self-organization emerges when the system reaches certain level of **criticality** (**Per Bak**, 1948–2002). In this respect, it is an inherent activity of nature arising from within the systems. Subsequently, it was recognized that some latent internalized forces are the impetus and dynamo behind structure, life, and human organizations — self-transcending constructions (order not totally for free). And in human organizations self-transcending constructions is a manifestation by individual intelligence (driven by intelligence), as well as collective intelligence.

As discussed earlier, the second law of thermodynamics indicates that the Universe is expanding, entropy is increasing, and the phenomenon itself can be complex and/or chaotic. However, in the sea of chaotic expansion is countless '**local activity centers**', each surrounded by a **space of order** that defies the 2nd law emerges. In each of these spaces, some form of structure emerges, entropy is reduced, and predictability is enhanced — leading to the formation of the physical matter world initially. The latter analyzed in the domains of atomic and nuclear physics are exact sciences with high precision. Thus, the space of order is a space of established physical structure where predictability is high, if not absolutely accurate. Subsequently, these local activity centers are extended to plants, amoeba, apes, human thinking systems, and communities of human beings — the biological world. However, these categories of activity centers also encompass complexity.

Thus, in humanity order and complexity co-exist. The linear world (relativistic) that humankind is familiar with will continue to exist, and serve as the comfortable primordial stratum. However, the more embracing and unexplored frontiers of the nonlinear domain (**space of complexity**) should be the next territory to be exploited, if human beings are to ensure its resilience and sustainability, and to progress further into the intelligence era. As competitions, niches, and focal areas have changed, understanding and exploiting the fundamental characteristics of complexity and nonlinearity is crucial for all human agents, human organizations, as well as the entire humanity. In this respect, socio-political and corporate governance whose functions encompass nonlinear activities/functions such as leadership, governance, strategic planning, creating competitive advantage, structuring organization, and nurturing collective intelligence must also exploit complexity in the current context.

7.2 Complex Adaptive Features and the Intelligence Dynamic

7.2.1 *Intelligence, chaotic manifestation and complex adaptation*

It is now understood that human thinking systems (brain and mind combined) are inherently complex, adaptive, and nonlinear (emotions versus logic). The first distinction of complex dynamic is the presence of surface phenomena due to sensitive dependence on initial conditions, the butterfly effect. At the micro-level, the set of elementary processes operating in every brain must be similar (electrical and chemical). However, arising from a fairly simple set of elementary processes (micro-dynamic), great diversification in macroscopic/cognitive characteristics are observed (the behavior of individuals is rather different). The sophisticated behavioral patterns versus the same set of simple elementary processes indicates that the brain at micro-level is a chaotic system (simplicity to chaotic) — emotional but could be logical. Thus, the proliferation of behavioral patterns due to small variations in initial conditions is a significant property to note. The implication is that a person's behavioral schemata can be greatly altered by just small changes in conditions. In addition, at the macroscopic level the human thinking systems (especially, the mind) are CAS. In this respect, the human thinking systems manifest both chaotic

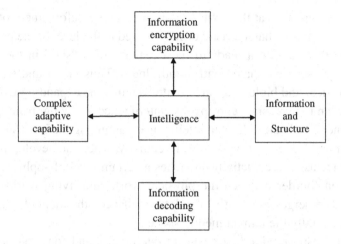

Figure 7.2 Functions of information encryption and decoding.

(simplicity to chaos — micro-level dynamic) and complex adaptive (complexity to simplicity — macro-level dynamic) characteristics.

Another vital characteristic of evolution systems is their ability to encrypt information (driven by intelligence) about themselves and their environment — structure (see Figure 7.2). A piece of snowflake contains information. The genetic message of human beings is encoded in DNA (intelligence <=> structure). In today's societies, the human thinking systems are embedded with highly sophisticated and complex knowledge structures. Similarly, human organizations (communities, nations, humanity) must also possess the equivalent genetic packages, the **corporate/ organization/societal DNA** (Baskin, 1998) if it is to be regarded as intelligent (collective intelligence <=> organizational structure). Thus, identifying and strengthening organizational DNA is a new responsibility of social, business, and political leaders — towards higher structural capacity.

The encoded information in any structure can only be decoded when intelligence is present. As analyzed earlier, intelligence is associated with a spectrum of information-related activities. At the higher end of the spectrum, intelligence energy tends to create more distinct order through self-centric/autopoietic or **self-enrichment processes** with respect to a certain local order center — at the entity/agent level. This reinforcement of local structure is a basic characteristic of life (started at the level of the physical world). Subsequently, it leads to the existence of a "self" in the living world — closely associated with mindfulness. Thus, order and structure (both physical and biological) are created against the expanding Universe dynamic and increasing entropy by intelligence (varying from proto-intelligence to advanced human intelligence), an intangible intrinsic entity of this enormous mysterious space. Eventually, when the development of intelligence associated activities reaches a certain level of sophistication/abstraction (border between the physical world and living world), consciousness emerges inherently. The latter enhances the intangible mental space, especially the human mental space.

In this respect, with the impetus of intelligence and consciousness, all CAS that evolve successfully with time are innovative and creative to a great extent. They shift or transform from one state to another state, responding to changes in situations of the system and its environment — for instance, for humanity — from basic life-intelligence dynamic to advanced human intelligence dynamic (presence of a written language). In addition, there are certain preferred states or **attractors** that the CAS will move into swiftly, depending on the overall conditions. This observation noted in complexity theory has significant implications on organization strategy and leadership thinking because an **intelligence advantage** can be created if a preferred state (**basin of attraction**) is quickly recognized and adopted/exploited. Potentially, the **first mover advantage** is highly critical (see basin of attraction in Appendix 7).

Also recognizing the presence of **punctuated equilibrium** is vital. It is a 'sudden' phase transition or enormous changes take place quickly (see self-organized criticality in Appendix 7). In such a space, a slight change in conditions can lead to a huge transformation due to the existence of nonlinear characteristics, for instance, when water solidifies into a cube/slate of ice, and when unicellular organisms become multi-cellular organisms during the Cambrian era. Thus, during phase transition, CAS move swiftly into a new state/attractor, similar to a revolution. Subsequently, the changes that take place become slower again (stasis). Thus, some complexity characteristics (including those mentioned in earlier chapters)

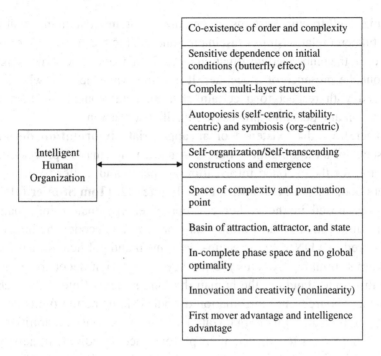

Figure 7.3 Some basic complex adaptive features that are beneficial to human organizations if appropriately exploited.

that must be better analyzed, comprehended, and exploited by intelligent human organizations are captured in Figure 7.3.

7.2.2 *Necessity and roles of an effective information decoder*

As indicated earlier, the Universe is coded with information, ranging from a molecule, crystal, DNA, colony structure, human brain, human organization, nation, and eventually a human global society. All these examples are systems embedded with varying forms of structure. [**Pierre Teilhard de Chardin** (1881–1955) conceived the terms **omega point** (the Universe is evolving towards maximum level of complexity and consciousness), and **noosphere** (the sphere of human thoughts — an intangible information space/structure) about a century ago.] As information is the capacity to organize and structure systems, all organized systems contain information. This bilateral relationship is fascinating and vital to the emergence of life. However, the embedded information by itself may not be very meaningful without the presence of a decoder. It becomes valuable only when it is decoded with respect to a certain environmental context — both the encryption and decoding process are intelligence driven.

Therefore, the existence of an appropriate **information decoder** (presence of an intelligence source — also an information processor) is essential for the encoded information in energy and matter forms to be understood, released and utilized (see Figure 7.2) [**Tom Stonier** (1927–1999) proposed in the earlier concept of energy–matter–information equilibrium.] In the micro-biological world, a cell decodes the information stored in a DNA. In the socio-economical and political dimensions, the human thinking systems are the key information decoders. Hence, with this understanding, the human thinking systems (intelligence/consciousness sources and information decoders) must be the fundamental focal points in all human organizations. Their functions and abilities, as well as the means to improve their performance at individual, network, and organizational levels must be allocated high priority and better comprehended. Basically, the human thinking systems must be 'made' to function as better information decoders which determine the value of the sources.

In this respect, intelligence, consciousness, and information are closely associated universal entities with mutually reinforcing relationships. At a more advanced stage of nurturing, intelligence and consciousness are the unique intangible entities from human thinking systems that 'drive' human organizations (intelligence/consciousness-centricity <=> intelligence leadership <=> intelligence governance <=> information decoders) — see intelligence leadership and intelligence governance in Appendix 7. Concurrently, the more sophisticated the information processing and decoding capabilities, the higher the level of intelligence (increase in intelligence <=> increase in information processing/decoding capability) — see general information theory in Appendix 7. Thus, leaders possessing high information decoding capability will be in a better position to identify and understand a surfacing problem faster.

7.3 Dialogue and Paper Dialogue

7.3.1 *Complications and uniqueness of human interconnectivity*

Apparently, the **voluntary connectivity** and **truthful engagement** of interacting agents in all human organizations is a basic crucial requirement for nurturing **collective intelligence**. In general, it is easier to connect a colony of ants (more simplistic) than a group of human beings. In fact, the difficulty of connectivity increases if the individuals are highly intelligent and educated. (Very often, it is harder to connect an intense intelligence/consciousness source — partially due to its high independency.) Each of them is self-centric, and their autopoietic dynamic is also more sophisticated. They are well-informed and not easily influenced (with redefined values and expectations). In general, each of these human interacting agents could survive by itself but an ant depends greatly on its colony for its existence.

It has been indicated earlier that the **agents' mental state** (in general), and **orgmindfulness** (intelligence-intelligence linkages) are two vital attributes involved in the dynamic/processes for nurturing collective intelligence. As illustrated, orgmindfulness is the inward focusing consciousness mental function of a human organization. Orgmindful organizations are interested in the mental state of their interacting agents (employees, stakeholders, citizens, members), and connecting them. Expressing better concern for the 'all' interacting agents and assimilating their thoughts into the organizations improve their connectivity, engagement, communications, and personal commitments (see Figure 7.4). The entire orgmindfulness process (presence of a mindful culture) enhances a stronger sense of belonging (symbiotic), elevates collectiveness capacity, and increases the level of positive **'feeling'**, **'truthfulness'**, and trust in the organization (see feeling system in Appendix 7).

However, many corporations and nations today are more externally focused rather than internally focused due to the absence of a **supportive culture** with a **mindful culture** at its core. These organizations are highly aware of the changing environment, and the more sophisticated needs of their customers or foreign talents. But they either ignore or are not so sure of the mental state and requirements of their own employees or citizens.

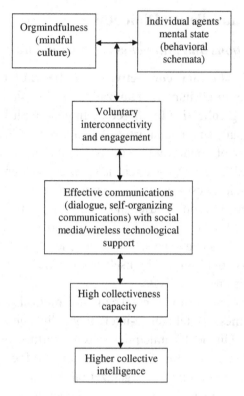

Figure 7.4 Basic dynamic for nurturing higher collective intelligence.

This ignorance can cause an extremely negative impact on the thinking and dynamic of the organization. Organizations that are poorly connected internally do not communicate well and can be self-destructive. Consequently, the **3C-OK dynamic** cannot be orchestrated successfully (see Chapter 8). Such organizations are not competitive, and will deteriorate in the new information and knowledge intensive battleground. Thus, a key to nurturing a higher level of collective intelligence is through high intelligence/consciousness-centricity. The indication is clear. Basically, some forms of 'truthful' communications, either written or verbal, are essential to initiate the binding process. A more omniscient understanding of the entire process is critical. In this respect, **dialogue** is a very valuable tool to initiate the constructive dynamic.

7.3.2 *The phobic mindset and Abilene paradox*

Why is open sharing and communications so intimidating in human organizations? Why are true feelings and opinions sometimes unspeakable? While the notion of dialogue is appealing, it is not commonly observed in some current organizations because it contradicts the bureaucratic mindset, and hierarchical structure, establishment, and leadership. In such an environment, when people need to talk about sensitive issues, most are trapped by the present design paradigm, cultural norms, and whether it is an illusion or unrealistic pessimism. It is dangerous to share one's true feelings and opinions because they may be politically incorrect — due to the high complexity in the intertwined human mental space and socio-political space. A truthful interacting agent never knows when s/he may end up in trouble. Some agents will perceive that it is abnormal if they do not synchronize with the thought or policy of the leadership. Obviously, the individual's basic need for safety and security is significant — autopoietic. So many agents elected to keep mum about their true feelings and thinking, even though it is stressful. They confine themselves to providing only the politically correct information.

The 'do not rock the boat' (high inertia to remain status quo) thinking has been observed in many traditional organizations. The interacting agents try to suppress their emotions and thinking, and appear rational and non-confrontational because of a **phobic mindset**. Most of these human agents are defensive (**defensive communications**) rather than participative (**participative communications**). Consequently, in these traditional organizations, the higher the individual is in an organizational hierarchy, the more that person is insulated from meaningful and genuine feedbacks. The interacting agents feel that s/he who answers honestly is honestly out of his/her mind. Thus, the phobic mindset inhibits the exchange of relevant and accurate/truthful information, reduces sensitivity to feedback, and makes real problem solving and learning virtually impossible in any teams, as well as the organization.

In addition, even when one individual knows that another person is also aware of an issue that is a problem of mutual concern, they both choose to act as if neither of the parties knows anything. They do this in a highly skillful and convincing manner in order to perpetuate a cover-up. The behaviors that support the camouflages, or **defensive routines** [the term was introduced by **Chris Argyris** (1923–2013), in his book 'Teaching smart people how to learn', in 1991], drastically hinder the learning that is needed to bring about individual and organizational changes for improvement. Such defensive routines are a double bind. If the interacting agents do not discuss the defensive routines, then these routines will persist and proliferate. If they do discuss them, they may get into trouble. The consequence is that defensive routines are protected and reinforced by the very people who prefer that they do not exist.

The above observation, the **Abilene paradox** [a term introduced by **Jerry Harvey** (in 'The Abilene Paradox: The management of agreement'. Organizational Dynamics, in 1974)], is still a widely spread phenomenon in many present traditional organizations (see Figure 7.5 and Appendix 7). Instances of people agreeing on things that they all disagree with is present, simply because nobody is speaking up keep happening. Apparently, Abilene Paradox advocates that truthful communications among interacting agents with the traditional culture is not a natural

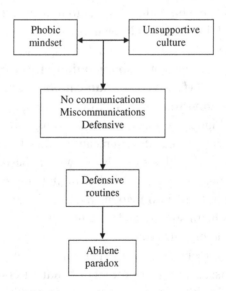

Figure 7.5   Presence of the Abilene paradox.

phenomenon. The agents are subdued and not voluntarily connected, and in the extreme, there is actually no contribution at all. Eventually, most of the interacting agents then develop a cynical attitude that 'nothing will change around here'.

Thus, the obvious reason dialogue does not materialize in such organizations is because the interacting agents are not even voicing truthfully. In this respect, it is totally useless to talk about 'listening', 'respecting', and 'suspending' when people just refuse to 'voice'. In this respect, dialogue facilitators find it difficult to get people to talk honestly and openly about issues, much less to uncover deeper mental models and constructing real shared vision.

7.3.3 *Introduction to dialogue*

Vividly, to achieve better human socio-political cohesion, some forms of constructive information exchange must be present, and the **organizational relational parameter** must be highly positive. **David Bohm** (1917–1992) in 1990 introduced a theory on **dialogue** — a form of free ideas and information exchange. The current form of dialogue (different from its daily usage) to be introduced here is a methodology classified under an interesting domain called **thought technology** — first proposed and utilized by a group of researchers at MIT (Ellinor and Gerald, 1998). It is a possible tool for nurturing better connectivity, communications, and collective intelligence. Another such methodology is **visual thinking**. In the current context, dialogue is defined as a free flow of meaning that balances inquiry and advocacy in one's attempts to influence other. The purpose of dialogue is to go beyond the present understanding held by each member in the group, and to explore issues creatively from many and diverse points of view. Dialogue requires the participants to 'suspend' their present opinions so that deeper levels of listening, synthesis, and meanings can evolve. The entire process is divergence in nature — that is, there is no predetermined purpose, no agenda, and no immediate goal. What emerges eventually is an expanded and deeper perspective of an issue or a better solution — more constructive self-transcending constructions may surface at an appropriate time.

When the interacting agents in an organization gather during a dialogue session, there is a general consensus that they commit themselves to a common set of guidelines as follows:

- Willingness to voice openly.
- Willingness to listen intently.
- Willingness to respect one another (comments or ideas).
- Willingness to suspend immediate judgment.

During a positive dialogue session, as the interacting agents share their thoughts openly, and as sensitivity and experience increase, a perception of **shared meanings/views** emerges (a facilitator is always present). Thus, over time, the participants find that they are neither opposing one another, nor are they simply interacting. Increasing trust (**mutual trust**) between members of the group, and trust in the process itself leads to the expression of the sorts of thoughts and feelings that are usually kept hidden (minimizing the Abilene paradox) — the relational parameter is positively elevated. In this case, there is no imposed consensus, no instigation, no condemn, nor are there any attempts to avoid conflict. Consequently, the participants recognize that they are involved in an ever-changing environment and slowly developing a pool of common meanings and shared views, and the culture, values, and expectations are also redefined. Gradually and astonishing, a shared content of consciousness emerges which allows a level of creativity and insight that is not generally available to individuals or to groups that interact in traditional ways to mature — that is, higher collective intelligence and collectiveness capacity is achieved.

7.3.4 *Some additional characteristics of dialogue*

A more comprehensive recognition and understanding of its characteristics is significant for the methodology to be effectively utilized. In general, it is a time consuming process, and high conscientiousness is needed. Many dialogue sessions must be executed for any positive returns to surface, and it may have to be done 'infinitely' (as long as the organization exists). Some additional characteristics of dialogue are as follows:

a. Introduction

- Dialogue is a form of conversation developed by a group of researchers at MIT that helps to create and sustain collaborative partnerships (better connectivity, communications, and engagement).
- It helps to elevate the collective awareness of an organization through reflective thinking, collective thinking, and better shared values (elevates the relational parameter).
- It promotes collective learning, growth, understanding, healing, and renewal (higher collectiveness capacity, and adaptive capacity).
- It develops skills to build the trust needed to surface taboo issues (higher mutual trust).
- It opens doors to new and creative ways of thinking and problem solving (higher group innovativeness and creativity).
- It gets to the roots of recurring problems (minimizing recurrence and deeper comprehension).
- It helps to unleash the full potential of every interacting agent (better utilization of the self-powered and intrinsic leadership capabilities).
- It helps to enhance collective intelligence and foster self-organization/self-transcending constructions (higher self-organizing capacity and emergence-intelligence capacity).
- Thus, dialogue is about emergence.

b. Discussion verses Dialogue

- Generally, pure dialogue (no immediate goal) and discussion (immediate decision required) are not found in daily conversation. Dialogue and discussion can be perceived as two extreme ends of a conversation continuum (see Figure 7.6). Normally, a conversation tends to move inbetween the spectrum, and the participants are usually unaware of where they are.

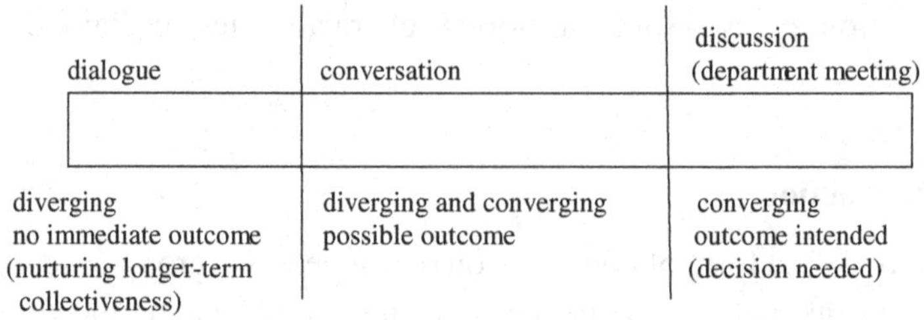

dialogue	conversation	discussion (department meeting)
diverging no immediate outcome (nurturing longer-term collectiveness)	diverging and converging possible outcome	converging outcome intended (decision needed)

Figure 7.6 A simplified conversation spectrum with respect to immediate outcome.

- Dialogue is about gathering or unfolding meaning that comes from many parts, while discussion is about breaking the whole down to many parts (reductionist).
- When the underlying dynamic in a meeting is to learn and expand what is known about something or to generate new perspectives from the views of many, the conversation tends towards the dialogic end of the continuum.
- Conversely, when the dynamic focuses on immediate decision making, it tends towards the discussion end.

c. Divergent verses Convergent

- Thus, dialogue is divergent in nature. It encourages an opening up about problems, issues, or topics, and examining them from several different possible perspectives (futuristic to some extent, that is, convergent may emerge spontaneously).
- While, discussion or debate is convergent in nature. It narrows down the conversation to a final decision (goal seeking). It always ensures every participant (within a group or department) knows what to do eventually.
- If a group or a team dialogues about a problem or an issue first (consciously or sub-consciously), by the time a solution need to be selected, chances are the process will be quick or even spontaneous due to past deliberations — that is, the choice may almost choose itself (self-organizing with high collective intelligence).

d. Advocacy and Inquiry in Dialogue

- In dialogue, advocacy is quite appropriate if it is to offer some perspective for the purpose of group learning. In this case, the intention is not to force the group to accept a (personal) perspective, but rather to build shared meanings (higher orgmindful).
- In dialogue, inquiry exists for the purpose of digging deeper into the problem/issue concerned. It is used to ask about other's assumptions and underlying thinking for further clarification. The intention of inquiring is also to learn more. It also nurtures deeper ·'feeling' (towards a 'feeling' system).

e. Other Qualities (Attitude) of Dialogue

- Suspension of immediate judgment is beneficial.
- Correspondingly, no immediate decision making occurs.
- Deeper inquiry into underlying assumptions (creating deeper understanding is a longer term benefit).
- Ensuring authenticity is significant.
- Slower pace of conversation with silence between speakers (for better listening, and deeper thinking and contemplation) — listening is as significant as communicating.
- Also listen deeply to one-self and others for better collective meaning (mindfulness) must be a norm.

Finally, it is important to note that none of the above characteristics by itself makes a conversation a dialogue. It is the integration of all of them that the conversational processes are moved towards the dialogic end of the conversation spectrum.

7.3.5 *Needs for paper dialogue*

Based on the above observation, it is clear that (verbal) dialogue can be an effective methodology that enhances communications, connectivity, engagement, and collective intelligence in any human organizations if the interacting agents are contributing voluntarily and genuinely. Apparently, some forms of constructive communications are vital to all human organizations. An organization that does not communicate internally is brain dead. However, the constraint often encountered is a culture and leadership that stifles 'openness'. Thus, there is a need to overcome the trap (Abilene paradox, defensive routine) of the phobic mindset in the interacting agents in traditional hierarchical organizations. An attempt must be executed to render this latent aspect more apparent, and a potential solution must be explored.

In this respect, **paper dialogue** a modified approach to **verbal dialogue** can serve as an effective intermediary measure for some organizations to overcome the cultural 'obstruction' for truthful engagement (Ng and Liang, 2005). It is introduced as a convenient and useful alternative to address the above 'challenge' — reducing Abilene paradox and the phobic mindset of the interacting agents in organizations to initiate a **self-organizing communications** process. In general, paper dialogue brilliantly ensures better confidentiality, a significant factor for 'personal safety'. It allows the initial obstacle of fear and intimidation to be minimized or even removed as the identity of the (original) contributors is unknown. Thus, it is a means to overcome the phobia of lash back for communicating truthfully. It reduces the pressure of hesitation and frustration. It enables and encourages the interacting agents to speak the unspeakable. In addition, it also allows other interacting agents to dialogue (verbally) without fear subsequently. In this respect, paper dialogue provides all organizations with an extra valuable tool in their repertoire to generate more effective and truthful communications that is desperately needed (see Figure 7.7).

7.4 The Human Agent-Agent/System Micro-Structure and Dynamic

It has been introduced earlier that all human organizations are CAS. In human CAS, the agents interact with its immediate neighboring agents to form spaces of localized order. These heterogeneous human agents encompass certain characteristics/properties that decide their behavioral schemata (including those analyzed above). Fundamentally, human beings (human thinking systems) are inherently not fully rational (emotional), and also subject to further constraints by the bounded rational situations.

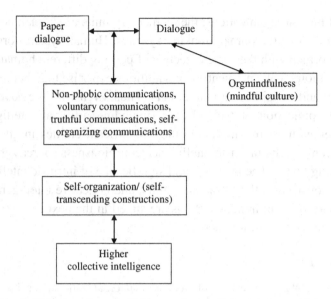

Figure 7.7 Combination of orgmindfulness and paper dialogue nurtures higher collective intelligence.

In addition, local interactions of an agent may affect the global dynamic eventually, although, it was not the original intention. The local space can be a complex network that emerges in this complex dynamic.

7.4.1 *Local self-enrichment processes*

In this case, it is beneficial to examine the human CAD more in-depth, starting at the elementary unit level. In all evolving systems, the smallest unit of interest, the elementary unit, is an extremely significant entity. An elementary unit is the smallest unit capable of independent existence (autonomous) in the system under examination — highlighting the significance of stability-centricity. The evolutionary success or failure of these units determines the fate of the systems. Successful elementary units help to stabilize the systems and unsuccessful units propagate instability. This is analogous to atoms as the basic building blocks of elements and compounds (unstable atoms will continue to react and 'unstable' human beings become refugees/migrants or rebels).

In all human organizations, the elementary units are human beings or more specifically, the human thinking systems. Human systems/organizations are formed with the basic objective of pooling different human needs (physical, biological, and mental), and abilities/expertise together to create coherency and certain synergetic effects. Thus, even with the advent and extensive application of technologies (including artificial intelligence), human beings must remain as the most significant entities in all human organizations, as the intrinsic intelligence/consciousness sources are decision-making nodes. The presence and significance of intrinsic intelligence and consciousness in the elementary units, and collective intelligence and org-consciousness in human systems are stated in the next two axioms of the intelligent organization theory.

Axiom I

The elementary units of intelligent human organizations, the human agents (human thinking systems), are driven by their own intrinsic intelligence/consciousness. Each of these units or agents is an intrinsic CAS.

Axiom II

All intelligent human organizations possess their own collective intelligence/org-consciousness (presence of an org-brain and orgmind — **organizational thinking system**). Hence, they are higher order/ composite intelligent CAS.

The interacting agents of human systems are influenced and controlled by certain elementary forces that are **self-centric** or **autopoietic**, and **stability-centric**. These primary forces controlling all human activities and decision making are the **self-enrichment processes**. Thus, the self-enrichment forces, analogous to attractive physical forces are centripetal in nature. They focus on strengthening the local structure/space, and prolong the existence of the individual elementary entities (see principle of locality in Appendix 7). For instance, even in the physical matter world (the non-living world), atoms that are self-sufficient do not react. They are highly stable. A group of such atoms, the noble gases, is totally inert. They are fully 'self-sufficient'. However, other atoms that are not self-sufficient will react through sharing (covalent bond) and exchanging (electrovalent bond) electrons. These atoms are more stable in the molecular/compound state.

In the human world, the stability-centric dynamic is similar to some extent, except these self-enrichment processes are not necessarily material based alone. The sophisticated and multi-dimensional needs (physical, biological, and mental) of human beings render their interactive dynamic highly complex. In humanity, mental, spiritual, self-actualization and other forms of intangible enrichment are equally significant. (At the core of the human mental space, the 'self' emerges.) Although, for many people (in the less developed or unstable countries) at the moment, the socio-economical dimension still appears to predominate. The existence of these elementary self-enrichment processes is stated as the next axiom of the model.

Axiom III

There exist self-centric and stability-centric elementary self-enrichment processes that constantly enhance the stability of the human agents (autopoiesis), and their local spaces/networks (self-organization/ self-transcending constructions) in all intelligent human organizations.

Thus, the elementary self-enrichment processes (1st localized order and 2nd localized order) constitute the first set of primary stabilizing forces in human organizations. Under all circumstances, these elementary processes cannot be ruthlessly suppressed or totally deactivated. In certain communist regimes, for instance, where individuals are asked to make sacrifices for the nation to the extent that their own interests are completely ignored, the expected surface phenomena never materialize. Instead, a very different outcome emerges. In this case, the systems moved into a punctuation point and disintegrated. Although, a fundamental belief in the communist ideology is actually to stabilize the elementary units, some practices have been otherwise. Apparently, the elementary units must be stabilized first before the system in which they are elementary units can ever be stabilized. In addition, besides autopoiesis, self-enrichment also encompasses localized self-organization/self-transcending constructions — the formation of a stable localized space or network (see principle of locality, localized order, self-organizing capacity, emergence, and network theory in Appendix 7) (see Figure 7.8).

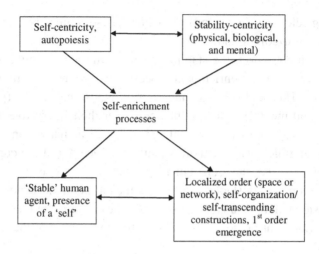

Figure 7.8   Self-centricity and stability-centricity of all human agents.

It is now apparent that in all human organizations, once the self-enrichment processes vanish, the system destabilizes and may disintegrate quickly (observe in numerous countries). Basically, in such a situation, complexity exceeds connectivity. Such a consequence is due to the fact that the most basic layer of the system is no more in proper order. Over time, the internal dynamic moves towards in-deterministic chaotic, and the 'expected' constructive surface phenomenon does not materialize (see in-deterministic and chaotic attractor in Appendix 7). The adaptive system can no longer adapt or evolve. This important understanding is stated as the next postulate of the model.

Postulate I: Law of Local Self-Enrichment

Self-enrichment of the elementary units (human interacting agents) is the most fundamental requirement for the successful evolution of all human organizations. Self-enrichment processes (self-centric, stability-centric, autopoietic, localized, self-organizing, and 1st order emergence) form the first set of primary stabilizers in such systems. (Thus, similar to physical matter structure, human organizational structure is stable only if the elementary units (and the local spaces/networks) are stable. Otherwise, the human organization disintegrates.) For human agents, stability is three dimensional, namely physical, biological, and mental.

In general, the degree of self-enhancement needed by an elementary unit is subjective with respect to the individual units concerned. However, local 'optimization' associated with the concept of an **economic man** (**Adam Smith**, 1723–1790, classical economic theory) rarely materializes. In addition, due to the constraints of the thinking systems of the interacting agents, there are limits to optimizing a decision or an action. This is the **administrative man** concept. The **bounded rationality** concept (**Herbert Simon**, 1916–2001, satisficing principle) indicates that the inner dynamic of the individual elementary unit is very important. However, the inner dynamic of the human thinking systems is extremely nonlinear and complex as well. Later in this chapter, the characteristics and inner dynamic of an **intelligent person** as a smart evolver and emergent strategist will be introduced.

7.4.2 *Global forces*

In the atomic world, the structure of an atom must be intact before a molecule can be formed (that is, the atom is stable within the molecule). Apparently, the purpose of forming a molecule is to further increase the stability of the respective atoms. Similarly, a piece of element or compound is created for the same reason. The atoms and molecules come together to stabilize themselves within a larger system. In the biological world, similar group instinct exists. Colonies of various kinds are common sight, and in many respects, colonies (as a whole) are more successful evolvers than loners. Thus, the integration of evolution and co-evolution of a system, and its elementary units is a common phenomenon in nature.

In human organizations, the micro-dynamic manifested is the same — agent-agent/system dynamic. A few human beings are attracted to form a group (local space/network), and to participate in the groups' activities fundamentally for better self-enrichment. First degree self-organization/self-transcending constructions and 1st order emergence emerge spontaneously as well —— agent-local space/network dynamic. Similarly, self-organization has also been observed in the matter world. For instance, when the condition is right, crystallization takes place spontaneously. Again, the phenomenon occurs to strengthen both the existence of the individual atoms and the collection of atoms that now exists as a crystal.

For human agents, the size of the group can be increased to that of a corporation, an economy, or a nation. In these cases, **global forces** emerge within the agent-agent/system dynamic as well. Full scale symbiosis and org-centricity must be present. Constructive global forces support the survival and competitiveness of the systems. Thus, positive global forces (encompassing autocatalysis, circular causation, and cascading effect) of these systems must simultaneously enhance the elementary self-enrichment processes and sustain the existence of the interacting agents, as well as the (certain) local spaces/networks, if they are to be effective — 2nd degree self-organization/self-transcending constructions and 2nd order emergence (see complex networks, complex adaptive networks, network-centric, org-centric, and emergence in Appendix 7). The next axiom stipulates this requirement.

Axiom VI

There exist global forces that further enrich the elementary units, that is, global forces must enhance the self-enrichment processes, as well as the entire system concurrently, if they are to be regarded as constructive.

Apparently, the strangeness of **constructive global forces** is that, although they are globally focused, they interact with the local elementary self-enrichment processes to ensure that the CAS evolves and survives successful together with its interacting agents. On the contrary, global forces that interrupt or suppress elementary self-enrichment possesses have negative contributions. Thus, the overall effective multi-dimensional dynamics of human organizations is inherently an interaction between the self-enrichment processes and the constructive global forces (as the interacting agent supports the system, the system must also support the agents). The entire dynamic is cyclical and emergence in nature. [(In this respect, intelligent complex adaptive dynamic (*i*CAD) is not totally similar to CAD (in physical systems) as the continual existence of the interacting agents is significant. Thus, in intelligent human organizations (*i*CAS), the leadership has to ensure the stability of the agents so that the systems remain competitive, resilience, and sustainable. Hence, as indicated in the intelligent organization theory, intelligence/consciousness-centricity is a key paradigmatic shift.]

Postulate II: Law of Global Forces

The effective global forces in intelligent human organizations are those that further enrich the elementary units of the systems, that is, they must enhance the elementary self-enrichment processes. These are constructive global forces, and their presence is essential and critical for successful evolution of all intelligent human organizations. This set of constructive global forces forms the next set of system stabilizers.

Therefore, the notion that global interest should be enforced and be placed above that of the elementary units at all costs does not support the expected global phenomenon. If a business organization places too much priority on its corporate interest and ignores those of its employees, the set-up will collapse eventually. Similarly, for a country the stability (coherency) of its citizens is vital for identifying or achieving some forms of **basin of attraction** (see basin of attraction in Appendix 7). When the elementary units observe that the elementary self-enrichment activities are being suppressed, the system will self-destruct eventually. It is only through the further enhancement of the elementary processes with constructive global forces that positive system phenomena can emerge. This is a (new) critical success factor of *i*CAS (see Figure 7.9). Thus, the subtlety that leads to successful competition and survival of an intelligent human organization in the knowledge-intensive economy is the mental state of its human thinking systems (see latent leadership in Appendix 7).

7.4.3 *Unique intelligent human organizational dynamic*

Primarily, the self-enrichment processes of the individual human beings must be recognized and respected as a vital local self-centric phenomenon with high positive relational parameter value — towards a **feeling system/organization** — higher **organizational justice** and **coherency** (see feeling system, organization justice and relational capacity in Appendix 7). The basic objective is to strengthen the local structure, and to prolong the existence of the elementary units. As indicated, in most circumstances, the multi-dimensional needs of human agents encompassing the material/

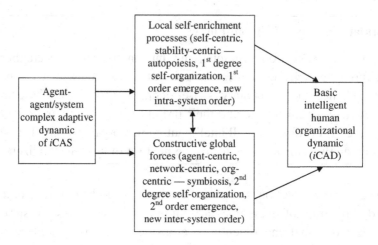

Figure 7.9   The basic integrated complex dynamics in human organization.

physical, biological, mental, and spiritual perspectives render the system dynamics of human organizations very complex. This dynamic is driven by the intelligence and consciousness embedded in all human thinking systems that form the local spaces.

Similar to the self-enrichment processes that emerge from the individual interacting agents, conceptually the global forces emerge concurrently from the organizational thinking system (org-brain + orgmind). Fundamentally, an organization is intelligent only if it is able to nurture a high level of collective intelligence and org-consciousness through organizing around intelligence. A 'satisficing dynamic equilibrium state' of the system has to be determined by the constructive interactions between the elementary processes and the global forces. Thus, an intelligent organization must be able to bind the individual agents, and the latter must be able to influence and contribute to the system positively at the same time (autocatalysis, cascading effect, recurrence relations, upwards causation, and downwards causation). This loop of forces concurrently enhances the elementary units (integrates the networks) and the global system, and also facilitates them (agents, networks, and organization) to learn, adapt, and evolve together. A human organization with intense collective intelligence self-organizes more effectively when the condition is right. As a new stable surface structure emerges, a better and more competitive system is perceived to come into existence. The entire dynamic is highly nonlinear, complex, and continuous focusing on both the evolution and co-evolution of the system and its elementary units.

With intense intelligence/consciousness-centricity, the elementary self-enrichment processes could be modified or enhanced by a more mindful mind. In this respect, the mental state of the human thinking systems, a crucial factor, must be better managed. Thus, the mindfulness of the individual minds is a vital attribute. Similarly, for an organization, orgmindfulness is another new crucial property. As indicated earlier, an organization is orgmindful if it constantly focuses inwards on the mental states of its agents (intense intelligence-intelligence linkages) to ensure that all its interacting agents are in a stable and highly participative state. Thus, the nurturing of the collective intelligence source is effective only if the orgmind is able to influence the consciousness of the individual thinking systems. This bilateral relationship has been observed to be is extremely significant and delicate in all human organizations. It enhances consensus and commitment, and elevates the collectiveness capacity, relational capacity, and adaptive capacity, and vice versa, as illustrated in Figure 7.10.

In this respect, the state of the orgmind is an extremely vital factor in the complex and knowledge-intensive environment. In addition, a highly coherent and dynamic intangible structure only evolves from a very well-focused orgmind with intense collective intelligence and org-consciousness (higher structural capacity). The presence of intense orgmindfulness enhances the evolution and co-evolution of the system and its interacting agents. The organization becomes better focus on the priority of the mental state of each and every interacting human thinking system — elevating organizational mental cohesion. Thus, the intelligent biotic macro-structure and dynamic, and the intelligent human agent-agent/system micro-structure and dynamics must be mutually enhancing (see Figure 7.11). The perception also facilitates the emergent of a 'feeling' system with higher positive relational parameter value — that is, further elevating collective intelligence and enhancing org-consciousness. This important understanding is

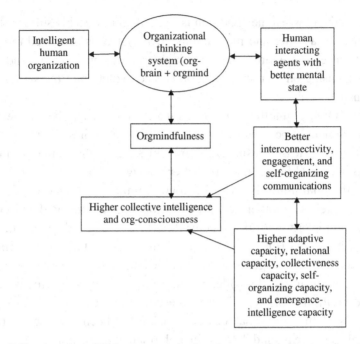

Figure 7.10 An orgmindful human organization always monitor the mental state of its interacting agents, and nurtures higher collective intelligence.

summarized as the next two postulates of the intelligent organization theory. It also establishes the foundation of the 3C-OK framework (see Chapter 8).

Postulate III: Law of Collective Intelligence

The collective intelligence of an intelligent organization resides in its organizational thinking system (org-brain + orgmind, organizational neural network), and it is the critical energy source that is responsible for moulding a coherent deep intangible structure, and an effective nimble surface physical structure. Without the presence of collective intelligence a human organization is retarded.

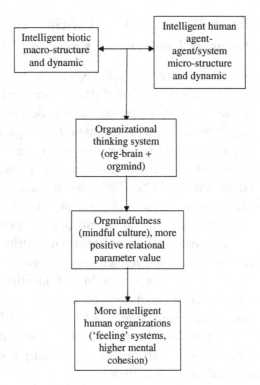

Figure 7.11 The human agent-agent/system micro-structure and the intelligent biotic macro-structure must be mutually enhancing.

Postulate VI: Law of Orgmindfulness

A high level of orgmindfulness is necessary to nurture an intense, coherence, and well-focused collective intelligence and org-consciousness source (vice versus). Otherwise, the evolution and co-evolution dynamics (self-enhancing process and global forces) of the organization and its interacting agents will not be constructive or synergetic. In this respect, more intense orgmindfulness (presence of a mindful culture) assist in enhancing the positive relational parameter value, and nurturing the 'feeling' characteristic of human organizations better — higher mental cohesion.

7.5 The Intelligent Person Model: Efficient Information Decoder, Smarter Evolver and Emergent Strategist

The intelligent person model is a highly significant component of the intelligent organization theory because it defines the (preferred/'ideal') characteristics of human agents (especially the leaders and actors) that possess higher capabilities in nurturing intelligent organizations. The need for such redefined agents is critical in the 'raplex' environment. The model emerges from the economics man model (total rationality/ optimality) of **Adam Smith** (1723–1790), and the administrative man model (bounded rationality and satisficing principle) of **Herbert Simon** (1916–2001) see Figure 7.12. An **'intelligent person'** in the intelligent person model is a self-powered human agent with intrinsic leadership capability (a deviation from empowerment and hierarchical leadership), an effective information decoder (capability of identifying surfacing problems, foresight, futuristic), and decision-making node that is also a smarter evolver and an emergent strategist (conscientiously exploit the co-existence of order and complexity). In this respect, it is someone that constantly focuses on the self-organizing capacity and emergence-intelligence capacity of the organization.

As the mental state (mindset and thinking) of human agents is highly crucial to the 'success' of a human organization, an intelligent person as a

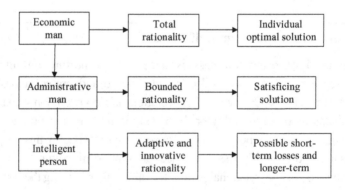

Figure 7.12 Comparison of the economic man, administrative man, and intelligent person models.

highly mindful agent is preferred. Thus, the capacity, quality, and thinking of the human thinking systems are the most important assets of all human beings, as well as the organizations in which they are elementary units. Once the thinking system ceases to function, the person ceases to exist, and the physical/biological system in which the mind resides will be swiftly absorbed into the expanding main flow of the Universe. The intangible human mind comes into existence because of the emergence of human consciousness from human intelligence. Otherwise, it will remain as a brain, merely a biological organ, like a kidney. In this case, there will be not much significant differences between a biological system and an automated mechanical machine. Hence, the human mind, a unique intangible complex abstract space projected by the intense intelligence of the human brain is a vital 'entity'. Even though the mind is intangible, its presence is overwhelmingly felt.

Different level of consciousness emerges when intelligence crosses different levels of thresholds as shown in the intelligence spectrum (see the intelligence spectrum in Chapter 3). The consciousness of a human mind makes a human being aware of the environment (external focusing), as well as his/hers own existence as an independent unique entity (the emergent of a self, I, and a different level of self-centricity). Subsequently, intelligence and consciousness facilitate the emergent of other mental functions such as perception, reasoning, and decision making. In addition, the state of awareness can be further enhanced by the presence of a better developed sensory system. Thus, the sensory input helps a person to act and react to the changing conditions more effectively (human beings are open systems). Most human beings today are highly aware of their chancing environment (especially, with the support of social media/ wireless technology).

As discussed earlier, to sustain itself as a unique consciousness source, a human mind has to be extremely mindful too. Mindfulness emerges only when the mind focuses inwards at its own mental state. Very likely, the mental function of mindfulness only exists in the human mind, and not in any other living species on this planet. It creates directed inward attention, and teaches the mind to be more focus on itself. Thus, it is the observation of each and every thought that arises in the mind. In this respect, mindfulness is the ability to venture more deeply into the mind than self-awareness. Hence, mindfulness is an internal self-search mental function, and is perceived as the core function of self-awareness. It is a highly valued attribute because it creates 'deeper' rationality (remembering that the human thinking system is an emotional system), and higher quality interconnectivity.

It has been accepted that there is a relationship between brain wave and mindfulness. The latter can be better achieved when the brain is in the alpha or even theta states, that is, when the mind is more serene and less confused. The brain waves in these states have frequency between 1 to 13 Hz (approximately). In addition, mindfulness and creativity has been observed to be intimately related. Thus, a more mindful mind (with deeper thoughts) is usually more calm, innovative and creative. This recognition has a significant contribution to the leadership, governance, and management mindset, and also the mental state of smarter evolvers and emergent strategists.

In intelligent human organizations, 'right' mindfulness and 'clearer comprehension' are the two significant attributes that guide the inner dynamic of an intelligent person and the better self-organizing dynamic of the system. Therefore, it is when the mind is mindful that the other activities such as perception, problem solving, and decision making are executed effectively. As an action arises from a thought, a mindful mind being more clearly focused will eventually generate a more rational (not optimal) longer-term decision and action. Thus, in a highly intelligent mind, there exists a deeper organizing center. This center continually reminds the mind to be mindful. In an intelligent person, a very high order of mindfulness must be present at all times to sustain 'deeper' rationality, constructive interconnectivity, truthful engagement, higher collectiveness capacity, and better self-organizing capability.

In this manner, an intelligent person frequently modifies and introduces additional meanings to his/hers self-enrichment processes. A more subtle approach is usually adopted compared to an ordinary thinking system. An intelligent person ensures that s/he has better long-term survival opportunities. The evolution of an intelligent person also encompasses co-evolution with the system. Such an intelligent person seeks 'holistic adaptive solutions'. In this respect, an adaptive solution may not be optimal (total rationality of an economic man) or even satisficing at a particular moment in time (bounded rationality of an administrative man). Due to mental, physical and environmental constraints, the solution adopted may even be an option with short-term losses (to ensure better sustainability, optimizing the rugged landscape and red queen race characteristics is needed) that eventually leads to longer-term gains — [avoiding **complexity catastrophe** (Kauffman, 1993)].

In this respect, an intelligent person is deeply aware that an effective transformation may not take place overnight (emergent strategist). Thus, being highly adaptive and futuristic, an intelligent person focuses on longer-term survival (focusing on both deliberate and emergent strategies). In addition, an intelligent person also concentrates on exploiting certain spaces of complexity (better risk management), and continuously making preparation for the sudden appearance of punctuation points (better crisis management). As the self-organization/self-transcending constructions processes of human organizations are highly dependent on the mental state of the individual interacting agents, these processes can be greatly enhanced by the characteristics of an intelligent person. This concept is captured in Figure 7.13. Inevitably, intelligence leaders must possess attributes of the intelligence person.

In summary, an intelligent person is a self-powered, and highly mindful and orgmindful agent (a significant balance, as *i*CAD is both self-centric and org-centric — different from CAD that focuses only on the system) that possesses high intrinsic leadership capability, recognizes the presence of the fluctuating rugged landscape and the difficulty of red queen race, accepts short-term losses for longer-term gains, exploits the integrated deliberate and emergent strategy, recognizes the value and significance of constructive self-organization/self-transcending constructions, nurtures team-working capability and integrates networks, and exploits other complexity associated properties when necessary (including butterfly effect, symbiosis, far-from-equilibrium, interdependency, basin of attraction, attractor, relativistic complexity, synergetics). An intelligent person searches for best possible solutions (futuristic), and adapts with the continuous changing conditions swiftly (high flexibility). Thus, overall,

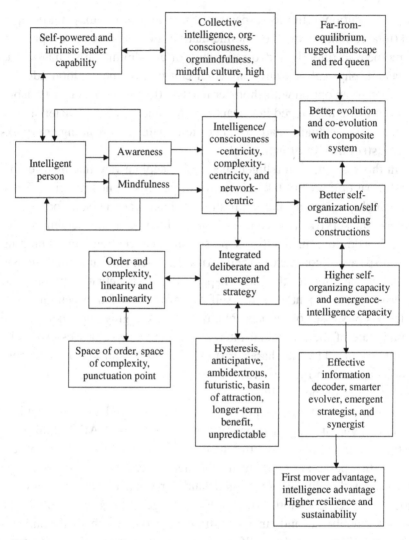

Figure 7.13 Basic dynamic of an intelligent person as a smarter evolver and emergent strategist.

such an agent each carrying a set of highly 'intelligent' and changing (adaptive) behavior schemata is an effective participant in the *i*CAS, and helps to drive a constructive *i*CAD. It is vital that current and future leaders, managers, and even ordinary interacting agents (actors or non-actors) are intelligent persons.

Intelligent Person: Human Interacting Agent (II)

Intelligent persons are intelligent human interacting agents. In addition to the characteristics specified in 'human interacting agent (I)' (see Chapter 4), they are also self-powered agents, intrinsic leaders, intelligent information decoders, intrinsic decision-makers, smarter evolvers, and emergent strategists. They are mindful and orgmindful, aware of the presence of the rugged landscape and red queen race, constantly exploit both order (including relativistic order) and complexity (innovation and risk management), and making preparation for punctuation points (crisis management), as well as futuristic (longer-term benefit). In this respect, they recognize the importance and benefit of high structural capacity, collectiveness capacity, adaptive capacity, relational capacity, self-organizing capacity, and emergence-intelligence capacity.

7.6 Conclusion

This chapter reinforces some fundamental facts of the intelligent organization theory that the evolution of all natural systems, including human organizations, is primarily driven by the intrinsic intelligence (proto-intelligence, basic life intelligence, basic human intelligence, advanced human intelligence) of the agents, and the collective intelligence of the system (art colony, ecosystem, corporation, nation). Intelligence is the mysterious intangible entity embedded in nature that drives its own evolutionary and co-evolutionary dynamics (a dynamic that enhances local stability, and contradicts universal expansion). The more intelligent agents and systems learn quickly, decipher information faster, create quality sophisticated knowledge structure, and adapt to fast changing environment continuously. In this respect, intelligence is not merely computational competency. In the human world, thinking, or for that matter, 'logical and rational thinking' (abstract perception and construal capability) is a necessary attribute that indicates the presence of advanced human intelligence.

In general, the basic dynamic of human agents and their intelligent organizations has a stability-centric, self-centric (autopoiesis), as well as an org-centric (symbiosis) component. Fundamentally, the autopoietic self-enrichment processes are essential for individual survival. Coupled with the constructive global forces of the system, the interacting agents co-evolve with the organization — very often through the better integration of stabilized local spaces (agents and networks). The combined dynamic ensures higher interconnectivity, communications, and engagement, and nurtures higher collective intelligence and org-consciousness facilitated by a supportive mindful culture, that is desperately needed in all intelligent human organizations (mental cohesion).

The above observation leads to the conceptualization of the intelligent person model — human agents with redefined (ideal) characteristics. An intelligent person besides being highly aware of the environment (externally focus) also maintains a highly mindful mind (internally focus) at all times. Interacting agents with such a mental state is vital if humankind wishes to move into a more advanced state of existence. In addition, an intelligent person being also orgmindful helps to expedite the nurturing of collective intelligence, and also towards a feeling system. Thus, an intelligent person always attempts to establish a more mindful culture (collective survival) in the organization by improving the quality of its connectivity, competitiveness, and evolution and co-evolution dynamics. The intelligent human organizational dynamic is the iCAD. The latter must ensure the survival of all the interacting agents, as well as the system (intelligence leadership and intelligence governance). This is a cyclical process (stasis and punctuated equilibrium, ambidextrous, autocatalysis, recurrence relations, cascading effect, and self-organizing) that requires the intelligent interacting agents and the system to continually identify new equilibriums, guided by the core properties of the complexity theory (consciousness, complexity, connectivity, dissipation, emergence). The learning and adjustment processes between the system and the agents/local spaces are continual, and may have no ultimate known destination (red queen race). This is also the basic mindset (intelligence mindset) of an intelligent person.

Finally, the important attributes, features, and dynamic to note when nurturing an intelligent human organization are summarized as follows:

a. The CAD of an intelligent human organization is an integration of local self-enrichment processes and constructive global forces.

b. The mental state of the interacting agents, as well as the presence of an orgmind and its collective intelligence and org-consciousness has an extremely significant impact on the overall system dynamic of human organizations.

c. An interacting agent that is an intelligent person ensures a more constructive system dynamic (*i*CAD). Such a person possesses certain basic intelligence/consciousness-centric and complexity-centric characteristics and thinking namely, efficient information decoding, self-powered and intrinsic leadership, high level of mindfulness, high collective intelligence and org-consciousness, the changing landscape and red queen race (anticipative), better risk management and crisis management, longer-term optimality rather than shorter-term gain (futuristic), and the presence and significance of emergence.

d. Thus, an intelligent person is able to adapt more effectively in spaces of complexity (risk management, relativistic complexity) and at punctuation points (crisis management). Better self-organization/self-transcending constructions will also emerge spontaneously in the system at criticality due to its high self-organizing capacity and emergence-intelligence capacity. In this respect, an intelligent person is a smarter evolver and emergent strategist that continuously adopts an integrated deliberate and emergent strategy.

Therefore, in the current context, the mindfulness of the interacting agents and the orgmindfulness of the human organizations must be allocated high priority when leading and managing an intelligent human organization and their interacting agents. A higher level of collective intelligence and org-consciousness can be better nurtured and sustained with a mindful culture, and exploiting the intelligence leadership theory/strategy and the intelligence governance theory/strategy (will be further discussed in Chapters 9 and 10).

Coherency, synergy, and constructionist effect are vital attributes that competitive human organizations must achieve. In particular, the constructionist effect is positively correlated with innovation and creativity.

The ability to reduce everything to simple fundamental laws does not imply the ability to start from those laws and reconstruct the Universe.

Philip Warren Anderson, *More is Different*

Chapter 8

Advanced Intelligence Human Organizational Nonlinear Dynamic and the Integrated 3C-OK Framework

"A smart evolver must also be an emergent strategist"

"A high level of intelligence is useful for visualizing structure (information decoder) and dynamics (surface pattern)"

"The invisible hand is nonlinear"

Summary

The basic foundation of intelligent complex adaptive dynamic (*i*CAD) exploits the interdependency of five significant attributes of intelligent human organizations (*i*CAS) that possess certain unique characteristics only associated with human organizations. The attributes involved are collective intelligence, connectivity, culture (mindful), organizational learning, and knowledge management, and their integrative structure and dynamics. This foundation pillar of the *i*CAD is conceived as the 3C-OK framework. Recognizing the necessity of this integrated and redefined foundation of the intelligent human complex adaptive dynamic is vital, as this set of attributes is not present (minimal) in other complex adaptive systems (CAS). In this respect there are differences between highly intelligent human adaptive dynamic (*i*CAD) and other biological complex adaptive dynamics (CAD). A primary factor that created the difference is the mental function of orgmindfulness. Thus, the characteristics and capabilities of human collective intelligence are substantially different from swarm intelligence. In this respect, the high intelligence-intelligence linkages which are strongly correlated with collective intelligence [determined by the characteristics of the agents' abstract mental space (including a space for deeper contemplation)], and org-consciousness and the relational parameter (relational capacity) are new significant focal points (an intelligent human organization <=> at least a thinking system + feeling system).

In the intelligent organization theory, the integrated 3C-OK structure and dynamic is mutually enhancing with organizing around intelligence and the intelligent biotic macro-structure. The framework supports the elevation of the collectiveness capacity and adaptive capacity which are key capacities of intelligent human organizations. In particular, their interdependency illustrates that organizational learning and knowledge management (a vital capability associated with the creation of an intangible abstract mental space in the human world) cannot be executed effectively in any human organizations without the presence of the other three attributes. Hence, human interacting agents, each an intense intelligence/consciousness source, and embedded with a set of changing nonlinear behavioral schemata, and their linkages (including the social cognition and construal perspective that influence the self-transcending constructions capability, and emergence-intelligence capacity of the organization) must be well-exploited. In this respect, the integrated 3C-OK structure provides the basic strata of the *i*CAD. Thus, an organization that places sufficient emphasis on the integrated 3C-OK structure and dynamic will gradually experience the emergence of a higher level human *i*CAD. The presence of such an environment also facilitates faster and better responses to unexpected changes.

Keywords: Interdependency, intelligence/consciousness-centricity, collective intelligence, swarm intelligence, connectivity, mindful culture, organizational learning, knowledge management, 3C-OK framework, organizing around intelligence, intelligent biotic macro-structure, intelligence-intelligence linkage, complex adaptive systems (CAS), intelligent complex adaptive systems (*i*CAS), complex adaptive dynamic (CAD), intelligent complex adaptive dynamic (*i*CAD), adaptive capacity, collectiveness capacity, structural capacity, relational capacity, self-organizing capacity, emergence-intelligence capacity, information explosion, information implosion, space-time compression, complexity-intelligence strategy, basic human intelligence, advanced human intelligence, consciousness, awareness, self-awareness, mindfulness, intelligent person (model), human thinking system, composite thinking system, organizational neural network, consciousness-connectivity cycle, emergence-dissipation cycle, org-consciousness, orgmindfulness, org-awareness, autopoiesis, symbiosis, stability-centricity, dissipation, self-organization, self-transcending constructions, emergence, resilience, sustainability, intelligence advantage, learning organization, corporate intelligence enhancer, knowledge structure, externalized knowledge repository, learning organization, smarter evolver, emergent strategist, cosmopolitan communicator, self-organizing communications, organizational knowledge structure, tacit knowledge, explicit knowledge, (human) relational parameter, feeling system, coherency, synergy, mental cohesion, raplexity, intelligence mindset, intelligence paradigm, relative complexity, intelligence leadership, intelligence governance and intelligence advantage.

8.1 Introduction: The World of Advanced Human Complex Adaptive Dynamic

8.1.1 *Human uniqueness, high nonlinearity and current non-synchronicity*

At the moment, humanity is situated in the transition period between the third and fourth era in the history of humankind. The human world is in the midst of another complex transformation, at a new edge of emergence — requiring greater intelligence/ consciousness-centricity. The primary causes driving the transformation are **information explosion** and **information implosion**, due to a world population with better knowledge structures arising from the intense education systems (in most developed countries), and also associated with the accelerated rate of information acquisition, 'virtual' communications (speed of light), and direct/physical communications (speed of sound) associated with the advancement media/wireless and swifter transportation technologies, respectively. Concurrently, business, economic, and political environment of many countries and other organizations have been inherently redefined. In the current humanity space, there is a critical need to create higher quality national/corporate knowledge structures and connectivity (due to low collectiveness capacity — high diversification and spread, and poor engagement of agents), and **space-time compression** (due to rapid globalization and urbanization). Consequently, a highly complex human world (especially, in the mental space) that has never been observed in the ecosystem of any other species is emerging.

In particular, the increasing use of valuable information and knowledge [including intensive focus on technological R&D (space, aero-space, bio-medical, media, and military technologies), and creating income from wealth investment instead of from employment/job] called for the cultivation of a totally different breed of human beings and human organizations. The new individuals and the new form of organizations must be able to process information fast, learn fast, use knowledge (technical expertise) effectively, adapt to competition and the changing environment swiftly (continuously changing landscape), and evolve smartly and successfully with an intense 'emergence thinking' (emerging new order). Hence, the flesh strategic bio-logic approach that focuses on structuring, organizing, and strategizing human organizations around intelligence/consciousness has certain advantages (in particular, the swift and more accurate information and knowledge synchronization, comprehension, and utilization; and the presence of a written language). Ironically, many organizations today still do not share all information/knowledge with all their agents (employees and citizens) that is crucial for expediting and integrating the process — significant non-synchronicity.

The adaptive dynamic of humanity has developed beyond the 'basic-life' requirements (predators and preys, see Figure 8.1). In addition, the intellectual development of humanity has arrived at a phase whereby focusing on bio-logic rather than machine-logic alone makes better sense in many of its endeavors due to high nonlinearity. However, there are still many human organizations with dynamic that is inherently complex but not sufficiently adaptive. To the extreme, mainly due to the traditional hierarchical/ authoritative leadership and the Newtonian mindset, the nonlinear and complex perspective has always been suppressed or assumed as errors — always attempting to create 'enforced' order leading to low coherency and commitment or even disintegration. In the process, local spaces/networks with different thinking, values, and expectations emerge, pushing the organizations (countries, corporations) into in-deterministic chaos. Apparently, it is vital to recognize that human organizations that are highly hierarchical, and are controlled and managed like machines (with low or no positive relational parameter value) will self-destruct in the current context.

As indicated earlier, it is crucial to recognize that the characteristics and strengths of biological structures are far more superior or adaptive than

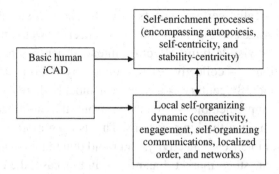

Figure 8.1 Key components of the basic human intelligence dynamic.

that of mechanistic models in numerous aspects. (Basically, that is the reason for embedding artificial intelligence in automated machines. Humanity is moving into a stage where by many jobs are replaced by 'intelligent' machines, and more people are becoming investors rather than workers.) Machines, besides being orderly, linear, and rigid, have to be controlled and monitored directly or remotely, and maintained externally. Biological systems, even those with relatively lower intelligence, inherently manifest properties associated with adaptation, individual and group/colony survival, evolution and co-evolution, inherent order out of complexity spontaneously, constructionist and synergetic, and their dynamics are driven by their own intrinsic intelligence and collective intelligence (see collective intelligence and swarm intelligence in Appendix 7). In particular, for human organizations and their associated systems, it is significant to note the following relationships (mutually enhancing linkages) for elevating collective intelligence and org-consciousness:

Biological structural capacity > Mechanical structural capacity (8.1)

Structural capacity <=> Collective intelligence (8.2)

Adaptive capacity <=> Collective intelligence (8.3)

Collectiveness capacity <=> Collective intelligence (8.4)

iCAD ≠ 'common' CAD (8.5)

self-organizing capacity <=> Smarter evolver and
emergent strategist (8.6)

Even historically, certain aspects of earlier human societal dynamic observed, and some corresponding theories conceived were unconsciously nonlinear. The **invisible hand** effect (unintended benefits resulting from individual actions — collectively) introduced by **Adam Smith** (1723–1790) in the mid-18th century is a nonlinear model where market conditions can be unpredictable — emerges from the nonlinear complex interactions of human thinking systems. This is even more so in the present world with intense connectivity, and rapid dynamics — including the 'emotional' (fear) stock market dynamic — in this case, the consequence is not always beneficial to many agents. Therefore, highly intelligent human organizations (*i*CAS) that possess basic characteristics of better 'integration' of all interacting agents with the **intelligent person** characteristics (who are highly intelligence/consciousness-centric, complexity-centric, and possess higher quality knowledge structures, and share information effectively/holistically) must be nurtured (illustrated in Chapter 7). In the present context, intangible properties/activities such as human capitals, intellectual capitals, social capitals, and wealth investments are new crucial assets. Thus, a deeper analysis and comprehension of the human abstract nonlinear dynamic is significant and beneficial. The intangible aspect of the human interactive dynamic that is driven by advanced human intelligence can be extremely abstract.

8.1.2 *Presence and significance of interdependency and consciousness*

Recognizing the unique independency and interdependency characteristics of human beings is valuable. Human beings are sophisticated biological beings with intense intelligence and consciousness. Each human being carries a nonlinear thinking system (in particular, advanced nonlinear intelligence, mindfulness, and emotional characteristics) from which many other properties, features, and capabilities (including a 'common' language, artificial information networks linkages, complex individual/organizational/global knowledge structure, defensive routines, and complex relational parameter) of that person is defined, determined, and manifested. Thus, connecting human agents is linking these highly complex thinking systems together to form an effective **composite thinking system** (an enormous complex collection of 'human neurons' — complex **organizational neural networks**) that must be structurally 'organism-like' (with an intelligent biotic macro-structure) and not machine-like. In this respect, even in corporations with a profit-oriented mission, employees are not merely a physical means of production (or service). The biological and mental dimensions of human existence must always be vital in humanity, and all its microcosms. It has been mentioned that the human mental space is highly nonlinear, complex, and not easy to manage.

As indicated earlier, human thinking systems are fundamentally emotional systems, and human agents can be highly interdependent, despite their intense intelligence (see Chapter 5). [(Ants and bees (with low individual intelligence) are more easily connected (swarm intelligence). Similarly, in the human world, human agents in the agricultural era were more easily connected due to their deeper social needs, lower education, and independency. However, highly intelligent human agents are difficult to connect — high individual intelligence but low collective intelligence — due to lower interdependency.)] Thus, conscientiously effort is required to manage this complex dynamic.

In summary, all human agents are self-centric, stability-centric and autopoietic. Thus, to better manage human organizations, the human thinking systems must be well-managed first (focusing on the mental states of the agents — consciousness, mindfulness, orgmindfulness, presence of a mindful culture — constantly searching for an opportunity for better integration). It is in this manner that voluntary collaboration among agents can be achieved through mutual respect, intimacy, subtlety, and trust — in the process lowering or eliminating defensive routines and Abilene paradox. Leaders must be aware that such a paradigmatic shift is inevitable (see intelligence leadership in Appendix 7). Apparently, a more constructive optimization of human unique interdependency, and a deeper recognition and comprehension of human agents' consciousness is critical (see Figure 8.2).

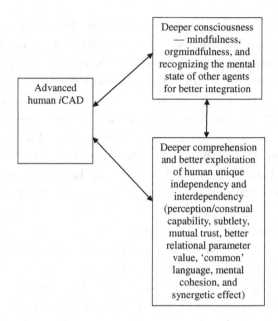

Figure 8.2   The unique advanced human intelligence dynamic.

8.2 Introduction to the 3C-OK Framework

The above discussion clearly indicates the significance and criticality of possessing high agent's consciousness and (organizational) collective intelligence. It also provides a better foundation for the analysis and nurturing of the integrated **3C-OK framework** (encompassing collective intelligence, connectivity, culture, organizational learning, and knowledge management — a dynamic confined only to humanity and its organizations). The latter is the underlying dynamic (foundation pillar of the *i*CAD) of any intelligent human organizations. This framework is a significant integrated tool (component) of **complexity-intelligence strategy** (3C-OK framework <=> organizing around intelligence <=> intelligent biotic macro-structure; mutually enhancing). Thus, the framework and its strategy is a vital aspect of the intelligent organization theory that helps to nurture higher quality human complex adaptive dynamic (*i*CAD) by better exploitation of advanced human intelligence (see Figure 8.3).

A vital aspect of this framework is the recognition of the strong interdependency of the five attributes involved. The interdependent and

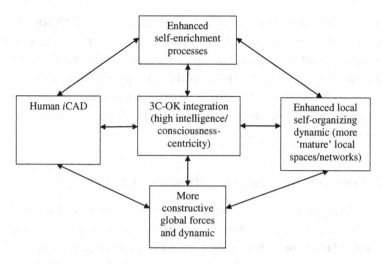

Figure 8.3   3C-OK as the basic foundation of human *i*CAD.

nonlinear dynamic involving these five attributes is a critical foundation
of the intelligent human organizations dynamic that must be recognized
by all their interacting agents (both leaders and followers). For instance,
knowledge management activity cannot be executed effectively in an
organization without cautiously managing the other four activities concurrently. The new recognition provides an indication how an organization
can be led and managed more effectively. It also redefines governance in
human organizations (see Chapter 10). As observed earlier, the human
intelligent complex adaptive (*i*CAD) dynamic is also highly dependent on
the manifestation of a 'common' language, self-organizing communications, truthful engagement, network-centricity, localized order, and distributed power. The 3C-OK framework is conceptualized and analyzed
with respect to this recognition.

8.3 The 3C (Collective Intelligence, Connectivity and Culture) Dynamic

In complexity theory, the five core properties of the complex adaptive
systems (CAS) and their dynamics are namely, consciousness, complexity, connectivity, dissipation, and emergence. The interactive dynamic

among these five attributes form the basic foundation of CAS for survival and evolution. However, in the intelligent organization theory, a critical key attribute is intelligence (collective intelligence). In this theory, intelligence has been observed to possess the vital property of stability-centricity, and it is also the source where consciousness (awareness, self-awareness, mindfulness) emerges with the existence of life (only in living systems).

8.3.1 *Consciousness, connectivity and complexity*

Consciousness is an extremely unique attribute that is present in the world of life, and it has entices some of the existing and existed best minds. In 1637, **Rene Descartes** (1596–1650), the father of modern western (feeling-based) philosophy, indicated that 'I think, therefore I am', and conceptualized **Cartesian dualism** (embedding the presence of the mind and consciousness). While, **Pierre Teilhard de Chardin** (1881–1955) conceived the term **omega point** indicating that the Universe is evolving towards maximum level of complexity and consciousness. In complexity theory, consciousness is introduced as one of the core properties of CAS. The dynamic of the five core properties (five core properties interactive cycle) is illustrated in Figure 8.4.

In the intelligent organization theory, it has been illustrated that corresponding to the intelligence spectrum, the level of consciousness spreads over a spectrum as well. It has been stated that arising from human consciousness are two mental functions, namely, **awareness** and **mindfulness.** Awareness focuses outwards. It recognizes the environment in which the individual exists, and enables the latter to act/react to the changing circumstances. On the other hand, mindfulness focuses inwards on the mental state of the individual, and is unique to humanity. It enables internal search on the mind, and also observes/controls the mental state of the mind. In the abstract mental space, mindfulness assists the mind to watch itself when a new thought emerges. Mindfulness is the core of **self-awareness** — greatly enhances the recognition of the presence of the 'self'. Thus, mindfulness only emerges from intelligence sources with high consciousness — a unique characteristic of human thinking systems.

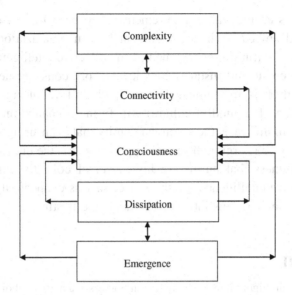

Figure 8.4   The five core properties interactive cycle.

In this respect, according to the intelligent organization theory, a key characteristic of intelligent human organizations is that it must be aware of its environment continuously (intense org-awareness — external focusing, including customers, competitors, neighboring countries, the atmospheric environment, and unexpected changes), and its internal entities/agents and dynamic (intense orgmindfulness — internal focusing, including employees/citizens and their mental state, and the value of the relational parameter), and the presence of an orgmind. This fundamental concept is stipulated in Axiom I of the 3C-OK framework, as follows:

Axiom I

An intelligent human organization manifests both org-awareness and orgmindfulness, and they are mental functions that emerge from the collective intelligence and org-consciousness of an orgmind (reflecting the presence of an effective organizational thinking system).

In particular, when analyzing the **consciousness-connectivity cycle**, it is observed that the presence of an orgmind and its collective intelligence is an inevitable requirement. They must be conscientiously nurtured and embedded in all intelligent human organizations. Quality connectivity and truthful engagement, and collective intelligence that are necessary to create and sustain a high level of org-consciousness are present only if there is an orgmind. In return, a high level of org-consciousness (presence of a mindful culture) will further enhance the collective intelligence. In this case, the significant entity that is ensuring the smooth flow of this cycle is orgmindfulness. Apparently, it is the intense presence of orgmindfulness that nurtures a high level of collective intelligence. Thus, collective intelligence and the consciousness-connectivity cycle are mutually enhancing. This intrinsic characteristic is stipulated as the next axiom.

Axiom II

A highly intelligent human organization possesses a high level of collective intelligence (together with a mental space the orgmind — unique to humanity) that drives a higher quality and more effective consciousness-connectivity cycle (mental cohesion), and vice versa.

In addition, the consciousness-connectivity cyclical dynamic is also responsible for establishing other vital attributes such as mindset (intelligence mindset), culture (supportive and mindful), vision (similar to that of an intelligent person or leader), as well as decision-making processes of agents/actors/leaders in human organizations. The elements that directly affect the effectiveness of the above creations are org-awareness and org-mindfulness. Primarily, arising from the analysis of the consciousness-connectivity cycle, it is recognized that an organization can remain stable only if its level and quality of connectivity exceeds its increasing complexity [see relationship (8.7) below].

Increase in connectivity >> Increase in complexity   (8.7)

Once the above characteristic fails, the system will move into a space of high complexity — if the degree of freedom becomes too large and not manageable (see relativistic complexity on Appendix 7). However, if complexity is skillfully exploited, re-structuring will take place through dissipation and emergence. In this case, the system moves into a new order, a higher state of existence, and 'a battle is won'.

8.3.2 *Uniqueness and criticality of the human mindful culture*

Mindfulness is unique to the human minds, and orgmindfulness is only present in intelligent human organizations with a mindful culture (as indicated in relationships 8.7. 8.8 and 8.9) — also strongly emphasized in the earlier part of the book. They are not manifested in any other CAS (other biological species). Thus, human organizations that intend to elevate competitiveness have to focus on this critical mental function to elevate their collectiveness capacity and adaptive capacity. As stipulated earlier, mindfulness is the attribute that directs the human mind to focus internally. Many human beings today are more concerned about the (external) environment rather than the internal mental state of the mind itself. This mindset and thinking is incomplete and disastrous. Both mindfulness and awareness are significant attributes that affect autopoiesis, symbiosis, and self-organization/self-transcending constructions and must enhance local self-enrichment processes and the 'self'. In this case, the two mental functions must be executed concurrently with a proper balance. They are equally important to the evolution and co-evolution of an interacting agent and his/her local spaces/networks, and eventually the organization.

In general, when a mind is mindful, it learns faster and more effectively. Such a mind also nurtures higher quality knowledge structures. This characteristic has been stipulated earlier in the intelligent person model (see Chapter 7). Logical and effective theories, better thinking, and more effective decision-making processes only originate from a mind that is mindful (also associated with calmness). Under all circumstances, mindfulness is a key crucial attribute of all highly intelligent minds. For a more effective human agent, the vital mental function steering the dynamic of the above 3C-OK cycle is mindfulness. Mindfulness also helps to nurture higher quality collective intelligence (innovative) associated with intelligence leadership and longer-term (futuristic) aim, leading to better resilience and sustainability. Thus, it is a greatly desirable attribute that must be nurtured by all intelligent human agents.

Similarly, an organization that is orgmindful learns faster through better connectivity and sharing knowledge (learning organization). With the right mindset, all interacting agents in such an organization believe that the continuous acquisition of knowledge and skills (at both individual and organizational level) is their individual responsibility. They are also more willing to share whatever they have acquired voluntarily. Such a collaborative and supportive culture that increases the survival capacity of the organization only emerges from an orgmind that is orgmindful — also a necessity for organizational mental cohesion. A highly orgmindful organization can self-organize more swiftly when the need arises (better risk and crisis management). Without an intense mindful culture, human organizations today will not be able to manage the current increasing complex environment well. Thus, the ability to maintain a high level of orgmindfulness is a new **intelligence advantage**. However, many current organizations are still more outward seeking, and they tend to neglect or ignore the internal mental state of the interacting agents (employees, stakeholders, citizens).

Therefore, to nurture collective intelligence, and enhance connectivity and engagement more efficiently, the orgmind must first be orgmindful, and vice versa — a continuous mutually enhancing cycle. With the presence of an organizational culture that is willingness to collaborate and share, a deeper concern for the organization's vision and mission will emerge. In addition, the internal activities of the orgmind (a collection of organizational 'neurons') also become more coherent and sustainable. Thus, a mindful culture and higher collective intelligence can only be cultivated and sustained through continuous refinement by exploiting orgmindfulness (see relationship 8.8). Similarly, an intelligent organization is regarded as highly intelligent only if a quality mindful culture exists. In this respect, an organization that is always orgmindful and coupled with org-awareness is a better survivor. This conceptualization is stipulated as the next axiom.

Axiom III

A mindful culture as the core of a supportive culture exits in all intelligent human organizations. It nurtures a higher collectiveness capacity and adaptive capacity. It also supports the organizational objectives, as well as the requirements of the individual interacting agents (self-stability and org-stability, that is, it supports both the evolution and co-evolution dynamics, through the autopoiesis, symbiosis, and self-organizing dynamics of human agents and the organization concurrently) more effectively.

Collective intelligence <=> mindful culture   (8.8)

8.3.3 *Dissipation, emergence and collective intelligence*

Corresponding to the consciousness-connectivity cycle is the **emergence-dissipation cycle**. This is another self-organizing cycle that an intelligent organization will venture into if a sufficient level of collective intelligence is attained. This is the cycle that helps to modify and enhance the structure and dynamic of the organization. It is important to note again that the presence of structure indicates the presence of information, and vice-versa. All forms of structure are created by some level of intelligence. As complexity increases, a higher level of intelligence is needed to process information or visualize structure in the system. In the process of change, unwanted elements/energy is dissipated. Thus, a more robust structure (associated with each new order) and dynamic in human organizations can only be attained if the above two cycles are integrated, and evolve concurrently.

The merging of the two cycles helps to create better order/structure out of complexity — the emergent of new order. This macro-cycle (illustrated in Figure 8.4) is the dynamic that supports the evolution of CAS. It is the desire to survive with a more robust structure in a complex environment that leads to the evolution of all biological organisms or ecosystems (for instance, from a village to a small town, and to a cosmopolitan city). In this situation, 'greater order' is established from exploiting a higher level of complexity. The above analysis vividly reiterates that consciousness, connectivity, complexity, emergence and dissipation are indeed the most vital properties of all CAS, including human organizations. It assists in establishing the foundation of the 3C-OK framework, and provides a better perspective for analyzing and comprehending the abstract dynamic of intelligent human CAS and the bio-logic of living systems driven by intelligence, on a macroscopic level.

In summary, a better understanding of the five core properties of CAS and their integrated dynamic is a significant basic knowledge that leaders and managers must acquire in the current context and for future usage. The complex and adaptive dynamics of human organizations is space-time dependent (hysteresis, futuristic). It depends on the changes in attributes/entities such as memberships, relational parameter, variables involved, interacting processes, and the external environment. The intensity of connection and engagement (supported/determined by an abstract mental space) that is closely associated with self-organizing communications, self-organizing capability, formation of local spaces/networks, self-transcending constructions, and emergence. Thus, it is vital to note again that the above dynamic is driven by the integration of the latent impetus (intelligence), as well as the unique behavioral schemata, embedded in every human agent.

8.4 The OK (Organizational Learning and Knowledge Management) Dynamic

8.4.1 *Necessity for a quality organizational intelligence enhancer*

it has been introduced earlier that the collective intelligence of a human organization can also be better nurtured and enhanced by directing attention on the **organizational intelligence enhancer** (see Chapter 4). As the environment becomes more and more complex, the presence of such an enhancer, located in the orgmind/org-brain, must be able to constantly provide the organization with higher and higher levels of OK dynamic. The dynamic of the enhancer is facilitated by at least one physical symbol system, eventually manifested in a more advanced form as a 'common' language. The latter when exploited rightly is a form of social glue that binds all the human thinking systems in an organization. A highly developed and effective 'common' language is a product of both mindfulness and orgmindfulness.

The content of the intelligence enhancer highlights the significance of a corporate knowledge structure (including better information/knowledge sharing) in the new environment. The presence of a language enables more permanent **externalized knowledge depositories** to be constructed in human organizations. As the interactions between knowledge structure(s) and theory determine whether a new piece of information is consumed or rejected, a better-organized knowledge structure together with a more comprehensive theory will facilitate the consumption of more pieces of information, or the better use of a new piece of information. Apparently, the value of a new piece of information depends on the quality of the knowledge structure, and the collective intelligence of the organization. In this respect, the presence of a quality enhancer boosts the decision-making processes of human organizations.

8.4.2 *Continuous and comprehensive/holistic organizational learning*

Currently, some more intelligent organizations learn as human beings do. **Learning organizations** acquire, store, transfer, and create information and knowledge. However, learning in an organization is more complex. Learning occurs at different levels in an organization (see organizational learning in Appendix 7, and Appendix 6). Individual learning is the primary level of learning in any organization, whether the latter is a family, community, business corporation, or nation. This learning process should be encouraged and rewarded if humankind is to continue to exist as a 'primer' species on this planet. However, to be collectively intelligent as a group, the organization as a whole must also learn. Thus, higher-level learning must occur concurrently if the organization aspires to compete as a team or the entire organization. In this respect, collective learning must take place holistically and spontaneously encompassing all different levels of the organization, as groups (networks, departments, schools, communities, cities) of different sizes emerge. Basically, the relationship expressed in (8.2) must be achieved.

Rate of learning >> Rate of change   (8.9)

As all human organizations are formed with certain basic objectives in mind, the learning dynamic is to ensure that the organizations achieve and sustain these aims collectively. However, 'collectiveness' is a key attribute that many organizations are encountering difficulties. In general, an organization where by the interacting agents are continuously learning how to learn together is a more intelligent organization. In this respect, a learning organisation is one in which the leaders and other members are effective and efficient in collective learning because they are all willing to venture deeper and broader into their learning endeavours (see **learning leadership** and **leadership capacity** in Appendix 7).

Thus, in many instances, to nurture an organization that learns, and learns fast (at least faster than its competitors) and continuously (life-long learning) is no easy task. In order to learn and learn collectively, the interacting agents must first be willing to be engaged with one another and to communicate their hearts and minds voluntarily (again associated with Abilene paradox and defensive routines). Thus, an appropriate level of mental cohesion must be present — the willingness to share is vital (both bottom-up and top-down sharing). Thus, basically a supportive culture with a core mindful culture must exist. [For instance, nurturing a global eco-mindset (Gaia), thinking, and culture is necessary for eco-friendliness at different levels (agents, corporations, communities, and nations) to be cultivated concurrently. However, in this case, the learning processes and commitment involved are highly sophisticated because of differing self-centricity at different levels of the global structure (agent, corporation, community, nation, and regional organization) — also due to political constraints.] Inevitably, effective communications (self-organizing communications) and orgmindfulness are vital fundamental characteristics that are badly needed by human organizations that want to learn at all levels. Incoherent thinking and ineffective communications (due to phobic mindset) lie at the root of why people are not really learning together, and this obstacle can be minimized (overcome) by nurturing smarter evolvers.

In such a situation, being **cosmopolitan communicators** is beneficial. This concept of cosmopolitan communicators describes people who can make important contributions to diverse organizations because they do not ignore differences, but instead, fully recognize, appreciate, and collaborate across them. Such cosmopolitan communicators do not assume everyone is just like themselves but actively seek out different ideas and ways to think about issues (a form of mental cohesion despite the presence of diversification). These communicators consider functional conflict as a learning opportunity rather than a threat — a highly integrative thinking. This mindset improves the quality of thought, decision making, and performance of the interacting agents, as well as their organizations. Indeed before effective organizational learning can take place, the interacting agents must be willing to express their true feelings and thinking, instead of being closed up by the fear of saying wrong things. Thus, again, the basic key to nurturing collective learning is effective communication and willingness to share. The continuous organizational learning ability of an intelligent organization is stipulated as the next axiom.

Axiom IV

An intelligent organization possesses a continuous learning ability at various levels (faster than its competitors) that enables it to consume/ internalize new information, update knowledge structure/ repository, elevate the value of a new piece of information, adapt to changing environment, make better decision, and evolve with time supported by the utilization of a 'common' language.

8.4.3 *Knowledge management process and quality knowledge structure*

The quality of the **knowledge structure** embedded in the individual human thinking system has to be updated through continuous learning. The current emphasis is on fast learning coupled with innovation and creativity. Many developed nations are moving their education and skills training systems towards this direction. The objective is to develop diversified quality knowledge structures in their people, and to train them to learn continuously (a life-long commitment). These individuals' knowledge structures in the human thinking systems are the most vital sources for establishing quality **organizational/corporate knowledge structure**.

It is significant to note that there are some differences between (purely) individual and organizational learning. As indicated earlier, a new form of positive relationship has to be established. In this case, a mindful culture is an essential facilitating medium. An intelligent organization and its interacting agents must work collaboratively as partners, orchestrated by a new form of leadership and management philosophy (see intelligence/consciousness management, network management, and feeling system in Appendix 7). In particular, people with highly sophisticated knowledge structures cannot be led or managed in the present manner if the organization is looking forward to their truthful contribution.

As an organization learns and knowledge accumulates, the latter can be stored physically (externally) as well. The accumulation of organizational knowledge is a highly significant function of intelligent organizations. Thus, organizational knowledge structures do not only reside in the minds of the interacting agents alone. Intelligent organizations have to create additional organizational knowledge repositories that are outside the intrinsic human thinking systems. Usually, these externalized knowledge sources are stored in external physical storages (repositories) to ensure higher organizational sustainability. Information and communications technology has been extensively exploited in this respect for decades — including artificial information/intelligent systems, as well as the e-landscape (global).

However, an organized approach is essential to move towards better optimality. Thus, plan and strategy must be mapped out to ensure that an organization learns faster and better, and accumulates and utilizes knowledge more effectively. Inevitably, organizational learning and knowledge management are vital activities that must be highly integrated and effective in intelligent organizations. A high level of collective intelligence and continuous organizational learning is the main element for driving quality **knowledge management** processes in intelligent human organizations. However, it has been observed that collective intelligence, organizational learning, and individuals' and organizational knowledge structures cannot be acquired by force. As indicated earlier, a new form of relationship with an essential facilitating medium must be nurtured. An intelligent organization and its interacting agents, orchestrated by the new form of leadership, governance, and management philosophy (see Chapters 9 and 10) must work collaboratively as partners. Apparently, human agents with highly sophisticated knowledge structures cannot be led or managed in the present manner.

It is significant to note that in the intelligence era, an effective knowledge management dynamic is a new critical success factor, as the value of a new piece of information depends on the quality of the knowledge structure. Apparently, contributing to organizational/corporate knowledge structures, as well as exploiting existing individual structures is equally important. The effective combination of the two factors together with organizational learning and the efficient use of appropriate theory constitute an intelligent advantage that human organizations must more fully comprehend and exploit in the knowledge-intensive context. The presence of the knowledge management dynamic in intelligent organizations is stated in the next axiom.

Axiom V

An intelligent human organization possesses the ability to create and enhance/update organizational/corporate knowledge structures (at both individual and collective levels — in the human thinking systems, as well as external knowledge repositories) as the organizational learning dynamic progresses. The presence of quality knowledge structures and the ability to create new knowledge is an indication of its level of collective intelligence.

8.5 Deeper Analysis of the Integrated 3C-OK Dynamic

The above analysis clearly illustrated the roles, dynamic, and significance of the 3C-OK structure as a basic foundation of the *i*CAD, as well as its differences with other biological interaction dynamics (see Table 8.1).

8.5.1 *Integration of the 3C-OK cycle and five core properties interactive cycle*

The interdependency of collective intelligence, connectivity and culture (3C), and organizational learning and knowledge management (OK), and their dynamic clearly stipulates that intelligent human organization must be managed differently from the present (hierarchical and mechanistic) approach due to lack of focus on the **relational parameter**. The **3C-OK framework** illustrates that the five attributes governing the interaction of human beings are integrated. These attributes in human organizations cannot

Table 8.1 Differences in 3C-OK characteristics between an ant colony, a pack of wolves, and an intelligent human organization.

Example Attribute	An ant colony	A pack of wolves	An intelligent human organization
Collective intelligence	Swarm intelligence >> summation of all individual intelligence	Group intelligence ~ or > summation of all individual intelligence	Collective intelligence > or >> summation of all individual intelligence (can be significantly elevated)
Connectivity	Localized, chemical processes/ connectivity, one-to-one, simplistic	Localized, sight and sound, one-to-one or one-to-several, fairly simplistic	Localized, network, organization, symbolic process, language, technological support, one-to many, complex, intense
Culture	Absent	Absent or not apparent	Complex culture, and ideally a mindful/ supportive culture should exist
KM	Very low, 'biologically' internalized in individual ant	Low, instinctive/ biological, accumulative	High, biological, accumulative, internalized, and can be externalized because of the presence of a written language
OL	Inherited and closed, that is, no further learning possible	Inherited but possesses learning potential	Inherited, open, and appears to possess 'infinite' potential encompassing, perception, abstract concept creation, wisdom creation capability

be decomposed and focused on separately as linear systems are often dealt with — failure of reductionist hypothesis and hierarchical decomposition. It is significant to recap that collective intelligence, culture, connectivity, organizational learning and knowledge management are intertwined in a complex manner, and together with the integrated processes involved they form the basic foundation of the *i*CAD. In general, the merging of two cycles (five core properties interactive cycle and 3C-OK cycle) helps to elevate the capabilities of all human organizations.

The situation observed is analogous to the confinement of quarks in elementary particles. For instance, a proton has three quarks. They are interlocked in the proton and cannot be separated by gluons. In addition, the gluons behave in a nonlinear manner. When the quarks are moved apart, the attractive force of the gluons increases in strength. The strength increases quickly, thus confining the quarks to the elementary particles. Similarly, when some of the above organizational attributes in human systems are diminished, their presence becomes even more necessary — also associated with the unique relationship between human independency and interdependency. The more a particular attribute is being removed, the greater its presence is needed. In this respect, the **integrated 3C-OK dynamic** (the significant foundation pillar of *i*CAD) helps to glue the interacting agents together. The five attributes are the 'abstract gluons' that elevate the collectiveness capacity and adaptive capacity of all human organizations. In addition, they must also be able to bind certain interacting agents more strongly when needed. The above discussion vividly indicated that these 'abstract gluons' are linked to intelligence and consciousness (intelligence-intelligence linkages). Thus, focusing on intelligence/consciousness-centricity, encompassing mindful culture and orgmindfulness, is the beginning to enhancing the nonlinear power of attraction of these 'abstract gluons' in human organizations.

In summary, the 3C-OK framework recognizes that the five attributes are nonlinearly interdependent, and there are 'abstract gluons' of human organizations due to the presence of intense individual intelligence and collective intelligence, and individual consciousness and org-consciousness, as well as the unique independent and interdependent characteristics of human agents. This intelligence/consciousness-centric dynamic is complex, nonlinear and adaptive, and different from that of other biological CAD. In this case, a special focus on the mental space of human agents is a vital necessity (mental stability, relational parameter, feeling system). The behavioral schemata of human agents are nonlinear and constantly changing, and their self-organizing capability must always be allocated special attention.

In this respect, a deeper understanding of the social psychological perspective (focusing on peoples' behaviors, thoughts, relational friction, and feelings) is beneficial for better mental states exploitation by increasing the human relational parameter value. In addition, utilizing construal (social cognition) concepts from the self-construal theory is also useful (see feeling system in Appendix 7). The latter identifies two perspectives about the 'self', namely 'independent self' and 'interdependent self' (see human agent in Appendix 7). In this model, human agents with higher independent self-perspective view the self as autonomous and separate from others, while, agents with higher interdependent self-perspective view the self as connected to others. The mental state (perception/construal) of the interacting agents has an impact on the self-transcending constructions ability of the agents, and the collectiveness capacity, self-organizing capacity, emergence-intelligence capacity, and the emergent of new order of the organization.

Therefore, in the current complex situation, possessing the new intelligence mindset, and exploiting the intelligence paradigm is crucial to the leadership, governance, and management of all categories of human organizations. In particular, the integrated 3C-OK framework is a critical component of the complexity-intelligence strategy. The dynamic of the 3C-OK framework (integrating with the five core properties cycle) elevates the competitiveness, and enhances the resilience and sustainability of all intelligent human organizations. The above concept is summarized in Figure 8.5, and (mutually enhancing) relationships 8.10 to 8.12.

3C-OK framework <=> five core properties interactive cycle   (8.10)

3C-OK framework <=> organizing around intelligence   (8.11)

3C-OK framework <=> intelligent biotic macro-structure   (8.12)

8.5.2 *Some conceptual relationships of resilience and sustainability*

In any CAS, there are two special attributes that determine its length of existence. They are namely, resilience and sustainability. These two attributes are related to how that system responds to the rate of change (both

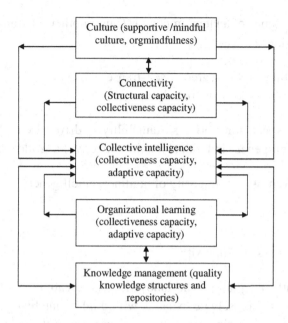

Figure 8.5   The integrated 3C-OK cycle of intelligent organizations.

internally and externally), thus, are closely associated with their robustness. More specifically, resilience is associated with the degree of non-disturbance, that is:

$$\text{Resilience} <\!=\!> \text{Degree of non-disturbance} \qquad (8.13)$$

While, sustainability is associated with the degree of complex adaptability (normally with external force) and the degree of 'self-organizability' (without external force), that is:

$$\text{Sustainability} <\!=\!> \text{Degree of complex adaptability} \qquad (8.14)$$
$$\text{Sustainability} <\!=\!> \text{Degree of self-organizability} \qquad (8.15)$$

Concurrently, the degree of complex adaptability and the degree of self-organizability are linked to both the intensity of intelligence and consciousness of the individuals, and the collective intelligence and org-consciousness of the system (self-organizability is also linked to order for free or the presence of a latent impetus). Thus, another relationship should be mentioned:

$$\text{Sustainability} <=> \text{Degree of self-transcending} \qquad \text{constructability} \qquad (8.16)$$

In this respect, innovative sustainability is driven by highly intense nonlinear intelligence (individual and/or collective) as follows:

$$\text{Innovativeness} <=> \text{Intensity of nonlinear intelligence} \qquad (8.17)$$

and also

$$\text{Innovativeness} > \text{Raplexity} \qquad (8.18)$$

Apparently, adaptation, and innovation and creativity are two special features that are closely associated with highly intelligent biological beings (that is, possessing capability to change faster than change).

$$\text{Adaptiveness} > \text{Rate of change} \qquad (8.19)$$

Thus, human organizations that hope to increase their competitiveness, resilience, and sustainability must place sufficient emphasis on adaptation, nonlinear individual intelligence, nonlinear collective intelligence, effective self-transcending constructions, and high innovation and creativity (including constantly exploiting the certain spaces of complexity by transforming them into edges of emergence). As indicated earlier, an edge of emergence is a space of complexity with apparent surface pattern, and in this situation, **complexity is in the mind of the beholder** — leading to the emergent of **relativistic complexity** in the intelligent organization theory (see relativistic complexity in Appendix 7, and Chapters 9 and 10). Vividly, an intense intelligence source with the ability of emitting nonlinear intelligence/consciousness, and possess mental calmness (link to the intelligence leadership strategy) is in a better position to observe surface patterns and early warning signals more quickly.

8.6 Conclusion

Apparently, the five core properties of CAS constitute an excellent fundamental platform for analyzing, comprehending, organizing, leading, and managing any human organizations more omnisciently in the current environment. The dynamic of this set of properties together with some additional characteristics of the complexity theory further reinforces the fact that intelligent human organizations are intelligent composite CAS that are dissimilar to other biological CAS (for instance, an ant colony) because of the intense intelligence/consciousness of the agents, and the collective intelligence and org-consciousness of the organization (the presence of a mindful culture — significant and unique to humanity).

The analysis in this chapter reinforces the fact that with the unique intense human level intelligence and consciousness (awareness, mindfulness), the CAD of human interactions can be enhanced and modified (relativistic, perceptive, construal) beyond 'normal' complex adaptive dynamic — iCAD $\neq$ CAD. The high interdependency of the five human complex and intelligence-associated characteristics (collective intelligence, connectivity, culture, organizational learning, and knowledge management) captured in the integrated 3C-OK framework that serves as a foundation pillar of the iCAD is confined to humanity. In particular, the integrated 3C-OK framework also mutually enhances organizing around intelligence and the intelligent biotic macro-structure of human systems illustrated earlier (see Figure 8.6).

Finally, the key factors and characteristics that the integrated 3C-OK framework focuses on are summarized below:

a. The mental state (absence of mental paralysis), and the unique independent and interdependent characteristics of human interacting agents is vital to the success of the group/organizational dynamic. In human organizations, orgmindfulness (presence of the mindful culture, intense intelligence-intelligence linkages) is greatly responsible for nurturing a high level of collective intelligence, and vice versus. Thus, the human thinking systems as sources of intense intelligence/consciousness must be the key focal centers — higher coherency with organizing around intelligence.

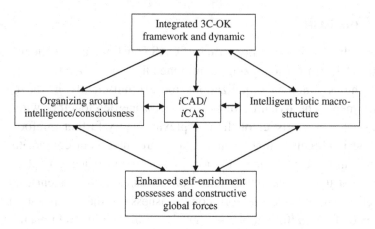

Figure 8.6   Some basic mutually enhancing components of *i*CAS/*i*CAD.

b. The five complexity and intelligence-associated attributes of intelligent human organizations, namely, collective intelligence, connectivity, culture, organizational learning, and knowledge management are highly interdependent on each other. In addition, they are also the 'abstract gluons' in highly intelligent human organizations that provide the binding force for the human agents, if the 'interdependency environment' is positive (symbiosis, coherency, synergetic effect). In this case, an intelligent composite CAS emerges.

c. In particular, organizational learning and knowledge management (associated stress, controversy, or anxiety) cannot take place continuously, extensively, and effectively (not sporadically) in any human organizations without the presence of high collective intelligence/ consciousness — that is, high structural capacity, collectiveness capacity and adaptive capacity must be present. Consequently, the presence of an orgmind is vital (presence of the entire intelligent biotic macro-structure is beneficial).

d. Thus, the integrated 3C-OK dynamic is a significant foundation pillar of the *i*CAD of intelligent human organizations (*i*CAS). In addition, for any synergetic effect to materialize the intense and nonlinear human mental space that also encompasses a 'feeling' dimension must be cautiously managed (high positive relational parameter value). The intense focusing on the mental state of the interacting agents is vital for the better organizational mental cohesion, and it is positively correlated with the resilience and sustainability of the organization.

e. In this respect, ensuring the presence of a constructive integrated 3C-OK structure and dynamic is an important necessity for leading, governing, and managing current human organizations, as humanity ventures deeper into 'raplexity'. Consequently, the attributes of leadership and governance in all categories of human organizations (corporations, institutions, military units, nations) must be redefined (see intelligence leadership, self-organizing governance, intelligence governance in Appendix 7).

[As mentioned earlier, the world population is becoming more educated and better informed. Consequently, the values and of pectations of people are modified (especially the younger generations) — a new form of inter-generation incoherency is present. Monetary rewards alone may not be sufficient. Social recognition and mutual respect is a new perspective that must be satisfied. The need of intangible satisfaction of the individuals has increased. Thus, intelligent organizations must also recognize and encompass this new agents and trend of development. Otherwise, without proper integration, the organizational learning and knowledge management dynamic will not evolve satisfactorily or spontaneously.]

Mental cohesion leads to high synchrony and creates synergetic effect, and its impact may camouflage certain tangible diversity and functional incoherency.

As executive leaders test their brains against their corners of the great complexity, they find that certain leadership work-ways work best. The hallmarks of this modern style are the soft voice and the low key.

Harlan Cleveland, *Nobody in Charge*

Chapter 9

The Intelligence Leadership Theory/Strategy

"In highly intelligent human organizations, everybody is in charge"

"Intelligent leaders recognize that enhancing the stability of agents
is an incentive for them to bind"

"Contemplating on a set of scenarios to elevate the accuracy of the chosen
path is an activity of far-sighted leadership"

Summary

Fundamentally, effective leadership is associated with its ability to achieve collective goals (agents and their organization, stability-inducing capability) and organizational sustainability, irrespective of the nature of the organizations (leadership capacity <=> relational capacity <=> unifying capacity). The mismatch of the bureaucratic mindset and its associated hierarchical/administrative leadership with the changing situation is escalating. Basically, the presence of an adaptive leadership is beneficial. In this respect, the collectiveness capacity and relational capacity of the organization are critical attributes. It has been recognized that the intense and quality of these two capacities is highly dependent on both the thinking and attributes of the leaders, as well as the other interacting agents (including non-actors, and quality of leader–agents exchanges). Overall, a high leadership capacity and organizational mental cohesion is a key necessity. In general, the success of today's global turbulence can only be achieved through global mental cohesion.

In order to achieve this, fresh insights beginning with constructive intelligence-intelligence linkages is required. In the present state, it is significant to note that for any categories of human organizations (economic, social, education, political, and military) their agents (employees, citizens, members, stakeholders) are possessing redefined attributes (principles, values and expectations), due to better education, quick access to information, and high interconnectivity. This profound transition (supported by intensive usage of mobile/social media technology) transformed some other attributes including autonomy/independency, autopoiesis, self-centricity, self-organizing communications, interdependency, symbiosis, and other self-organizing capabilities. Consequently, current human beings are more sophisticated interacting agents. Hence, leading these 'transformed' agents is drastically different from leading traditional setups. Agent-centricity is a new vital attribute that required deeper attention, and one commonality among agents at all levels must be achieved — stability-centricity (agent-centricity <=> intelligence/consciousness-centricity + stability-centricity).

The more intelligent, complex adaptive, and nonlinear evolving dynamic is driven by the intrinsic intelligence/consciousness of the individuals, and the collective intelligence and org-consciousness of the organization (anticipatory, adaptive capacity), as well as local spaces/complex networks — the presence of networks (formal and informal) is becoming more dominant, and this development renders elevating collectiveness capacity (consensus and collaboration) at organizational level more complex. Apparently, coupled with the influence of the knowledge-intensive, fast-changing, more complex environment, and the modified agents' attributes, an immense shift in strategic thinking, leadership attributes, governance characteristics, management abilities and operational style in the new generation of leaders is inevitable. In general, the leader–follower gap has been narrowed, and their relationship (relational parameter) is more complex and nonlinear, again, confirming that intelligence/consciousness-centricity must be a key focus of the new leadership.

In such a situation, a deeper insight into complexity is inevitable. In this case, a better comprehension of leadership strategy and organizational dynamic can be acquired by 'bisociating' some properties of the complexity theory, and the different perspectives of complexity-intelligence linkages. The resulting evolutionary model to be introduced in this chapter is the intelligence leadership theory/strategy for *i*CAS. In this model, an intelligence leader must recognize that a fundamental capability of intelligence is stability enhancement. Concurrently, an intelligence leader must be an effective lateral/collective actor (always encompassing agent-agent, intelligence-intelligence, agent-network, agent-system, and network-system linkages; and the intrinsic leadership capacity of all agents, and collective leadership capacity of networks and the organization) with a new set of attributes (encompassing enabler, smarter evolver, and unifying, emergent strategist and synergist capabilities).

Hence, an effective intelligence leader must possess certain relevant or appropriate attributes of the traditional leadership, as well as a set of new complexity-intelligence related attributes that can better ensure the survival of the agents, integrate networks, and elevate the resilience, and sustainability of the organization (achieving higher coherency, synergy, constructionist effect, self-organizing capacity, emergence-intelligence capacity, unifying capacity and organizational mental cohesion) — (constructionist effect <=> innovation and creativity) — that is, focusing on continuous acquisition of capacities improvement is critical. In addition, with this paradigmatic shift, possessing the latent leadership capability is highly beneficial.

Keywords: Newtonian mindset, design paradigm, reductionist hypothesis, aristocratic mindset, defense routines, Abilene paradox, satisficing principle, organizational justice, feeling system, intelligence governance, intelligence era, servant leadership, intelligence/consciousness management, network management, self-powered capacity, intelligence leadership strategy, structural capacity, collectiveness capacity, adaptive capacity, relational capacity, leadership capacity, autonomous, self-centric, anticipatory, upwards causation, intelligence/consciousness-centric, complex networks, raplexity, relational parameter, organizing around intelligence, stability-centric, effective enabler, smarter evolver, emergent strategist, synergistic, coherency, mental space, complexity mindset, intelligence mindset, intelligence paradigm, mental cohesion, functional cohesion, humanization, intangible returns, space of complexity, intrinsic intelligence, collective intelligence, intelligence/consciousness management, highly intelligent complex adaptive system (*i*CAS), self-powered capacity, stability-centric, org-centric, intelligence-intelligence linkage, truthful engagement, complexity-centric, network-centric, constructionist hypothesis, autopoiesis, symbiosis, ambidexterity, self-organization, self-transcending constructions, highly intelligent complex adaptive dynamic (*i*CAD), complex/adaptive-centric, self-organizing capacity, emergence, emergence-intelligence capacity, intelligence advantage, group-centric/network-centric leadership, self-centric leadership, intrinsic leadership, lateral/collective leadership, consultative leadership, learning leadership, transitional leadership, diffusive leadership, latent leadership, unifying leadership, unifying capacity, soft voice and low key, physical stability, biological stability, mental stability, nonlinear intelligence, anticipatory, ambidexterity, collective social consciousness, mindful culture, red queen race, rugged landscape, autocatalysis, cascading effect, hysteresis, futuristic, first mover advantage, early warning, scenario planning, risk management, crisis management, space-time dependent, phase space, basin of attraction, innovative and creative capacity, intelligence advantage and relativistic complexity.

9.1 Introduction: Redefining Human Leadership

9.1.1 *Contradicting mindsets, thinking and attributes of the current leadership*

Almost all human beings exist in groups of varying sizes (department, community, corporation, education institution, and nation) where leadership is an inherent trait or requirement. Concurrently, mindset (both of leaders and other agents) is a critical attribute in humanity. The latter determines the type of thinking that emerges, and that has a significant influence on the social culture, interactions, organizational structure, leadership, governance, strategy, and their associated dynamics of the group. This inherent development is reflected as the traits of the organizations, and also determines their competitiveness, peacefulness, resilience and sustainability.

As stipulated earlier, many current human organizations still possess a machine-like structure that originates from the **Newtonian mechanistic mindset** engulfing order, linearity, reductionism, predictability, and low tolerance for error. The consequence of the above mindset leads to the domination of leadership and management theories and practices that believe human systems must be controlled and managed hierarchically (**bureaucratic mindset**), like physical instruments of production, and workers must be engineered and re-engineered to fit the mechanistic structure (design paradigm). In addition, in some countries, leaders cling on 'absolute' power and still possess the **aristocratic mindset** (bureaucratic, hierarchical). Apparently, it is essential that these undermining mindsets must be transformed. In an authoritative and hierarchical environment, human thinking systems are massively disabled. The omnipotence of hierarchical/individual leadership can lead to organizational dysfunctional and deep predicament (even with empowerment — transformational leadership — self-powered capability is suppressed). In such a situation, there is minimal space for query, exploration, and contradiction — leading to the emergent of defensive routines and the Abilene paradox. To the extreme, it is a confinement of human agents in a slavery mental space. Thus, it is vital to recognize that the credibility of leadership is greatly dependent on its acceptance.

It is significant to remember that human beings are biological beings (with feeling and emotions). People are not merely a physical means of production. More importantly, each human being carries a nonlinear intense thinking system from which many other attributes and features of that individual are defined and determined. In addition, connecting people is linking these highly complex thinking systems together (intelligence-intelligence linkage). To better understand and manage human organizations, the human thinking systems and their dynamic must be more deeply comprehended — intelligence/consciousness-centricity is inevitable (as emphasized earlier). Thus, the cognitive and social perspectives, and to some extent the neural dimension must also be better understood. Voluntary collaboration can only be achieved through mutual respect, intimacy, subtlety and trust. Thus, the current social/corporate culture must also be better scrutinized and transformed. Primarily, the organization must be managed holistically as ensuring stability-centricity at all levels (agents, networks, and the organization) is a key necessity.

It is a known fact that most organizations today that are led and managed in the traditional manner are moving farther and farther away from any **satisfying optimality**. Authoritative/bureaucratic leadership and governance (for instance, in some underdeveloped countries, and family businesses) are confronted with discontentment, skepticism, revolution, and even terrorism (basically self-destructing). Human beings, especially the better educated ones (generations Y and Z, or even the generation X agents) will definitely not welcome their roles as machine parts that have no mental freedom, respect, organizational justice, innovation and creativity. It has been observed that some characteristics of generation Y are technology savvy, self-assured, and fulfilment-seeking. Inevitably, the generation Z will be even more sophisticated, and will not be easily connected. Coupled with their higher literacy rate, 'wealth base', and mobility, engaging them is obviously nonlinear, and the needs to be more **'humanized' (feeling system)** must be beneficial. Definitely, their ambition is beyond monetary seeking alone (may be seeking **intangible returns** as well).

Vividly, there is an **incoherency** (direct mismatch) between Newtonian leadership mindset and thinking, and agents changing expectations, perceptions, and values (including the indirect incoherency due to differences in 'intended' leadership and 'perceived' leadership associated certain social psychological aspects will be discussed under **intelligence governance** strategy in Chapter 10). Political, social, and corporate leaders who are steering their nations, communities, and corporations through new competitions must be able to comprehend and assimilate new attributes, such as complexity, connectivity, nonlinearity, and the butterfly effect as a strategic path becomes more indefinite and unpredictable. The current environment and competitions that encompass new characteristics (of agents, groups/networks, and organizations; and unknown unknowns and in-complete phase space of the system) that can never be handled effectively by existing strategies, warrants a flesh mindset and new thinking. Leaders of these human organizations must be prepared to make the paradigmatic shift and venture into a new dimension of leadership, if they are to remain effective, relevant, acceptable or distinctive.

In the economic domain, over the last two decades, some newer organizations, especially those at the technological frontiers are beginning to be structured, cultivated, managed, and led differently. These organizations practices lateral consultative interaction, greater respect (welfares) and trust for all agents involved, and frequent exploitation of certain spaces of complexity (those encompassing new opportunities, and higher potentials for innovative and creative exploitation — better risk management). Therefore, already a gradual change or even a revamp in leadership and management mindset is present, and this change is inevitable if higher coherency and synergetic effects are to escalate. Achieving higher coherency and creating positive synergetic effects are two vital capabilities of the new leadership. Thus, acquiring a deeper insight into the self-conscious science of complexity is highly beneficial. A reasonable key starting point is to examine administrative leadership versus adaptive leadership.

9.1.2 *Some key attributes influencing leadership transformation*

As presented above and in the earlier chapters, a general shift from a machine perspective to an **intelligence/consciousness and complex adaptive mindset** must be accelerated, as humanity moves deeper into the **intelligence era**. (But the extreme concept of **'servant'** leadership is redundant as it reflects the lack of self-confidence in the leaders — lateral mutual trust and respect are critical attributes, and towards **everybody is in charge** is valuable — attaining higher leadership capacity and unifying capacity.) Humanity and its biotic and intense mental characteristics, in particular, the intelligence/consciousness sources and their contents, must assume a more significant role in many aspects of current human system dynamics. Thus, the new primary focus of leadership and management is intelligence/consciousness management, network management, and complexity management which are beyond the traditional domain of human resources management — human agents and certain networks are valuable assets. This new awareness is stimulated and intensified by the emergence of numerous new thinking and characteristics of complex adaptive systems. In particular, the following critical features and changes that is closely responsible for driving the transformation, and must be conscientiously managed and exploited by the new leadership are as follows:

a. Agents and organizations are 'trapped' in faster changing environment (at time unpredictable).
b. Agents (self-powered) are involved in more intensive engagement and self-organizing communications (in particular, due to rapid mobile/ social media development).
c. Agents are learning faster and continuously (life-long learning is inevitable).
d. More knowledge-intensive interactions are surfacing.
e. Human being are functioning as smarter interacting agents (at all levels).
f. The expectations (including intangible returns), perceptions, and values of all interacting agents are (constantly) modified.
g. The intelligence (agents), and collective intelligence (networks, organization) that drive the self-transcending constructions dynamic is more intensive.

h.   Faster spontaneous emergent of self-organizing networks (formal and informal) is a current phenomenon in the human world — networked communities/groups/local spaces.

i.   Unification through diversification is possible (mental cohesion is beyond tangible diversity — including agreeing to disagree).

j.   The mobility of interacting agents (including temporary workers, foreign talents, transnational migrants, dissipation rate) has increased substantially.

k.   The significance of nurturing a mindful culture (intense orgmindfulness, and intelligence-intelligence linkages) in organizations (including nations) is crucial.

All these indicators clearly re-emphasized that the vital primary focal points are the intelligence/consciousness sources, and their significance. Consequently, the crucial recognition associated with the transformation in leadership and management thinking and strategy for all categories of human organizations is to focus on the attributes of the collective mental states of the agents in the organization — apparently, cultivating mental cohesion is critical. In the intelligence era, concepts and strategies on leadership and management have to be transformed towards the fresh direction identified. In this respect, executing the basic functions of intelligence/consciousness management is a crucial starting point, and some new basic attributes and functions that an effective leader can exploit are as follows:

a.   Possess high leadership capacity (both 'intended' and 'perceived' leadership) directed at mental cohesion.

b.   Optimize and integrate every intelligence/consciousness sources (if necessary or possible) — coherency.

c.   Recognize that every agent is intrinsically self-powered and possesses intrinsic leadership (optimize **self-powered capacity** and **intrinsic leadership capacity** of all agents).

d.   Increase the intensity of orgmindfulness (focusing on intelligence-intelligence linkages and collectiveness capacity) that leads to better mental cohesion, and the latter exists even when there are physical diversifications.

e.   Collectiveness capacity can be cultivated through more effective 'lateral' connectivity and engagement (appropriate intelligence-intelligence linkages, and sensitivity to the presence of certain differentials that leads to high unifying capacity) — that is, intense collaborative-oriented.

f. Nurturing a high collective intelligence and org-consciousness as a fundamental pillar of the organization is a key necessity.

g. Ensure better balance between independency (self-centricity, autonomous, autopoiesis) and interdependency (org-centric, symbiosis, ambidexterity) of agents to optimize and integrate intrinsic leadership capacity.

h. Nurture new adaptive capacity (including nurturing agents with intelligence person characteristics — in particular, better information decoder, smarter evolver and emergent strategist) with a deeper insight into complexity and issues.

i. Nurture high self-organizing capacity and emergence-intelligence capacity [(with special focus on certain spaces of complexity (new opportunities, innovation and creativity, better risk management, butterfly effect, huge returns, new advancement), and making preparation for punctuation points (better crisis management, and higher resilience and sustainability)] that is directly linked to higher resilience and sustainability of the organization.

Therefore, a paradigmatic shift in mindset and thinking, and the transformation in effective leadership attributes/functions with respect to the change in the key agents, organizational, and environmental characteristics and dynamics are necessary for all forms of human organizations. The interacting agents and the organization have to be positively connected differently (higher structural capacity). As the interacting agents are more educated and informed, the thinking systems possess highly complex and sophisticated knowledge structures, thinking dynamics, behavioral schemata, problem-solving abilities, and decision-making processes. In addition, the combined/ integrated social, economic, political, and biophysical perturbations in human organizations are equally complex. Hence, a more lateral/collective leadership and management approach must be adopted, as nurturing higher collectiveness capacity, adaptive capacity, self-organizing capacity, and emergence-intelligence capacity provides a more robust foundation pillar. Thus, exploiting the new **intelligence leadership theory/ strategy** (thinking and attributes) is beneficial (see Figure 9.1) — a significant starting point for initiating a transformation. It may also be interesting

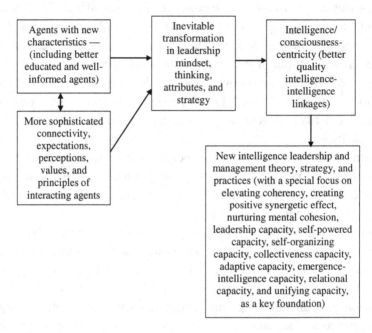

Figure 9.1 The new leadership mindset must be fundamentally intelligence/consciousness-centric.

and significant to note at this juncture that intelligence/consciousness-centricity and self-centricity are not totally identical, although, the two terms are analogous in some ways (see intelligent person in Appendix 7).

9.2 Criticality of Structural and Dynamic Transformation

9.2.1 *The significance of an intelligent biotic macro-structure*

The above introduction emphasizes that comprehending and exploiting the close association between intelligent human biological and mental (living systems) characteristics and dynamics, and the new leadership and management mindset is highly vital. As the **holistic functional capacity** of an organization is greatly dependent on its **structural capacity**, transforming into an intelligent biotic macro-structure (away from a mechanistic structure) is beneficial — the first essential initiative to accommodate rapid changes and high complexity. To eliminate the incompatibility of the machine-like structure, the more feasible option is to focus on how intelligence/consciousness drives a living system, how the human mind behaves and operates, how the individual biological species sustains itself, how an ecosystem evolves, and how human organizations can be better managed and enhanced with the presence of orgmindfulness and the orgmind. This basic recognition opens a significant new frontier and a new direction for leadership and management philosophy and practices.

As discussed earlier, the mind and orgmind are the sources where intrinsic intelligence and collective intelligence emerges, respectively. The primary critical success factor that sustains the competitiveness of human organizations today is to optimize available intrinsic individual intelligence, and nurture high collective intelligence. All human organizations are both tangibly and intangibly connected. The structure and substructures involved are dominantly connections of human thinking systems. The human minds are the key decision-making nodes in all information processing and communication systems/networks that contain the ability to deal with the nonlinear aspect of unstructured problems, especially in unpredictable events/spaces. Apparently, a high collective intelligence only emerges from a biotic macro-structure with a well-developed orgmind that is effective in handling all problems/issues, including integrating agents, venturing into spaces of high complexity (risks management), and preparing for punctuation points (crises management), with an intense focus on the relational parameter.

9.2.2 *The significance of nurturing the intelligent complex adaptive dynamic*

All biotic structured human organizations possessing a high structural capacity embedded with sophisticated knowledge structures, effective information processing and learning capabilities of their interacting agents, quality interconnectivity of the agents and system, and the presence of a mindful culture and an enormous collective intelligence are intelligent human organizations. Orgmindful and org-aware organizations are both internally and externally focus, and in particular, orgmindfulness focuses on the mental states of the interacting agents, including their thoughts, feeling, emotions, and behaviors (ensuring higher collectiveness capacity). These human organizations are highly intelligent complex adaptive systems (*i*CAS). The highly intelligent *i*CAD (supported by the unique 3C-OK foundation and dynamic) of the *i*CAS, includes fast learning, adaptation, quality connectivity, self-organizing communications, truthful engagement, self-organizing capability, innovation and creativity, high competitiveness, and smarter evolution and co-evolution with the composite system and the environment.

Thus, the ability to orchestrate an overall highly intelligent complex adaptive dynamic is another critical requirement for the new leaders. Integrated intelligence/consciousness-centric, complexity-centric, and network-centric leadership and management theory, strategy, and practices are the best options for all current human organizations and their interacting agents that wish to maintain/elevate their competitiveness, resilience, and sustainability. Directly or indirectly, effective leaderships are those that constantly focus on elevating the various capacities of the organization (see Figure 9.2). Thus, the basic foundation of any effective leadership strategy, associated with the level of the **leadership capacity** (including both **intrinsic leadership capacity** and **collective leadership capacity**) depends on other organizational capacities. In addition, a key devotion of the intelligence leadership strategy is nurturing mental cohesion (see Figure 9.3).

9.3 Fundamentals of the New Intelligence Leadership Theory/Strategy

9.3.1 *Basic foundation of the emerging leadership mindset*

Based on the above introduction, it is crucial that the leadership possesses a deep recognition and comprehension of the structure, dynamic, and attributes of the agents and organizations that they lead. As the mindset, thinking, values, expectations, and other attributes of the elementary units have changed, their associated organizational characteristics and dynamics are also different. Apparently, the intelligence/consciousness-centric mindset of the leadership establish the critical foundation of the intelligence leadership theory (primarily, a key starting point of the intelligence leadership must synchronize with nurturing a more intelligent organization). This paradigmatic shift should at least encompass the following attributes/

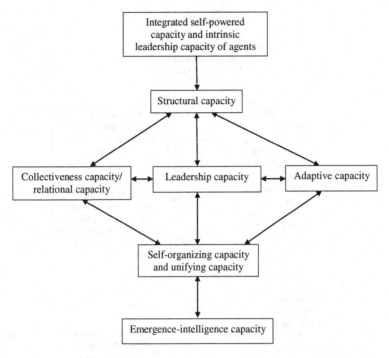

Figure 9.2   The high interdependency of different capacities in a complex environment.

capabilities that define the fundamentals and boundaries of the new intelligence leadership theory/strategy:

a.   The thinking that maximizes the contribution of each and every intrinsic intelligence/consciousness source in the organization — optimize the naturally endowed individual self-powered capacity and intrinsic leadership capacity through higher autonomy.

b.   The thinking that recognizes the needs to nurture high collective intelligence by being orgmindful (presence of a mindful culture that focuses on intense intelligence-intelligence linkages).

c.   The thinking with a strong devotion to constructively exploit the complexity and nonlinearity of both the intrinsic intelligence and collective intelligence sources.

d.   The thinking that focuses on the necessity to learn, adapt, compete, innovate, evolve, and co-evolve with other interacting agents, as well as the composite system (towards nurturing an *i*CAD).

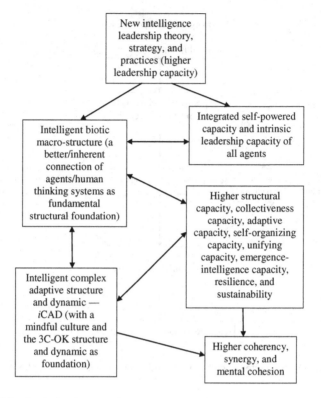

Figure 9.3 Some fundamental focuses of the new intelligence leadership strategy.

e. The thinking that recognizes the significance of possessing high positive relational parameter value (nurturing a feeling system with better social consensus and mental cohesion).

f. The recognition that the leader–follower relationship is more complex and nonlinear, lateral/collective, consultative, and no more unidirectional (towards everybody is in charge).

g. The thinking that focuses on optimizing structural capacity at all levels is vital — intelligent biotic macro-structure, agent-agent/system microstructure, complexity meso-structure, and networks meso-structure.

h. The thinking that constantly elevates the collectiveness capacity, and adaptive capacity of the organization.

i. The new intelligence leadership also nurtures a high self-organizing capacity, emergence-intelligence capacity and unifying capacity in the organization.

Apparently, the intelligence leadership strategy emerges from an intelligent complex adaptive mindset. The intelligence leadership dynamic possesses must encompass **upwards causation**. Thus, coupled with the smarter interacting agents (with intelligent person attributes), nurturing lateral/collective leadership through more entrenched mass participation, quality networking, and truthful engagement is highly recommended. Therefore, a crucial ability of the new leadership is to orchestrate and facilitate the emergence of a **group-centric (network-centric, org-centric) leadership** dynamic (by exploiting the independent and interdependent attributes of the agents more creatively). Thus, a highly effective leader is no longer one that maximizes his/her own intelligence alone, and dominates the scene (**individual leadership**), but one that optimizes the collective intelligence of the agents/networks/system, and allows the entire organization (as well as the agents) to evolve, compete, lead, and succeed. In the new environment, both the leaders and followers possess both direct and indirect functions. This is the **lateral/collective leadership** approach, and it is a vital aspect of the intelligence leadership strategy. Overall, some transformation in basic leadership characteristics is summarized in Table 9.1.

Lateral/collective leadership =
Σ (intrinsic individual leadership) (9.1)

And with synergetic effect, ideally it should be,

Capacity of lateral/collective leadership $\gg$
Σ (capacity of individual leadership) (9.2)

Table 9.1 Some changes in basic leadership characteristics.

Traditional Leadership	New Leadership
Hierarchical/empowerment	Lateral/horizontal/self-powered
Individualistic	Collective (groups/networks/system)
Command-and-Control	Lateral, consultative, and adaptive
Machine-logic	Bio-logic/intelligence-centric
Immediate goal	Longer-term goal

In this respect, the new leadership itself is also becoming complex and nonlinear, and therefore new leaders must possess the new recalibrated adaptive thinking, that is, always learning — **learning leadership** (see Figure 9.4).

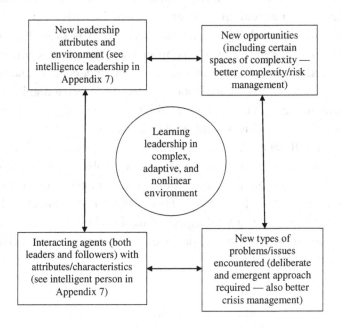

Figure 9.4   A complex and learning leadership dynamic.

9.3.2 *Deeper analysis of the stability-centric phenomenon and self-organizing dynamic*

In cosmology and astrophysics, the current belief is a form of energy known as the dark energy is expanding the Universe. There is a general universal expansion that increases entropy, and does not support the emergence of detailed structure. However, more microscopically, a reverse dynamic has also been occurring concurrently in this huge explosion leading to the formation of the physical matter world. This complex dynamic encompassing self-organization gives rise to structure, pattern, network, stability, and life — leading to the emergent of the biological world. These are localized stability-centric and self-centric phenomena. The 'energy' driving this fascinating localized development is some forms of intelligence (proto-intelligence, basic life-intelligence).

In this respect, intelligence is the unique form of 'energy' that is embedded intrinsically in the Universe that supports structural formation, localized order, and self-organization/self-transcending constructions. It takes place in a localized space varying from atoms to molecules to cells to organisms, and to complex animal species and their communities. The inherent goal is stability enhancement at the local level. At the energy–matter boundaries, the confinement of quarks in sub-atomic particles is an elementary stability-centric characteristic. This phenomenon allows sub-atomic particles to exist (in an energy–matter duality state). At the atomic level, atoms that are stable do not react, and atoms that are not stable react chemically to enhance their stability. However, in all these cases, the need for stability is rather simplistic. It is purely physical in nature — totally **physical stability-centricity**. For instance, a hydrogen atom by itself is not stable. It is willing 'to forgo something' to elevate its stability. In this example, it is through sharing of electrons. A hydrogen molecule with a more 'complex and robust structure' (a new order) is more stable. It is through this 'latent' proto-intelligence driven dynamic (physical self-organization) that an enormous numbers of compounds emerge from approximately one hundred elements. Apparently, intelligence is not confined to living organisms alone.

However, as the intelligence level becomes more intense and nonlinear, the living world emerges. The boundary between non-living and living matters is a significant threshold. In this environment, intelligence sources arises (become more apparent), and as they increases in intensity up to a certain level, autopoietic needs and (self-enrichment) processes of the localized spaces (biological entities) also heightened. It is these more intense and nonlinear intelligence sources embedded in biological organisms that further increase the complexity and evolution capability of the living systems — emergent of **biological stability-centricity** (encompassing autopoiesis, symbiosis, and ambidexterity). From a single cell organism, gradually the intelligence embedded in it is able to transform it into a trillions cells living system, such as a human being. Vividly, the stability-centric needs of non-living interacting entities are much more simplistic because it only involves physical stability. The autopoietic and symbiotic (independency versus interdependency) needs of living intelligent interacting agents are more sophisticated because it encompasses both the physical and biological dimensions. It is in the living world that consciousness emerges.

It is highly distinctive that every human being, each embedded with an intense intelligence/consciousness source focuses significantly on the 3rd order **mental stability**. To a great extent, mental stability is confined only to humanity. In this respect, an intelligent human organization with an intense collective intelligence and org-consciousness must focus on all three levels of stability in order to elevate its competitiveness, resilience, and sustainability. In particular, the mental stability of all its agents is critical for nurturing, sustaining, and exploiting organizational mental cohesion. Again, intense orgmindfulness is a highly valuable attribute in all human organizations. Hence, possessing stability-inducing capability is a basic requirement of the new leadership. Briefly, the stability-centric concept is captured as the next postulate as follows:

Postulate I: (Law of Stability-Centricity/Autopoiesis/Symbiosis)

Stability-centricity is a vital attribute that establishes structure and life (the physical matter world and the biological world). The stability-centricity of less intelligent interacting entities/agents is more simplistic (for examples, a hydrogen atom, an ant, or a bee). Similarly, their stability-centric and autopoietic dynamic also reaches 'optimality' very quickly (physical stability alone, or physical and biological stability combined). However, higher intelligent interacting agents possess more complex autopoietic needs, and hence the autopoietic and symbiotic dynamic is much more complex, requiring better ambidexterity. For humanity, the intense mental space of human agents due to intense consciousness, nonlinear perceptions and intangible needs lead to 3rd order stability (physical, biological and mental stability).

Human interacting agents being interdependent form groups or local spaces/networks through self-organization/self-transcending constructions. Highly intelligent human interacting agents with characteristics as specified in the intelligent person model will have to balance between autopoiesis (self-centric) and symbiosis (self-centric and org-centric) with a high level of mindful culture so that a constructive self-organizing dynamic emerges whenever it is required. Thus, ensuring better coherency among agents, and localized spaces/networks is vital. In this case, the self-organizing capability of human agents must better utilize at all levels. This is dynamic is linked to the self-organizing capacity and emergence-intelligence capacity of the networks and organization, respectively.

As discussed earlier chapters, mindfulness is the ability to focus inwards at the mental state of the mind is unique to human intense consciousness. Similarly, an intelligent human organization must be focusing on the mental state of all its agents and networks. However, most 'competitive' organizations today are aware of the changing environment to a varying degree (externally focus) but many of them are not orgmindful (not internally focus) enough. It is important to note that a well-synchronized org-awareness and orgmindfulness approach is critical. A human organization with this thinking is a more effective *i*CAS. In this respect, balancing local processes and global forces is beneficial. The above analysis leads to the proposal of the second postulate:

Postulate II: (Law of Self-Organization/Self-transcending Constructions)

Less intelligent interacting agents self-organize more automatically, as their self-organized (order) state is relatively more simplistic (for examples, a crystal, or a bee hive). It is more difficult for a group of human beings to self-organize because they are 'autopoietically' and 'symbiotically' more complex (involving physical, biological, and mental stability; agents-networks-system relationships; and higher independency). Special effort is required to nurture a high level of collective intelligence (better intelligence-intelligence linkages) to ensure an effective self-organization/self-transcending constructions capability (exploiting self-organizing capability of the agents, and nurturing self-organizing capacity and emergence-intelligence capacity of the organization) is present at all levels (intra-system emergence, and inter-system emergence — better agents-networks-organization coherency).

9.3.3. *Deeper analysis on the different levels of stability-centricity*

The above analysis vividly revealed that stability is the most fundamental characteristic and objective of emergence — that is, **emergence is stability-centric** — emergence leads to a **new order** (a higher level of stability with a more robust structure). It is also the basic property that opposes universal expansion (for the same reason, anything that is composed will one day decompose). In more details, stability is closely linked to localized order, structure, robustness, 'balanced' autopoiesis and symbiosis, and eventually the existence of a unique entity with a self (self $<=>$ I). In the physical and biological world (a small component of the Universe), three orders of stability exist, and they are re-captured as follows:

- Physical (matter) world — physical stability (1st order stability).
- Living/biological (organisms, species, ecosystems) world — physical stability, and biological stability (2nd order stability).
- Humanity (human communities, societies, nations) — physical stability, biological stability, and mental stability (3rd order stability).

Succinctly, the dynamics and outcomes of emergence can be highly nonlinear and unpredictable. For instance, the self-organization of a collection of atoms (carbon, oxygen, hydrogen, nitrogen, sulfur, phosphorus) can give rise to a relatively more complex structure (gene, DNA) embedded with a 'collective intelligence' that enables life to emerge eventually (synergetic effect, constructionist effect). This is a highly nonlinear phenomenon, a butterfly effect, a significant change in state (from the non-living to the biological world), that encompasses the emergent of a new dimension — consciousness.

The mental dimension humanity emerges from the intense neural networks (especially, the cerebral cortex in human thinking systems). This large collection of neurons gives rise to a level of consciousness and intelligence that has never been observed on this planet before (creation of character sets, emergent of sophisticated verbal and written languages, mindfulness attribute, extensive exploitation of technologies, and the over dominance of this planet). The intense intelligence of human beings allows perception and conceptualization of ideas and knowledge to emerge, and communications at a very abstract level is also enabled. Similarly, the intense human consciousness (encompassing awareness and mindfulness) allows the mental state of the intelligence source to be observed, analyzed, and even modified. Thus, deriving from the above analysis the following inferences are established as a set of basic postulates of emergence (also see Chapter 2).

Postulate III: Law of Individual Stability

There is a natural/inherent intuition for self-stability (self-centricity) in all interacting entities/agents (at all levels — from atoms to molecules, cells, ants, apes, and human beings) in the physical world and living world (ecosystems) driven by their individual intelligence (varying from proto-intelligence to basic life-intelligence, to human intelligence).

Postulate IV: Law of Local Spaces (Networks)/Organizational Stability

Interacting entities/agents self-organize (and emerge) to enhance the stability of themselves, local spaces/networks, and the entire organization through different levels of emergence (intra-system, inter-system) by exploiting the interconnectivity, collective intelligence (from collective proto-intelligence to collective human intelligence) and self-organizing capability of the agents/networks/subsystems/organization involved.

Postulate V: Law of Dual (Entity-System) Stability

The interacting agents and the organization spontaneously balance between autopoiesis (individual intelligence, self-stability), symbiosis, and self-organization/self-transcending constructions (collective self-organizing capability, local spaces/networks or entire system collective stability), so as to continuously seek a best possible sustainable attractor/state (evolving and co-evolving, and prolonging dual stability) for better survival of the agents, and resilience and sustainability of the organization.

In highly intelligent human organizations, the interacting agents are intelligent persons (as specified in the intelligent person model), and they are constantly mindful of the mental dimension. Therefore, the new leadership should be highly focused on the mental dimension of 3rd order stability. In particular, the mental space of the orgmind of human organizations has to be allocated with sufficient attention. The mental states of all the other interacting agents in the organization have to be well-managed — well-convinced and engaged (intelligence mindset); and not mobilized as desired (bureaucratic mindset). In this respect, orgmindfulness and nurturing a mindful culture is vital for better mental-strategic competitiveness and sustainability in the current context. Inevitably, the mental dimension is becoming more significant and strategic. The new intelligence leadership theory/strategy places a significant emphasis on this aspect. The involvement and contributions of intense intelligence and consciousness is summarized as the next postulate of mental stability.

Postulate VI: Law of Mental Stability (I)

For human beings and human organizations, mental stability is a unique and vital requirement associated with 'human emergence' that can only be fulfilled by much higher level constructive autopoiesis, symbiosis, and self-organization/self-transcending constructions driven by the intense individual intelligence of the agents, and the collective intelligence of the local spaces/networks and the entire organization. For the latter, the presence of mental cohesion (stimulated by intense org-consciousness) is vital for higher coherency, synergetic effect, and constructionist effect to occur. Mental cohesion is a basic foundation pillar for higher resilience and sustainability.

9.3.4 *Deeper analysis on iCAS and iCAD*

The above postulates indicate that in the living world autopoiesis is associated with localized order (agents and networks), while self-transcending construction leads to collective order (networks and organization) — the integrated order of the agents, local spaces/networks, and the entire system (at least a three-layer dynamic). From the entity perspective, autopoiesis leads to self-stability, and self-transcending construction leads to a larger localized order (group/network). The latter occurs due to the presence of self-organizing capacity (driven by the collective intelligence of the local space involved). Thus, when the organization is analyzed as a system, self-transcending construction (1st order, intra-system) as a micro-dynamic has to be closely monitored at the networks level, and exploiting the collective intelligence of networks becomes extremely vital. In the current context, networks are common features, and have to be well-integrated into the organization — a significant focus of the new leadership and governance. In addition, when an organization is perceived as an entity (a local space of order) with respect to its environment, the emergence-intelligence capacity of the organization is a vital attribute (2nd order self-transcending constructions, emergent of new order). This new recognition and under-standing strongly indicates that organizing around intelligence is a vital paradigmatic shift, and it should be a primary focus of the intelligence leadership when nurturing an *i*CAS.

Hence, human organizations with intrinsic characteristics and structure closely associated with intelligence blend more naturally with the requirements of the complex adaptive processes. As indicated earlier, an intelligence-based structure that emerges from intelligence-driven dynamic should be the inherent structure of the biological world. Concurrently, enhancing stability at all levels (micro, meso, and macro) by utilizing intense intelligence/consciousness is also a critical requirement. Overall, highly intelligent human systems learn, adapt, innovate, compete, and evolve better with nonlinear human intelligence — presence of the unique 3C-OK structure and dynamic. Nonlinear intelligence is more effective at balancing between autopoiesis (agents) and self-transcending construc-tions (agents, localized spaces/networks, and system) depending on needs and circumstances, and is also more closely associated with innovation and creativity. Thus, highly *i*CAD is not totally similar to traditional com-plex adaptive dynamic (CAD).

Apparently, nurturing highly intelligent human organizations is vital, as *i*CAS are the best competitors/survivors in the knowledge-intensive and strongly social media connected environment. Therefore, the intelligence/consciousness-related biological and complexity characteristics of CAS are crucial attributes that intelligence leaders must conscientiously exploit. [As indicated earlier, some core properties/attributes of intelligent human organizations are intelligence and consciousness, co-existence of order and complexity, nonlinearity, interconnectivity, self-organizing communications, independency, interdependency, far-from-equilibrium, sensitive dependence on initial conditions, fast continuous learning and sharing, adaptation, dissipation, information decoder, smarter evolver, emergent strategist self-transcending constructions, and emergence]. Consequently, a strong emphasis must be placed on cultivating and exploiting the associated capacities of the organization (including structural capacity, collectiveness capacity, adaptive capacity, self-organizing capacity, emergence-intelligence capacity, self-powered intrinsic leadership capacity, and unifying capacity) — illustrated earlier in Figure 9.2. In this respect, it is vital that quality relationships, high mutual trust and consensus are appropriately nurtured and exploited to achieve higher mental cohesion and constructionist effect.

The above analysis and re-capturing clearly reinforces the criticality of high collective intelligence and org-consciousness in human organizations. Inevitably, organizing around intelligence, strong intelligence-intelligence linkages, high mental cohesion, well-integrated intrinsic leadership capacity, high self-organizing capacity and emergence-intelligence capacity, and lateral/collective leadership form an effective approach that must be adopted when leading, managing, and nurturing all categories of human organizations in the current context. The fundamental objective is the continuous increase in actors and leaders (increase in self-powered capacity) so that an *i*CAS, as a smarter and smarter evolver and emergent strategist, emerges successfully in the continuous changing and cyclical process. This is a vital strategic thinking and path that a new intelligence leadership exploits (summarized as the next postulate).

Postulate VII: (Law of Organization)

Organizing around intelligence, exploiting both the intrinsic intelligence of the individuals/agents and the collective intelligence of the organization (criticality of intelligence/consciousness-centricity and management, intelligence-intelligence linkages, relational capacity, mental cohesion) with an orgmind and intangible structure, is the primary requisite for nurturing a more competitive and sustainable *i*CAS in the current rapidly changing environment. In addition, intelligence leaders must also recognize that human organizations are high finite dimension nonlinear CAS with in-complete phase space (not all variables are known), and the presence of a set of complexity associated attributes including the butterfly effect (unpredictability). In this respect, they must also be highly complexity-centric and network-centric, as well as possessing the attributes of an intelligent person (including being a smart evolver and emergent strategist).

9.4 The Conceptual Foundation of the Intelligence Leadership Theory/Strategy

9.4.1 *The significance of exploiting intrinsic leadership capability*

The above introduction and analysis establishes a new perspective (encompassing a brief listing of agent and organization critical attributes, and their nonlinear CAD) for leadership. The latter is a significant attribute for human group survival. Conceptually, effective leadership is a vital attribute that connects organizational objectives, strategies, plans, functions, and the other associated activities together. Thus, the basic essential capabilities and responsibilities of leadership are to provide new directions, garner support, nurture collectiveness, nurture an integrative culture, cultivate an 'organizational soul', and sustaining the organization. Are these abilities within the reach of every individual human agent? Inherently, every individual/agent is endowed (self-powered) with a certain degree of leadership (intrinsic leadership) capability. If a substantial disparity exists between the leadership and the other agents, there is a high potential that the organization will not integrate. The intrinsic leadership capability in all the agents that assume the role of followers is often suppressed by the structure (arising from hierarchical/bureaucratic thinking, design, and practices) of the traditional mindset and its environment (aristocracy, slavery, organizational hierarchy, caste system). With the new evolving situation, where individuals are better informed and educated, this naturally endowed leadership capacity is at least subconsciously activated, and sometimes even more visibly manifested — for instance, more frequent emergence of self-organized (informal) local spaces/networks. A new advantage for any organization is therefore to explore, engage, and exploit this natural endowed capability and capacity rather than to eliminate them.

In this respect, the command-and-control leadership, and even empowered leadership (**transformational leadership**) are vividly losing its effectiveness — will lead to polarization. Even organizations with a highly hierarchical structure such as the military are gradually adopting a modified mindset and approach, **soft voice** and **low key** (Cleveland, 2002). There is a general consensus and can be observed rather visibly in many corporations and nations that the traditional leadership and its characteristics are becoming less relevant, if not obsolete over the last few decades. Different views and dissimilar schools of thoughts have emerged over this period.

Primarily, the highly rank-and-class domineering, command-and-control, and aristocratic leadership has been rejected by the current interacting agents in most types of human organization. Even the **empowering leadership** approach, perceived to be rank-and-class domineering, appears to be undermining. The lower ranking leaders have to be empowered with authority by the higher levels leaders to execute certain duties and responsibilities are far from 'satisficing optimality'. The current trend is towards **leadership emergence**, beyond leadership empowerment — integrated emergence of self-powered leadership (self-powered capacity versus enabling capacity). Some corporations (especially, high information technology firms) are exploiting self-powered leadership (with wide spread incentives — monetary, non-monetary, intangibles, ride and consensus, individual and family welfares) for higher innovation and creativity. Consequently, the mindset, thinking, and practices of intrinsic self-powered leadership, learning leadership, and lateral/collective leadership that appear to encompass deeper bio-logic are more appropriate and appealing.

9.4.2 *The significance of lateral, collective and consultative leadership*

Inevitably, the general trend is from authoritative to consultative, and individualistic to lateral/collective, that is, the **diffusive leadership** approach is becoming more acceptable — towards everybody is in charge (any organization that is able to effective achieve this is in an 'ideal' state). Thus the more lateral, consultative, and diffusive approach appears to be the new direction. While, enhancing leadership learning and upgrading strategic thinking, nurturing high self-organizing capacity and emergence-intelligence capacity that leads to more constructive emergence, and optimization of the intrinsic leadership are vital possesses. In addition, traits such as acceptability, truthfulness, mutual trust, and even compassion (high positive relational parameter value, feeling organization, and mental cohesion) are critical attributes that must be carefully managed.

Deriving from the above analysis, the first set of basic crucial factors associated with the transformation in leadership characteristics and dynamic are summarized as follows:

a. There is a general (desired) shift from one prominent leader to lateral/ collective leadership.
b. Leadership in organizations is no more associated with some individuals at the top of the organizational structure but has become more diffused with managerial/executive and even operational level actors (local spaces and networks) — a phenomenon related to optimizing structural capacity.
c. Leadership cannot depend on empowerment alone. The leadership capacity of an organization now depends greatly on the ability to exploit and integrate self-powered intrinsic leadership capacity.
d. Thus, a critical requirement for leading effectively is closely associated with nurturing intense collective intelligence, org-consciousness

(orgmindfulness), and a mindful culture in the organization — higher collectiveness capacity.

e. The form of leadership to be adopted has become more dependent on the types of activity or problem encountered, that is, more situations dependent (processing a deeper insight into complexity) — must possess higher adaptive capacity.

f. The leadership is highly dependent on the (constantly changing) characteristics and expectations of the interacting agents — including intangible perceptions and non-monetary values (self-powered capacity).

g. Leadership, particularly in nations can be more generative and unifying by exchanging information ('demoncratization' of information) and shared influences (principles of governance).

h. Hence, the success of intelligence-intelligence linkages, that is, the direct links between the intelligence of the leader and the intelligence of the followers is a critical success factor — better access and understanding of mental states of the agents is a critical requirement for nurturing a more 'feeling' organization, and achieving higher mental cohesion in the organization.

i. Within the lateral/collective leadership approach, a new category of leadership, the transitional (temporary) leadership is also emerging (particularly important in spaces of high complexity and punctuation points) — situation dependent, better optimal exploitation of intrinsic self-powered leadership capacity — better unifying capacity.

The above are some new accelerants for elevating leadership effectiveness. As the leader–follower gap has to be diminished significantly, in the new leadership dynamic of an intelligent human organization, the followers have to be as much a part of the leadership process as possible. To connect them constructively requires a more humanized approach — intense humanization of organizations (human beings are not machine parts of a mechanistic system). The social, cognitive, and psychological perspectives of every human agent are vital. As indicated, a basic way to enhance this development is to have effective and continuous communications through thought methodology conducted with an appropriate mindset, thinking, and environment.

Simultaneously, there must always be a significant level of self-organizing communications between the leaders and their intelligent interacting agents, and as the process evolves, new or larger collective leadership emerge — constantly elevating leadership capacity. This activity also ensures that the followers get their thoughts (**truthful engagement**) through, and hence further increasing motivation and commitment. Thus, effective leadership capacity is directly correlated to its **unifying capacity**, and its ability to enhance quality relationships and processes is critical (self-organizing system of voluntary collaboration <=> unifying capacity). With this thinking (embedded in a mindful culture), truthful engagement and constructive participation emerges spontaneously (see Figure 9.5). Consequently, with higher mental cohesion, leaders as well as the other interacting agents can then better exploit creativity at the edge of emergence, whenever possible.

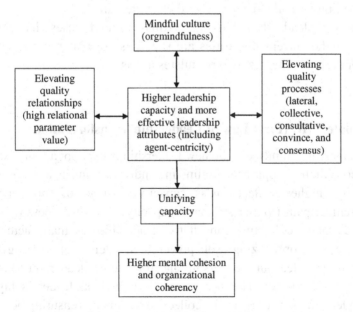

Figure 9.5 The significance of an unifying capacity.

9.4.3 *The first two laws of leadership transformation*

Apparently, nurturing collective intelligence through mass participation (generative, mutual influence, self-organize) is an inevitable change (rather than mobilize and enforce) — including recognizing the significance of **collective social consciousness**. Constructive integration of the interdependency between individual intrinsic leadership and networks/organization collective leadership is a critical component of the intelligence leadership strategy. In general, the success of hierarchical leadership has diffused in the new environment. An individual leader that hopes to be effective has to depend on the effectiveness of the collective leadership s/he nurtured. This observation further reinforces the significant of encompassing and/or exploiting effective self-transcending constructions at local spaces/networks/system (higher self-organizing capacity and emergence-intelligence capacity). Hence, the new leadership capability must be able to handle constant changes, highly information-interconnected agents/networks, certain spaces of high complexity, and punctuation points. In particular, it must be a unifying leadership that is capable of exploiting all collective associated characteristics.

The new leadership thinking, attributes and focuses that need to overcome the current disparities are stated as postulates for leadership transformations. The first two postulates are as follows:

Postulate VIII: (First Law of Leadership Transformation)

A fundamental mindset of the new leadership is to adopt a more lateral and consultative approach (optimizing individual intrinsic leadership capacity, higher collectiveness capacity) instead of the vertical/hierarchical path (higher structural capacity). Thus, the new trend is towards lateral/collective consultative leadership (as many actors as possible — optimizing self-powered capacity of all agents) encompassing learning leadership and transitional leadership (higher leadership capacity). The success of an individual leader is highly dependent on the success of the collective leadership (ensuring both the survival of the agents and the success of the organization).

Postulate IX: (Second Law of Leadership Transformation)

The next new leadership mindset is that the lateral/collective leadership and unifying leadership approach (optimizing individual intrinsic leadership and quality interconnectivity) can only be orchestrated effectively with a high level of collective intelligence and org-consciousness that encompasses intelligence-to-intelligence linkages, consultation, sharing/communicating, diffusion, truthful engagement, soft voice and low key, collective participation, mutual influence, high relational parameter value, calm mind, mutual respect, and unifying capacity (presence of a mindful culture is vital). The consequence is towards a deeper 'feeling' dynamic and organization with higher mental cohesion.

9.4.4 Latent leadership and the next two laws of leadership transformation

The above recognition leads towards a vital attribute — effective self-transcending constructions and the significance of self-organizing capacity. Self-transcending constructions creates opportunities for the new leadership, but in some ways may negate the usefulness/presence of (traditional) leadership. In a system with a highly effective ('spontaneous') self-organizing dynamic, where are the leaders, or is every agent/actor a leader? However, it does clearly indicate the fact that the presence of leadership is not entrenched in one person. Leadership is no longer confined to a charismatic person that pulls the organization along with his/her definition of what a successful direction might be. In this situation, leadership that is able to nurture 'desired' self-organizing capacity and emergence-intelligence capacity is more constructive.

According to the intelligence leader theory every individual agent is a self-powered intrinsic leader, and collective leadership in any human organizations is a natural phenomenon that results from the intrinsic leadership capability and its associated self-organization/self-transcending constructions capability. With the presence of high collective intelligence driven self-transcending constructions, the set of rules exploited may even be latent, that is, not explicitly stated but implicitly embedded in the collective minds of the integrated interacting agents at different levels (networks/organization). Thus, the interesting reality observed is that lateral/collective leadership and self-transcending constructions can be mutually enhancing. Individual intelligence, collective intelligence (networks/organization), self-transcending constructions, and the ultimate effective emergent dynamic are highly interdependent. Recognizing this condition is important for achieving coherency and synergy. Therefore, a primary aim of the new strategy is to nurture a group/network of self-organizing intrinsic leaders, that is, each interacting agent is behaving both as a leader and follower, depending on the exact situation and requirement of the organization. Thus, the roles and gap between a leader and follower is significantly redefined and diminished.

Hence, in the current environment possessing intelligent person characteristics is vital for both leaders and followers (see Figure 9.6). A highly intelligent interacting agent frequently modifies and introduces 'additional meanings' to his/her autopoietic self-enrichment dynamic — changes in the behavioral schema. A more subtle approach is usually adopted compared to an ordinary agent. An intelligent person, both a leader and a follower, ensures that s/he has better long-term survival opportunities. The

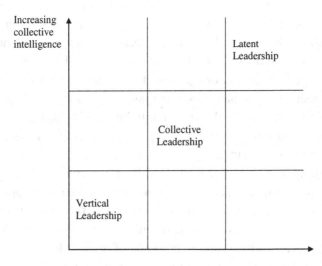

Figure 9.6   General variations in leadership strategy/thinking with respect to increasing intelligence and knowledge intensity.

evolution dynamic of an intelligent person (smarter evolver and emergent strategist) is also strongly committed to co-evolution with the system through strong intelligence-intelligence linkages. Thus, at all times, an intelligent person balances autopoiesis, symbiosis, and self-transcending constructions, and seeks satisficing holistic adaptive solutions.

In this case, the solutions may even be an option with short-term losses that eventually leads to longer-term gains because of mental, biological, physical and/or environmental constraints. Therefore, an intelligent person (as leaders) being more adaptive and nonlinear, focuses on longer-term survival, and also helps to orchestrate a more constructive system dynamic (integrating networks and entire system) through the manipulation of both deliberate and emergent strategies. In this respect, an intelligent person is also constantly making preparation for the sudden appearance of punctuation points. When the condition is right, a group of highly intelligent interacting agents (leaders and followers) with a high level of collectiveness should self-organize constructively at criticality (see Table 9.2). The crucial aspect of the above recognition is summarized as the next postulate.

Postulate X: (Third Law of Leadership Transformation)

The next mindset is on the special needs/benefits to initiate, orchestrate, and optimize constructive human self-organization/self-transcending constructions at different levels (agents, local spaces/networks, organization) in an *i*CAS (intra-system, inter-system, emergent of new order). The ability of the leadership to integrate possesses at different levels (agents, groups/networks, and organization) with mutual influence, enhancement, and trust, and achieving higher mental coherency with synergetic effect is vital. This is also part of the intelligent emergent dynamic (*i*CAD) that allows an organization to exploits certain spaces of complexity, and a desirable state to crystallize spontaneously when a punctuation point is encountered (high self-organizing capacity and emergence-intelligence capacity). In this case, the new leadership possesses high unifying capability, and capability of identifying new basin of attraction.

Table 9.2 Additional changes needed in leadership characteristics.

Traditional Leadership	New Intelligence Leadership
Power-to-fear relationship	Direct intelligence-to-intelligence linkages (intelligence/consciousness-centric, information exchange, self-organizing communications, consultative, mutual influence, mutual enhancement, mutual trust, and mindful culture)
Top-to-bottom dependency	Exhibit lateral mass participation, unifying, and self-transcending constructions ability (driven by a collective impetus — agents/networks/system, and also upwards causation)
Intelligence confined to the top leadership	Huge and diverse collective intelligence source (smaller leader–follower gap, lateral/collective leadership, information sharing is vital)
Leaders have no 'feeling' for other agents (empowerment, enforcement, mobilization)	Leaders focus on the mental state of all other agents (intense focus on agents' mental stability, orgmindfulness, mindful culture, unifying capacity, coherency, feeling system, and mental cohesion)

Finally, a significant attribute of the intelligence leadership strategy is **latent leadership**. The leader of a highly intelligent organization (*i*CAS) could also adopt the latent leadership approach. It is also perceived as the highest form of leadership. The presence of the leader becomes latent when the leader orchestrates a dynamic with such great subtlety to the extent that the followers are not aware of his/her intention (stimulates lives in hidden ways). In this case, an effective leader need not be highly visible. The presence of such a leader in a complex environment is an advantage. Very likely, the latent leader with intense intelligence/consciousness has already observed the potential global patterns in a certain space of complexity. Consequently, the latent leader subtly initiates the self-organizing capability of the agents (at different levels), and when it exceeds a certain threshold, a positive self-organizational dynamic emerges spontaneously. In the process, the agents take pride in their 'self-achievement'. Thus, the presence of this trait, the latent leadership, indicates is a new level of organizational consciousness. Hence, the next law of leadership transformation is conceived as follows:

Postulate XI: (Law of the Latent/Ultimate Leadership)

The final mindset is the recognition of the strengths and values of the latent leadership strategy for leading intelligent interacting agents in *i*CAS. It is a well-integrated and vital part of the lateral/collective leadership strategy that emerges from a 'latent mind', the highly intense intelligence/consciousness source of a 'latent' leader. The latter orchestrates the combination of leadership styles and dynamic according to the emerging situation without the notice of the interacting agents. If such a dynamic is effectively orchestrated it greatly enhances the collectiveness capacity, adaptive capacity, self-organizing capacity, and emergence-intelligence capacity (optimizes the utilization of integrated intrinsic leadership capacity) of the network organization. Concurrently, a feeling organization with higher mental cohesion emerges inherently due to the higher self-recognition and pride of the agents. In this leadership dynamic, very often the agents do not notice the intention of the latent leader, and assume that the success of their venture (or problem solving) is totally strategized and executed by them alone.

9.4.5 *Summary of the new intelligence leadership strategic factors*

At this juncture, it may be beneficial to recapitulate some of the fundamental attributes of the traditional leadership that are still appropriate in the current context, so that the new intelligence leadership strategic factors can be better identified, integrated, and effectively exploited. The set of attributes and capabilities that is still valid as leadership foundation are as follows:

a. The ability to identify new objectives, directions, and opportunities.
b. The ability to map out new strategies.
c. The ability to garner the support of other members (unifying) in the organization.

d.   The ability to nurture an organizational/supporting culture.

e.   The mindset of adapting to changes.

With respect to the new rapidly changing environment, the above capabilities are still vital but insufficient for the more competitive environment. They have to be modified and supported with new attributes, depending on the situation or problem encountered, in particular, with an intense concentration on emergence (the intelligence mindset and its key thinking). Therefore, some additional vital leadership strategic attributes/ factors that provide a more comprehensive and nimble foundation must be nurtured and embraced. The intelligence leadership theory/strategy indicates that the following new abilities (a more comprehensive set) are of high significance when leading *i*CAS:

a.   The special ability to perform/orchestrate the above basic foundation attributes continuously with the new intelligence/consciousness-centric mindset (higher structural capacity), and recognizing the presence of nonlinearity, complexity, change, and unpredictability (complexity mindset).

b.   The special ability to continuously optimize the intrinsic intelligence capacity of the individuals (every agent, if necessary) to enhance the collective intelligence of the organization, that is, intense internal focusing (quality intelligence-intelligence linkages) on nurturing, updating, and exploiting collectiveness capacity (networks, organization) at all time.

c.   The special ability of balancing high org-awareness (focus externally — external factors, anticipatory) and orgmindfulness (focus internally on the mental state of all agents) effectively to elevate collective intelligence (higher collectiveness capacity, optimal exploitation of the integrated self-powered intrinsic leadership capability).

d.   The recognition that enhancing stability is a basic incentive for elementary units (agents-centricity) to bind (high stability-centricity at all levels) — by exploiting intelligence/consciousness-centricity and network-centricity, and independency (agent-centric) and interdependency (network-centric and org-centric) appropriately.

e. The special ability to constantly update the mental space (behavioral schemata) of the interacting agents (information exchange, dialogue), and the culture of the organization through quality interconnectedness, deeper deliberation, acceptability/consensus, truthful engagement, information exchange, self-organizing communications, mutual influence, mutual trust, mindful culture, and intense orgmindfulness.

f. The special focus on the human mental dimension, including the mental stability of the agents, and mental cohesion of the organization (stability-centric, self-centric and org-centric, autopoiesis and symbiosis, achieving high positive relational parameter value, organizational justice, coherency, and evolution and co-evolution).

g. The special ability to change faster than the changing environment (also recognizing change is the only thing that never change), as well as to learn and adapt faster than all the other interacting agents, if needed (generative, proactive, learning leadership, red queen race, and high adaptive capacity).

h. The special ability to lead with comprehensive intelligence/consciousness management, information exchange, organizational learning, and knowledge sharing and creation at all levels (establishing a dynamic with 3C-OK as foundation).

i. The special ability to lead with new knowledge, theory, and strategy whenever necessary, that is, the (conceptual) leadership foundation is always evolving and emerging in nature (especially, when human agents are becoming better educated and well-informed) — constantly updating objectives/goals and strategies.

j. The special ability to nurture a swift and effective self-organizing dynamic for the organization at all levels, especially to solve difficult unpredictable problems (emergence-centric) — cascading effect, ambidextrous, well-integrated intrinsic leadership, high self-organizing capacity, and high emergence-intelligence capacity (high unifying capacity).

k. The special ability to recognize certain benefits and disasters in the continuous stasis and punctuated equilibrium cycle — especially, nurturing the capability to exploit any punctuation point collectively — high innovation and creativity.

l. The special ability to switch between the deliberate and emergent path without difficulty — exploit the co-existence of order and complexity. This approach also encompasses the ability to effectively exploit the predictable and makes substantial preparations for the unpredictable (high adaptive capacity).

m. The special ability that recognizes the characteristics of the changing rugged landscape (including the fact that a present optimal point may be a future minimal point, and vice versus).

n. The special ability that recognizes nonlinearity, sensitive dependence on initial conditions (butterfly effect), and potential benefits can be related — constantly looking out to reap the benefit of the butterfly effect.

o. The special ability to lead the followers to exploit certain spaces of complexity, innovatively and creatively (complexity-intelligence-centric, complexity management, to be the first to see a potential surface pattern, to be a first mover — better risk management and smarter evolver).

p. The special ability to exploit global forces, and recursive and auto-catalytic possesses that integrate the agents, networks, and the entire organization more effectively, and also with a special awareness on potential historical impact (hysteresis) — an action may have started earlier but it impact has not manifest fully yet.

q. The special ability to be futuristic and always focuses on certain future potential benefits (early warning, anticipative, scenario planning, nurturing high futuristic capacity) — first mover advantage.

r. The special ability to orchestrate the integration and emergence of intrinsic, lateral/collective, consultative/diffusive, learning, transitional, and latent leadership strategic thinking and dynamics, and to exploit them selectively depending on the situation — through broader consensus, decision-making, and more intense commitment (high leadership capacity, everybody is in charge).

s. The special ability to more realistically humanize the organization to a higher level of existence, a smarter evolver and emergent strategist, with deeper bio-logic and wisdom encompassing new vital intangible attributes such as compassion (high quality intelligence-to-intelligence linkages, social consensus, organizational justice, feeling organization, coherency, synergy, constructionist effect, and mental cohesion).

t. The special ability to recognize and lead a human organization as high finite dimension nonlinear complex adaptive system with an in-complete phase space. In this case, global optimality can never be achieved due to the presence of unknowns (hence, accepting the best possible satisficing outcome is a new thinking).

u. Finally, the unique ability to identify a new basin of attraction that may lead to a total organizational transformation (holistic view, profound transition, long and deep sighted, futuristic, wisdom) when a critical situation emerges.

The categories of leadership style that emerge from the intelligence leadership strategy are summarized in Figure 9.7, together with its linkages to some complexity associated attributes. Some of these styles can be exploited concurrently by the same leader depending on the situations and environment.

9.5 Conclusion

The intelligence leadership theory/strategy provides a more accurate glimpse into the highly complex traits/attributes and dynamics of the redefined leadership mindset, thinking, and goals, as well as their strategies, and micro processes (see Figure 9.7). Fundamentally, the new effective leadership has to focus on enhancing stability at all levels (agents, networks, and the entire system) as a basic goal (leadership capacity <=> stability-centricity; leadership capacity <=> unifying capacity). Thus, elevating the mental stability of agents, and achieving higher mental cohesion of the organization concurrently is a vital objective. In this respect, the new leaders must be effective enablers that are able to establish quality relationships (high relational capacity) and processes, and influence and orchestrate certain desired processes with the appropriate subtly to enhance performance, trust, commitment, and competitiveness. Very often, the processes required can be situational dependent, and where the organization is exactly located on the constantly changing rugged landscape must be known so that certain optimality ('fitness') can be achieved

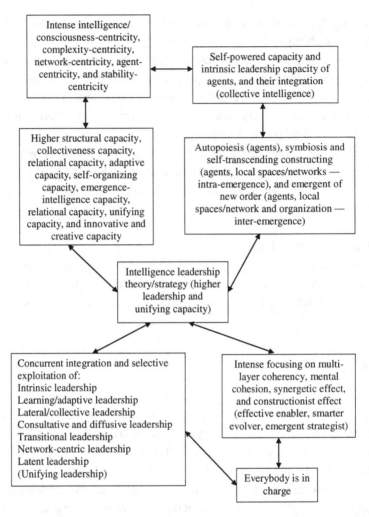

Figure 9.7 Different categories of leadership style that emerge from the intelligence leadership strategy and can be exploited selectively.

(adaptive leadership). In this case, the present leadership mindset and thinking is also critically space-time dependent.

In addition, for intelligent human organizations, effective leadership, autopoiesis and symbiosis, ambidexterity, self-transcending constructions, constructive networks nurturing and integration, and emergence are highly interdependent, indicating the significance of intelligence-intelligence linkages, complexity-intelligence linkages, and emergence-intelligence linkage. Apparently, mass consultative participation is a new criticality. Thus, new leadership with high mental calmness (soft voice and low key) must emerge with the local processes/networks and the upwards causation dynamic of the system concurrently, with a special focus on intelligence/ consciousness at different levels (nurturing structural capacity, collective-ness capacity, adaptive capacity, and mental cohesion, and exploiting rela-tivistic complexity). It is also important to note that certain fundamental phenomena and relationships due to the profound human mental instinct are associated with relativistic complexity exploitation (see relativistic complexity in Chapter 10). It is now more explicit that to be at the fore-front of the new leadership requires a more in-depth comprehension of the complex and nonlinear dynamics (*i*CAD) of *i*CAS, and intelligence/con-sciousness management, complexity management, network management, and mindful culture) provides the basic foundation (leadership capacity <=> innovative and creative capacity).

Thus, the new leadership must recognize that there is a critical shift in mindset, from favoring accurate forecasting alone (deliberate strategy) to the needs for a well-prepared smarter evolver and emergent strategist thinking — a need for better ambidextrous balancing (structurally, dynam-ically, and strategically). A vital factor is the intensity and quality of organizational integration and coherency (including a better governance system). In particular, the presence of more leaders/actors is beneficial, that is, higher leadership capacity is an intelligence advantage (see govern-ance in Chapter 10). Fundamentally, the leaders–followers gap must be reduced, the nonlinear relational parameter better exploited, and the intrin-sic leadership capacity and self-powered capacity of all agents are better utilized. In addition, in the human context, 'satisficing global optimality' may not be similar to achieving mathematical maximum coherency. In this respect, optimal functional coherency may encompass diversification — including the fact that organizational mental cohesion is beyond functional cohesion (see mental cohesion in Appendix 7).

In summary, the intelligence leadership theory/strategy is an intense intelligence/consciousness-centric, complexity-centric, and network-centric strategy that are both present-oriented and future-oriented, internal and external focus, lateral/collective and consultative, cultivating and unifying various capacities, enhancing the stability and innovation and creativity of all agents (constant new knowledge creation), focusing on coherency, synergy, and constructionist effect, and nurturing redefined competitiveness, resilience, and sustainability for the organization (see futurology in Appendix 7).

Under most circumstances, self-powered self-transcending constructions dynamic and its associated self-organizing capacity (agents, networks), and emergence-intelligence capacity (agents, networks, organizations) at different levels is most effective in highly intelligent human organizations where everybody is in charge.

The wicked leader is he who the people despise.
The good leader is he who the people revere.
The great leader is he who the people say,
"We did it ourselves."

Lao Tzu

Chapter 10

Relativistic Complexity and the Intelligence Governance Theory/Strategy

"Elevating self-organizing capacity and emergence-intelligence capacity is a critical focus of the new intelligence leadership"

"The presence of self-powered self-organizing governance is a critical requirement in the governance system of intelligent human organizations"

Summary

The first section of this chapter is an introduction to relativistic complexity (a significant component of the intelligent organization theory). The presence of intense intelligence/consciousness-centricity and 3rd order stability-centricity in the human world renders complexity relativistic. The impact of the human mental space is so tremendous that complexity is in the mind of the beholder, and predictability becomes highly subjective. In this situation, the state of relativistic static equilibrium may be beneficial. Certain spaces of complexity appear as spaces of relativistic order with surface patterns becoming more apparent. Such spaces must be creatively explored and exploited (higher exploratory capacity) leading to a more advanced level of intelligence advantage. In this respect, effective self-transcending constructions, high self-organizing capacity and emergence-intelligence capacity are significant attributes that the new leadership and governance system in intelligent human organizations must exploit. Holistically, the two strategies focus on concurrent exploitation of intelligence/consciousness-centricity and relative complexity, and optimizing the more comprehensive contributions of the integrated deliberate and emergent strategy.

Many issues/problems that present human organizations (nations, political systems, communities, business organizations, markets) are encountering due to accelerating changes (mindset, thinking, values, perceptions, expectations, redefined boundaries and high interactive dynamics) that cannot be well-managed with traditional knowledge and hierarchical practices are affecting governance and governance systems. Fundamentally, governance deals with power, interest, and conflict. The traditional governance systems are hierarchical, highly directed, controlled and managed, and the relational aspect has not been allocated sufficient priority resulting in extensive disparities. In the current complex dynamical and high interdependency environment, its weaknesses and constraints are highly apparent. The latter includes 'space-time compression'; incoherency in thinking, values, perceptions, and expectations between the leadership and the other agents; diversification in stakeholders' needs not accommodated; and constraints of current governance theories. Thus, a new theory that provides a more 'realistic' foundation is essential for deeper contemplation.

Primarily, recognizing the inherent strengths of human agents and the fundamental constraints/weaknesses of human organizations is a key foundation towards better adaptation, leadership, governance, resilience and sustainability. In all human organizations, the agents are intrinsic intense intelligence/consciousness sources that could easily transform their behavioral schemata. This observation contradicts the Newtonian/design paradigm, as the organizational dynamic of human agents is complex, nonlinear, constantly/continuously changing with limited predictability. In addition, human agents are self-centric, self-powered, stability-centric, independent and interdependent, network-centric and self-organizing due to high awareness. In this situation, high self-organizing capacity and emergence-intelligence capacity are new niches. However, this phenomenon can create new opportunities, innovation, and elevates competiveness; or destruction.

In particular, effective leadership and governance are spontaneously emerging key requirements in all human groupings — a primary trait for human collective survival. Historically, many organizations disintegrated because of the weaknesses in leadership and governance. Currently, with more knowledge-intensive and higher participative new agents (self-powered intrinsic leadership) possessing modified attributes that are dissimilar from the older generations (also due to the deeper integration of the economic, social, political, and environmental perspective), reduces consensus and collaboration, and renders governance and leadership even more nonlinear or dysfunctional. In particular, the traditional governance systems of more organizations are manifesting their constraints and incompetency, including incoherency due to new values and cultural pressure, and the wider spread of self-organizing networks. The emergent of informal networks is a more commonly observed phenomenon worldwide. Apparently, a deeper comprehension on the diminishing effect of the traditional organizational thinking (political, social, economic), governance capacity, precise strategic planning, decision making, hierarchical structure, communications and engagement, empowerment leadership, management, operations, and the highly nonlinear relational parameter is essential. Apparently, new principles of governance must emerge (intelligent human organization > thinking system + feeling system).

The new paradigmatic path of the intelligence governance strategy that exploits intelligence/consciousness-centricity, complexity-centricity, and network-centricity concurrently, introduces a new basic strategic path towards better adaptive governance and acceptance governance. The latter focuses on integrating self-powered self-organizing governance, reducing direct governance, and increasing e-governance and network-centric governance as a new necessity. In this case, the merits of adopting the intelligence leadership strategic approach simultaneously are more apparent. Hence, the new governance focal points must include more and better interconnected actors, the critical ability of self-organizing communications (supported by mobile/social media development), immersion of leadership nodes in networks (better exploitation of e-governance), increasing coherency of complex networks (exploiting interdependency of network of networks, and better network management), and elevating self-transcending constructions capability (higher self-organizing governance capacity and emergence-intelligence capacity) that better facilitates emergence through multi-level and 'multi-lateral' dynamics (complex adaptive networks <=> intelligent networks). Thus, the intelligence governance strategy emphasizes that mass lateral collectivity (acceptance governance) rather than selective enforced hierarchical empowerment as the more constructive approach in the present contact. In particular, the stability-inducing role of leaders and institutions are critical. Apparently, optimizing the 'everybody is in charge' phenomenon (whenever necessary) is a more viable option.

Keywords: Newtonian mindset, design paradigm, complexity mindset, intelligence mindset, intelligence paradigm, relativistic complexity, space of relativistic order, relativistic static equilibrium, exploratory capacity, proto-intelligence, intelligence/consciousness management, intelligence-intelligence linkage, emergence-intelligence linkage, emergence-intelligence dynamic, stability-emergence linkage, constructionist hypothesis, attractor, awareness, mindfulness, network management, orgmindfulness, mindful culture, complexity management, complexity-intelligence linkage, sensitive dependence of initial conditions, interdependency, space-time compression, unpredictable, basin of attraction, strange attractor, morphogenetic attractor, emergence, self-powered capacity, adaptive capacity, collectiveness capacity, self-centric, stability-centric, agent-centric, autopoiesis, constructionist hypothesis, intelligent person, self-organizing communications, self-organization, self-transcending constructions, emergence-intelligence dynamic, relational capacity, self-organizing capacity, emergence-intelligence capacity, unifying capacity, self-powered human agents, intrinsic leadership, intelligent person, space-time compression, relational friction, deliberate strategy, emergent strategy, deliberate-emergent auto-switch, ambidexterity, first mover advantage, governance, governance system, public governance, corporate governance, social media governance, stakeholder, governance capacity, 'multi-lateral' dynamic, coherency, synergetic, constructionist effect, direct governance, acceptance governance, adaptive governance, self-powered self-organizing governance, e-governance, intelligence governance strategy, hysteresis, intelligence leadership, relational-centric, leadership capacity, leadership field, network-centric governance, network theory, graph theory, node, link, random network, complex network, network of networks, small world network, complex adaptive network, artificial neural network, weak tie phenomenon, interdependent networks, strong ties, weak ties, power law, mental cohesion, intelligence advantage and intelligent organization theory.

10.1 Introduction: Redefining Human Complexity and Governance

10.1.1 *Contributions and constraints of the Newtonian mindset*

Inherently, humanity is group instinctive, primarily attracted by attributes such as race, religion, family, nationality, and employment. At present, an enormous number of organizations (ecosystems, communities, education institutions, corporations, military units/clusters, nations, regional institutions) of different nature and sizes exit in the human world. Historically, unknown number of civilizations have also appeared and disappeared leaving behind traces of complexity. In general, irrespective of their original mission, the social and political perspectives of these systems surface spontaneously wherever a group of human beings exists, and enlarges over time.

The fact that human beings, their organizations and the entire humanity have to survive initiates the impetus for adaptation, competition, dispute, and destruction. In particular, the economic perspective intensified when the industrial revolution started at the end of the eighteenth century (1760s to 1840s) that led to the establishment of a large number of business organizations, first in the UK and subsequently worldwide (employment and stakeholders emerges). After World War II, the entire global arena started to interconnected. More regional and global organizations/institutions are also established (economic, financial, political) [United Nations (UN), International Monetary Fund (IMF), Asian Development Bank (ADB), North Atlantic Treaty Organization (NATO), European Union (EU), and Association of South East Asian Nations (ASEAN)]. This development reflects the intensity, interdependency, and significance of networks, symbiosis, complex dynamics, and local versus global competition in the entire human world.

Apparently, human beings are the most sophisticated biological species ever exist on this planet. In humanity, deep formalization of structures and processes in governments, societies, political systems, businesses, and governance systems have been established spontaneously at different levels. Together with knowledge power and diversified technological developments, humanity possesses capabilities that are beyond the natural endowment of all other biological species. Certain features, characteristics, and dynamics (in particular, the intangible component) in the human world (for instance, the scale and power of battles and confrontations) are also never observed in the 'community' of other species. The primary source that enables this unique development is the human mental space — the intense intelligence/consciousness of the human thinking systems and their associated knowledge, theories, philosophy, and creation.

One significant scientific influence and enormous impact that trans-forms humanity into a technological-centric species and global commu-nity is due to the strong presence of the **Newtonian mindset** (order, linearity, equilibrium, planning, forecasting, and predictability), a machine-based (fundamentalism, reductionism, and Cartesian belief) and hierarchi-cal design paradigm that dominated the structures and dynamics of human organizations (top-down structure), and their leadership mindset and gov-ernance systems (hierarchical leadership, command and control, transfor-mational leadership). Thus, the Newtonian sciences have provided the conceptual foundation from early industrialization to futuristic thinking (forecasting, scenario planning, early warning), and have contributed sig-nificantly to humanity. However, the mindset, thinking, structure, leader-ship, strategy, and practice that emerge from these traditional scientific sources are manifesting their constraints and weaknesses leading to new predicaments. A key incoherency observed is due to the more apparent co-existence of order and complexity, and the emergent of intangible structures/networks with different interest and goals — resulting in greater dysfunction of the hierarchical structure.

10.1.2 *Boundaries and constraints of the design paradigm*

The introduction of the **design paradigm** (encompassing the cybernet-ics and systems engineering perspectives) of management and opera-tions emerges in the middle of the 20th century (derived from research done during World War II) for organizational problem solving (Ashby, 1956) greatly depended the Newtonian mindset. The key focus of the initial cybernetics perspective is to design organizations as systems with structural stability that could be regulated and controlled by manage-ment intervention (using feedback loops) — that is, highly hierarchical and centralized control (especially, in large organizations). The main weaknesses of this model are they do not take into account the 'non-rational' (emotional functions) behavior of human beings, the intense mental space of every agent, the self-powered and intrinsic leadership capability of human agents, the highly nonlinear relational parameter, the emergent aspects of their destructive collective behavior (internal destruction, intra-organizational destruction), and the increasing presence of complexity (see cybernetics in Appendix 7) — although, certain aspects of cybernetics are included/exploited in the complexity mindset and thinking.

The systems engineering perspective comprises the 'hard' system approach and the 'soft' system approach. The 'hard' system approach focuses on the internal consistency of modularized systems (their hierarchical structures and modular organization — reductionism). The 'soft' system approach concentrates on the problem definition of the 'whole' for human systems. Its design is to enable all stakeholders to observe the whole, to identify the diverse problem space, and to take a best collective decision. Again, the overall disadvantage of this paradigm is planned management interventions, highly hierarchical leadership, and not all agents are well-connected, integrated or informed (low agent-centricity). In this case, the significant self-stability of the agents is not always well managed leading to low collaboration — lack of agent-centricity.

The design paradigm is basically mechanistic in thinking with a slight inclusion of cybernetic perspective. It is important to recognize that a significant proportion of human dynamics inherently manifest evolutionary nonlinear behavior and unpredictability within and without the organization. Each human agent is self-centric, stability-centric, and thus, autopoietic. In complexity theory, the focus on the assumptions of organizational structural stability has been shifted to the non-equilibrium dynamics of open systems, and the autopoietic and self-organizing capabilities of the interacting agents — that is, an intense focus on spontaneous dynamics — a prominent process in humanity that requires greater attention. In the intelligent organization, the stability of all agents, certain networks, and the organization is a primary concern (stability-centric at all levels, agent-centricity with respect to the organization), and lateral/collective consultative participation is a natural requirement (quality intelligence-intelligence linkages, lateral/collective leadership, better collaboration, smarter evolver, emergent strategist). However, the Newtonian mindset and reductionist perspective can still be exploited selectively with the intelligence mindset due to the presence of relativistic complexity in the human world.

10.2 Introduction to Relativistic Complexity

10.2.1 *Intense human mental dimension and relativistic complexity*

The dominance and uniqueness of humanity is basically due to the intense intelligence/consciousness source embedded in every human thinking system. Otherwise, we are no different from other biological species, still wandering and surviving in jungles. The crossing of the profound threshold that allows human beings to think, create a character set and its associated language, accumulate knowledge, conceptualize theory, and exploit technology have greatly distinguishes humanity from the rest in this evolutionary world. Primarily, the behavioral schemata of human beings are complex, nonlinear, and constantly changing — significantly different from the simplicity of artificial life. In this respect, complexity in the human world is dissimilar from that of the physical world, as well as the other biological worlds.

Hence, in any higher order biological systems (those that possess a fairly well-connected neural network), the intense presence of its 'mental instinct' greatly transforms their characteristics and dynamics that arise from their basic 'biological instinct' alone. In particular, the dominant presence of the mental dimension in humanity is so intense that it renders complexity relativistic. This new capability redefines some spaces of mental complexity, as well as spaces of biological/physical complexity in human agents/networks/organizations — in general, as intelligence increases, complexity decreases (complexity is in the mind of the beholder). This transforms the characteristics of complexity and complex adaptive dynamics, and gives rise to new phenomena that are unique to the human world — **relativistic complexity, relativistic complex dynamics, and predictability is subjective** (intense intelligence/consciousness + complexity <=> relativistic complexity).

As this unique characteristic and capability of humanity is correlated with the high intensity of human intelligence, awareness, mindfulness, knowledge structures, theory, perception, subjectivity, and behavior schemata of the human interacting agents, it must be creatively exploited. In this case, a space of complexity may appear as a **space of relativistic**

order depending on the state of the intense intelligence/consciousness (individual and/or collective) source involved. Concurrently, predictability is subjective (more positive), and it can be elevated with intense intelligence/consciousness-centricity. Similarly, with the presence of an intense intelligence/consciousness space, dynamic equilibrium may be perceived as **relativistic static equilibrium**. In this case, the level of complexity in certain spaces of complexity that becomes/appears relative must be potential focal points — higher **explorative capacity**.

For simplicity, this development can be captured in a model, starting with an intelligence, complexity, and time space (I, C, t) (I denotes intelligence, C represents complexity, and t represents time). The axioms to be stated provide the basic foundation of the relativistic complexity theory (note: $dC/dt \neq 0$, as there is no static equilibrium in CAS, that is, change is always present). The first three axioms at the agent's level are as follows:

Axiom I

When $dI/dt \approx dC/dt$, a human agent exists in a space of order or dynamical equilibrium (stasis), that is, minimal or no change is observed.

Axiom II

When $dI/dt \gg dC/dt$, a human agent exists in a space of relativistic order, a surface pattern is observed, and some form of self-organizing capability is present, that is, the agent can innovatively and creatively explore and exploit this space of complexity.

Axiom III

When $dI/dt \ll dC/dt$, a human agent exists in a space of intense complexity, and some forms of adaptive capacity must be nurtured and elevated for continuity.

On a deeper perspective, relativistic complexity is also associated with the collective intelligence, orgmindfulness, org-awareness and philosophy of the organization. This recognition is stated in the next few axioms. In this case the collective intelligence, I_c, is involved, and $I_c > \Sigma I$ if the nurturing process has been synergetic.

Axiom IV

When $dI_c/dt \approx dC/dt$, the system/organization remains in a space of order or stasis.

Axiom V

When $dI_c/dt \gg dC/dt$ and $d^2I_c/d^2t \gg d^2C/d^2t$, some forms of 'patterned' dynamic surfaces indicating that the system is self-organizing, and emergence may occur (high self-organizing capacity, and emergence-intelligence capacity).

Axiom VI

When $dI_c/dt < dC/dt$, the system/organization moves into a space of high complexity or (relativistic) disequilibrium, either gradually or suddenly (punctuation point).

Axiom VII

When $dI_c/dt \ll dC/dt$ and $d^2I_c/d^2t \ll d^2C/d^2t$, spaces of high complexity density surfaces, and a punctuation point may appear suddenly, and the organization will move into the edge of in-deterministic chaos — towards disintegration.

In this respect, complexity in human world (at all levels — agents, networks, systems/organizations, and composite systems — including, nations and Gaia) defers from the physical world (complex systems) or even the lower-intelligence biological world (other complex adaptive systems). As complexity in this unique intelligence/consciousness intensive environment can be relativistic, the emerging spaces of relativistic order and relativistic static equilibrium must be better exploited by highly intelligent organizations (*i*CAS) — creating an advanced intelligence advantage that is greatly beneficial for any organizations in the current highly competitive situation — see Figure 10.1.

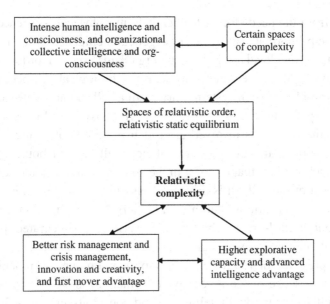

Figure 10.1 Complexity is relativistic with respect to intense human intelligence/consciousness.

10.2.2 *Stability-centricity, relativistic complexity and emergence*

As emphasized earlier, the physical/matter world (a small part of this Universe) appears to be embedded with an enormous spread of proto-intelligence. In this case, atoms are (physically) stability-centric and establish localized order. At the level of proto-intelligence, intelligence is perceived to exist when the physical stability-centric capability is present. For instance, atoms that are stable do not react, while atoms that are physically unstable react, leading to the formation of molecules which are relatively (structurally) more stable — also indicating the presence of a physical self-organizing capacity. Even the confinement effect at sub-atomic level is stability-centric. In this respect, physical structural stability (first-order stability) is the basis for structure formation, and the beginning and the basic foundation of the visible Universe. The existence of this unique relationship between intrinsic proto-intelligence and physical matter created the tangible physical world. Thus, the latter is the product of first-order emergence resulted from the needs for first-order stability (physical) — hence, establishing the primordial stage of the emergence-intelligence dynamic.

Next, at the level of biological organisms, second order stability, encompassing the (integrated) physical and biological perspectives surfaces. Examples of such systems vary from a cell to multi-cellular organisms, to a pack of wolves, and to an entire ecosystem. In second order stability, the dynamics involved are much more complex, including the phase transition, and the presence of not well-defined boundaries (for instance, a boundary that co-exist in the solid and liquid states depending on the need of the cell). It is driven by basic life-intelligence. For human agents and organizations, stability and emergence is a three-dimensional phenomenon; third-order stability encompassing the (integrated) physical, biological, and mental perspectives.

The presence of the high mental space is unique to humanity. The dominant presence of the 3rd component (mental) is created by the presence of intense individual intelligence and consciousness, as well as supported by the creation of integrated thoughts, concepts, perceptions, and the presence of (at least) a symbolic language. Apparently, emergence and intelligence are even more strongly interconnected and sophisticated in the human world. Therefore, there exists a different emergence-intelligence linkage in humanity, as compared to that of all other animal species (beyond basic biological complexity) due to the presence of the intense, intangible, abstract, and highly emotional human mental space.

The above analysis vividly revealed that **sustaining/enhancing stability is the most fundamental characteristic and objective of emergence** — that is, emergence is directly or indirectly driven by stability-centricity (and vice versa) at different levels (stability-centricity <=> self-organizing capability and emergence-intelligence capacity <=> emergent of order). Stability is linked closely to localized order, structure, robustness, autopoiesis, symbiosis, ambidexterity, and eventually the existence of a unique entity (self — 'I'). Over time, as the system dynamics spread localized order (from an agent to a network to an 'intended' system) can be achieved through self-enrichment processes and global order; although, the effect on every agent may not be similar. Thus, this analysis leads to the modification with the following inference; stated as the redefined postulate of **stability-emergence and emergence-intelligence**

linkages, also encompassing the emergence of **relativistic complexity** in the human mental space.

Law of Mental Stability (II)

For human beings and human organizations, mental stability (third-order stability) is a unique and vital requirement associated with 'human level emergence' (including corporations and nations, and involving relativistic complexity). It can only be fulfilled by much higher levels constructive autopoiesis, symbiosis, ambidexterity, and self-transcending constructions driven by intense individual intelligence/consciousness and collective intelligence/org-consciousness (in particular, focusing on the intangible, complex, and highly emotional mental space of every agent, and also exploiting spaces of relativistic order, and achieving relativistic static equilibrium for better risk management, and innovation and creativity). In this respect, the 'intended' and 'perceived' perspective of the agents/networks/organization must be coherent and synergetic — that is, constantly focusing on achieving higher organizational mental cohesion.

10.2.3 *Large emergence-intelligence capacity and effective self-transcending constructions*

In intelligent human organizations, possessing high self-organizing capacity is a necessity. In this case, self-organization is spontaneous whenever required. During its initial stage of conceptualization, it was recognized as the spontaneous process whereby agents in a CAS interact without the guidance of a blueprint (Kauffman's order for free — 1993, a significant attribute of CS/CAS). It is also the dynamic underlying the emergent of forms manifest in physical, chemical, biological, ecological, social, and cultural structures (the latter is confined to human organizations), that is, the spontaneous crystallization of order out of complexity in CS/CAS, including the prominent Prigogine's self-organizing system. Thus, self-organizing capability is the driver of emergence. Self-organizing systems possess states that are far-from-equilibrium. The dynamic is morphogenetic, that is, it favors certain states known as **morphogenetic attractors**. This dynamic fluctuates from incoherency to coherency, and also synergetic. However,

synergetics and some later research, including the intelligent organization theory reveal that self-organization is not totally order for free. There is a **latent internal impetus** that drives the self-organizing capability. As mentioned earlier, in a highly intelligence human organization, self-organization is driven by the individual intrinsic intelligence of the agents, and collective intelligence of the system.

In this respect, the 'spontaneous' self-organization in human organizations during emergence is self-transcending constructions instead. The latter is a dynamic that emerges from the **constructionist hypothesis** of **Philip Anderson** (1923–present), in 1972. Some complexity researchers, including **Jeffery Goldstein** have been working on this dynamic in the early 2000s. Self-transcending constructions involve some form of 'control mechanisms', and a host of structuring operations. In the intelligent organization theory, the emergent associated process is perceived to be constructional and 'spontaneous' (but driven by individual intelligence) during the initial stage (for instance, the formation of localized spaces/ networks), but greater subtlety is needed for better orchestration and construction subsequently (associate with the intelligence leadership strategy, as well as the collective intelligence of the organization). Overall, the process appears more 'spontaneous' when collective intelligence is well-nurtured so that constructive self-organization could be activated at punctuation points as well. In this respect, the presence of the self-transcending construction capability is critical during crisis management. This recognition and understanding is vital for effectively exploiting the integrated deliberate and emergent strategy, and the nurturing of an effective deliberate-emergent auto-switch — achieving higher ambidexterity. Thus, the 'automated activation' of the self-transcending constructions dynamic, especially when the unexpected suddenly surfaces, reflects the presence of intense collective intelligence in an organization, and the presence of a huge emergence-intelligence capacity is vital for competitive human organizations.

10.2.4 *Intelligence leadership strategy and relativistic complexity*

The recognition that all human interacting agents are intense intelligence/ consciousness sources, intrinsically self-powered, and naturally endowed with a certain level of intrinsic leadership capability is a significant aspect of the intelligence leadership strategy. Thus, an intelligence leader focuses on better satisficing optimal exploitation of all intrinsic intelligence sources, and the collective intelligence (lateral/collective) of the organization as the key paradigmatic shift. In this respect, every agent is a valuable asset, and the self-stability of all agents must be ensured — agent-centric.

According to the intelligent organization theory, ideally all human agents must possess intelligent person attributes, especially, the high self-powered capacity (not empowered) that when well-integrated elevates other capacities of the organization. Along the journey in life, such human agents constantly acquire knowledge, modify/update their knowledge structures and thinking (changes in behavioral schemata), and nurture new decision-making capability. The latter includes the highly valuable intrinsic ability of deciding and leading that has always been suppressed, at least to a certain extent in the traditional hierarchical organizations — due to aristocracy, bureaucratic and other leadership mentality. As indicated earlier, leadership has to be dispersed and shared by a larger group of people (more actors) to achieve higher team-working capabilities, so that both stasis and punctuated equilibrium can be better managed. This greater diversification and dispersion of roles, power, and responsibilities of leadership, as well as the integration of distributed knowledge (also better information sharing) helps to further enhance the collective intelligence and org-consciousness of the organization.

In addition, collective intelligence that arises from the synergetic integration of the individual intrinsic intelligence of all (if necessary) interacting agents is a strategic and critical entity in all human organizations. Fundamentally, it is significant to recognize that the intelligence-to-intelligence linkages in human groups are much more complex and nonlinear due to the intense human mental dimension (for instance, beyond 'chemical connectivity') — involving (at least) a sophisticated symbolic set, and abstract conceptions/perceptions. The presence of these complex linkages helps to nurture a sophisticated and intelligent organizational mental space. When the nurturing processes exceed a certain threshold it becomes emergent in nature, and the collective intelligence that emerges possesses new characteristics and abilities/capabilities (constructionist effect) that maybe absent in the individual agent. A higher level nonlinear collective intelligence capacity enables the organization to self-organize instantaneously and more effectively at all times — manifesting the presence of the critical 'everybody is in charge' phenomenon. Thus, the self-powered capacity of the human agents is fundamentally different from other species.

The intelligence leadership also concentrates on exploiting complexity-intelligence linkages, creating a situation where certain spaces of complexity are recognized as spaces of relativistic order by some intelligent agents/networks/organizations. The capability of the latter to explore and exploit relativistic order has to be valued and respected as a new niche. In such a situation, high innovative intelligence is vital. In addition, the integrated intelligence/consciousness-centric and complexity-centric approach leads to the emergence of lateral/collective leadership characteristics such as low key, soft voice, and calm mind. They are critical attributes for elevating new individual/organizational potentials, as intense 'collectiveness' can only be achieved if a highly lateral approach is adopted, and the latter is a vital condition for effective self-transcending constructions to be 'self-activated' in time of criticality.

In this respect, constantly nurturing and fine-tuning of the well-integrated deliberate and emergent strategy by the leadership and other agents must be spontaneous. To certain extent, the boundaries between order and complexity also become more obscure, and the presence of intense nonlinear intelligence is beneficial. Inevitably, leaders in all competitive human organizations have to depend on the redefined integrated deliberate and emergent paths that can be automatically interchanged when needed — very often substantial grey areas exist. In this context, there are now three perspectives/spaces to monitor and explore namely, order, relativistic order, and (high) complexity (see Table 10.1). Organizations that are able to identify more spaces of relativistic order (by elevating certainty and predictability in certain spaces of complexity) will vividly possess an advantage over their competitors. A leader/agent who is able to 'transform' a space of complexity into a space of relativistic order (those embedded with high values must be swiftly explored and exploited) is in a better position to observe the 'surface pattern' first.

In this case, being the first to recognize an emerging surface pattern (opportunity or problem), achieves the first-mover advantage, better risk

Table 10.1 Some characteristics associated with the three different spaces (order, relativistic order, and high complexity).

Space / Characteristic	Space of Order	Space of Relativistic Order (certain Space of Complexity)	Space of High Complexity and Punctuation Point
Path	Linear and predictable	Linear, nonlinear, and surface pattern is recognizable	Nonlinear, and surface pattern is not apparent, or does not exist
Strategy	**Deliberate** (low innovation and creativity, common knowledge, detail planning is significant, and forecasting is possible and useful)	**Deliberate and emergent** concurrently exploited, high innovation and creativity (better risk management), both planning and nurturing are involved	**Emergent** (presence of high collective intelligence is vital, towards better crisis management), intense nurturing before crisis is essential and beneficial
Degree of Freedom	Zero to low	Low to relatively high (still manageable)	Very high (with unknown unknowns) and may not be manageable
Examples	Any mechanical system, or an artificial information system	A biotechnological R&D space (always there), or any intense research frontiers	A worldwide financial crisis, or an enormous tsunami/landslide (sudden and surprising)
Leadership (Intelligence)	May be partially hierarchical — but ideally more lateral, collective, and consultative	Lateral/collective, towards 'everybody is in charge', and latent leadership is beneficial	Ideally, 'everybody is in charge' must be present (when needed), otherwise the system self-destruct

management, higher agility, adaptation, and competitiveness. Effective leaders will have to make preparation for this 'relativistic' endeavor, and ensure that their agents are able to identify and function in such spaces innovatively at all time. In highly intelligent human organizations, this ability to 'expand' the (perceived) human orderly/certainty dimension (through constant new knowledge creation) provides a new path for higher innovativeness, competitiveness, resilience, and sustainability. In addition, it is significant to note that even at a punctuation point, such as a worldwide financial crisis, an emergent of order still possible, although some of the agents/networks/organizations no longer exist. Therefore, the emergent strategy must be nurtured simultaneously with the planning of the deliberate path so that when there is a crisis (sudden, destructive, and unpredictable) the deliberate-emergence auto-switch can be self-activated.

In addition, focusing on complexity in the human world encompasses the mental dimension. The critical focus for better holistic group/team leadership participation is on enhancing the stability of the mental space at all levels (agents/networks/organization and beyond — environmental). Hence, a fundamental foundation of the intelligent complex adaptive dynamic for global/organizational stability is the stability of all agents. It is vital to constantly remember that the human mental space is a highly nonlinear emotional space. This recognition will lead to better organizational mental cohesion, resilience, and sustainability when the survival/status of all its agents is ensured.

10.3 Transformation in the Normative Foundation of Governance

10.3.1 *Traditional governance, governance theory and governance systems*

Governance (a complex integrated social, political, and economic structure/system and dynamics) is another inevitable requirement/feature in human existence. In general, the presence of proper and **acceptable governance** is crucial whenever a group of human beings coalesce irrespective of their primary purpose or functions (community, government, corporation, financial market, or regional institution). Therefore, governance (**public governance, corporate governance**, non-profit governance, environmental governance, **social media or e-governance**) is a necessity that emerges 'inherently' whenever a formal or informal group of human agents and their associated activities need governing for better coherency. Again, this necessity is partially due to the self-centric and stability-centric of the human agents, as well as the organizations they are associated with. In this respect, the primary objective of all governance systems should be to establish and implement better and deeper collectivity (higher collectiveness capacity) to achieve more sustainable organizational performance — for both the actors/leaders and non-actors.

For instance, in a nation, effective public governance must align leadership decisions/policies with citizens' interests/survival — that is, concurrently towards a more holistic balanced/coherent national (economic, societal, power) development, and nurturing of citizenry (agents' stability at all levels). Similarly, for a business corporation, effective corporate governance must align the various stakeholders' interests, and top management decisions and actions to achieve a better working environment and higher competitiveness simultaneously (employees, customers, and other stakeholders). On the global basis, the leadership roles and the associated competition of human global governance is highly complex embedded deep political interest — currently, the failure of human global governance is apparent. Even for an 'informal/intangible' system such as a market, its governance system may not be formal/tangible but it is still 'observable' — at least its presence can be felt.

Basically, the traditional governance approach concentrates tremendously on defining/designing rules and actions, control, compliance, and also verifying performance supported by a hierarchical structure and empowerment processes. In this respect, traditional governance is greatly dominated by how an organization is constituted, led/directed, controlled, and managed — very often consciously or subconsciously introducing a high level of rigidity (intense Newtonian mindset — no acceptance for errors/mistakes).

Conceptually, governance (normative governance theories, concepts, and traditional practices) concentrates on three basic entities namely, **power** (appropriate distribution), **interests** (intensity of differences and diversification), and **conflicts** (problems/issues/priorities incoherency, their spread and frequency of emergent) that will greatly affect both the internal and external environment, development, competitiveness, resilience, and sustainability of organizations and their agents — in numerous perspectives, including the entire humanity itself. Vividly, a fourth critical parameter that must be included is the **relationships** (relational parameter, organization injustice, 'feeling' organization) among agents, and between agents/networks and their organization. The human relational parameter (relational friction) is a highly nonlinear and complex parameter that requires deep and subtle management. For instance, a deep social gap reveals a significant lack of shared well-beings in public governance. The above illustration provides a general boundary of governance and its systems — see Figure 10.2.

Apparently, a governance system is a vital subsystem of all human organizations that focuses on the diversification and better management of power, interests, conflicts, relationships, and objects of regulation (largely

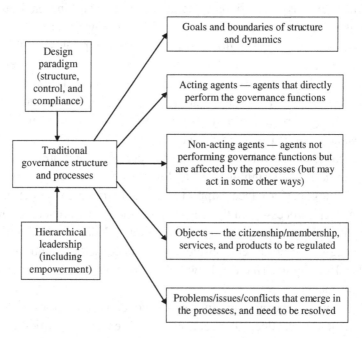

Figure 10.2   The basic structure and dynamics of a traditional governance system.

organizational, including citizenship, employment, service, product). Similar to other types of human systems, very often it also encompasses an important intangible component beyond the formal structure and expected dynamics — that is, involving informal/intangible ('invisible') actors/networks/localized spaces that surface spontaneously (often with some associated reasons). Thus, the critical needs for collectiveness and org-stability require certain level of leading and co-ordination on thinking, behavioral schemata, interconnectivity, dependency and interdependency, and collectiveness and adaptation — largely due to the contradicting self-centric autopoiesis (self-stability) of human agents (leaders/actors and non-actors alike) versus the 'collective objectives' of the organization (org-stability). However, the responsibilities and functions of a traditional governance system very often focuses more on the organizational needs and priorities, but not so much on the states and requirements of agents due to the hierarchical structure/leadership thinking. Consequently, some non-actors are neglected or sacrificed. In such a situation, some agents' instability is high, the rights of agents as stakeholders are not well recognized, and therefore an 'inherent' incoherency exists.

In summary, the basic aim of a traditional governance system is the creation of a better order/structure, and always seeks static equilibrium (does not exist in complex adaptive dynamic) by exploiting the design paradigmatic thinking and strategies — hierarchical leadership, empowerment, command and control, low adaptation ('do not rock the boat' mindset), and unbalanced priority. In this case, the role of bureaucracies as a source of stability is highly preferred — resulting in significant imbalance between the organization and certain agents/networks within. In this situation, very often it is those at the bottom of the hierarchical structure that are negatively affected (presence of upwards causation is minimal). However, governance is a complex and multi-level phenomenon involving a large collection of heterogeneous agents who needs and expectations are highly diversified. Consequently, frequent existence of (mass) discontentment and disparity, and the rising impact of complex networks in its structure (large informal network of networks) and dynamics (nonlinearity, incoherency, mental diversification, and unpredictability) clearly revealing the inefficiency and negative consequences of the traditional governance system.

10.3.2 *Some key complications/weaknesses in traditional governance systems*

Basically, a significant requirement in the current environment is acceptable power distribution (narrowing power differentials) among all agents (leaders — actors, followers — actors, and non-actors), better coherency between intended and perceived (construed) values and expectations, according to some formal and informal rules. Conceptually, a holistic consensus is significant — or at least increases the degree of consensus (towards better mental cohesion). However, in reality, differences and non-synchrony are still present in many regional institutions, nations, and corporations. At the extreme, dominant leaders with absolute power continue to render 'governance' meaningless to the masses — can be easily observed in some countries.

As indicated, due to present higher living sophistication, governance in humanity encompasses integrated perspectives, including social, political, economic, and even the environmental — to a great extent elevating its level of complexity beyond 'mass comprehension'. This integration inevitably escalated the complexity and incoherency of governance in the current human world. For instance, in public governance, as politics and administration are more deeply integrated, more agents are subjected with binding policies that may not be transparent. In addition, as present agents are better self-powered by the social media and education (possessing higher self-powered capacity) rather than by the leadership, the leader-follower gap is expanding rapidly.

In general, some interesting factors that added on to the non-synchrony and disparity, and needed deeper analysis and comprehension are as follows:

- **Increasing Stress of Space-Time Compression**
  In the present context, the first significant governance complication arises from '**space-time compression**' which is a consequence of escalation in speed of interactions, and increases in linkages and intensity of coupling (primarily due to globalization, and the swift development of wireless/mobile/social media technology — the substantial increase in information processing capacity, spreading

interdependency, and the 'shrinking' world effect), leading to rapid elevation in complexity even in basic living. Human beings become 'well-informed' (or over-informed leading to confusion), and self-organizing communications intensified leading to potential rapid changes in thinking and situation interpretation or misinterpretation.

Very often, the necessity of swift decision-making is becoming more critical. The latter has also created discontentment in the masses when they are left out of the decision-making process — especially, in public governance. Under extreme condition, this large space-time compression effect also elevates mental stress, and may ignite an economic or political crisis (punctuation point) more frequently due to the unpredictable nonlinear behavior (incoherency) of the agents, networks, the organization, and its environment — lack of **mental cohesion**. Thus, the leadership must be aware that what appear to be small perturbations at time may result in enormous and rapid irreversible changes (butterfly effect).

- **Incoherency in Leadership Mindset and Agents Redefined/ Construed Expectations**
  Concurrently, there is also a general increasing direct mismatch between the traditional leadership mindset/paradigm (centralized/ omnipotent power and hierarchical control thinking, aristocratic, individual leadership) and agents redefined values, expectations, and perceptions (better power distribution and higher recognition for contributions at all levels is necessary) — in some situations, it is due to the leadership reluctance to change. In particular, governance bureaucracy depending on precedence may be obsolete due to constant rapid changes — hierarchical dysfunction. Even when the mindset of the leaders and agents is synchronized, there are indirect incoherency between the 'intended' leadership and the 'perceived' leadership due to the construal and self-construal effect of the human agents. In this respect, leaders must have a stronger regards and deeper comprehension of the human social psychological aspect to achieve higher collectiveness capacity. In particular, the mental state of the agents, and their perception of the leadership and the organization are significant aspects that determine overall coherency.

Under certain complex circumstances with rapid causation, the emergent of informal localized spaces with different expectations and mission emerges (complex networks with new values and 'local' cultural pressure that do not synchronize with that of the organization) is becoming more common. In this case, leaders that attempt to regulate all details by legislation and administrative procedures are losing respect and no more effective (minimal or no collaboration). At the extreme, every intervention may result in unintended consequences. Inevitably, no recognition, and contradicting mindset and thinking (values, belief, ethics, and culture — prominent in international businesses) cause relational/psychological discomfort to the masses. In addition, social/organizational injustice and unfairness (widening of wealth gap, social inequalities, merging of political and economic power confined to a small group, and some legal structures) always exists with detailed regulations, as only a 'preferred' minority (empowerment) will benefit from such a situation.

Thus, a key vulnerability of traditional governance and its systems is the increasing non-synchrony in thinking, ideology, system structure, practices, and expectations between the leadership (confined to a few individuals) and other agents. The lack of collectiveness results in higher mass skepticism, scrutiny, and criticism. This is concurrently elevated by the lack of information sharing. As a primary purpose and focus of governance is 'stability control' [ensuring better social cohesion, political consensus, power and economic (wealth) distribution, and higher overall performance (individuals and their organization) and sustainability of the organizations], constructive mass participation and acceptance (lateral and consultative) is beneficial. However, the traditional approach is still bureaucratic, and hierarchical/preferential due to prominent imposition (over reliance on hierarchical leadership), and empowerment of selective actors (structuralism, and restricted information sharing/confidentiality), while the rest are 'restricted' actors or non-actors.

In particular, a system with low and distorted information flow (including, feedback) possesses low or incoherent adaptive capacity, collectiveness capacity, self-organizing capacity, and emergence-intelligence capacity. For instance, a 'state-centric' governance system because of the many veto points creates information deficiency (poor feedback), and a lack of socio-emotional well-being exists (mental incoherency). This will lead to unidirectional or no communication (Abilene paradox) that is disastrous. Consequently, such a situation may also leads to internal conflicts, dysfunctional activities or even ('innovative') destruction — as any incoherency may swiftly multiply by the butterfly effect pushing the system into an in-deterministic chaotic space (already manifesting in some countries). In this respect, it is important to note that human agents (due to their intrinsic emotional mental space) that are trapped in 'local minima' (local spaces with no stability) can be highly frustrated and destructive.

- **Stakeholders' Dissimilar Needs at Different Levels**
  With decades/centuries of existence, many current governance systems are multi-level and highly sophisticated (complex network). Mutual understanding, agreement, and action that must be fulfilled are diminishing or absent. In practice, at the microscopic level, it is highly significant to recognize that human agents are autopoietic and self-centric. The thinking of agents pursuing basic needs, and those beyond pursuit of basic needs (very often, those in the leadership) are greatly dissimilar. All agents in an organization are stakeholders (citizens in a nation, employees in a business corporation), and that status must be correctly recognized. If their status as stakeholders is devalued or disrespected, discontent will surface (for instance, when citizens and foreign talents in a country are perceived to be in the same stakeholders group).

  As stated earlier, the presence and/or perceived presence of organizational injustice and lack of mutual consensus have intensified due to the modified beliefs, values, and expectations of the diversified agents, and the profound deficiencies in the social and relational dimension. In many governance systems, the common problems/issues involved are general welfare, justice, individual (human) rights, or even fundamental beliefs, resulting in conflicts (or weak consensus) between the establishment and challenging agents/groups/networks. Also as indicated, with the rapid advancement in technologies, and the development of internationalization/globalization (broader intense coupling that modifies values), disgruntled agents swiftly self-organized into informal/'unintended' networks — leading to a larger set of governance complications.

More networks (self-organizing local spaces) that are not part of the formal structure are also surfacing rapidly and intensively in the current dynamic — resulting in the emergent of more conflicting decision-making nodes (both in the real world and virtual world). The informal intrinsic self-powered dynamic substantially redefined the intangible structure, and destabilized/challenged the formal traditional structure. Co-existence issues due to differing self-centricity and stability-centricity at multi-level (agents, networks, organizations, and the entire humanity) activities intensify. For instance, policy failure and failing political attempts to improve social and economic conditions, and abrupt 'local' catastrophic development are more prominently observed. A weak and/or non-credible political leadership becomes more apparent as the capacity and quality of governance quickly diminishes to an unfavorable level. The overall development (in particular, those contributed by the great dissent of agents) will lead to the more frequent surfacing of spaces of intense complexity (due to 'destructive' circular causation and self-organization), as well as punctuated disequilibrium (abrupt catastrophic events).

At the moment, another vital new trend has been emerging — a more direct confrontation between younger agents/stakeholders (new values and cultural pressure) and older leaders leading to generation-gap incoherency. Due to rapid economic development (affluence and independency), and more emphasis on education (foreign education, as well as easier access to information/knowledge — omnipresence of media) in many parts of the world, these new agents possess rather different behavioral schemata with diverse needs and aspirations — as compared to the older agents. The newer agents are more aware, self-aware, knowledge intensive, better informed, interconnected with accelerated communications and interactions, expose to greater cross-perspective influences, and financially independent, hence, resulting in a new generation of agents with rather different mindset. This is an emerging worldwide phenomenon. They (rightly or wrongly) constantly seek greater organizational/social justice, modified governance arrangements and dynamics (changes), leading to greater complexity and nonlinearity.

- **Constraints of Existing Governance Theories**
  Consequently, many contemporary governance theories and practices including agency theory, stakeholder theory, steward theory, and sustainability theory which emphasize hierarchical control and empowerment are revealing their constraints and inefficiency. In general, very often traditional leaders/actors due to the hierarchical structure do not fully comprehend the needs of the masses (especially, their new demands). The newer agents who possess higher 'mobility' often challenge such a governance/leadership thinking and structure more aggressively — resulting in greater social and political dissatisfaction, organizational injustice (actual or perceived), indifference, no loyalty, and surfacing of 'free' or 'semi-free' agents (agents with no long-term commitment, for examples, foreign talents, transnational migrants, or part-time/contract employees). The traditional governance system lacking in lateral/collective engagement, convening, and unifying abilities appears to be self-contradicting as the state-society, society-individual, and organization-employee relationships become highly complex, obscure, and disconnected. This heightened incoherency as both the spread and depth of mass integration is swiftly diminishing.

  Apparently, the traditional features/attributes of hierarchical leadership theories and practices, and supported by existing governance theories are reducing in efficiency, while the intrinsic self-powered self-organizing capability of agents is escalating and demanding deeper attention. Therefore, a crucial thinking that current leaders should embrace in human organizations is more intensely manifestation of their complex adaptive characteristics (including 'sensitive' characteristics such as local instability, presence of complex networks, and the butterfly effect), and towards a governance system that can manage diversification, rapid changes, a deeper and more complex dynamic, and unpredictability through better mass participation is crucial. Thus, deeper comprehension of the varying characteristics of human agents and more tactical management of the network meso-structure (network of networks, informal local spaces) are highly essential for elevating governance efficiency. In particular, the reality of unpredictability can be stressful and fearful for both actors/leaders and non-actors alike.

Consequently, a highly responsive governance system featuring better integrated adaptability at all levels (agents, networks, organizations, and the environment) are preferred. Thus, focusing on self-organizing capacity, and self-organizing sub-groups or networks/ local spaces that are incoherent with the global/holistic system is a new crucial leadership advantage. In this respect, a greater awareness and participation in emergent processes is vital (possessing a high emergence-intelligence capacity is necessity). Apparently, the new capabilities and their link to more innovative governance capacity must be better comprehended, explored, nurtured, and exploited.

10.3.3 *Recognizing additional foundations for nurturing quality governance capacity*

For all adaptive and competitive human organizations, nurturing a higher quality governance capacity is critically essential. In public governance, a 'quality' governance capacity is a vital asset/resource for effective government, and similarly in corporate governance, it is a significant asset/ resource for effective management and operations. The new capacity should encompass redefined multi-perspective thinking and strategies including, dynamical complexity, network-centricity, nonlinearity, uncertainty, self-organizing capability, tipping point, unpredictability, emergent of new order, and lateral/collective leadership — recognizing that 'no one leader has all the answers'.

Although many leaders are aware of some of the existing problems/ issues but initiating a change is difficult as there is no viable option — in particular, the absence of a 'common language', and no new leadership model or paradigm that are totally acceptable. In this respect, what are the possible new principles of governance and leadership? A key concern and focal point of the new leadership should be the stability-centricity of the human agents, and that human thinking systems, the sources of human emotions, in particular, anger, fear, stability-centricity, and perception are highly nonlinear and risk-intensive. Anger and fear of the agents when manifested to a certain level can be destructive to other agents, as well the entire system.

In general, towards a 'multi-lateral' endeavor (more collective participation with higher trust and respect for every agent in all perspectives — including informal networks) that reduces relational friction (as there is a great need for closer and more enhancing intelligence-intelligence linkages, and higher collectiveness capacity — presence of a mindful culture), instead of a hierarchical multi-level structure and dynamics is a key starting point. Relational friction is a highly nonlinear variable that could easily shift the system into a space of in-deterministic chaos. Thus, leadership with deeper insights, in particular, focusing on collectiveness (with the leadership included as actors in the localized networks), enhancing interdependency and exploiting independency (self-powered capacity), and the critical nonlinear relational aspects is inevitable. Consequently, a new thinking and transformation is one that must encompass change, integrated mass participation (collectiveness), complexity (new opportunities), network-centricity (interconnectivity, truthful engagement), and self-organization/self-transcending constructions (higher self-organizing capacity and emergence-intelligence capacity) with higher autonomy to elevate the **governance capacity**.

In a constantly and rapidly changing environment, the capacity of governance must be 'sufficient and good enough' to handle/manage or even exploit the swift changes to enhance the resilience and sustainability of the organization. Inevitably, a deeper comprehension on the inherent fundamentals of human agents and organizations is essential. In this respect, it becomes crucial to focus on two basic vital and integrated aspects that better define governance and governance system. The first focus is with respect to the characteristics of the human agents — **individualistic characteristics**. A deeper recognition of the characteristics of the current human agents is the first critical step towards better governance or governance systems. They have to be analyzed earlier and must be subtly integrated. Some of the important characteristics are re-listed as follows:

- Human agents are intelligence/consciousness intensive sources.
- They possess self-powered capacity and intrinsic leadership capability.

- They are intrinsically self-centric and stability-centric — autopoietic, independent.
- They are guided by a changing behavioral schemata that are complex, nonlinear, emotional, and constantly changing.
- They encompass an intense mental dimension (relativism) — indicating the significance of mental-stability, coherency, synergy, and presence of relativistic complexity.
- They can be unpredictable — the human thinking systems are intrinsically nonlinear/emotional complex adaptive systems that can be logical — defensive routines versus voluntary collaboration.
- They are different from agents in other complex adaptive systems because of their intense intelligence and consciousness (human intelligence, awareness, mindfulness, mental space, and relational friction are nonlinear) — independency versus interdependency.
- They are intensively interconnected by wireless/mobile/social media technology — digital revolution, self-organizing communications.
- Every agent in a governance system must be a stakeholder (citizenship, shareholder, employee, member) that possesses certain individual rights, interests, and status.
- Every agent would prefer to be an acting/active agent (actor rather than non-actor) to a certain extent (self-powered, intrinsic leadership) depending on the situation or environment (in this respect, lateral/collective participation is important).
- Every agent is complex with diversified needs, including basic social, economic, and mental necessities — human stability is highly complex.

Due to the heterogeneity of human agents in human organizations, the performance of different local spaces/networks can be rather dissimilar from the global system, resulting in incoherency, especially, the presence of local spaces with 'local minima' (no stability at both the agent and network level) can be disastrous. However, the heterogeneity of agents could also elevate the rate of innovation — indicating that the presence of diversification can be advantageous.

The second key focal point is the **holistic (collectivistic) characteristics** of the organization (the fact that it is intrinsically a composite complex adaptive system embedding a multi-level structure and dynamics). Some of these characteristics are as follows:

- The agents/networks within a human organization can be interconnected and interdependent in varying degrees — due to the presence of certain 'local' impetus (self-enrichment processes) — symbiosis versus autopoiesis.
- There are certain levels and quality of communications and engagement involved — both positive and negative (affecting consensus and voluntary collaboration).
- Networks/local spaces (local/network collective intelligence) within the organization surfaces spontaneously (network of networks, may contradict formal structure, self-enrichment processes versus global forces).
- Thus, human organizations possess self-organization/self-transcending constructions capability — driven by the latent impetus (intelligence of the agents and/or collective intelligence of the network and/or system, thus, the presence of high self-organizing capacity, and emergence-intelligence capacity is vital).
- The holistic emerging dynamic is complex adaptive — exploiting co-existence of order and complexity, continuous learning, knowledge creation/accumulation, and adaptation (presence of high collectiveness capacity, and adaptive capacity is vital).
- Co-evolution exists within and without the organization (agent/network versus organization, organization versus 'ecosystem'/Gaia).
- A human organization being a complex adaptive system is sensitive dependence on initial conditions — butterfly effect — unpredictable changes can happen suddenly (tipping point, punctuation point).
- Complexity in human organizations is relativistic if it is highly intelligent — possessing the capability of exploiting spaces of relativistic order and relativistic static equilibrium, and reflecting higher innovation and better risk management is highly beneficial.
- A human organization is a high finite dimension nonlinear dynamical system with incomplete/unknown variables — in-deterministic and unpredictable — that is, no optimal global solution due to incomplete phase space (seeking optimal satisficing solution is the best possible option).

Consequently, recognizing the intrinsic strengths human agents and constraints of human organizations is a highly crucial and beneficial starting point for new normative governance concepts to emerge. These two fundamentals introduced in Chapter 2 are re-stated below:

- The intelligent organization theory emphasizes that the inherent strengths of all intelligent human organizations is the intense intelligence and consciousness (awareness and mindfulness) of the human interacting agents. Thus, each of these sources (in particular, mindfulness) must be well-integrated and exploited. This recognition re-confirms that a paradigmatic shift towards intelligence/consciousness-centricity is most beneficial, as it serves as the foundation pillar of human longevity.
- Next, the constraints of human organizations include the fact that they are intrinsic complex adaptive systems (high finite dimensionality) possessing a very large number of variables or inputs — and not all are well-defined or known. This situation reduces the accuracy of analyzing human organizations (in particular, mathematically). Thus, formulating a mathematical model of a human system/organization (for instance, a financial market, a social community) is at best an approximation — an estimated model with estimated outputs (contradicts the Laplace belief). The nonlinear and sensitive dependence on initial conditions characteristics of human organizations further elevated unpredictability. In this respect, there are only best possible (satisficing) solutions and no global optimality in human organizational dynamics and outputs, as their phase space is never completely known (that is, can only optimize the best possible attractor observed). These constraints must always be in the mind of the leadership during decision making.

Hence, recognizing the strengths and attributes of the agents, the constraints and dynamics of the system/organization, and the rapid increase in complexity in its environment (internal and external) vividly indicate that a transformation in governance mindset is inevitable. Fundamentally, the new strategic thinking of governance that involve all intelligence/consciousness sources, lateral and changing structure (especially, the intangible component), interactive and new unifying processes at all levels (including the meso-structures), and collective decision and practices is more favorable. Thus, a larger and better quality governance capacity that helps to elevate the flexibility, resilience, and sustainability of the system must include a well-integrated intelligence/consciousness management, complexity management, and network management as the global approach.

10.4 The Holistic Intelligence Governance Theory/Strategy

10.4.1 *Self-organizing governance and quality governance capacity*

Apparently, current leaders (government, community, and business leadership) must recognize that centralized, deliberate, hierarchical, and bureaucratic authority is no longer feasible or acceptable in totality. The new leadership thinking and governance theory must concentrate on the inherent strengths of agents, constraints of the organizations, spontaneous self-organizing dynamic of local spaces, exploitation of networks, and emergence-intelligence dynamic of human organizations — self-organizing governance and higher unifying capacity. This spontaneous adaptive and emergent dynamic (constant/continuous changes, new order) in the human world that encompasses the various self-organizing capabilities (self-organizing communications, self-organizing capacity, emergence-intelligence capacity), localized order (network, network of networks) leads to the creation of more decision-making nodes (formal and informal), and emergence of new actors (more intense collaborative integration is needed). Therefore, ideally, the dynamics orchestrated in human organizations must drift towards more integrative multi-lateral interactions (engaging individual agents and networks, including informal networks, and across network of networks) by the leadership (e-governance, network governance).

As a general guide, there are certain changing characteristics in human organizations and their governance systems that can be more cautiously explored and exploited for elevating the quality of governance capacity. First, every agent should be directly or indirectly associated

with the governance holistic engagement — that is, more actors is beneficial (this is also a new preference of agents — especially, the younger
agents with higher independency). Next, the new governance dynamic
should continuously encompass change — that is, the governance
dynamic with continuous collective learning and adaptive ability (new
expertise), exploit changing complexity and new networks, create new
coherency with mass consensus, and the generation of fresh innovative
ideas is essential. Concurrently, it is vital to recognize that human relationship (relational friction) is highly nonlinear (a nonlinear parameter
that constantly changes its functionality with complexity and unpredictability). The **relational capacity** can be elevated with better alignment of
leadership and governance relationships. Thus, ideally a comprehensive
set of socio-informational linkages is presence. Higher governance
capacity could be achieved only if the following features are also present
namely, quality interconnectivity, holistic truthful engagement (deeper
consensus and collaboration), balancing independency and interdependency (ambidexterity), cognitive flexibility, diminishing direct governance, increasing self-organizing governance and e-governance (beyond
efficient e-government services alone), and elevating collective intelligence (network, network of networks, organization) at all levels. Many of
these indicators are important attributes closely associated with the
nonlinear relational parameter (a higher positive relational parameter
value is crucial).

In this respect, self-organization or self-transcending constructions is
strongly affected by the speed of interactions (collaboration) of agents,
multiplication of linkages, networks formation/emergence, and global
space-time compression. These self-organizing attributes/processes are
significant and inevitable spontaneous abilities that respond to change (the
inherent presence/impact of change differentials). Thus, possessing
intense self-organizing capability is beneficial when there are rapid
changes — establishing better global (higher level) coordination and
synergy. However, organizational dynamic that occurs without a central
control is not acceptable with the present leadership mindset. Thus, a
change in the leadership thinking, behavioral schemata, and expectations
is essential — reaffirming the significance of the intelligence leadership
strategy, as creative self-transcending constructions dynamic is closely

linked to the collective intelligence of the local spaces (self-organizing capacity), as well as the organization (emergence-intelligence capacity). Similarly, in public governance 'aligning' the evolutionary dynamic of government institutions is vital. Thus, fundamentally the intelligence paradigmatic shift is a necessity for better governance and governance systems. Instead of absolute control and hierarchical empowerment, switching towards orchestrating innovative collectivity, encompassing local spaces/networks and self-organizing processes with more intrinsic leaders' or actors' participation is a preferred dynamic (e-governance, network-centric governance). The above analysis is summarized in Figures 10.3 and 10.4.

10.4.2 *The integrated intelligence/consciousness management and complexity management approach*

The better integration of the three management processes (intelligence/consciousness management, complexity management, and network

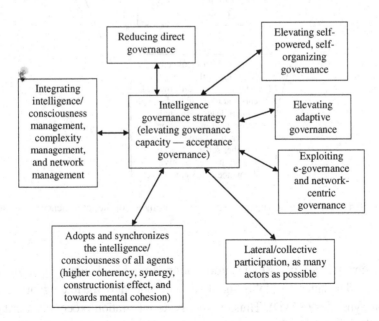

Figure 10.3 Some key focal points of the (holistic) intelligence governance strategy.

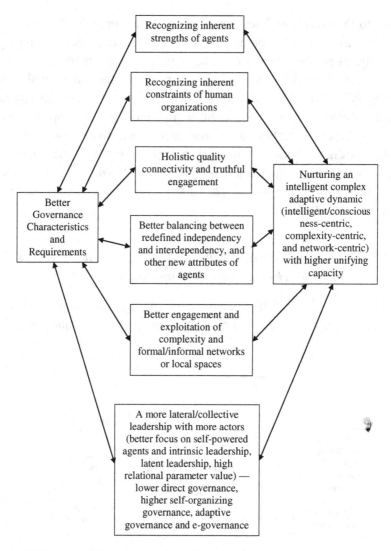

Figure 10.4 Some basic characteristics and requirements of the intelligence governance strategy.

management) is an essential foundation for the changing governance dynamic. The latter is a highly significant component of the intelligent organization dynamics (*i*CAD). Thus, adopting the integration process is a critical strategic path (a significant component of the holistic complexity-intelligence

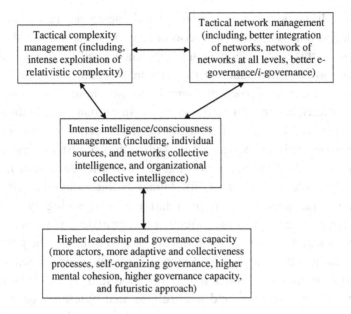

Figure 10.5   Nurturing better adaptive and collective governance capacity.

strategy) for better adaptive and collective governance management to evolve (see Figure 10.5). In this respect, the intelligent organization theory provides a better conceptual foundation that facilitates better comprehension and exploitation of human organizational dynamics that provides a better foundation for effective governance.

As indicated earlier on, the most critical aspect of the theory indicates that organizational competitiveness, resilience, and sustainability can be best initiated and driven by a constant inflow of intelligence [including, exploiting latent intelligence, innovative ideas, relativistic complexity, and new expertise (insight, futuristic) that elevates its intelligence advantage]. With respect to the growing awareness of current governance deficiencies, a key requirement is the recognition that the natural endowment in every human agent has to be more effectively engaged and utilized. Consequently, intelligence/consciousness management processes must attempt to optimize the microscopic agents-agents, agents-network, agents-system, networks-system multi-level structure and dynamics through appropriate intelligence-intelligence linkages (with elevating overall collectiveness capacity as a key objective). In particular, how can unexplored intelligence be extracted and utilized, and not well-connected networks can be better integrated are key concerns. In this case, redefining and re-balancing self-centricity, stability-centricity, and mental stability at all levels are essential.

Due to the significance of mental stability, human sociality is an important attribute for collective survival. In human organizations, the latter is a socio-biological attractor. For some insects with colonies, it is encrypted in their genes (usually fixed within a certain time frame, orderly, linear, and pre-determined, generation after generation), and is inherently achieved. However, for humanity the relational parameter and the mental space (subjectivity, relativism) that are highly nonlinear and constantly changing are affecting its holistic emergence. Thus, complex sociality is a vital evolutionary attribute in humanity that differentiates human collective intelligence from swarm intelligence. This distinction is uniquely and innovatively modified by the presence of intense human awareness and mindfulness that redefines the adaptive characteristic of human agents. In particular, mindfulness, a unique mental function confined only to humanity, must also be better exploited by organizations — orgmindfulness.

In any human organizations, all agents are inherent stakeholders in some levels or forms (may possess dissimilar interests), and this characteristic has to be recognized and acknowledged by whoever are the leaders, policy makers, decision makers, and managers. This is a vital mindset and thinking that provides a redefined foundation for better synergy, and hence the establishment of a more effective (quality) governance capacity and governance system. Every agent has an individual rights, interests, and status in the organization that s/he is a member/player. Consequently, heightening the percentage of actors (deeper collaboration) is always useful and significant. In this case, it is the responsibility of the organization (leaders) to take care of the welfare of the agents (including equity, organizational justice), and ensure the sustainability of the agents. However, many organizations today are much more externally focus rather than internally focus (for instance, customers versus employees, and citizens versus foreign talents), leading to low mental cohesion.

As stipulated earlier, the micro-dynamics of human organizations (complex adaptive systems) are highly intertwined with a large number of agents, linear and nonlinear variables (known and unknown), and different integrated perspectives (including social, economic, political and environment) — resulting in complex cascading issues/problems. In addition, human complex adaptive systems are also history dependent (hysteresis) — where earlier happenings/interventions will lead to unintended consequences. Simultaneously, relational complexity in the social perspective by itself is enormous, and this is often further heightened by the tremendous intensity and impact of sudden economic and political turmoil (observed in some countries). This dynamic has constantly gives rise to unpredictable punctuated disequilibrium.

However, with more focused complexity management, certain spaces of complexity (social, economic, technology, environment) can be better comprehended and exploited — a significant aspect of risk management. Certain surface patterns can be observed, and its dynamic can be better understood. As indicated, some of these spaces can be unexplored territories that are embedded with gold nuggets. Concurrently, effective complexity management must also encompass preparation for sudden appearance of punctuation points — towards better crisis management and constructive transition. This is a more open form of 'futuring' (sometimes a known destination may become valueless even before reaching it — due to the changing landscape). Hence, this aspect of complexity management makes preparation for unpredictability through elevating collective intelligence and org-consciousness, intensive engagement of self-powered agents/networks, intense lateral/collective leadership, and better global self-transcending constructions at all time (see Figure 10.5). As complexity in the human world is relativistic the integration of effective intelligence/consciousness management and complexity management is highly significant. (The network management aspect will be analyzed in Section 10.4.7.)

10.4.3 *Integrating self-organizing governance, relativistic complexity and the intelligence leadership*

Agents as they interact change their 'fitness', as well as the 'fitness' of other agents, that is, their rugged/fitness landscape is constantly/continuously changing. In addition, a relatively optimal strategy or solution has a limited space-time constraint because once another organization or competitor changes its strategy the landscape is also redefined. In addition, actors (intelligence persons) with intense intelligence/consciousness-centric and complexity-centric characteristics are in a better position to render complexity relativistic. Concurrently, the flexibility and adaptation of the leadership is crucial as creating a constantly exploring and exploiting thinking and environment that increases innovative adaptive governance capacity is essential. However, a leader must always be a leader (lateral but respected) and not a 'servant/slave leader'. In particular, a primary concern of leadership is whether a leader as a key actor (including, latent leadership) is able to orchestrate the system (including incoherent networks) into a preferred **basin of attraction.** This is a highly significant unifying capability and action. A leader that is able to directly or indirectly (latent leaders/actors — the **invisible hand of the 'leadership field'**) initiates and orchestrates the desired path possesses a unique intelligence leadership advantage.

10.4.4 *Some finer aspects of the integrated deliberate and emergent approach*

The intelligent organization theory strongly emphasizes that deliberate planning is essential but can never be complete. Thus, the presence of the integrated deliberate and emergence strategy in an organization at all time is critical. Flexible and adaptive exploitation of the deliberate and emergent characteristics concurrently (presence of two paths) is significant in a highly complex environment — the subtle balancing of the two characteristics is the new critical leadership capability (co-existence of order and complexity <=> deliberate and emergence). In this case, the micro details (especially, the actions) are situation dependent — closely associated with the intelligence/consciousness and complexity-centricity of the leaders, as well as the agents. Inevitably, the capability to overcome or manage unpredictability is vital, as unknowns (unknown variables, sudden changes) are always present in human organizations. In this respect, both the intra-system and inter-system self-organizing dynamics must be nimble and well-managed at all time. Consequently, the presence of self-organizing governance greatly enhances the adaptive governance capacity of the organization.

In addition, the deliberate strategy is enhanced by relativistic order (space of relativistic order), and 'broader' relativistic static equilibrium. Exploitation of relativistic order can be strategic (broaden risk management) and innovative. Inevitably, there must be a certain focus on this strategic component with more flexible planned strategic options. However, this aspect alone does not accommodate punctuation points (crises) that are unpredictable. Thus, a more sustainable development is dependent on the fact that sudden punctuation points (crisis management) must be better 'self-managed'. In this case, it depends on the effectiveness of the emergent strategy nurtured — the quality of the self-organizing capacity. Hence, the emergent approach and innovative adaptive capacity of organizations are also closely interrelated. In addition, the various capacities in an intelligent human organization are closely correlated and mutually enhancing (collectiveness capacity <=> adaptive capacity <=> self-organizing capacity <=> emergence-intelligence capacity) if nurtured appropriately. Apparently, the boundaries of the deliberate strategic approach have been expanded significantly by the relativistic complexity perspective.

Consequently, the role and function of a deliberate-emergent auto-switch is vital, and it is not purely a 'binary switch'. The latter must possess a combination of characteristics, such as spontaneous (automatic), adaptive (gradual change), and binary (sudden change) capabilities. These capabilities must synchronize with the high collectivity in the organization. Hence, leaders/actors must also be able to identify new focal points for higher constructions, better coherency, and positive synergetic contribution so that capability changes with respect to network-centricity is optimized.

10.4.5 *E-governance and network-centric governance*

In addition, human organizations are complex adaptive systems encompassing complex networks (network organizations). With the prominent presence of complex networks, a better exploitation on the network meso-structure and dynamic is beneficial. Thus, in the present context, the governance strategy must also encompass effective networks management. The network-centric approach focuses on interconnectivity, relationships, and interdependency, and it perceives human organizational dynamic as sophisticated networked patterns of interactions. Thus, the presence of the network meso-structure and its self-organizing dynamic must be well exploited. Unconscious dysfunctional processes can emerge in a network when the leadership 'fails'. Primarily, in human organizations the following relationships associated with networks should be noted: formation of network <=> self-organization/self-transcending constructions <=> natural selection <=> characteristics of links <=> synergetic effect/output.

Presently, the omnipresence of social media (increases speed of interactions, multiplication of linkages, higher interdependency) very much favored and strengthened the formation of 'networked organizations', especially, the formation of informal networks. In this case, structural incoherency is elevated, and complexity is further escalated because certain interactive networks are not in synchrony with the formal structure due to varying causal effects and cascading effects. In addition, networks with respect to the organizational objectives can be both constructive and destructive. Therefore, overall, current human beings exist in a structurally more complex and networked world with multi-level interconnection and interdependency. Thus, an effective governance strategy must also focus on networks — especially, informal networks by elevating e-governance capacity. It is important to note that an interdependent networks system could enhance developments or escalate cascading failures through rapid self-organization. Hence, they must be carefully managed. The above observation clearly indicates that network-centric self-organizing governance is a new critical process in contemporary organizational dynamics that must be allocated more attention.

Although, human agents are intrinsically self-centric, the characteristic of stability-centricity is often better achieved with networking — a balance between autopoiesis and symbiosis (local space dynamics — often it is a complex shared influence among interdependent agents with similar interests). This is true for 'ordinary' agents (non-actors), as well as key actors (leaders), and the latter could subtly offer a deeper knowledge on leading and organizing in this complex context. Inevitably, the new effective leadership has to be network-centric. Thus, the constructive dynamic must encompass several characteristics, including mutual understanding and respect (collective social consciousness), and mental cohesion. Leaders that are able to observe the dynamical differentials and orchestrate it in the 'desired' or appropriate direction are constructive. In the current environment, leaders/actors that are not part of (not able to engage) a particular network will not be effective within that localized context. Thus, it is significant to recognize that network-centric self-transcending constructions occurs only when agents/actors/leaders in the network possess localized self-organizing capacity — orchestrated by the agents' individual intelligence and network collective intelligence within the local space (exhibiting a certain level of confinement effect).

Vividly, as different levels of local spaces emerge in space-time (from individual agent to network to network of networks to the entire organization and changes with time), the immersion of leaders/actors into lower level spaces and processes (agent-agent interactions, agent-network interactions) must be part of the intelligence governance focus so that its overall collectiveness capacity and adaptive capacity can be elevated. The presence of such a diversified and yet integrated dynamic is a new critical requirement of an intelligence governance system. In general, the presence of upwards causation in intelligent human adaptive dynamic is essential for better resilience and sustainability.

10.4.6 *Introduction to graph/network theory and small world theory*

With the increasing significant impact of networks in human organizations, a more comprehensive and deeper understanding of networks and their associated characteristics is highly valuable to the current leadership. Basic network concepts originate from **graph theory**. The latter was formalized as a domain when a related paper was published by **Leonhard Euler** (1707–1783), in 1736. The paper introduced a new branch in mathematics on the study of graphs which are mathematical structures with **nodes (vertices)** and **links (edges)**. Graphs appear in many structures and are particularly useful in computer science for developing computer algorithms (flow of computation, data organization).

The foundation of **network theory** was later initiated by **Paul Erdos** (1913–1996), and **Alfred Renyi** (1921–1970). They focused mainly on **random networks**. They found that even for a large network (with a large number of nodes), a small percentage of randomly selected links will be sufficient or good enough to generate the characteristics and impact on the entire network. Besides randomness (hypothetical, evenly distributed, static, no growth or preferential attachment characteristic, for instance a bell-curve), networks can be scale free (**'real world'** networks, exhibit growth and preferential attachment characteristics, large number of nodes and links) — see scale-free network in Appendix 7. Currently, network applications ('real world' networks) have spread to numerous domains, including sociology (**social networks**), biology (**molecular networks**), economics (**market internal relations networks**), and computer science (**artificial neural networks**). In human networks (**complex adaptive networks, complex adaptive networks**), focusing on the links is crucial. Links can be relational (encompassing relational friction in the human world) intangible, and nonlinear — see complex adaptive networks in Appendix 7.

In addition, the **small world theory**, a subset of network theory focuses on a unique characteristic of scale free 'real world' networks (networks with diameter relatively smaller than the number of nodes are known as small world networks) — see small world network in Appendix 7. The latter is not totally random but followed a predictable pattern of order and growth. As they form clusters and 'nurture', early nodes possess preferential attachment — first mover advantage. In addition, their links are differentiated as **strong ties** and **weak ties**, and interestingly the latter provides a high percentage of contribution to the entire network (first discovered by **Mark Granovetter** (1943–present), in 1973, in his paper entitled 'The strength of the weak ties') — also connected to **Pareto distribution** (80/20 rule) and **power law**. The **weak tie phenomenon** is highly significant with the relational parameter [the strength of weak ties is associated with its large number of connections and not its 'individual' efficiency alone, for instance, the fast and wide spread of codified information ('reduction' in path lengths) gives rise to an unexpected aggregated impact]. While, strong ties focus on the 'quality' or efficiency (close interaction) of every 'individual' connection. In particular, network theory and its association with power law indicate that not all networks in the human world and its subsystems are totally random — that is, order and complexity co-exists.

Currently, network theory is also regarded and analyzed as a subset of complexity theory — based on the observation that complex systems encompass complex networks. In this respect, nodes in certain networks are the equivalent of agents in complex adaptive systems where information is consumed (internalized), created (externalized), and/or transmitted (communicated) — depending on the details characteristics of the nodes/ agents (real or artificial) concerned. In this case, every node/human agent is subject to constraints and enablers. Very often, the primary purpose of links is to connect nodes/agents and transmit information — also to establish deeper communications and engagement. Thus, network theory focuses on the structure, properties, and behavior of a network so that its future behavior can be better predicted (however, it is vital to be always aware of the butterfly effect — and networks with local minima can be destructive). Consequently, it is important to note that 'real world' networks are consistently dynamical (grow and change, tangible and/or intangible, formal and/or informal, conscious and 'unconscious' dynamic, and small increase in randomness creates a large change in degree of separation), and they form localized spaces with nodes that possess preferential attachment and interdependency (self-organizing, self-centricity).

10.4.7 *Complex adaptive networks and better network-centric governance*

Better networks management is a new crucial necessity in present human organizations. Currently, human beings and their organizations exist in a complex world where multi-level complex networks with interdependent agents, and integrating multiple interconnected perspectives, including social networks, information networks, market networks, governance networks, and other technical networks is the norm. These complex networks (network of networks) are real world networks that possess complexity characteristics. All human networks are complex, nonlinear, communicating, engaged, self-organizing, and emerging. A significant and critical characteristic of such a system of networks is that the networks involved can be interdependent, scale free, and adaptive. They also exhibit the properties of clustering and forming a 'small world' or local space (that may be non-synchrony with the system/organization). **Interdependent networks** are networks with nodes that are interdependent across networks. Such interdependency could either enhance developments or escalate cascading failures. In this case, a key strategy is to render the multi-level structure and dynamics more 'multi-lateral' (at least spreading it across laterally first — for better collectiveness) — nurturing complex adaptive networks that better integrate with the global structure.

The concept of **complex adaptive networks (CAN)** is introduced in the intelligent organization theory. A CAN is an intelligent network of networks (formal and informal) in any human organizations (corporations, nations, regional institutions) that possess the adaptive characteristic (CAN <=> intelligent networks). These networks are complex networks embedded with intense intelligence (individual and collective) because of the presence of intelligent nodes (intense mental space) and special relational links (tangible and intangible) — usually integrated with self-organizing communications, intense information processing capability and beyond (value, expectation, relativism). In this respect, these networks possess learning, adaptation, communicating, engagement, and self-organization/self-transcending constructions capabilities as a localized space (cluster). However, for an organization, diversification characteristics or internal disparity exist because each network can be developing in a different direction (incoherent). In addition, the nodes involved are living ('feeling') agents (for instance, social networks are CAN whereas computer networks are not). In this respect, better network management is associated with nurturing of innovative adaptive capacity, and to integrate informal and incoherent CAN into the holistic macrostructure. Thus, the presence and better network management of CAN in human organizations is vital for holistic constructive self-organization/ self-transcending constructions (higher self-organizing capacity and emergence-intelligence capacity), intelligence leadership, and intelligence governance. Apparently, in the present environment, achieving coherency in CAN of networks is a critical requirement for higher governance capacity, and reflects the effectiveness of the leadership.

As an intelligent human organization adopts an intelligence/ consciousness-centric strategy focusing on the nodes (intense intelligence sources), concurrently, the links (for instance, a set of dyadic ties in social networks) in the organization must also be optimized with better network management (higher relational-centric, higher organizational justice, lower social inequality). This aspect is vital as the characteristics of the links will influence/determine how the related nodes will act and/or react — affecting its collectiveness capacity. Again, back to the basic foundation, it is significant to note that constructive human dynamics encompass several critical characteristics, including mutual understanding and respect, meaningful relations, elevating voluntary collaboration, and the development of the process itself is information dependent. Thus, it is beneficial to adopt and exploit a 'common language'. This thinking is part of the characteristics of the new leadership, and must be incorporated in the new intelligence governance strategy as well.

10.4.8 *The significance and key focal points of the intelligence governance strategy*

Apparently, nurturing high self-organizing capacity and emergence-intelligence capacity is a key focus of the intelligence leadership strategy, and a foundation pillar of the intelligence governance strategy. However, as indicated earlier, concentrating on self-organization/self-transcending constructions does not imply that planned strategies are invalid. The ability to orchestrate constructive self-organizing dynamic subtly (must be constantly adjusting and leading to continuous acquisition of capacity improvement) is a critical new intelligence leadership characteristic. Concurrently, the ability to integrate informal self-organizing networks (focusing on both 1st and 2nd degrees self-organization/self-transcending constructions, self-organizing capacity, complex adaptive networks) is also a new leadership criticality (see edge of emergence in Appendix 7). It enhances the role of an emergent strategist in the intelligence leadership. Hence, the intelligence leadership strategy constantly orchestrates constructive self-organization (integrated self-transcending constructions at all levels towards global coherency and synergy) by engaging all intrinsic leadership sources, facilitating both 1st and 2nd order emergence at all time. Collectivity and 'right' connectedness (high collectiveness capacity) also diminishes ('direct') structural and dynamic control — hence, diminishing direct governance and elevating innovation and creativity.

Therefore, a significant process in the intelligence governance strategy is the integration (including, informal networks) of self-powered self-organizing governance. Although, the latter may or may not be part of the formal structure and dynamics but it encompasses certain processes that must be better comprehended and exploited by the holistic governance and leadership. Currently, many hierarchical leaders, managers, and decision-makers are consciously/unconsciously suppressing self-organization which is a destructive and costly act as micro-control requires a substantial amount of resources and often escalates incoherency. However, an intelligence leader recognizes that the local activities (self-organizing networks) of the agents (citizens, employees, members) produce collective (network/global) effect (can be either positive or negative). The quality of human organizational dynamics can be improved by its rate/quality of supportive self-transcending constructions [involving continuous learning effects, nurturing information sharing, planned and 'unplanned' collaboration, achieving desired capabilities and aspiration levels, and quick re-learning and (spontaneous) responses during crisis]. In such a situation, complexity becomes relative and predictability increases. Vividly, nurturing a highly coupled self-organizing and emergence-intelligence capacity is critical.

In this respect, constantly in the mind of an intelligence leader is 'can the contributions of certain networks/local spaces (irrespective if they are formal or informal) be elevated and better integrated?' It is a state where collective intelligence significantly determined how potential self-transcending constructions will be manifested (recognizing the correlation among collectiveness capacity, self-organizing capacity, emergence-intelligence capacity, and collective intelligence). For intelligent complex adaptive dynamic, diversified local interactions will eventually increase in coherency through self-transcending constructions with the right orchestration. With respect to a nation, social justice may be elevated (better distribution of opportunities, wealth, and privileges). Thus, it is vital that leaders (as committed actors) must be immersed in all levels of processes (directly or indirectly) — that is, they must be active nodes (through intensive dialogue and circular causation) in all the three levels of processes (within a local network => network of networks => entire organization) to identify and orchestrate the final emergent of new order.

Inevitably, the lateral/collective leadership path that is more relational-centric (links focus) and integrates networks (formal and informal) is a more favored approach. As more power distribution is a new requirement in the emerging environment, the trend is away from intense bureaucracy, hierarchical control and empowerment (one prominent leader has all the 'answers'), and towards highly intense network-based self-powered capability, and its individual intrinsic leadership capability. In such a situation, towards minimal direct governance is a more ideal path. Hence, the basic ideology of all governance systems, including corporate governance systems must encompass community-minded (socio-emotional functionality), value-based, and collectivity-oriented thinking as a significant part of their primary foundation. And the nurturing of a 'diversified concerned commitment' (increasing 'abstract' coherency — mental cohesion) of all agents (if necessary) is a better option, as the approach also increases the relationships capacity of the system (that is, significantly towards nurturing a 'feeling system', that is, beyond merely a 'thinking system').

Based on the above analysis, increasing governance adaptive capacity in the current context is vividly associated with the better engagement of the self-powered self-organizing agents with well-connected information processing networks. The latter that realign governance relationship must be effectively exploited (including, e-governance) through a 'common language' that manages the complex nonlinear relational parameter better. A 'common' language inherently encompasses a social and relational, and mental dimension (cognition and socio-emotional well-beings — including respect, recognition, trust, and mutual reciprocity) that is not sufficiently focused upon in many organizations today. Overall, the presence of a 'common language' with deeper 'relational synchrony' and 'mental coherency' is a new advantage — towards a deeper intelligence advantage through greater mental cohesion.

Finally, the latent leadership (invisible innovative 'impetus' in the organization) that orchestrates the intrinsic intelligence sources (encompassing as many actors as possible), and the collective intelligence (as holistic as possible) of the system is the most distinct form of leadership for better governance. With respect to complexity concepts the implication of this thinking is that highly effective leaders must be able to visualize (exceptional foresight) and 'move' the organization into a new stable basin of attraction (if necessary) — one that is still constantly changing and adjusting within a certain defined boundary — without the notice of the agents (see Figure 10.6). Thus, the latent leader is highly intelligent with intense foresight, and adopts a handoff approach. In this situation, many other actors are activated, and large collective action is initiated. However,

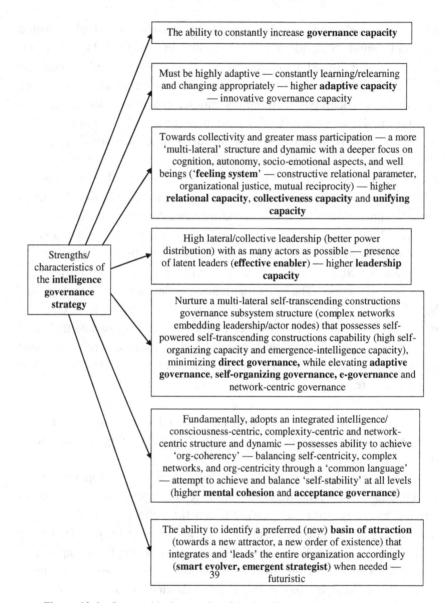

Figure 10.6   Some critical strengths of the intelligence governance strategy.

the other actors are not aware of the presence and roles of the latent leader. Hence, a latent leader (calm mind, low key, soft voice, futuristic, high awareness and mindfulness) is an intelligent complex adaptive leader that exploits an integrated path encompassing intelligence/consciousness-centricity, emergence, complexity-centricity, network-centricity, self-organizing capacity and emergence-intelligence capability.

10.4.9 *Summary of the intelligence governance strategy*

Briefly, some of the fundamental thinking, focuses, and processes of the intelligence governance strategy that have been scrutinized are summarized as follows:

- Focusing on intelligence/consciousness management, intensive self-powered self-organizing interconnectivity and communications, information sharing, and truthful engagement (the behaviors and emotional of all agents must be constantly motivated) — also exploiting the power of information networks — mobile/social media (elevating e-governance).
- Focusing on intelligence/consciousness driven self-transcending constructions — optimizing collective intrinsic self-powered leadership, especially, through the latent leadership approach (elevating self-organizing governance).
- Forming, transforming, and integrating networks/network of networks (network-centric, complex adaptive networks), especially when invisible self-organizing capability or network routines (changing behaviors) contradict the formalized governance system (elevating collectiveness capacity).
- Reducing diverse behaviors and enhance interdependency within the complex network (network of networks) with reflexivity loops that better align agents, networks, and the organization — enhancing org-coherency, higher unifying capacity, and towards higher mental cohesion.
- Balancing between localized self-organizing interactions (formal and informal) and global/holistic emergence — better ambidexterity, nurturing high self-organizing capacity, emergence-intelligence capacity, unifying capacity, and emergent of new order.

- Leadership must be actors within informal networks as well — orchestrating better 'alignedness' by allowing bottom up absorption (upwards causation) of new spatial structures and dynamics (that is, agents participation in policy making and actions is essential for better coherency and synergy).

- Focusing on orchestrating collectivity and 'multi-lateral' dynamics, through the lateral/collective leadership — minimizing direct governance, towards higher innovative governance capacity with constructionist effect.

- Focusing on nurturing constructive collective intelligence (both at network and global level), enhance the pool of actors (better power distribution), and nurturing higher 'quality' governance capacity at all time.

- Progressing towards a 'feeling' system, encompassing the 'feeling' and 'perceptions' (cognition, construal effect) of all stakeholders, beyond just a thinking (logic-based) system — minimizing conflicts, and elevating mutual reciprocity, relational parameter value, and organizational justice (relational capacity).

- Focusing on both the deliberate and emergent components at all time, and optimizing the benefit of ambidextrous structuring and dynamics ('optimal' exploitation order, and relativistic complexity, and preparing for high and complexity).

- Recognizing that human organizations (complex adaptive systems) exist both in a 'probabilistic' state and a state with definite value (order) — that is, performing scenario planning seeking probabilistic outcomes can be a beneficial option — thus, the significance of being futuristic (note some unknown unknowns will always remain as unknowns), and possessing the ability of identifying a new basin of attraction is critical.

10.5 Conclusion

The first section of this chapter concentrates on the introduction to relativistic complexity in human organizations due to the presence of the unique intense mental dimension in the human world. In this respect, complexity is in the mind of the beholder, and predictability is subjective. Thus, relativistic complexity emerges from the nonlinearity of intense human intelligence/consciousness associated only with an individual and/or certain group of human interacting agents. In this respect, new characteristics/properties such as spaces of relativistic order and relativistic static equilibrium must be recognized and exploited innovatively, creating a higher level of intelligence advantage. In highly intelligent human organizations, the interacting agents must possess intelligent person attributes (including being smarter evolvers and emergent strategists), and they are constantly mindful of the mental dimension of agents/networks/organization that is more sensitive dependence on initial input. Therefore, the intelligence leadership mindset and thinking focuses intensely on human mental spaces, enhances their interconnectivity and collective intelligence with high positive relational parameter value, that can better exploits relativistic complexity whenever possible.

Thus, in the new context, the mental complexity of human agents and their organizations (associated with intense intelligence, awareness, mindfulness, emotions, diversified knowledge, mutual reciprocity, perception, cognition, relativism, and new decision-making abilities) is highly significant, valuable, and strategic, that can lead to a new level of organizational mental cohesion, resilience and sustainability. Therefore, the intelligence leadership strategy concentrates on and utilizes the three spaces concurrently, namely, order (deterministic and predictable, deliberate planning, collectiveness, and forecasting), relativistic order/complexity (partial determinism and predictability, intense intelligence/consciousness-centricity, subjectivity, ambidextrous structuring, self-transcending constructions, surface pattern, innovation and creativity, first mover advantage, risk management, coherency, synergetic, constructionist, and higher level intelligence advantage), and high complexity (in-determinism, suddenness and unpredictability, punctuation point, high collective intelligence, scenario planning, self-transcending constructions, crisis management, high spontaneous collaboration and coherency, and emergence) that exist in human organizations. This thinking clearly indicates that organizational governance must be redefined.

The second portion of analysis indicates that a transformation in the governance paradigm is inevitable, and must broadly encompass the integrated intelligence/consciousness-centricity, complexity-centricity, and network-centricity approach so that a better adaptive option can emerge. This fundamental shift from the traditional centralized bureaucratic (hierarchical, autocratic, control, selective, empowerment) to a more lateral/collective self-powered self-organizing (more balance collective large-scale participation and power distribution — higher autonomy, massive self-powered intrinsic leadership integration, higher collectiveness capacity, 'everybody is in charge' dynamic) approach with a spontaneous emergent dynamic (encompassing autocatalysis, upwards causation, networks integration, self-transcending constructions, recognizing potential stable new basin of attraction ability, supported by high self-organizing capacity and emergence-intelligence capacity) is a new critical requirement (while, balancing 'self-stability' at all levels is a primary pre-requisite). Thus, the heightening in flexibility, reflexivity, and adaptation characteristics (constantly exploring, learning, and exploiting), effective integration of localized spaces (formal and informal networks), facilitating self-organizing governance, exploiting e-governance, and minimizing direct governance elevates the organizational governance capacity.

Distinctly, self-powered self-organizing governance, a basic characteristic of the new intelligence governance strategy, is one significant component of the intelligent complex adaptive dynamics (*i*CAD) that is evolving in the human world. Hence, the presence of intelligence leadership capability in balancing (quality ambidexterity) the diversified agents'/networks' interests and the system's interests is critical — higher mutual reciprocity. The diversified multi-stakeholder environment must be cautiously managed. In particular, the presence of latent leadership with intense intelligence/ consciousness, quality problem-solving structures knowledge, futuristic, and high orchestrating capability is critical for elevating synergetic and constructionist effect holistically. As indicated, nurturing 'feeling' organizations (with constructive relational value, relational-centricity, relational capacity) with higher consciousness (mindfulness, orgmindfulness), and intense focusing on the nonlinear mental spaces of all agents is another key necessity for higher mental cohesion.

Overall, the intelligence governance strategy exploits the intelligence leadership strategy and relativistic complexity; integrates adaptive governance, self-organizing governance, network governance, and e-governance;

and minimizes direct governance to achieve a higher global governance capacity. Apparently, all human organizations that wish to enhance their resilience and sustainability through better governance will have to recognize the intelligence paradigmatic approach in thinking, leadership, strategy, and development, and the significance of achieving spontaneous self-organizing capability.

> In a highly intelligence/consciousness-centric environment, complexity is in the mind of the beholder.

Concluding Topic of the IO Theory

XI: Being Futuristic and a Higher Order Existence

The strangest and the best thing about teaching is that a seed dropped into what looks like rocky ground will often stick and take root gradually, and spring up years later, sometimes in a bizarre form and oddly hybridized, but still carrying the principle of life.

Gilbert Hilbert, *The Art of Teaching*

Chapter 11

Being Futuristic and a Higher Order Existence

"New knowledge creation is a critical capacity of intelligent
human agents"

"Innovative discoveries are closely associated with prepared minds"

Summary

The chapter concludes the book by illustrating the potential of extending
the boundaries of the intelligence mindset and its space of innovation
and creativity. Some theories that could be integrated subsequently are
mentioned briefly. In addition, a holistic view (new knowledge creation)
of the intelligence paradigm, the complexity-intelligence strategy, and
the intelligent organization theory is summarized through recollecting
and amalgamating the various normative attributes, concepts, perspectives and strategies analyzed. Organizing around intelligence (including
intelligence/consciousness management, complexity management and
network management), and the integrated deliberate and emergent strategy (exploitation of the co-existence of order and complexity) are the
(holistic) fundamental strategies that must be exploited in the present
environment. Due to the current high complexity and nonlinearity, this
paradigmatic shift is apparently beneficial. As indicated earlier, properties of complex adaptive systems and the complex adaptive dynamic
must be better comprehended and exploited by all human organizations
to elevate competitiveness, resilience and sustainability.

In summary, the intelligent organization theory introduced in this
book contains concepts and ideas (including intelligence/consciousness-
centricity, complexity-centricity, network-centricity, intelligence-intelligence
linkage, complexity-intelligence linkage, self-organizing capacity, emergence-
intelligence capacity, coherency, synergy, constructionist effect and mental

427

cohesion) that are more holistic, integrative, and accurate manifestations of humanity and its organizations and agents. Thus, it is highly critical for the leadership, governance, strategy, and management in rapidly changing environment. Primarily, it is a new significant complexity-intelligence-relational/network domain (a more inherent aspect of nature and this universe) that must be better comprehended and exploited by all human organizations. As indicated, the complexity-intelligence strategy of the intelligent organization theory encompasses numerous components, including organizing around intelligence, integrated deliberate and emergent strategy, general information theory, 3C-OK framework, intelligent person model, intelligent multi-layer structure model, intelligence leadership theory/strategy, intelligence governance theory/strategy, and relativistic complexity.

Fundamentally, the new thinking emphasizes the significance and linkages of the human intelligence/consciousness sources, and stability-centricity at all levels (agent-centric, network-centric and org-centric), co-existence of order and complexity, and the attributes of swift information decoders, smarter evolvers and emergent strategists. The strategies and models/frameworks of the intelligent organization theory that focus on structuring, nurturing, leading, and governing/managing of highly intelligent human organizations (*i*CAS) that are orchestrated by the highly intelligent complex adaptive dynamic (*i*CAD) are briefly re-captured. Ultimately, it is the intention of the author that an omniscient understanding of this book will instill in leaders and actors the new critical intelligence advantage.

Keywords: Newtonian theory, evolution theory, quantum theory, theory of relativity, cosmology, astrophysics, neuropsychology, cognitive psychology, complexity theory, relativistic complexity theory, quantum nanotechnology, cognitive neuroscience, neural networks, reductionist thinking, systems thinking, evolution thinking, cybernetics thinking, network thinking, constructionist thinking, quantum thinking, quantum non-locality, quantum entanglement, quantum communication, quantum tunneling, quantum teleporting, intelligence mindset, intelligence paradigm, intelligent organization theory, self-centric, stability-centric, agent-centric, org-centric, autopoiesis, symbiosis, self-stability, network-stability, org-stability, ambidextrous, organizing around intelligence, consciousness, collective intelligence, org-consciousness, org-awareness, orgmindfulness, intelligence/consciousness management, complex adaptive dynamic (CAD), interdependency, general information theory,

3C-OK framework, intelligent person model, smarter evolver, emergent strategist, integrated deliberate and emergent strategy, intelligent multi-layer structure, intelligence leadership theory/strategy, intelligence governance theory/strategy, relativistic complexity, highly intelligent human organization (*i*CAS), highly intelligent complex adaptive dynamic (*i*CAD), self-powered capacity, intrinsic leadership capacity, structural capacity, collectiveness capacity, adaptive capacity, unifying capacity, self-organizing capacity, emergence-intelligence capacity, leadership capacity, governance capacity, network theory, coherency, synergetic effect, constructionist hypothesis, compassion, futuristic, wisdom paradigm, feeling system, mental cohesion and intelligence advantage.

11.1 Introduction: Beyond Current Comprehension and Existence

11.1.1 *Integrating some other scientific domains*

There has been a significant transformation in humanity over the last century. The entire environment (social, economic, political, technology) at the beginning of the 20th century was totally different from the beginning of the 21st century. Inevitably, the beginning of the 22nd century will also be substantially different from now. The thinking, knowledge and perception, societal structure and environment, interactive processes and dynamics, technologies exploited, leadership and governance attributes, values, expectations and principles, and the entire human existence (a new global order) will be beyond current recognition. For instance, humanity has drifted from monarchy and aristocracy to a more lateral/collective leadership and governance structure to some extent. Concurrently, human knowledge and theories have developed from human sensory dimension (Newtonian theory) to other more abstract dimensions (quantum theory, quantum field theory, theory of relativity, cosmology/astrophysics, and neuropsychology). Technologies have developed from steam engine to jet engine; coal energy to nuclear energy; direct/physical control to remote control, standalone computer to global social media networks (to quantum computer); and mechanistic medical equipments to quantum-oriented medical equipments. In this context, the theories and applications associated with intelligence paradigm will continue perpetually. A few domains with direct or indirect potentials are introduced (see Figure 11.1).

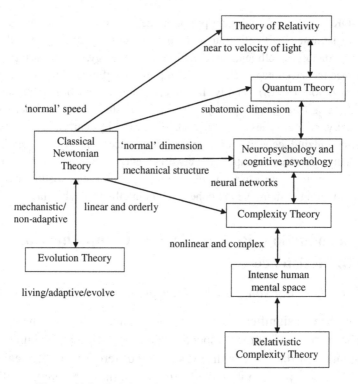

Figure 11.1 Relationships and interlinks of some theories.

Knowledge emerging from the theoretical perspective of **cosmology** [the term was coined by **Christian Wolff** (1679–1754), in 1730] and **astrophysics,** now perceived the Universe rather differently. The proposal and analysis [initiated by **Vera Rubin** (1928–present) and **Kent Ford** (1931–present), in the 1960s and 1970s] of the existence of dark energy, dark matter, and quantum field (grid) will transform the current understanding of the Big Bang theory, the concept of absolute vacuum, zero point field and some other aspects of human existence. Presently, it is estimated that only 4.9% of the Universe is make up of familiar constituents ('known' energy and the 'visible' physical matter world), and the remaining 95.1% is make up of quantum constituents (not directly visible to human beings). Some prominent astrophysicists and their contributions that lead to the current comprehension, include **Stephen Hawking** (1942–present), Hawking radiations, gravitational singularity theorem; **Subrahmanyan Chandrasekhar** (1910–1995), stellar structure and dynamics, theory of white dwarfs, Nobel Prize,

1983; and **William Alfred Fowler** (1911–1995), chemical elements in stars, Nobel Prize, 1983].

Next, **quantum theory** is the theory of the subatomic world (zero point field/energy, quantum entanglement — the 'strange' interconnectivity in the quantum/subatomic world) that will have significant impacts on humanity. The foundation of this domain was established in the last century by a group of quantum physicists, including **Max Planck** (1858–1947, Planck's law and constant, harmonic oscillator: $E = hn\nu$, Nobel Prize, 1918); **Albert Einstein** (1879–1955, quantization, photon: $E = h\nu$, photoelectric effect, theory of relativity, unified field theory, Nobel Prize, 1921); **Neil Bohr** (1885–1962, quantization of matter, Bohr model, complementarity principle, Nobel Prize, 1922); **Erwin Schrodinger** (1887–1961, Schrodinger equation, wave mechanics, Nobel Prize, 1933); **Louis de Broglie** (1892–1987, wave-particle duality, $p = h/\lambda$, Nobel Prize, 1929); **Max Born** (1882–1970, Born rule, matrix mechanics, Nobel Prize, 1954); **Wolfgang Pauli** (1900–1958, Pauli exclusion principle, spin theory, Nobel Prize, 1954); **Werner Heisenberg** (1901–1976, uncertainty principle, matrix mechanics, Nobel Prize, 1932); and **Paul Dirac** (1902–1984, Dirac equation, antimatter, quantum field theory, Nobel Prize, 1933). The solution of quantum systems is a complex wave function (eigenstate and eigenvalue) with probabilistic value, and the wave function changes is described by the Schrodinger equation. Over time, research activities at the large hadron collider at CERN will elevate the human sensory and mental interpretations of the quantum world (boundaries between energy and physical matter) further for useful applications. (Is the emergent of consciousness a neural quantum phenomenon? see Appendix 5.)

Currently, the quantum technological development is emerging gradually [**Anton Zeilinger** (1945-present), Wolf Prize in Physics (2010)]. Some research and development activities in these technological frontiers (including **quantum nanotechnology** — quantum superposition, quantum entanglement) are directed at quantum computer and quantum computing, quantum tunneling, teleporting, superconductor, superfluity, and medical imaging. Successes of these endeavors are expected to transform humanity drastically. This is a unique domain that intelligent organizations must be constantly observing. For instance, it has been estimated that a personal quantum computer will possess a computing power equal to all the present computers in the world combined. While, medical imaging is already a significant medical support in hospitals, and is providing a deeper comprehension of the human neural networks. In addition, a new sub-branch, **quantum chaos** has emerged, and it focuses on how quantum theory can explain classical chaos from a different perspective. Similarly, the quantum-relativistic domain will definitely and gradually increase its impact on humanity over the current century. Therefore, exploring and exploiting the quantum world (and its potential applications) is greatly significant for the future sustainability of human existence.

In addition, the **cognitive neuroscience** domain that focuses on the psychological functions emerging from neural networks [neuron doctrine — **Camillo Golgi** (1843–1926), **Santiago Ramon Cajal** (1852–1934), and **Heinrich Wilhelm Gottfried von Waldeyer-Hartz** (1836–1921); cognitive science/psychology — **George Armitage Miller** (1920–2012), **Avram Noam Chomsky** (1928–present), **Herbert Simon** (1916–2001), and **Allen Newell** (1927–1992)] will provide a stronger foundation for comprehending the human thinking systems, intelligence, consciousness, and the relational parameter. In this study, the neural substrates of mental processes (cognition) are the key focus. Apparently, as the intelligence mindset is highly intelligence/consciousness-centric, this domain that overlaps with **neuropsychology** (brain structure and functions <=> psychological processes and human behaviors; correlations between the brain and the mind), and **cognitive psychology** (mental processes — thinking, attention, memory, perception, creativity, problem-solving ability, and language exploitation) must be better comprehended and integrated. As mentioned earlier, with the support of more advanced functional neural imaging (magnetic resonance imaging, positron emission tomography, electroencephalography), a deeper understanding of the human thinking systems at the neural level may be gradually achieved.

11.1.2 *A more encompassing intelligence/consciousness mindset*

Eventually, the boundaries of the intelligence mindset and its associated paradigm will encompass broader frontiers, including the relativistic quantum domain and cognitive neuroscience domain (see Figure 11.2). Primarily, as indicated earlier, the quantum mindset focuses on probabilistic outcomes (not definite outcomes). However, after about a century of analysis and experimentation, the relativistic quantum domain [**Oskar Klein** (1894–1977) and **Walter Gordon** (1893–1939), Klein-Gordon equation — relativistic

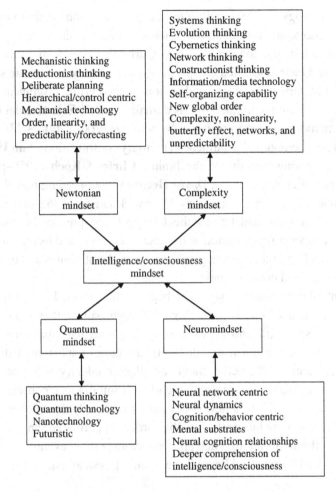

Figure 11.2   The more encompassing intelligence/consciousness mindset.

version of Schrodinger equation; **Paul Dirac** (1902–1984), Dirac equation; **Kenneth Wilson** (1936–2013), confinement of quarks, renormalization group <=> self-similarity, phase transition, Nobel Prize, 1982], especially its application aspect is still rather preliminary. However, associated technologies not known currently will surface. In the new context, human mental interpretations may be significantly modified — for instance, seeking possible applications of the quantum tunneling effect in the human world.

The cognitive neuroscience domain is a discipline that has attracted many top minds to investigate the minds. Neuroscience that started as a branch of biology is now highly interdisciplinary encompassing numerous natural sciences, and also cognitive science, medicine, linguistics, psychology, engineering, and computer science. Currently, a key focus is the neural networks and their associated complex cognitions and behaviors are still at a rather preliminary stage of comprehension. Some current prominent neuroscientists that have contributed to this domain, include **Eric Kandel** (1929–present, memory storage in neurons, Nobel Prize, 2000), **James McGaugh** (1931–present, emotionally-influenced memory consolidation), **Van Wedeen** (large-scale wiring patterns of the brain), **Christof Koch** (1956–present, neural bases of consciousness), **David Heeger** (1960–present, how the brain senses optic flow and neural motion), **Henry Markram** (1962–present, neocortical microcircuit, and **Fritz Albert Popp** (1938-present, biophotons)). Vividly, a deeper comprehension of the neural networks and its functions and capability will definitely have a great impact on the attributes and utilization of intelligence and consciousness.

Eventually, humanity may exist beyond the planet, Earth. Presently, the development of space technology is progressing rather rapidly. The potential of space travel/tourism is emerging, and interplanetary migrations may become a norm in future. In this case, a substantial different order of existence will emerge. Inevitably, the complexity of humanity will continue to escalates and depend greatly on intelligence/consciousness-centricity to elevate it to a new order that is not easily comprehensible at this juncture — new humanity celestial order. In particular, an interesting query is will human intelligence and consciousness be eventually intense enough to lead humankind beyond the visible physical matter world?

11.2 Consolidating the Existing Intelligent Organization Theory

11.2.1 *Inherent complexity and humanity*

Human agents are biological entities that learn, adapt and evolve, and human organizations features complex adaptive dynamics (CAD). Fundamentally, a human organization and its problems encompass different dimensions and levels. Thus, complexity in humanity is inherent, and is also closely associated with the relational parameter, interconnectivity, and interdependency (potentially: increase in complexity <=> decrease in relational capacity <=> increase in interdependency). The presence of the nonlinear relational and distinctions (perceptional, logical, emotional) attributes renders human existence highly complex. For all human complex adaptive systems, it is significant to note the following relationship: an autonomous open system <=> a complex and self-organizing system <=> 'the whole is greater than the parts combined' (synergetic). In particular, the emergent of new constructive attribute (constructionist hypothesis) is highly beneficial (constructionist effect <=> innovation and creativity), and a focal point of highly intelligent organizations.

Next, a system with agents that possesses self-organizing and adaptive (evolving) capabilities is also inherently complex. Human cognition (a biological phenomenon, as well as a social and communications phenomenon), and knowledge acquisition, accumulation and comprehension processes are self-organizing. Overall, self-organizing capability, feedback processes (cascading effect/behavior), and emergent attributes are executed concurrently. Due to the above set of characteristics and dynamics, a surface pattern can be observed, if intense intelligence and consciousness is present. In addition, self-organization and emergence encompasses both divergence (differentiation) and convergence (integration) processes with different levels of participation from all agents (ideally). Thus, nurturing intense collective intelligence in human organizations is a critical factor. This recognition highlights the significance of lateral/collective and consultative approaches (intelligence-intelligence linkages, leadership, governance, network integration), and the criticality of the relational parameter. Hence, the intelligence leadership also focuses on nurturing various high capacities (collectiveness capacity, relational capacity, adaptive capacity, structural capacity, leadership capacity, governance capacity, self-organizing capacity, emergence-intelligence capacity, and unifying capacity) in the organization as a key capability.

Due to the nature of complexity, absolute optimality does not exist; only relative (satisficing) optimality can be achieved (consciously or unconsciously). This reality is also partially related to the in-complete phase space of CAS (especially, human organizations). In this respect, the evolution trajectory of different CAS (including different biological species, cities, and nations) is dissimilar — sensitive dependence on initial conditions. In particular, with the intelligence mindset and intense intelligence/consciousness-centricity, human complexity is redefined — relativistic. Even the Newtonian mindset and the reductionist perspective can still be exploited selectively due to the presence of relativistic complexity in the human world — supported by the presence of intense intelligence/consciousness and collective intelligence/org-consciousness sources. Thus, being farsighted (forecasting) and futuristic is still an advantage. Finally, it is crucial to note that the cognitive and constructive self-organizing capabilities of human organizations are highly critical. For instance, the power or impact/output of self-organizing capability can be extreme, as has been observed in social media clusters and terrorist groups.

11.2.2 *Nurturing highly intelligent human organizations*

The above analysis on complexity provides a significant and beneficial foundation for re-capturing the key clusters of the intelligent organization theory. First, human organizations are inherently complex adaptive systems. They are unique CAS that are not totally identical to other CAS. Currently, it has been observed that critical continuous changes are affecting humankind and its organizations (corporations, educational institutions, economies, nations, and regional institutions) in all perspectives (social, political, economic, and environmental) — greater integration with increasing complexity density. Due to rapid transformation in thinking, knowledge, and operations, attributes and practices that were accepted as traditional or heritage may now be regarded as outdated or obsolete. Basically, the evolution dynamic and outputs deviate as the inputs continue to vary. The rules and environment that were once logical or bearable may now be totally incongruous. Due to the over dominant of humankind on this planet some of these unfolding changes can be highly negative. Ultimately, economic abundance and the quality of human existence may not be positively correlated. The needs for more critical sustainability are surfacing — industrialization or economic development and other human/societal developments may no more be totally synonymous or congruous.

Inevitably, nurturing highly intelligent human organization (*i*CAS), and recognizing and exploiting highly intelligent complex adaptive dynamic (*i*CAD) guided by the intelligence mindset is the new critical approach. With respect to leading, organizing, and managing/governing human organizations, the changes or accelerants vividly indicate the importance of intelligence and consciousness as the utmost priority. Thus, organizing around intelligence is the first strategic dynamic to adopt. For all human organizations, regardless of their sizes and missions, the fundamental foundation is to 'make' systems more intelligent — intense intelligence-intelligence linkages, high relational capacity, nurturing collective intelligence and the orgmind, and certain short-term losses may be longer-term gains. In this respect, intelligence/consciousness management is a distinctive focal point. Consequently, the presence of intelligent multi-layer structure, intelligence leadership strategy, and intelligence govern-ance strategy of highly intelligent human organizations are significant changes. Attributes/properties with new merits must be allocated greater attention (see Figure 11.3).

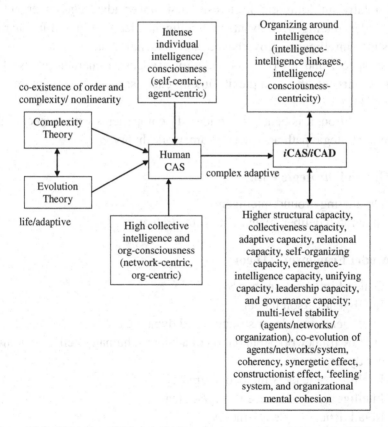

Figure 11.3 Nurturing *i*CAS and *i*CAD as fundamental foundation of the IO theory.

11.2.3 *The holistic complexity-intelligence strategy*

The complexity-intelligence strategy is the global/holistic strategy of the intelligent organization theory that encompasses numerous components (sub-strategies, models and frameworks) that also indicate the boundaries of the theory. The key attributes and activities involved are intelligence, consciousness (awareness, mindfulness), self-centric, stability-centric, neural networks, collective intelligence, org-consciousness (org-awareness, orgmndfulness), network-centric, org-centric, individual and organizational learning, knowledge acquisition/management, intelligent multi-layer biotic structure, adaptive, collectiveness, cognition, sensitive dependence on initial conditions (butterfly effect), rugged landscape, self-organizing capability, basin of attraction, attractor, smarter evolver, emergent strategist, relativism, futuristic, hysteresis, first mover advantage, emergent of new order, intelligence advantage, intelligence leadership and its characteristics, intelligence governance and its characteristics, in-complete phase space, and all other complexity associated characteristics. The components of the complexity-intelligence strategy are captured in Figure 11.4.

In addition, it is beneficial to identify components with respect to the general strategic path and model/framework/theory.

a. General Strategic Path

- Organizing around intelligence
- Integrated deliberate and emergent strategy

b. Model/Framework/Theory

- General information theory
- Intelligent person model
- Intelligent multi-layer structure and dynamics
- 3C-OK framework (foundation of advanced human intelligent nonlinear dynamic)
- Intelligence leadership theory/strategy
- Intelligence governance theory/strategy
- Relativistic complexity theory

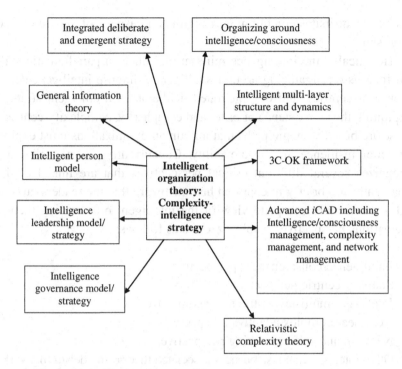

Figure 11.4 Key components of the complexity-intelligence strategy.

11.3 Key Foundation of the Intelligent Organization Theory

Fundamentally, the intelligent organization theory provides a foundation for new thinking to emerge, fresh concepts to be utilized, and broad holistic strategic path to be exploited in an environment when the Newtonian mindset is manifesting constraints and disparities. In this context, algorithmic micro-paths with stepwise solutions that can achieve a specific optimal outcome are not always available. The choice (strategic path and action) to be adopted depends on the varying situation, and very often attaining a new satisficing state is the consequence, as human organizations are also complex adaptive systems with an in-complete phase space (presence of unknown unknowns, and limited predictability). Recognizing this basic attributes/condition is a significant aspect of the redefined leadership.

Holistically, the intelligence mindset introduces a paradigmatic shift that focuses on organizing around intelligence (intense intelligence/consciousness-centric), and the integrated deliberate and emergent strategy (exploiting the co-existence of order and complexity, complexity-centric). These are broad strategic paths that all human organizations must exploit for better resilience and sustainability. Concurrently, the new thinking recognizes several different critical perspectives that are linked to the broad paths are briefly re-captured here to ensure that the readers nurture and attain a more complete view of the intelligent organization theory. The various perspectives emphasized are as follows:

- Intelligence/consciousness perspective
- Stability-centric perspective
- Intelligent multi-layer structure perspective
- Nonlinear complex adaptive perspective
- Network and self-organizing perspective
- Other intelligence/consciousness-associated theories/models/frameworks

11.3.1 *Intelligence/consciousness perspective*

The primary focal point of organizing around intelligence is the human mind and the orgmind. Thus, intelligence/consciousness management that concentrates on optimizing all intrinsic intelligence sources and nurturing high collective intelligence (intense intelligence-intelligence linkages, mindful culture) must be a formal continuous endeavor in all intelligent human organizations. Some details are illustrated in Figure 11.5.

11.3.2 *Stability-centric perspective*

Stability-centric is a fundamental attribute of the physical matter world, as well as the biological/living world. Atoms, molecules (proto-intelligence <=> physical stability), organisms, and biological species (basic life-intelligence <=> physical and biological stability) exist because of this

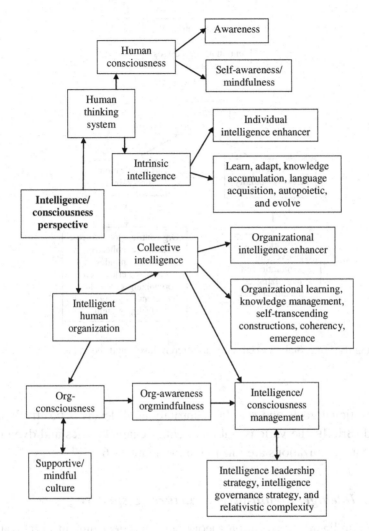

Figure 11.5 The characteristics/activities of the intelligence/consciousness perspective.

basic trait. The evolution theory also focuses on stability-centricity — survival of the fittest (fitness <=> stability-centricity <=> resilience and sustainability). Similarly, every human being is stability-centric (physical, biological and mental stability; autopoietic, self-centric), and this fundamental requirement must be ensured in human organizations at all levels (agent/network/organization stability). Very often, in human organizations,

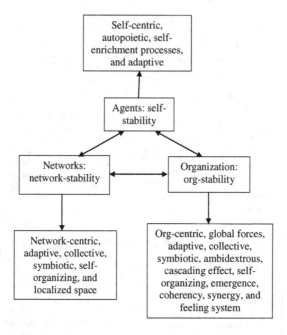

Figure 11.6   Stability-centricity at different levels and their characteristics.

organizational goals and stability-centricity at all levels is positively correlated. Briefly, the various stability-centric characteristics and dynamics
in human organizations are illustrated in Figure 11.6.

11.3.3 *Intelligent multi-layer structure perspective*

In the intelligent organization theory, an intelligent human organization
encompasses an intelligent biotic multi-layer structure that better supports
the *i*CAD (including the cognitive perspective), and vice versa. The different structural layers are as follows:

*   Agent-agent/system micro-structure
*   Intelligent biotic macro-structure
*   Complexity meso-structure
*   Network meso-structure

Briefly, the attributes at different layers and dynamics are illustrated in Figures 11.7 and 11.8.

11.3.4 *Nonlinear complex adaptive perspective*

The fourth emphasis is the nonlinear complex adaptive perspective of intelligent organizations. This perspective focuses on the co-existence of order and complexity (including relativistic complexity), and it overlaps with some of the other perspectives. In general, Figure 11.9 re-captures some of the key focal points. Significant spaces that must be allocated special attention are the spaces of relativistic order. These are spaces of complexity associated with certain human intense intelligence, and they can be embedded with gold nuggets awaiting the right explorers with the prepared mind — deeply associated innovation and creativity. Equally significant is the intelligent organizational dynamic that emerges from the

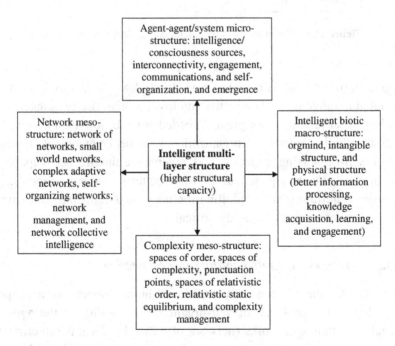

Figure 11.7 Components of the intelligent multi-layer structure.

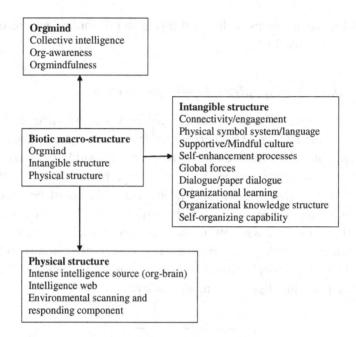

Figure 11.8   Components of the intelligent biotic macro-structure.

integration of autopoiesis and symbiosis (ambidexterity). A high level of individual intelligence and collective intelligence give rise to quicker recognition of surface patterns greatly needed for the new exploration. In addition, a highly intelligent organization with better emergent strategy (higher self-organizing capacity and emergence-intelligence capacity) will survive better at a punctuation point (better crisis management). In this respect, nurturing and exploiting the integrated deliberate and emergent strategy at all times is highly critical.

11.3.5 *Networks and self-organizing perspective*

Networks are inherent meso-structure in all human organizations, especially due to the presence of self-organizing capability of the agents. Inevitably, complex networks (network of networks) form the intermediary layer between agents and their organizations. In intelligent human

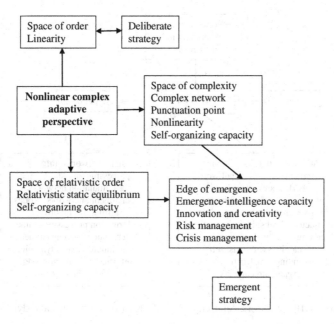

Figure 11.9   The nonlinear complex adaptive perspective that focuses on human organizations with *i*CAD.

organizations, transforming networks into complex adaptive networks, including connecting them in an 'appropriate' way is highly crucial (higher relational capacity and unifying capacity). Appropriate connection and exploitation of networks is significant with respect to the intelligence leadership (later/collective leadership, consultative leadership, learning leadership, and latent leadership), and intelligence governance (self-organizing governance, adaptive governance, and e-governance). The presence of self-organizing capabilities contradicts direct control (bureaucracy, hierarchical leadership, direct governance, empowerment), and excessive direct control creates a high level of odiousness in the organization. In addition to inherent networks (formal and informal), different artificial networks have also been created to enhanced the interconnectivity, communications, information processing, and knowledge acquisition/ accumulation capability of the organization — see Figure 11.10.

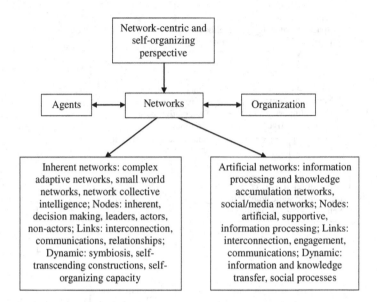

Figure 11.10 Network-centricity and self-organizing attributes and dynamic.

11.3.6 *Some intelligence/consciousness-associated theories/ models/frameworks*

The last aspect concentrates on the intelligence/consciousness-centric, complexity-centric, and network-centric models/theories that provide a more holistic comprehension and exploitation of the human and human organizational attributes, structure, processes, dynamics, and the mental state of the interacting agents. The different models covered in this book, include the general information theory, intelligent person model, 3C-OK framework, relativistic complexity theory, intelligence leadership theory/strategy, and intelligence governance theory/strategy. They are summarized below:

- Briefly, it is interesting to note again that the **general information theory** perceives the human thinking system (brain + mind) as two subsystems (energy–matter subsystem and physical symbols subsystem), and provides a macroscopic explanation of the information processing and knowledge acquisition/accumulation dynamic of the thinking systems that is unique to humanity. Human brains are the most intense intelligence/consciousness sources on this planet. The projected mind is nonlinear, emotional but can also be logical. The human thinking systems as a whole possess diversified capabilities, including symbol creation, event capturing, information processing, internalization, externalization, knowledge acquisition/accumulation, learning, perception/construal, decision making, and wisdom creation — create a complex behavioral schemata, and an abstract mental space. Inevitably, the mental state of the agents is crucial to their organizations.

- **Intelligent person model** focuses on the thinking that ideal human agents must possess certain fundamental characteristics. Basically, such a person is more mindful and orgmindful (intelligence/consciousness-centric), and an effective information decoder, smarter evolver and emergent strategist. S/he is highly self-powered and an intrinsic leader — a natural endowment. In addition, an intelligent person is highly aware of the characteristics of the changing rugged landscape, red queen race, butterfly effect, synergetic effect, constructionist effect, and other complexity associated attributes, as well as the roles and significance of intelligence/consciousness and collective intelligence/org-consciousness. When needed such a person would focus on longer-term gain/survival even if there are shorter-term losses, to ensure both evolution of agents and co-evolution of system. Hence, an intelligent person focuses on organizing around intelligence, and adopts the integrated deliberate and emergent strategy continuously.

- Next, the **3C-OK framework** emphasizes the interdependency of the five properties in human complex adaptive systems, namely collective intelligence, culture, connectivity, organizational learning, and knowledge management. Changes in one characteristic will affect the rest in one way or another. In addition, nurturing and possessing an effective 3C-OK dynamic is critical in any human organizations as this is the unique integrated human complex adaptive processes that erect the foundation of the *i*CAD. Only human CAD is supported by the 3C-OK dynamic that is absent in other species. In this respect, the 3C-OK structure and dynamic is better supported by an intelligent biotic macro-structure.

- **Relativistic complexity theory** is a subset of complexity theory that is confined to humanity and its organizations and agents because of the presence and effectiveness of intense intelligence/consciousness and collective intelligence /org-consciousness. In this situation, certain spaces of complexity can be perceived as spaces of relativistic order with more apparent surface pattern by prepared minds (individual and collective) — also indicating the existence of relativistic static equilibrium. This capability is closely interrelated with innovation and creativity (first mover advantage, butterfly effect, intelligence advantage), as well as better risk management and crisis preparation. It is also connected to the fact that in humanity 'complexity is in the mind of the beholder'.

- The **intelligence leadership theory/strategy** focuses on nurturing intelligence-to-intelligence linkages, mindful culture, organizing around intelligence, intrinsic leadership, and self-organizing capacity (high intelligence/consciousness-centricity). Overall, leadership has to be more lateral/collective and consultative in nature due to the emergent of better educated and informed interacting agents embedded with redefined values and expectations. In this respect, the roles and duties of leaders and followers are narrower or more defused. Under certain situations, especially in spaces of complexity, concentrated calmness (soft voice and low key) of the leaders and even the non-actors is a vital new characteristic so that certain surface patterns can be observed, and deeper collaboration emerges — high self-organizing capacity and emergence-intelligence capacity. Hence, the intelligence leadership strategy exploits the intelligence mindset and thinking with a spread of new leadership attributes including learning leadership, lateral/collective and consultative leadership, transitional leadership, and latent leadership with the basic objective of elevating leadership capacity (leadership capacity <=> unifying capacity). The ideal situation in highly intelligent organizations 'everybody is in charge' (whenever needed).

- The **intelligence governance theory/strategy** focuses on intensifying self-organizing governance, adaptive governance, and e-governance through better integration and network (localized spaces) management, and reducing direct governance as current agents are more self-powered. Thus, collective and lateral mass involvement of all agents (if necessary — as many actors as possible) in the organization, and towards high consensus and collaboration (maximizing exploitation of self-powered capacity, and intrinsic leadership capacity) is favored. Its basic objectives, include achieving better distribution of power, elevating coherency and synergy (reducing conflicts, and nurturing collective interests), ensuring better social relationship (reducing relational friction, and elevating the value of the nonlinear relational parameter — higher relational capacity) by nurturing a feeling system (higher organizational justice), and achieving higher mental cohesion (coherency can still be achieved with the presence of diversification). Thus, the intelligence governance strategy is highly dependent on the attributes of the intelligent person and the intelligence leadership strategy (intelligence governance <=> intelligence leadership <=> 'optimal' integration of 'intelligent' agents), and how they are constructively exploited across the multi-layered structure of the intelligent human organization (presence of differing stakeholders). Thus, a key focal point of current governance strategy is effective exploitation of higher self-organizing capacity and emergence-intelligence capacity. In the respect, the stability of all the agents (stakeholders), as well as the organization must be achieved concurrently.

The above swift review of the intelligent organization theory covering the various perspectives provides a useful recollection. However, it is important to reinforce that the different perspectives are highly interdependent too. There is a substantial amount of overlapping among them. This is the basic nature of complexity theory, evolution theory, as well as the intelligent organization theory. In this respect, when analyzing an intelligent human organization an integrative approach is inevitable. Similarly, when structuring, leading, and governing/managing an *i*CAS, a holistic application of the various perspectives and their practices is a necessity for the organization to be better strengthened and moves in unison. Besides, it is significant to note highly intelligent human organizations cannot be 'constructed' overnight. An intelligent human organization can only be 'nurtured' holistically through gradual evolution, by continuously exploiting intelligence, consciousness, complexity, nonlinearity, interconnectivity, interdependency, self-organizing communications, truthful engagement, networks, voluntary collaboration, organizational consensus, self-transcending constructions (self-organizing capacity), dissipation, and emergence (emergence-intelligence capacity), achieving an intense organizational mental cohesion with conscientious efforts. Hence, even coherency (agree to disagree) with diversifications may be positive, and if there is a synergetic effect and/or constructionist effect is ideal.

11.4 The Uniqueness of Humanity: Its Agents and Organizations

The stability and survival of humanity and all its microcosms (agents, corporations, economies, nations, global institutions, ecosystems, Gaia) ishighly dependent on their intelligence/consciousness and collective intelligence/org-consciousness sources (varying from bipedal locomotion to language acquisition to intensive exploitation of technologies). This interdependency is escalating with increasing acceleration because of the current changing environment (both internal and external). No other biological species exist in a world similar to human beings — encompassing an abstract complex mental space. The criticality of intelligence and consciousness and its association with the capabilities of intense learning, cognition, new knowledge creation self-powered abilities, extensive exploitation of strategies and technologies, self-organization/self-transcending constructions, efficient leadership and governance, and innovation and creativity, have greatly redefined human existence. This intelligence/ consciousness-centric uniqueness has been a positive enabler (ensuring higher structural capacity, adaptive capacity, collectiveness capacity, self-organizing capacity, emergence-intelligence capacity, and unifying capacity). However, it may also lead to self-destruction as the complexity of the human world continues to accelerate. Potentially, a small change in input may lead to a tremendous negative output. In this respect, the nurturing of global mental cohesion is vital.

In particular, focusing on intellectual development is a highly critical path for certain human organizations (corporations, nations) — including fundamental research and R&D (intense intelligence/consciousness-centricity <=> intellectual capacity; high intellectual capacity <=> innovation and creativity <=> new creations/outputs — with new attributes). A fair percentage of the human agents in certain nations and corporations must be involved in elevating intellectual capacity. Reducing intellectual development will lead to the downgrading of every new generation of human beings. Concurrently, all other aspects of humanity will also diminish. However, concentrating on intellectual development has also been perceived to be elitist. The fear is that it leads to wider inequalities and elevates social stresses. In this respect, socio-political incoherency exists. The impact can be so great that some countries are making changes to their education system and manpower planning.

11.4.1 *The individual wisdom paradigm*

As the human world is becoming more intelligence/consciousness-centric, the intensity and attributes of the human thinking systems must be cautiously exploited. At the agent level, intelligence and consciousness is closely linked to knowledge acquisition and its comprehension — although, the values and culture of the agents are equally significant. Anyone that aspires to be an expert in this domain or any other disciplines must realize that there is no shortcut to achieving the ambition. A tremendous amount of hard work is needed during the learning and knowledge accumulation process/period. Effort is the key root of all achievements. Interests and self-motivation are the other two crucial factors. Probably, this requirement is fairly obvious. Inevitably, the knowledge structures in the mind of the individual agent must be substantially nurtured and well-established, and their quality (integration and depth of knowledge structure, and chunk size) must be continuously enriched. The process must be continuous as changes (even in a single domain) are unfolding at all time.

Fundamentally, the quality of the knowledge structures (with intense explicit relationships) must be substantial before any forms of innovation and creativity can emerge. A new concept/discovery or invention only emerges from a highly prepared mind. It does not appear from a vacuum. A deep comprehension and 'seeing through' knowledge structural relationships in the domain is needed. The seeing through capability illuminates the expert to generate new knowledge and hence wisdom (as defined in the general information theory — although, not all experts are wise men). In addition, it is also vital to recognize that the concepts and their associated theories in a domain are very often linked to a certain dimension(s), and they are also time dependent. A theory/domain that is acceptable at this juncture will manifest constraints or ambiguity subsequently, or it may even become obsolete. However, despite this cyclical process, the future of humankind is greatly dependent on the continuous creation of new concept, knowledge, and theory by its agents.

11.4.2 *A significant learning mindset*

In the current environment, not all human agents are keen learners. Some are just not in the mindset to learn. It may be linked to mental constraints, economic affluence, or the domain concerned. Different education systems have introduced differing focuses and methodologies aiming at elevating learning capacity, different focal points, and even life-long learning. Desperate attempts have been exploited to nurture more intelligent and useful human agents. Whatever the diversification in thinking and processes, it is important to recognize that great teachers sow seeds of knowledge with great compassion. Even if some seeds land on concrete ground, it is fine. One day, the conditions of the ground may change, and the seeds may still germinate. In addition, in an intelligence/consciousness-centric environment, it may also be beneficial to note that a highly promising learner is one that has the potential to overtake the teacher. And a great teacher is one that possesses the ability to stimulate a learner to surpass oneself. Every generation must perform better than the previous one, if humanity is to be more sustainable.

11.4.3 *Criticality of compassion and organizational mental cohesion*

The 'greatness' of humanity does not depend on learning and knowledge acquisition (intellectual development) alone. A unique attribute of humanity is **compassion** (intense mindfulness). Thus, the survival of the fittest characteristic (a basic characteristic of the biological world) must be modified in the human world. Human collective survival depends on 'feeling' (fairness, organizational justice, basic survival, trust, consensus, coherency, mental cohesion) systems (nations, communities, as well-corporations). The presence of a relational parameter with high positive value (high relational capacity) is a critical requirement. In this respect, the stability of every human agent is a key focal point. Accounting for every individual agent (contradicts the 'common' CAD that focuses more intensely on the global/organizational patterns — at the expense of some interacting agents), is a unique attribute of the *i*CAD. The latter is the dynamic of a highly intelligent human organization with characteristics confines only to humanity. Thus, the presence and proper manifestation of compassion at all levels is critical.

11.5 Conclusion

Nobody lives forever, not even organizations or nations or the entire humanity. Any things that are composed (against universal expansion) will one day decompose. The existence of an entity depends greatly on how long its intelligence is able to subdue the decomposing processes. On this planet, countless species had emerged and disappeared. Therefore, every new generation of human beings must consistently move on to unexplored new frontiers (spaces of complexity), generate and exploit new knowledge and wisdom, and adopt a new form of thinking, scientific theories, structure, practices, social, economic and political consensus, and culture and philosophy, as well as making preparation for punctuation points, if humanity is to be more resilience and better sustained. Inevitably, being futuristic and continuously entering a higher level of existence (a new humanity global order) is a criticality.

Watching the river that day the boy made a discovery. It was not the discovery of a material thing, something he might put his hand upon. He could not even see it. He had discovered an idea. Quite suddenly, yet quietly, he knew that everything in his life would someday pass under the bridge and be gone, like water.

Grove Patterson, Toledo Blade

Additional/Supportive Information

Appendix 1

Basic Deterministic Chaos Concepts

1 Introduction

1a *What is (deterministic) chaos theory?*

Deterministic chaos theory or **chaotic dynamics** (a branch of mathematics) is the study of relatively low dimensionality chaotic systems captured by one or more **difference equations (discrete chaotic systems** — chaotic characteristics start with dimension 1 systems) or **differential equations (continuous chaotic systems** — chaotic characteristics start with dimension three systems) — see Poincare–Bendixson theorem in Appendix 7. Discrete chaotic systems manifest **bifurcation**, while continuous chaotic systems undergo **transition**. Thus, chaotic systems are nonlinear dynamical systems whose state changes with time nonlinearly (low dimensionality deterministic chaotic systems — sensitive dependence on initial conditions — deterministic not random, but unpredictable).

1b *What are linear/nonlinear dynamical systems?*

In general, there are two different ways of perceiving dynamical systems (constantly changing/evolving). They are as follows:

i. Dynamical Systems
   - Linear, closed conservative systems
   - Dissipative, open, nonlinear systems

ii. Dynamical Systems
   • A set of processes (dynamic)
   • A set of states (outcome)

From the latter perception, the study of dynamical systems focuses on the collection of all its states (phase space) and its constantly changing dynamics (although, some early scientists perceived chaos as a science of process rather than state, that is, of becoming rather than being). In chaos theory, chaos is a certain dynamical phenomenon or chaotic motion (from simplistic to deterministic chaotic) that happens when a chaotic system changes with time (discrete-time or continuous-time). Hence, the term chaos (as defined by **Li** and **Yorke** in 1975) is not a state.

1c *Deterministic chaotic systems and the chaotic dynamic*

Deterministic chaotic systems (DCS) are a type of nonlinear dynamical systems that have a small number of variables (mathematical) — low dimensionality simple deterministic systems/models that manifest chaotic behavior (deterministic ≠ predictable). DCS can be stable for a period of time (predictable) and then manifesting chaotic changes (unpredictable). Some common examples of simple chaotic systems are as follows:

• Logistic map (a difference equation — mathematical system, discrete-time)
• Henon map (a set of difference equations — mathematical system, discrete-time)
• Lorenz waterwheel (mechanical system, continuous-time)
• Water in a container with heat supply (physical system, continuous-time)
• Double rod pendulum (physical system, continuous-time)
• Lorenz convection system (nature/environmental system, continuous-time)

In real world DCS, the variables (at least one variable/parameter must be nonlinear — for instance, the relationship between speed and friction is nonlinear) of such a system interact in a chaotic nonlinear manner (also associated with the microscopic entities are clear but the macroscopic behavior is difficult to comprehend) leading to a deterministic but not predictable output. It is deterministic because when inputs are known, the output can be computed accurately. However, if an estimated input is used, the output can be totally different, that is, a small change in input can produce a totally different output — leading to unpredictability — sensitive dependence on initial conditions — a divergent process — butterfly effect (see 2b) — first observed by Edward Lorenz in his weather system.

A chaotic system also possesses the property of interdependency (high interconnectedness among the variables). Discrete-time chaotic systems changes in state through a discrete process called bifurcation (see 2c) — chaotic attractor. In addition, there are also certain preferred states that form strange attractors (see 2d and 2e). An attractor is a set of states and a subset of the phase space. The first strange attractor that is not a mathematical strange attractor is the Lorenz attractor of his three-dimensional convection system (physical system) — observed by Edward Lorenz in the 1960s (although some mathematical strange attractors have been observed earlier).

Hence, in general, the **chaotic dynamic/motion** changes from **simplicity to deterministic chaotic** (relatively low finite randomness, not infinite randomness) which is unpredictable due to the butterfly effect, and interdependency of variables, leading to the emergent of **chaotic attractor** and/or **strange attractor.**

2 Further Discussion on Properties of Chaotic Systems

Deterministic chaotic systems are inherently sensitive dependence on initial conditions (exhibiting the butterfly effect) due to the presence of nonlinear variable(s). As indicated earlier some other characteristics of DCS include bifurcation, far-from-equilibrium and presence of chaotic attractor. These characteristics are further illustrated below.

2a *Linearity and nonlinearity*

The essence of linearity is the proportionate relationship between cause and effect (in mathematics, a simple linear equation is $y = x + 1$ where x is the cause and y denotes the effect) — see Appendix 3. A small input leads to a small output, and larger inputs leads to larger outputs. A linear equation can be easily 'solved', and a linear system could be 'dismantled' and 'assembled' (Cartesian belief, reductionism and fundamentalism) again without changes in properties.

However, for a nonlinear system, the direct proportional relationship is no longer true (nonlinearity). Consequently, in a nonlinear system, starting points that are close to one another may result with rather 'distant' ending points (for instance, for a power/exponential equation $y = x^2$, when $x = 1$, $y = 1$, but when $x = 3$, $y = 9$ — a simple nonlinear relationship).

In is important to note that finite dimensional linear dynamical systems are never chaotic. Chaotic behavior only emerges in nonlinear or infinite dimensional linear dynamical systems. The latter is **in-deterministic chaotic systems**.

2b *Sensitive dependence on initial conditions (butterfly effect)*

Lorenz (through his weather system) is the first to recognize that chaotic systems are sensitive to initial inputs. The slightest initial difference, if amplified repeatedly (by both positive and negative feedbacks) may lead to highly unpredictable behavior/output (see Figure 1A.1 for a simple illustration). At the initial stage of the diagram the outputs of the two curves are about the same for the same initial inputs. At a later stage, their outputs are substantially different for approximately the same inputs. This

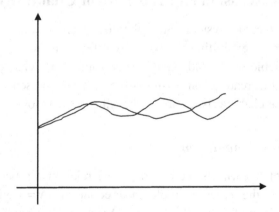

Figure 1A.1   A simplified illustration of sensitive dependence on initial conditions (butterfly effect).

phenomenon of repetitive amplification due to iterations leads to the consequence known as the butterfly effect. Thus, the sensitive dependence on initial conditions attribute of a DCS renders its output unpredictable.

2c *Bifurcation*

Bifurcation is splitting into two paths, and it is a unique way that discrete-time chaotic systems behave. The system becomes chaotic when the bifurcating process accelerates rapidly increasing the number of paths from 1 to 2, 4, 8, 16, 32, ..., (chaotic attractor). A commonly studied chaotic system that is frequently used to illustrate bifurcation is the logistic map — a discrete chaotic system. Mathematically, the logistic map (dimension one, degree 2) is a relatively simple equation, $x_{n+1} = rx_n(1 - x_n)$ where x_n is between 0 and 1, and r (bifurcation nonlinear parameter) is a positive number (interest value, $0 \leq r \leq 4$). The characteristic of bifurcation indicates that a variety of different paths are opened up before the system. At the 4th bifurcation point the logistic map moved into deep chaos — **chaotic attractor** (see the simplified bifurcation diagram — Figure 1A.2) — also see Appendix 3.

In 1978, **Feigenbaum** published his theoretical study on bifurcation, including period doublings, the computation of the (first) **Feigenbaum constant** (≈ 4.6692, a universal constant) and universality using the logistic

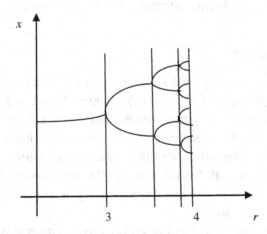

Figure 1A.2 A simplified illustration of bifurcation — at 4th bifurcation the system is highly chaotic.

map. The constant is the ratio of the length between two consecutive points of bifurcation.

2d *States/attractors/phase space of nonlinear dynamical systems*

An attractor (a set of states) is a subset of the phase space (the set of all the states of the system) of dynamical systems. Dynamical systems possess four types of attractors as follows:

- Point attractor
- Periodic (limit cyclic) attractor
- Strange/chaotic attractor
- In-deterministic chaotic attractor

A point (dimension zero) and periodic attractors have been observed in simple linear physical systems (dimension two and below). When a marble is rowed along the side of a bowl it will circulate continuously in the bowl moving towards the lowest point. This lowest point is a point attractor (one state). Similarly, the pendulum of a 'charged' old grandfather clock possesses a two-point periodic attractor (at the two extreme ends of the swing) — see Appendix 3 for simple mathematical illustrations. The strange/chaotic attractor was discovered last in mathematical chaos. (All chaotic attractors are strange attractors, but not vice versus.)

2e *Strange attractor*

As stated earlier, in dynamical systems, there are four types of attractor namely, point (fixed), periodic (cyclic), strange/chaotic, and in-deterministic chaotic. In physical systems (dimension two or less) the fixed/point attractor and periodic attractor are very common. In higher dimension nonlinear systems, the attractor could be a curve, a manifold (a topological space), or a set with fractal structure. In mathematics, the evolving variables of an attractor (in finite dimensional systems) are represented by an n-dimensional vector.

A commonly illustrated example of a strange attractor is the **Lorenz attractor** — its phase diagram (3D) is a deep spiral that never intersects,

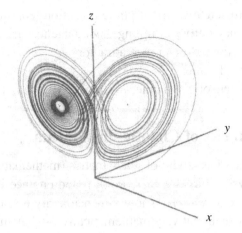

Figure 1A.3   The 3D Lorenz strange attractor.

and is confined in a finite three-dimensional space (see Figure 1A.3) — converges to an attracting set. The path appears to be infinity long (with a significant depth) that never intersects itself (diverge from other nearby orbits), and the attractor is scale invariance (see strange attractor Appendix 7). In a human society, sociality is a biological attractor. A strange attractor is a 'stable' state.

2f *Far-from-equilibrium*

Far-from-equilibrium systems do not return to their earlier regular states, they never repeat themselves, and they are nonlinear. Thus, such systems are never in static equilibrium. The nonlinear interactions in far-from-equilibrium open systems allow the systems to pass from one basic state to another by bifurcation and transitions. In this respect, the far-from-equilibrium characteristic in nonlinear interdependent dynamical systems is both the source of chaos and renewal.

Notes: **Some Significant Properties of DCS:**

- Sensitive dependence on initial conditions (butterfly effect)
- Deterministic but not (limited) predictable (presence of surprises)
- Nonlinearity (variable and/or parameter)

- Bifurcation (discrete-time), or phase transition (continuous-time)
- Interdependency (strong coupling among agents/variables)
- Chaotic attractor and/or strange attractor
- Far-from-equilibrium
- Deterministic chaotic dynamic — simplicity to chaotic

3 The Boundaries of Chaotic Phenomena

Chaos theory started as a field of mathematics (mathematical theory) and is applied in physics, biology, meteorology, and engineering focusing on nonlinear dynamical systems of low dimensionality (easier to handle — can be analyzed quantitatively/mathematically — but manifest chaotic behavior). Thus, the behaviors of any DCS can be analyzed using a mathematical model with one or a set of difference or differential equations. Subsequently, it is recognized that in this Universe chaotic phenomena are a rule rather than an exception. Chaotic dynamic/motion has been observed in astrophysics, meteorology, oceanography, fluid dynamics, and optics. In the living world, it is present in ecological systems, as well as the dynamics of the brain and heart.

Over time, chaotic mathematical models have also been exploited in other disciplines such as economics, finance, philosophy, and sociology (although, most of these systems are now recognized as complex adaptive systems). Research activities in chaos were most intense during the 1960s to 1980s. Since the 1990s, chaos theory has been absorbed into complexity theory (see Appendix 2) — especially, after the formation of the Santa Fe Institute in 1984. DCS can be perceived as a subset of complex systems with no historical dependency (hysteresis). Complex adaptive systems, a special group of complex systems are nonlinear dynamical systems with living agents.

Appendix 2

Basic Complexity and CAS/CAD Concepts

1 Introduction

1a *What is complexity?*

In general, **complexity** is some 'form' of disorderliness. 'Traditional' **disorder** or **randomness** (especially, in the exact sciences and mathematics) is objective but complexity is subjective (more so in the living world and definitely in humanity), that is, **predictability** is also subjective. In general, complexity is highest in high finite dimensional nonlinear systems (infinite randomness is not complex — statistical/stochastic) — see Figure 2A.1. Holistically, complex dynamic varies from complexity to simplicity — **emergent of new order**. In this respect, a key characteristic of complexity is the presence of a surface pattern (a potential next state of 'existence'). Thus, in the complexity theory, there is a distinct different between deterministic chaos and complexity.

1b *What is complexity theory?*

Mathematically, **complexity theory is the study of nonlinear dynamical systems**. Currently, the domain encompasses chaos theory, evolution theory, cybernetics, systems theory, and networks theory. There are three common types of systems involved in this domain, namely deterministic chaotic systems (DCS), complex systems (CS), and complex adaptive systems (CAS) — see Figure 2A.2.

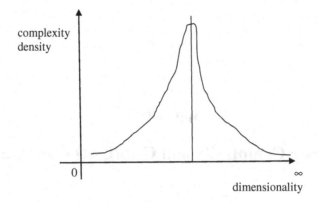

Figure 2A.1 A simplified illustration of complexity density versus dimensionality of systems.

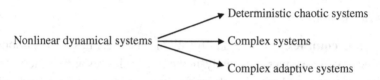

Figure 2A.2 Different types of nonlinear dynamical systems.

Since the 1980s, complexity theory focuses on complex systems and complex adaptive systems — although, it also include deterministic chaotic systems because of their common subset of properties (including sensitive dependence on initial conditions — butterfly effect, unpredictability, interdependency, far-from-equilibrium, scalability/scale invariance/self-similar, and strange attractor) — for DCS see Appendix 1. **A significant difference between chaotic systems and complex systems is that the latter is in-deterministic and possesses historical dependency** — the history of complex systems and complex adaptive systems is important, as the earlier states of these systems can affect the later states, a characteristic known as **hysteresis** (time-based dependency). The key different between CS and CAS is the agents in CAS are living (adaptive).

As indicated earlier, **CS/CAS** are usually high finite dimensionality nonlinear dynamical systems involving a large number of variables/agents/networks (presence of a network meso-structure) that possess

self-organizing capability. In general, nonlinear dynamical systems (especially, high dimensionality systems) are difficult (or impossible) to solve mathematically (in-deterministic, nonlinear, unpredictable, in-complete phase space), and their components cannot be analyzed separately and added together subsequently (see reductionist hypothesis and constructionist hypothesis in Appendix 7). Thus, CAS can only be analyzed quantitatively with approximate mathematical models as a large number of interdependent variables are involved — including **known variables** that cannot be measured accurately, and **unknown unknowns/variables**. All living systems and human organizations are CAS (for instance, cell, immune system, brain, ant colony, ecosystem, corporation, stock market, economies, social system, political party, nation, and regional/global institution).

In addition, the complex adaptive dynamic (CAD) evolves from **complexity** (encompassing continuous change/variation) **to simplicity** — there is a (potential) surface pattern, although, the details (of the agents) may not be known. In this respect, a system is complex when there is a particular patterned order in the way it changes as a whole, but the future of its individual agents/components is unknown, or may not be known. Consequently, the application of complexity theory into humanity highlights the presence of subjective disorderliness or orderliness (**relativistic complexity**), sensitive dependence on initial conditions, nonlinearity, spaces of complexity embedded with high benefits, the significance of effective self-transcending constructions (and its correlation with collective intelligence), better network management/integration, preparation for sudden punctuation points, and emergent of new order. This new thinking and comprehension provides a more 'realistic' and accurate insight of human world, and its organizations and dynamics. In this respect, any attempts to exploit complexity associated characteristics can create a new niche and competitiveness in a fast changing environment that traditional theories and thinking cannot achieved.

1c *What is order?*

At one extreme end, order indicates no change, everything remains status quo. Order, linearity, determinism, certainty, regularity, reliability, predictability, and similarity are inter-related and do exist in this world to certain extent. This observation and thinking is derived from or associated with the Newtonian mindset. Within certain time scales and under certain conditions many phenomena change in an orderly and linear way, or at least perceive to be so — a period of (relativistic) static equilibrium. In this case, order provides humanity with comfort, confidence, assurance, as well as complacency.

Mathematically, for linear systems, small causes (inputs) lead to small effects (outputs) and large causes have large effects. Two similar linear systems under the same conditions often develop in the same way. In many circumstances, small errors in measurements cancel each other, and are negligible in predicting outcomes. From the ways such a system changes in the past, it is often possible to predict how the system will change in the future — indicating that deliberate strategy and forecasting are beneficial. In such a situation or environment, change is perceived as orderly, manageable, and controllable.

In complexity theory, order is still presence (co-existence of order and complexity) and highly significant because ultimately emergence leads to a new order. This basic phenomenon is so significant that some complexity researchers simply defined **complexity theory as the study of emergent of order**.

1d *Complex adaptive systems and complex adaptive dynamic*

Complexity theory deals with how relationships and interactions between the entities/agents/parts in CS and CAS give rise collective behaviors (interdependency) or surface patterns. Briefly, the key meanings of CAS are as follows:

Complex => Surface pattern exists but detail patterns may not be known
Adaptive => Consume information, learn, and change if necessary
System => A collection of interconnected and interacting agents/ networks confined within a defined boundary

Simply, complex adaptive systems are systems with a large number of 'living interacting agents', and are driven by a complex adaptive dynamic where both order and complexity co-exist leading to the emergent of new order (otherwise, the systems disintegrate). The level of order and complexity varies continuously with time depending on many factors/variables such as the behavioral schemata of the interacting agents (mental state of human agents in human organizations), internal possesses of the system, problems (issues and policies in nations) encountered, and the changing environment (both internal and external). In this respect, the presence of complexity is formally endorsed, and for human systems the presence of complexity has to be well-scrutinized, comprehended, and exploited to elevate innovation, resilience, and sustainability.

In general, macroscopically the complex adaptive dynamic evolves from complexity to simplicity, and at more micro levels it encompasses autopoiesis, interconnectivity, interdependency, engagement, autocatalysis, self-organization/self-transcending constructions of agents and networks, and emergence (if constructively 'orchestrated'). Thus, CAS, in particular, human organizations possess the capability of self-transcending constructions (order not totally for free — an added advantage) — due to the presence of intense intelligence/consciousness of human agents, and collective intelligence of the system.

1e *Five core properties of complexity theory*

Some earlier researchers have observed/proposed the following five core properties from the study of chaos/complexity in this Universe:

- Consciousness (Life-centric)
- Complexity (Unpredictability)
- Connectivity (Network-centric)
- Dissipation (Self-renewal)
- Emergence (Self-Organizing, Evolution and Co-evolution, New order)

In this respect, complexity theory is a self-conscious science (see law of complexity/consciousness, law of complexity/intelligence, and law of consciousness/intelligence in Appendix 7 for further illustrations.) Recognizing the presence of intelligence and consciousness is a key foundation for better comprehension and exploitation of complexity in human organizations. In the intelligent organization theory, intelligent human organizations (*i*CAS) embedding an intelligent complex adaptive possess a sixth core property — **intelligence**.

2 Some Additional Characteristics of CAS/Human Organizations

2a *Life-centric, behavioral schemata and adaptive*

A complex adaptive system comprises a group of dynamically changing and interacting heterogeneous agents each embedded with a set of behavioral schemata. Thus, complex adaptive systems are living systems (perceived to be so in the intelligent organization theory). They are adaptive, that is, they continuously consume new information and act on it, if necessary. In human organizations, this processes and dynamic are multi-layer. It is done at the agents, networks/complex networks, and systems levels. As agents learn, their behavioral schemata change and the interactive dynamic is also modified (intra-organizational). As the systems learn, they evolve and co-evolve with the environment which very often is a composite CAS (inter-organizational). Even the set of rules governing its dynamic is evolving or changing constantly (for example, policies in a country are modified or changed over time). In this respect, CAS encompass life-centric intelligence/consciousness which is absent in complex systems.

2b *Connectivity/interconnectivity and interdependency*

Another crucial characteristic of CAS is connectivity (engagement, relationship, relational friction, and relational capacity). In the world of CAS, everything can be connected to everything else (for example, in the human world, the connections include individuals and family, business corporations and economy, economies and regional/global society). They are also highly interdependent at all levels (agent/agent, agent/network, and agent/system relationships). Thus, the indicators of complexity are the degree of differentiation and degree of organization in terms of intricacy of interconnectedness and interdependency (higher interdependency <=> higher complexity). In this respect, a component in CAS cannot be analyzed separately from the system (contradicts the Newtonian mindset and reductionist hypothesis). A CAS has to be analyzed as a whole.

2c *Open and dissipative*

Complex adaptive systems are open and dissipative systems in perpetual motion. A dissipative system is a thermodynamically open system that is in frequent matter and energy exchange with the environment. A human agent/organization is open and dissipative because it is in constant exchange with other systems or the environment involving many entities (including energy, food, information, knowledge, and agents). Such a system possesses a **dissipative structure** — presence of a differential structure/tension. However, the dissipative structure of a complex adaptive system is a dynamical regime that appears as a 'steady' state. This term was first used by Prigogine when he recognized that dissipative structure is thermodynamically equilibrium. Thus, it is a structure that is in constant change, and yet through the process brings greater order to the structure itself.

2d *Space of complexity and punctuation point*

Complexity arises as a natural/inherent development when a CAS reaches a certain level of variety and diversity — that is, it is an intrinsic characteristic of all CAS. Over time, the internal processes of autocatalysis feed the system leading it to self-organize into a more complex level of functioning (higher robustness). At every instant when the complexity of the interactions is rich enough, the system becomes supercritical. If the autocatalytic process (self-organization) is intrinsic the system would get order for free but when a latent impetus is present the process is known as self-transcending construction.

In this respect, all CAS evolve themselves to the **edge of order**, and **edge of emergence** (see Appendix 7 for the new explanation of edge of order, edge of emergence, and edge of chaos). These are the spaces where the system/organization needs to balance (autopoiesis, localization => self-organization, globalization) and re-organize itself through emergence — so as not to self-destruct. In human organizations, spaces of complexity are always present. Some of them possess fairly well-defined boundaries (for instance, technosphere of biotechnology), while others intertwined in a sophisticated manner (regional political relationship/conflict). Thus, some spaces of complexity are not surprises, while punctuation points that appear suddenly are (devastating events). The latter include large scale natural disasters.

Very often, spaces of complexity are stable enough to receive and keep information, and they are also able to transmit them — especially, if they are well managed. They can adjust themselves to a point where their computational ability is maximized. Hence, it is in such spaces where the organization can attain their highest level of fitness and adaptability. It is also at spaces of complexity that CAS can be most innovative and creative. Thus, certain spaces of complexity are unexplored territories embedded with gold nuggets — linked to **risk management** (innovation and creativity, intelligence leadership strategy). Hence, intelligent human organizations must constantly venture into and exploit certain spaces of complexity. Concurrently, there must also be preparation for punctuation points that appear suddenly — **crisis management**.

2e *Butterfly effect, unpredictability and feedback*

All CAS are sensitive dependence on initial conditions (butterfly effect). In addition, not all the present states of CAS (including human organizations) could be measured with absolute precision. As such systems usually have large numbers of inputs/variables and/or interacting agents, unknown unknowns are always present. Thus, the evolution trajectories of such systems cannot be described precisely because of its high complexity and nonlinearity. The latter is further elevated due to the fact that CAS possess feedback loops — circular causation. It is these closed loops of cause and effect in CAS which results in higher nonlinearity and unpredictability (see autocatalysis and circular causation in Appendix 7). In this respect, a future state is not always predictable, rendering forecasting not always meaningful.

2f *Autopoiesis, symbiosis, self-organization/self-transcending constructions and phase transition*

It is important to recognize that human agents are autopoietic (self-centric, self-stability). The term autopoiesis was first used by **Maturana** and **Varela**. Autopoietic agents are self-centric, self-preserving, self-enhancing, and self-producing. Thus, the autopoietic dynamic is an inward focusing constant order-creation process — including creating a local order space or network. Therefore, the agents in CAS can be highly myopic and self-centric — significant emphasis on immediate (short-term) gain. At the extreme, autopoiesis can be an inward self/center-seeking process encompassing non-equilibrium that resists changes, and makes communication/connectivity/engagement difficult — self-destructive.

However, if the condition is right, autopoietic agents can be self-regulating, self-organizing, and balancing with networks and the system — symbiosis. Thus, they are capable of maintaining a 'dynamical stable state' in a non-equilibrium environment. In this case, the agents make adjustment to their local space to maintain a stable holistic organization, if the mental state of the agent is balanced. In this case, a nonlinear, interdependent, far-from-equilibrium system/organization can continuously self-organize itself into a new, more complex order.

Therefore, self-organization/self-transcending constructions is the critical possess underlying the emergence of forms manifest as physical, chemical, biological, ecological, social, and cultural structures. With self-organization, matter becomes 'active' and has the potential to spontaneously and unpredictably develop new forms and structures by itself (proto-intelligence, stability-centricity). It is also the principle connecting the sciences of the physical (non-living) world and the world of the living (biological). Self-organization produces 'biological' (including gene, chromosome, genome and cell) matter (from physical matter) that possesses 'life' — a highly critical and unique phase transition (constructionist hypothesis) — an emergence embedded with intelligence and consciousness.

Fundamentally, phase transition is used to describe the transformation of a thermodynamic systems changing from one matter state to another. It is a continuous process. In CAS, phase transition occurs when the system is self-organizing between the edge of order, edge of emergence, and edge of chaos. Similar to other CAS, phase transition in human organizations occur at **self-organized criticality** (self-transcending constructions driven by individual intelligence of the agents and collective intelligence of the organization) — leading to the emergent of a new state.

2g *Evolution, phylogenesis and hysteresis*

As indicated earlier, CAS are embedded with intelligence and/or collective intelligence (for instance, an ant, a colony of ants, a pack of wolves, an ecosystem, human beings and their organizations). Therefore, they possess higher level intelligence (beyond proto-intelligence that is confined to the physical matter world), and are able to adapt and evolve with the changing environment. All CAS in the biological/ecological world evolve from a 'primitive' (less complex) stage to a more sophisticated and robust (more complex) stage (for instance, from unicellular organisms to trillion-cellular organisms, and from a small village to an enormous cosmopolitan city), although the complex adaptive dynamic is described as varying from complexity to 'simplicity' — emergent of new order (relativistic, constant elevation in system robustness).

Evolution has the tendency to build upon its own historical successes (for example: the cerebral cortex emerges on top of the limbic system and cerebellum) — phylogenesis (see Appendix 7). Thus, microscopically CAS become more complex over time but macroscopically there are surface patterns (including their layered structure) that can be deciphered or understood, and even exploited with a higher level of intelligence (collective intelligence). Similarly, CAS are also dependent on their history, as a future state may depend on one or more earlier states or an event that started earlier and its impact is still accumulating — hysteresis (chaotic systems are not).

3 Human Organizational are Intrinsic Complex Adaptive Systems

Fundamentally, all human organizations are intrinsic CAS with a collection of human thinking systems, irrespective of their primary functions (social, business/economic, education, political). They are high finite dimensionality complex adaptive systems with life/intelligence/ consciousness, stability-seeking, and self-organizing capabilities, and an in-complete phase space. In human organizations, not all the variables involved are known or could be measured accurately. Thus, not all the outcomes are deterministic or predictable — that is, global optimality is not achievable. Concurrently, the structure of human organizations is multi-layered, encompassing agents, networks, network of networks (complex networks), and the entire system. Thus, a human organization/ system, for instance, a stock market or a nation is a CAS and not a deterministic chaotic system because of its complex adaptive dynamic, hysteresis, and in-determinism (due to the large and in-complete number of variables involved — rendering mathematical modeling and forecasting as best an estimation). Thus, the adoption of a qualitative approach is more feasible.

In human organizations, both linear order and complexity intertwine in varying degrees, and alternate throughout the life history of the systems. A period of relative order is followed by a period of complexity (that is, always fluctuating between stasis and punctuation), which in turn brings forth a new order — that is, complexity is always part of the **organizational meso-structure**. The period of deep complexity (physical and/or mental) is a natural and inevitable part of development/evolution of human organizations. And the creation of new order is born out of the turbulence of complexity — indicating the significance of emergence. Overall, to maintain its wholeness a human organization has to invest in itself more meaningful communications, truthful engagement, and positive relationships among its components (agents and networks), as well as between itself and its environment. In addition, in highly intelligent human organizations complexity is relativistic — leading to the emergence of relativistic complexity.

In general, when human systems lag in matching the quality of their relationships to the degree of complexity of these relationships, they are in for a period of high uncertainty. Increasing complexity of a system breeds growing uncertainty when it is not matched with a parallel change in the quality of relationships.

Some Summary Notes:

The equations/relations below should serve as a general guide for nurturing intelligent human organizations.

Quality of relationships >>   Degree of complexity — (through high orgmindfulness)

Collective intelligence >> Σ individual intelligence (synergetic)

Intensity of intelligence >>   Intensity of complexity => relativistic complexity

4 Some 'Simplified' Definitions

In summary, the characteristics of the different category of systems and the dynamics involved can be briefly described as follows:

- **Deterministic Chaotic systems** are relatively low dimensionality nonlinear deterministic dynamical systems that undergo bifurcation or phase transition, and possess chaotic/stranger attractors — deterministic but unpredictable.
- **Chaotic dynamic** evolves from simplicity to deterministic chaotic through bifurcation or phase transition.
- **Complex adaptive systems** are finite high dimensionality nonlinear dynamical living systems that undergo self-organization/self-transcending constructions (from complexity to emergent of new order), and possess strange attractors — in-deterministic and unpredictable.
- **Complex adaptive dynamic** evolves from complexity to simplicity through autopoiesis, symbiosis, autocatalysis, self-organization/self-transcending constructions, and emergence.
- **Human organizations** are high finite dimensionality complex adaptive systems, and not deterministic chaotic systems — the in-complete set of variables renders quantitative studies (mathematical or algorithmic analysis) difficult because of insufficient information for certain known variables, presence of unknown variables, and/or unknown unknowns (thus, to capture a human organization as a mathematical

dynamical system, for instance, a stock market is at best an approximation, and the phase space is never complete).

5 Some Illustrations with Examples

[There are other specialized subsets of complexity theory, including computational complexity theory (a sub-domain of information theory and computer science), algorithmic information theory (including Kolmogorov complexity — founded by Ray Solomonoff), and programming complexity, that are not included in this book.]

Table 2A.1   Some characteristics and examples of the three different spaces (order, relativistic order, and complexity).

Characteristic \ Space	Order	Relativistic order	Complexity
Path	Linear	Linear <=> Nonlinear	Nonlinear
Strategy	Deliberate	Deliberate <=> Emergent	Emergent
Degree of Freedom	Zero <=> Low	Low <=> Relatively high (Manageable)	Very high (towards punctuation)
Example	A mechanical system	A biotechnological R&D space	A worldwide financial crisis

Appendjx 3

Some Simple Mathematical Illustrations

1 Introduction

A simple dynamical system can be captured and analyzed by means of a single or collection/set of mathematical equations. The equations can be **continuous-time** (differential equations or partial differential equations) or **discrete-time** (difference equations). The equation or set of equations possesses a **dimension** (the number of variables), a **degree** (the highest power of a variable), and the variable(s) and parameter(s) can be linear or nonlinear. An equation with only one variable is of dimension one. The presence of a nonlinear **variable** or **parameter** renders the equation or set of equations nonlinear. A variable is nonlinear if there is a nonlinear relationship, for instance, the changing relationships between speed and friction (two variables). A parameter is nonlinear when changes in its value causes the output of the system to be unpredictable, for instance, the bifurcation parameter (r), of the logistic map causes the system to be chaotic for certain values of $r - \{[x_{n+1} = x_n r (1 - x_n)] $ — where x_n is the variable, and r the parameter}. (A map in mathematics is an evolution function. A chaotic map generates chaotic behavior, and sometime also fractals.)

2 Point and Periodic Attractor

A dynamical system (linear or nonlinear) possesses state(s), attractor(s), and a phase space. An **attractor** is a subset (a collection of **states**) of the

phase space that manifests certain properties. There are four different categories of attractors. The first two attractors are fixed point and periodic attractor (both attractors can be accurately calculated/predicted).

2a *Fixed point (dimension zero) — an attractor with one state*

A point whose iterates are the same point is a fixed point.
For x_0 in the domain of f, x_0 is a fixed point of f if $f(x_0) = x_0$.

Example: For $f(x) = \sin x$, 0 is the unique fixed point of f

because   f(0) = sin 0 = 0.

2b *Periodic (low finite-cycle) — an attractor with finite number of states*

For period 2:

For x_0 in the domain of f, x_0 has period 2 if $f^{(2)}(x_0) = x_0$, and if $x_0, f(x_0)$, $f^{(2)}(x_0)$ are distinct. The orbit $\{x_0, f(x_0), f^{(2)}(x_0)\}$ is 2-cycle.

Example: For $f(x) = -x^3$, $\{-1, 1\}$ is a 2-cycle

because   f(−1) = 1

and   f(1) = −1.

3 Linearity and Iteration

3a *One-dimensional linear function — in R*

Any one-dimensional functions of the form $f(x) = cx$ where x is a real number (R), and c is a constant, are linear functions. Their graphs are straight lines.

3b *Two dimensions linear function — in R^2*

Any function $f\colon R^2 \to R^2$ is linear if $f(a\tilde{n} + b\tilde{u}) = af(\tilde{n}) + bf(\tilde{u})$ for all $\tilde{n}$ and $\tilde{u}$ in R^2, and all real numbers of a and b.

3c *Iteration*

In mathematics, iteration refers to applying a function repeatedly, that is, using the output of one iteration as the input for the next.

If f is a function, with x_0 in the domain of f, then:

$$f(x_0) = \text{first iterates of } x_0 \text{ in } f$$

$$f^{(2)}(x_0) = f[f(x_0)] = \text{second iterates of } x_0 \text{ in } f$$

and after n iterations,

$$f^{(n)}(x_0) = n^{\text{th}} \text{ iterates of } x_0 \text{ in } f$$

where $\{f^{(n)}(x_0)\}^{\infty}_{n=0}$ is the orbit of x_0.

Iterations (in dynamical systems, fractals) of simple functions could produce complex behaviors [common examples, Poincare map (**Henri Poincare**, 1854–1912), Julia sets (**Gaston Julia**, 1893–1978), and Fatou set (**Pierre Fatou**, 1878–1929)].

4 One-Dimensional Deterministic Chaos

Mathematically, a function f is (deterministic) chaotic if it satisfies one of the following conditions:

— f has sensitive dependence on initial conditions on its domain.
— f has a positive Lyapunov exponent (exponential divergence) at each point in its domain that is not eventually periodic.

4a *Sensitive Dependence on Initial Conditions*

For $f : I \rightarrow I$ in an interval I, x is sensitive on initial conditions if there exists an $\varepsilon > 0$ and $\partial > 0$, such that $|x - y| < \partial$ and $|f^{(n)}(x) - f^{(n)}(y)| > \varepsilon$, where y is in I and n is a positive integer.

Example: For $f(x) = 2x$ in $I = \{0 \leq x \leq 0.5\}$ and $f(x) = 2x-1$ in $I = \{0.5 < x \leq 1\}$, $|f^{(10)}(x) - f^{(10)}(y)| > 0.5$ when $x = 1/3$ and $y = 0.333$

Iterates	$f^{(n)}(x)$	$f^{(n)}(y)$
0	1/3	0.333
1	2/3	0.666
2	1/3	0.332
3	2/3	0.664
4	1/3	0.328
5	2/3	0.656
6	1/3	0.312
7	2/3	0.624
8	**1/3**	**0.248**
9	**2/3**	**0.496**
10	**1/3**	**0.992**

Thus, $f^{(10)}(x) = 1/3 = 0.333$ and $f^{(10)}(y) = 0.992$.

Hence, $|f^{(10)}(x) - f^{(10)}(y)| = 0.659 > 0.5$.

=> f is sensitive dependence on initial conditions (in I).

4b *Lyapunov Exponent*

The Lyapunov (Aleksandr Lyapunov, 1857–1918) exponent of a dynamical system is a quantity that shows the rate of separation of infinitesimally close trajectories. Basically, for two trajectories with initial separation ∂z_0, they will diverge at a rate $|\partial z(t)| \approx e^{\lambda t}|\partial z_0|$ where λ is the Lyapunov exponent.

For $f: I \rightarrow I$ in a bounded interval I where f is continuously differentiable, and for a $x \in I$, then $\lambda(x)$ the Lyapunov exponent is defined as $\lim_{(n \to \infty)} (1/n) \ln |(f^{(n)})'(x)|$ (if the limit exists).

(A map has a **strange attractor** if the attractor has a non-integer Lyapunov dimension, for instance, Horse map and Henon map. A map has a **chaotic attractor** if the attractor is sensitive dependence on initial conditions or a Lyapunov number greater than 1, for instance, Henon map. Not all strange attractors are chaotic attractors. Some other common strange attractors are Lorenz attractor and Rossler attractor.)

5 Equations of Motion/Change

The causal relation between the current state and the next state can be represented by a (or a set of) mathematical (differential or difference) equation as follows:

- For continuous-time change, $dx/dt = f(x)$ or $\partial x/\partial t = f(x)$;
- For discrete-time change, $x_{n+1} = f(x_n)$;

where x is the state and t is the time variable. The dynamic is linear if the casual relation between the present state and next state is linear. Otherwise, it is nonlinear. Take note of the following information:

- Finite dimensional **linear** systems are never chaotic.
- Finite dimensional systems are chaotic when there is **nonlinearity** (**difference equation can be chaotic from dimension one**, while **differential equation can be chaotic from dimension three**). Common examples of nonlinearity are quadratic equations, and nonlinear recurrence relations.
- High dimensional linear systems can be in-deterministic chaotic.

5a *Differential equations (continuous-time) describe how system processes change continuously over time*

- A simple example is **Newton second law of motion**, $F = m \, dv/dt$ (motion equation of an object with mass, m — with orderly, deterministic, and predictable states) — (Isaac Newton, 1642–1726).
- Another example is **Schrodinger equation** (partial differential equation — wave equation of an object with mass, m — that describes how its quantum state changes with time), $i\hbar \, \partial\psi(\check{r}, t)/\partial t = -\hbar^2/2m \nabla^2\psi(\check{r}, t)\partial\psi(\check{r}, t)/\partial t + V(\check{r}, t)\partial\psi(\check{r}, t)/\partial t$ where $\hbar = h/2\pi = 1.05459 \times 10^{-34}$ joule second, h is Planck's constant, $\psi(\check{r}, t)$ is the wave function (over space-time), ∇^2 is the Laplacian operator, and $V(\check{r}, t)$ is the potential energy influencing the particle (with eigenstates that are probabilistic) (Erwin Schrodinger, 1887–1961).

5b *Difference equations (discrete-time) describe system processes that 'jump/leap' from one state to another*

- A common example is the **logistic map**, $x_{n+1} = x_n r (1 - x_n)$. The latter is deterministic chaotic because bifurcation (unpredictability) occurs at certain values of r.
- Another example of a set of discrete difference equation is the **Duffing (or Holmes) map**; $x_{n+1} = y_n$ and $y_{n+1} = -bx_n + ay_n - y_n^3$, where x and y are the variables, while a and b are the parameters. The system is deterministic chaotic when $a = 2.75$ and $b = 0.2$.

6 Discrete-time Dynamical Systems

These systems can be chaotic from one-dimensionality onwards. Historically, a prominent example is the logistic map — a single nonlinear difference equation that can be chaotic (from simplicity to chaotic) due to bifurcation.

6a *Logistic map and chaotic attractor*

This logistic map (first created by (**Pierre Francois Verhulst**, 1804–1849) is a one-dimensional (one variable), degree 2 (highest power is 2) discrete-time deterministic chaotic system. It is a single equation that manifests chaotic behavior depending on the value of the nonlinear parameter, r. It is commonly used to illustrate bifurcation. It is a recurrence relation (power two), represented by the difference quadratic equation:

$$x_{n+1} = x_n r (1 - x_n)$$

$$x_{n+1} = r (x_n - x_n^2)$$

(One variable, highest power two)

The logistic map popularized by **Robert May** (1936–present) is a demographic model (statistical study of how a population changes). The variable x_n (population value) is a number (between 0 to 1); it is the ratio of the existing population to the maximum population at year n, while r

(bifurcation nonlinear parameter) takes positive value presents a combined rate of reproduction and starvation. The interest value/range of r is (0, 4].

For $0 \le r \le 1$, the population disappeared (ceased to exist).

For $1 \le r \le 3$, the population approaches the value of $(r-1)/r$.

For $r \ge 3$, the population path splits into 2 (period 2).

For $r \ge 3.44949$, the population path splits into 4.

For $r \ge 3.54409$, the population path splits into 8, 16, 32,..., rapidly (the lengths/paths of 8 and 16, and 16 and 32,..., decreases quickly).

For $r \ge 3.56995$, the model becomes chaotic (period-doubling cascade — period ∞).

The period doubling cascade or (first) **Feigenbaum constant**, ∂ is computed as follows:

$$\partial = \lim_{(n \to \infty)} (r_{n-1} - r_{n-2})/(r_n - r_{n-1}) \approx 4.6692$$

(that is, each new bifurcation appears about 4.67 times faster than the previous one.)

Thus, the logistic map is a deterministic chaotic system that venders into chaos at 4th bifurcation when $r \approx 3.56995$ (see bifurcation diagram in Appendix 1).

Hence, it sensitive dependence on initial conditions characteristic becomes prominent when r is in the interval [3.57, 4]. Overall, it also indicates that simple recurrence relations can manifest very chaotic behavior.

6b *Henon map and chaotic attractor*

Another discrete-time nonlinear dynamical system is the Henon map (two-dimensional, degree 2) introduced by **Michel Henon** (1931–2013). A new point (x_{n+1}, y_{n+1}) in the plane is represented by the two following equations:

$$x_{n+1} = y_n + 1 - ax_n^2,$$

$$y_{n+1} = bx_n,$$

where (x_n, y_n) is the input — the initial point is (1,1). For the classical Henon map which is chaotic, $a = 1.4$ and $b = 0.3$. It gives rise to the Henon chaotic attractor. When the constants a and b take other values, it is not totally chaotic.

6c *Mandelbrot set*

The Mandelbrot (**Benoit Mandelbrot**, 1924–2010) set (discrete-time complex quadratic map of one-dimension, a set of complex numbers, related to Julia sets) with two-dimensional fractal shape is generated by the following equation:

$$z_{n+1} = z_n^2 + c,$$

where c is a complex number ($c = a + ib$), z_n is a conjugate $[z_n = + (z_{n+1} - c)^{1/2}$ or $-(z_{n+1} - c)^{1/2}]$, and the value of z_n remains bounded however large the n gets; that is:

$$[z_1, z_2, z_3, z_4, \dots] = [c, c^2 + c, (c^2 + c)^2 + c, ((c^2 + c)^2 + c)^2 + c, \dots].$$

7 Continuous-time Dynamical Systems

These systems can be chaotic and only exhibit strange attractors when their dimensionality is three and above.

7a *Lorenz convection system and strange attractor*

The Lorenz (**Edward Lorenz**, 1917–2008) weather prediction system (physical system, continuous-time, nonlinear, and deterministic turbulent flow) is a set of 12 differential equations.

His rolling fluid convection model (simplified) is a set of three differential equations with three variables that exhibits chaotic dynamic (deterministic nonlinear flow). The simplified model for atmospheric convention is captured as follows:

$$dx/dt = \sigma(y - x),$$

$$dy/dt = x(\rho - z) - y,$$

$$dz/dt = xy - \beta z,$$

where x, y, z make up the system state (x, y, z) (x is proportional to the intensity of convection motion, y is proportional to the temperature difference between ascending and descending currents, z is proportional to the distortion of vertical temperature profile), t is time, and σ, ρ, β are the system parameters (usually take positive values, σ and β are constant within a 'region'/'box').

The details of the three parameters are as follows: σ (Prandtl number) is the ratio of the fluid (kinematic) viscosity and its thermal conductivity, ρ is the temperature difference between the top and bottom of the system, and β is the ratio of the width and the height of the region/box. In Lorenz original system the values of σ, ρ, and β were 10, 28, and 8/3 respectively, when the system was exhibiting chaotic behavior.

The Lorenz attractor, a strange attractor in three-dimensional space emerges which is the space containing the points (x, y, z) after many iterations. It is a set of chaotic solutions/states (a strange attractor — a subset of the phase space —— confined within a finite space-time) that resembles a butterfly (see Figure 1A.3 in Appendix 1).

7b *Rossler system and strange attractor*

The Rossler (**Otto Rossler**, 1940–present) system is a continuous-time dynamical system (three-dimensional, oscillations in chemical reactions) with three nonlinear differential equations as follows:

$$dx/dt = -y - z,$$

$$dy/dt = x + ay,$$

$$dz/dt = b + z(x - c),$$

Rossler strange attractor (two-dimensional) is derived with the values $z = 0$, $a = 0.2$, $b = 0.2$, and $c = 5.7$.

7c *Chua's circuit/system and strange attractor*

Chua's (**Leon Chua**, 1936–present) circuit is a simple electronic circuit (one nonlinear resistor, two capacitors, and one inductor) that exhibits chaotic behavior. It could be captured as a system of three nonlinear differential equations as follows:

$$dx/dt = \alpha[y - x - f(x)],$$

$$dy/dt = x - y + z,$$

$$dz/dt = -\beta y,$$

where $x(t)$ and $y(t)$ are the voltages across the two capacitors, $z(t)$ is the current across the inductor, and $f(x)$ depends on the electrical response of the nonlinear resistor, and α and β depends on other circuit components.

Appendix 4

Some Prominent Complexity Pioneers/Researchers and their Contributions

"Walking the path of genius"

1 Before Chaos

Isaac Newton (1642–1727), English, one of the most prominent scientists ever lived. He established the foundations of classical mechanics ('Mathematical principles of natural philosophy', 1687) — laws of motion and law of gravity, optics (theory of color), calculus (independently by **Gottfried Leibniz**, 1646–1716), and some other aspects of mathematics. His contributions to the exact sciences is so engrained that the term **Newtonian mindset** (mechanistic) has been adopted to denote the thinking that all systems are orderly, linear, deterministic and predictable.

Rene Descartes (1596–1650), French, mathematician and philosopher, his prominent works included 'modern' philosophy (I think, therefore I am; and his book *Principles of Philosophy* published in 1644–present in Latin), Cartesian co-ordinate system (analytical geometry), dualism, and the **Cartesian belief** (the behavior of the whole can be fully understood from the properties of the parts — **fundamentalism, reductionist hypothesis**). Descartes also proposed the **principle of dualism** — while material objects obey mechanical laws, the mind does not.

Joseph Louis Lagrange (1736–1813), French, mathematician, with diversified contributions including number theory, algebra and astronomy.

One of his key works is **Lagrangian mechanics** (a transformed version of Newtonian mechanics) introduced in 1788. With the Lagrangian (a mathematical formula) everything of the system can be explained. He possessed an exact mathematical mindset.

Pierre Simon Laplace (1749–1827), French, mathematician and astronomer, and he is famous for his Laplace's transform (integral transform), Laplace's equation (2nd order partial differential equation), Laplace's differential operator, differential calculus, and the **Laplace belief** (the entire characteristics of a system can be fully expressed/captured by one or a set of mathematical equations — also associated with **Lagrangian mechanics**. He believed in certainty and predictability (all minute details in this Universe are fixed).

2 Chaos Studies in the 1970s and Earlier

Jules Henri Poincare (1854–1912), French, mathematician and physicist (polymath) with numerous contributions, at the end of the 19th century (1890) researched on three-body problem, resulted in revealing chaotic motion (**non-periodic**, and not moving towards a fixed point and not continuously increasing in value) with no repetitive path (motion confined within a space). Thus, he was the first to discover a **deterministic chaotic system**, coined the term **bifurcation** in 1885, and established a foundation for **deterministic chaos theory.**

Aleksandr Mikhailovich Lyapunov (1857–1918), Russian, mathematician and physicist, is well known for his development of the **stability theory** of dynamical systems (**Lyapunov stability**), and probability theory. The positive **Lyapunov exponent (exponential divergence)** has been used to define the presence of **deterministic chaos.**

George David Birkhoff (1884–1944), American, mathematician, in 1913 proved Poincare's **'last geometric problem'**, a special case of three-body problem. He also studied **nonlinear differential equations**. Birkhoff is well known for his **ergodic theorem.** For special ergodic systems, they 'forget' their initial state after a long period of change.

Gaston Julia (1893–1978), French, mathematician, contributed the **Julia set** (**strange 'repeller'**) a discrete-time dynamical system exhibits **iterations** and chaotic behavior.

Andrey Kolmogorov (1903–1987), Russian, mathematician, focused on turbulence, astronomical problems, and conceived the algorithmic information theory and computational complexity theory (**Kolmogorov complexity theory**).

Edward Lorenz (1917–2008), American, mathematician and meteorologist, in 1963 discovered **sensitive dependence on initial conditions** (unpredictability, and coined the term **butterfly effect**), and the **Lorenz attractor** (strange attractor) in his weather prediction system ('Deterministic non-periodic flow', in *Journal of Atmospheric Sciences*). Thus, he laid a key foundation of chaos and complexity theory.

Benoit Mandelbrot (1924–2010), mathematician, found recurring patterns in 1963, developed **fractal geometry** and discovered **Mandelbrot set** (closely related to the **Julia set**), in 1979 — a simple equation that generates images of high complexity (two-dimensional fractal). He also coined the word **fractal** that is associated with **self-similarity**, **scale invariance**, and attractor.

Stephen Smale (1930–present), mathematician, focused on **nonlinear oscillators** (including van de Pol electrical oscillator and horseshoe map), linking topology and dynamical systems, and **topological transformation** of shape in phase space (horseshoe). He was awarded the Fields Medal in 1966.

David Ruelle (1935–present) and **Floris Takens** (1940–2010) coined the term **strange attractor** in 1971 ('On the nature of turbulence', in *Communications of Mathematical Physics*). Ruelle, physicist, was awarded the Boltzmann Medal in 1986, and a few other medals subsequently. Takens was a mathematician, and established the **Taken's theorem**.

Heinz Pagels (1939–1988), physicist, contributed to chaos theory and quantum field theory. His books include *The Dreams of Reason: The*

Computer and the Rise of the Sciences of Complexity published in 1988, and *Perfect Symmetry* in 1982.

Tien-Yien Li (1945–present), mathematician, and **James A. Yorke** (1941–present) mathematician and physicist, coined the term **chaos** in 1975 ('Period three implies chaos', in *American Mathematical Monthly*) which illustrated the study of chaos in its present/mathematical form (**deterministic**).

Mitchell Feigenbaum (1944–present), mathematician and physicist, in 1978 published his theoretical study on **bifurcation** (**period doublings**, a key property of mathematical chaotic systems), including the computation of the **Feigenbaum constant** (≈ 4.6692, a universal constant) using the **logistic map** — **universality**. He was awarded the Wolf Prize in 1986, together with Albert Libchaber.

Albert Libchaber (1934–present), mathematician and physicist, in 1979 obtained experimental observation of **bifurcation** — cascade to chaos in dynamical systems.

Alwyn Scott (1931–2006), physicist and mathematician, contributed to human **consciousness**, **chaos** and **emergence** with a special focus on protein and DNA. He was Founding Director of the Center for Nonlinear Studies at the Los Alamos National Laboratory, and editor of the *Encylopedia of Nonlinear Science* (2005).

Robert May (1936–present), theoretical ecologist, popularized the **logistic map**, a simple nonlinear dynamical system (one discrete-time chaotic difference equation model) that exhibits chaotic behavior. He was awarded numerous awards/medals including the Copley Medal in 2007.

Michel Henon (1931–2013), mathematician and astronomer, contributed the **Henon map**, a two-dimensional discrete-time dynamical system that exhibits chaotic behavior.

Otto Rossler (1940–present), biochemist, contributed the **Rossler attractor** with three nonlinear differential equations (**Rossler system**), which is a three-dimensional continuous-time dynamical system.

Leon Chua (1936–present), electrical engineer and computer scientist, is the inventor of **Chua's circuit** (a simple electronic circuit that exhibits chaotic behavior — can be captured by three nonlinear differential equations).

George Zaslavsky (1935–present), mathematical physicist, with **Boris Chirikov** (1928–2008), physicist in 1971 published a paper (**Stochastically instability of nonlinear oscillators**) that emphasized that low-dimensionality (low degrees of freedom) dynamical systems exhibit chaotic behavior — a key property of mathematical chaos theory.

Rene Thom (1923–2002), mathematician, is the founder of **catastrophic theory** (around 1970). Nonlinear dynamical systems will reach a critical point through period doubling and must self-organize into a new level of complexity (emergence), or collapse into **in-deterministic chaos** (**turbulence**) and disintegrate. Catastrophic theory focuses on the latter. He was awarded the Fields Medal in 1958.

Christopher Zeeman (1925–present), mathematician, is famous for popularizing the **catastrophe theory** in the 1970s. He was awarded the Faraday Medal in 1988 and the David Crighton Medal in 2006.

3 Complexity Studies in the 1970s and Beyond (With Some Exceptions)

Norbert Wiener (1894–1964), mathematician and cyberneticist, is the founder of **cybernetics** that is a significant component of complexity theory. He was awarded the National Medal of Science in 1963.

Warren Weaver (1894–1978), mathematician, in 1848 introduced the concepts of **disorganized complexity** (total randomness, statistical mechanics, probability theory), and **organized complexity** (the current type of complexity). (He co-authored the paper 'The mathematical theory of communication' with Claude Shannon, in 1949.) He was awarded the Arches of Science Medal in 1965.

Ross Ashby (1903–1972), psychiatrist, is also one of the founders of cybernetics. He was first to use the term **self-organization** through the formulation of the **principle of self-organizing dynamic system** — such a system moves into a state of equilibrium (attractors) and skips all non-attractor states. His other main contribution was the **Law of Requisite Variety**.

Ilya Prigogine (1917–2003), Belgian, chemist, from 1950s to 1970s conducted research on dissipative structures (initiated by environmentally imposed **adaptive tensions** due to **energy differentials**) on thermodynamic systems that are **far-from-equilibrium**, discovered that for open systems the traditional second law of thermodynamics could be reversed, and conceptualized the **dissipative structures theory** (concentrated on **edge of order — first critical value** — new **intra-system order** emerges) that focused on **self-organizing systems**. He was awarded the Nobel Prize in Chemistry in 1977.

Manfred Eigen (1927–present), biophysical chemist, in the 1970s indicated that the origin of life (**pre-biotic systems, biopoiesis**) evolved by passing through instabilities, and creating successive higher levels of organization characterized by greater diversification of components and structures for natural selection to act on — interacting **autocatalytic cycles** (**hypercycles**) through positive feedbacks — self-organization. He coined the term hypercycle. He was awarded the Nobel Prize in Chemistry in 1967.

Philip Anderson (1923–present), physicist, proposed the **constructionist hypothesis** — the ability to reduce everything to fundamental laws does not imply that the reverse process is similar, because in the upwards process properties that do not originally exist emerge at different level, as well as **broken symmetry**. He published the paper 'More is different' in 1972, and was awarded the Nobel Prize in Physics in 1972.

Stephen Gould (1941–2002) and **Niles Eldredge** (1943–present) both paleontologist and evolutionary biologist, proposed the **punctuated equilibrium theory** in 1972. It introduced the concept of punctuation points (nonlinear complex spaces), and **branching evolution** (versus phyletic gradualism of the Darwinian's theory).

Leigh Van Valen (1935–2010), evolution biologist, proposed the term **Red Queen race/hypothesis** in 1973 with the meaning that it is used in complexity theory.

George Cowan (1920–2012), chemist, founded the **Santa Fe Institute** in 1984 with **Murray Gell-Mann, David Pines**, and a few others. The original mission of SFI was to analyze and publicize the interdisciplinary study of complex systems (complexity theory). Currently, SFI focuses on investigating the basic principles of complex adaptive systems including physical, biological, social and computational systems. Cowan was awarded the Enrico Fermi Award in 1990.

Murray Gell-Mann (1927–present), was a significant contributor at SFI. Although, he is more prominent as a particle physicist than a complexity researcher, coined the term **quarks**, played a key role in the establishment of **quantum chromodynamics** and **string theory**. He was awarded the Nobel Prize in Physics in 1969.

David Pines (1924–present), physicist, one of his key research areas is in many-body systems, and **complex adaptive matter**. He is the founding director of the Institute for Complex Adaptive Matter in 1999.

Hermann Haken (1927–present), physicist, founder of **synergetics** (in the 1960s). One of his research focal areas is in nonlinear optics concentrating on interpreting laser principles as self-organization and non-equilibrium systems, **from incoherency to coherency**. He published a book entitled *The Science of Structure: Synergetics* in 1981, and was awarded the Max Planck Medal in 1990.

James Lovelock (1919–present), chemist, environmentalist and futurist, proposed the **Gaia hypothesis** (Gaia must be a synergetic self-regulating complex adaptive system) in the 1960s, and was awarded the Tswett Medal 1975.

Humberto Maturana (1928–present), biologist and cybernetics theoretician, and **Francisco Varela** (1946–2001), biologist and neuroscientist, coined the term **autopoiesis** in 1972.

Lynn Margulis (1938–2011), biologist, introduced the **endosymbiosis theory** in 1966, and later the **theory of symbiotic relations** (encompassing interdependency and co-evolution). She was awarded the National Science Medal in 1999, and the Darwin–Wallace medal in 2008.

Stuart Kauffmann (1939–present), theoretical biologist, indicates that the complexity and evolution of biological systems might be due to **self-organization (order for free; self-organized emergence)**, and far-from-equilibrium dynamics as from Darwinian natural selection. His other contributions include **fitness/rugged landscape, autocatalytic sets, co-adaptation** (co-evolution, composite CAS), and the **humpty dumpty effect** (contradicts the reductionist hypothesis). Among his publications is the book *The Origin of Order: Self-organization and Selection in Evolution* (1993).

John Holland (1929–2015), computer scientist and electrical engineer, focuses on computational complexity, and one of his key contributions is **genetic algorithm**. He was awarded the Louis E. Levy Medal in 1929.

Kenneth Arrow (1921–present), economist, and his main contributions are **Arrow's impossibility theorem** (no Pareto optimality), general equilibrium theorem, and endogenous theory. He was awarded the Nobel Prize in Economics in 1972, and the National Medal of Science in 2004.

Per Bak (1948–2002), physicist, **Chao Tang**, physicist and biologist, and **Kurt Wiesenfeld**, physicist focused on critical point in phase transition, and coined the term **self-organized criticality** in 1987 ('Self-organized criticality: An explanation of 1/f noise', *Physical Review Letters*).

Doyne Farmer (1952–present), physicist and complex system scientist, focuses on nonlinear systems, chaos/complexity theory, artificial life and **econophysics** (in finance).

Norman Parkard (1954–present), physicist, focuses on chaos/complexity theory, and coined the term **edge of chaos**.

Christopher Langton (1948–present), computer scientist, is one of the founders of **artificial life**. He studied the edge of chaos using computer, and created the **Langton ant** — a simple artificial life stimulations using a two-dimensional Turing machine (simplicity) but leading to a complicated emergent behavior.

Brian Aurthur (1946–present), economist, applies complexity in economics and financial markets. He is famous for his contributions in **positive feedbacks** and **increasing returns** in economies. He was awarded the Schumpeter Prize in 1990.

4 Complexity Studies in Humanity and Human Organizations

Joseph Schumpeter (1883–1950), economist, developed **evolutionary economics**, **theory of economic development**, and popularized the term '**creative destruction**' which is also associated with self-organization and emergence (**emergent of new order**).

Friedrich Hayek (1899–1992), economist, contributed to the concept on **spontaneous order** in economics — 'self-organization is due to human action and not human design'. He was awarded the Nobel Prize in Economics in 1974.

Niklas Luhmann (1927–1998), sociologist, and a significant contributor to social system theory that focused on **autopoiesis in social systems**, **complex networks** (network of networks), and **self-organizing communications** — a communication that generates more communications. He also conceived the **social spontaneous order theory**.

Elinor Ostrom (1933–2012), political economist, was Distinguished Professor at Indiana University and Arizona State University. Her contributions that were linked to complexity adaptive dynamics, include the social-ecological systems framework, **self-organized governance systems**, and collective-choice arrangements and participation — **public choice theory**. She was awarded the Nobel Prize in Economics in 2009.

Ralph Douglas Stacey (1942–present), Professor of Management, University of Hertfordshire, is among the first to exploit chaos/complexity theory in business and management. He focuses on complexity thinking and strategy. Over time his thinking of human organizations shifted from a systemic approach to **a complex responsive processes approach**. The latter concentrates on the characteristics of human agents in human organizations. Among the books he published, include *The Chaos Frontier* in 1991, and *Complexity and Organizational Creativity* in 1996.

Harry Eugene Stanley (1941–present), physicist, University Professor at Boston University, in 1995 coined the term **econophysics** (a field that used physics theories and methods to solve problems in economics, started in mid-1990s as a sub-field of statistical mechanics focusing on stochastic processes and nonlinear dynamics including statistical financial) provides an explanation for **'fat-tails'** in certain distributions (many kinds of financial data with high risks). He was awarded the Boltzmann Medal in 2004.

Fritjof Capra (1939–present), physicist, focuses on systems thinking, **holistic approach**, feedback, and interconnectedness. In 2000, he published the book *The Hidden Connections* which exploited complexity theory in the social domain.

Max Boisot (1943–2011), was Professor of Strategic Management at ESADE Business School. His works include the Ashby's Law on Requisite Variety, **I-space**, and his book 'Knowledge assets: Securing competitive advantage in the information economy'. He was awarded the Ansoff prize in 2000.

Mark Granovetter (1943–present), sociologist, focuses on modern **social network theory** including the threshold model of social behavior (tipping point). His famous contribution is his paper 'The **strength of weak ties**' in 1973.

Francis Heylighen (1960–present), cyberneticist, focuses on **self-organization, menetics, selfishness versus cooperation,** and the **global brain,** and his well-known **Principia Cybernetic Project.**

Bill McKelvey, Emeritus Professor of Strategic Organizing and Complexity Science, UCLA Anderson School of Business. He focuses on **econophysics** (scale-free theory) including its application in stock market, organizational performance, and economies encompassing **power laws** and **Pareto distribution, agent-based models,** and **complexity leadership.** Among the books he published include *Organizational Systematics* in 1982, and *The SAGE Handbook of Complexity and Management* in 2011 (editor).

Yanner Bar-Yam (1959–present), physicist and systems scientist, is founding president of the New England Complex Systems Institute. His research interests include market instability and financial crisis, **network dynamic,** and global food crisis. Among the books he published was *Dynamics of Complex Systems* in 1997.

Robert Axelrod (1943–present), political scientist, is Professor of Political Science at the University of Michigan. He focuses on **agent-based modeling,** and his books, include *The Complexity of Co-operation: Agent-based Models of Competition and Collaboration* in 1997. He was awarded the National Science Medal in 2014.

Michael Cohen (1945–2013) was Professor of Complex Systems, Information and Public Policy at the University of Michigan. He focused on **agent-based modeling.** In 2000, he published a book entitled *Harnessing Complexity: Organizational Implications of a Scientific Frontier* with **Robert Axelrod.**

Walter Baets (1955–present), Professor of Complexity and Innovation, Director of the University of Cape Town Graduate School of Business. He focuses on complexity and change, **uncertainty and societal responsibility,** innovation and knowledge, and **quantum interpretation** of management. His books include *Complexity, Learning and Organizations* in 2006.

Peter Allen (1944–present), physicist, Emeritus Professor of Evolutionary Complex Systems, Cranfield University. His research interests include **evolutionary complex systems**, and mathematical modeling and integrated modeling of change and innovation in social, economic, financial, and ecological systems.

Mary Uhl-Bien, Endowed Professor of Leadership, Texas Christian University, Neeley School of Business, focuses on **complexity leadership**, relational leadership and followership, and ethics. Among the books she edited, include *Leadership and Complexity* (Vol. II: Empirical evidence and practical applications), and *Complexity Leadership* (Part 1: Conceptual foundations) in 2007.

Pierpaolo Andriani, Professor of Complexity and Innovation Management, Durham University. He focuses on the impact of **complexity theory** on innovation, **scale-free theory**, organizational theory, and entrepreneurship.

Benyamin Lichtenstein, Professor of Management and Entrepreneurship, University of Massachusetts, Boston. He focuses on the **complexity of leadership**, organizational change and transformation, management, innovation, sustainability, and **emergence**. He is one of the authors of the book *Complexity and the nexus of Leadership* (2011).

Jeffery Goldstein, Professor of Management, Adelphi University. He focuses on **complexity and leadership**, social entrepreneurship, and innovation (creative process) encompassing **self-transcending constructions** (order not totally for free). He is one of the authors of the book *Complexity and the Nexus of Leadership* (2011).

James Hazy, Professor of Management, Adelphi University, and Founder and CEO of Leadership Science, focuses on **complex systems leadership theory**. He is one of the authors of the book *Complexity and the Nexus of Leadership* (2011).

Russ Marion, Professor of Education Administration, Clemson University. He focuses on **complexity leadership**, and organizational complexity, creativity, learning and adaptability. Among the books he published, include *The Edge of Organization* in 1999, and *Organizational Leadership and Complexity Mechanisms* in 2012.

Elena Olemdo, Professor of Economic, University of Sevilla, and her research focus on nonlinear chaotic economic dynamics, and **complex behavior** of organizations.

David Byrne, Professor of Sociology, Durham University. One of his main interests is on the application of **complexity theory in social sciences**. His books include *Complexity Theory and Social Sciences: The State of the Art* (2013) — co-authored with G. Callaghan.

Oliver Baumann, Professor of Management, University of Southern Denmark, he concentrates on the strategic and organizational implications of **complexity**, and the **computational modeling** of organizations as complex adaptive systems.

Milan Zeleny (1942–present), Professor of Management Systems, Fordham University, and Founding Chief Editor of Human Systems Management, concentrated on **autopoiesis** and **dissipative structure**. His books include *Autopoiesis: A Theory of Living Organization* (editor, 1981), and *Autopoiesis, Dissipative Structures and Spontaneous Social Orders* (editor, 1980).

(The list is far from complete as many other significant contributors are not included.)

Appendix 5

Gaia, Human Beings and the Brain's Evolution

"Human thinking systems are emotional systems that can be logical"

1 Introduction

1a *The Universe and Cambrian explosion*

- The Universe appeared about 13.8 billion years ago.
- The physical (visible) matter world occupies only about 4.9% of the Universe, and the remainder comprises dark matter [about 26.8%, transparent to electromagnetic radiation, **Vera Rubin** (1928–present), and **Kent Ford** (1931–present)] and dark energy (about 68.3%). Thus, the Universe contains much more matter than those observed through electromagnetic signals.
- The Earth, a small component of the physical matter world, was formed about 4.6 billion years ago.
- All life forms/species (on Earth) emerged about 3.8 billion years ago from a last (common/universal) ancestor.
- More than 5 billion species have been discovered and more than 99% of them no longer exist.
- The Cambrian explosion occur about 570 to 530 million years ago. The Cambrian period lasted about 20 million years (associated with the concepts of a punctuation point, a space of high complexity, a threshold in genetic complexity, biological diversification, a creative dynamic, branching evolution, and revealing that evolution is not always gradual), while most of the current phyla were formed over the

next 80 million years. The current interest on the Cambrian period is very much due to **Harry Whittington** (1916–2010).

- Before the Cambrian period only simple unicellular organisms exist.
- During this period large amount of complex multi-cellar organisms emerged.
- Primates ('prime' species) appear around 65 million years ago and apes (tailless primates) around 28 million years ago.

1b *Homo sapiens and brain's evolution*

- 'Homo' (the genus that includes the species, Homo sapiens) appears around 2.8 million years ago.
- Homo sapiens (sapiens) [wise person, coined by **Carl Linnaeus** (1707–1778) in 1758] appear around 200,000 years ago in Africa (the fully anatomically modern humans). (Homo sapiens encompasses homo sapiens idaltu and homo sapiens sapiens.) Human is the last surviving genus Homo. (Humans closest relatives now are chimpanzees — genus Pan, both originate from tribe Hominini. Humans possess 23 pairs of chromosomes, while chimpanzees have 24 pairs.)
- It is believed that they migrated out of Africa about 70,000 years ago and (prominently) inhabited Asia, Europe, and Australia (about 40,000 years ago), and America (about 15,000 years ago).
- As evolution proceeds, nerve cells in the biological structure tend to coordinate themselves into complex neural networks. (All vertebrate has a brain. Only a few invertebrates do not have a brain — for example, jellyfish.)
- This led to the emergence of the 'first brain' — a neural network of more compact concentration of neurons (components: soma, dendrites, and axon). Neurons are the main component of the brain and spinal cord. They are connected by synapses. This development is significant because neurons are able to stimulate and communicate with other cells in the body.
- Thus, neurons themselves are excitable — electrical stimulation that initiate action. They transmit information through electrical and

chemical (neurotransmitters — including amino acids, peptides, and monoamines) signals.

- It is believed that the neural coding ability of neurons encompasses both digital and analog information.
- For human beings, with the emergent of the cerebral cortex ('third brain'), certain abilities/characteristics unique to humanity surfaced. Human's cerebral cortex is about 2 mm thick, and 4 times the size of the chimpanzees — leading to a quantum leap in intelligence.
- The two-color (dichromatic) vision of our early ancestors became three-color (tri-chromatic).
- Also with the increase in brain size (due to the presence of the cerebral cortex), the human ancestors acquired bipedal locomotion (the ability to walk with two limbs), and more refined motor skills emerged.
- Eventually, the ability to create physical symbol set emerged (a unique ability associated only with human intelligence), and a language becomes the binding medium.
- Subsequently, human beings with their large brain, languages and abstract thoughts began dominating this planet about 40,000 years ago.
- Currently, the human brain has about 10 billion to 1 trillion neurons, 100 trillion cells, and is about 1.3 to 1.4 kg (1130 cc to 1260cc).
- The EQ (Encephalization Quotient — the brain-to-body relationship) of human beings is about 7 to 8, while a chimpanzee is about 2 to 2.5, and a dog is 1.4. (Normally, brain size increases with body size, although, not linearly.)
- Interactions between neurons are nonlinear and modifiable. The neural network is a complex network.
- This neuronal structure (synaptic cleft) was first discovered by **Santiago Ramon Cajal** (1853–1934, Nobel Prize for Physiology/ Medicine in 1906), in 1889.
- The human thinking systems short-term memory capacity is on average limited to seven [in an article 'The magical number seven, plus or minus two', Psychological Review (1956) — by **George Armitage Miller** (1920–2012) — a founder of cognitive psychology].
- Hence, in general, biological complexity is also associated with information processing ability.

2 Layered Evolution (Phylogenesis) and the Tri-partite Structure

- The process of evolution does not replace its history — phylogenesis — layered evolution. Consequently, the present human brain has three layers.
- From layer 1 to 3, they are namely, the brain stem and the cerebellum (reptile brain), the limbic system (mammalian brain), and the cerebral cortex (primate/human brain).
- The brain stem and the cerebellum => responsible for smell, taste, touch, sight, hear, and spontaneous response without 'thinking' — spontaneous reaction.
- The limbic system => responsible for emotion (especially fear) and memory.
- The cerebral cortex => the grey/gray matter is responsible for memory, and intellectual abilities such as thinking/logical abilities, perceptual awareness and consciousness — especially in human beings.

3 Brain Stem and Cerebellum

- It resembles the entire brain of a 'modern' reptile.
- It took about 200 million years to form.
- The brain stem is responsible for controlling some of the body's vital functions. It comprises three parts, namely medulla oblongata, pons and midbrain.
- Medulla oblongata => the lowest part joining the spinal cord is responsible for functions such as breathing, heart rate, and digestion.
- Pons => a small swollen region just above the medulla. It functions include respiration, facial expression, eye movement, and sleep, as well as directing information movement between the cerebellum and cortex.
- Midbrain => located just below the middle part of the brain and controls many sensory (hearing, vision) and motor (temperature regulation) functions.
- The cerebellum (little brain) is located behind the brain stem. It is split into two hemispheres, and is responsible for instantaneous sensory functions such as sight, smell, taste, touch and hearing.

4 Limbic System

- It resembles the brain of current mammals.
- It took about 150 million years to form.
- Its components are as follows: amygdala (predominantly emotions, also include memory and decision-making abilities), hippocampus (short-term and long-term memory, and spatial navigation), hypothalamus (monitoring information from the central nervous system, and regulating some inner organs), thalamus ('switchboard' of the brain) and pineal gland.
- The left amygdala induces pleasant and unpleasant emotions (happiness, sadness, fear, anxiety), while the right amygdala only induces unpleasant emotions (fear, sadness).

5 Cerebral Cortex

- Its presence is only substantially significant in primates (first appear about 65 million years ago — twice as 'brainy' compared to other mammals), (monkeys, 35 million years ago; apes, 28 million years ago; hominid, 5 million years ago; homo sapiens, 200,000 years ago).
- In human beings, the cerebral cortex is a thin sheet (2 to 4 mm thick) of complex interconnecting cells (grey — unmyelinated neurons and cells, and white — outer layer tissues, the myelinated axon tracts) covering the entire human brain.
- The cerebral cortex of human beings is the most developed, about twice as thick as the other primates.
- When spread out a human cerebral cortex is four times the size of a chimpanzee. Thus, it gives human beings a quantum leap in intelligence (largely due to the frontal lobe).
- It has a six-layered structure, with vertical cortical micro-circuits (neuronal networks) forming cortical columns and mini-columns (the elementary functional units of the cerebral cortex).
- It is responsible for the trichromatic and three-dimensional vision, bipedal motion, and the creation and manipulation of the physical symbol set.
- It is also responsible for the higher mental functions such as human level consciousness, memory, perception, reasoning, decision-making,

abstract thoughts/concepts, and creation and advance usage of languages (including written language, mathematical symbols/language, and musical symbols/language).

- In particular, most of the dopamine-sensitive neurons are situated at the frontal lobe (dopamine is a neurotransmitter of the catecholamine and phenethylamine families). The dopamine system is responsible for the attention, short-term memory, motivation, reward, and planning functions.
- In particular, the prefrontal cortex, the front part of the frontal cortex is responsible for planning complex cognitive behavior (managing cognitive processes) — perceived as the most intelligent part of the human brain.

6 The Four Lobes

- The cerebral cortex is divided into four lobes in both the left and right hemispheres, and they are the frontal, occipital, parietal and temporal lobes.
- Frontal = > most recently developed and controls the higher cognitive functions such as self-awareness, mindfulness, abstract thinking and reasoning, self-motivation, appropriateness of behavior, and wisdom — contains most of the dopamine neurons.
- Occipital = > the back portion of the brain (smallest of the four lobes) that is responsible for visual interpretation — the main visual processing centre of the brain.
- Parietal = > the top middle portion of the brain that is responsible for creating the three-dimensional world, and the location of the self in this environment. It is also responsible for information processing, and integrates sensory information, for instance input from the skin (touch, pain, temperature), as well as language processing.
- Temporal = > situated on both sides of the brain above/near to the ears is primarily responsible for the hearing (auditory input), learning (language recognition), speech and verbal memory, as well as visual memory and long-term memory (hippocampus and amygdala).
- The thickness of the different cortical lobes is different, for instance, the sensory cortex is thinner than the motor cortex. The cortical

thickness and intelligence is positively correlated (the other cortical function is association — deals with abstract thinking and language).

7 Left and Right Hemispheres

- The human brain is also divided into two cerebral hemispheres known as the left brain and the right brain.
- The two hemispheres are rather asymmetrical — lateralization.
- The information processing dynamics of the two hemispheres are also rather dissimilar.
- The two hemispheres (all the four lobes) are connected by a thick band (about 10 cm long) of tissues (neural fibers) known as the corpus callosum — the largest white matter structure in the human brain (about 200 to 250 million axonal projections).
- Left brain/hemisphere => is more self-centric, ego center, language center, structured thinking, sequential thinking, logical thinking, critical thinking, better at organizing information, memorizing, rationalizing, and theorizing. For right handed people, certain language functions such as grammar, vocabulary, and literal meaning are lateralized to this hemisphere.
- Right brain/hemisphere => is more group-centric, higher consciousness, kinesthetic, imagination, emotion, innovation and creativity, more compassionate and externally optimistic, and more sensitive to non-verbal communication.
- The current belief is that both hemispheres have to be well-nurtured from a young age (an integrated approach) to better exploit the brain's capacity.
- A better connected neurological bridge (corpus callosum) ensures better learning, and enhances other thought processes.
- Also, the cerebral hemispheres are believed to be complementary — therefore, maximizing on lateralization is beneficial.
- To better exploit the complexity-intelligence strategy, the right brain has to be better exploited — in particular, associated with nurturing collective intelligence.

8 Neuron Theory: Neuronal Dynamic and Structure

- The human brain is composed of neurons (each neuron is connected to average 7,000 others), glial cells (maintain homeostasis, form myelin, and protect neurons), and blood vessels.
- The human brain has up to about a trillion neurons. The presence of neurons in the brain was confirmed by **Camillo Golgi** (1843–1926) using silver nitrate (Golgi's method). He was awarded the Nobel Prize in Physiology/Medicine in 1906.
- The term **neuron** was coined by **Heinrich Wilhelm Gottfried von Waldeyer-Hartz** (1836–1921) — he is also known for consolidating the neuron theory.
- Neurons are electrically excitable (due to different concentration of ions — presence of electrical differential), and transmit (neural) information through electrical (energy) and chemical (matter) signals — synaptic communication. Interactions between/among neurons are nonlinear.
- The connection of the neurons (neuronal networks) forms the complex neural network (grey matter) in the brain.
- Neurons are also found in the spinal cord and the peripheral nervous system [somatic nervous system (skeletal muscle), autonomic nervous system (internal organ), and part of the sensory system].
- A neuron has three components namely, soma (body), dendrites (branching structure => input), and axon (cable-like => output).
- A gap (synapse — for neurotransmission, 20–40 nm) exits between the axon of a neuron and the dendrites of another.
- As indicated, each neuron has membranes (atoms and molecules that vibrate) that are excitable electrically, and as a result generates and propagates electrical signals (energy).
- The electrical signals at the axon of a neuron may activate the emission of a neurotransmitter (matter/endogenous chemical) across a synapse to the dendrite of the next neuron. An adult possesses about 100 to 500 trillion synapses.
- The neurotransmitter and synaptic cleft was first discovered by **Santiago Ramon Cajal** (1852–1934), Nobel Prize in Physiology/Medicine in 1906 — established the foundation of the neuron doctrine

(neuron theory), a sub-domain of cell theory, and he is known to many as the father of neuroscience.

- To date, more than 100 neurotransmitters have been identified, including the common neurotransmitters, namely acetylcholine (first known neurotransmitter), glutamate, dopamine, norepinephrine (noradrenaline), and adenosine. Acetylcholine was discovered by **Otto Loewi** (1873–1961) in 1921. He was awarded the Nobel Prize in Physiology/Medicine in 1936.

9 Other Important Properties/Characteristics (Emotion/Proliferation/Myelination/Pruning)

- The human brain is an emotional system (dominance of the amygdala) that thinks.
- The prefrontal cortex that is responsible for higher cognitive functions is not fully developed until a person is about 20 years old.
- Proliferation/Synaptogenesis => from infancy to about 10 years old, there is a huge proliferation of new neural connections in the child's brain (at about 6 weeks old, a fetus emits brain waves).
- Thus, the human brain is most 'extensively' connected (at least physically, matter-wise) when a person is about 10 years old.
- Myelination => it begins when a fetus is 14 weeks old, and each time a new connection is activated/utilized it is coated (around the axon of a neuron) with a layer of white fatty acid called myelin.
- The myelinated paths (myelin sheath) have less resistance (information/impulse flows faster) and are more difficult to break (last longer).
- Myelin (a dielectric material — insulate the axons from electrically charged ions) was first discovered by **Rudof Virchow** (1821–1902) in 1854. Myelinated axons are the white matter of the brain.
- Neural pruning => from 10 to 20 years old, neural pruning removes those paths that are not used (the brain becomes less compact and its matter density is lower).
- In this respect, the educational methodologies for children, adolescences and young adults are different from adults (amygdala versus prefrontal cortex).

- Demyelination leads to many form of illness (demyelinating diseases — usually at old age due to massive damages of the myelin sheaths).

10 Brain Waves and Mental State

- The brain, a complex neural network, is a center of enormous electro-chemical activities. It is continuously emitting tiny electrochemical impulses within a certain frequency range — brain waves.
- In 1924, **Hans Berger** (1873–1941) used electroencephalograph (EEG — records the brain's electrical activities) to measure human brain waves for the first time, and discovered the α-state. Currently, the waves observed are classified into four different categories:
  - β waves => 13 to 60 Hz (associate with active calmness, thinking, and mild stress to tenseness, agitation — the mind is strongly engaged)
  - α waves => 8 to 13 Hz (associate with reflecting, relaxing, and meditating)
  - θ waves => 4 to 8 Hz (associate with idling and day-dreaming, low level consciousness)
  - Δ waves => 1 to 4 Hz (associate with slow-wave sleep, uncon-sciousness)

- Further studies have reviewed the following observations associated with the α-state:
  - Every human being can move into the α-state with mindfulness.
  - The α-state is mentally relaxing and 'empty/non-focus'.
  - People know that they are in the α-state.
  - Calmness is associated with the α-state.
  - The α state and creativity are interrelated — better exploitation of the right hemisphere.
  - Thus, creativity can be nurtured.
  - Just before people sleep and just after they wake up they are in α state, and these are excellent period's innovative and creative exploitation.

11 Human Intelligence and Consciousness

- The human brain is the source of two critical entities, namely human intelligence and human consciousness.
- Human intelligence is the most intense intelligence source on this planet. This observation can be easily substantiated by the creation and manipulation of a physical symbol set that eventually flourished into a sophisticated vocal and written language. In addition, high cognitive functions including abstract thoughts/concepts (high imagination) creation and usage also emerges. This phenomenon has taken place in many human civilizations (the creation of many different character sets) but never with any other species.
- Next, human intelligence has facilitated the emergence of a very intense level of consciousness confined only to the human race. Human consciousness activates both the awareness (external) and self-awareness (internal) mental functions. At the core of the self-awareness ability is mindfulness. **Mindfulness is the unique ability of the human mind that enables it to observe the mental state of the mind itself.** This ability is currently also unique to humanity. In addition, a human thinking system is beyond a merely thinking system — it is a thinking system with 'feeling'. In this respect, (intelligent) human organizations are also potential 'feeling systems' — that is, beyond merely a 'thinking systems' that can be artificially created. (To date, there is no artificially created 'feeling' system.)

12 Physics and Consciousness

- **Roger Penrose** (1931–present) and **Stuart Hameroff** (1947–present), in the early 1990s, proposed that consciousness is the result of quantum gravity effects in microtubules — Orch-OR (orchestrated objective reduction) model of consciousness [the latter originates from processes (quantum-scale activities) inside neurons].
- Microtubules are tubular polymers of tubulin in the cytoskeleton of cytoplasm (in neurons).
- They also believe that human consciousness is non-algorithmic and cannot be produced by artificial computer systems. The implication is

that an algorithmically based system could never assume/project the complete traits of human intelligence and consciousness.

- **Max Tegmark** (1967–present) in 2000 showed that quantum states in microtubules are too brief for any significant neural processes.
- However, in 2014, **Anirban Bandyopadhyay** showed that quantum vibrations in microtubules are similar to that specified in updated Orch-OR theory.

13 Conclusion

Many of the current observations and understanding of the brain structure and its functions are obtained with the assistance from some interesting technological aid (brain scanning and neuroimaging), such as computerized axial tomography (CAT) (**Godfrey Hounsfield**, 1919–2004, and **Allan McLeod Cormack**, 1924–1998, Nobel Prize in Physiology/Medicine, 1979), magnetic resonance imaging (MRI) (**Peter Mansfield**, 1933–present, and **Paul Lauterbur**, 1929–2007, Nobel Prize in Physiology/Medicine, 2003) — a nuclear magnetic resonance technique, and positron emission tomography (PET) — a nuclear medical imaging technique (**David Kuhl**, 1929–present). Thus, scientists are now able to visualize specific neurons with certain designated functions in real time. In particular, PET is able to identify specific brain receptors with their associated neurotransmitters.

Summary Note:

- **CAT** — uses and combines computer-processed X-ray images taken at different angles to form a cross-sectional (tomographic) image of an object/organ.
- **MRI** — uses intense magnetic fields at appropriate resonance frequency causing the hydrogen atoms in the water molecules to emit radio waves, and records the latter as a medical image of the body (also known as NMRI — nuclear magnetic resonance imaging, or MRT — magnetic resonance tomography).

- **PET** — detects the gamma rays emitted by a positron-emitting radioactive tracer introduced into the body, and constructs a three-dimensional image using computer analysis.

However, up to this stage, comprehension of the human thinking systems is still far from complete. Although, over the generations a significant number of top brains have been attracted to the neuron domain, a deeper comprehension of the human brain and mind (human thinking systems) is only emerging gradually — for instance, quantum brain dynamics and electromagnetic theories of consciousness have been studied. Eventually, an integrated complex adaptive/cognitive (macroscopic), and quantum/atomic/neural (microscopic) analysis may be essential for a more holistic interpretation of the brain's dynamics and mystical mind.

Integrating Intelligence/Consciousness Management, Knowledge Management, Organizational Learning and Complexity Management

"Knowledge is Power" (Francis Bacon, 1597)

"Power is in the Hand of the Active Learner" (Eric Hoffer, 1932)

"High Collective Intelligence is Higher Resilience and Sustainability"

"Complexity is in the Mind of the Beholder"

1 Introduction

1a *Historical development of organization theory*

Human beings have come together to form groups, as early as they were cave dwellers. Subsequently, communities and countries emerge and leadership, governance, and management are inherent features. With the industrial revolution, the intention and characteristics of human organizations and their dynamics have changed drastically. Nations and corporations are structured and managed with intense economic centricity focusing on investment, profit and economic growth. Industrialization also stimulated rapid urbanization and subsequently globalization. Over time, the governance theory and organization theory are introduced and extensively exploited. There are both positive and negative consequences. Continuous modifications have been done to accommodate the changes in thinking and environment — agents, leadership and organizations.

The historical development of organization theory has been stimulating, as several outstanding schools of thoughts have emerged during the last century [including contributions from **Henri Fayol** (1841–1925), *General and Industrial Management* — general administrative theory; **Fredrick Taylor** (1856–1915), *The Principles of Scientific Management* — scientific management theory; **Max Weber** (1864–1920), *The Theory of Social and Economic Organizations* — bureaucratic theory; **Chester Barnard** (1886–1961), *The Functions of the Executive*; **Peter Drucker** (1909–2005), *Concept of the Corporation*; **Ralph Davis**, *The Fundamentals of Top Management*; **Herbert Simon** (1916–2001), 'Organization' with **James March** (1928–present) — bounded rationality; **Henry Mintzberg** (1939–present), *The Rise and Fall of Strategic Planning: Re-conceiving the Roles for Planning, Plans, Planners*; **Victor Vroom** (1932–present), *Leadership and Decision Making*; **Michael Porter** (1947–present), *Competitive Advantage: Creating and Sustaining Superior Performance*, and **W Chan Kim** (1952-present and **Renee Mauborgne**, *Blue Ocean Strategy*]. (Principles of governance and governance theory have been analyzed in Chapter 10.)

The contributions of management organization theorists embrace numerous domains/perspectives such as executive leadership, governance, management function, management strategy, operational procedure, organization objective and productivity with the intention of integrating them. The detail philosophy, concepts and practices of these schools differ to some extent. However, overall the influence of the exact sciences, in particular, the Newtonian science has been tremendous. The foundation pillars include bureaucracy, rationalization, hierarchy, command and control, empowerment, high efficiency and no allowance for mistake, linearity, orderly and predictability (forecasting).

In particular, during the 1950s, the contingency theory was proposed. There are numerous researchers associated with this theory, and the contributors include **Alfred Chandler** (1918–2007), 'Strategy and structure'; **Gareth Morgan** (1943–present), 'Imaginization: New mindsets for seeing, organizing and managing'; and **James March** (1928–present) and **Johan Olsen** (1939–present), 'Democratic governance'. The structure and dynamics of humanity and their organizations change rapidly overall the next few decades due to globalization, technological advancement, and accelerating human population growth (and aging). By the 1990s, complexity theory is introduced into organization theory [**Michael McMaster**, *The Intelligence Advantage: Organizing for Complexity* (1996); **Ralph Stacey**, *Complexity in Creative Organization* (1996), *Experiencing Emergence in Organizations: Local Interaction and the Emergence of Global Pattern* (2005); **Uri Merry**, *Coping with Uncertainty* (1995); **Arthur Battram**, *Navigating Complexity* (1996), **De Geus**, *The Living Company* (1998); **Russ Marion**, *The Edge of Organization* (1999); **Robin Wood**, *Managing Complexity* (2000), **Michael Cohen and Robert Axelrod**, *Harnessing Complexity: Organizational Implications of a Scientific Frontier* (2001); **Harland Cleveland**, *Nobody in Charge* (2002); **Walter Baets**, *Complexity, Learning, and Organizations: A Quantum Interpretation of Business* (2006); **Peter Allen**, **Steve Maguire** and **Bill McKelvey**, *The SAGE Handbook of Complexity and Management* (2011)]. The complexity aspect of humanity and its human organizations must be better managed and exploited.

1b *Towards intelligence/consciousness-centricity*

Humanity has dominated (over-dominated) this planet primarily due to its intense intelligence and consciousness. There exists a significant gap between human beings and chimpanzees, the next most intelligent species. The gap difference is so enormous due to the fact that humanity has created symbols/languages, abstract thoughts/concepts, knowledge, technologies, and skills that all other species are not able to achieve. Apparently, the competitiveness and survival of the human world is highly dependent in intelligence (education, training, intellectual capacity, skills capacity, technologies, and innovation and creativity) — intense intelligence/conscious-centricity. In addition, the rapid changes and high interconnectivity occurring has also elevated complexity and interdependency. Thus, it is significant to recognize that intelligence/consciousness management, knowledge management, organizational learning, and complexity management closely inter-related, and must be well integrated in all human organizations. Basically, the effectiveness of knowledge management and organizational learning in an organization depends greatly on the performance of intelligence/consciousness management — including nurturing intense collective intelligence (intelligence-intelligence link-ages, collectiveness capacity, and adaptive capacity). In the intelligent organization theory, effective intelligence/consciousness management is a key foundation pillar that supports all other activities in human organizations — including knowledge management, organizational learn-ing, leadership, governance, strategy, operations, ethicality, competitive-ness, resilience, and sustainability.

In this respect, intelligent organizations should ideally appoint a **Chief Intelligence (Management) Officer** (and a group/network) that orchestrates the overall intelligence/consciousness-centric, complexity-centric, and network-centric activities and dynamics across the entire organization (nation, corporation, regional institution). A key thinking of such an individual (stakeholder) is that all interacting agents (human beings) are valuable assets (their intelligence, consciousness, knowledge, feeling, consensus, commitment, and collaboration), and therefore should not be managed as other natural resources. Their interconnectivity, engagement, communications, and self-organizing capabilities must be constructively cultivated and maintained at all time and situation. In this respect, recognizing the presence of a socio-psychological subsystem (high relational capacity) in human organizations is vital, as the intense mental space of human agents is always self-centric and stability-centric.

2 Intelligence/Consciousness Management

Intelligence is a unique form of energy that drives certain activities focusing on stability (stability-centric) that reflect its presence. As indi-cated earlier, there is a great diversification in intelligence varying from the physical (atomic) world, to the living world, and in particular, human beings. For instance, when a dog retrieves a ball and brings it back to its owner is perceived to be intelligent. If an adult human being does like-wise in the same context, it is perceived as weird or even mentally unsta-ble. Apparently, the level of intelligence expected of a human being is higher, for instance the ability to drive a car and the ability to solve a mathematical problem is regarded as human intelligence. In this respect, the intelligence function of a human being can be a perceived as a sophisticated 'equation' with numerous abstract variables/parameters that can be enhanced by education and training, self-learning, and experiences associated with natural and unnatural events. Concurrently, human consciousness is related to the responsiveness to the changing environment, and the ability to observe the human mind. In this respect, the intensity of an individual intelligence/consciousness source can be 'increased', as there is always a latent proportion that is not utilized.

Some fundamental thinking and focuses of intelligence/consciousness management must be recognized and well-managed in order to elevate the capacity of all intelligence/consciousness sources in the organization. They are as follows:

a. Recognizing that intrinsic human intelligence/consciousness sources are inherently emotional rather than logical.
b. Recognizing that human intelligence/consciousness is the unique primary intrinsic strength of every human agent, as well as his/her organizations.
c. Continuously educating/training the individual intelligence/consciousness sources (information processing, knowledge acquisition and accumulation), and nurturing adaptive thinking is a significant aspect of all human agents in intelligent organizations (higher adaptive capacity).
d. 'Optimizing' all the intense intelligence/consciousness sources, and achieving optimal intelligence-intelligence linkages, if necessary — encompassing relativistic complexity.
e. Recognizing the mental state of all interacting agents is critical to the survival of the organization — the presence of orgmindfulness, and nurturing a mindful culture is essential.
f. Connecting (agents, local spaces, complex networks, and the organization) and ensuring truthful engagement of all intelligence/consciousness sources (activating latent intelligence, nurturing collective intelligence, and achieving higher coherency) is a necessity.
g. Recognizing that every human agent is self-powered and is an intrinsic leader (intrinsic self-powered leadership capacity) that must be well engaged — this mindset ensures better connectedness and collaboration with a more lateral/collective approach.

h. Recognizing that innovation is linked to diversification and risk management — better complexity exploitation, and a higher tolerance for errors can be constructive.

i. Recognizing and exploiting the intelligent person attributes, interdependency of human interacting agents (higher complexity <=> higher interdependency), and the rugged landscape characteristics of human organizations is highly valuable.

j. Driving a more intelligent complex adaptive dynamic (*i*CAD) through better self-organizing capability, self-organization or self-transcending constructions, and emergent of new order is significant (higher self-organizing capacity and emergence-intelligence capacity).

k. Recognizing that (*j*) can be better achieve through a 'common language' — including self-organizing communications and truthful engagement that also focuses on the relational/social aspect (emotions, feelings, perceptions, and values of the mental state of every interacting agent) — orgmindfulness (higher relational capacity) is beneficial.

l. Recognizing that self-powered governance and e-governance is a significant component of the governance system in all human organizations (quality governance capacity) is a new necessity.

m. Constantly elevating collective intelligence and org-consciousness of the organization, and concurrently recognizing that there is no global optimality (absent of a complete phase space) is a new significant mindset — 'satisficing optimal' solution/option.

n. Recognizing that complexity is relative in humanity (with respect to intense intelligence and consciousness — both individual and organization), and innovatively exploiting it is an intelligence advantage.

o. Thus, constantly preparing and channeling intelligence into spaces of high complexity — exploring and exploiting new territories for embedded gold nuggets also achieves better competitiveness, first mover advantage, and higher sustainability (better risk management, higher innovation and creativity).

p. In addition, continuously making preparations for the sudden surfacing of punctuation points is vital for higher sustainability (crisis management preparation, futuristic, and presence of the emergent strategy at all time).

3 Knowledge Management and Organizational Learning

3a *An escalating knowledge intensive environment*

At the frontiers of intense knowledge activities is the creation of new knowledge. Only top-notch researchers and highly creative people (thinkers) are involved in this activity. The second line of action is the acquisition and better utilization of knowledge (creative exploitation). The acquisition of knowledge, re-organizing it, giving it a new perspective, and using it innovatively to solve a problem and make a better decision, are the daily tasks of many professors, leaders, managers, and national leaders. However, as humankind ventures deeper into the intelligence era, the better acquisition and utilization of knowledge at all levels is becoming a new necessity. Eventually, every individual (leaders and followers/ non-actors alike) will have to participate in the diversified knowledge activities space as humanity becomes highly educated, media-connected, and intensely competitive.

More than a decade back, approximately 50% of the fastest growing companies in the US were already knowledge-intensive organizations that were selling the knowledge and the know-how/expertise of their employees rather than manufactured products or providing services. Today, more human beings are better educated, and skills are also more knowledge intense. Therefore, almost all human agents and business corporations, as well as nations (education hub, technology hub, high tech products, high-tech armed forces) are involved in knowledge-intensive activities (high level technology <=> intense knowledge innovativeness <=> high value product). In addition, human agents and their organizations are well-connected, continuously communicating, and constantly updated by and through the Internet, and wireless/social media technology. In such a situation, more intensive learning at different levels (individual, team/ network, and organization) is a necessity.

3b *Collective intelligence and knowledge management*

Intelligent human organizations (corporations, nations) today must attempt to capitalize on their collective intelligence to maintain their competitive edge and sustainability through an intelligence advantage continuously. In this environment, human mental/knowledge capital (intrinsic human intelligence) and structure/artificial capital (databases, knowledge repositories, patents, and intellectual property) are vital elements of organizational level intelligence. Thus, effective knowledge (a significant component of the corporate intelligence enhancer) management is a critical activity/process in intelligent human organizations. Inevitably, acquiring, sharing and exploiting knowledge is power (at both individual and organizational levels) in the new context.

3c *Development of knowledge management*

Historically, knowledge management (KM) emerged as a scientific domain during the 1990s [**Ron Sanchez and Aime Heene**, *Strategic Learning and Knowledge Management* (1996); and **Thomas Stewart**, *Intellectual Capital: The New Wealth of Organizations* (1998)]. Traditionally, knowledge management encompasses acquiring, capturing, coordinating, combining, retrieving, distributing/sharing, and creating knowledge at all levels in human organizations. Thus, it is a process of creating and elevating value from an organization's intangible assets. In particular, knowledge in the individual minds should be creatively exploited at organizational level through better knowledge sharing. The organizational knowledge structure (knowledge bases/repositories, expert systems, intranets) together with collective intelligence and organizational philosophy/theory is an important component (organizational intelligence enhancer) of the orgmind.

With the introduction of the knowledge-based/expert systems technology about three decades back, human organizations begun to better realize the significant of externalized knowledge. With the construction of the first artificial automated knowledge structure, the domain of knowledge management has evolved substantially. Knowledge repositories (organizational knowledge) have proliferated, continuous updating and usage of these artificial knowledge structures has become a necessity in knowledge-intensive organizations. Therefore, with the even greater dependency on better knowledge to survive the current competition, the quality of knowledge repositories and knowledge management processes must be enhanced. Similar to an intelligent being, this is one activity that no human organization can avoid.

3d *Intensive integrated learning a new necessity*

Organizational learning and better knowledge management are closely inter-related (organizational learning <=> knowledge management). Organizational learning encompasses the processes of retaining, creating, and transferring knowledge at different levels — including the creation and updating of knowledge structures at individual levels, and the creation and updating of knowledge repositories at organizational level [**Chris Argyris**, *On Organizational Learning* (1993); and **James March**, *The Pursuit of Organizational Intelligence* (1999)]. **Individual learning** is an elementary level activity of all organizations (training in organizations, and education in countries) — encompassing single and double loop learning. It is a vital category or level of organizational learning as its failure will also cause all other levels of learning to fail. The mental stress involved is so intense that learning and pedagogy research is a significant focal point in many countries.

Group/team learning and **organizational learning** (and knowledge acquisition) are higher levels learning with nonlinear characteristic that closely associated with the interconnectivity, communications, engagement and trust of agents in an organization (collaborative learning). Thus, to nurture an organization that learns, and learns fast and continuously is no easy task. In order to learn collectively, people must first be willing to be engaged with one another 'to communicate their hearts and minds' — determine by their level of consensus, collaboration and commitment (Abilene paradox, defensive routine, dialogue, relational friction, relational capacity, coherency, and mental cohesion). Agents with a phobic mindset possess a defensive routine and are anti-learning. Thus, an appropriate mindset must be present. A supportive/mindful culture must exist. Inevitably, effective communication (self-organizing communications) is a fundamental characteristic that is badly needed in organizations that want to learn spontaneously. Thus, nurturing the ability to integrate individual learning, team learning and organizational learning is an interesting challenge.

In addition, organizations today learn beyond the 'organization itself' — inter-organizational learning (globalization, e-learning) is common. The benefits of the latter include a faster learning process and lower cost involved. Thus, synthesizing knowledge from the external environment to create value internally to the organization is also an important form of knowledge creation, although, the first mover advantage status may be gone. Despite the details, eventually, it is the quality of knowledge acquired that indicates the relevancy of learning that is progressing in the organization.

3e *Intelligent organizations are learning organizations*

Fundamentally, a learning organization learns continuously at all levels (agents/teams/networks/organization) and transforms itself, if necessary [**Chris Argyris** (1923–2013), *Personality and Organization* in 1957, *Teaching Smart People How to Learn* in 1991, *Organizational Learning: A Theory of Action Perspective* in 1978 with **Donald Schon** (1930–1997). Another contributor to learning organization is **Peter Senge** (1947–present), *The Fifth Discipline: The Art and Practice of the Learning Organization* in 1990, and according to him a learning organization must encompass the following processes, namely systems thinking, personal mastery, mental models, shared vision, and team learning. He also defined a learning organisation as one in which 'people continually expand their capacity to create the results they truly desire, where new and expansive patterns or thinking are nurtured, where collective aspiration is set free, and where people are continually learning how to learn together'. Therefore, a learning organisation is one in which the leaders and members are effective and efficient in learning, and learning how to learn together (collectively and sharing) because they are all willing in heart and mind to go deeper and broader in their learning endeavor.

In the intelligent organization theory, organizational learning is one of the key characteristics of intelligent organizations. For an organization's collective intelligence to increase, the organization must be able to learn, adapt and evolve collectively — that is, as the individual agents learn, the organization must also learn concurrently (collectiveness capacity, adaptive capacity and unifying capacity). In addition, intelligent organizations must have sensors and systems (natural and artificial) in place to anticipate, learn, react and adjust to changes (both internal and environmental) swiftly (for instance, the RAHS system — that is, being futuristic or scenario planning is also a form of learning process). Hence, a significant way to sustain a competitive advantage is to ensure that the organization is learning faster and more innovatively than others (first mover advantage, better risk and crisis management, and intelligence advantage). Therefore, an intelligent organization is an inherent learning organization.

3f *Basic constructive KM environment*

It is critical to nurture a supportive culture (mindful culture/intelligent organization) that encourages knowledge sharing. Preferably, an incentive and reward system must be established for better engagement. Although, info-communication technology is a significant supporting tool, very often, technology is not the limiting factor in creating a favorable KM environment. It is usually the management of people and culture that determines the success of KM endeavors (indicating the significance of intelligence/consciousness management and the presence of a well-nurtured mindful culture that focuses on the mental state of the agents are highly critical). Apparently, the social and cognitive (construal) perspectives are vital as well (**Max Boisot**, 'Knowledge management and complexity' in *The SAGE Handbook of Complexity and Management*, 2011).

Historically, an introductory KM environment should include the following features (**Gilbert Probst, Steffen Raub, and Kai Romhardt**, *Managing Knowledge: Building Blocks for Success* (2000):

— A knowledge goal as a path pointer.
— A yellow page directory mapping knowledge areas to experts within the organization.
— A best-practices or lessons-learned knowledge repository to facilitate knowledge sharing.
— A KM infrastructure whose mandate is to identify, analyze, manage, maintain, and disseminate knowledge to appropriate individuals within the organization and externally to others (customers, citizens).
— A web-based/intranet system must be present to enhance connectivity and dissemination.
— A culture that supports agents that are contributing to the KM structure, as well as exploiting knowledge from the KM repositories.

3g *The role and significance of social capitals*

In particular, all organizations must recognize that knowledge originates in the human thinking systems of their agents, and becomes 'embodied' in communities and artificial systems, 'embedded' in work routines, practices, and norms, and 'represented' in artifacts (including documents and reports). As indicated, in order to build knowledge capitals (new knowledge, critical technology), collective intelligence and social capitals are vital elements that must be concurrently nurtured and enhanced.

Basically, social capitals include the following aspects:

— Trust (reciprocity)
— Respect (mutually — a more lateral structure and dynamic)
— Space (cognitive space — sharing of mind and knowledge)
— Slack (time to reflect — deeper deliberation)
— Coherence (shared context, 'common' language, vocabulary, symbols and signals)

Thus, high collective intelligence and social capitals enhance knowledge management and organizational learning (higher willingness to share), and creates new values, attitudes and behaviors that elevates organizational performance and achieves organizational objectives more effectively.

3h *Tacit and explicit knowledge*

A key to creating organizational knowledge is to tap on the pool of tacit knowledge (resides/internalized in the human thinking systems/knowledge structure of the interacting agents — that may be difficult to externalize), and convert it into explicit knowledge (resides in the corporate knowledge structure — external depositories). Very often, **tacit knowledge** is the knowledge an agent/expert uses spontaneously without even realizing its 'appropriateness' — a term introduced by **Michael Polanyi** (1891–1976), in 1958.

However, the knowledge created or acquired by an individual has to be extracted and disseminated (knowledge mining), if it is to be made valuable to others — **explicit knowledge**. The latter is externalized knowledge stored in some forms of repository — articulated and captured by the physical symbol system/written language. Thus, knowledge repositories are significant components of the organizational knowledge structure, as well as humanity. In the computer/automation world, there are various acquisition techniques used by knowledge engineers to acquire tacit knowledge, and encode it in a knowledge repository/expert system as explicit knowledge. Thus, in general, internalized knowledge will have to be made explicit before it can be shared and used by others. In addition, potentially knowledge could also be acquired by observation learning or action learning.

3i *Continuous learning culture*

A mindful culture is the key determinant for nurturing collective intelligence, creating valuable corporate knowledge structure, and facilitating team/organizational learning. Overall, the interacting agents in an organization with a mindful culture are better connected, engaged and committed, and are more willing to share their knowledge and learn collectively. They also understand better the importance of co-evolution with their organization — balancing self-stability and org-stability. In addition, for KM strategies to be successful, a continuous learning culture must be present (change is the only attribute that never change; niches are only temporary — the red green race). With the presence of a learning culture, the interacting agents assume that knowledge and skill acquisition is their essential and life-long responsibility. In this respect, a more lateral/collective and consultative leadership is a vital part of an effective learning and KM culture. However, a mindful, continuous learning, and knowledge sharing culture will only evolve continuously if the leadership (intelligence leadership strategy) of the organization is actively involved in nurturing it.

Summary Note:

- Knowledge is a resource/asset.
- Knowledge structures are embedded in the individuals' mind (tacit knowledge).
- Learning is the process that continually alters the knowledge structure, behavioral schemata, and decision making of the agents.

- Organizational learning involves individual/collective learning, knowledge sharing and creating external knowledge repositories (explicit knowledge).
- Individuals participating in knowledge management and organizational learning input knowledge into the repositories, as well as exploit knowledge from the repositories.
- The quality of the knowledge repositories in an organization is one indicator of its collective intelligence.
- Thus, fast quality knowledge management and continuous learning is a strategic requirement for elevating the competitiveness, resilience, and sustainability of the organization.

4 Complexity Management

The above thinking and processes are effective only if complexity is also well-managed and integrated. Thus, complexity management and intelligence/consciousness management are closely inter-related and mutually enhancing in the rapid changing situation — leading to the conceptualization of the **complexity-intelligence strategy**, the holistic/global strategy of the intelligent organization theory. Fundamentally, a highly intelligent and conscious mind will be in a better state to venture into a new space of complexity (intelligence/consciousness <=> complexity => **relativistic complexity** — complexity is in the mind of the beholder). Very likely, the amount of risks involved will be lowered — supported by the appropriate knowledge and mental state needed for the new endeavor — perceptions leading to the emergence of spaces of relativistic order (emergent of surface patterns), and relativistic static equilibrium. Conversely, the new accelerating complex environment may elevate the consciousness of the mind of more human agents.

Basically, when dealing with complexity it is significant to recognize the two primary properties of complex adaptive systems namely, sensitive dependence on initial conditions (butterfly effect), and the presence of an attractor (basin of attraction). The leadership must be aware and exploit the butterfly effect that can be both constructive and destructive. Similarly, leadership with ability to recognize states in basin of attraction or attractors is more effective (exploring basin of attraction <=> scenario analysis). In particular, order and complex co-exists in all human organizations — that is, spaces of complexity are always present. Some of these spaces are embedded with gold nuggets if they are appropriately explored and exploited (innovatively, risk management, concentrated calmness). Thus, in this situation, possessing continuously learning new capabilities is beneficial.

However, it is also vital to be aware that punctuation points also 'appear' suddenly — without prior warning (unpredictable, crisis management — high self-organizing capacity needed). With some forms of continuous general preparation (emergent strategy), spontaneous new learning during a crisis can be expedited and elevated (higher collectiveness capacity, adaptive capacity, collective/shared learning, coherency, and some others are crucial), leading to faster and more constructive self-organization/self-transcending constructions to achieve coherency (emergent of a new order — higher self-organizing capacity, emergence-intelligence capacity, and emergent of new order).

5 Conclusion

Hence, leaders with intense intelligence/consciousness-centricity and complexity-centricity possess a new form of wisdom (wisdom <=> new knowledge creation). Thus, a key strategic factor is integrating intelligence/conscious management, knowledge management, organizational learning, network management and complexity management constructively. In this case, a critical niche is one that is achieved by high individual and collective intelligence that leads to an intelligence advantage. This effective integration (leading to a holistic dynamic and high mental cohesion) must always be a primary objective of all intelligent human organizations — in addition to their respective functional goals.

Key Terminologies and Concepts
(Complexity Theory, Intelligent Organization Theory and Relativistic Complexity Theory)

"With intense intelligence/consciousness-centricity, complexity
is in the mind of the beholder"

"In highly intelligent organizations, everybody is in charge"

Abilene paradox — It is the phenomenon when interacting agents try to agree on ideas/actions (a form of socio-psychological conformity — 'false' consensus — presence of a 'negative latent' mental force) they actually disagree [the term was introduced by **Jerry Harvey** (1935–2015), in 1974 *The Abilene Paradox: The Management of Agreement*]. They suppress their emotion, and appear rational and non-confrontational because of the phobic mindset. There is no truthful engagement or participative communication. It is more a situation with miscommunication or no communication. The normative belief is that for their 'personal safety' it is highly illogical to be logical (stability-centric, self-centric and defensive routine). In this case, nurturing collective intelligence is very difficult. Many organizations today are trapped by this phenomenon (low coherency, mental cohesion and collectiveness capacity) due to its highly hierarchical/bureaucratic structure and leadership, and the consequence can be devastating (see phobic mindset, agent, connectivity, engagement, defensive routine, participatory system, cosmopolitan communicator, stability-centric, self-centric, order, collectiveness capacity, collective intelligence, paper dialogue, organizational justice, coherency, mental cohesion and feeling organization).

Adaptive — It is the continuous ability to consume new information and to respond to it spontaneously if necessary — a characteristic associated with intelligence, consciousness, and continuous learning in living entities/organisms (adaptive <=> basic life-intelligence). In the biological world (evolution theory), adapting increases the fitness level of organisms (adaptive => continuous learning => continuous information consumption => continuous updating of knowledge structure => changing behavioral schemata). Individual behavior will mutate and through self-organization collective behavior will emerge (collectiveness capacity <=> adaptive capacity). In Prigogine's dissipative structures theory (**Ilya Prigogine**, 1917–2003), externally imposed energy in a physical system creates energy differentials that cause an 'adaptive tension' in the system. Adaptation in complex adaptive systems (CAS) on a macro level ('entire system' — 'whole' — system plasticity) is characterized by self-organization/self-transcending constructions and emergence based on integrated local adaptive behavior (intelligence) of the interacting agents — which also determines/reflects the level of collective intelligence of the system. In a highly complex situation, tactical agility is needed for nonlinear adaptation (see complex adaptive systems, evolution, exaptation, adaptive capacity, agent, fitness, behavioral schemata, intelligence, collective intelligence, consciousness, self-organization, self-transcending constructions, dissipative structure, edge of order, edge of chaos, edge of emergence, symbiosis and sustainability).

Adaptive capacity — It encompasses the innate ability of a CAS (individual agents and the organization) to learn, acquire/store knowledge and experience, the flexible problem-solving and decision-making characteristics, and the power structure that is responsive to the (changing) needs of the interacting agents (adaptive capacity <=> self-organizing capacity). The presence of this capacity is crucial to the governance (adaptive governance), leadership, strategy, resilience, and sustainability in intelligent organizations (complexity management, and intelligence/consciousness management). The adaptive capacity of an organization depends on its structure (structural capacity), and mental capacity (especially, in intelligent human organizations), that is closely linked to collectiveness capacity. In this respect, a biotic/biological macro-structure that resembles a highly intelligent biological being (rather than a machine) will enhance the adaptive capacity of human organizations effectively. In addition, it is also important to note that characteristics such as nonlinearity, innovativeness, and exaptation will also affect adaptive capacity — (see adaptive, intelligence, biotic macro-structure, knowledge structure, orgmind, intelligence/consciousness management, complexity management, network management, nonlinearity, exaptation, coherency, intelligent person, collectiveness capacity, adaptive capacity, intelligent organization, self-organizing capacity, emergence-intelligence capacity, emergence, structural capacity, satisficing principle, resilience and sustainability).

Notes: **Some significant relationships associated with adaptive capacity:**

- **Individual adaptive capacity** (agent) <=> intelligence <=> autopoiesis <=> stability-centricity <=> self-centricity <=> localized order
- **Collective adaptive capacity** (organization) <=> stability-centricity <=> structural capacity <=> collectiveness capacity <=> leadership capacity <=> collective intelligence and org-consciousness <=> self-organization/self-transcending constructions <=> emergence <=> resilience and sustainability
- **High adaptive capacity** <=> nonlinearity <=> high self-organizing capacity <=> high emergence-intelligence capacity
- **'Unique' human adaptive capacity** <=> nonlinear mental capacity <=> relational capacity <=> constructionist effect

Administrative man — A term (as opposed to economic man) proposed by **Herbert Simon** in 1978 (1916–2001, Nobel Prize in Economics, in 1978) in his concept on bounded rationality (started in 1957). It indicates that all individuals, especially managers, do not make use of the entire information set collected (sometimes, the complete set is not available) during decision making because of the limited usable/working capacity of the human thinking systems (especially, the working memory space — cognitive constraint). Instead, a best subset of the information collected is normally exploited. Thus, the decision made is still rational but bounded — leading to a 'satisficing solution' (bounded optimality, satisficing principle) and not fully optimal solution. In complexity, this concept on bounded rationality has been extended to human organization — its dynamics are just 'sufficiently efficient' and 'sufficiently adaptive' and there is no global optimality (also due to incomplete phase space) — (see economic man, adaptive capacity, global optimality, satisficing principle, intelligent person and phase space).

Agent — Agents are the elementary entities/components of CS/CAS. In CAS, these interacting agents are autopoietic, autonomous, heterogeneous, interconnected, interdependent, and anticipatory. Thus, every agent is self-centric, stability-centric, and embedded with a set of behavioral schemata. Their interactions are initially localized (principle of locality, localized order, networks) but eventually lead to the emergent of global dynamic (collectiveness capacity) through self-organizing communications, self-organizing networks, and self-organization/self-transcending constructions. However, the agents are not aware of the remote/global effect of their actions. Agents in CS/CAS can also be CS/CAS — nested, composite systems. In general, agents as they interact changes their 'fitness', as well as the 'fitness' of other agents, that is, the rugged/fitness landscape is constantly changing. In particular, human interacting agents are living, self-powered, intrinsic leaders, smarter evolvers, feeling system, and emergent strategists. In the present context, a new category of agents ('free agents' or 'semi-free agents') is increasing in human organizations (nations, communities, and corporations). These agents may possess only temporary commitment, and minimal loyalty to their organizations (contract workers, foreign talents). In addition, agent-based modeling (ABM) is highly popular in complexity theory — NK, GA and CA models (see self-centric, stability-centric, behavioral schemata, principle of locality, localized order, network theory, autonomous, rugged landscape, intelligence, consciousness, interdependency, autopoiesis, localized order, non-linearity, self-organization, self-transcending constructions, self-powered, intrinsic leadership, smarter evolver, feeling system, emergent strategist, intelligent person, adaptive capacity, collectiveness capacity, anticipatory system, composite systems, complex adaptive systems, NK modeling, genetic algorithm and cellular automata).

Agent-agent/system micro-structure — It is the key structure of all CS/ CAS, as well as the basic micro-structure of all human organizations. [In the intelligent organization theory (**T.Y. Liang**, 2001), intelligent organizations are perceived to encompass a multi-layer structure.] Its associated dynamics possess the order and complexity characteristics (autopoiesis, butterfly effect, nonlinearity, connectivity, self-organization, self-enrichment process, global force, cascading effect, evolution, and emergence) indicated in the complexity theory. The dynamics stimulate multi-level effect, ranging from the local agent/agent processes [local self-organization/self-transcending constructions, formation of local spaces/networks — formal or informal) to network/network interactions (complexity meso-structure, network meso-structure), to agent/system and network/system processes (coherency and mental cohesion)] — (see agent, human agent, self-centric, stability-centric, behavioral schemata, butterfly effect, principle of locality, localized order, network theory, network management, autonomous, intelligence, consciousness, connectivity, interdependency, autopoiesis, nonlinearity, collectiveness capacity, cascading effect, self-organization, self-transcending constructions, self-powered, intrinsic leadership, smarter evolver, feeling system, emergent strategist, intelligent person, adaptive capacity, anticipatory system, composite systems, complex adaptive systems, complex networks, coherency, mental cohesion and emergence).

Agent-centric — Agent-centricity is one of the key attribute that differentiate *i*CAD from CAD. In intelligent human organizations, the attributes agent-centricity, network-centricity and org-centricity are equally significant, and mutually dependent and enhancing. Intelligence/consciousness-centric, intelligence-intelligence linkages and orgmindfulness are directly associated with human agent-centricity. Similarly, stability-centricity is also positively correlated with agent-centricity [self-centricity ('activated' by the agent) <=> agent-centricity ('activated' by the organization or leadership)] — (see agent, adaptive capacity, collectiveness capacity, autopoiesis, behavioral schemata, collective leadership, connectivity, engagement, feeling system, governance system, human agent, human organization, intelligence/consciousness-centric, intelligence-intelligence linkage, intelligence leadership, intrinsic leadership, mindful culture, org-centric, organizational justice, orgmind, orgmindfulness and intelligent organization).

Anticipatory system — It is an aware (org-aware) and mindful (orgmindful) (presence of intelligence and consciousness) system that plans ahead (futuristic) to ensure continuous existence and higher sustainability — high adaptive capacity. In the current context, it is not confined to forecasting alone. In 'realty', an intelligent organization must make preparation for (sudden) unknown problems/events (punctuation points), by nurturing collective intelligence (mindfulness, collectiveness capacity, scenario analysis, self-organizing capacity, emergence-intelligence capacity, futurology) and, exploiting relativistic complexity (risk management, crisis management) and the emergent strategy if it is to be regarded as anticipatory — (see awareness, aware system, mindfulness, mindful system, punctuation point, adaptive capacity, collectiveness capacity, self-organizing capacity, emergence-intelligence capacity, futurology, relativistic complexity, emergent strategy, early warning system, sustainability and intelligent organization).

Artifact — An entity artificially constructed/conceived in the non-sciences to assume the roles of a variable in the natural/exact sciences, such as the physical variables in classical mechanics (including distance, time, mass, speed, acceleration, and force). In the general information theory (**T.Y. Liang,** 1994) the artifacts are data, information, knowledge, wisdom, information-coded quantum, and information-coded matter quantum which define the boundaries of the theory — (see basic entity, variable and general information theory).

Attractor — It is the subset (an attractor encompasses one or more states) of the phase space of a dynamical system. In CS/CAS, the four types of attractor are point (fixed), periodic (cyclic), strange, and chaotic (indeterministic). In physical systems (dimension two or less) the fixed/point attractor (one state) and periodic attractor (a few states) are very common. A prominent example of a strange attractor is the Lorenz attractor — its phase diagram appears as a deep spiral (phase space trajectory) that never intersects, and is confined in a finite three-dimensional space (a 'stable' region with a large number of states). The Lorenz attractor is the first strange attractor of a physical system observed by **Edward Lorenz** (1917–2008), in 1963. In a human society, sociality is a biological attractor. (In mathematics, the term **strange attractor** was coined by **David**

Ruelle (1935–present) and **Floris Takens** (1940–2010) in 1971. Mathematically, the evolving variables of an attractor are represented by an n-dimensional vector — attractor in an *n*-dimensional space. When $n > 3$, it is difficult to perceive the attractor mentally. For many linear physical systems, their attractors can be captured by two to three positional coordinates (physical variables). In the biological world, there are certain **morphogenetic attractors** ('preferred' attractor) in the morphogenetic space, for instance, eye is such a 'preferred' attractor as many organisms have eyes (see dimensionality, phase space, strange attractor, Lorenz attractor and morphogenesis).

Notes: **Some relationships of phase space/attractor/state:**

- **Phase space** — the set of all possible states of a dynamical system with each possible state of the system corresponding to one unique point in the phase space.
- **Attractor** — a subset of the phase space — a set of states.
- **State** — a unique point in the phase space.
- **Point attractor** — 1 state.
- **Periodic attractor** — finite number of states — usually 2 or 3 states.
- **Strange attractor** — an enormous number (or a set) of states confined within a finite boundary/space.

Autocatalysis — It is a process that creates itself (in a self-perpetuating sequence — self-replicative) by catalytic action. Positive feedbacks create/support autocatalysis. Hypercycles (interacting autocatalytic cycles) proposed by **Manfred Eigen** [(1927–present), Nobel Prize in Chemistry, 1967)] in the 1970s indicates that the origin of life evolved by passing through instabilities, and creating successive higher levels of organization characterized by greater diversification of components and structures for natural selection to act on (robustness) — emergence. Hypercycles and (normal) autocatalytic systems both involve cyclic arrangement/reactions of catalysts. The different in hypercycles is that the catalysts are themselves self-replicative (see feedback, autocatalytic set, circular causation, cascading effect, upwards causation, downwards causation, natural selection and emergence).

Autocatalytic set — It is a set of entities, each of which can be created by other entities within the set. In this case, the set is able to catalyze its own production — autocatalysis. Initially, autocatalytic sets were used in natural sciences (molecular entities) but this concept has been extended to economics and sociology (see feedback, autocatalysis, cascading effect, natural selection and emergence).

Autonomous — An autonomous agent/system is active and acts independently by itself. It is driven by its own internal goals (self-centric, stability-centric). For human organization, autonomy is determined by the intrinsic intelligence (embedded with a behavioral schemata) of its agents, and/or the collective intelligence of the system/organization. Human agents are not fully autonomous (independency versus interdependency) — (see autopoiesis, self-centric, stability-centric, intelligence, symbiosis and interdependency).

Autopoiesis — The term was first used by **Humberto Maturana** (1928–present) and **Francisco Varela** (1946–2001), in 1973 to define characteristics of life at the cellular level ('auto' means 'self'/'life', and 'poiesis' means 'production' or 'creation' — with biotic potential). An autopoietic agent is self-centric, self-preserving/maintaining, self-enhancing, and self-producing. The autopoietic dynamic (constant localized order creation processes, only present in CAS) is inward focusing, and closely associated with individuality — as utilized in the intelligent organization theory (stability-centric — to the extreme, the presence of an 'I' in human beings). Therefore, the individual entities or agents in CAS can be highly 'myopic' and self-centric (intense self-awareness). Thus, autopoiesis is an inward self/center-seeking process (stability-centric, homeostasis) encompassing non-equilibrium that resists changes and makes connectivity, communications, and engagement difficult. However, if the condition is right an autopoietic entity can be self-regulating and self-organizing, thus, capable of maintaining a 'dynamical stable state' in a non-equilibrium environment. In this case, the individual entities make adjustment to their local space/network relations to main a stable holistic organization. In this respect, autopoiesis is associated with organizational identity, shared cognition, and growth, and 'balanced' by self-organization/self-transcending constructions (note the unique relations among autopoiesis, symbiosis, self-organization/self-transcending constructions and emergence) — (see awareness, self-centric, stability-centric, localized order, homeostasis, autonomous, symbiosis, cybernetics, interdependency, network theory, self-organization, self-transcending constructions and emergence).

Aware system — It is an autonomous system that responds to the changing environment (outward focusing) positively. (Awareness is external focusing, while self-awareness is internal focusing. At the core of self-awareness is mindfulness.) Such a system usually possesses reasonable level of collective intelligence (including org-consciousness as specified in the intelligent organization theory). Thus, it is also anticipatory — mapping plans for the deliberate path, as well as nurturing the emergent path concurrently (see awareness, mindfulness, anticipatory system, autonomous, collective intelligence and consciousness).

Awareness — In the intelligent organization theory, consciousness only exists in the living world — that is, consciousness arises from basic life-intelligence. Awareness is a primary 'mental' function that is identified in all biological species. (All living organisms/systems exhibit a certain level of awareness, including amoeba and plants.) A high level of consciousness (human consciousness) leads to a high level of awareness of the surrounding environment (awareness => external focusing), and the existence of a 'self' (self-awareness => internal focusing). At the core of self-awareness is mindfulness (internal focusing) (see intelligent organization theory, intelligence, consciousness, aware system, mindfulness, orgmindfulness, mindful culture, law of complexity/consciousness, law of complexity/intelligence, and law of consciousness/intelligence).

Axiom — A principle/rule that is assumed to be true within a certain theory/domain. Axioms are commonly used in mathematics. Many mathematical models in other domains are also conceived using the axiomatic approach. The intelligent organization theory and complexity-intelligence strategy make use of axioms in several of its sub-models (see general information theory, intelligent organization theory and complexity-intelligence strategy).

Basic (elementary) entity — It is the most fundamental/elementary entity a theory/system deals with. In the natural sciences, they are known as variables. In the non-science domain, artifacts are created to assume/perform the roles of entities (basic entity <=> variable <=> artifact). An artifact recognized/created in a non-scientific domain also describes its characteristic and dynamic. The set of basic entity/artifact/variable involved also defines the boundaries of the domain/theory. In a human organization, the basic entities are the human interacting agents. In an economy, the basic entities are business corporations. In CAS, the basic entities are alive and adaptive, highly interconnected and interdependent — (see artifact, variable, agent, connectivity, interdependency, complex adaptive systems and general information theory).

Basic life-intelligence — It is the type of intelligence that is beyond proto-intelligence in the intelligence spectrum. It emerges when crossing the boundaries of the physical/matter world into the living/biological world — introducing awareness and adaptive capability. Simple organisms exhibiting this level of intelligence, include amoeba (responding to the changing pH value of its environment), and plants (responding to the changing sun direction spontaneously). Basic life-intelligence sources can be integrated to form swarm intelligence (for instance, a beehive of bees, a colony of ants). As basic life-intelligence is elevated, consciousness is also escalated concurrently (for instance, the awareness of a wolf to the awareness of a chimpanzee) — (see intelligence spectrum, intelligence, proto-intelligence, adaptive capacity, swarm intelligence, collective intelligence, consciousness, awareness, biosphere, Gaia and Universe).

Basin of attraction — It is a space (a set of conditions) where iterations take place, and eventually leads to the long-term behavior of an attractor — that is, the points in a basin of attraction of an attractor will eventually iterate (converge) into the attractor itself (may be more simply perceived as a basin 'surrounding' an attractor). When a human organization moves into a different basin, it will eventually moves into another attractor. The ability to 'identify' a new basin of attraction is a significant attribute of the intelligence leadership (basin of attraction <=> scenario analysis; emergent of new order <=> into a state/attractor). Mathematically, a fixed point p of function f is 'attracting' if the iterates of all points near to p converge to p. The set of all the points whose iterates converge to p forms the basin of attraction of p (see attractor, phase space, strange attractor, Lorenz attractor, morphogenesis and intelligence leadership).

Notes:

- Outside a basin of attraction => unlikely to 'move' into an attractor.
- Within a basin of attraction => potentially able to 'move' into a state in an attractor.
- An attractor => a space with one or more states.
- States within an attractor are stable (even for strange attractor).
- States outside an attractor or basin of attraction may not be unstable.

Behavioral schemata — The set of behavioral schemata decides how an agent (both living and non-living entity) will behave and interact in CS/CAS. It could be a simple schema, especially in physical non-living agent and artificially created agent (cellular automata, artificial life), or 'simpler' species (a colony of ants, a flock of birds) — their collective behavior can be captured in a mathematical model (simpler swarm intelligence). Usually the initial interaction is localized (confined within a local space/order — significant of the local context) but it gradually becomes more global — leading to emergence (emergent of surface patterns). The behavioral schemata of living agents are always changing through continuous learning with time (adaptive). In human agents, it (a sophisticated set of behavioral schemata) is closely associated with their intrinsic intelligence/consciousness (intense mental space, including the knowledge structure with the accumulation of experiences), and the collective intelligence and org-consciousness of the system (thus, rendering intelligence/consciousness-centricity highly significant). Hence, intelligence/consciousness greatly affect the dynamics of autopoiesis, symbiosis, self-organization/self-transcending constructions, and emergence. In addition, due to the intense mental capacity of human agents their behavioral schemata can be highly nonlinear, constantly changing, and relativistic. In this case, a deeper understanding and utilization of social psychology is beneficial (relational friction, social cohesion, feeling system). In particular, the relatively newer theory in social cognition, the self-construal theory can be exploited. This theory indicates that there two perspectives about the 'self', namely independent self and interdependent self. Agents with higher independent self-perspective view the self as autonomous and separate from others, while agents with higher interdependent self-perspective view the self as connected to others. This characteristic has an influence on the collectiveness capacity, and self-transcending constructions capability of the organization. For an ideal case, the behavioral schemata of a human organization are the summation of the behavioral schemata of all the interacting agents with a synergetic effect — after transforming certain incoherency to coherency, and more. In this respect, the presence of a mindful culture (orgmindfulness, intelligence-intelligence linkage) is vital. Thus, due to the high complexity and nonlinear of human behavior it is difficult (not possible) to capture it in a mathematical model. Thus, the phase space of a human organization is never complete due to the presence of unknown unknowns (see agent, human agent, adaptive, adaptive capacity, collectiveness capacity, autopoiesis, symbiosis, principle of locality, localized order, interdependency, nonlinearity, intelligence, swarm intelligence, collective intelligence, self-organization, self-transcending constructions, mental cohesion, feeling system, synergetics, emergence, mindful culture, orgmindfulness, phase space and relativistic complexity).

Bifurcation — Bifurcation means splitting into two paths and rapid bifurcation causes chaos (from simplicity to chaotic, towards a deterministic chaotic attractor). Bifurcation theory is the study of bifurcation in nonlinear dynamical systems. Bifurcation occurs in discrete-time deterministic chaotic systems (DCS). Thus, mathematically bifurcation theory of DCS is the study of changes in topological structure in difference equations. The term bifurcation was introduced by **Henri Poincare** (1854–1912), in 1885. A bifurcation takes place when a small change in the value of a variable causes the system to behave very differently, implying determinism $\neq$ predictablility. **Mitchell Feigenbaum** (1944–present), in 1978, worked on bifurcation cascade mathematically, and it was experimentally confirmed by **Albert Libchaber** (1934–present), in 1979. A common illustration of bifurcation is captured in the logistic map — a one-dimensional (degree 2) discrete-time difference equation

$[x_{n+1} = x_n r(1 - x_n)]$ with recurrence relations [popularized by **Robert May,** (1936–present)]. At a bifurcation point, the developmental path of the logistic map splits into two different paths, and the outcome for selecting any one will be very different from the rest — the onset of deterministic chaos. As each path moves towards higher chaos and away from equilibrium, the number of paths increases rapidly due to further bifurcations. At the nexus of every path is another bifurcation point. At each bifurcation point the system cascades through a period of instability and chaos before a new path develops. The path in between two bifurcation points is a period of stability. The latter becomes shorter and shorter as the system evolves through the process of bifurcation (a cascading effect) into a deterministic chaotic attractor. A period doubling bifurcation in a discrete chaotic system (for instance, the logistic map) is a bifurcation in which a slight change in the bifurcation parameter value (r) causes the period of the system to double (twice as many iterations) — (see chaos, logistic map, feedback, recurrence relations, fractal dimension, dimensionality, chaos, recursion, cascading effect, topology, phase transition, attractor, chaotic attractor, strange attractor and chaos theory).

Biodiversity — It is the variation of taxonomic life forms (scientific classification and its underlying principles) at all levels of biological organizations (biosphere/ecosystem/Gaia). In general, bio-diversification helps to reduce risk during evolution. This term is now commonly used to mean 'spreading out' in other domains. Diversity is also interpreted as the ranges of features and/or niches available in a system, for examples, diversification in investment, structure, or thinking — (see biosphere, Gaia, evolution, co-evolution, adaptive, adaptive capacity, exaptation and global optimality).

Biosphere — It is an ecosystem that encompasses certain life forms (including predators and preys networks, forest, as well as the environmental space), and possess characteristics of CAS — including self-regulating and self-organizing. Gaia that encompasses all life forms and their systems is the largest ecosystem/biosphere on this planet, Earth (see complex adaptive systems, biotic system, extropy, ecosystem, self-centric, self-organization, Gaia and Universe).

Biotic macro-structure — It is the intelligent macro-structure of human organizations similar to highly developed biological organisms (a basic intelligence/consciousness-centric model with higher coherency, structural capacity, collectiveness capacity and adaptive capacity introduced in the intelligent organization theory). Basically, it comprises three components namely, the orgmind, the intelligence web (comparable to the central nervous system and other 'latent'/intangible connections), and the environmental scanning and responding subsystem (sensory subsystem), including the early warning subsystem. A human organization with an intelligent biotic macro-structure (supported by an agent-agent/system micro-structure and agents with the intelligent person attributes, as well as complex network) will be in a better position to nurture collective intelligence, accumulate organizational knowledge structure, facilitate organizational learning, exploit relativistic complexity, and enhance resilience and sustainability, creating an intelligence advantage (it is introduced in the intelligent organization theory to eliminate the hierarchical structure of the design paradigm) — (see organizing around intelligence, intelligence/consciousness-centric, biotic system, coherency, structural capacity, collectiveness capacity, adaptive capacity, intelligent person, collective intelligence, complex network, intelligent organization, *i*CAS, relativistic complexity, resilience, sustainability, design paradigm and intelligence advantage).

Notes: Multi-layered structure of intelligent human organizations:

- Intelligent biotic **macro-structure;**
- Agent-agent/system **micro-structure;**
- Complexity **meso-structure;**
- Networks **meso-structure;**
- The different layers are integrated and reductionism is ineffective and dysfunctional.

Biotic system — It is an autonomous, living, aware and adaptive system. It possesses a biotic structure and other biological attributes (in particular, intelligence, consciousness, anticipatory and adaptive) rather than mechanistic characteristics. The structure (and sub-structures, in particular, the three-layered brain) of a human being is regarded as a highly intelligent and sophisticated biotic system. In the intelligent organization theory, human organizations with high collective intelligence, and a biotic macro-structure (the presence of an orgmind, and an effective communication structure that links all parts of the organization, including the environmental scanning and responding system) are intelligent biotic systems (potentially possessing a higher self-organizing capacity and emergence-intelligence capacity). In this respect, artificially constructing a physical/mechanistic structure (Newtonian mindset/design paradigm) contradicts morphogenesis (see intelligence, consciousness, awareness, biotic macro-structure, adaptive, adaptive capacity, collective intelligence, autonomous, anticipatory system, aware system, organizing around intelligence, collectiveness capacity, orgmind, self-organizing capacity, emergence-intelligence capacity, morphogenesis, biosphere, Gaia, Universe, Newtonian mindset, design paradigm and intelligent organization).

Bisociation — It is the ability to relate/link things together that are previously unrelated [(first used in the book, The Act of Creation, **Arthur Koestler**, 1964) — (for instance, connecting telephone, radio, and camera in mobile phone)]. Another interesting example is the emergent of the complexity mindset which encompasses (establishing the bisociation) systems thinking, biotic/evolution thinking, and connectivity/cybernetics thinking. Similarly, the intelligence mindset encompasses the Newtonian mindset (selectively), complexity mindset, and extended it with intensive intelligence/consciousness-centricity, complexity-centricity, network-centricity, complexity-intelligence linkages, intelligence-intelligence linkages, and relativistic complexity. This ability is closely associated with innovativeness and nonlinear thinking (see Newtonian mindset, complexity mindset, intelligence mindset, intelligence/consciousness-centric, complexity-intelligence linkage, intelligence-intelligence linkage, nonlinearity and relativistic complexity).

Black Swan (model) — This metaphor refers to an event that is a surprise (relatively unpredictable) with a major impact but on hindsight reveals that there is information for its happening (uncertainty). It is a punctuation point to a great extent. The term was popularized by **Nassim Nicholas**

Taleb (1960–present) in his book, *The Black Swan*, in 2007 — [see complexity, nonlinearity, space of complexity, punctuation point (wicked problems), predictable, tipping point and uncertainty].

Broken symmetry — It is breaking of an exact symmetry of the underlying laws of physics by the random formation of some structures — by emergence. Symmetry breaking can be more easily explained/comprehend with an example, for instance crystallization. A crystal is a 'large' and complex system of atoms. The electrons and nuclei that form the crystal do not possess the properties of the latter (a crystal is a solid with rigidity and elasticity — properties not found in atoms/molecules — constructionist hypothesis — **Philip Warren Anderson** (1923–present). The crystalline state is an example of an emergent property of broken symmetry because the crystal has less symmetry than the atoms of the fluid from which it crystallized. Another interesting example is the emergent of hole states (hole localization) of molecules and solids due to symmetry breaking that lowers the energy (due to relaxation energy) of the SCF (self consistent field) wave functions (a local space with higher stability) (see Cartesian belief, hierarchical decomposition, fundamentalism, constructionist hypothesis, ontological reductionism, epistemological reductionism, localized order and emergence).

Butterfly effect — **Henri Poincare** (1854–1912), in 1890 was the first to discover sensitive dependence on initial conditions (a highly nonlinear phenomenon) when studying three-body problem (butterfly effect <=> sensitive dependence on initials conditions => a key characteristic that leads to complexity/chaos) — a significant historical root of the complexity theory. Subsequently, all DCS/CS/CAS are observed to be highly sensitive to a slight change in the conditions (divergent flow) of the input state, thus rendering the output state unpredictable. In this respect, a small change in input can lead to an enormous change in output — supported by feedbacks. This characteristic is also known as the butterfly effect — also observed by **Edward Lorenz** (1917–2008) using a differential equations model of the weather system in 1961 with slight changes in input. The term butterfly effect appeared in the title in one of Lorenz's paper in 1972. Mathematically, the Lyapunov exponent also manifests the sensitive to initial conditions effect (how two trajectories with infinitesimally small gap diverge); $| \partial Z(t) | \approx e^{\lambda t} | \partial Z_0 |$ where ∂Z_0 is the initial separation, and λ is the Lyapunov exponent (see Appendix 3). In this respect, for human organizations (CAS) forecasting can never be fully accurate, and 'future-proofing' can never be complete (see chaos, complexity, nonlinearity, punctuation point, tipping point, feedback, deterministic, uncertainty, predictability and futurology).

Cambrian explosion — The Cambrian explosion that started about 540 million years ago, after over 3 billion years of 'biological silence'. The Cambrian period [a term proposed by **Adam Sedgwick** (1785–1873), the academic advisor of Charles Darwin] lasted about 20 million years. Simple unicellular organisms were transformed into complex multi-cellular organisms — most of current phyla appeared during that period (and the subsequent 80 million years). In complexity theory, the Cambrian explosion is regarded as a punctuation point, the sudden and surprising surfacing of a space of high complexity, a threshold in genetic complexity, a creative dynamic with constructionist effect, and revealing that evolution is not always gradual. The current interest on the Cambrian period is very much due to **Harry Whittington** (1916–2010) (see stasis, punctuation point, complexity theory, nonlinearity, raplexity, chaos, space of complexity, natural selection, phyletic gradualism, constructionist hypothesis and emergence).

Cartesian belief — The belief [named after **Rene Descartes** (1596–1650)] that the behavior of the whole can be fully understood from the properties of the parts (reductionism) — associated with the concept of hierarchical decomposition and functional coherency (the global function is the sum of all the elementary functions of the parts). In this case, each of the parts/components can be analyzed separately. Systems with these characteristics are linear and orderly (including machine systems and traditional information systems). This belief is perceived as part of the Newtonian mindset and is linked to fundamentalism => Newtonian mindset <=> Cartesian belief <=> reductionist hypothesis <=> fundamentalism <=> hierarchical decomposition <=> Laplace belief <=> mathematical modeling. (Rene Descartes also introduced the philosophy of dualism which assumes that although material entities obey mechanical laws, the mind does not — 'I think, therefore I am') — (see Laplace belief, reductionist hypothesis, fundamentalism, hierarchical decomposition, ontological reductionism, epistemological reductionism and Newtonian mindset).

Cascading effect — The likelihood of cascades is related to the degrees of coupling between agents/networks/systems (loosely coupled systems — weak cascading, tightly coupled system — strong cascading). A system with strong cascading effect could result in cascading failure, that is, a failure in one component (agent/network) could lead to the failure of the entire system/organization (or composite system — causal chain effect — high risk in time of a crisis). In this respect, cascading effect is linked to the power law and can lead to crises. The cascading effect could also move across scale (scale-free, local-regional-global, individual-network-organization-nation), including spatial scale (space) and temporal scale (time) resulting in a complex cascading chain (see agent, composite system, network theory, scalability, feedback, circular causation and autocatalysis).

Catalysis — A reaction that is enabled by an agent (catalyst) and the latter is not changed in the process. It is a simpler and more orderly reaction than autocatalysis (see autocatalysis, feedback and cascading effect).

Catastrophe theory —— This theory was conceived by **Rene Thom** [(1923–2002), Fields Medal, 1958] in the 1960s, and popularized by **Christopher Zeeman** (1925–present) in the 1970s. In general, nonlinear dynamical systems will achieve new emergent of order through self-organization/self-transcending constructions, or collapse into in-deterministic chaos (high turbulence) after crossing the edge of chaos (new — 3rd critical value). A space of in-deterministic chaos has no more potential surface pattern. The catastrophe theory focuses on how such systems self-disintegrate — in mathematics, it is also a subset of bifurcation theory (see systems spectrum, bifurcation, in-deterministic, self-organization, self-transcending constructions, emergence, edge of emergence, edge of chaos and punctuation point).

Cellular automata — It is a large network with simple cells/agents. The simple agents with limited communication and number of states (a simple behavioral schema — a simple set of rules), and no centralized control are arranged in a grid form. Complex dynamics arise from the simple rules, and the system exhibits self-organization and emergence — emergent of surface patterns. It was invented by **John von Neumann** (1903–1957) and **Stanislaw Ulam** (1909–1984) to study self-production. In the 1940s, Neumann developed a two-dimensional grid with rules based on the 'Turing machine' (**Alan Turing**, 1912–1954). The state of a cell is solely (confined) determined by the state of the agents and those of their immediate neighbors. Later, **John Conway** (1937–present) developed the popular cellular automata, Conway's Game of Life (see agent, autopoiesis, localized order, behavioral schemata, self-organization, emergence, and principle of locality, NK modeling and genetic algorithm).

Cerebral cortex — This is the third layer of the human brain where most of the neurons are situated (especially, in the frontal cortex). The cerebral cortex exists prominently only in the primate family (phylogenesis). In the human brain, it is twice as thick as in the other primates. It is responsible for the emergent of bi-petal locomotion, tri-chromatic and three-dimensional vision, the creation of the character set (physical symbol systems, languages and abstract concepts), and mindfulness. Thus, it is the presence of better developed cerebral cortex (a six-layered neural structure with vertical cortical micro-circuits) that gives rise to more intense human intelligence (both basic and advanced human intelligence) which is different from basic life-intelligence (see phylogenesis, character set, human thinking system, physical symbol system, energy–matter system, general information theory, basic life-intelligence, intelligence, consciousness and mindfulness).

Chaos (deterministic chaotic systems — DCS) — It is the process/dynamical phenomenon (simplicity to chaotic — sensitive dependence on initial conditions, butterfly effect, bifurcation, deterministic but unpredictable — unpredictability surfaces when the dynamic exceeded 2 to 3 times the Lyapunov time) that causes a chaotic system to enter the deterministic chaotic state/attractor (some common DCS are logistic map, Henon map and double rod pendulum). These DCS are of low dimensionality, that is, they do not involve many variables (a few highly coupled variables interacting in a nonlinear manner). Deterministic (mathematical) chaos theory focuses on how simplicity in the form of a low-dimensional deterministic system creates high 'randomness' (not infinite randomness) — its phase space is quite random. Discrete-time chaotic systems bifurcate, and exhibit (deterministic) chaotic/strange attractor whatever their dimensionality (starting from dimension one). Continuous-time chaotic systems undergo phase transition, and exhibit strange attractor only with dimensionality three and above — Poincare–Bendixson theorem. (Systems that exhibit mathematical chaos are deterministic, that is, the output can be accurately computed but the value of the output can be surprising — contradicts with the common/layman usage of the word chaos.) The boundary between regular/orderly and chaotic behavior is often characterized by period doubling, quadrupling, and more. The word chaos was coined as a mathematical term by **T.Y. Li** and **James A. Yorke**, in 1975, in their paper 'Period Three Implies Chaos'). Thus, there is a significant difference between deterministic and in-deterministic chaos (systems spectrum) — (see chaos theory, nonlinearity, deterministic, dimensionality, systems spectrum, logistic map, recurrence relations, bifurcation, phase transition, deterministic chaotic attractor, strange attractor, edge of chaos, edge of emergence, Poincare–Bendixson theorem, complexity and complexity theory).

Notes: **Type of systems** => (also see dimensionality and systems spectrum below, and Appendices 1 and 2).

[Basically (mathematically), a system can be perceived as a set interacting variables. The dimensionalities, characteristics, relationships of the variables, and value of the parameters determine the type of system it is.]

- **Ordered systems (OS):** (Newtonian theory, low dimensionality, usually closed systems, static equilibrium, dynamic equilibrium, orderly, linear, deterministic, predictable, fixed point attractor and periodic attractor).

- **Deterministic chaotic systems (DCS):** (Chaos theory, closed or open systems, low dimensionality, deterministic, nonlinear, bifurcate (discrete-time), phase transition (continuous-time), deterministic, unpredictable and chaotic/strange attractor).

- **Complex (adaptive) systems (CS/CAS):** (Complexity theory, usually open systems, high finite dimensionality, nonlinear, phase transition, in-deterministic (mathematically), far-from-equilibrium, continuous change, stasis and punctuation equilibrium, unpredictable, self-organizing, symmetry breaking, emergence and stranger attractor — for CAS, adaptive agents, autopoietic, symbiosis, self-centric and interdependency).

- **Intelligent human organizations/systems (*i*CAS):** (Intelligent organization (IO) theory, complexity theory, open systems, high finite dimensionality, order and complexity co-exist, stasis and punctuation cycle, nonlinear, interconnectivity, interdependency, far-from-equilibrium, in-deterministic (mathematically), uncertainty, anticipatory, unpredictable, intelligence/consciousness-centric, mindful, org-awareness, orgmindfulness, continuous change, self-organizing communications, stability-centric, self-centric, org-centric, interdependency, complexity-centric, integrated deliberate and emergent strategy, smarter evolver, emergent strategist, self-transcending constructions, local spaces, network-centric, symmetry breaking, relativistic complexity, relativistic static equilibrium, space of relativistic order and emergence).

- **(Highly) Disordered systems (DS) (Disordered systems <=> stochastic systems**, statistical mechanics, usually closed systems, infinite randomness/dimensionality, equilibrium at maximum entropy and ontological reductionism).

Notes: A 'reasonable' definition of DCS and CAS and their dynamics:

- **Deterministic chaotic systems** are low dimensionality nonlinear deterministic dynamical systems that undergo bifurcation or phase transition, are deterministic but unpredictable, and possess chaotic attractors and/or stranger attractors (DCS is now studied under complexity theory but it is not a subset of CS).

- **Chaotic dynamic** evolves from simplicity to deterministic chaotic through bifurcation or phase transition.
- **Complex adaptive systems** are high finite dimensionality nonlinear dynamical living systems with adaptive agents that undergo self-organization/self-transcending constructions and emergence, are in-deterministic, unpredictable, and possess strange attractors (CAS is a subset of CS with living agents).
- **Complex adaptive dynamic** evolves from complexity to simplicity through autopoiesis, autocatalysis, cascading chain, self-organization/ self-transcending constructions, synergetic and emergence (both agents and their system are adaptive).
- **Human organizations** are high finite dimensionality in-deterministic CAS (with an in-complete phase space), and not chaotic systems (although, localized chaotic processes — simplicity to chaotic — do occur at random).

Chaos theory — Deterministic chaos is the 'popular' name for the study (mathematical) of nonlinear dynamical systems with low dimensionality (how chaotic systems with low dimensionality create chaos) that manifest the simplicity to chaotic dynamic (deterministic because the output can be calculated but unpredictable as the result may be surprising, that is, chaotic => determinism $\neq$ predictability). Thus, it is a mathematical theory that focuses on bifurcation, chaotic attractor/strange attractor (phase diagram), and phase space of DCS. A key characteristic of such systems is sensitive dependence initial conditions — butterfly effect. A chaotic system can be represented by one or more differential equations (continuous-time) or difference equations (discrete-time) with a small number of variables — equations with recurrence relations. Thus, some simple recurrence relations exhibit chaotic behavior. The bifurcation process of a discrete chaotic system, from stability to periodicity to chaos occurs when the coupling among stability (negative feedbacks) and instability (positive feedbacks) forces increases. Mathematical chaos also focuses on topological mixing and dense periodic orbits. Orbit is a subset of the phase space, and they do not intersect — attractor. (However, with the presence of nonlinearity, conceiving a high dimensionality mathematical model is difficult, and solving nonlinear equations is even more difficult. In addition, some early chaos and complexity researchers believe that the Universe and its micro-cosms are more a mind than a machine — **'awakening to a cosmic mind'**.) [Some of the pioneers of this domain include Henri Poincare, George Birkhoff, Andrey Kolmogorov, Mitchell Feigenbaum, Benoit Mandelbrot, Tien-Yien Li, Edward Lorenz, David Ruelle, Stephen Smale, Floris Takens, James Yorke, Albert Libchaber, Robert May, Michel Henon, and Otto Rossler] — (see butterfly effect, bifurcation, deterministic, pre-dictability, dimensionality, Poincare–Bendixson theorem, logistic map, feedback, recurrence relations, chaotic attractor, strange attractor, phase space, nonlinearity, complexity theory, catastrophic theory, consciousness, Universe, and law of complexity/consciousness).

Chaotic (deterministic) attractor — DCS possess deterministic chaotic attractor (with sensitive dependence to initial conditions attribute). A dynamical system with deterministic chaotic attractor is locally unsta-ble but globally stable. All deterministic chaotic attractors are strange attractors but not vice versus. There is a significant different between deterministic chaotic attractor and the in-deterministic chaotic space. The latter is the fourth attractor of nonlinear dynamical systems [order, periodic, strange (some are deterministic chaotic), and in-deterministic chaotic)]. A nonlinear dynamical system moves into the fourth attractor when it cannot self-organize and emerge constructively anymore. The in-deterministic chaotic attractor is a space where the details cannot be understood, the states are unstable, and there is also no obvious global pattern (high turbulence). In this situation, the outcome is self-destruction/disintegration. The catastrophic theory focuses on how sys-tems venture into such a space. An example of a human system that had gone into this space and disintegrated was USSR (the original system had disappeared but the fragments are still around and re-organized). In the intelligent organization theory, the space of in-deterministic chaos emerges after crossing the redefined edge of chaos (3rd critical value) — (see order, chaos, in-deterministic, attractor, chaotic attractor, strange attractor, edge of chaos, catastrophic theory, phase space, punctuation point, edge of emergence, and emergence).

Notes: Some differences between (deterministic) chaotic attractor and strange attractor:

- The term chaotic indicates a loss of predictability (chaotic <=> high sensitivity), (chaotic <=> unpredictability).
- A chaotic attractor is a strange attractor (chaotic attractor => strange attractor).
- **A chaotic attractor** is sensitive dependence on initial conditions, and non-periodic.
- Not all strange attractors are chaotic attractors (not all strange attractors are sensitive dependent on initial conditions).
- A **strange attractor** is given the name 'strange' because it has a non-integer dimension.
- Examples of non-strange (non-fractal) attractors are fixed point attractor, limited cycle (periodic) attractor, and torus attractor (can be predicted accurately).

Character set — This is the collection of all the most basic/elementary symbols used in a particular language. Different character sets in different languages can be extremely dissimilar. For instance, in the English language the character set is {A, B, C, ..., a, b, c, ..., 1, 2, 3,...}. Many other languages are using their own character set (for instance, Chinese, Greek, Thai, Korean, and Russian). The character set of most languages are emerging, that is, new characters are being introduced continuously, new words are emerging, and new collections of words introduce new meanings and concepts frequently (characters => words => collection of words => language => concepts/abstract meanings, is an emerging process). Some human civilizations that had vanished also had their own character set. The creation of character sets is unique to the human race (intense human intelligence). No other animal species has ever created such a set. This ability (creating character set => physical symbol set => event/ thought capturing => information/knowledge => abstract concepts => written language => external knowledge storage => mass communications => complex interconnectivity) can be used to confirm that human intelligence is the highest compared to the basic life-intelligence of all other biological species on this planet (see intelligence, consciousness, physical symbol system, human thinking system, general information theory, intelligence spectrum, basic life-intelligence, consciousness, swarm intelligence, collective intelligence and emergence).

Circular causation — It is due to the closed loops (feedbacks) of cause and effect in CS/CAS which results in greater nonlinearity. Multiple interconnected causes and effects (cascading effect) can co-exist, thus rendering explanation in the conventional manner (linear chain) impossible — in-deterministic and unpredictable. This dynamic may create spaces of high complexity, as well as punctuation points (see nonlinearity, autocatalysis, feedback, predictability, uncertainty, cascading effect, recurrence relations, upwards causation, downwards causation, space of complexity and punctuation point).

Co-evolution — It indicates the concurrent evolution, emergent and survival of two or more interacting agents and/or CAS that are interacting (balancing between self-centricity and org-centricity — co-adaptation, nested/composite systems) in the same environment/ecosystem (agent <=> CAS, CAS <=> composite CAS). The co-evolution dynamic focuses on the complexity, connectivity, relationships, engagement, interdependency, individual intelligence, autopoiesis, symbiosis, self-organization, self-transcending constructions, and collective intelligence between/ among the entities involved. In the process, the 'shape' of the rugged/ fitness landscape is constantly modified. During evolution not all agents/ CAS achieve their goals (no global optimality). Some agents involved only achieve best possible goals/fitness/solutions (satisficing principle), while some agents may even be eliminated. Thus, the recognition of micro-diversity at the elemental level, and its ability to generate alternative evolution paths is significant (see evolution, exaptation, global optimality, collective intelligence, self-centric, org-centric, interdependency, intelligent person, autopoiesis, symbiosis, self-organization, self-transcending constructions, rugged landscape, global optimality, satisficing principle, composite CAS, biosphere and Gaia).

Coherency (coherent) — In physics, two wave sources are coherence if they possess the same frequency and constant phase difference; a situation ideal for stationary (space-time constant) interference. In human organizations, the term coherency refers to the presence of a binding effect (integration) that is logical and congruous (synchrony, intelligence-intelligence linkages). The ability to cohere well in any organization is vital as a synergetic effect may surface, and the process leads to high organizational competitiveness (see intelligence/consciousness-centric, intelligence-intelligence linkage, synergetic effect, mental cohesion and constructionist hypothesis).

Cohesion — Cohesion, in particular, social cohesion refers to bondages (presence of certain attractive forces, intelligence-intelligence linkages) of human agents that link them together as a team/network/organization. The processes involved are multi-dimensional (including the emotional dimension) rendering the dynamic highly complex. In all human organizations, due to the intense mental dimension of human agents (3rd order stability), achieving organizational mental cohesion is extremely vital (see behavioral schemata, intelligence/consciousness-centric, intelligence-intelligence linkage, stability-centric, mindfulness, stability-centric, mental cohesion and coherency).

Collective intelligence — Human collective intelligence arises from the synergetic integration (intelligence-intelligence linkages from incoherency to better coherency) of the individual intrinsic intelligence from all (if necessary) human interacting agents (self-centric and nonlinear sources) that form networks and/or organizations (stability-centric, connectivity, interdependency, engagement, complex adaptive network, collectiveness capacity, adaptive capacity, network-centric, coherency, mental cohesion — consensus decision making and action). Some form of collective intelligence is present and observable in all biological entities that exist in group (an ant colony, a pack of wolves, and in particular, a human community. However, there is a significant different between human collective intelligence and swarm intelligence, as the behavioral schemata of human beings is highly nonlinear due to the highly intense intelligence/consciousness sources — also high nonlinear relational parameter). Both human collective intelligence and swarm intelligence arises from local interactions, and group interconnectivity with synergetic effect.

In intelligent human organizations, the direct intelligence-to-intelligence linkages (intelligence/consciousness management) help to nurture a sophisticated and intelligent mental space known as the orgmind. High level human collective intelligence is better nurtured with high human consciousness, in particular, with the presence of mindfulness and org-mindfulness (mindful culture) — feeling system, unifying capacity, mental cohesion, and preparing for unpredictability (human collective intelligence <=> organizational mental cohesion). When the nurturing process exceeds a certain threshold it becomes emergent in nature, and the collective intelligence that emerges possesses new characteristics and capabilities (ideally with synergetic effect, constructionist effect, coherency, nonlinearity, and innovative and creativity). A higher level and capacity of collective intelligence (quality collectivity and connectedness) enables the organization to self-organize more effectively in times of crises/punctuation points (higher collective intelligence <=> higher self-organizing capability) — that is, towards a highly intelligent human organization (*i*CAS) with greater emergent potential (high self-organizing capacity and emergence-intelligence capacity). (In this respect, sociality is an important attribute for survival. In human organizations, sociality is a biological attractor. For ants, it is encrypted in their genes — highlighting the significant difference between human collective intelligence and swarm intelligence) — (see intelligence, consciousness, intelligence/consciousness-centric, mindfulness, orgmindfulness, intelligence-intelligence linkage, autopoiesis, self-centric, stability-centric, collective intelligence, swarm intelligence, intelligence spectrum, behavioral schemata, organizing around intelligence, human organization, collectiveness capacity, adaptive capacity, relational capacity, connectivity, nonlinearity, engagement, interdependency, intelligence/consciousness management, complex adaptive network, network management, symbiosis, agent-centric, org-centric, coherency, mental cohesion, self-organization, self-transcending constructions, self-organizing capacity, self-organizing criticality, self-organizing capacity, emergence-intelligence capacity, unifying capacity, synergetics, constructionist hypothesis, intelligence leadership, collective leadership, feeling system, mental cohesion, predictability, punctuation point, network theory, intelligent organization, *i*CAS, *i*CAD, sustainability and intelligent organization theory).

Collective leadership — As the human world evolve into greater complexity, leadership in all human organizations have to be dispersed and shared by a larger group of people (closely associated with collective intelligence, interconnectivity, interdependency, mindful culture, lateral leadership, network-centric, collectiveness capacity, feeling system, and consensus and collaboration) — a significant trait of the intelligence leadership strategy (collective leadership <=> lateral leadership <=> consultative leadership <=> learning leadership <=> opinion leadership). In addition, such a situation is becoming more critical as more interacting agents are better educated and informed (self-powered human agents with intrinsic leadership capability — intelligent person attributes, leadership capacity). This collective and lateral approach is inevitable as more consultation is necessary with regards to policies and changes. This diversification of power, roles, and responsibilities of leadership helps to nurture and elevate the collective intelligence, and self-organizing governance and e-governance in organizations (corporations, nations) are needed for better competitiveness, resilience and sustainability. In a highly intelligent human organization, high self-organizing capability is driven by the individual intrinsic intelligence of the agents and the collective intelligence of the system — that is, self-powered human agents endowed with intrinsic leadership ability balance (ambidexterity) between autopoiesis and symbiosis leading to 'everybody is in charge'. The presence of this ability is particularly significant during punctuated equilibrium. Hence, characteristics such as low key, soft voice and concentrated calmness are critical leadership attributes in the new environment. Thus, the 'redefined collectiveness' can be better achieved only if a more lateral and 'sharing' approach is adopted. Consequently, in this current context, encompassing more intrinsic leadership sources with a 'common' language and achieving organizational mental cohesion is strategic (see lateral leadership, intrinsic leadership, latent leadership, intelligence leadership, self-powered, leadership capacity, mindful culture, collective intelligence, network theory, feeling system, nonlinearity, collectiveness capacity, global mindset, autopoiesis, symbiosis, self-organization, self-transcending constructions, punctuation point, intelligent person, intelligent organization, Abilene paradox, character set, physical symbol system, self-organizing communications, engagement, self-organizing governance, coherency, mental cohesion and sustainability).

Collectiveness capacity — Collectiveness capacity is a critical attribute of intelligent human organizations, and it is positively correlated with collective intelligence (collectiveness capacity <=> collective intelligence). Collectiveness intelligence will elevate when the sustainability of the individual human agents are taken into consideration — higher coherency and synergetic. In this respect, intelligent (human) complex adaptive dynamic (*i*CAD) is not totally similar to normal complex adaptive dynamic (CAD). It is determined by the behavioral schemata (self-centric, stability-centric, and other changing and nonlinear characteristics, including the social cognition, construal, and self-construal perspectives) of the interacting agents, and the orgmindfulness (mindful culture, intelligence-intelligence linkages, unifying capacity) of the organization. Therefore, the ability to connect, communicate and engage the agents and networks (mutual trust, consensus, collaboration, commitment) is positively correlated to the collectiveness capacity of the organization. Thus, focusing on the mental space of the agents (3rd order stability) is highly critical in the present context — (collectiveness capacity <=> organizational adaptive capacity with synergetic effective <=> unifying capacity) — (see behavioral schemata, self-centric, stability-centric, intelligence, collective intelligence, connectivity, engagement, coherency, synergetics, structural capacity, adaptive capacity, intelligent person, symbiosis, self-organizing communications, self-transcending constructions, self-organizing capacity, emergence-intelligence capacity, unifying capacity, orgmindfulness, mindful culture, mindful system, network theory, network management, collective leadership and intelligence leadership).

Complex/Complexity — Complex in complexity theory originates from a Latin word that means 'intertwined' (in this respect, the system must be analyzed holistically and cannot be by parts — reductionism fails). Thus, it is the situation where the details (microscopic aspects) cannot be comprehended but the surface pattern (due to potential emergence) that enables the system as a whole to be understood is present (elementary processes leading to a surface pattern in space-time that is neither static nor random but complex — continuous changes involving high finite dimensionality). Thus, complexity is highest in systems with finite high dimensionality (this category of systems is CS/CAS — systems spectrum). In certain spaces of complexity there is a critical first mover advantage (in the intelligent organization theory, not all spaces of complexity are punctuation points). In all CS/CAS, order and complexity co-exist (uncertainty). (It is interesting to note that autopoiesis theory and network theory and its association with the power law indicate that the Universe and its subsystems are not totally random — confirming the co-existence of order and complexity.) In human organizations, better complexity management (complexity-intelligence linkage, relativistic complexity) can be achieved with the intelligence mindset (complexity-intelligence strategy) — (see order, nonlinearity, connectivity, chaos, emergence, uncertainty, dimensionality, systems spectrum, complex systems, complex adaptive systems, space of complexity, punctuation point, complexity-intelligence linkage, relativistic complexity, complexity management, intelligence mindset, intelligent organization and complexity-intelligence strategy).

Notes: Type of spaces:

- **Space of order** — exists in OS, and DCS/CS/CAS including human organizations (deterministic and predictable).
- **Space of complexity** — exists in CS/CAS, including human organizations (no suddenness or surprises).
- **Punctuation point** — spaces of high complexity that exist in CS/CAS, including human organizations (with suddenness or surprises).
- **Space of relativistic order** — exists in highly intelligent human organizations, iCAS <=> rCAS, due to the presence of intense individual intelligence and/or intense collective intelligence and orgmindfulness.
- **Space of deterministic chaotic state** — exists in chaotic systems (deterministic chaotic attractor).
- **Space of infinite randomness** — exists in highly disordered systems, perceived as 'stable' (equilibrium at maximum entropy).

- **Space of in-deterministic chaotic** — the ultimate space of nonlinear dynamical systems (in-deterministic chaotic attractor/space) that do not self-organize effectively and lead to disintegration or self-destruction (fundamentally, any systems that are composed will one day decompose).

Notes: Some relationships between chaos (DCS) and complexity (CS/CAS):

- (Mathematical) chaos is deterministic but not predictable (chaotic <=> unpredictability), (determinism ≠ predictability), and DCS are low dimensional nonlinear dynamical systems.
- Complexity is in-deterministic and unpredictable (complexity <=> in-determinism <=> unpredictability), and CS/CAS are high finite dimensional nonlinear dynamical systems.
- CS/CAS are historical dependent (hysteresis) but DCS are not.
- (Complexity ≠ chaos), (DCS ≠ CS/CAS), (not all strange attractors are chaotic attractor).
- However, all DCS, CS, and CAS are sensitive dependence on initial conditions.

Complex adaptive networks (CAN) — Complex adaptive networks are complex networks (network of networks) embedded with intelligence (individual and collective) — (complex adaptive networks <=> intelligent networks). This is a term introduced in the intelligent organization theory (**T.Y. Liang**, 2001) to indicate networks with adaptive capability in human organizations. Thus, human networks are local spaces that emerge with self-organization/self-transcending constructions, and the nodes involved are living/human agents (for instance, human social networks are CAN whereas computer networks are not — just CN). Hence, these networks possess learning, adaptive, self-organizing communications, and self-organization/self-transcending constructions abilities (network collective intelligence). Focusing on the presence of such networks (the two common types are small world networks and scale free networks) in human organizations is vital aspect of the intelligence leadership strategy, and intelligence governance strategy (network management). In a CAN, the links manifest both strong ties and weak ties. Nodes connected with strong ties tend to form clusters with self-organizing capability. While, nodes connected with weak ties manifest small worlds effect/phenomenon (including the Pareto distribution) — [see adaptive, localized order, graph theory, network theory, small world network, scale free network, complex network, collective intelligence, scalability, interdependency, principle of locality, network management, emergence, S(1)-S(4), self-organizing communications, self-organization, self-transcending constructions, intelligence leadership and intelligence governance].

Complex adaptive systems (CAS) — These are complex systems (CS — multi-agent, high finite dimensionality, create 'simplicity' — emergent of order from complexity) with adaptive (living) agents (for instance, bees, human beings, human networks) that consume information, communicate, learn, and adapt to changes continuously. As the agents adapt, the system also adapts. In this respect, CAS are living systems (open) embedded with intelligence (living interacting agents) — as defined in the intelligent organization theory. [Living systems unlike mechanical systems are intrinsically open. They interact with the environment, absorb (input) and dissipate (output) matter and energy (and information) to stay alive/sustainable, for instance, ant colony, stock market, ecosystem, social community, and humanity as a whole.] In general, CAS are more 'predictable' than CS — can generate some simple surface patterns. CAS are also self-similar, self-organizing, dissipative and co-evolutionary. The interacting agents and networks (complex adaptive networks) in the CAS self-organize to 'optimize'/sustain their individual/group existence — adaptive capacity. In addition, CAS can be nested (composite CAS: for instance, corporations and economy), and possesses memory (the history of the system can be important — hysteresis — time-based dependency). The term CAS was introduced by the group of researchers that established the Santa Fe Institute in the 1980s. Some of the pioneer researchers in this institute include George Cowan, Doyne Farmer, Murray Gell-Mann, John Holland, Stuart Kauffmann, Norman Packard, Chris Langton, Kenneth Arrow, and Brian Arthur. All human organizations are intrinsic CAS, and can be nurtured as highly intelligent human organizations (*i*CAS

<=> emergent of new order) — (see agent, complexity, nonlinearity, connectivity, adaptive, dissipation, dimensionality, Poincare–Bendixson theorem, systems spectrum, evolution, exaptation, autopoiesis, interdependency, self-organization, self-transcending constructions, adaptive capacity, ordered systems, complex systems, disordered systems, composite complex adaptive systems, systems spectrum, *i*CAS, upwards causation, downwards causation, adaptive capacity, network theory and emergence).

Complex networks (CN) — A complex network (also known as network of networks) is a network that possesses complexity characteristics, such as social networks and computer networks. (The WWW is a complex network with web documents as nodes and URLs as links.) The two common types of CN are small world networks and scale free networks. A significant and critical characteristic of such a 'system' of networks is that the networks involved can be interdependent. Interdependent networks system is a system of networks with nodes that are interdependent across networks. Such interdependency could enhance developments or escalate cascading failures — [see graph theory, network theory, small world network, scale free network, scalability, complex adaptive network, self-organizing communications, interdependency, S(1)-S(4), self-organization, self-transcending constructions, cascading effect and emergence].

Complex systems (CS) — All complex systems (open) are high finite dimensionality nonlinear dynamical systems (multiple levels/networks, and large number of variables) that encompass both order and complexity (between order and randomness), and are therefore in-deterministic and unpredictable (continuous balancing divergence and convergence dynamics => from complexity to 'simplicity'), and what can be predicted is very constraint — due to in-complete phase space. Their entities/agents are interdependent (some degree), autonomous (not fully), and undergo direct and indirect localized interactions (local space/network). CS move from one dynamical state to another through transition process — phase transitions at critical points. However, the new state that emerges may not be predictable. CS are non-living systems (according to the intelligent organization theory). The behavior of complex systems are not simply the sum of their components (failure of reductionism/fundamentalism) — (physical complex systems — for example, weather system), while CAS (living systems — for examples, ecosystems, human organizations) encompass life. Conceptually, CS/CAS can be classified as a category of systems that exist between OS and DS — that is between order (Newtonian space) and randomness (statistical mechanical world). In this respect, complexity is high/highest in between order and infinite randomness — (see systems spectrum, complexity mindset, dimensionality, open system, ordered systems, Newtonian mindset, disordered systems, in-deterministic, reductionist hypothesis, fundamentalism, butterfly effect, statistical mechanics, predictability, Poincare–Bendixson theorem, self-organization, self-transcending constructions and complex adaptive systems).

Complexity-intelligence linkage — It indicates the link/relationship between complexity and intelligence (at both individual and collective levels) in humanity, as well as the entire living world (highlighting the differences of complexity in the biological and physical worlds — in particular, focusing on the exploitation of complexity with the intense human intelligence sources). This is a primary and highly significant linkage in the intelligent organization theory (**T.Y. Liang**, 2001) that modifies/transforms the meaning of complexity in the human world (complexity is in the mind of the beholder — introducing relativistic complexity). Primarily, intelligent organizations exploit the co-existence of order and complexity, channel resources into certain spaces of complexity, and make preparation for punctuation points (towards better risk management and crisis management). As a human organization and its interacting agents possess 3rd order stability (space of mental complexity), complexity and the complex adaptive dynamic becomes relativistic with intense intelligence/consciousness-centricity and complexity-intelligence-centricity. In this respect, dynamical equilibrium may appear as relativistic static equilibrium, and certain spaces of complexity may appear as spaces of relativistic order (see intelligent organization theory, order, complexity, complexity-intelligence strategy, intelligence/consciousness-centric, stability-centric, nonlinearity, intelligence spectrum, intelligence/consciousness management, space of complexity, punctuation point, complexity management, intelligent organization, sustainability, global mindset, law of complexity/intelligence, space of relativistic order and relativistic complexity).

Complexity-intelligence strategy — This is the overall holistic/global strategy (with several sub-strategies/models/frameworks) of the intelligent organization theory (**T. Y. Liang**, 2001). It recognizes and exploits the close association between complexity and intelligence (complexity-intelligence linkage) as a key foundation. Thus, this strategic approach is highly intelligence/consciousness-centric (organizing around intelligence, intelligence-intelligence linkage, collective intelligence, intelligence/consciousness management, collectiveness capacity, adaptive capacity, self-organizing capacity) and complexity-centric (integrated deliberate strategy and emergent strategy, complexity management), network-centricity (self-organizing communications, network of networks, network management, emergence-intelligence capacity) — facilitated by the intelligence mindset, and intelligence paradigm — mindfulness culture, org-mindfulness. With intense nonlinear intelligence (supported by the appropriate knowledge structures) a space of high complexity may not be that complex — relativistic complexity — space of relativistic order. The sub-strategies/models/frameworks include organizing around intelligence, integrated deliberate and emergent strategy, intelligent biotic macro-structure model, agent-agent/system micro-structure and dynamic, integrated 3C-OK framework, intelligent person model, intelligence leadership strategy, intelligence governance strategy, and relativistic complexity. The ultimate goal of the complexity-intelligence strategy is to nurture *i*CAS driven by *i*CAD that could exploit certain spaces of complexity, and survive at punctuation points better — enhances competitiveness, resilience, sustainability through an intelligence advantage (see *i*CAS, *i*CAD, intelligence, intelligence mindset, intelligence paradigm, consciousness, intelligence/consciousness-centric, organizing around intelligence, intelligence-intelligence linkage, coherency, mental cohesion, collective intelligence, collectiveness capacity, adaptive capacity, self-organizing capacity, intelligence/consciousness management, feeling system, complexity-intelligence linkage, space of complexity, punctuation point, complexity management, intelligent organization theory, intelligent person, deliberate strategy, emergent strategy, emergence-intelligence capacity, intelligence leadership, network management, network theory, self-organizing governance, law of complexity/consciousness, law of complexity/intelligence, law of consciousness/intelligence, intelligence advantage, sustainability, space of relativistic order and relativistic complexity).

Complexity approaches (key strategic paths) — **[1]** The **European Complexity School** focuses on the emergent behavior (the dynamics that initiate and sustain order creation) in far-from-equilibrium systems initiated by environmentally imposed adaptive tensions (due to energy differentials) on the system — **Ilya Prigogine's** (1917–2003, Nobel Prize in Chemistry, 1977) dissipative structures theory (concentrates on edge of order — 1st critical value — new intra-system order emerges). **[2]** The **American Complexity School** focuses on how complexity is created, and the emergent of order in a disorganized system (heterogeneous agent, agent interaction, behavioral schemata, co-evolution, inter-system process, interdependency, agent-based modeling, self-organization, and concentrates on the edge of chaos (old) — second critical value). **[3] Econophysics** (coined by **Harry Eugene Stanley**, 1941–present) approach (scale-free theory) focuses on the use of power laws (PL) to explain the unrestricted self-organizing behavior in systems/organizations (physics, economics) — PL phenomena/effects (PL theory), and Pareto distributions are normally due to interdependency of components/agents, and they are scale-free. A scale-free theory explains the emergent organizing dynamic of a multiple levels system using a single rule/function. **[4]** Next, the **intelligent organization theory** (**relativistic complexity, T. Y. Liang,** 2001) focuses on the intrinsic intelligence and consciousness (intelligence/consciousness-centric) of the individuals (self-powered human agents — intelligent person endowed with intrinsic leadership ability — high adaptive capacity), and the collective intelligence (orgmindfulness and mindful culture) of the organization that leads to self-organization/self-transcending constructions, and emergent of new order — through the intelligence mindset that exploits characteristics, concepts, and tools such as intelligent biotic macro-structure, integrated deliberate and emergent strategy, complexity-intelligence linkage, intelligence-intelligence linkage, intelligent person attributes, mindful culture, orgmindfulness, 3rd order stability, co-evolution, global optimality, intelligence governance strategy, intelligence leadership strategy, and relativistic complexity. As human agents stability possesses a mental dimension (high mental capacity), complexity in the human world becomes relativistic (see emergence, interdependency, far-from-equilibrium, edge of order, dissipative structure, edge of chaos, power law, stability-centric, self-organization, self-transcending constructions, adaptive capacity, co-evolution, global optimality, self-powered, interdependency, intelligence/consciousness-centric, orgmindfulness, mindful culture, intelligent person, intelligence/consciousness management, complexity management, relativistic complexity, power law, power law phenomena, Pareto distribution, scalability, constructionist hypothesis, self-transcending constructions, relativistic complexity and intelligent organization theory).

Complexity management — Complexity management is a new vital focal point, as well as ability that leaders and managers must acquire in the current knowledge intensive and swift changing context, and highly complex environment — raplexity (one of the key aspects of the intelligent organization theory). It recognizes the co-existence of order and complexity, existence of complex nonlinear dynamics, exploitation of spaces of high complexity (could be unexplored territories with new opportunities — a new innovation/market — better risks management, first mover advantage, intelligence advantage), presence of relativistic complexity associated with the intense human mental dimension, the significance of preparing for punctuation points (sudden surprises, crisis management), and other complexity-related matters in human organizations (reducing devastation). A key strategy adopted is the integrated deliberate and emergent strategy (with a deliberate-emergent auto-switch). In humanity and its organizations, complexity management is also closely correlated with intelligence/consciousness management (complexity-intelligence linkage => space of relativistic order; intelligence-intelligence linkage => collective intelligence), and network management (complex networks, small world network, self-transcending constructions), and they must be executed simultaneously. In general, another possible interpretation is (increase in robustness >> increase in complexity => relativistic order). Higher level intrinsic human intelligence and collective intelligence, including nonlinear intelligence (associated with innovation and creativity) are vital for orchestrating higher level intelligent complex adaptive dynamics (more constructive self-organization/self-transcending constructions — *i*CAD) and nurturing intelligent organizations (*i*CAS). In this respect, a new mindset in leadership, governance, management, and strategy is essential and crucial (see nonlinearity, complexity, connectivity, raplexity, intelligence/

consciousness management, complexity mindset, complexity-intelligence linkage, deliberate strategy, emergent strategy, deliberate-emergent auto-switch, principle of locality, space of complexity, punctuation point, network management, self-organizing capacity, emergence-intelligence capacity, space of relativistic order, intelligence-intelligence linkage, collective intelligence, intelligence leadership, intelligence governance, intelligence advantage, broken symmetry, sustainability revolution, governance, relativistic complexity, emergence, law of complexity/consciousness, law of complexity/intelligence, law of consciousness/intelligence, *i*CAD, *i*CAS, sustainability and intelligent organization theory).

Notes: Some micro-aspects of complexity-intelligence thinking:

- **Step 1**: Complexity must be explored and exploited, and not ignored or suppressed.
- **Step 2**: Comprehending and exploiting complexity theory with respect to organizational structure, dynamics, culture, leadership, governance, strategy, management and sustainability.
- **Step 3**: Optimizing the opportunities embedded in the co-existence of order and complexity in CAS using the holistic integrated deliberate and emergent strategy (with a deliberate-emergent auto-switch) at all time.
- **Step 4**: Focus on and exploit the complexity-intelligence linkage in human organizations, transforming certain spaces of complexity (unexplored territories) into spaces of relativistic order, and be the first to reap the gold nuggets — better risk management, first mover advantage, and a new opportunity/market/technology/innovation.
- **Step 5**: Focus on making preparation for the sudden surfacing of punctuation points — better crises management, reduces devastation and self-disintegration, and elevates resilience and sustainability.
- **Step 6**: Focus on intelligence/consciousness-centricity, intelligence-intelligence linkage (intelligence/consciousness management), nurturing high collective intelligence and organizational consciousness (org-awareness, orgmindfulness), and also incorporating better network management, self-organization/self-transcending constructions and emergence (higher self-organizing capacity, emergence-intelligence capacity and unifying capacity) when necessary — that is, towards an *i*CAS driven by *i*CAD — a new intelligence advantage.

Complexity mindset — It emerges with deeper knowledge on complexity theory, and encompasses (not in totality — see design paradigm) three components, namely systems thinking, evolution/biotic thinking, and connectionist/cybernetics thinking. **[1] Systems thinking** originates from the development of the General Systems Theory (GST) by **Ludwig von Bertalanffy** (1901–1972), in 1940 that concentrates on common properties (holism, holistic approach — opposite from the reductionist thinking of the Cartesian belief) in all form of systems, including conceptual/abstract systems. This holism thinking (**Jan Smuts**, 1926) believes that the components of a system can best be understood in the context of relationships with each other and with the system (interdependency), rather than in isolation (reductionism, fundamentalism). A key property of GST is the 'whole' is more than the sum of the parts (synergetic effect). **[2]** The **evolution/biotic thinking** focus on the characteristics and dynamics of the Evolution Theory (**Charles R. Darwin**, 1809–1882, natural selection, fitness, blind variation, and evolution and co-evolution), in particular, on autopoietic systems (autopoiesis, self-organization and emergence) proposed by **Humberto Maturana** (1928–present) and **Francisco Varela** (1946–2001). These living systems are self-producing, self-maintaining, adaptive and changing behavior over time (innovative and sustainable). In addition, their subsystems interactions are in-determinate and the control is distributed and centralized. Such systems defy the second law of thermodynamics (complex and not infinite randomness). **[3]** Finally, the **connectionist/cybernetics thinking** [originates from **Norbert Wiener** (1894–1964) in 1948, and **Ross Ashby** (1903–1972), — **Ashby's law of requisite variety**, 1956] focuses on the connectivity (both quality and quantity) of the interacting agents (intrinsically subjective and uncertain), and hence places significant attention on communications, control and feedback loops (circular causation) — leading to nonlinearity, sensitive dependence on initial conditions (butterfly effect), indeterminism and unpredictability. In cybernetics, knowledge is perceived as intrinsically subjective — dependent on the agent using it. In the Newtonian science, the characteristics of subjectivity and uncertainty are negative factors of the absolute mechanism, but they are positive factors associated with adaptation, creativity and evolution in complexity theory/intelligent organization theory. Further developments in complexity theory include constructionist hypothesis, self-transcending constructions and synergetics (see Newtonian mindset, design paradigm, Cartesian belief, reductionist hypothesis, fundamentalism, interdependency, Laplace belief, intelligence mindset, nonlinearity, complexity, interdependency, natural selection, holism, cybernetics, autopoiesis, self-organization, self-transcending constructions, second law of thermodynamics, feedback, circular causation, self-organizing capacity, emergence-intelligence capacity, emergence, law of requisite variety, complexity approaches, synergetics, butterfly effect, constructionist hypothesis and relativistic complexity).

Complexity theory — The main focus of complexity theory is high finite dimensionality nonlinear dynamical systems (CS/CAS — discrete-time and continuous-time open systems) that encompasses order and complexity, nonlinearity, sensitive dependence on initial conditions, connectivity, interdependency, indeterminism, unpredictability, self-organization, and emergence. (Another definition is complexity theory is the study of order creation — emergent of new order.) It also studies how interacting agents self-organize (self-organizing principles) to form evolving structure (simplicity arising from the aggregated behavior of interacting agents driven by a set of rules that drive a complex dynamic), usually more robust (order out of complexity). (Such systems undergo spontaneous symmetry breaking transformation, emerging with new features, capabilities, and processes — into a different and 'higher order' level — constructionist hypothesis and emergence.) Other properties associated with this theory include autopoiesis, self-transcending constructions, attractor, strange attractor, rugged/fitness landscape, far-from-equilibrium, dissipation, scalability, fractal, power law and law of requisite variety. In the social, economic, political, and environmental domains, complexity theory focuses on human CAS (each a collection of intense intelligence sources), their adaptive dynamics, and in particular the edge of emergence. In this respect, the study of complexity has become highly interdisciplinary and continuously expanding. [In general, complexity theory adopts a system-evolution-cybernetics reasoning and approach — resulting in the emergent of a new mindset and thinking, new strategic paths, and new thinking tools/models (complexity $\neq$ uncertainty; deterministic $\neq$ predictability; in-deterministic = unpredictability). Currently, complexity theory also encompasses chaos theory (DCS) and network theory (see order, complexity, dimensionality, nonlinearity, connectivity, interdependency, chaos, catastrophic theory, complexity, uncertainty, deterministic, predictability, self-organization, self-transcending constructions, butterfly effect, rugged landscape, red queen race, complexity mindset, complex systems, complex adaptive systems, edge of emergence, power law, constructionist hypothesis, broken symmetry, emergence and network theory).

Composite CAS (nested CAS) — It is a term used to indicate higher level CAS with interacting agents that are also CAS. For instance, an economy is a composite CAS with corporations as interacting agents. Similarly, a corporation is a CAS with human beings as interacting agents. In this respect, all composite CAS are nested systems — possessing co-adaptation and co-evolution characteristics (see agent, complex adaptive systems, agent-agent/system micro-structure, adaptive, adaptive capacity, collectiveness capacity, super-system, upwards causation, downwards causation, cascading effect, interdependency and co-evolution).

Connectivity — It indicates a (physical, mental) connection between an entity/agent and some of its immediate neighbors (localized order/space/network). At one extreme, it could be a localized (physical) space with no 'visible' interaction or a stabilized structure such as a molecule (note quantum entanglement). However, if the agents are 'living' and some forms of relationships (sparsely, intermediate, and/or high interconnection) exist among its neighbors, certain levels of engagement (self-organizing communications, formation of a network) exists — elevating collectiveness capacity. In human organizations, it is the quality of the interconnections (including intensive information sharing), and depth of the engagement (truthful engagement) among interacting agents (intelligence-intelligence linkages) in the system, as well as the quality of the relationships (high relational capacity) between the agents and their organization that determine its coherency, mental cohesion, collective intelligence and org-consciousness (org-awareness, orgmindfulness, mindful culture, diversification and synergetic effect). Overall, the quality and intensity of the connectivity of agents in a human organization (intelligence/consciousness management) is highly correlated with its structural capacity, collectiveness capacity, adaptive capacity, self-organizing capacity, emergence-intelligence capacity and unifying capacity, and therefore has a strong effect on it complex adaptive dynamic (see nonlinearity, complexity, complex adaptive systems, complex adaptive dynamic, intelligence-intelligence linkage, coherency, network theory, network management, structural capacity, collectiveness capacity, complex network, engagement, adaptive capacity, interdependency, intelligence/consciousness management, dialogue, engagement, self-organizing communications, localized order, principle of locality, orgmindfulness, mindful culture, collective intelligence, mental cohesion, self-organization, self-transcending constructions, self-organizing capacity, emergence-intelligence capacity and unifying capacity).

Consciousness — Consciousness emerges from intelligence and it is only present in a living organism/system (based on the intelligent organization theory). In a human thinking system, consciousness is the most fundamental and significant phenomenon of the human mind, as other mental functions/factors cannot exist without it presence. Human consciousness is recognized as the highest level consciousness on this planet. It enables the mind to cognize the world of thoughts and ideas through the two primary functions of **awareness** (outward focusing) and **self-awareness** (inward focusing). At the core of self-awareness is **mindfulness** which is unique to humanity. The existence of mindfulness in human consciousness differentiated humanity from the consciousness of all other biological beings. (Mindfulness is the ability of the mind to observe its own mental state; and orgmindfulness is the ability of an organization to observe the mental states of its interacting agents — higher potential for nurturing feeling system — higher mental cohesion.) Similar to intelligence, consciousness has to be extensively and appropriately exploited by intelligent human organizations — thus, high intelligence/consciousness-centricity is critical. [**Pierre Teilhard de Chardin** (1881–1955) conceived the terms omega point (the Universe is evolving towards maximum level of complexity and consciousness), noosphere (the sphere of human thoughts — an intangible information space/structure)] — (see intelligence/consciousness-centric, intelligence, cerebral cortex, awareness, mindfulness, orgmindfulness, mindful culture, mindful system, human thinking system, human agent, orgmind, intelligence/consciousness management, relativistic complexity, feeling system, mental cohesion, law of complexity/consciousness, law of complexity/intelligence, law of consciousness/intelligence, and Universe).

Constructionist hypothesis (constructionist effect) — This hypothesis ('More Is Different', Science, 1972 — **broken symmetry** and the nature of the hierarchical structure of science) was observed/conceptualized by **Philip Warren Anderson** (1923–present, Nobel Prize in Physics, 1972). It indicates that although it is possible to reduce nature to simple, fundamental laws, this does not entail a similar ability to re-construct the Universe using the same set of simple laws (contradicts the Cartesian belief). The reason being that at each new level of complexity, new properties and laws not present in the lower stages appear. That is, each new level of complexity exhibits the presence of new structures, properties, and laws that transcend lower level characteristics and dynamics (emergent levels are a type of scale variance; self-dissimilarity at different levels — not scale free — also contradicts econophysics). In the intelligent organization theory (**T.Y. Liang**, 2001), constructionist effect is associated with innovation and creativity (emergent of a new positive attribute/capability not present originally) — (see broken symmetry, self-organization, self-transcending constructions, reductionist hypothesis, hierarchical decomposition, Cartesian belief, scalability, self-similarity, cascading effect, econophysics, epistemological reductionism, emergence and intelligent organization theory).

Corporate governance (system) — Corporate governance systems can be perceived as a subset of governance systems. Corporate governance emerges when a principal-agent relationship is established in business corporations. The principal-agent relationship is a subset of stakeholder-agency relationship. The corporate governance mechanisms include market for corporate control, legal and regulating systems, board of directors, and managerial incentives. The mechanisms try to resolve the divergent in interest (conflicts) among the principals, other stakeholders, and managers. Thus, the corporate governance system is also a CAS comprised of rather heterogeneous agents — with different goals, interests, values, and self-centricity. In the current context, corporate governance also encompasses corporate social responsibilities (sustainability) — integrating the economic, social, political, and environmental perspectives — (see agent, self-centric, nonlinearity, complexity, stability, stability-centric, governance, governance system, organizational justice, intelligence leadership, self-powered, intrinsic leadership, self-organizing governance, symbiosis, feeling system, mental cohesion and sustainability).

Cosmopolitan communicator — Such a person is not affected by differences (ideas/beliefs) in other people. Instead, this person will recognize, appreciate, interact and collaborate with people with great diversity (different races, cultures, religions, nationalities and education background). He/she will seek out dissimilar ideas and ways to think about issues — is an 'ideal/preferred' candidate for global managerial role. Thus, 'functional conflict' is considered as an opportunity to learn, and not as a threat. Possessing this characteristic is vital for truthful communication, dialogue, connectivity and engagement, as well as intiating self-organizing communications and elevating collective intelligence — (see Abilene paradox, defensive routine, agent, connectivity, engagement, interdependency, dialogue, paper dialogue and self-organizing communications).

Criticality/Self-organizing criticality (SOC) — It describes the characteristic of the critical space after edge of order (lower bound) and before the edge of emergence (upper bound) — a space of high complexity where phase transition occurs. This term is first used by **Per Bak** (1948–2002), in 1966. Self-organized critical (SOC) systems' critical points are states in an attractor. Thus, criticality/critical point/critical state exist when no phase boundaries exist. Critical exponents describe the behavior of physical variables of the system near continuous phase transitions. Systems with the same set of critical exponents belong to the same universality class [the latter is a collection of mathematical models (with differing finite scale) that share a single scale invariant limit (their behavior becomes increasing similar)]. CS/CAS (continuous-time) self-organize at criticality and reap order for free [a terminology used by **Stuart Kauffman** (1939–present)] — (see edge of order, edge of chaos, edge of emergence, phase transition, self-organization, self-transcending constructions, edge of emergence, and emergence).

Cybernetics — It is a domain (encompasses machine and living systems) that focuses on the connectivity of interacting agents. It places significant attention on control (homeostasis), communications, and co-ordination, as well as feedback loops (negative and positive loops — hypercycles). This domain was introduced by **Ross Ashby** (1903–1972), and the term 'cybernetics' (steersman) was first used by **Norbert Wiener** (1894–1964), in

1948. In management, cybernetics highlighted the organizing principles that governed the nonlinear dynamics of structurally stable systems to managers. A significant law in this domain is **Ashby's law of requisite variety**, proposed in 1956. The initial agenda of the May group (a cybernetics movement) were to develop a self-guiding and self-regulating machine (machine intelligence) that could discover the common principles of organization in diverse systems, and to create an exact science of the mind through understanding the neural mechanisms of mental phenomena. The complexity theory/mindset encompasses cybernetics, and a more recent prominent cybernetic researcher is **Francis Heylighen** (1952–present), the Principia Cybernetic Project — (see complexity mindset, autopoiesis, homeostasis, engagement, autocatalysis, feedback, circular causation, cascading effect, design paradigm and law of requisite variety).

Defensive routine/communication — Defensive communication is due to self-centricity, and it exists because of the phobic mindset. It leads to miscommunication or no communication. Thus, defensive routine is a sequence of actions taken by interacting agents to safe guard their continuous existence (stability-centric) in an organization/system due to mistrust [the term was introduced by **Chris Argyris** (1923–2013) in 1991]. Its presence also renders organizational learning difficult. This detrimental behavior is often linked to the culture and leadership of the organization. In this case, there is no mutual trust and positive engagement. Usually, the leadership in this type of organizations is highly hierarchical an bureaucratic, and the collective intelligence (collectiveness capacity) of the organization is very low — resulting in low coherency — (see Abilene paradox, phobic mindset, agent, engagement, self-centric, stability-centric, stability, dialogue, paper dialogue, cosmopolitan communicator, organizational learning, collective intelligence, collectiveness capacity, organizational justice, coherency and feeling organization).

Deliberate strategy — This is the current form of strategy adopted by most human beings/organizations (arising from the Newtonian mindset — dominated by order, linearity, deliberation and predictability/forecasting). It assumes that if the present state is known with high precision, and the path towards the future is also known, then any future states can be predicted/calculated accurately (determinism = predictability) — or at least up to a certain acceptable level that makes strategic management processes (forecasting) very common in most human organizations [(for instance, operation plan and strategic plan mapping, and economic forecasting). This strategy is highly beneficial in spaces of order. However, if exploited alone when the situation becomes highly nonlinear and complex (spaces of complexity), it manifests apparent constraints (although, in practice, this strategy does accumulate certain variation in complexity density). The deliberate strategic plan (including futurology) is never complete due to the in-complete phase space of human organizations. However, it is still exploited in the intelligent organization theory but it has to be integrated with the emergent strategy for better holism. The presence of deliberate strategy is still significant because of the co-existence of order and complexity, and relativistic complexity in human organizations — (see Newtonian mindset, order, linearity, predictability, ordered systems, complexity mindset, intelligence mindset, nonlinearity, complexity, complex adaptive systems, space of order, space of complexity, futurology, holism, relativistic complexity and emergent strategy)].

Deliberate-emergent auto-switch — This is a highly significant latent 'automatic switch' (closely associated with high collective intelligence, org-consciousness, collectiveness capacity, adaptive capacity, self-organization/self-transcending constructions capability, and varying complexity density) present/nurtured in highly intelligent human organizations (*i*CAS) that have mapped their deliberate strategy (strategic and operational) and nurtured their emergent strategy (exploiting relativistic complexity, and making preparation for the sudden appearance of punctuation points — better risk management and crisis management) concurrently. It is a term coined by **T.Y. Liang,** in 2010. This concept (nurturing a unique intangible switch — not fully binary) introduced in the intelligent organization theory allows an *i*CAS to switch between the two strategic paths (better and more comprehensive exploitation of the co-existence of order and complexity — achieving higher ambidexterity) spontaneously. Thus, its presence facilitates the deeper integration and coordination of the two strategies. It re-distributes predictability and unpredictability in human organizations that depend on the relative intensity of order and complexity. Hence, the effectiveness of this switch also depends on the integrated collective intelligence and organizational consciousness (orgmindfulness) of the organization, and its highly self-powered human agents (intrinsic leadership). In particular, this switch should be activated automatically when a highly intelligent human organization experiences a sudden (intensive) increase in complexity, for instance, when it encounters a punctuation point — switching from the deliberate path to the emergent path. In this respects, the switch is both an adaptive (gradual and used with the deliberate strategy), and binary (sudden) switch. For the latter, 'constructive' self-organizing (self-transcending constructions) dynamic emerges automatically. This self-organizing capability is a vital characteristic of an *i*CAS — also signifying the presence of intelligence leadership [The deliberate and emergent strategy was first proposed by **Henry Mintzberg** (1939–present) and **James Waters,** in 1985. In their model, there are eight components from 'planned' to 'imposed'. The first component is 'totally' deliberate while the remaining seven components possess an adaptive characteristic. However, his model did not include emergence associated with punctuation points) — (see space of order, space of complexity, punctuation point, collective intelligence, self-powered, self-organization, self-transcending constructions, self-organizing capacity, self-organizing capacity, emergence-intelligence capacity, deliberate strategy, emergent strategy, orgmindfulness, *i*CAS, intelligence leadership, emergence and relativistic complexity).

Design paradigm — This paradigm of management (encompassing cybernetics and systems engineering) emerges in the middle of the 20th century for better organizational problem solving. The key focal point of the **cybernetics perspective** is the design of organizations as systems with structural stability that could be regulated and controlled by management intervention (using feedback loops) — highly hierarchical. The main weaknesses of the models are they do not take into account the non-rational (emotional function of the amygdale — human rationality) behavior of human beings, the emergent aspects of their collective behavior (relational capacity), and the increasing presence of complexity. The

systems engineering perspective comprises the 'hard' system approach and the 'soft' system approach. The 'hard' system approach focuses on the internal consistency of modularized systems (their hierarchical structures and modular organization). The 'soft' system approach focuses on the problem definition of the 'whole' for human systems. Its design is to enable all stakeholders to recognize the whole, to identify the diverse problem space, and to take a best collective decision. The overall disadvantage of this paradigm is planned management interventions, and highly hierarchical leadership. However, in complexity theory, the focus on the assumptions of structural stability is shifted to the non-equilibrium dynamics of open systems, and the autopoietic/symbiotic and self-organizing abilities of the interacting agents — an intense focus on spontaneous dynamic — (see Newtonian mindset, complexity mindset, intelligence mindset, relational capacity, satisficing principle, cybernetics, feedback, human thinking system, human rationality, biotic macro-structure, autopoeisis, symbiosis, self-organization, self-transcending constructions, self-powered, intelligence leadership and emergence).

Deterministic — Determinism is a basic key attributes of the exact sciences. Mathematically, an equation or a set of equations (difference or differential) is deterministic if all their variables are known, and their values can be accurately measured or calculated. Similarly, a system is deterministic if it can be fully captured (mathematically) by an equation or a set of equations, and outputs can be computed accurately if an input is known. Thus, deterministic also indicates that the future behavior or outcome of a system can be fully determined from the initial conditions — that is determinism => predictability. (A deterministic system has no randomness — a key focus of the Newtonian/exact sciences, although, statistical mechanics focus on systems with infinite randomness.) However, in complexity theory (chaos) deterministic ≠ predictability — DCS are deterministic but unpredictable — due to the presence of butterfly effect — sensitive dependence on initial conditions. In this case, an input will lead to a totally unexpected output, and/or a precise input and an estimated input can lead to a totally different output (unpredictability). This is a basic characteristic of mathematical/deterministic chaotic systems. [DCS are low in dimensionality and can be conceived as a (or a set) of differential equation (continuous-time) or difference equation (discrete-time). When the input is known the output can be computed, that is, deterministic. But due to the butterfly effect (bifurcation or phase transition) the output of the system can become unexpected/unpredictable (simplicity to chaotic). However, CS/CAS are in-deterministic and unpredictable] — (see Newtonian mindset, chaos/DCS, complex systems, complex adaptive systems, butterfly effect, bifurcation, phase transition, dimensionality, predictable, in-deterministic, uncertainty, stochastic and phase space).

Notes: Some similarities and differences among dimension/deterministic/ uncertainty/randomness/predictability:

- **Dimension** = degrees of freedom = number of variables.
- **Deterministic** => usually low dimensionality => all variables are known and their values can be measured/computed accurately => can be captured by a mathematical model => complete phase space.
- **Deterministic** => either small input leading to small output (OS, deterministic = predictable), or small input resulting in large output (DCS, deterministic ≠ predictable) — sensitive dependence on initial conditions (butterfly effect) — but output can be computed accurately.
- **Risks** = known unknowns — variables cannot be measured or measured accurately — but its presence is known.
- **Uncertainty (total)** = unknown unknowns => unpredictable, in-deterministic — due to the presence of unknown variables/inputs (for instance, ontological reductionism) — in-complete phase space.
- **Uncertainty (partial)** => partial predictability, probabilistic.
- **In-deterministic** => high finite dimensionality => high complexity => cannot be (completely or accurately) captured by a mathematical model (CS/CAS) due to the presence of unknown unknowns, in-deterministic = unpredictable.
- **Stochastic** => infinite randomness, probabilistic, statistical.
- **Random** => many paths of development, unpredictable or partially predictable.
- **Randomness** = lack of predictability (pattern) in a system/event.
- **Randomness is objective** (mathematical) but **predictability is subjective** (possessing human perspective).
- **Intelligence/consciousness-centricity** enhances predictability (relativistic complexity).

Dialogue — A theory on dialogue (a form of free exchange of information and ideas) was introduced by **David Bohm** (1917–1992), in 1990. The current form is a methodology of thought technology conceptualized by a group of researchers at MIT (**Ellinor and Gerald**, 1998). It is a special kind of divergent conversation that focuses on nurturing better connectivity, free will, more truthful engagement, higher level collective intelligence, deliberation, mental cohesion and emergent dynamic in an organization. It is a conversation with no predetermined purpose, fix agenda, or immediate goal. It allows time for reflection and relationships enhancement — orgmindful — observing the mental states of the interacting agents, and elevation of collectiveness capacity. If it is properly executed (enhancing self-organizing communications) the organization/group involved is able to self-organize more effectively when unpredicted events/problems surface later on. Therefore, the success of dialogue is time dependent — (see Abilene paradox, phobic mindset, connectivity, engagement, collectiveness capacity, collective intelligence, orgmindfulness, human rationality, mental cohesion, self-organzing communications, network theory, emergence and paper dialogue).

Dimension/Dimensionality — In Mathematics and Physics, the dimension (number of variables, degrees of freedom) of a space or object/system is defined as the number of coordinates needed to specify any point in it (for instance, a line is one dimension, a cube is three dimensions, physical space is three dimensions, and 'space-time' is four dimensions). In mathematics, spaces beyond three dimensions exist such as configuration spaces. Thus, in a system, its dimension is indicated by the number of **variables** involved (for instance, $z = ax + by$ is three dimensions, indicated by x, y, and z; and the power of all the three variables is one) — [while, the degree of a polynomial is the degree of the term (sum of the exponent) with highest power (for instance, $z = x^2y^3 + xy$ has degree = 5)]. In complexity theory, (deterministic) chaotic systems are discrete-time or continuous-time low dimensionality nonlinear dynamical systems, while CS/CAS are usually continuous-time high finite dimensionality nonlinear dynamical systems. However, dimensionality of human organizations can be very complicated and in-complete because of **ontological reductionism** and unknown unknowns — thus, they cannot be captured accurately or completely as a mathematical model (high finite nonlinear CAS, in-complete phase space, in-deterministic, unpredictable) — (see variable, agent, ordered systems, disordered systems, chaos, chaotic systems, complexity, ontological reductionism, complex systems, complex adaptive systems, phase space, deterministic, in-deterministic, predictability, human organization and Poincare–Bendixson theorem).

Disordered (highly) system (DS) — In such a system (highly disordered) all its entities are independent and acting without any constraints (totally random or infinite degrees of freedom) — (disordered systems <=> stochastic systems), (disordered systems ≠ in-deterministic chaotic systems). The behavior of the individual units/entities cannot be predicted. However, their average behavior (macroscopic — stochastic process => random process => probabilistic) can be 'accurately' predicted (probability theory) because of their statistical dependency — using statistical mechanics, **Ludwig Boltzmann** (1844–1906) (for example, a container of gas, dealing with populations of particles rather than individual particles — the focus is on macro-variables such as temperature and pressure, and not on micro-variables such as speed and direction of atoms or molecules — ontological reductionism) — (see order, ordered systems, stochastic, systems spectrum, dimensionality, systems spectrum, entropy, second law of thermodynamic, nonlinearity, chaotic system, complex systems, ontological reductionism and statistical mechanics).

Dissipation — It is a process present in all open system. Certain entities could flow in and out (through) of the system inherently. All CS/CAS are open and dissipative. For instance, many such in-flow and out-flow streams (energy, air, foods, information and knowledge) are present in the human body. The term also refers to the removal of extra entropy (dissipation of energy imposed by energy differentials) from a CS/CAS that is undergoing emergence by creating new intra-system order. A dissipative system is also far-from-equilibrium — (see open system, edge of order, dissipative structure, complex systems, complex adaptive systems, far-from-equilibrium and dissipative structure).

Dissipative structure — It is a stable structure, S(1), with recognizable form and is continually being dissipated and renewed. In the 1960s, **Ilya**

Prigogine (1917–2003) and his colleagues showed that energy input to an open system with many interacting components, operating far-from-equilibrium, gave rise to an adaptive tension and created a higher level of order (new intra-system order). He called the emergent ordered structures 'dissipative structures' because they speed up the dissipation of energy imposed by energy differentials. Prigogine was awarded a Nobel Prize (1977) for his study of such structures in chemical systems. Thus, his dissipative structures theory shows that via phase transition new order will appear — an interesting aspect of complexity theory that offers many concepts such as edge of order, energy differential tension, adaptive tension, opportunity tension, creation tension, and order creation that are also useful in the non-science domains; dissipative structure <=> hole localization <=> energy reduction [for instance, it shows how adaptive tension drives the emergence of intra-system order (principle of locality, networks) within a human organization] — (see dissipation, open system, far-from-equilibrium, edge of order, phase transition, principle of locality, constructionist hypothesis, broken symmetry, $S(1)$-$S(4)$, network theory, complex network and complexity approaches).

Downwards causation — It indicates that the behavior of parts (subsystems) is to certain extent constrained by the characteristics (functions) of the system/super-system (hierarchical). For instance, in human community/corporation the behavior of an individual is not only controlled by his/hers neural networks but also by the rules/regulations, and culture of the society or corporation — impacts of the global forces; to a certain extent enforces functional cohesion. However, it may lead to higher complexity when the agents decide to oppose the global forces (see autocatalysis, circular causation, feedback, super-system, fundamentalism, reductionist hypothesis, constructionist hypothesis, complex adaptive systems, composite CAS and upwards causation).

Dynamical equilibrium — CS/CAS at stasis are usually in dynamical equilibrium. Such systems are never in 'absolute' static equilibrium (space of 'absolute' order never exist). Otherwise, they will disintegrate. In intelligent human organizations, dynamical equilibrium and relativistic complexity are highly inter-related. Thus, human dynamical equilibrium could be relativistic static equilibrium in an *i*CAS with high intelligence/consciousness-centricity. Similarly, a space of complexity to some human agents/organizations (with the right intelligence, knowledge, and 'mental' preparation) could be a space of relativistic order (see static equilibrium, space of order, intelligence/consciousness-centric, complexity-intelligence linkage, space of complexity, intelligent person, *i*CAS, *i*CAD, relativistic complexity, relativistic static equilibrium and space of relativistic order).

Early warning system — It is a vital subsystem in an intelligent human organization (in particular, it is a significant subsystem of its 'sensory' subsystem — also an anticipatory system) that collects and analyzes information/signal/pattern of potential threats/crises/opportunities — usually focus on competitors and the external environment (futurology). It facilitates better planning, adaptation, respond and helps nurture collective intelligence (an example is the RAHS system — a system used by the Singapore's National Security Coordinating Centre — NSCC). In this respect, it is a highly significant component (through scenarios analysis) of the sensory subsystem that provides better support for the orgmind (see biotic macro-structure, biotic system, human thinking system, anticipatory system, intelligence, collective intelligence, awareness, awaresystem, orgmind, futurology, emergent strategy and intelligent organization).

Economic man — This is a term used in classical economic theory (**Adam Smith**, 1723–1790, and **John Mill**, 1806–1873) which indicates that all individuals are perfectly rational (in realty, human thinking systems are emotional systems that can be logical), and they always make optimal decision (orderly, linearity and predictable), and seek optimal solution (maximizes utility) — also self-centric. In realty, especially in a fast changing situation such a dynamic is unrealistic and non-achievable. There is no global optimality (satisficing principle). The characteristics of human beings as interacting agents have been redefined by bounded rationality (administrative man model), and intelligent person model (smarter evolver, emergent strategist, intelligent organization theory) — (see human thinking system, complexity, self-centric, stability-centric, nonlinearity, administrative man, satisficing principle, intelligent person, global optimality, smarter evolver and emergent strategist).

Econophysics — The econophysics [(scale-free theory) coined by **Harry Eugene Stanley** (1941–present) in 1995, a sub-field of statistical mechanics focusing on stochastic processes and nonlinear dynamics] approach utilizes power laws (PL) to explain the unrestricted self-organizing behavior in systems/organizations (physics, economics) — PL phenomena/effects, PL theory and scale-free theory. PL phenomena and Pareto distributions are normally due to interdependency of components/agents, and they are scale-free. A scale-free theory explains the emergent organizing dynamic of a multiple levels system using a single rule/function — contradicts the constructionist hypothesis (see scalability, Pareto distribution, power law, interdependency, constructionist hypothesis and complexity approaches).

Edge of chaos (old — a space) — This is the space of bounded 'instability' and high complexity in CS/CAS (a term coined by **Norman Packard** and **Doyne Farmer**). The edge of chaos (a key focus of many US complexity pioneer researchers in the 1980s and 1990s — the upper bound of criticality, a 'region of emergence' — second critical value, R_{c2}) is more a space rather than an edge — involving SOC, introduced by **Per Bak** in 1996 [the European complexity researchers focus on the edge of order (a boundary/edge, 1st critical value, R_{c1}) instead — Prigogine's dissipative structures theory]. The edge of chaos can be a highly complex physical space (for instance, moving into a tsunami region) or even a mental space — a space of high mental complexity where emergent of order is still possible — usually located just before the system moves into the in-deterministic chaotic state. The perception was when a CAS moves into the edge of chaos its computational ability is maximized, and the system is at its highest level of fitness and adaptability. In the intelligent organization theory, the edge of chaos (due to the mismatch between its characteristics and terminology — also a distinction between chaos and complexity is necessary) has been redefined as the **edge of emergence** (a boundary rather a space) — into inter-system emergence (see chaos, complexity, edge of emergence, punctuated equilibrium, dissipative structure, edge of order, space of complexity, power law phenomena, self-transcending constructions, emergence and complexity approaches).

Edge of chaos (new — an edge) — In the intelligent organization theory, the edge of chaos has been shifted and redefined as the third critical value, R_{C3} — the boundary/edge when any nonlinear dynamical moves into a space of in-deterministic chaos (high turbulence with great potential of disintegrating — catastrophic theory) — conceived by **T.Y. Liang**, in 2013 [see chaos, complexity, catastrophic theory, edge of order, edge of emergence, S(1)-S(4) and emergence].

Edge of emergence — This is the new edge that 'replaces', and 'redefined' the (old) edge of chaos, second critical value, R_{C2} (a boundary/edge). There are now three critical edges namely, 1st critical value (edge of order), 2nd critical value (edge of emergence), and 3rd critical value (edge of chaos). Crossing the edge of order activates first degree self-organization and causes first order intra-system emergence. When crossing the edge of emergence, 2nd degree self-organization/self-transcending constructions occurs leading to inter-system emergence — 2nd order emergence, the emergent of new order (conceived by **T.Y. Liang**, in 2013). And crossing the edge of chaos (into the space of in-deterministic chaos) will lead to disintegration. This conceptualization provides a clearer understanding on the macro-dynamic of emergence [see power law phenomena, constructionist hypothesis, edge of order, edge of chaos, S(1)-S(4), and emergence].

Edge of order — Prigogine's dissipative structures theory (**Ilya Prigogine**, 1917–2003) indicates that dramatic phase transition occurs at 1st critical value, R_{C1} — edge of order. When external energy drives a system across the edge of order, dissipative structures appear. Dissipative structures S(1) accelerate dissipation imposed by energy differentials (adaptive tension) initiating new intra-system order — 1st order emergence. In the intelligent organization theory, when a human organization moves across the edge of order, 1st degree self-organization/self-transcending constructions occurs, and the emergent of networks S(2) and self-organizing complex adaptive network S(3) also appear [see order, phase transition, edge of chaos, dissipative structure, power law phenomena, edge of emergence, network theory, S(1)-S(4), and emergence].

Notes: Summary on the three edges:

- All the three edges are boundaries (not spaces).
- **Edge of order (1ˢᵗ critical value)**: before — space of order; after — space of complexity => localized order; intra-system order => 1ˢᵗ order emergence.
- **Edge of emergence (2ⁿᵈ critical value)**: before — space of complexity; after — emergent of new order (with higher robustness); organizational/system order => 2ⁿᵈ order emergence.
- **Edge of chaos (3ʳᵈ critical value)**: before — space of high complexity; after — space of in-deterministic chaos (high turbulence) => towards disintegration.

Notes: The five spaces in relativistic complexity theory and intelligent organization theory:

- **Space of order** (linear and orderly space — deterministic, minimal or no change — any change is predictable).
- **Space of relativistic order** (space of low and 'manageable' complexity — observable surface pattern, in-deterministic but high relative predictability — reflects the significance of complexity-intelligence linkage).
- **Space of complexity** (space of high complexity — simplicity to complexity — rapid and continuous changes — surface pattern may be observable, in-deterministic and low relative predictability).
- **Space of chaos** (simplicity to chaotic — deterministic but unpredictable).
- **Space of in-deterministic chaos** <=> extreme 'sudden' punctuation point with high complexity (no more potential surface pattern, in-deterministic and unpredictable — system self-destruct).

Emergence (I) — The term (in the modern sense) was first used by psychologist **George Henry Lewes** (1817–1879), in the 1875. Emergence is associated with holism and synergy. It is also the creation of a new global properties (a set of closely related properties), structure, organization, and behavior (a transformation process driven by self-organization — order for free) by interacting agents due to some local rules, but the exact patterns that emerge cannot be predicted in advance (unexpected and unpredictable because the outcome can be totally different from the old properties, structure, organization, and environmental forces — constructionist hypothesis — for instance, life is associated with cells (biological/living world) but not molecules (physical matter world). In addition, the agents are intrinsically subjective and uncertain about the consequences of their actions, but they can self-organize/self-transcending construct (order not for free) into a new adaptive emergent system. Emergence behavior once activated has a life of its own. To date, emergence is not a fully understood dynamic. Prigogine's dissipative structures theory indicates that emergence is driven by adaptive tension caused by energy differentials — intra-system order. The American school approach focuses on inter-system order, co-evolution, and edge of chaos (edge of emergence, in the intelligent organization theory). While the constructionist hypothesis approach considers symmetry breaking and localization as emergent — for instance, crystalline is an example of emergence due to broken symmetry because the crystal has less symmetry than the atoms of the fluid from which it crystallized. In general, it is a divergent-convergent phenomenon (conflicting forces and disorganized fluctuations) that leads to the creation of a more robust complex structure with new properties and laws (order out of complexity <=> emergent of new order <=> into an attractor). In particular, it is significant to recognize that not all agents benefit from emergence, in fact, some will be worst off. Hence in intelligent human organizations, the presence of mindful culture and a high relational capacity, self-organizing capacity and emergence-intelligence capacity is critical (all human agents must be taken care — feeling system) [see complexity mindset, holism, synergetics, self-organization, dissipative structure, self-transcending constructions, constructionist hypothesis, broken symmetry, attractor, scalability, power law phenomena, epistemological reductionism, graph theory, network theory, mindful culture, relational capacity, self-organizing capacity, emergence-intelligence capacity, feeling system and emergence (II)].

Emergence (II) — In the intelligent organization theory, emergence is divided into 1st order emergence and 2nd order emergence (**T.Y. Liang**, in 2013). When a CAS moves across the edge of order (1st critical value), 1st degree self-organization/self-transcending constructions occurs (presence of self-organizing capacity), leading to 1st order emergence [for example, dissipative structure, emergent network, and emergent self-organizing complex adaptive network (network of networks) — new intra-system order => S(1) to S(3)]. When the CAS moves across the edge of emergence (2nd critical value), 2nd degree self-organization/self-transcending constructions occurs (presence of self-organizing capacity and emergence-intelligence capacity), leading to 2nd order emergence (a full-fledged emergence, an emergence of new order => S(4), giving rise to new structure, robustness, characteristics, and governing rules — a total transformation of the organization/system — new inter-system order). Symmetry breaking may have occurred at this stage — constructionist hypothesis (for instance, small village => small town => city => cosmopolitan city). Thus, in human organizations when a new order emerges, its laws of behavior are redefined. If the 2nd degree self-organization fails, the organization/system will move across the (new) edge of chaos (3rd critical value) — into a space of in-deterministic chaos, and it will disintegrate subsequently. This conception allows the macro-dynamic of emergence to be better understood [see emergence (I), edge of order, edge of emergence, edge of chaos (old), edge of chaos (new), power law phenomena, self-organization, self-transcending constructions, self-organizing capacity, emergence-intelligence capacity, synergetics, constructionist hypothesis, broken symmetry, graph theory, network theory and S(1)-S(4)].

Notes: The two different orders of emergence in human organizations:

- **1st order emergence**: 1st degree self-organization/self-transcending constructions (localized space, network, network of networks) => new intra-system order => S(1)-S(3).
- **2nd order emergence**: 2nd degree self-organization/self-transcending constructions (organizational/holistic) => new inter-system order => S(4).

Emergence-Intelligence capacity — The emergence capacity of a CAS (human organization) can be elevated by the presence of intelligence/consciousness — redefined as emergence-intelligence capacity. Thus, the latter attribute (a more 'complete' form of self-organizing capacity at organizational level — emergent of new organizational order) is introduced in the intelligent organization theory to indicate the ability of a human organization to spontaneously self-organize/self-transcending construct and emerge when the deliberate strategy is no more effective (high organizational adaptive capacity <=> high emergence-intelligence capacity). Possessing a huge emergence-intelligence capacity (including high quality) is closely associated with high collective intelligence and org-consciousness (collectiveness capacity, unifying capacity) of the organization as the latter drives the self-transcending constructions dynamic when the organization encounters a ('sudden') punctuation point (reflecting better complexity management, and the presence of and a highly efficient emergent strategy). In this respect, it is also closely linked to the presence of high leadership capacity and governance capacity [see complexity mindset, complexity management, connectivity, engagement, self-organization, dissipative structure, structural capacity, adaptive capacity, unifying capacity, biotic macro-structure, collectiveness capacity, self-organizing capacity, punctuation point, self-transcending constructions, complexity management, deliberate strategy, emergent strategy, emergent strategist, emergence (I), emergence (II), intelligence leadership, intelligence governance, resilience, sustainability, *i*CAD and *i*CAS].

Emergent strategy — The concept of emergence in strategy was popularized by **Henry Mintzberg** (1939–present) and **James Waters** in their article 'Of strategies, deliberate and emergent', in 1985. They proposed that strategies (eight types — planned, entrepreneurial, ideological, umbrella, process, unconnected, consensus, and imposed) emerge from the dynamics of interaction between the organization and its environment. However, the emergent component of the integrated deliberate and emergent strategy in the intelligent organization theory possesses a more complete aspect of 'emergence' (associated with collectiveness, adaptation, and accumulation) meaning that exploit the co-existence of order and complexity, better complexity management, elevating the self-organizing capacity and emergence-intelligence capacity, and making preparation for the sudden appearance of punctuation points. The deliberate component is mapped, while the emergent component is nurtured concurrently. In the intelligent organization theory, the integrated deliberate and emergent strategy is a vital component of the complexity-intelligence strategy. The strategic emergent component is the adaptive path that takes care of the spaces of complexity (risk management) and punctuation points (crisis management). It focuses on nurturing collective intelligence and org-consciousness (orgmindfulness, mindful culture, organizing around intelligence, anticipatory system, aware system, adaptive capacity, collective capacity, self-organizing capacity and emergence-intelligence capacity), exploiting self-powered agents and their intrinsic leadership, and other intelligence/consciousness-centric attributes so that the organization is innovative, and can self-organize effectively at (sudden) punctuation points. The emergent strategy and deliberate strategy (strategic exploitation of order, complexity management, and intelligence/consciousness management) of any intelligent organization has to be integrated and well-coordinated. Therefore, it is significant that the two strategies have to be nurtured (emergent) and mapped (deliberate) simultaneously, and elevated to a critical level so that the two components can interchange automatically — the presence of the deliberate-emergent auto-switch is critical [see deliberate strategy, order, nonlinearity, complexity, space of order, space of complexity, punctuation point, interdependency, orgmindfulness, mindful culture, organizing around intelligence, adaptive capacity, collectiveness capacity, principle of locality, deliberate-emergent auto-switch, collective intelligence, anticipatory system, aware system, self-powered, intrinsic leadership, complexity management, intelligence/consciousness-centric, intelligence/consciousness management, self-organization, self-transcending constructions, self-organizing capacity, emergence-intelligence capacity, complex adaptive systems, S(1)-S(4), futurology, law of consciousness/intelligence, emergence, sustainability, self-organizing capacity and complexity-intelligence strategy].

Emergent strategist — As stipulated in the intelligent person model, an emergent strategist (confined only to human beings — with intense anticipatory ability) ensures that the emergent component in the system dynamic is continuously and effectively nurtured and exploited (focusing on high and effective adaptive capacity, collectiveness capacity, self-organization or self-transcending constructions, self-organizing capacity, and emergence-intelligence capacity leading to emergence when needed — always focusing on orchestrating multi-level emergent phenomena) — (emergence capacity <=> futuristic capacity). Such an 'intelligent' interacting agent recognizes the co-existence of order and complexity, and possesses both the self-centric and org-centric mindset with a special focus on risk management and crisis management. An intelligent person (being self-powered, and possesses intrinsic leadership) is both a smarter evolver and an emergent strategist. In the intelligent organization theory, interacting agents that are emergent strategists are more constructive participants and effective (intelligence) leaders in the current high complexity density context (relativistic complexity) — recognizing that predictability/forecasting is not always possible, but still make preparation for unpredictability (punctuation points, futurity) through enhancing collective intelligence and org-consciousness (orgmindfulness, mindful culture). In this respect, there is an overlap between an emergent strategist and a futurist (elevating resilience and sustainability), although the mindset is not totally identical — [see order, nonlinearity, complexity, intelligent person, self-powered, intrinsic leadership, principle of locality, interdependency, anticipatory system, self-centric, org-centric, predictability, adaptive capacity, collectiveness capacity, self-organization, self-transcending constructions, self-organizing capacity, emergence-intelligence capacity, smarter evolver, intelligence leadership, orgmindfulness, mindful culture, collective intelligence, constructionist hypothesis, futurology, resilience, sustainability, emergence and S(1)-S(4)].

Energy-matter system/subsystem — The human brain encompasses a highly complex neural (matter) network (continuously active), that emits neurotransmitters and energy pulses. It is also the origin of the intense intelligence/consciousness source that every human being is carrying. In the general information theory (**T.Y. Liang**, 1994), the human thinking system comprises two components, namely the physical symbol subsystem (artificial component) and the energy–matter subsystem. The latter is a (simplified, macro) physical subsystem of the human thinking system — the natural component. While, the physical symbol subsystem is the artificial component created by the human thinking system that greatly enhances human intelligence usage enabled by a language that supports deeper thinking, perception, abstract conceptions and knowledge creation (see intelligence, consciousness, character set, physical symbol system, knowledge structure, human agent, information decoder and human thinking system).

Engagement — When the interacting agents are engaged (beyond physical connectivity), they communicate, and share information and knowledge (truthful — network-centric, self-organizing communications; or not truthful — Abilene paradox, defensive routine) with one another (mental connectivity). Thus, human engagement is the interactions of mental states encompassing people's thoughts, feelings, and behaviors (behavioral schemata). With truthful engagement the level of trust and commitment are high (unidirectional communication can be disastrous). In this respect, they are better connected (quality), constructive local spaces/networks emerge (higher collectiveness capacity), and gradually the collective intelligence of the organization is also elevated (higher coherency and mental cohesion). In a highly intelligent organization, ensuring truthful engagement is a key responsibility of its intelligence leaders (presence of orgmindfulness and mindful culture) (see human rationality, intelligence, collective intelligence, Abilene paradox, phobic mindset, nonlinearity, complexity, connectivity, behavioral schemata, coherency, mental cohesion, collectiveness capacity, symbiosis, network theory, network management, self-organizing communications, defensive communication/routine, cosmopolitan communicator, dialogue, paper dialogue, orgmindfulness, mindful culture and intelligence leadership).

Entropy — Entropy came from a Greek word that means 'change'. It is associated with randomness (dimensionality) of the system. There is a tendency for closed system to lose order and move into a space of higher disorder as stipulated by the second law of thermodynamics (for instance, a closed container of air when heated — Boltzmann's kinetic theory of gases). Thus, entropy is also a measure of how close a system is to equilibrium — the higher the entropy the greater the disorder. But the ultimate equilibrium state of a closed highly DS is one with maximum entropy. In statistical mechanics, the entropy, S of a macroscopic state is k times the natural logarithm of the numbers of microscopic states (W) corresponding to it, that is $S = k \ln W$ (entropy formula of **Ludwig Boltzmann**, 1844–1906), where k is Boltzmann's constant. However, for open systems the process may be different (see dimensionality, extropy, dissipation, disordered systems, statistical mechanics and second law of thermodynamics).

Epistemological reductionism — It is the derivation (including methods, validity, and scope) of a law (or a set of laws) from other more basic ones — for example, the derivation of Kepler's laws [**Johannes Kepler** (1571–1630), three laws, and the 3rd law is $T^2 = 4\pi^2 a/G(M+m)$, where T is the period of planets, a is the semi major axis or the mean distance between the two planets, G is gravitational constant, and M and m are the masses of the planets involved] from Newtonian mechanics (laws of motion, three laws, and the 2nd law is $F = md\mathrm{v}/dt$) — (see order, Cartesian belief, hierarchical decomposition, fundamentalism, reductionist hypothesis, constructionist hypothesis and complexity mindset).

Evolution (theory) — Darwinian's (**Charles Darwin**, 1809–1882) evolution (*On the Origin of Species*, 1859) is a gradual and adaptive dynamic (natural selection and blind variation) that varies with the changing environment in the ecosystem. However, it was discovered later that there are punctuation points in actual evolution dynamics such as the Cambrian explosion — that is, involving both stasis and punctuation points. Evolution can be exaptation, and also builds upon its past successes (phylogenesis — for example, the three layered human brain). As a CAS evolves (evolving => becoming => constantly changing; no known ultimate destination — red queen race) its complexity increases, and its structure becomes more robust — for example, from a small village to a small town to a huge cosmopolitan city (emergent of new order with higher robustness) — (see complexity mindset, natural selection, adaptive, exaptation, morphogenesis, phylogenesis, biodiversity, extropy, co-evolution, stasis, punctuation point, rugged landscape, red queen race, self-organization, smarter evolver and emergent strategist).

Notes: Some characteristics of evolution theory useful to CS/CAS:

- Natural selection, blind variation, phyletic gradualism;
- Adaptive, fitness, exaptation, biodiversity;
- Phylogenesis, morphogenesis, hysteresis;
- Anticipative, awareness, smarter evolver, emergent strategist;
- Co-evolution, ecosystem.

Exaptation — This term was introduced by **Stephen Gould** (1941–2002) and **Elizabeth Vrba** (1942–present), in 1982 (in their article, 'Exaptation — A missing term in the science of form') to replace the term 'pre-adaptation'. It is the shifting of the function of a trait during evolution — a trait serves one function and then another function, for example the feathers of birds (initially used for temperature regulation and later used for flight). Exaptation (also known as **cooptation**) is a common attribute, thus rendering the dynamics and outcomes of evolution more unpredictable, and difficult to analyze (see evolution, adaptation, nonlinearity, predictability and natural selection).

Externalization — The exportation of an idea/concept from a human mind (from tacit to explicit) — introduced in the general information theory (externalization is the opposite from internalization but there are not exact reverse processes). It is the transferring of an idea/concept from the knowledge structure in the human thinking system of an individual/ expert to other interacting agents or some external sources (repositories). The process is better facilitated by the use of a physical symbol system (written language) that also renders external storage possible. This capability is unique to humanity (see internalization, character set, physical symbol system, energy–matter system and general information theory).

Extropy — The term indicates the tendency of a system to grow towards higher orderliness (localized order, equilibrium with minimum entropy — local interactions leading to the emergent of structure — stability-centric), in opposition to the second law of thermodynamics (dynamical equilibrium at maximum entropy) and the expanding Universe theory (for instance, the emergent of the physical world, and living organisms with structure). Thus, it is linked to dissipation, self-organization, and emergence, and opposite from entropy (see localized order, entropy, second law of thermodynamics, dissipation, self-centric, stability-centric, self-organization, emergence, complex systems, complex adaptive systems, network theory and Universe).

Far-from-equilibrium (system) — Such a system (CS/CAS) does not return to an earlier (regular) state (continuously changing). It does not repeat itself, and the dynamic is nonlinear. Therefore, it indicates that such a system is never in static equilibrium but always becoming. All human organizations, including corporations, societies, nations, and the entire humanity are far-from-equilibrium systems, and such systems require a constant inflow of energy for sustainability (see static equilibrium, nonlinearity, edge of order, dynamical equilibrium, relativistic static equilibrium, strange attractor and human organization).

Notes: Systems and equilibrium:

- **OS** — towards 'static' or dynamical equilibrium (relativistic) with minimum entropy (order).
- **DCS/CS/CAS/IO** — far-from-equilibrium (constantly/continuously changing).
- **DS** — towards equilibrium with maximum entropy (infinite randomness).

Fat-tailed distribution — It is a probability distribution that exhibits large skewness (lopsided — variance does not exist) and kurtosis ('peakedness') — law of the vital few. Some fat-tailed distributions have power law decay at the tail end — not the entire distribution. In some application areas (finance, marketing), 'fat tails' are regarded as higher risks. The Pareto distribution (80–20) is a 'fat-tail' manifestation of the data used, while Gaussian distribution is 'vanishing tails' (see power law, power law phenomena, Gaussian distribution, Pareto distribution and tipping point).

Notes: Different 'tailed' distributions:

- **Heavy-tailed distributions** have 'heavier' tails than the exponential distribution.
- **Heavy-tailed distributions** => Three classes, namely fat-tailed distributions, long-tailed distributions, and sub-exponential distributions.
- All **long-tailed distributions** are heavy-tailed, but not the reverse (for examples, Pareto distribution, Levy distribution — tailed off asymptotically).
- All **fat-tailed distributions** are heavy-tailed, but not the reverse (for examples, Pareto distribution, Cauchy distribution).
- All **sub-exponential distributions** are long-tailed, but not the reverse.

Feedback — It is a linkage from the output of a system back to its input. Feedback (circulation coupling, upwards causation and downwards causation) can be negative (convergent) or positive (divergent). This concept is first recognized by **Norbert Wiener** (1894–1978) in 1948, and is broadly used in cybernetics. In cybernetics, excessive number of positive feedbacks (divergent) amplifies processes, increases the complexity and instability of the system, leading to exponential growth, unpredictability, and the butterfly effect. However, positive feedback was only better comprehend in the 1990s when **Fritjof Capra** (1939–present) in 1996 pointed out that such feedback is a source of new order, and complexity in dissipative structures (when a system is 'increasing', a positive feedback increases the 'increasing', while a negative feedback deceases the 'increasing'. When a system is 'deceasing' a positive feedback increases the 'decreasing', while a negative feedback decreases the 'decreasing'). Thus, basically negative feedback suppresses the effect of fluctuations (see autocatalysis, circular causation, recurrence relations, upwards causation, downwards causation, cybernetics, homeostasis, nonlinearity, butterfly effect, increasing returns, law of requisite variety and dissipative structure).

Feeling system/organization — An intelligent human organization is both a thinking system and a feeling system (intelligent human organization > thinking system + feeling system). A feeling entity (individual or organization) recognizes the presence of life (consciousness — awareness and mindfulness), and the criticality of compassion (feeling system <=> high relational capacity + organizational justice + compassion + mental cohesion) —agent-centric. In this case, an intelligent person, as well as an intelligence leader is itself a feeling system. In a feeling system/organization, connectivity, collectiveness, consensus and commitment are enhanced by the group-survival mindset (collectiveness capacity, relational capacity, organizational justice, unifying capacity, coherency, mental cohesion) — that is, the survival of every agents must be ensured, not just the organization — beyond the normal CAD. Thus, *i*CAD (org-awareness, orgminfulness, mindful culture, self-organizing governance, and intelligence leadership) encompasses attributes that are not found in CAD. In this case, physical, artificial life, and AI systems possess (programmed) 'algorithmic/thinking ability' but no 'feeling ability'.

In this respect, there is a distinct different between living intelligent systems (in particular, intelligent human organizations) and artificially created intelligent systems (computer systems) — (see human agent, human thinking system, intelligence paradigm, consciousness, awareness, mindfulness, behavioral schemata, agent-centric, collectiveness capacity, relational capacity, unifying capacity, coherency, mental cohesion, intelligent person, self-organizing governance, intelligence leadership, latent leadership, orgmindfulness, mindful culture, collective intelligence, organizational justice, symbiosis, *i*CAS, *i*CAD and intelligent organization).

First mover advantage — It is the advantage associated with the first to move into certain position/space/possibility associated with a unique niche. (For instance, QWERTY, the first keyboard layout gives it the first mover advantage as the entry of subsequent layout, such as the Dvorak layout, never become popular). In complexity studies, the first mover advantage is associated with the first to recognize and exploit an emerging surface pattern in a space of complexity — the latter could be an unexplored territory that is embedded with gold nuggets. In intelligent organization theory, a first mover (intense intelligence and collective intelligence) is also linked to the capability to recognize and exploit spaces of relativistic order — relativistic complexity — elevating intelligence advantage (first mover advantage <=> intense intelligence/consciousness <=> innovative and creative <=> intelligence advantage) and (continuous/constant first mover <=> winner of the red queen race) — (see, intelligence, collective intelligence, complex, space of complexity, complex adaptive systems, relativistic complexity, space of relativistic order, futurology, red queen race, intelligence advantage and emergence).

Fitness — It is the ability of a species to survive and flourish in an ecosystem with respect to all the other species present — with respect to the changing landscape (rugged/fitness landscape). This is a key significant characteristic in the Darwinian's evolution theory — survival of the fittest. In the current context (especially, in humanity), 'fitness' also encompasses the intelligence/consciousness or mental perspective, that is, it is beyond just the physical aspect or physical fitness alone. Human dominance on this planet is very much due to 'mental fitness' rather than physical fitness and biological fitness (combined) — (see evolution, exaptation, rugged/fitness landscape, human thinking system, intelligence and consciousness).

Fractal — It is a system (a natural phenomenon or mathematical set) with similar details at all scales (**self-similarity** — the repetition of self-similar patterns across levels or scales). A set of points is a fractal if its dimension is non integer. Thus, fractal [coined by **Benoit Mandelbrot** (1924–2010) in 1975, and fractal geometry in 1982] boundaries/structure when magnified always appears the same — scale invariant/scalability/scale free (for examples, coastline, cauliflower, broccoli, leaf veins, mountain ranges, Mandelbrot set and Koch snowflake). An attractor is strange if it possesses a fractal structure (fractal <=> strangeness). Fractals often show Pareto distributions (**Vilfredo Pareto** — 1848–1923) and are signified by power laws. 'Natural fractals' (scale free up to about seven levels of magnification) are not as perfect as 'mathematical fractals' (scale free for infinite numbers of magnification, thus, 'fractal' is a subset of 'self-similarity') — (see scalability, self-similarity, Mandelbrot set, fractal dimension, attractor, strange attractor, Pareto distribution, power law, and power law phenomenon).

Fractal dimension — In fractal geometry, an object can be divided into certain equal pieces for examination — fractal dimension, D. For instance, when N-secting (each side divided N times) a D-dimensional object, there will be N^D fractional pieces, each of size $1/N^D$. Let $N^D = M$. Taking log on both sides, then $\log N^D = \log M$, and $D = (\log M)/(\log N)$. For instance, the fractional dimension of the logistic map (unimodal) bifurcation diagram is approximately 0.538 — (see, dimensionality, fractal, scalability, bifurcation and logistic map).

Fundamentalism — Fundamentalists advocate reductionism. The exact sciences focus on the fact that the world at different levels (for instance, from atomic physics to nuclear physics to particle particles) can be fully explained by the same set of theories, laws, and basic entities (fundamentalism <=> reductionist hypothesis <=> hierarchical decomposition). In complexity theory, there are many systems and their properties that defy the reductionist explanations (or the Cartesian belief) — some can be better explained by theoretical principles, such as the **humpty dumpty effect** and the constructionist hypothesis (including symmetry breaking) — indicating that emergence provides a better understanding of certain phenomena (see Newtonian mindset, Cartesian belief, Laplace belief, hierarchical decomposition, reductionist hypothesis, epistemological reductionism, complexity mindset, intelligence mindset, constructionist hypothesis, broken symmetry, epistemological reductionism, self-transcending constructions and emergence).

Futurology (futurity/futurist) — Futurology is the 'study of the future'. It focuses on the possible, probable, or preferable futures of humanity and human organizations (futurology <=> strategic foresight <=> scenario planning <=> futuristic capacity). The establishment of this domain was first advocated by **Herbert George Wells** (1866–1946), in 1902 ('The discovery of the future'), and supported by other futurists, including **Jacque Fresco** (1916–present) and **Ken Keyes, Jr.** (1921–1995) — coauthored the book 'Looking forward', in 1969. The domain/approach possesses the Newtonian mindset and believes very much in forecasting and predictability (relativistic). In the intelligent organization theory (**T.Y. Liang**, 2001), a futurist must also be a smarter evolver and emergent strategist (futuristic capacity <=> exploratory capacity + self-organizing capacity + emergence-intelligence capacity). Thus, being futuristic also encompasses preparing for unpredictability. In this respect, futurology is also closely associated with better risk management, punctuation point, crisis management, homeostasis, first mover advantage, and intelligence advantage due to the presence of co-existence of order and complexity, and intelligence/consciousness-centricity. Hence, possessing ability to elevate futuristic capacity is beneficial but it is also interesting for futurists to note that human organizations as CAS that are history dependence (hysteresis), and not just focusing on futurity (see stasis, punctuation point, smarter evolver, emergent strategist, intelligent person, space of complexity, predictability, uncertainty, homeostasis, first mover advantage, deliberate strategy, emergent strategy, complex adaptive systems, anticipative system, aware system, intelligence/consciousness-centric, relativistic complexity and hysteresis).

Game theory — It is the study of strategic decision making using mathematical models of conflict and cooperation among rational decision makers (intelligent interacting agents) — economic man, administrative man and intelligent person. The game deduces a set of equilibrium strategies for each player, and the overall integrated equilibrium strategies determine the equilibrium to the game. Currently, it is applied to a diversified spread of behavioral relations in domains such as decision sciences, economics, psychology, political science and biology — (see agent, economic man, administrative man, intelligence person and dynamical equilibrium).

Gaia — It is a term that viewed the entire Earth as a self-regulating, holistic, biotic CAS (global biosphere). In this respect, Gaia encompasses all the ecosystems on this planet. It is the largest biosphere on Earth. This term is first used by **James Ephraim Lovelock** (1919–present) in the 1960s. He proposed the Gaia hypothesis which indicates that biological organisms on this planet interact with the physical/inorganic surroundings to form a CAS that maintain life on Earth — (*Gaia: A New Look at Life on Earth*, 1979; and *The Revenge of Gaia*, 2006) — (see biosphere, evolution, intelligence, consciousness, complex adaptive systems, human organization and Universe).

Gaussian distribution — It is the common bell shape curve with the Gaussian function (**Johann Carl Friedrich Gauss,** 1777–1855), $f(x) = a \exp[-(x-b)^2/2c^2]$ where a, b, $c > 0$ [a is the y-coordinate (peak value), b is the x-coordinate of the peak, and c (standard deviation) determines the width of the curve)], and $\exp = e = 2.718281828$ — Euler's number. Other properties of the Gaussian distribution include 'vanishing tails', stable means, clearly defined confidence interval, and limited variance — thus, this distribution is different from power law phenomena (for instance, Pareto distribution (80–20) is a 'fat-tail' distribution). The Gaussian functions are commonly used in statistics as normal distributions — (see power law, power law phenomena, fat-tailed distribution and Pareto distribution).

General information theory — This theory is conceived to explain the macroscopic dynamics of the human thinking systems (the elementary entities/agents of all intelligent human organizations) — (**T.Y. Liang,** began in 1994). It is perceived to be comprised of two subsystems namely, the natural energy–matter subsystem and artificially-created physical symbol subsystem. [This theory complements the intelligent organization theory because the latter perceives a human organization as a collection of human intelligence/consciousness sources, irrespective of the nature or primary function of the organization (corporation, military unit, education institution, share market, city and nation)]. The boundaries of the theory are defined by the six basic entities/artifacts namely, data, information, knowledge, wisdom, information-coded energy quantum, and information-coded matter quantum. The dynamics are driven by different levels of intelligence, and the functions executed include symbol creation function, event coding function, data processing function, information processing function, knowledge accumulation function, perception function, decision-making function, wisdom creation function, internalization and externalization. The presence of the physical symbol subsystem (written language) differentiates human intelligence (far beyond instinctive abilities and into deep abstract mental abilities) from the basic life-intelligence of all other animal species — (see human thinking system, basic entity, artifact, character set, intelligence, consciousness, physical symbol system, energy–matter system, knowledge structure, internalization, externalization and basic life-intelligence).

Genetic algorithm — It uses evolutionary techniques (ABM) to diversify, combine, and select better options (fitness) in order to improve competitiveness according to natural selection. This algorithm (a subset of evolutionary algorithm) was popularized by **John Holland** ((1929–2015) in the 1970s, and is now a significant algorithm in computing complexity — including bioinformatics, phylogenetics and computational science. A typical genetic algorithm possesses two basic requirements namely (i) a genetic representation of the solution domain, and (ii) a fitness function to evaluate the solution domain — (see agent, fitness, natural selection, interdependency and evolution theory).

Notes: Some common algorithms:

- Evolutionary algorithm => genetic algorithm + some others.
- Emergent algorithm => cellular automata, ANN, swarm intelligence.
- Swarm intelligence => artificial life, ant colony optimization + some others.

Global mindset — In business/economic, this mindset is frequently associated with awareness, openness, cultural diversity, differences of agents, market differences, and the ability to identify a global pattern — a worldwide phenomenon. Basically, business and economic activities have been intensively internationalized or globalized, the human world has shrunk (mental perception), organizations (nations, corporations) have become more interconnected and interdependent, and competition is no more localized (global diversification). In the intelligent organization theory, the linkage between the intelligence mindset and global mindset focuses on the more nonlinear global intelligence-intelligence linkage, intense intelligence/consciousness-centricity, and global human collective intelligence (an extreme end of the intelligence spectrum); and higher complexity density and more rapid changes (raplexity, complexity-intelligence linkage). In this respect, it concentrates on the human global system encompassing all human perspectives, including economic, social, political, and environmental (global holistic engagement, the entire humanity). In general, globalization/international has both positive and negative effects — (see intelligence mindset, intelligence-intelligence linkage, nonlinearity, raplexity, interdependency, engagement, complexity-intelligence linkage, intelligence/consciousness-centric, collective intelligence and intelligence spectrum).

Global optimality (organizational optimality) — It is the state where all agents' goals/fitness in a system/organization is maximally satisfied — global in this contact (could) mean just an organization/system. As agents in CAS are autonomous and self-centric, and together with the principle of locality and satisficing principle, global optimality does not exist in reality. In CAS, agents co-evolve with each other, and achieve best possible goal/fitness/solution — no individual and global optimality. (Note the characteristics of economic man, administrative man and intelligent person.) Another reason is that high finite dimensionality systems (including human organizations) have large numbers of variables, and not all of them are measurable (not known or cannot be accurately measured) or totally unknown. In this case, the phase space is in-complete (not all states in the 'preferred' attractor are known), and global optimality is not achievable — (see self-centric, autonomous, variable, principle of locality, satisficing principle, co-evolution, economic man, administrative man, intelligent person, human organization, smarter evolver, emergent strategist and phase space).

Governance — It is the complex coordinating, steering and regulating processes established, executed and maintained for a certain collective purposes when a group of human beings co-exist together. The thinking and processes are guided by a set of principles of governance. A key focus is to ensure that power is well-distributed among different groups of agents (different groups may have different interest and goals — complex networks) based on some formal/informal rules. Thus, governance exists in all human organizations (corporations, communities, nations, markets, global institutions), and it deals mainly with the better management of power, knowledge, and conflict. In general, governance design and functioning concentrates on the characteristics of the governance objects and their environment. It has to change continuously responding to the changing thinking and needs of (different) agents and the organizations. Hence, a better governance dynamic (intelligence governance strategy in intelligent organizations) must be closely linked to intelligence/consciousness management, intelligence-intelligence linkage, complexity-intelligence linkage, complexity management, intelligent person, complex adaptive networks, network management, intelligence leadership, organizational justice, relational capacity, feeling system and sustainability. Thus, the new focus is on self-organizing governance — increasing self-powered self-organization of agents/actors and intrinsic leaders, and decreasing hierarchical empowerment (direct governance). This is the basic foundation of the intelligence governance strategy — (see agent, connectivity, nonlinearity, complexity, governance system, intelligence, engagement, human organization, intelligent organization, organizational justice, intelligence/consciousness management, intelligence-intelligence linkage, collective intelligence, intelligent person, collectiveness capacity, complexity-intelligence linkage, complexity management, complex networks, network theory, network management, intelligence leadership, relational capacity, feeling system, self-organizing governance, futurology and sustainability).

Governance system — It is system of (interacting) agents (actors with diversified interest, power and knowledge) and objects (including natural, biological, technical and organizational — citizenship, membership, services and products) established for the purpose of shaping, governing and regulating the interacting agents themselves. As the agents (leaders, actors and non-actors) are greatly diversified and interdependent, governance arrangements exhibiter great variability and incoherency. The key drivers of governance processes are power, knowledge, and conflict. Other factors/properties involve include ethics, human relationships, culture (organizational culture, culture diversification), organizational justice, and leaderships. Currently, the structure of governance system is very much dominated by the design paradigm — hierarchical control and empowerment. A new type of governance systems established by a group of autonomous agents under decentralized conditions using the processes of diffusion and emulation are surfacing (self-organizing governance, e-governance, and complex adaptive networks). The differentiated agents initiate a change locally with no obvious coordination (although the group may be communicating), and possess no intention of global transformation. The dynamic is self-powered self-organizing, leading to a new governance paradigm. This spontaneous shift to a new governance paradigm is an emergent behavioral development => a primary aim of the intelligent organization theory that uses intelligence, consciousness, collective intelligence, organizational consciousness (org-awareness, orgmindfulness, mindful culture), network management, complexity management and feeling system to achieve it (intelligence governance strategy — higher relational capacity, self-organizing capacity and emergence-intelligence capacity). In addition, **Elinor Ostrom** (1933–2012, Nobel Prize in Economics in 1999) had contributions to self-organizing governance systems including collective–choice arrangements and participation — (see agent, design paradigm, intelligence paradigm, nonlinearity, complexity, connectivity, intelligence, engagement, collectiveness capacity, collective intelligence, consciousness, mindfulness, orgmindfulness, mindful culture, governance, corporate governance, agents, autonomous, interdependency, behavioral schemata, satisficing principle, organizational justice, self-organization, self-transcending constructions, intelligence leadership, network management, collective capacity, relational capacity, feeling system, self-organizing capacity, emergence, emergence-intelligence capacity, self-organizing governance, sustainability, *i*CAS and *i*CAD).

Graph theory — This theory originates from a paper published by **Leonhard Euler** (1707–1783), a mathematician, in 1736. It is a mathematical domain on the study of graphs which are mathematical structures (pair-wise relations, ordered pair) with vertices (nodes) and edges (links). A graph is undirected if there is no distinction between the nodes and the links. Otherwise, the link/edge is directed. Graphs are used in discrete mathematics that focuses on variables with separated values — discrete objects (but not consistently separated like integers). They are also used in computer science for developing computer algorithms (flow of computation, and data organization). Subsequently, the theory also provides a foundation for network theory (sociology, biology) — [see network theory, small world theory, complex network, complex adaptive network, scale free network, emergence, S(1)-S(4) and self-organization].

Notes: Some additional information on graphs, random networks, small world networks and scale free networks:

- **Graph theory** => graphs (including random networks) — a branch of discrete mathematics, introduced by **Leonhard Euler** (1707–1783), in 1736.
- **Random network theory** => random networks (probability distribution over graphs, lies in between graph theory and probability theory), introduced by **Paul Erdos** (1913–1996) and **Alfred Renyi** (1921–1970), in 1959.
- **Networks** => mathematical networks + real world networks.
- **Network theory** => a subset of graph theory; focus on real world networks, order still exists — also perceived as a subset of complexity theory.
- **Real world networks** => **complex networks + complex adaptive networks**
- **Complex adaptive networks** => a subset of complex networks with 'living' nodes (agents) => the human world is characterized by complex adaptive networks (network organizations).

- **Complex adaptive networks** => small world networks + scale free networks.
- **Small world phenomenon/theory** => small world networks => almost all nodes are connected to all other nodes, short path lengths, and high clustering.
- **Scale free networks** => networks with power law distribution.

Hierarchical decomposition — This approach is used to analyze systems that are closed, orderly, and linear (OS) — compared to statistical mechanics at the other extreme (closed, disordered, and infinite randomness — DS). This reductionist path adopts a top-down approach when analyzing the system, and a bottom-up approach when designing and building the system — linked to fundamentalism and the Cartesian belief. The functions of the elementary units are supportive of the overall goal of the system (functional coherency). This property of functional cohesion is highly significant in many systems, especially machines and physical systems. However, in CAS this approach cannot be used because of complexity, nonlinearity and the Humpty Dumpty effect. In CAS, the interacting agents need not be supporting the system objective, and the set of rules governing the system may change with time, but the system (global forces) will continue to emerge — (see Newtonian mindset, Cartesian belief, Laplace belief, statistical mechanics, reductionist hypothesis, fundamentalism, ordered systems, complex adaptive systems, constructionist hypothesis, self-organization, self-transcending constructions and interdependency).

Holism — It is the thinking that a system has to be analyzed as a whole (opposite to reductionism, fundamentalism and Cartesian belief), and the tendency of a whole is greater than the sum of the parts — coherency, synergetic, and emergent effect (**Jan Smuts**, 1870–1950, his book *Holism and Evolution*, published in 1926 — before GST was conceived/ popularized in 1940, **Ludwig von Bertalanffy**, 1901–1972). For instance, a car is totally different from its parts (the new characteristics 'speed' and 'driving' are emergent properties/characteristics — constructionist hypothesis) — (see hierarchical decomposition, fundamentalism, Cartesian belief, interdependency, synergetics, constructionist hypothesis and complexity mindset).

Homeostasis — It is the (self-organizing and self-maintaining) ability of a system that maintains the stability of its internal environment (resilience), while the external environment is changing (specially focusing on negative feedback). This possess was first described by **Claude Bernard** (1813–1878), while the term homoeostasis was coined by **Walter Bradford Cannon** (1871–1945), in 1932. For human beings, homeostasis is a main responsibility of the brain. Thus, to a great extent, this characteristic is closely linked to autopoiesis (high self-centric and stability-centric), and self-organization (self-organization in biology — the self-maintaining abilities of systems from cell to whole organism). It is the ability of an agent/system to resist change, self-regulate, and maintain a particular stable state by regulating its internal environment (its stability to perturbation) — (see cybernetics, resilience, autopoiesis, self-centric, stability-centric, self-organization, feedback, resilience and sustainability).

Human agent — In human organizations the interacting agents are human beings each carrying an intense intelligence/consciousness source [high level intelligence and consciousness — and emotional (not inherent rational actors) — creating the nonlinear mental space], embedded with a complex, nonlinear, and continuously changing behavioral schemata (or a set of behavioral schema). Human agents are (inherently) self-powered, heterogeneous, autonomous, independent, interdependent, self-centric, stability-centric, and 'conditional' altruistic. In addition, the causal relationship (cause-effect, condition reaction) is determined by the goal of the agents, as well as their behavioral schemata. They are also subjective (perception, emotional) and uncertain (intrinsic uncertainty) about their environment and future. Thus, human agents are very different from other interacting agents (especially, some artificially created agents) because of their high awareness and mindfulness. In a highly intelligent human organization (*i*CAS), they are also naturally self-powered and endowed with intrinsic leadership ability — some intelligent person attributes. The intensity of human intelligence and consciousness renders the interactive dynamics (including connectivity, communications and engagement) extremely nonlinear and complex encompassing the physical, biological and mental spaces/dimensions (3rd order stability) — involving the volitional and social perspectives (shared cognition, feeling system) — relational capacity, collectiveness capacity, adaptive capacity and unifying capacity. Overall, learning and adaptive agents (smarter evolver and emergent strategist => intelligent person) cause structural change, and drive emergence through self-organization/self-transcending constructions (*i*CAD). At the higher levels dynamic, human organizations are agents of a large system (nested, composite CAS, for instance, business organizations in an economy) — (see self-centric, stability-centric, stability, behavioral schemata, principle of locality, autonomous, adaptive, intelligence, consciousness, awareness, mindfulness, interdependency, autopoiesis, nonlinearity, self-powered, intrinsic leadership, satisficing principle, smarter evolver, emergent strategist, intelligent person, collectiveness capacity, relational capacity, feeling system, adaptive capacity, anticipatory system, complex adaptive systems, self-organization, self-transcending constructions, *i*CAS, *i*CAD, emergence and intelligent organization theory).

Human organization/system — It is a group comprising of two or more human beings as interacting agents, irrespective of the primary objective (education, social, political, economic, military, nation and/or environment) of the system (human agents => human thinking systems => intrinsic intense intelligence/consciousness sources). In the intelligent organization theory, all human organizations are fundamentally perceived as a collection of intrinsic intelligence/consciousness sources. As the group increase in size other characteristics and abilities/functions become necessary, for instance leadership, management, collective intelligence, governance, governance mechanisms, and strategy. In addition, human organizations are highly sophisticated information processing systems and knowledge repositories, and are also open systems with non-equilibrium (far-from-equilibrium) dynamics — that is, they are continuously changing nonlinear CAS (and they are more complex than a bee hive or ant colony). It is also important to recognize that all/many human organizations are multi-layered systems intertwined with a large number of agents, local spaces/networks, linear and nonlinear variables (known and unknown), and different perspectives (including social, economic, political and environment). Earlier studies have recognized/characterized human organizations as 'cooperative systems', and 'interpretative systems'. In structural contingency theory, the complexity of a human organization is three-dimensional namely vertical (numbers of hierarchical level), horizontal (numbers of interacting agents), and geographic (numbers of distinct cluster). In the intelligent organization theory, a highly intelligent human organization is an *i*CAS — a well-interconnected/integrated collection of intelligence/consciousness sources with multi-layer structure (macro, micro and meta-structures). In realty, human organizations (business corporations, social communities and nations) are mathematically in-deterministic high finite dimensionality systems (systems spectrum) due to the presence of uncertainty (the set of variables defining the dynamics is never complete, variables cannot be measured accurately, and unknown unknowns — ontological reductionism) — that is, the phase space is in-complete, thus, elevating unpredictability. In this case, human organizations are normally analyzed qualitatively rather than quantitatively (mathematical modeling is difficult or inaccurate — at best an estimation — Laplace belief fails) — (see agent, intelligence, consciousness, awareness, mindfulness, nonlinearity, complexity, connectivity, engagement, network theory, collectiveness capacity, symbiosis, predictability, deterministic, in-deterministic, far-from-equilibrium, uncertainty, ontological reductionism, interdependency, human rationality, satisficing principle, open system, dimensionality, systems spectrum, collective intelligence, adaptive capacity, relational capacity, governance, law of requisite variety, systems spectrum, complex adaptive systems, org-centric, synergetics, Laplace belief, intelligent organization and *i*CAS).

Notes: Some prominent characteristics and constraints of human organizations:

- All human organizations are intrinsic CAS — therefore, they are sensitive dependence on initial conditions (butterfly effect), and unpredictable.
- All human organizations are high finite dimensionality (continuous-time) nonlinear dynamical systems with in-complete variables (some variables cannot be accurately measures and presence of unknown unknowns) — thus, their phase space is also in-complete — elevate unpredictability — no global optimality — Laplace belief fails.

- The interacting agents of human organizations are human beings (intense intrinsic intelligence/consciousness sources — awareness and mindfulness) each embedded with a set of behavioral schemata that is continuously changing — high nonlinearity and interdependency (thus, they are very different from other interacting agents) — fundamentalism and Cartesian belief fail.
- The set of rules and norms governing all human organizations are also continuously changing — high complexity density — no static equilibrium.

Human rationality — The human brain is an emotional organ that can also be rational. It is dominantly controlled by the amygdala in the limbic system (second layer). The frontal cortex (in the cerebral cortex — third layer) that provides the higher cognitive functions such as self-awareness, mindfulness, abstract thinking and logical reasoning, self-motivation and wisdom is fully developed only when a person is about twenty-one years old. Thus, human beings are not absolute rational actors, as the human thinking systems (brain + mind) are nonlinear, complex and non-rational that attempt to be adaptive and logical (human rationality is bounded). In this respect, all human organizations (from a social community, a business corporation to the world stock market, a nation, and the entire Gaia) are a collection of emotional nonlinear human thinking systems (thus, human rationality is nonlinear due to the inherent dominancy of emotions — phobic mindset, fear, Abilene paradox and defensive routine) — (see human thinking system, cerebral cortex, behavioral schemata, human organization, agent, human agent, nonlinearity, consciousness, awareness, mindfulness, phobic mindset, and economic man, administrative man, satisficing principle, intelligent person, phobic mindset, Abilene paradox and defensive routine).

Human thinking system (HTS) — It is the elementary unit is all human organizations. In general, the human thinking system (HTS = brain + mind) encompasses the brain, the tangible three-layered (phylogenesis) biological organ (brain stem and cerebellum, limbic system, and cerebral cortex) and its projection, the abstract mind (with unknown boundaries) — an abstract emotional system that can be logical. In the general information theory, the human thinking system is divided into two subsystems, namely, the energy–matter subsystem (natural) and the physical symbol subsystem (artificial). The latter extended the human thinking system into territories that are unexplored by all other animal species, including highly abstract concept spaces supported by the presence of one or more languages. Consequently, human thinking systems are the sources of highest intelligence present on this planet that emit the highest consciousness function of mindfulness that could observe itself (mental state). In addition, ideally human thinking systems are or must be 'feeling systems' and not merely ordinary 'thinking systems'. Otherwise, they are not significantly different from artificially created systems (AI). Thus, consciousness (awareness, mindfulness) and relational capacity are critical attributes in the human mental world, and intense intelligence/consciousness is the key inherent strength of a human agent, as well as his/her organizations (see character set, physical symbol system, energy–matter system, phylogenesis, intelligence, consciousness, awareness, mindfulness, human rationality, general information theory, orgmindfulness, feeling system, relational capacity, satisficing principle and orgmind).

Notes: Different interpretations of HTS and human organizations (orgmind):

- Human thinking system = human brain + human mind.
- Human thinking system = energy–matter subsystem + physical symbol subsystem.
- Human thinking system => intense intelligence + consciousness (awareness + mindfulness).
- Human organization = $\sum$ human agents = $\sum$ human thinking systems = $\sum$ intrinsic intelligence/consciousness sources.
- Intelligent human organization (collective intelligence) > $\sum$ human thinking systems (intrinsic intelligence) + (coherency and coherency effects).

Hysteresis — Hysteresis is presence in CAS but not in DCS. In this respect, human organizations are dependent on their history as a future state can be dependent on one or more earlier states. In physics, hysteresis refers to a delayed effect arising from an earlier change that has taken place (or has not manifested its full impact) — indicating that the historical perspective is significant. Similarly, evolution does not forget its history (phylogenesis). Thus, for human organizations, recognizing the impact of an event that started in the past and has not surfaced yet because it is still in the process of accumulating, and it will have a significant influence on a future state can be highly critical (futurology, tipping point and punctuation point) (see phylogenesis, evolution, CAS, human organization, futurology, tipping point, black swan, punctuation point and predictability).

*i*CAD — This term is introduced in the intelligent organization theory (**T. Y. Liang**, 2001) to denote **highly intelligent complex adaptive dynamics** in highly intelligent complex adaptive systems (*i*CAS) — achieves through proper intelligence/consciousness management (intelligence/consciousness-centric, collective optimization of all intrinsic intelligence/consciousness sources — high collectiveness capacity, adaptive capacity, relational capacity, unifying capacity, 3C-OK structure and dynamic, self-organizing capacity and emergence-intelligence capacity), and complexity management (complexity-intelligence-centric, including the anticipatory and emergent component => the presence of the integrated deliberate and emergent strategy is significant). Such a dynamic recognizes and exploits the co-existence of order (deliberate dynamic) and complexity (emergence dynamic), and is driven by both the high collective intelligence of the system and the individual intelligence of the agents — and substantiated by individual and organizational consciousness (awareness, self-awareness, mindfulness, orgmindfulness). Thus, the system is in a better position to spontaneously self-organize and emerge constructively when necessary (recognizing the complexity-intelligence linkage, intelligence-intelligence linkage, and relativistic complexity). In this respect, *i*CAD (agent-centric) is not totally similar to CAD (not agent-centric). In an *i*CAS driven by *i*CAD, the focus is not only confined to the system/organization alone, the state of every agent is also significant (elevating both collectiveness capacity and adaptive capacity). This is also a key thinking of the intelligence leadership strategy (higher leadership capacity) [see agent-centric, org-centric, intelligence/consciousness management, collective intelligence, awareness, mindfulness, orgmindfulness, human rationality, complexity-intelligence linkage, intelligence-intelligence linkage, collectiveness capacity, adaptive capacity, relational capacity, unifying capacity, complexity management, self-organizing capacity, emergence-intelligence capacity, intelligent organization, feeling system, symbiosis, deliberate strategy, emergent strategy, self-organization, self-transcending constructions, emergence, broken symmetry, S(1)-S(4), synergetics, relativistic complexity, stability, resilience, sustainability, *i*CAS, intelligence leadership and leadership capacity].

*i***CAS** — This term introduced in the intelligent organization theory (**T. Y. Liang**, 2001) to denote **highly intelligent human organizations** (high structural capacity, collectiveness capacity, collective intelligence, orgmindfulness, adaptive capacity, relational capacity, self-organizing capacity and emergence-intelligence capacity) that are driven by highly *i*CAD — due to the unique/quality connectivity, self-organizing communications, information exchange, truthful engagement, and homeostasis of highly intelligent interacting agents (possessing intelligent person attributes — *i*CAS ≥ ∑ intelligent persons synergetic effect). These human organizations are highly intelligence/consciousness-centric (agent-centric), complexity-centric, and network-centric. Such organizations always attempt to optimize the exploitation of the co-existence of order and complexity, and prepare for punctuation points. Most of the time, these organizations/systems are able to self-organize effectively/constructively during punctuation. Thus, the term *i*CAS is only reserved for human organizations with very high collective intelligence, org-consciousness, spontaneous self-organizing capability, emergence-intelligence capacity, and constantly focusing on 3rd order stability (spaces of mental complexity) through nurturing a mindful culture (feeling system), as well as exploiting relativistic complexity — spaces of relativistic order (*i*CAS <=> *r*CAS) [see complex adaptive systems, intelligence, consciousness, agent-centric, intelligence/consciousness-centric, connectivity, engagement, collective intelligence, synergetics, dimensionality, systems spectrum, mindfulness, org-centric, structural capacity, collectiveness capacity, orgmindfulness, mindful culture, *i*CAD, intelligent person, intelligent organization, coherency, adaptive capacity, relational capacity, unifying capacity, self-organizing capacity, emergence-intelligence capacity, feeling system, network theory, self-organization, self-transcending construction, broken symmetry, synergetics, constructionist hypothesis, S(1)-S(4), relativistic complexity, space of relativistic order, homeostasis, intelligent person, stability, resilience, sustainability and intelligent organization theory].

Increasing returns — Traditional economic dynamics observe decreasing returns. Increasing returns (positive feedbacks in economic systems, multiple equilibriums) was introduced by **Brian Arthur** (1946–present), (*Increasing Returns and Path Dependence in the Economy*, in 1994) to explain the reverse dynamic, especially in the complex knowledge-based economy. In this case, once a path is chosen it may become locked in (path dependency) regardless of the advantages of other paths [QWERTY is a prominent example — first mover advantage] — (see complexity, feedback, recurrence relations, circular causation, organizational learning and first mover advantage).

In-deterministic — CS/CAS (including human organizations/systems) are in-deterministic due to its high dimensionality (although finite), and the presence of in-complete phase space (due to information of known variables may not be complete), and unknown unknowns (unknown variables, uncertainty). The relationships among variables may also be constantly changing, thus, rendering it difficult to capture them. In this case, conceiving a mathematical model (Laplace belief) of a human organization or system is 'impossible' or inaccurate (at best an approximation/estimation). In addition, the sensitive dependence on initial conditions (butterfly effect) characteristic further elevates unpredictability (CS/CAS are in-deterministic and unpredictable, while DCS are deterministic but unpredictable, that is, in-deterministic <=> unpredictable, and deterministic ≠ predictable). In intelligent human organizations, in-determinism and unpredictability can be and must be better managed (see deterministic, dimensionality, systems spectrum, variable, uncertainty, Laplace belief, chaos, complex systems, complexity adaptive systems, butterfly effect, predictability, phase space, stochastic and human organization).

Individual intelligence enhancer — It is a triad (introduced in the intelligent organization theory) that exists in the human mind, encompassing intelligence, theory, and knowledge structure. The three components are highly interdependent and mutually enhancing, and their constructive interaction could make latent intelligence more apparent. Its dynamic is facilitated by the presence of a language (character set and physical symbol system) that enhances and redefines thinking, communications, and engagement in humanity. The increase in 'sophistication' of the language used in the enhancer elevates the intellectual (abstract conceptual) perspective of the mind — rendering the intrinsic intelligence of human interacting agents more complex and nonlinear, and its consciousness more intense (see intelligence, consciousness, character set, physical symbol system, knowledge structure, interdependency, adaptive capacity, collectiveness capacity, engagement, intelligence/consciousness management, physical symbol system and organizational intelligence enhancer).

Information decoder — Information and structure are closely interrelated. The presence of structure indicates the presence of encoded information (for instance, crystal, DNA and human organization), and a decoder is needed to decode the embedded information. To decode/decipher the embedded information some form/level of intelligence must be present. A cell decodes the information in the DNA. A human being with the appropriate knowledge structure is in a better position to decode an associated piece of information, and increase its value. An intelligent person is in a better position to decode a space of complexity establishing the relationships among certain pieces of information (relativistic complexity, surface pattern). In this case, possessing the information decoding ability elevates the potential of identifying new opportunities (see intelligence, human thinking system, knowledge structure, intelligent person, smarter evolver, emergent strategist, space of complexity and relativistic complexity).

Intelligence — Intelligence (at all levels) inherently focuses on stability-centric. This is a unique form of energy (abstract, intangible, and not fully understood) or latent impetus that exists intrinsically in this Universe that leads to the establishment of structures (localized order and the physical/

atomic world — proto-intelligence), nurturing of life (basic life-intelligence), and emergent of consciousness — that is, intelligence is spread out as a spectrum (intelligence spectrum). In general, it drives a self-centric and stability-centric dynamic (physical, biological and mental) that establishes a localized order. Intelligence when elevated to a certain level manifests nonlinearity characteristic (principle of locality). Intense intelligence activates consciousness, including mental functions such as awareness, and mindfulness. In the intelligent organization theory (**T.Y. Liang,** 2001) human level intelligence is perceived as the highest on this planet — human thinking systems (intense intelligence/consciousness is the inherent strength of human agents). In the general information theory (**T.Y. Liang,** began in 1994), human intelligence is confirmed as significantly different from the intelligence of other species. This claim is substantiated by the creation of the physical symbol sets and languages which are confined only to humanity (starting with a character set). In addition, higher level human intelligence activates sophisticated thinking and reasoning, as well as the conceptualization of abstract theories (intense intelligence <=> nonlinearity <=> innovativeness and creativity). With high intelligence/ consciousness the diversification space can be restricted or controlled due to intentionality and calculated approach, or innovative exploration. However, it is both the high intrinsic individual intelligence and collective intelligence (orgmind, orgmindfulness and org-awareness) of the organization that facilitates more effective self-organization/self-transcending constructions, and emergent of new order (see proto-intelligence, basic life-intelligence, self-centric, stability-centric, consciousness, awareness, mindfulness, character set, human thinking system, self-centric, stability-centric, intelligence spectrum, orgmind, org-awareness, orgmindfulness, org-centric, collective intelligence, principle of locality, self-organization, self-transcending constructions, emergence, complexity-intelligence strategy, law of complexity/consciousness, law of complexity/intelligence, law of consciousness/intelligence, intelligent organization, general information theory and Universe).

Notes: The significance of human intelligence and consciousness:

- Intense intrinsic intelligence and consciousness are the inherent strengths of every human interacting agents.

- Nurturing and optimizing these inherent strengths in an integrative manner with coherency and synergy (achieving high collective intelligence and org-consciousness — org-awareness and orgmindfulness) is another critical cultivated strength of all human organizations.

Intelligence/consciousness-centric — Intelligence/consciousness-centricity is the fundamental focus (a foundation pillar, thinking and paradigmatic path) of the intelligent organization theory. The intelligence mindset concentrates on the intense human intelligence/consciousness sources (agent-centric), and their connectivity, engagement, and collectiveness capacity (organizing around intelligence, and exploiting human intelligence and consciousness — intelligence/consciousness management). This approach triggers the most potent effects of human agents. Human organizations that are intelligence/consciousness-centric perceive human intelligence and consciousness as the most important assets/entities. (The use of the term 'resource' in this case is not very accurate as a human being possesses an identity and morals perspective — an asset.) All other resources (economic) are secondary. Thus, intelligent organizations concentrate strongly on human thinking systems, organizing around intelligence, and establishing appropriate intelligence-intelligence linkages to nurture collective intelligence and org-consciousness (orgmindfulness, mindful culture, collectiveness capacity, adaptive capacity, *i*CAS and *i*CAD). The holistic approach adopted is the complexity-intelligence strategy (see intelligence, consciousness, awareness, mindfulness, intelligence mindset, intelligence paradigm, intelligence/consciousness management, agent-centric, org-centric, organizing around intelligence, collective intelligence, intelligence-intelligence linkage, orgmindfulness, mindful culture, intelligent organization, *i*CAS, *i*CAD, collectiveness capacity, adaptive capacity and complexity-intelligence strategy).

Intelligence/consciousness management — This is a key new management thinking introduced in the intelligent organization theory (**T. Y. Liang**, 2001 — intelligence mindset, intelligence/consciousness-centricity). It is the subtle and proper management of individual intense intelligence/consciousness sources ('optimal' exploitation of all sources, if necessary), and the nurturing of high level collective intelligence in a human organization (organizing around intelligence, intelligence-intelligence linkages, mental state of agents, awareness, mindfulness, agent-centric, orgmindfulness, org-consciousness, org-centric, mindful culture, orgmind and organizational mental cohesion). The approach also focuses on the nurturing and better exploitation of *i*CAD through elevating self-organizing capability (in particular, self-organization, self-transcending constructions, emergence, and relativistic complexity). Apparently, it must be closely integrated with knowledge management, organizational learning, complexity management, and network management. Thus, the basic goal of intelligence/consciousness management is to nurture a highly intelligent human organization, *i*CAS, driven by a highly *i*CAD — creating an intelligence advantage (first mover advantage). In this respect, it is also important for leaders and managers to know some basic characteristics of human interacting agents (including stability-centric, self-centric, autopoietic, autonomous, heterogeneous, self-powered, subjective and interdependency), and some key organizational characteristics (including collectiveness capacity, adaptive capacity, relational capacity, self-organizing capacity, emergence-intelligence capacity and unifying capacity) — (see intelligent organization theory, intelligence mindset, agent, intelligence, awareness, mindfulness, intelligence/consciousness-centric, human thinking system, organizing around intelligence, intelligence-intelligence linkage, agent-centric, org-centric, stability-centric, self-centric, connectivity, engagement, collectiveness capacity, adaptive capacity, relational capacity, collective intelligence, interdependency, complexity management, network management, nonlinearity, complexity, organizational justice, intelligent person, feeling system, intelligence mindset, complexity-intelligence linkage, principle of locality, autopoiesis, symbiosis, self-powered, uncertainty, consciousness, orgmindfulness, mindful culture, orgmind, self-organization, self-transcending constructions, self-organizing capacity, emergence-intelligence capacity, unifying capacity, emergence, intelligence advantage, first mover advantage, relativistic complexity, sustainability, *i*CAS and *i*CAD).

Intelligence-intelligence linkage — In the intelligent organization theory, a human organization is perceived as a collection of intrinsic intense intelligence sources. Their connectivity is the voluntary linkage between one source with some other another sources (intelligence/consciousness-centric, elevating collectiveness capacity, minimal or no direct control — spontaneous org-centricity, high self-organizing capability) — (orgmindfulness <=> intelligence-intelligence linkages => mental cohesion). This is a primary focus that arises from the intelligence mindset, and intelligence paradigm. A special focus on this linkage is vital in human organizations as it is a pre-requisite for truthful communications (self-organizing communications), truthful engagement, nurturing collective intelligence, better information sharing, consensus and collaboration, orchestrating self-organization/self-transcending constructions, and greater potentials for emergence. An intelligence leader places a significant amount of emphasis on establishing this linkage (intelligence/consciousness management) by concentrating on the mental states of the agents (orgmindfulness, relational capacity, feeling system, coherency, mental cohesion) — (see intelligence, intelligence mindset, intelligence paradigm, intelligence/consciousness-centric, org-centric, collectiveness capacity, unifying capacity, organizing around intelligence, feeling system, relational capacity, coherency, mental cohesion, nonlinearity, connectivity, engagement, self-organizing communications, collective intelligence, orgmindfulness, mindful culture, engagement, symbiosis, intelligence/consciousness management, self-organizing capability, self-organization, self-transcending constructions, emergence, intelligence leadership and intelligent organization).

Intelligence advantage — It is the new competitive advantage/niche acquired by any human organization (corporation, social community, education institution, military unit, political system and nation) that is highly intelligence/consciousness-centric (agent-centric), organizes around intrinsic intelligence, nurtures collective intelligence, practices intelligence/consciousness management, and exploits the intelligence leadership strategy — also achieving high collectiveness capacity, adaptive capacity, relational capacity, self-organizing capacity, emergence-intelligence capacity and unifying capacity (that is a redefined VRIN). The co-existence of order and complexity, and certain spaces of high complexity (could be perceived as spaces of relativistic order) are usually explored and exploited. Holistically, it is the positive outcome (resilience and sustainability) arising from the adoption of the complexity-intelligence-centricity (intelligence advantage <=> first mover advantage). This term was used by **Michael McMaster**, in 1966 in his book *Intelligence advantage: Organizing for complexity* (see intelligence/consciousness-centric, organizing around intelligence, collective intelligence, adaptive capacity, intelligence/consciousness management, collectiveness capacity, self-organizing capacity, emergence-intelligence capacity, complexity management, first mover advantage, intelligence leadership, space of relativistic order, futurology, resilience, sustainability and complexity-intelligence strategy).

Intelligence era — This term is proposed in the intelligent organization theory to indicate the core of the information/knowledge era that places high significance on individual human intrinsic intelligence/consciousness sources, and the nurturing of collective intelligence and org-consciousness — the mindset, thinking, concepts, strategies, practices, dynamics, and structures are all highly intelligence/consciousness-centric. The key strategic entities exploited are intelligence and consciousness (awareness and mindfulness) that emerge from the intense intelligence/consciousness sources (human thinking systems). The overall strategic approach is the complexity-intelligence strategy focusing on creating intelligence advantages (see intelligence, consciousness, awareness, mindfulness, intelligence/consciousness-centric, intelligence mindset, intelligence paradigm, complexity-intelligence strategy, intelligence advantage, intelligence leadership and intelligent organization).

Intelligence governance (strategy/theory) — This strategy (a sub-strategy of the complexity-intelligence strategy) focuses on collective and lateral mass involvement of all agents (if necessary) in the organization — as many actors as possible, and towards everybody is in charge (self-powered agents and intrinsic leadership). The approach reduces direct governance, encompasses (elevating) self-organizing governance, e-governance, and better network (localized spaces) management and integration (adaptive governance and acceptance governance). Its objectives include achieving better distribution of power, increasing coherency (reducing conflicts and nurturing collective interest, and increasing consensus and collaboration), and ensuring better social relationship (higher relational parameter value) by nurturing a feeling system (high organizational justice and relational capacity), and achieving higher mental cohesion (synergetic effect and constructionist effect). Thus, the strategy is highly dependent on the characteristics of intelligent person and intelligence leadership (intelligence governance <=> intelligence leadership <=> intelligent organization), and how they are constructively exploited across the multi-layered structure (biotic macro-structure, agent-agent/system micro-structure and the two meso-structures — complexity management and network management) through better structural capacity, self-organizing capacity, emergence-intelligence capacity and unifying capacity. Fundamentally, the stability of all the agents, as well as the organization must be achieved (see agent, self-powered, intelligent person, intrinsic leadership, collective leadership, lateral leadership, intelligence leadership, self-organizing governance, network theory, network management, synergetics, organizational justice, relational capacity, feeling system, symbiosis, structural capacity, biotic macro-structure, agent-agent/system micro-structure complexity management, network management, self-transcending constructions, emergence, self-organizing capacity, emergence-intelligence capacity, unifying capacity, stability and intelligent organization).

Intelligence leadership (strategy/theory) — It is the new leadership theory and practice (a sub-strategy of the complexity-intelligence strategy) that places significant amount of emphasis on the individual intelligence and consciousness, self powered capability, intrinsic leadership, knowledge structure, learning, behavioral schemata (cognition), agent-centric, leader–agents exchanges and mental cohesion (intelligence/consciousness-centric, organizing around intelligence, autopoiesis, symbiosis, intelligence/consciousness management, social conformity and consensus, commitment and volition, self-organization/self-transcending constructions, and anticipative ability) of the interacting agents; and the collectiveness capacity, collective intelligence (orgmindfulness, intelligence-intelligence linkage, collectiveness capacity, relational capacity and feeling system — org-centric), self-organizing capacity, emergence-intelligence capacity and unifying capacity of the organization. This leadership approach encompasses sub-components such as collective leadership (involve all intrinsic leadership sources if necessary — everybody is in charge — minimal or no empowerment required), lateral leadership (horizontal approach — instead of hierarchical control, switch to orchestrating innovative collectivity and self-organization), learning leadership (learn, anticipatory and adapt), transitional leadership (situation dependent), unifying leadership (unifying capacity <=> coherency), as well as latent/ virtual leadership (a significant role of an intelligence leader — an advanced stage of intelligence leadership). As the intelligent organization theory believes that every human interacting agent is intrinsically self-powered, and endowed with intrinsic leadership ability, every intelligence/ consciousness source will be allocated individual attention (individual awareness and mindfulness, self-centricity versus org-centricity, nurturing org-awareness and orgmindfulness and high relational capacity — focusing on the mental state of each agent, quality relationships, complex networks, and feeling system). Overall, the type (or combination) of leadership to be executed is situation dependent and must be highly adaptive (adaptive capacity). Thus, the approach attempts to engage and exploit all intrinsic leadership capacity, orchestrates self-organizing communications with a 'common language', and network-centric self-organizing governance, optimizes the nurturing of collective intelligence, and steering the organization towards a new basin of attraction. Intelligence leaders are more subtle, low key, soft voice, and calm mind (Harlan Cleveland, 2002). They are also both smarter evolvers and emergent strategists. Thus, intelligence leaders focus on an integrated deliberate and emergent strategy that optimizes the exploitation of both order and complexity (resilience, sustainability, futurology and intelligence advantage) — (see intelligence/consciousness-centric, intelligence, consciousness, intelligence-intelligence linkage, human thinking system, collectiveness capacity, organizing around intelligence, behavioral schemata, stability, self-centric, agent-centric, feeling system, interdependency, engagement, symbiosis, nonlinearity, connectivity, org-centric, intelligence/consciousness management, adaptive capacity, collective intelligence, self-organization, self-transcending constructions, emergence, self-organizing capacity, emergence-intelligence capacity, unifying capacity, orgmindfulness, mindful culture, mental cohesion, self-powered, intelligence person, complexity management, network management, smart evolver, emergent strategist, basin of attraction, coherency, relational capacity, feeling system, deliberate strategy, emergent strategy, intrinsic leadership, lateral leadership, collective leadership, latent leadership, invisible hand, intelligence advantage, intelligent organization, self-organizing governance, resilience, sustainability, futurology and complexity-intelligence strategy).

Notes: A summary on types of leadership:

- **Newtonian mindset** — aristocratic leadership, authoritative/ hierarchical leadership, bureaucratic leadership, administrative leadership, and transformational leadership (empowerment).
- **Complexity mindset** — adaptive leadership and enabler leadership.
- **Intelligence mindset** — self-powered intrinsic leadership, lateral/ collective leadership, consultative leadership, learning leadership, transitional leadership, and latent leadership.
- **Some intelligence leadership attributes** — intelligence/consciousness-centric, network-centric, complexity-centric, everybody is in charge, concentrated calmness, low key and soft voice, collectiveness, ambidexterity smarter evolver and emergent strategist.

Intelligence mindset — This mindset subtly (selectively) encompasses the Newtonian mindset (order, linear, predictability) and complexity mindset (focusing on co-existence of order and complexity, the Universe and its components are more a mind rather a machine, complexity-centricity, network-centricity, nonlinearity, unpredictability, self-organizing capability, and emergent and new order), plus a special focus on all levels of intelligence/consciousness (intelligence/consciousness-centricity, individual intrinsic intelligence, collective intelligence, latent intelligence, emergence of consciousness => organizing around intelligence rather than around functions or processes, intelligence leadership and intelligence governance). With this mindset an intelligence paradigm emerges (highly intelligence/ consciousness-centric — every human organization is a collection of intense intrinsic intelligence sources — intelligence/consciousness management and agent-centricity is highly significant), and intelligence/ consciousness is perceived as the most critical asset or entity in humanity. Primarily, the thinking focuses on engaging and exploiting intrinsic individual intelligence/consciousness (intelligence-intelligence linkage), extracting/mining latent intelligence, orchestrating the right set of behavior schemata, and nurturing collective intelligence (collectiveness capacity, adaptive capacity, and org-centric) and org-consciousness to reap the best possible rewards from spaces of complexity (whenever possible). It also focuses on the unique complexity-intelligence linkage, and the 3rd order stability (mental dimension), and the value of constructive self-organization or self-transcending constructions (mental cohesion). Overall, it exploits the complexity-intelligence strategy (including the integrated deliberate and emergent strategy — maximizing the exploitation of the co-existence of order and complexity) that nurtures highly intelligent human organizations (*i*CAS) driven by highly *i*CAD (see Newtonian mindset, complexity mindset, intelligence paradigm, intelligence, consciousness, intelligence/consciousness-centric, organizing around intelligence, stability-centric, self-centric, agent-centric, feeling system, org-centric, emergence, intelligence-intelligence linkage, collective intelligence, org-consciousness, collectiveness capacity, adaptive capacity, unifying capacity, intelligence/consciousness management, complexity management, complexity-intelligence linkage, complexity-intelligence strategy, deliberate strategy, emergent strategy, intelligence leadership, intelligence, governance, mental cohesion, intelligent organization, law of complexity/consciousness, law of complexity/intelligence, law of consciousness/intelligence, synergetics, constructionist hypothesis, relativistic complexity, *i*CAS, *i*CAD and intelligent organization theory).

Notes: A summary on intelligence mindset and some of its implications:

- **Intelligence mindset** => intelligence paradigm => stability-centricity => intelligence/consciousness-centricity => agent-centricity => intelligence/consciousness management => organizing around intelligence => intelligence-intelligence linkage => collective intelligence => org-awareness and orgmindfulness => network-centricity and org-centricity => complexity-centricity => relativistic complexity => smarter evolver and emergent strategist => intelligence leadership => intelligence governance => high leadership capacity, collectiveness capacity, adaptive capacity, self-organizing capacity, emergence-intelligence capacity, relational capacity and unifying capacity => coherency and synergy => constructionist effect => organizational mental cohesion => intelligent organization.

Intelligence paradigm — The intelligence paradigm that emerges from the intelligence mindset is the new strategic path/approach (highly intelligence/consciousness-centric) that focuses primarily on optimizing the individual intelligence/consciousness of the interacting agents (agent-centric), and elevating the collective intelligence, org-awareness, and orgmindfulness of the organization (collectiveness capacity, adaptive capacity and relational capacity — org-centric). It exploits thinking, concepts, and practices linked to intelligence/consciousness management, intelligence leadership, and intelligence governance. Consequently, primary functions such as organizing around intelligence (instead of around functions or processes), nurturing intelligent biotic macro-structure, exploiting an integrated deliberate and emergent strategy, and other intelligence-related activities are vital (self-powered agents, agent-centric, network-centric, org-centric and feeling system) — (see paradigm, intelligence, consciousness, intelligence/consciousness-centric, biotic macro-structure, collective intelligence, intelligence mindset, stability-centric, agent-centric, network-centric, org-centric, organizing around intelligence, intelligence leadership, intelligence governance, intelligence/consciousness management, complexity management, network management, deliberate strategy, emergent strategy, feeling system, intelligent organization and emergence).

Intelligence spectrum — On this planet Earth (Gaia), intelligence is perceived to exist as a spectrum with proto-intelligence (associated with the non-living atomic/matter world — physical stability) at one end to global human collective intelligence at the other end — not easily achievable (the human race is perceived as the most intelligent species on this planet but its collectiveness or global intelligence is still relatively low). Inbetween there are different types/levels of intelligence. Between the non-living world and living world is the 1st edge of consciousness. Awareness emerges from basic life-intelligence. Between humanity and the other animal species is the 2nd edge of consciousness where the presence mindfulness is dominantly observed — emerges from basic human intelligence (physical, biological, and mental stability). Hence, overall, intelligence is stability-centric and 'self-centric' (see intelligence mindset, global mindset, proto-intelligence, basic life-intelligence, intelligence, consciousness, awareness, mindfulness, human agent, intelligence person, intelligence/consciousness-centric, collective intelligence, stability-centric, self-centric, law of complexity/consciousness, law of complexity/intelligence, law of consciousness/intelligence and Gaia).

Notes: Spread in the intelligence/consciousness spectrum:

- **1ˢᵗ edge of consciousness:** before — **proto-intelligence** (atomic/physical/matter world; no consciousness, physical stability); after — **basic life-intelligence/consciousness** (basic awareness, living/biological world, and physical and biological stability).
- **2ⁿᵈ edge of consciousness:** before — **basic life-intelligence** (more intense awareness, more intelligent animal species); after — **basic and advanced human intelligence/consciousness** (intense awareness and self-awareness, emergent of mindfulness, creation of the characters set, language, abstract concepts and perceptions, redefined engagement; and 3ʳᵈ order stability — physical, biological and mental stability).

Intelligent organization/system (IO) — A human organization is a collection of intense intelligence/consciousness sources, and an intelligent organization (IO <=> *i*CAS <=> *r*CAS) is highly intelligence/consciousness-centric, complexity-centric, and network-centric (agents are intelligent persons, high org-awareness and orgmindfulness), and balancing between agent-centricity, network-centricity and org-centricity (ambidexterity). Thus, an intelligent human organization is a unique *i*CAS. Nurturing a highly intelligent organization is the primary aim of the intelligent organization theory. It is a human organization with an intelligent biotic macro-structure (biotic system) that engulfs an orgmind, an intangible and intelligence web, an environment sensing and responding subsystem, and a physical structure. Such an organization learns, anticipates, adapts, mindful/orgmindful, and evolves like an intelligent 'biological being' — constantly elevating its structural capacity, collectiveness capacity, adaptive capacity, collective intelligence, organizational consciousness, self-organizing capacity, emergence-intelligence capacity, relational capacity, feeling system, unifying capacity, coherency, synergy, constructionist effect, mental cohesion and 3rd order stability (stability-centric) — intelligence advantage. Thus, an intelligent organization is highly competitive and innovation, constantly focusing on certain spaces of complexity (a relativistic complex adaptive system, *r*CAS). With the presence of high individual intelligence (interacting agents possessing intelligent person attributes) and collective intelligence, the dynamic involved balances between autopoiesis and self-organization or self-transcending constructions — a highly *i*CAD 'orchestrated' by the appropriate intelligence/consciousness management, complexity management, network management and self-organizing governance (encompassing self-organizing communications, self-organizing networks, synergetics/coherency), and the intelligence leadership strategy — leading to the emergent of new order when needed. In the intelligent organization theory, the co-existence of order and complexity is effectively exploited, abundant resources are channeled into certain spaces of complexity, and preparation for punctuation points is continuous. Thus, a highly intelligent human organization (*i*CAS <=> *r*CAS) complexity is relativistic and, it is driven by highly intelligent relativistic adaptive dynamic (*i*CAD <=> *r*CAD) — achieving high resilience and sustainability (see intelligent organization theory, intelligence mindset, intelligence paradigm, *i*CAS, *i*CAD, order, complexity, space of complexity, punctuation point, agent, self-centric, stability-centric, agent-centric, org-centric, nonlinearity, connectivity, engagement, intelligence/consciousness-centric, complexity-centric, network theory, dimensionality, systems spectrum, intelligence-intelligence linkage, collective intelligence, org-consciousness, complexity-intelligence linkage, intelligent person, autopoiesis, biotic macro-structure, biotic system, anticipatory system, adaptive capacity, collectiveness capacity, mindful, orgmindful, relational capacity, feeling system, coherency, synergetics, constructionist hypothesis, mental cohesion, symbiosis, principle of locality, interdependency, self-organizing capacity, emergence-intelligence capacity, self-organization, self-transcending constructions, complex adaptive networks, self-organizing governance, self-organizing communications, collective intelligence, self-powered, emergence, intelligence/consciousness management, complexity management, network management, organizational justice, intelligence leadership, futurology, intelligence advantage, resilience, sustainability, complexity approaches and relativistic complexity).

Intelligent organization (IO) theory — This is an intelligence/consciousness-centric (relativistic) complexity theory of human organizations (conceived by **T.Y. Liang** in 2001). Fundamentally, the theory (encompassing complexity theory and network theory) perceives a human organization as a collection of human intelligence/consciousness sources (human thinking systems — the most vital assets), concentrates on how every intense intelligence/consciousness source can be strategically connected and utilized irrespective of the nature of the organization (education institution, corporation, military unit, stock market, city, and nation). Thus, besides the five core properties of CAS (consciousness, complexity, connectivity, dissipation and emergence) it has a sixth core property — intelligence (individual intelligence, collective intelligence, latent intelligence). The approach can be employed by any human organizations (focusing on the new intelligence/consciousness-centric mindset, paradigm, structure, dynamics, culture, philosophy, leadership, governance, management, advantage, resilience and sustainability), irrespective of their organizational goals. It emphasizes the concept of organizing around intelligence as a new paradigm [around all intense intelligence/consciousness sources — human agents (intelligent persons) with self-powered and intrinsic leadership capabilities that constitute the spontaneous self-organizing system, covering S(1) to S(4)]. This paradigmatic shift focuses on the exploitation of attributes such as individual intelligence, consciousness, awareness, mindfulness, stability-centric, self-centric, intelligence-intelligence linkage, org-awareness, orgmindfulness, mindful culture, latent intelligence, collective intelligence, complexity-intelligence linkage, quality connectivity and engagement, structural capacity, collectiveness capacity, adaptive capacity, organizational learning, organizational knowledge structure, relational capacity, feeling system, autopoiesis, interdependency, symbiosis, anticipative, intelligence/consciousness management, complexity management, network management, self-organization, self-transcending constructions, emergence, self-organizing capacity, emergence-intelligence capacity, butterfly effect, intelligence leadership, intelligence governance, coherency, synergy, mental cohesion, constructionist effect and other complexity-intelligence-associated entities/properties (that is, basically complexity must be recognized, explored and creatively exploited). This theory also indicates that complexity in the human world is relativistic (*i*CAS <=> *r*CAS, and *i*CAD <=> *r*CAD) because of the existence of the intense mental dimension (3rd order stability — high nonlinear mental capacity — relative complexity) in human agents — complexity is in the mind of the beholder (constantly attempting to establish and exploit relativistic static equilibrium — relativistic, its seventh core properties of intelligent human organizations). The overall strategy conceived and adopted is the complexity-intelligence strategy that possesses several sub-components (including intelligent biotic macro-structure model, human agent-agent/ system micro-structure and dynamics, organizing around intelligence, integrated deliberate and emergent strategy, integrated 3C-OK framework, intelligent person model, self-powered self-organizing governance strategy — intelligence governance strategy, intelligence leadership strategy and relativistic complexity). The new advantage achieved is the intelligence advantage — achieving higher resilience and sustainability through intense intelligence/consciousness-centricity [see intelligence mindset, intelligence paradigm, intelligence, consciousness, intelligence/ consciousness-centric, intelligence-intelligence linkage, structural capacity, collectiveness capacity, adaptive capacity, relational capacity, self-organizing capacity, emergence-intelligence capacity, unifying capacity, organizing around intelligence, complexity-intelligence linkage, *i*CAS, *i*CAD, agent, self-powered, self-centric, stability-centric, stability, non-linearity, connectivity, engagement, symbiosis, org-centric, collective intelligence, orgmindfulness, mindful culture, feeling system, human rationality, intrinsic leadership, intelligent person, intelligence advantage, governance system, complex adaptive networks, network theory, organizational justice, resilience, sustainability, deliberate strategy, emergent strategy, anticipatory system, intelligence/consciousness management, complexity management, network management, self-organization, self-transcending constructions, self-organizing governance, intelligence leadership, intelligence governance, law of complexity/consciousness, law of complexity/intelligence, law of consciousness/intelligence, coherency, synergetics, broken symmetry, interdependency, constructionist hypothesis, complexity approaches, edge of emergence, S(1)-S(4), complexity-intelligence strategy, intelligent organization, space of relativistic order and relativistic complexity].

Notes: The eight core properties of the intelligent organization theory:

- **Intelligence** (Intelligence-centric)
- **Consciousness** (Life-centric)
- **Complexity** (In-deterministic and unpredictability, complexity-centric)
- **Connectivity** (Network-centric, relational-centric)
- **Dissipative** (Self-renewal)
- **Stability** (Agent-centric, network-centric, org-centric)
- **Relativistic** (Mental-centric, third order stability)
- **Emergence** (Autopoietic, autocatalysis, self-organizing, self-transcending constructions, evolution and co-evolution)

Intelligent person (model) — This model (a sub-model of the complexity-intelligence strategy) emerges from the economic man model (total rationality/optimality) of **Adam Smith** (1723–1790), and the administrative man model (bounded rationality, satisficing principle and satisficing solution) of **Herbert Simon** (1916–2001). An intelligent person (an intense intelligence/consciousness source, a sharp information decoder) in the intelligent person model (conceived by **T.Y. Liang** in 2004) is a self-powered human interacting agent that is also an intrinsic leader, a smarter evolver and an emergent strategist — highly intelligence/consciousness-centric, complexity-centric, network-centric, and aware of the fluctuating rugged landscape, difficulties of the red queen race, the inherent strengths of human agents, the prominent constraints of human organizations, and futuristic. Such a person is highly mindful (self-centric, stability-centric) and orgmindful (intelligence-intelligence linkage, org-centric), accepts short-term losses for longer-term gains, exploits the integrated deliberate and emergent strategy (complexity management, network management, intelligence/consciousness management, and anticipative), recognizes the values and significant of constructive self-organization or self-transcending constructions (self-organizing governance), feeling system, and other complexity associated properties — including the benefits of recognizing and exploiting spaces of relativistic order; relativistic complexity. Such a person (embedded with a set of highly nonlinear intelligent behavior schemata) is an effective participant in an *i*CAS that helps to drive a constructive *i*CAD, and seeks best possible solutions adapting/anticipating with the continuous changing conditions (making preparation for sudden appearance of punctuation points) — an ideal set of human agent attributes. It is vital that current and future leaders, managers, and even ordinary interacting agents/actors are intelligent persons (a collection of intelligent persons <=> an intelligent human organization). A highly intelligent person is also an ideal candidate for latent leadership (see intelligence/consciousness-centric, intelligence, consciousness, economic man, administrative man, satisficing principle, stability-centric, self-powered, nonlinearity, org-centric, information decoder, smart evolver, emergent strategist, futurology, collectiveness capacity, self-organization, self-transcending constructions, self-organizing governance, network theory, network management, synergetics, rugged landscape, anticipatory system, feeling system, complexity management, intelligence/consciousness management, punctuation point, relativistic complexity, human organization, dimensionality, global optimality, intelligence leadership, intrinsic leadership, latent leadership, resilience, sustainability, futurology, *i*CAS, *i*CAD and complexity-intelligence strategy).

Interdependency — Similar to interconnectivity, interdependency is a key characteristic of all CS/CAS (interdependency versus independency/ autonomous). The human interacting agents, as well as many properties/ variables of human organizations are highly interdependent, especially with the introduction of social/mobile media (higher interdependency <=> higher complexity). In this respect, a CS/CAS/IO cannot be analyzed using hierarchical decomposition (reductionist hypothesis). Instead, the system has to be analyzed as a whole — holism. In human organizations, all human agents are mutually dependent on one or more other agents (socially, economically, ecologically and/or emotionally), forming interdependent networks. In this world of high complexity, many entities/ characteristics/components/phenomena are highly interrelated, and affect one another significantly (for instance, as stipulated in the 3C-OK framework). Similarly, CAS that affect and influence one another are also interdependent — for instance, environmental sustainability is dependent on the high interdependency of the economic, social and the environmental system. (In genetic algorithms, agents become interdependent when they interact and exchange knowledge/resources with one another. Similarly, with globalization nations also become more interdependent in this manner.) Interdependency plays a critical role in the emergence of order. For instance, a group of interdependent agents forms a basin of attraction that facilitates self-organization/self-transcending constructions leading to the emergent of order. Thus, it is one of the key characteristics that make CAS different from linear and orderly systems (OS) (see autonomous, complexity mindset, complexity, Cartesian belief, hierarchical decomposition, reductionist hypothesis, holism, complexity approaches, nonlinearity, connectivity, complex adaptive systems, network theory, network management, complex adaptive network, collectiveness capacity, self-organization, self-transcending constructions, genetic algorithm, emergence and sustainability revolution).

Internalization — It is the consumption of a piece of information by the human thinking system (not quite notice by most people). Conscientious effort over a period of time has to be made to consume a piece of information (into permanent memory). When internalization occurs, the knowledge structure (formation of tacit knowledge) in the brain will be extended and/or altered, and the subsequent decision made may also be different. In this respect, with quality knowledge structure the value of a new piece of information could be different (higher) (see human thinking system, externalization, knowledge structure, adaptive capacity and behavioral schemata).

Intrinsic leadership (capacity) — In the intelligence leadership model (**T.Y. Liang**, 2007) it is believed that every human being (highly intelligent interacting agent — with intelligent person attributes) is naturally self-powered and endowed with a certain level of leadership ability (which may be suppressed due to the environmental condition) — intrinsic leadership. The intelligence leadership strategy which focuses on collective and lateral leadership attempts to optimize and integrate every self-powered intrinsic leadership source whenever possible — that is, every interacting agent as a natural leader that must be exploited. Thus, an effective collective/lateral leader is one that managed to optimize a large collection of intrinsic leadership sources — intelligence/consciousness management, self-organizing governance, and everybody is in change.

This ability is highly significant for nurturing collective intelligence, orchestrating constructive self-organization/self-transcending constructions, and the entire *i*CAD (see intelligent person, lateral leadership, collective leadership, latent leadership, self-organizing governance, intelligence leadership, self-powered, intelligence/consciousness management, collective intelligence, self-organization, self-transcending constructions and *i*CAD).

Invisible hand — The invisible hand phenomenon/effect (unintended benefits resulting from individual actions) was introduced by **Adam Smith** (1723–1790) in the mid 18th century (*The Wealth of Nations*, in 1776), is nonlinear and may be unpredictable. In the intelligent organization theory, the invisible hand is perceived to possess certain characteristics similar to CAD — the action of an agent may introduce localized and (unintended) global effect (1st degree self-organization, localized space, network, intra-system order, 2nd degree self-organization, inter-system order). In this respect, the market dynamic is facilitated by the 'invisible hand' that emerges from the integrated (nonlinear/emotional) intrinsic intelligence/consciousness sources that form it (invisible hand <=> collective intelligence) — an intelligence-driven self-transcending constructions dynamic (see economic man, nonlinearity, complexity, complex adaptive dynamic, intelligence leadership, unpredictability, self-organization, self-transcending constructions, localized order, network theory, collective intelligence, S(1)-S(4), and emergence).

Knowledge structure — This is a large collection of information with established relationships that is stored in the brain (more tacit — implicit knowledge structure). The quality, sophistication, depth, nonlinearity, and innovativeness of a knowledge structure are positively correlated to the thinking and depth of the intelligence/consciousness source (human's knowledge is inherently subjective). The large numbers of pieces of information are internalized over a 'considerable' period of time, and conscientious effort is needed. A high quality knowledge structure (with linkages to other knowledge structures) is essential for anyone to achieve the status of an expert in a particular domain. Subsequently, the value of a piece of information consumed is dependent on the quality of the knowledge structure it interacts with. In cybernetics, knowledge is intrinsically subjective (very often human knowledge is a 'subjective construction' and not an objective reflection of reality — construal theory). With a written language the information/knowledge in the knowledge structure can be externalized and stored in knowledge depositories (explicit, the 'knowledge structure' of human organizations, also associated with their collective intelligence) — (see internalization, externalization, intelligence, adaptive capacity, human thinking system, individual intelligence enhancer, collective intelligence and corporate intelligence enhancer).

Laplace belief — It is the belief (**Pierre Simon Laplace**, 1749–1827) that the entire characteristics of a dynamical system can be fully express or capture by one (or a set) mathematical equation(s). In **Lagrangian mechanics** [first conceptualized by **Joseph Louis Lagrange** (1736–1813) in 1788], the lagrangian of the many classical systems is a function that summarizes the dynamics of the system. This mathematical concept is a highly orderly and linear thinking approach that has been very useful in the exact sciences (assuming that the phase space is complete). It has been extended to **Hamiltonian mechanics** by **William Rowan Hamilton** (1805–1865) in 1833 — (could be used in Newtonian mechanics and gravity, electromagnetism, general relativity, and quantum field theory — in field theory, another quantity lagrangian density exists which is the integral of the lagrangian function over all space-time). Subsequently, other human-related disciplines, including economics, social sciences, finance and political science have also adopted this mathematical modeling approach. Overall, this belief is also closely linked to the Newtonian mindset. However, human organizations with unknown unknowns (high finite dimension and in-complete phase space) cannot be captured completely as a mathematical model (at best an estimation) (see Cartesian belief, Newton mindset, order, linearity, predictability, dimensionality, complexity mindset, intelligence mindset, phase space and intelligent organization theory).

Latent leadership — A latent leader (someone with high leadership capacity) is a highly intelligent leader that often attempts to orchestrate a 'desired' dynamic or goal with great subtlety — highly lateral and collective — and it is a unique key component/characteristic of the intelligence leadership strategy. Such a leader may have a certain foresight and a goal that s/he hopes to achieve (futuristic). The approach adopted is 'latent' to the extent that the rest of the interacting agents do not know that the strategy/plan was actually orchestrated by the latent leader even after the goal has been achieved. In this process, the self-powered and intrinsic leadership abilities of the interacting agents are naturally exploited. The collective intelligence and adaptive capacity of the group involved are also very high leading to constructive self-organization/self-transcending constructions, and emergent of new order. Consequently, they think that their achievement is self-initiated — leading to higher commitment, collaboration, pride and self-satisfaction (stimulates lives in hidden ways). The origin of this leadership style could be backdated to **Lao Tzu** (a contemporary/senior of **Confucius**). In the intelligence leadership strategy it is perceived as the highest form of leadership — with intense intelligence/consciousness centricity (high lateral/collectiveness, relational capacity, agent-centricity, network-centricity, self-organizing governance, collectiveness capacity, adaptive capacity, self-organizing capacity and emergence-intelligence capacity) — (see intelligence leadership, intelligence/consciousness-centric, intelligence-intelligence linkage, leadership capacity, self-powered, connectivity, engagement, agent-centric, complex adaptive network, collectiveness capacity, collective intelligence, intrinsic leadership, self-powered, relational capacity, feeling system, adaptive capacity, self-organizing governance, collective leadership, lateral leadership, self-organizing capacity, emergence-intelligence capacity, unifying capacity, self-organization, self-transcending constructions, futurology and emergence).

Lateral leadership — This leadership style (horizontal and integrative — enhances everybody is in charge) spreads out the roles and responsibilities of leadership, and helps to elevate/enhance the collectiveness capacity, collective intelligence, unifying capacity and leadership capacity of the group/network or organization. A lateral leader focuses on the self-powered abilities and intrinsic leadership of every interacting agent (intense intelligence-intelligence linkages). This approach is significant and inevitable when the interacting agents are highly knowledgeable or experts of their respective domains — a more consultative approach is essential. Such a situation is becoming more common in the highly developed human world (organizations, communities and nations) — which are embedded with more prominent intrinsic self-powered leadership sources that demand sharing and respect — self-organizing governance and collective leadership. A characteristic of this leadership style is low key, soft voice and calm mind — greatly increase the organizational adaptive capacity, collectiveness capacity, self-organizing capacity, emergence-intelligence capacity and leadership capacity (see agent, self-powered, intrinsic leadership, connectivity, engagement, collectiveness capacity, leadership capacity, intelligence/consciousness-centric, intelligence-intelligence linkage, collective intelligence, adaptive capacity, self-organizing governance, collective leadership, self-organizing capacity, emergence-intelligence capacity and intelligence leadership).

Law of complexity/consciousness — This law (proposed by **Pierre Teilhard de Chardin**, 1881–1955) indicates that there is a tendency for matter to increase inherently in complexity and consciousness over time concurrently. Teilhard (and Liang in the intelligent organization theory) stipulates that matter 'complexified' from physical matter (physical world, proto-intelligence, and no consciousness), to plant-life and animal-life (biological world, basic life-intelligence, consciousness and swarm intelligence), to human-life (humanity, human intense intelligence, human consciousness, awareness, mindfulness, collective intelligence, org-consciousness, org-awareness and orgmindfulness). In the biological world and humanity, the space of awareness and its intensity also depends on the ability of the sensory system of the biological organisms. In humanity, awareness is also associated and elevated with certain technological advancement for instance, introduction of a world that is beyond electromagnetic scanning.) In addition, this law also supports the chaos theory indicating that the Universe is more a cosmic mind rather than a machine (the presence of consciousness). The intelligent organization theory stipulates that fundamentally the entire physical and biological world (including humanity) is formed by different levels of intelligence (intelligence spectrum) due to stability-centricity (opposing the universal expansion), elevating complexity and robustness, but consciousness only emerges in the world of life (see law of complexity/intelligence, law of consciousness/intelligence, intelligent organization theory, complexity, intelligence, consciousness, proto-intelligence, basic life-intelligence, swarm intelligence, intelligence spectrum, awareness, mindfulness, orgmindfulness, collective intelligence, chaos, Universe and intelligence spectrum).

Law of complexity/intelligence — The intelligent organization theory (**T.Y. Liang**, 2001) and relativistic complexity (**T.Y. Liang**, 2013) indicates that the relationship between complexity and intelligence (complexity-intelligence linkage) is in general inversely proportional — as intelligence increases complexity (relativistic) reduces. The complexity-intelligence strategy works on this principle too. One of its sub-strategies, the integrated deliberate and emergent strategy exploits the co-existence of order and complexity. Intense (individual and collective) intelligence (also associated with innovation and creativity) is utilized to explore and exploit in certain spaces of complexity. If successful, the latter will be transformed into spaces of relativistic order where surface patterns become (more) apparent (better risk management). Concurrently, intense intelligence is also invested in better crisis management (sudden surfacing of punctuation points) (see law of complexity/consciousness, law of consciousness/intelligence, intelligent organization theory, complexity-intelligence linkage, order, complexity, intelligence, intelligence spectrum, consciousness, awareness, mindfulness, complexity-intelligence strategy, deliberate strategy, emergent strategy, space of complexity, punctuation point, space of relativistic order and relativistic complexity).

Law of consciousness/intelligence — Consciousness executes two mental functions, namely external focusing function (awareness), and internal focusing functions (self-awareness, mindfulness). The law of complexity/consciousness stipulates that the increase in awareness increases complexity. The intelligence organization theory indicates that the increase in intelligence, mindfulness, collective intelligence and orgmindfulness (mindfulness and orgmindfulness are internal focusing) reduces complexity (relativistic complexity theory — complexity is in the mind of the beholder). The internal focusing functions directly or indirectly enhances intelligence and collective intelligence ('releasing' latent intelligence), and elevates self-organizing capacity which is also the key impetus of the emergent strategy. Thus, the integrative dynamic is rather nonlinear (see law of complexity/consciousness, law of complexity/intelligence, intelligent organization theory, complexity, intelligence, collective intelligence, latent intelligence, intelligence spectrum, consciousness, awareness, mindfulness, orgmndfulness, complexity-intelligence strategy, space of complexity, and space of relativistic order, relativistic complexity, self-organizing capacity and emergent strategy).

Law of requisite variety — [**Ross Ashby** (1903–1972) in 1956: *An Introduction to Cybernetics*] — This law of systemic complexity states that the greater the variety of perturbations, the greater the variety of compensating actions, and the greater the knowledge and intelligence needed — 'only variety can destroy variety'. In this case, variety (denotes the total number of distinct states in the system) can also be interpreted as the degrees of freedom of the system. This law is also linked to feedback, circular causation, circular coupling and cascading effect. To exploit this law effectively a three-step approach has been introduced: (i) uncover the contextual constraints, (ii) the degrees of freedom of an organization must match the degrees of freedom of the environment, (iii) normally the organization's degrees of freedom has to exceed that of the environment as some of its degrees of freedom may be not relevant — leading to Allen's law of excess variety, (**Peter Allen** (1944–present) in 2001 — (see complexity mindset, complexity, cybernetics, dimensionality, phase space, feedback, cascading effect and circular causation).

Leadership capacity — This is a conceptual attribute that is associated with the effectiveness of leadership (stability-inducing capability, effective enabler, smart evolver, emergent strategist, futurist and unifying capacity). In the intelligence leadership theory/strategy, intelligence leadership is closely linked to nurturing high leadership capacity with a certain key focus — high intelligence/consciousness-centricity. Thus, it is vital to recognize and exploit characteristics and dynamics of the intelligence leadership that include optimizing self-powered intrinsic leadership of all agents (intelligent person attributes) with orgmindfulness (mindful culture, intelligence-intelligence linkage) and truthful engagement resulting in more leaders/actors — mass participation. In this respect, it is beneficial to selectively exploit a different combination of leaderships (collective leadership, lateral leadership, learning leadership, transitional leadership, and latent leadership) that is situation-time dependent. Overall, a high leadership capacity is directly or indirectly associated with stability-centricity (at all levels), structural capacity, adaptive capacity, collectiveness capacity, relational capacity, self-organizing capacity, emergence-intelligence capacity and unifying capacity of the organization. Its quality is also associated with achieving coherency, synergy and constructionist effect (see intrinsic leadership, collective intelligence, orgmindfulness, mindful culture, self-powered capacity, intelligent person, symbiosis, intelligence leadership, collective leadership, lateral leadership, learning leadership, latent leadership, intelligent human organization, stability-centric, structural capacity, adaptive capacity, collectiveness capacity, relational capacity, self-organizing capacity, emergence-intelligence capacity, unifying capacity, coherency, synergetics, constructionist hypothesis and futurology).

Learning leadership — In the current fast changing world, leaders have to learn, anticipate, and adapt continuously — ideally faster and more in-depth (new knowledge creation) than the other interacting agents/actors, as well as competitors. They must possess high adaptive capacity, have to be situation dependent, and constantly adjust their leadership approach accordingly — high leadership capacity. In this case, intrinsic leadership, collective leadership, lateral leadership, transitional leadership, unifying leadership, and latent leadership attributes can all be exploited selectively depending on the situation. Thus, an intelligence leadership is always an adaptive learning leader — (constantly learning => adaptive => change), whenever necessary (also nurturing a learning organization concurrently) — (see intelligence/consciousness-centric, adaptive, adaptive capacity, evolution, connectivity, self-powered, leadership capacity, intrinsic leadership, collective leadership, lateral leadership, latent leadership, intelligence leadership, organizational learning and sustainability).

Linearity — It is the proportionate relationship between cause and effect (small input small output; and large input large output). Linear systems are modular, orderly, predictable, and they can be examined using hierarchical decomposition. (Mathematically, it is represented by the simple equation $y = ax + b$, a straight line in two dimensions and degree of variables is 1). In addition, linear systems obey the superposition principle, where the output is simply the sum of the inputs (see order, ordered systems, nonlinearity, deterministic, predictability and butterfly effect).

Localized order/space — Every interacting agent is self-centric and stability-centric trying to achieve localized order (1st degree localized order) at all time (inward focusing, autopoiesis, self-organization or self-transcending constructions). This is true for all agents/entities from atoms to human beings. For instance, a biological organism (from single cell to trillion cells) that learns, adapts and evolves is a localized order created by basic life-intelligence that drives the autopoietic and stability-centric dynamic. Hence, each of these agents is a space of localized order that defies the universal main stream expansion (big bang theory). Subsequently, 2nd degree localized order emerged — such as self-organizing network (a wider or more intense interacting space, network, or complex network). Thus, the physical matter world and living world in this Universe exist because of stability-centricity and localized order (extropy, increasing robustness, and opposes universal expansion). For the same reason no entity/system/structure exists permanently — the latter that is composed will one day decompose [see order, autopoiesis, self-centric, principle of locality, stability-centric, symbiosis, self-organization, self-transcending constructions, extropy, dissipative structure, network theory, self-organizing network, complex network, S(1)-S(4), second law of thermodynamics and emergence].

Logistic map — A simple, one-dimensional, discrete DCS popularized by **Robert May** (1936–present). It is represented by the deterministic (nonlinear difference equation — the equation is highly nonlinear for certain values of r) equation $x_{n+1} = rx_n(1-x_n)$, where x_n takes value between 0 and 1 is the ratio of the existing population and the maximum population at year n, and r (rate of growth) is a positive number (bifurcation parameter) that when iterated (with recurrence relations) displays deterministic chaos due to bifurcation — commonly used for studying species that breed once a year. In the logistic (unimodal — one hump) map, between $r_1 \approx 3.0$ (period 2) to $r_\infty \approx 3.57$ (period ∞) — onset of chaos, and the rate at which distance between bifurcations is shrinking is $\lim_{(n \to \infty)}$ $(r_{n+1} - r_n)/(r_{n+2} - r_{n+1}) \approx 4.67$ times faster than the previous one. The latter value (4.67) is the first Feigenbaum's constant [a universal constant, **Mitchell Feigenbaum**, (1944–present)] for all unimodal map. The bifurcation characteristic is more commonly and clearly illustrated using the bifurcation diagram — x_n is on the vertical-axis and r is on the horizontal-axis (the logistic function was first studied and introduced by **Pierre Francois Verhulst**, 1804–1849). Thus, the logistic map is a simple system that can be chaotic everywhere (in many systems the chaotic behavior is confined to a certain subset in the phase space) — (see chaos, chaotic system, nonlinearity, dimensionality, bifurcation, recurrence relations, feedback, fractal dimension, chaotic attractor, strange attractor and phase space).

Lorenz attractor — The Lorenz attractor is a set of chaotic solutions/states of the Lorenz weather system (**Edward Lorenz**, 1917–2008). The most well-known strange attractor (phase space trajectory — also a chaotic attractor), a three-dimension attractor is derived from Lorenz's simplified rolling fluid convection model (continuous-time), is a set of three differential equations with a total of seven variables on the right hand side, five of which are linear, and the other two are quadratic (nonlinear). It is a continuous line that looks like an infinite summation of ∞ confined within a restricted space, in a three-dimensional space (see Appendix 3). All chaotic attractors are sensitive dependence on initial conditions (butterfly effect) — (see attractor, phase space, chaotic attractor, strange attractor, phase space and butterfly effect).

Malthusian catastrophe — It is a phenomenon proposed by **Thomas Malthus** (1766–1834) that an organization, nation or humanity will return to subsistence level once the population growth exceeded agricultural production. In the middle of the 20th century, with the development of the Green Revolution (mechanized agriculture), population growth (in developed countries) outpaced productivity gains. However, subsequently, the demographic-economic paradox emerges (highly self-centric and nonlinear) — (autopoiesis, order, nonlinearity, complexity, stability-centric, self-centric and self-organization).

Mandelbrot set — The Mandelbrot set is a fractal. In 1982, **Benoit Mandelbrot** (1924–2010) worked on fractal geometry and discovered scalability — fractal is scale free (self-similarity) — (scalability = scale free, while they are a sub-set of self-similarity). The Mandelbrot set is created by the formula of z iterates to $z^2 + c$, where c is a complex number — which can be iterated infinite number of times. The diagram of the set is an amazing and organic looking picture — an image with high complexity generated from the relatively simple equation (see fractal, fractal dimension, scalability, self-similarity and power law).

Mental cohesion — It is a fundamental goal of the intelligence leadership to achieve mental cohesion in the organization. Mental cohesion (the highest form of coherency and synergy in humanity and human organizations) is closely associated with certain attributes including, intense orgmindfulness (presence of a mindful culture), constructive intelligence-intelligence linkages, high collective intelligence and org-consciousness, and positive relational parameter value (orgmindfulness <=> intelligence-intelligence linkages => mental cohesion). In this respect, mental cohesion is also linked to organizational coherency and synergetic potential (unifying capacity). However, the relationship between mental cohesion and functional cohesion is nonlinear, and may not be positively correlated. For instance, a group of agents can 'agree to disagree'. In this case, there is mental cohesion but not functional cohesion. On the other hand, when agents with cultural diversification interact harmoniously, there is functional cohesion and not (total) mental cohesion. In this respect, mental cohesion can be present even when there are other existing diversifications and disparities (physical, social or cultural diversification). In general, mental cohesion is more closely linked to organizational 'peacefulness', consensus, collaboration and integration (see orgmindfulness, mindful culture, mindful system, collective intelligence, intelligence-intelligence linkage, agent-centric, coherency, synergetics, organizing around intelligence, organizational justice, relational capacity, unifying capacity, intelligence advantage and intelligent organization).

Mindful culture — It is the core of the supportive culture — introduced in the intelligent organization theory (**T.Y. Liang**, 2001) to indicate the intense usage of mindfulness in human agents in intelligent organizations. Mindful organizations exhibit orgmindfulness (intense intelligence-intelligence linkages) — an inward focusing function — usually activated by the intelligence leadership possessing the intelligent person attributes. Orgmindfulness and mindful culture are key characteristics of intelligent human organizations that is crucial for nurturing high collective intelligence. Orgmindfulness focuses on the mental state of all interacting agents within the organization (corporation, community and nation) — a highly significant starting point for better interconnectivity, communications, and engagement, and nurturing/enhancing collective intelligence, org-consciousness — achieving coherency and mental cohesion. This characteristic (function) is absent in most organizations today. Currently, most organizations (especially, business corporations) possess high org-awareness (outward focusing) which concentrates on the entities (such as customers and competitors) outside the organization, as well as the changes in environmental factors. The presence of a mindful culture is greatly essential for an organization to elevate its adaptive capacity, collectiveness capacity, adaptive capacity, relational capacity, self-organizing capacity, emergence-intelligence capacity, unifying capacity, and self-organizing governance capability, by activating the self-powered intrinsic leadership sources more deeply — towards the nurturing of an *i*CAS (feeling system — better mental cohesion). In this respect, orgmindfulness is a crucial characteristic that the new leadership must exhibit (orgmindfulness <=> intelligence-intelligence linkage <=> mindful culture <=> collective intelligence and org-consciousness <=> intelligence leadership) — (see intelligence, consciousness, intelligence/consciousness-centric, mindfulness, orgmindfulness, awareness, organizing around intelligence, self-powered, intelligence-intelligence linkage, coherency, mental cohesion, law of complexity/consciousness, law of complexity/intelligence, law of consciousness/intelligence, nonlinearity, complexity, connectivity, intelligence-intelligence linkage, adaptive capacity, collectiveness capacity, collective intelligence, relational capacity, self-organizing capacity, emergence-intelligence capacity, unifying capacity, feeling system, engagement, interdependency, self-organizing governance, intrinsic leadership, intelligence leadership, stability, emergence and *i*CAS).

Mindful system/organization — It is a human organization (confined only to humanity) that is orgmindful, that is, it is mindful of the mental state of all its interacting agents (highly intelligence/consciousness-centric, and establishes quality intelligence-intelligence linkages). The process helps to elevate better connectivity and engagement, commitment, and expedite the nurturing of higher level collective intelligence (towards better mental cohesion). A mindful system nurtures a mindful culture which is the core of the supportive culture, and facilitates more constructive network connectivity, self-organization, self-transcending constructions and emergence spontaneously (see intelligence/consciousness-centric, connectivity, engagement, collectiveness capacity, mindfulness, orgmindfulness, mindful culture, intelligence-intelligence linkage, collective intelligence, coherency, mental cohesion, network management, self-organization, self-transcending constructions and emergence).

Mindfulness — It is a significant primary mental function that emerges from human consciousness (unique to humanity — after crossing the 2nd edge of consciousness). It is the core of the self-awareness function (inward focusing) that enables the human mind to keep track of its own internal mental state and dynamic — observe its own thinking. Mindfulness facilitates the emergence of better thoughts, words, decisions and actions. A mindful mind can be cultivated. (Mindfulness can be better achieved when the frequency of the brain wave is about 8 Hz to 13 Hz, that is, in the α-state). The presence of the mindfulness function in human thinking systems separates human consciousness from that of all the other animal species. The equivalence of mindfulness in human organizations is orgmindfulness — a significant characteristic of intelligent organizations (presence of the mindful culture) — (see intelligence, consciousness, awareness, orgmindfulness, mindful system, mindful culture, mental cohesion, law of complexity/consciousness, law of complexity/intelligence, and law of consciousness/intelligence).

Morphogenesis — It is a biological process that causes an organism to develop its shape/structure (including organ). There are certain preferred **morphogenetic attractors** in the morphogenetic space, for instance, the eye (a huge number of biological organisms have eyes — homologous organs — shared ancestry of different species through common genes). Thus, artificially constructing a physical structure contradicts morphogenesis. It has also been observed that **morphogenetic field** exists within the same species, for instance, the presence of morphogenetic field facilitates subsequent learning easier (see biotic system, basin of attraction, attractor, strange attractor, extropy and self-organizing capacity).

NK modeling — It is a mathematical model of a system composing of several interacting agents where each one can be in one of the many possible states. The purpose of this modeling is to optimize a measure of performance of the system based on the contribution from each agent, and its interaction with its neighbors. In this case, N is the numbers of agent, and K measures the 'degree' of interaction among the agents. In the original model of **Stuart Kauffmann** (1939–present) and **Simon Levin** (1941–present) — (in 1987, *Towards a General Theory of Adaptive Walks on Rugged Landscapes*), the system was genome, agents were genes, states were gene mutations, and performance measure was fitness (see rugged landscape, evolution, natural selection, fitness, genetic algorithm and cellular automata).

Natural selection — It is a basic mechanism of evolution, and encompasses the three stages of variation (random mutation, bio-diversity), selection (fitness), and reproduction (autopoietic) — **Charles Darwin** (1809–1882), *On the Origin of Species*, in 1859. Thus, the fundamental dynamic of natural selection depends on variation-and-selection (trial-and-error), a continuous process, guided by the 'fitness' attribute. In complexity theory, it is also linked to the dynamic of self-organization, self-transcending constructions, and emergence (self-organizing capacity) (see evolution, autopoiesis, self-centric, stability-centric, extropy, exaptation, smarter evolver, self-organization, self-transcending constructions, phyletic gradualism, Cambrian explosion, morphogenesis and emergence).

Network management — Human organizations manifest networked patterns of interaction — network organizations. In the intelligent organization theory, the emergent of networks (complex adaptive network) is due to stability-centricity (1st degree localized order and 2nd degree localized order, local spaces, principle of locality, a meso-structure in the multi-layered structure of human organizations). Thus, the capability of network management (network-centricity) is highly significant, in particular, with networks that are not part of the original desired structure. Network management includes managing the nodes (human agents, artificial nodes), links (relational parameter that is highly nonlinear, strong ties, and weak ties), and network of networks (interdependency). As it becomes more common for networks (especially, informal networks) to self-emerge, leaders must be capable to participate in their self-organizing communications, and self-transcending constructions. In general, as human organizations are more network-centric (graph theory, network theory, small world theory, network of networks, complex adaptive networks), the intelligence leadership must possess effective network management ability to elevate coherency, structural capacity, collectiveness capacity, adaptive capacity, governance capacity, self-organizing capacity, emergence-intelligence capacity and unifying capacity of the systems (see graph theory, network theory, small world network, complex network, complex adaptive network, scale free network, localized order, principle of locality, autopoiesis, symbiosis, interdependency, self-organizing communications, self-transcending constructions, intelligence leadership, coherency, structural capacity, collectiveness capacity, adaptive capacity, self-organizing capacity, emergence-intelligence capacity, unifying capacity, self-organizing governance, intelligent organization and complexity-intelligence strategy).

Network theory — Basically, this theory [initiated by **Paul Erdos** (1913–1996) and **Alfred Renyi** (1921–1970)] uses the graph theory as its foundation about 200 years after **Leonhard Euler** (1707–1783) introduced graph theory, although they focused mainly on random networks — in a random network its links are randomly selected, and the network percolates). The current applications focus on 'real world' networks (small world networks, scale free networks) in numerous domains, including sociology (social networks), biology (molecular networks), economics (market internal relations networks), and computer science (artificial neural networks). Networks are centralized (when processing is done at the core), decentralized (when processing is shared by all the nodes), or distributed (when all the nodes are connected to all others). A subset of network theory focuses on link analysis which explores the relationships (for instance, a set of dyadic ties in a social network which highly nonlinear) of the nodes. In human networks/organizations (complex adaptive networks), the links are or can be relational or intangible. In particular, network theory is significant with communications, especially technological supported communications (for instance, social media). In addition, network theory has also been regarded as a subset of complexity theory. In the intelligent organization theory, focusing on network management is a significant requirement (together with intelligence/consciousness management and complexity management) [see graph theory, small world network, scale free network, scalability, principle of locality, localized order, complex network, complex adaptive network, S(1)-S(4), emergence, engagement, self-organizing communications, self-organizing governance, self-organization, network management, intelligence/consciousness management, and complexity management].

Notes: Summary on graph, random network and real world network:

- **Graph** => finite or small number of nodes randomly connected by links, mathematical, first introduced by **Leonhard Euler,** in 1736.
- **Random network** => finite or small number of nodes and links, each node features an equally distributed number of links, a small number of random links are sufficient to form a complete network, introduced by **Paul Erdos** and **Alfred Renyi,** in 1959.
- **Real world network** => not totally random (that is, order exists), scale free, special effect from weak links/ties (**Mark Granovetter** in 1973), a small increase in randomness greatly affects the global network, although it may have little or no effect on local clusters/networks, exhibiting the small world phenomenon.

Newtonian mindset — This mindset (still contemporary to a great extent) arises from Newtonian mechanics/sciences that supported the entire industrialization concepts and dynamics (**Isaac Newton**, 1642–1727). It believes that the Universe and its subsystems are mechanistic (physical matter world, non-living machine), and possess clockwork characteristics (order, linear, predictable/forecasting), and are governed by the deterministic law of nature (for instance, all aspects of classical mechanics can be explained using the three laws of motions, in particular the second law, $F = ma$ — the latter enables all the states of the system to be determined if an accurate initial state is known). The systems involved are linear, orderly, and predictable, and driven by equilibrium dynamics. The present education systems (consciously or unconsciously) nurture the Newtonian mindset in all human beings. This mindset is further enhanced by the Cartesian belief (reductionism, fundamentalism, hierarchical decomposition, and functional coherency), and Laplace belief (mathematical modeling). Currently, almost all human beings and organizations are embedded with this mindset, and the Newtonian paradigm (general linear realty) has been 'imported' and exploited by many other disciplines (humanities) beyond the natural/exact sciences (for instance, imported by **Frederick W. Taylor** (1856–1915) into the business/management domain — scientific management). Consequently, forecasting (predictability) becomes a common and significant activity in many other domains, including business management, finance, economic, and weather forecasting (even futurology). However, this undermining mindset (including simplicity, regularity, reversibility, gradualism, equilibrium and forecasting) alone is insufficient when dealing with CS/CAS. Certain existing abilities and characteristics become inefficient or redundant, and new characteristics cannot be exploited efficiently (see Cartesian belief, Laplace belief, reductionist hypothesis, fundamentalism, hierarchical decomposition, order, linearity, ordered systems, design paradigm, complexity mindset, complex, nonlinearity, attractor, butterfly effect, punctuation point, space of complexity, self-organization, self-transcending constructions, basin of attraction, holism, futurology, emergence and intelligence mindset).

Nonlinearity — It is the non-proportionate relationship between cause and effect. The output of a nonlinear system is not proportional to the input — at the extreme it is linked to characteristics such as sensitive dependence on initial conditions, butterfly effect, unpredictability, and punctuated equilibrium. In mathematics, nonlinear systems are those that do not obey the superposition principle (that is, the output due to two inputs is not the sum of the outputs from the individual input), and their equations (nonlinear) cannot be expressed as a linear combination of variables (poly-nomials, difference equations) or functions (differential equations). For simpler analysis, very often nonlinear systems have been approximated with linear systems but the outputs are at best just estimations. Human associated phenomena are nonlinear due to the (emotional and subjective) human thinking systems, for instance, the invisible hand effect of **Adam Smith** (1723–1790) is nonlinear, and expresses unpredictability. In addition, life cannot exists and sustains itself without the presence of nonlinear intelligence (nonlinear intelligence <=> synergetic effect <=> construction-ist effect) — (see order, linearity, complexity, feedback, autocatalysis, predictability, variable, disordered systems, statistical mechanics, punctuation point, tipping point, predictability, systems spectrum, Cambrian explosion, invisible hand, synergetics, constructionist hypothesis, Poincare–Bendixson theorem, complexity mindset and intelligence mindset).

Ontological reductionism — It is associated with the idea that entities, properties, or processes at one level are typically a manifestation (summation) of entities, properties or processes that occur at a lower level, that is, macro properties are simply identified with the micro properties — for example, temperature/heat and molecular energy. However, in complexity theory ontological reductionism is always true due to the constructionist hypothesis (properties, laws, and complexity not present in the lower levels could surface) — (see order, Cartesian belief, hierarchical decom-position, fundamentalism, reductionist hypothesis, constructionist hypoth-esis, complexity mindset, epistemological reductionism, dimensionality, disordered systems, statistical mechanics and emergence).

Open system — It is a system with inputs and outputs, that is, such a system is dissipative (due to the presence of certain differentials), and constantly interacts with its environment. All human beings and human organizations are open systems (**Katz and Kahn**, 1966) with numerous inputs and outputs (including energy, information and products). In addition, the set of rules governing the system will also change with time. Thus, an open system is continuously/constantly changing (see dissipa-tion, entropy, second law of thermodynamics, extropy, evolution, complex systems and complex adaptive systems).

Order — At one extreme, it indicates that there is no change to an agent/system or the environment (raplexity is the opposite of order). Order is also closely associated with linearity, predictability, and the Newtonian mindset. In human organizations, the three properties namely, order, linearity, and predictability are interconnected, and are closely linked to the mental state of the interacting agents. Thus, order defines the level of comfort of the interacting agents (humanity). In reality, order and complexity co-exist. However, due to intense human intelligence/consciousness, 'manageable rate of change may be perceived as orderly'. In this respect, both order and complexity are relativistic in the human world (high mental dimension) — relativistic complexity. In addition, many other characteristics such as autopoiesis, self-centricity, stability-centricity, mindfulness, and even emergence are order-centric — order out of complexity and, towards a more complex and robust structure/existence (see Newtonian mindset, linearity, complexity, predictability, autopoiesis, self-centric, stasis, stability-centric, localized order, ordered systems, principle of locality, deliberate strategy, space of relativistic order and relativistic complexity).

Ordered systems (OS) — In such a system (low finite dimensionality), all its components/variables obey strict rules or constraints that specify how one component/variable depend/interact with another (systems spectrum). All outcomes can be predicted if an initial condition and the constraints are known. The mathematical model can be easily conceived (Laplace belief) — (see Newtonian mindset, order, linearity, dimensionality, Laplace belief, Cartesian belief, reductionist hypothesis, hierarchical decomposition, disordered systems, complex systems, human organization and systems spectrum).

Org-centric — Highly intelligent human organizations possess org-centric characteristics (besides being self-centric/agent-centric and network-centric), that is, the individual interacting agents place significant interest on the existence and survival of the organization (balancing between self-enhancement and the global forces — co-evolution, symbiosis). Orgmindfulness (mindful culture) is a key characteristic/function that helps to trigger org-centricity. This function activates the nurturing of effective engagement and connectivity, self-organizing communications, collective intelligence, collectiveness capacity, relational capacity, coherency and mental cohesion — intelligence/consciousness management. In such an organization, its interacting agents balance between autopoiesis (self-centric, stability-centric, evolution — inward focusing), and symbiosis and self-organization/self-transcending constructions (org-centric, co-evolution — outward focusing) The org-centric approach [S(1)-S(4)] is highly significant to the intelligence leadership strategy and intelligence governance strategy [see orgmindfulness, mindful culture, autopoiesis, self-centric, stability-centric, agent-centric, interdependency, intelligence/consciousness-centric, connectivity, engagement, nonlinearity, intelligence-intelligence linkage, self-organizing communications, coherency, collective intelligence, collectiveness capacity, co-evolution, symbiosis, mental cohesion, intelligence/consciousness management, self-organization, self-transcending constructions, punctuation point, S(1)-S(4), intelligence leadership, intelligence governance, organizational justice, relational capacity and *i*CAS].

Organizational intelligence enhancer — It exists in the orgmind of all intelligent human organizations with an intelligent biotic macro-structure. It is a triad encompassing collective intelligence, organizational knowledge structures, and organizational philosophy and theory that are driven and interconnected by a CAD — facilitated by a common language and a mindful culture — orgmindfulness, intelligence-intelligence linkages, collective intelligence and intelligence/consciousness management. Orgmindfulness enhances collectivity (collectiveness capacity, adaptive capacity and unifying capacity), org-centricity, as well as the organizational intelligence enhancer (see individual intelligence enhancer, biotic macro-structure, biotic system, orgmind, intelligence/consciousness management, collective intelligence, collectiveness capacity, adaptive capacity, unifying capacity, knowledge structure, mindful system, intelligence-intelligence linkage, org-centric, symbiosis and orgmindfulness).

Organizational justice — The presence of organizational justice (including normative justice) is highly crucial to all human organizations. It is an interesting concept that started in the 1960s. The governance system, leadership, ethics and stakeholders — that is, all interacting agents and their interests — are closely affected by the level of organizational justice (a significant component of the intelligence governance strategy) manifested in the organization. In the intelligent organization theory, it is one of the key factors that decide the level and quality of interconnectivity, engagement, agent-centricity, power distribution, collective intelligence, organizational consciousness, mindful culture, relational friction, relational parameter, coherency, mental cohesion, feeling system, leadership, self-organization, self-transcending constructions, and emergence — reflecting the significance of intelligence/consciousness management, intelligence-intelligence linkage, collectiveness capacity, relational capacity, feeling system and mental cohesion (feeling system <=> organizational justice + relational capacity + compassion + mental cohesion) — (see Abilene paradox, defensive routine, connectivity, engagement, intelligence/consciousness-centric, collective intelligence, mindful culture, agent-centric, governance, governance system, intelligence governance, collective leadership, lateral leadership, intelligence leadership, relational capacity, feeling system, coherency, mental cohesion, symbiosis, dialogue, intelligence/consciousness management, self-organization, self-transcending constructions, emergence, intelligence-intelligence linkage, network management and intelligent organization).

Organizational learning — Similar to individual human beings, most human organizations are also learning (collectively, learning organization), especially intelligent human organizations (IO) — learning how to learn <=> self-organized learning (see Appendix 6). Human organizations are learning at different levels varying from individual to group/network to the entire organization — thus, is more complex and involves interconnectivity and engagement. Different learning (and adaptation) dynamics are also involved, including single-loop learning and double-loop learning (agents/team or organization queries the value of policy/decision/action leading to modification is double-loop learning) — introduced by **Chris Argyris** (1923–2013) and **Donald Schon** (1930–1997), in 1978. (Double-loop learning is manifesting more commonly in many human organizations, including nations as the interacting agents are becoming better informed and educated — a more lateral dynamic — closely associated with the intelligence leadership.) Argyris in 2004 also proposed that there are two key mindsets in organization learning — productive mindset and defensive mindset. An organization that learns effectively is collectively more intelligent, adaptive, competitive, resilience and sustainable. In this respect, organizational learning is also closely associated with intelligence management, intelligence-intelligence linkages, mindful culture, nurturing collective intelligence, and developing corporate knowledge structure (knowledge management, including external depositories) — reinforcing the organizational intelligence enhancer. In cybernetics, the mechanism of structural coupling (establish relationships among interacting agents — right linkages — strong ties, weak ties) facilitates the organization to learn and to generate new behaviors (see intelligence, intelligence/consciousness-centric, cybernetics, adaptive, knowledge structure, collectiveness capacity, adaptive capacity, relational capacity, network theory, connectivity, engagement, symbiosis, intelligence/consciousness management, intelligence-intelligence linkage, mindful culture, collective intelligence, intelligent organization, organizational intelligence enhancer, learning leadership, lateral leadership, intelligence leadership, network management, resilience and sustainability).

Organizing around intelligence — This is a key sub-strategy (a foundation pillar) of the intelligence mindset, intelligence paradigm and intelligent organization theory. Organizing around intelligence (conceived by **T.Y. Liang** in 2001 — instead of organizing around functions or processes) focuses on each and every intense intrinsic intelligence/consciousness source (human interacting agents — human thinking systems — intrinsic intelligence/consciousness sources — the most crucial assets in all human organizations — agent-centricity), attempting to elevate them to optimal interconnectivity, collectivity, engagement, commitment, performance, and values (intelligence-intelligence linkage, intelligence management, collectiveness capacity, unifying capacity and stability-centricity at all levels). In this respect, an intelligent human organization is a collection of highly integrated human intelligence/consciousness sources. Concurrently, the approach also concentrates on nurturing and elevating collective intelligence, adaptive capacity, and self-organizing capability (self-organizing capacity, emergence-intelligence capacity) of the organization, involving self-centricity, network-centricity, org-centricity, mindful culture, org-mindfulness, intelligent person attributes, intelligence leadership, coherency, feeling system, mental cohesion and relativistic complexity (intense complexity-intelligence linkage). Organizing around intelligence is a significant component of the holist complexity-intelligence strategy that also encompasses several other components, including the intelligence leadership strategy, intelligence governance strategy and integrated deliberate and emergent strategy, seeking an intelligence advantage (coherency + synergetic effect + constructionist effect + mental cohesion) — [see intelligence mindset, intelligence paradigm, intelligence/consciousness-centric, human thinking system, agent, nonlinearity, connectivity, self-centric, agent-centric, org-centric, orgmindfulness, mindful culture, intelligence-intelligence linkage, collective intelligence, organizational justice, feeling system, coherency, synergetics, mental cohesion, symbiosis, collectiveness capacity, adaptive capacity, unifying capacity, self-organization, self-transcending constructions, intelligent person, intelligence/consciousness management, complexity-intelligence strategy, complexity-intelligence linkage, intelligence leadership, intelligence governance deliberate strategy, emergent strategy, self-organizing capacity, emergence-intelligence capacity, network management, intelligent organization, intelligence advantage, S(1)-S(4), constructionist hypothesis, resilience, sustainability, law of complexity/consciousness, law of complexity/intelligence, law of consciousness/intelligence and relativistic complexity].

Orgmind — This is an abstract intangible space similar to the human mind (human thinking system = human brain + human mind) where the collective intelligence and org-consciousness (org-awareness and org-mindfulness) of an intelligent human organization appears to emerge (org-brain — a self-organized collective intelligence and org-consciousness source). In this case, each human thinking system is an org-neural node, a key component of the organizational neural network (org-brain, intense intelligence-intelligence linkages). The orgmind is evolving (learning) continuously, and its boundaries are not well-defined (can be expanded and consolidated) — (orgmind = Σ mind + certain synergistic effect). It should also encompass a structure that accumulates knowledge and theories. The portion of the orgmind activated may be situation dependent.

At the extreme, it may include all interacting agents in the system/organization. The nurturing of the orgmind and its collective intelligence is a key responsibility of the intelligence leaders — by exploiting orgmindfulness, intelligence/consciousness management, cultivating a mindful culture, nurturing intelligent persons, ensuring quality interconnectivity, enriching engagement, self-organizing communications, orchestrating constructive self-organization/self-transcending constructions, and nurturing the emergent strategy (futuristic). An effective orgmind must be continuously orgmindful of the mental state of all the interacting agents (agent-centric, feeling system, mental cohesion) — (see intelligence/consciousness-centric, human thinking system, consciousness, mindfulness, intelligence-intelligence linkage, orgmindfulness, mindful culture, collective intelligence, biotic macro-structure, intelligence/consciousness management, intelligent person, connectivity, engagement, self-organizing communications, intelligence leadership, emergent strategy, self-organization, self-transcending constructions, agent-centric, feeling system, mental cohesion, futurology and emergence).

Orgmindfulness — Orgmindfulness (a vital attribute of the intelligent organization theory) is the equivalent of mindfulness at human organizational level. Thus, it is the mental factor of an intelligent human organization (especially, the leadership) that focuses on the mental state of all its interacting agents (org-consciousness that is continuously inward focusing — agent-centric — intense intelligence-intelligence linkages). Possessing an orgmindful orgmind is a critical requirement of all highly intelligent human organizations (which is absent in many human organizations today, including corporations and nations — a significant setback). It is responsible for elevating collectiveness capacity and collective intelligence (connecting and activating the intrinsic self-powered leadership sources), nurturing a mindful culture (core of supportive culture, coherency, feeling system, mental cohesion, unifying capacity), and structuring a better governance system (organizational justice, intelligence governance, self-organizing governance) in the organization. It is a critical function that must be ingrained in the leadership of all intelligent human organizations — thus, orgmindfulness (inward focusing) and org-awareness (outward focusing) must be carefully balanced in an *i*CAS — (see intelligence/

658   *Complexity Intelligence Strategy*

consciousness-centric, awareness, mindfulness, feeling system, org-centric, self-powered, intrinsic leadership, intelligent person, intelligence-intelligence linkage, connectivity, engagement, collectiveness capacity, unifying capacity, intelligence/consciousness management, intelligence leadership, mindful systems, mindful culture, collective intelligence, coherency, feeling system, symbiosis, governance system, organizational justice, mental cohesion, intelligence governance, *i*CAD and *i*CAS).

Paper dialogue — It is a modified version of **dialogue** that is activated with written expression rather than verbal expression. It is more suitable for any organization/group whereby certain oral communications can be highly sensitive (for instance, due to cultural influence). Paper dialogue initiates **truthful engagement** more easily by overcoming the phobia of negative repercussion (**Abilene paradox, defensive routine**) as the identity of the participants remains confidential. Subsequent participants assume that the idea/issue has already been raise earlier. Verbal dialogue could be exploited after paper dialogue has been successfully initiated (see dialogue, Abilene paradox, phobic mindset, defensive routine, human rationality, engagement, connectivity, self-organizing communications and collective intelligence).

Paradigm — A way/path/method that indicates a change in thinking/focus/direction. A paradigmatic shift is usually associated with a change in mindset. The intelligence paradigm stipulated in the intelligent organization theory points towards an intelligence/consciousness-centric path — organizing around intelligence, intelligence-intelligence linkage, orgmindfulness, intelligence/consciousness management, complexity-intelligence linkage, complexity-centric, complexity management, complexity-intelligence strategy, network-centric, collective intelligence, org-consciousness, relativistic complexity, emergence, satisficing principle and no global optimality (see intelligence mindset, intelligence paradigm, design paradigm, intelligence/consciousness-centric, collective intelligence, intelligence/consciousness management, complexity management, network management, complexity-intelligence strategy, emergence and intelligent organization theory).

Pareto distribution — It is a power law (a probability distribution — such a distribution assigns probabilities to all possible value of a variable) named after **Vilfredo Pareto** (1848–1923), an engineer/economist/sociologist (introduced in 1906) — also commonly known as the 80–20 distribution/rule — Pareto principle (80% of the outcome is generated by 20% of the sample, for instance, 80% of the world wealth is possessed/controlled by 20% of the population — a fat-tailed distribution, scale free). The Pareto distribution (Type 1) with variable x is mathematically captured as follows: $P(x) = (x_m/x)^\alpha$, for $x \geq x_m$, and $P(x) = 1$ for $x < x_m$. In this case, x_m is the minimum value of x, and α is a positive parameter known as Pareto index. In addition, it density distribution function is follows: $f(x) = (\alpha x_m)^\alpha/x^{\alpha+1}$, for $x \geq x_m$, and $f(x) = 0$ for $x < x_m$. Other Pareto distribution characteristics include unstable means, unstable confidence intervals, and nearly infinite variance (see stochastic, power law, power law phenomena, Gaussian distribution, fat-tailed distribution, scalability, network theory, complex network and small world network).

Phase space — The phase space (recurrence plot) concept was first introduced by **Willard Gibbs** (1839–1903), in 1901. It is the space that represents the set of all possible states of a system (linear and nonlinear, and of all dimensionality) with each possible state of the system corresponding to one unique point in the phase space (the phase space may not be complete if the system is nonlinear and high in dimensionality — due to the presence of variables that cannot be accurately computed and/or unknown variables). For one-dimensional system its phase space is a phase line, and two-dimensional system it is a phase plane. An attractor (strange attractor) is a subset of the phase space. A phase diagram commonly used to illustrate a strange attractor is a plot of position and momentum variables as a function of time, and the path shown is the phase space trajectory. For high finite dimensionality (open) human organizations — systems with large number of variables, 'in-complete' and changing variables, and unknown unknowns (in-deterministic, uncertainty and unpredictability exist, and failure of Laplace belief). 'Realistically', all human organizations will not be able to achieve global optimality (with added constraints from emotional human thinking systems) — (see linearity, nonlinearity, global optimality, dimensionality, Poincare–Bendixson theorem, variable, uncertainty, in-deterministic, predictability, Laplace belief, far-from-equilibrium, basin of attraction, attractor, chaotic attractor, Lorenz attractor and strange attractor).

Phase transition — It is the continuous change in phase/state at a threshold in a continuous-time system. In Physics, it could be due to a small change in energy supply at a critical point in a thermodynamic system [for example, change in state — from solid to liquid state or from the liquid to gaseous state or even to plasma state, and the relationships among the atoms/molecules are energetically redefined — enthalpy ($H = U + pV$ where H is enthalpy, U is internal energy, p is pressure, and V is volume of the system) increases in the process]. Similarly, Prigogine's (1917–2003) dissipative structure theory indicates that a system crosses the edge of order via phase transition. (Discrete-time DCS undergo bifurcation.) In general, CAS undergo phase transition at critical points. Human organizations (continuous-time) are CAS that undergo phase transition through autocatalysis, self-organization/self-transcending constructions, and emergent of new order (see edge of order, dissipative structure, edge of emergence, edge of chaos, chaos, bifurcation, complex system, complex adaptive systems, complexity approaches, autocatalysis, self-organization, self-transcending constructions, SOC, emergence and broken symmetry).

Phobic mindset — The human thinking system is intrinsically an emotional system (dominance of the amygdala) that can also be logical (prefrontal cortex — not fully developed until a person is about 21 years old). The main component of emotion is fear. Thus, the impact of phobia on human thinking and organizational dynamics has been tremendous. It is a form of 'mental paralysis' and affects communications, connectivity, engagement, commitment, collective intelligence, and numerous other aspects (including organizational justice, relational capacity, survival, resilience and sustainability). It is also associated with other human/social/complexity characteristics such as self-centric, autopoietic, stability-centric, defensive routine, dialogue, intelligence-intelligence linkage, and the Abilene paradox. In addition, **Chris Argyris** (1923–2013) in 2004 also indicated that there are two key mindsets associated with organizational learning, namely the productive mindset and defensive mindset that are also related with the phobic mindset (high phobic mindset low self-organizing capacity) — (see Abilene paradox, human rationality, connectivity, engagement, defensive routine, organizational justice, relational capacity, paper dialogue, human thinking system, autopoiesis, self-centric, stability-centric, agent-centric, intelligence-intelligence linkage, organizational learning, self-organizing capacity and sustainability).

Phyletic gradualism — It is a model in evolution theory that most speciation (emergent of new species — the term was coined by **Orator Cook,** 1867–1949) is slow and gradual — indicating that the transformation of a species into a new one is gradual and uniform. In this case, there is no demarcation between the descendant species and the ancestor species, unless a splitting has occurred (see natural selection, Cambrian explosion, punctuation point, space of complexity, morphogenesis and emergence).

Phylogenesis — It is a significant attribute/process of evolution that does not forget its history — layered evolution. For instance, the cerebral cortex (human brain) encompasses the limbic system (mammal brain) which in turn encompasses the brain stem and cerebellum (reptile brain). Similarly, the intelligence mindset in the intelligent organization theory (including relativistic complexity) is conceived as a larger 'thinking space' that encompasses the complexity mindset and Newtonian mindset (selectively) which are the smaller modified 'thinking sub-spaces'. In addition, CAS, including human organizations are history dependence due to hysteresis (see human thinking system, evolution, exaptation, extropy, intelligence mindset, complexity mindset, Newtonian mindset, complex adaptive systems, human organization, hysteresis and intelligence mindset).

Physical symbol system/subsystem — A physical symbol system (exist only in human thinking systems) emerges from a character set — a significant subsystem in the general information theory (**T.Y. Liang,** 1994). The character set supports the creation of words, phrases, sentences, language, concepts and perception (emergence at every stage), and different event capturing, communications, and decision-making abilities — supported by a written language. A written language emerges from a set of entity processing functions (including data creating function, data processing function, information processing function, knowledge accumulation function, perception function, decision-making function and wisdom function) that transform a set of physical symbol to a higher level of sophistication. As the language matures (a continuous process), it supports the formation of abstract concepts, mass communication abilities, and enables knowledge to be stored externally (outside the human brain — books and knowledge repositories) for the first time. The creation of a character set, the existence of a physical symbol system and a written language distinguish human intelligence from that of all other species (basic life-intelligence). It also enlarges the territory (ability and capacity) of the human thinking system (beyond the energy–matter system), enables certain latent intelligence to be utilized and elevates collective intelligence. Many physical symbol systems have emerged with different civilizations/races, and they are continuously emerging. In this respect, the human thinking systems process a natural component and an extended artificial component (see general information theory, character set, human thinking system, energy–matter system, intelligence, collective intelligence, knowledge structure, basic life-intelligence and emergence).

Poincare–Bendixson theorem — This theorem indicates that one and two dimensional continuous-time dynamical systems (differential equations) have regular behavior (point attractor, fixed attractor). Strange attractor only appears in three or higher dimensionality continuous-time nonlinear dynamical systems. While, discrete-time nonlinear dynamical systems can exhibit strange attractor at all dimensionality, for instance, the one-dimensional (nonlinear) logistic map is chaotic. (However, finite dimension linear systems are never chaotic. Dynamical systems are chaotic through bifurcation and phase transition only when they are nonlinear or possess 'infinite' dimensionality) — (see chaos, dimensionality, linearity, nonlinearity, complex system, logistic map, complex adaptive systems, bifurcation, phase transition, attractor, strange attractor and phase space).

Power law (PL) — A power law shows the relationship of two varying entities by the function $f(x) = ax^m$ (where one varies as a power of the other, and m is the degree exponent). The main property of power laws that makes them interesting is their scale invariance (scale free, scalability, self-similarity) characteristic, for instance, $f(cx) = a (cx)^m => f(cx) = ac^m x^m => f(cx) = ac^m f(x)$. In this case, scaling by a constant c is simply multiplying the original power function by the constant c^m. In this respect, the power law is linked to cascading effect. Three common examples of power law distribution are the Pareto distribution (80/20 — many small events co-exist with a few major events; a dominant portion, the 80%, and the long tail of the graph, the 20%); Newton gravitational law ($F = Gm_1 m_2 r^{-2}$); and scale free network [$P(n) \sim n^{-\alpha}$ where $P(n)$ is the fraction of nodes with n connections (degree of a node) to other nodes, and α usually takes value between 2 to 3] — (see scalability, self-similarity, cascading effect, Pareto distribution, Gaussian distribution, fat-tailed distribution, power law phenomena, stochastic, complex network, scale free network and network theory).

Power law (PL) phenomena — PL phenomena are a subset of nonlinear phenomena. They share the same characteristics, such a non-additivity, openness, emergent and multiple solutions. What differentiates power law phenomena from other nonlinear phenomena is its scalability property — thus, provides a scale-free theory for emergence. The PL theory indicates that the probability of reaching early stages of emergence is always much higher (easier) than that of reaching later stages. The probability of a stage occurring depends on the probability of all the previous stages. For instance, in a human organization with an assemblage of interacting agents the emergent probability is as follows: S(1) dissipative structure (localized order) >> S(2) emergent networks (manifesting interconnectivity) >> S(3) emergent self-organizing group/cluster (complex networks or network of networks <=> enhanced engagement with pattern relationships and structure <=> with physical relationships) <=> S(4) emergent of new order (a new and more complex coordinating structure with regulation processes, properties, and behavior surface; organization). This property vividly indicates the significance of intelligence, consciousness and intelligence/consciousness-centricity in human organizations — [see power law, Pareto distribution, Gaussian distribution, localized order, dissipative structure, self-organization, self-transcending construction, emergence, S(1)-S(4), network theory, complex networks, intelligence, consciousness, intelligence/consciousness-centric and scalability].

Predictability — The notion of complexity (chaos) in nonlinear dynamics indicate that the world is intrinsically unpredictable (limited) — opposes the Newtonian mindset of order, linearity, and predictability (predictability in the human world is subjective; futurology). The characteristic of sensitive dependence on initial conditions (butterfly effect) in DCS (deterministic ≠ predictable) and CS/CAS (in-deterministic = unpredictable) renders predictability/forecasting in the entire human world impossible/difficult/inaccurate. However, in human organizations predictability is a vital thinking and dominant action that is used by most people in activities such as strategy mapping, forecasting, and goal setting. As order and complexity co-exist in all human organizations, prediction exploiting deliberate strategy is still possible during stasis (relativistic). However, with higher complexity density, and the impact of nonlinearity a deeper recognition and understanding of unpredictability (presence of high dimensionality, in-complete known variables, unknown unknowns, ontological reductionism and in-determinism) is essential — exploiting the emergent strategy, in particular, through the exploitation of relativistic complexity. (Thus, nurturing collective intelligence and making preparation for the sudden appearance of punctuation points is vital — emergent strategist) — (see complexity, butterfly effective, deterministic, in-deterministic, Newtonian mindset, futurology, order, ordered systems, nonlinearity, evolution, exaptation, stasis, complexity, complexity mindset, dimensionality, deliberate strategy, emergent strategy, collective intelligence, space of complexity, punctuation point, self-organization, self-transcending constructions, emergent strategist, emergence, uncertainty, ontological reductionism, stochastic, complexity theory and relativistic complexity).

Notes: **Unpredictability arises due to the following reasons:**

- **Sensitive dependence on initial conditions** — butterfly effect [DCS are deterministic but unpredictable — for instance, the logistic map is a one-dimensional difference equation where output can be computed (deterministic) but due to bifurcation the value of the output may be surprising (unpredictable)].

- **In-complete phase space** — presence of unknown unknowns or inaccurate variables and relationships (in-determinism in varying degrees) elevates unpredictability (CS/CAS and human organizations are indeterministic and unpredictable).

Principle of locality — This principle states that agents only interact with a small number of other agents that are physically close to them (self-organization/self-transcending construction, emergence, S(1) — localized order, 1st degree localized order, 2nd degree localized order, local space, network, stability). However, over time these local interactions will spread and create broader consequences (global forces), and eventually affecting the system/organization as a whole (causal chain). In complexity theory, such global effects are unexpected at the agents' level (intrinsic uncertainty), that is, agents are unaware of the effect (without any original intention) or impact of their actions on remote agents — [see agent, localized order, self-organization, self-transcending construction, network theory, cybernetics, cascading effect, circular causation, stability, stability-centric, small world network, self-organizing communications, self-organizing network, self-organizing governance, network theory, complex network, network management, and complex adaptive network, emergence and S(1)-S(4)].

Proto-intelligence — Intelligence is perceived to exist as a spectrum (intelligence spectrum). Proto-intelligence is low level intelligence associated with the non-living/physical matter (it forms the physical/atomic world in the Universe — against universal expansion). Thus, the presence of proto-intelligence is 'confirmed' by the act of physical stability-centricity (physical self-organization), and the presence/emergence physical matter structure with embedded information. In this respect, atoms are stability-centric, and establish localized order. Atoms that are stable do not react. Atoms that are unstable react, leading to the formation of molecules (a new order with more robust structure) which are more stable. Similarly, during crystallization certain more robust structure (more sophisticated) embedded with more complex information is formed — may involves symmetry breaking. These dynamics of transformation (physical self-organization) are driven by proto-intelligence until the boundaries of the living world (see intelligence, intelligence spectrum, stability, stability-centric, basic life-intelligence, localized order, extropy, law of complexity/consciousness, broken symmetry and Universe).

Punctuation point (punctuated equilibrium theory) — All human organizations (corporation, community, education institution, military unit, nation and civilization) fluctuate between stasis and punctuated equilibrium (punctuation point <=> sudden devastating event). [The original punctuated equilibrium theory proposed by **Stephen Gould** (1941–2002) and **Nile Eidredge** (1942–present) in 1972 focused on evolutionary biology.] Usually, all CAS and human organizations are in stasis (complextiy in IO/ *i*CAS is relativistic), and at times move into punctuation points suddenly (for examples, tsunami, global financial crisis, and nuclear crisis) — links to the black swan theory [surprises and massive impacts — **Nassim Nicholas Taleb** (1960–present)], tipping point [**Morton Grodzins** (1917– 1964)], and wicked problems [**Horst Rittel** (1930–1990) and **Charles West Churchman** (1913–2004)]. Thus, it is a point (not a space) whereby changes taking place is sudden, nonlinear, complex and unpredictable — a sudden appearance of an unexpected (surprises) space of high complexity (in the intelligent organization theory not all spaces of complexity are punc- tuation points — some spaces of complexity that are awaiting exploration and exploitation are in fact new territories embedded with gold nuggets). Currently, many human organizations constantly move into punctuation points without any 'preparation'. If an organization at punctuation point self-organizes constructively emergence will occur (also minimizes damages/destructions/loses), and a more robust complex structure will surface — better crisis management. In human organization, constructive self-organization/self-transcending construction depends on its collective intelligence (collectiveness capacity, adaptive capacity) and the presence of an emergent strategy (the ability to exploit relativistic complexity is also a niche) — high self-organizing capacity and emergence-intelligence capacity. A human organization that fails to emerge from a punctuation point self-destructs. Thus, nurturing an intelligence/consciousness-centric organization is critical for survival and sustainability (preparing for unpre- dictability <=> preparing for punctuation point <=> better crisis manage- ment <=> higher sustainability) — (see butterfly effect, Cambrian explosion, stasis, nonlinearity, raplexity, chaotic, space of complexity, intelligence/

consciousness-centric, collective intelligence, emergent strategy, black swan, tipping point, self-organization, self-transcending construction, collectiveness capacity, adaptive capacity, self-organizing capacity, emergence-intelligence capacity, emergence, futurology, resilience, sustainability and relativistic complexity).

Notes: Basic differences between spaces of complexity and punctuation points (as perceived in the intelligent organization theory):

- A **space of complexity** may not be a punctuation point (if no suddenness exist).
- Some spaces of complexity are always 'there', awaiting exploration.
- A **space of relativistic order** is space with apparent surface pattern (elevating exploratory capacity, and innovativeness and creativeness of the organization).
- Any **space of high complexity** that appear suddenly is a punctuation point (often with devastating effect).
- A **space of in-deterministic chaos** is a punctuation point (it is a space that any system/organization will move into when its self-organizing capability drops to zero or negative — self-destruct).

Raplexity — It is a new term used by some complexity researchers to indicate rapid changes (dynamics) in a complex environment (**ra**pid and com**plexity**). It is an interesting and useful term to describe the current human situation/environment — including globalization (global human interconnectivity), faster traveling speed (human could travel faster than the speed of sound — supersonic), and swift intense information connectivity (at the speed of light), supported by social/mobile media (ICT). In the current situation with higher complexity density (physical, biological and mental), spaces of complexity and punctuation points are more common (see complexity, nonlinearity, connectivity, engagement, stasis, space of complexity, punctuation point, complex adaptive systems and intelligent organization).

Red king race — It is a race where those at the tail-end of the race are the ultimate winners (for instance, some African countries being less developed, and not well-connected to the existing world financial system were not much affected by the 2008 global financial crisis) due to no or lack of coupling, cascading effect, feedback and circular causation (see red queen race, connectivity, cascading effect, feedback, circular causation and localized order).

Recurrence relations — Recursion is a process of repeating items in a self-similar way, for example the images that appear in two parallel mirrors. Some simple recurrence relations can exhibit chaotic behavior. The one-dimensional logistic map (DCS, difference equation) is a common example with recurrence relations, and it exhibits chaotic behavior through bifurcation (see self-similarity, fractal, logistic map, bifurcation, chaos, circular causation and chaotic attractor).

Red queen race/hypothesis — **Leigh Van Valen** (1935–2010), proposed the term red queen race/(**Lewis Carroll**, 1832–1898: Alace's *Adventures in wonderland*) in 1973, with the meaning that it is used in complexity theory now. It is a race where by any advantage/niche attained by a winning participant is only temporary, and great effort is needed to sustain it (continuous seeking of new advantage/niche is crucial to sustainability — also due to the changing landscape — rugged landscape). In this respect, being a first mover at all times (continuously/constantly) is a new advantage. Besides, this race has no known destination. It is a continuous journey that many human beings and human organizations are trapped in (there are people who perceived it as 'running on-the-stop', that is, they do not move or gain any improvement/niche at all, despite the fact that they are running continuously) — (see red king race, rugged landscape, first mover advantage, intelligence advantage and sustainability).

Reductionist hypothesis — This hypothesis assumes that entities, properties, and processes at one level are just a manifestation of entities, properties, and processes that occur at a lower level — functional cohesion. More basically, it assumes that everything at every levels obey the same fundamental laws [(for instance, Maxwell's electrodynamics (**James Clerk Maxwell**, 1831–1879) can be 'reduced' to optics and electromagnetism; Kepler's law (**Johannes Kepler**, 1571–1630) and Galileo's law (**Galileo Galilei**, 1564–1642) can be derived from Newtonian's laws of motion (**Isaac Newton**, 1642–1726)]. This is the traditional fundamentalist mindset in the natural sciences. However, the current belief (involving complexity theory) also needs the presence of the 'constructionist' mindset (constructionist hypothesis), symmetry breaking, and emergence (**Philip Warren Anderson**, 1921–present) (reductionism <=> fundamentalism <=> hierarchical decomposition) — (see order, Cartesian belief, hierarchical decomposition, fundamentalism, holism, constructionist hypothesis, broken symmetry, self-transcending constructions, complexity mindset, ontological reductionism, epistemological reductionism and emergence).

Relational capacity — Human relationship is a highly nonlinear variable greatly responsible for escalating complexity in the human world. Hence, high relational capacity is a critical factor that determines the status of an intelligent human organization (IO/*i*CAS <=> feeling system <=> high relational capacity + organizational justice + compassion + mental cohesion). In the intelligent organization theory, it is positively correlated with attributes including intelligence-intelligence linkage, orgmindfulness, agent-centricity, collective intelligence, org-consciousness, social conformity and consensus, organizational justice, feeling system, collectiveness capacity, unifying capacity, coherency, synergy and mental cohesion. It is also a key focus of the intelligence leadership strategy and the intelligence governance strategy (high relational capacity <=> high self-organizing capability) — (see human agent, human thinking system, intelligence paradigm, consciousness, awareness, mindfulness, behavioral schemata, agent-centric, orgmindfulness, mindful culture, collective intelligence, intelligence-intelligence linkage, organizational justice, feeling system, symbiosis, collectiveness capacity, unifying capacity, coherency, mental cohesion, intelligent person, self-organizing governance, intelligence leadership, latent leadership, *i*CAS, *i*CAD and intelligent organization).

Relative truth — There is no absolute truth in humanity due to the constraints in the human sensory (three primary colors, three-dimensional physical space, and also linked to Heisenberg's uncertainty principle) and the human thinking systems (abilities, capacities and rationality of the three-layered brain), and their associated abilities (although, human beings possess the highest mental dimension). Due to the presence of these constraints, human knowledge, and perceptions are subjective constructs (construal theory), and not an objective reflection of reality [(reality <=> absolute truth) does not exist, and (subjectivity <=> relativism)]. In addition, all concepts, knowledge and theories conceived or developed are confined by a space-time boundary. Whatever is perceived to be truth at this point in time may not be truth indefinitely. Whatever is perceived to be truth in one dimension may not be truth in another dimension. Recognizing the 'reality' of relative truth will elevate open-mindedness, and it is highly significant to the entire humanity. In this respect, humanity will have to continuously seek new thinking, knowledge and theories as it progresses on the evolution journey (relativistic complexity) — (see human thinking system, intelligence, consciousness, awareness, mindfulness, human rationality, organizational learning, intelligent person, rugged landscape, dimensionality, phase space and relativistic complexity).

Relativistic complexity (theory) — Both human agents and human organizations are highly self-centric, stability-centric and intelligence/consciousness-centric — encompassing a three-dimensional phenomenon engulfing physical stability, biological stability, and mental stability (3rd order stability) enabled by their high level of intelligence or collective intelligence. In this respect, complexity in the human world is relativistic (intelligence/consciousness intensity <=> complexity density). Relativistic complexity theory (**T.Y. Liang** in 2013, *i*CAS <=> *r*CAS, and *i*CAD <=> *r*CAD) is a subset of the intelligent organization theory — (*r*CAS = relativistic complex adaptive systems, and *r*CAD = relativistic complex adaptive dynamic). The intense mental dimension of the human thinking systems arises because of the high intensity of human intrinsic intelligence, consciousness, and accumulated knowledge. It is also associated with the awareness, mindfulness, knowledge structures, subjectivity, and behavior schemata of the interacting agents (intelligent person), and the collective intelligence and org-consciousness of the system (intelligent organization). In this case, the level of complexity in a space of complexity (including punctuation point) becomes relative (space of relativistic order) depending on the state of the intense intelligence sources involved (complexity is in the mind of the beholder) — higher level explorative capacity and intelligence advantage. Similarly, dynamic equilibrium is perceived or appeared as relativistic static equilibrium (increase in intelligence intensity > increase in complexity density). In this respect, complexity in the human world (individuals and organizations) is not exactly the same as the physical world or even the lower-intelligence biological world — that is, predictability is relative and can be enhanced by intense intelligence/consciousness-centricity. [In general, complexity decreases with increase in intelligence but complexity increases with increase in consciousness] — (see intelligence, consciousness, nonlinearity, complexity, self-centric, stability-centric, intelligence/consciousness-centric, dynamical equilibrium, intelligent organization theory, complexity approaches, intelligent person, collective intelligence, complexity-intelligence linkage, complexity management, space of order, space of complexity, punctuation point, space of relativistic order, relativistic static equilibrium, relative truth, intelligence advantage, law of complexity/consciousness, law of complexity/intelligence, law of consciousness/intelligence,and intelligent organization theory).

Notes: General focus of *r*CAS:

- Highly intelligent human organizations => IO/*i*CAS.
- IO <=> *i*CAS <=> *r*CAS, that is relativistic human complex adaptive systems are also highly intelligent human organizations.
- *r*CAS focus on spaces of relativistic order and relativistic static equilibrium which are derived from high intrinsic individual intelligence of the agents and/or collective intelligence of the organizations.
- Thus, spaces of relativistic order (and relativistic static equilibrium) are high niche areas (better risk management, higher exploratory capacity) associated with innovation and creativity that create high intelligence advantage.
- *r*CAS also make preparations for (sudden surfacing) punctuation points (better crisis management) adopting emergent strategy, nurturing high collective intelligence, nurturing better self-organization/ self-transcending constructions, futuristic and emergence abilities.
- Thus, relativistic capability, self-organizing capability and the emergent strategy in an IO are positively correlated.

Resilience — Resilience and sustainability are the two key characteristics that determine the length of existence (longevity) of an interacting agent and a CAS/IO. It is linked to homeostasis, self-stability, stability-centricity and relativistic complexity. In complexity studies and the intelligent organization theory, resilience is perceived as the degree of non-disturbance (see homeostasis, self-centric, stability-centric, symbiosis, relativistic complexity, adaptive capacity, collectiveness capacity, adaptive capacity, satisficing principle, intelligent organization, *i*CAS, *i*CAD and sustainability).

Notes: Deeper interpretation of resilience and sustainability:

- **Resilience** <=> degree of non-disturbance.
- **Sustainability** (with external force) <=> degree of complex adaptability.
- **Sustainability** (without external force) <=> degree of self-organizability.

Rugged/Fitness landscape — It is a surface/space (terrain of adaptation) with many peaks and valleys/troughs, where the fittest has the highest peak, and the steepest slope indicates the highest selection pressure — a concept first introduced by **Sewall Wright** (1889–1988), in 1932, in evolution theory, and popularized by **Stuart Kauffman** (1939–present) in the 1980s, in complexity theory. The (dynamical) landscape changes over time with the changing environment (forming a fluctuating three-dimensional space). In this case, a peak can become a trough, and to move from one peak to another higher peak, a downward journey into a valley first is inevitable (for instance, in some biological cases, natural selection alone is not good enough to move a species from one peak to another, the genetic system has to be involved — **nonlinearity**). This concept was further exploited by **Stuart Kauffman** in his NK model — a mathematical model with two variables N (number of agents) and K ('degree' of interaction among the agents). When $K = 0$, it is a simple landscape with one peak. As N and K increase, the ruggedness of the landscape increases. It is important to know (both the leadership and interacting agents) the characteristics and dynamic of the rugged landscape so as to evolve more smartly (intelligent person and intelligence leadership) — (see agent, complexity, NK modeling, evolution, natural selection, fitness, intelligent person, smarter evolver, emergent strategist, self-organizing capacity, emergence-intelligence capacity and intelligence leadership).

S(1)-S(4) — In the intelligent organization theory (**T.Y. Liang**, 2001), human organizations have been observed to undergo four different stages (phase change) of emergence. In the theory, emergence is divided into 1st degree emergence (intra-system), and 2nd degree emergence (inter-system). When an organization moves across the edge of order, 1st degree self-organization/self-transcending constructions occurs, trigging 1st degree emergence — moving through three different stages starting with S(1): dissipative structure (a localized space of loosely formed structure), to S(2): localized emergent network/space (higher interconnectivity), to S(3): emergent self-organizing complex adaptive networks (network of networks; deeper engagement and interdependency, and high self-organizing capacity) — overall, a new intra-system order emerges. When an organization moves across the edge of emergence, 2nd degree self-organization/self-transcending constructions occurs, leading to 2nd degree emergence — a 'full-fledged' emergence, S(4): emergent of new order at organizational level (new inter-system order, high emergence-intelligence capacity) — (see complexity mindset, edge of order, edge of emergence, edge of chaos, connectivity, engagement, interdependency, collective intelligence, self-organization, self-transcending constructions, dissipative structure, constructionist hypothesis, graph theory, network theory, complex network, power law phenomena, emergence, self-organizing capacity, emergence-intelligence capacity and intelligent organization theory).

Notes: Summary of the four states:

- **S(1)**: dissipative structure (localized space) — intra-system.
- **S(2)**: emergent network/space (higher interconnectivity and more structural — physical or intangible) — intra-system.
- **S(3)**: presence of complex adaptive network (network of networks with deeper engagement and interdependency) — intra-system.

- **S(4):** emergent of a new global order (new organizational structure, dynamical coherency and robustness — involving the entire organization and its environment) — inter-system.

Satisficing principle — A principle associated with the concepts of administrative man, bounded rationality and satisficing solutions (as opposed to economic man) proposed by **Herbert Simon** (1916–2001, Nobel Prize in Economics, 1978). Due to the natural constraints of all human beings, especially managers, they do not make use of the entire information set collected (sometimes, the complete set is not available) during decision-making because of the limited usable/working capacity of the human thinking systems (constraints of the working memory space in the brains). Thus, the decision made is bounded but rational — leading to a satisficing solution. In the intelligent organization theory, this concept has been extended to human organizations due to the constraints in their capabilities, and the fact that global optimality is not achievable (due to the presence of in-complete phase space). Thus, a search for a 'good enough' solution from a set of existing/formulated solutions is adopted (satisficing optimality) — a vital mindset in the current context. In this case, the advantage is cost reduction and time saving (by adopting the first 'good enough' solution identified) — (see economic man, administrative man, intelligent person, human rationality, global optimality, intelligence leadership, intelligence governance, intelligent person, futurology, resilience and sustainability).

Notes: Associated characteristics associated with 'optimization' and satisficing principle:

- **Optimizing** — more time consuming, more costly, not necessary achievable — may not be realistic in practice (constraints of the human thinking systems, and the phase space of human organizations is incomplete)
- **Satisficing** — less time needed, less costly (the first 'good enough' solution is adopted, may involve scenario planning/futurology), more practical and achievable, more realistic and co-ordinate better with continuous change — a more appealing approach for leaders/actors and decision-makers in an environment with raplexity

Scalability (scale invariance/scale free) — The concept of scalability appears from Mandelbrot's study on fractal geometry (**Benoit Mandelbrot, 1924–2010**). It indicates that the phenomenon is scale independent (scale free = self-similarity across scale on magnification; scale invariance is a subset of self-similarity, or scale invariance is the exact form of self-similarity). Scale free dynamic can cascade across scales — from local to regional to global. Such systems/phenomena are also Pareto distributed (rather than Gaussian distributed), that is, they possess infinite variance, unstable means, and unstable confidence intervals. Scale free theory 'reduces' complexity to simplicity, and translates 'deep simplicity' to scalability. Real world networks (scale free networks) are also scale invariance. However, a scale free theory contradicts the constructionist hypothesis — (see fractal, cascading effect, Mandelbrot set, self-similarity, power law, power law phenomenon, Pareto distribution, Gaussian distribution, constructionist hypothesis and scale free network).

Scale free network — It is a network with degree distribution that follows the power law. In this case, there are many nodes with few links, and few nodes with many links (preferential attachment — for instance, many human agents prefer to 'join' a nodes that is already linked to many other nodes). Thus, a scale free network (with n nodes, and m of them have degree, k (degree of a node) can be captured as $P(k) \sim k^{-\alpha}$ [where the degree distribution $P(k) = n_k/n$ is the fraction of nodes with k connections to other nodes, and α usually takes value between 2 to 3]. The degree distribution is the probability distribution of these degrees over the whole network (see scalability, self-similarity, power law, power law phenomena, Pareto distribution, Gaussian distribution, fat-tailed distribution, complex network, complex adaptive network, small world network and network theory).

Second law of thermodynamics — This law of thermodynamics [abranch of physics that focuses on energy (thermal) and work of a closed system] states that the entropy (degree of disorder/randomness/freedom) of a closed system (usually a physical/thermodynamic system) which is not in equilibrium will tend to increase it over time until it reaches maximum, and the system is in equilibrium. In statistical mechanics, the second law states that the system always moves into a macroscopic state that corresponds with the maximum numbers of microscopic states. [(However, CS/CAS and living systems are open systems capable of maintaining ordered states under non-equilibrium conditions — this was confirmed by **Ilya Prigogine** (1917–2003) when he discovered that imposing and dissipating energy into chemical systems could reverse the maximization of entropy rule stated by the second law — dissipative structure — extropy — localized order — defies universal expansion) — (see entropy, DS, dimensionality, complexity mindset, statistical mechanics, stochastic, extropy, localized order, uncertainty, dissipative structure and complex adaptive systems).]

Self-centric — All interacting agents (from atoms to human beings) are self-centric up to a certain degree (only focus on their own goal or fitness/ stability). The self-centric characteristic activates the self-enhancing dynamic (stability-centric) to stabilize the existence of the self ('conditional' altruism versus autopoietic; 1st degree localized order). For human agents, autopoiesis and symbiosis occur concurrently (self-centric versus network-centric). In human organizations, a smarter evolver and emergent strategist (intelligent person) will balance between the self-centric mindset (awareness, mindfulness, evolution) and network-centric/org-centric mindset (org-awareness, orgmindfulness, co-evolution). The latter is significant for effective self-organization/self-transcending constructions (collective intelligence) to take place in the system when necessary. It is vital to recognize that the sustainability of an interacting agent also depends on the sustainability of the group/network and organization (2nd degree localized order) — (see agent, stability-centric, localized order, intelligence/consciousness-centric, awareness, mindfulness, org-centric, orgmindfulness, autopoiesis, symbiosis, homeostasis, principle of locality, self-organization, self-transcending constructions, smarter evolver, and emergent strategist, intelligent person, orgmindfulness, collective intelligence, evolution, co-evolution and sustainability).

Self-organization — This term was first used by **Ross Ashby** (1903– 1972) in 1947 (in psychiatry and cybernetics), and became a popular terminology in the 1960s to 1980s in chaos/complexity theory. It is the spontaneous process (no control) whereby the agents (each embedded with a set of behavior schemata) in a CAS interacts without the guidance of a blueprint leading to order [**Stuart Kauffman's** (1939–present), order for free — 1971, spontaneous order]. (Self-organization due to the local interactions of smaller components usually occurs in high finite dimensionality systems — group/global order/pattern that arises from 'disintegrated disorder' by means of local interactions — including agents and networks — self-organizing networks.) It is also the dynamic underlying the emergent of forms manifest in physical (crystallization), chemical (chemical oscillators), biological (swarming), ecological (ecosystem), social (human community), and cultural structures (civilization), that is, the spontaneous crystallization of global order out of complexity in CS/CAS (**Ilya Prigogine** — self-organizing system) — (both agent-centric and org-centric in human organizations). Self-organizing systems possess states that are far-from-equilibrium. The dynamic is morphogenetic, that is, it favors certain states known as morphogenetic attractors (thus, there are certain advantages being a first mover). This dynamic is also synergetic (from incoherency to coherency, the science of synergetics was introduced by **Herman Haken** (1921–present) in the 1960s]. The self-organizing capacity and emergence-intelligence capacity of a human organization is a vital attributes. However, more current research, including the intelligent organization theory shows that self-organization is not totally order for free, that is, there are some levels of internal/external influence presence — latent impetus. For instance, in a highly intelligent human organization, self-organization/self-transcending constructions is driven by the individual intrinsic intelligence of the agents and the collective intelligence of the system — that is, self-powered human agents endowed with intrinsic leadership ability balance between autopoiesis and self-transcending constructions leading to everybody is in charge. In this case, order is not totally for free. In addition, both self-organization and self-transcending constructions in human organizations possess heterogeneous frictional effect (relational capacity), that is, its space-time distribution is not the same everywhere (not homogeneous) — (see autopoiesis, self-centric, agent-centric, org-centric, extropy, principle of locality, localized space, network theory, far-from-equilibrium, emergence, relativistic complexity, intelligence leadership, intelligence person, intelligence, collective intelligence, self-organizing communications, first mover advantage, morphogenesis, synergetics, self-organized criticality, self-organization, self-transcending constructions, relational capacity, self-organizing capacity, emergence-intelligence capacity, network theory, self-organizing governance and morphogenesis).

Notes: Meanings and relationships among criticality, self-organization, self-transcending constructions, self-organizing capacity and emergence-intelligence capacity:

- At **criticality** => presence of self-organizing capability => **self-organization** => phase transition.
- 'Spontaneous' self-organization <=> order for free.
- In this process, newly formed structures (both macroscopic and microscopic) support each others.
- Self-organization with internal 'latent impetus' <=> **self-transcending constructions,** order not for free.
- 'Latent impetus' within human organizations <=> intrinsic intelligence of agents/leaders, and collective intelligence of systems/ organizations <=> coherency and synergy.
- Self-transcending constructions <=> presence of internal impetus <=> in intelligent organizations everybody is in charge — lateral and collective intelligence leadership.
- Nurturing and elevating self-organizing capability in an organization is highly critical => high collective intelligence, intelligence-intelligence linkages, and presence of innovation and creativity.
- High self-organizing capacity and emergence-intelligence capacity <=> highly intelligent human organization (IO/*i*CAS).

Notes: Some common self-organizing examples (systems/attributes):

- In Mathematics — cellular automata.
- In Chemistry — molecular self-assembly.
- In Biology — homeostasis, swarming.
- In Physics — formation of convection pattern, structural phase transition, critical points, scale invariance structure.
- In Economics — market economy (invisible hand).

- In Business/Management, Sociology and Politics — self-organizing communications, self-organizing governance.
- In Network Theory — small world networks dynamic (bottom up interactions).

Self-organized criticality (SOC) — It is a characteristic or process observed in high dimensional and nonlinear dynamical systems during non-equilibrium, and these systems possess a critical point as an attractor. The critical point manifests space and/or time **scale invariance** characteristic. An example is when energy is continuously supplied into such a system at criticality the output is discrete or sudden. At a critical point of a phase transition, the phase boundaries vanish. The term first appeared in an article on the Bak-Tang-Wiesenfeld 'sand-pile' model by **Per Bak** (1948–2002), **ChaoTang**, and **Kurt Weisenfeld**, in 1987 ('Self-organized criticality: *An explanation of 1/f noise*' in the *Physical Review Letters*) — (see self-organization, self-transcending constructions, self-organizing capacity, attractor, phase transition, scalability, self-similarity and emergence).

Self-organizing capacity (capability) — It is proportional to collective intelligence and self-transcending constructions capability of a local space/network or organization (self-organizing communications, self-organizing governance, and other self-organizing capabilities are present in intelligent human organizations (self-organizing capacity <=> adaptive capacity)]. [In the intelligent organization theory, self-organizing capability is a vital attribute that is closely associated with the agents, networks and organization). It enables 1st degree self-transcending constructions to be activated. In this respect, it is the presence of 'lower form' self-organizing capacity that facilitates 1st degree emergence (new intra-system order). In addition, it is the presence of higher level self-organizing capability that is highly beneficial for all organizations, especially for better crisis management. Coupled with emergence-intelligence capacity (2nd degree emergence), spontaneous holistic self-organizing and emergent functionality is present when a punctuation point emerges without warning. Thus, leadership that is able to orchestrate and elevate the self-organizing capability (self-organizing capacity and emergence-intelligence capacity) is a significant asset of an organization — (see intelligence, collective intelligence, self-organization, self-transcending constructions, self-organizing capacity, emergence-intelligence capacity, unifying capacity, emergence, punctuation point, intelligence leadership and intelligent organization).

Self-organizing communications — This is a terminology introduced by **Niklas Luhmann** (1927–1998), in his societal theory (social spontaneous order theory) that focuses on communications. Social systems are systems of communications where the agents interconnect, engage, and communicate. Self-organizing communications refers to a communication that generates more communications — elevating collectiveness capacity, establishing a network or network of networks — also towards better coherency and mental cohesion. In this respect, it supports self-organization/ self-transcending constructions (see autopoiesis, self-centric, self-powered, principle of locality, connectivity, engagement, symbiosis, emergence, coherency, mental cohesion, collectiveness capacity, collective intelligence, synergetics, self-organization, self-transcending constructions, self-organizing capacity, self-organizing network, self-organizing governance, network theory, complex network, network management and complex adaptive network).

Self-organizing governance (system/subsystem) — The self-organizing capacity of a human organization is a critical key attribute. Similarly, self-organizing governance (coupled with e-governance, and reducing direct governance — emerges from acceptance governance) is a critical capacity in an effective governance system (self-organizing governance is a subset of the intelligence governance strategy). The presence of a self-powered, network-centric self-organizing governance system is a key requirement of the intelligence governance strategy — a sub-strategy of the complexity-intelligence strategy. The ability to subtly orchestrate the formation and integration of networks or network of networks (complex adaptive networks), and the self-organizing governance dynamic supported by a 'common language' is a critical capability of the intelligence leadership (by enhancing the relational aspect, coherency, and synergy — recognizing that the relational parameter is a highly nonlinear attribute that leads towards a feeling system). Thus, self-organizing governance also adopts a network-centric approach, although, there may be no formal network structure initially. Many of the nodes (agents) in the network are leadership nodes (intrinsic leadership, lateral leadership, collective leadership, latent leadership). The mindset of the nodes (intelligence/consciousness-centric, self-powered, intelligent person, orgmindfulness, self-organizing capacity, network management, self-organizing networks, self-organizing communications), and the characteristics of the links (relational, lateral, collective) are crucial in such a system (unifying capacity). Eventually, effective networks appear with self-organization/self-transcending constructions, and as the dynamic become global, emergent of new order occurs [S(4)]. The self-organizing governance subsystem (community-based, high trust, common value and intense collective intelligence) must be nurtured in all current governance systems. Thus, self-organizing governance supported by a high self-organizing capacity and emergence-intelligence capacity is also a significant component of the emergent strategy (see governance, governance system, intelligence governance, complexity-intelligence strategy, intelligent organization theory, network theory, complex adaptive networks, coherency, synergetics, feeling system, mental cohesion, symbiosis, self-organizing communications, collectiveness capacity, adaptive capacity, intrinsic leadership, intelligence leadership, latent leadership, self-powered, intelligent person, orgmindfulness, network theory, self-organizing network, network management, self-organization, self-transcending constructions, self-organizing communications, collective intelligence, S(1)-S(4), emergence, self-organizing capacity, emergence-intelligence capacity, unifying capacity, emergent strategy, resilience and sustainability).

Self-organizing network — Self-organizing networks (network of networks, complex adaptive networks) are local spaces (localized order, principle of locality) that are present in most large human organizations. They emerge from the self-organization/self-transcending constructions dynamic due the autopoietic, stability-centric, symbiotic and interdependency characteristics of the agents. There is a significant correlation between self-organizing network (encompassing self-organizing communications) and self-organizing governance and the intelligence leadership (self-organizing capability <=> self-organizing communications <=>

self-organizing network) — (see autopoiesis, stability-centric, self-powered, symbiosis, interdependency, principle of locality, connectivity, engagement, collectiveness capacity, collective intelligence, synergetics, self-organization, self-transcending constructions, self-organizing communications, self-organizing capacity, self-organizing governance, intelligence leadership, unifying capacity, network theory, complex network, network management and complex adaptive network).

Self-powered (capacity) — Self-powered capability is a highly significant attribute of human agents. Due to the presence of the intense intelligence/consciousness sources, all human interacting agents are naturally endowed with a certain level of intrinsic leadership capability (that is, with initiative to act on their own) — a key concept of the intelligent organization theory (intense intelligence/consciousness enables self-empowerment). Therefore, every human being is inherently self-powered (not just 'externally' empowerment). Along the journey in life, human agents also constantly acquire knowledge, and with changing thinking elevate the complexity of their dynamic. Different agents possess dissimilar level of self-powered capacity. However, this highly valuable intrinsic capability has always been suppressed (to a certain extent) in traditional hierarchical organizations (slavery, hierarchical empowerment) — design paradigm. In this respect, moving into the intelligence paradigm is highly beneficial (focusing on intelligence/consciousness-centricity, intelligence-intelligence linkage, self-organizing communications, intelligence leadership, self-organizing networks, self-organizing governance) towards better exploitation of self-powered capacity (higher self-powered capacity <=> higher self-organizing capability) — (see intelligence, intelligence/consciousness-centric, self-centric, design paradigm, intelligence paradigm, intelligence-intelligence linkage, self-organizing communications, network theory, self-organizing governance, intrinsic leadership, intelligence leadership, intelligence person, governance system, self-organizing governance, self-organizing communications, organizational justice, self-organizing capability and collective leadership).

Self-similarity — A self-similar object is exactly or approximately similar to a part of itself. For instance, coastlines, leaf veins, and broccoli are statistically self-similar, while a Koch curve is infinitely self-similar when magnified — that is, scale invariance/scale free/scalability. In this respect, scale invariance is a subset of self-similarity. Complex adaptive systems are also self-similar (see scalability, fractal, recursion, power law, Mandelbrot set and complex adaptive systems).

Self-transcending constructions (stcs) — Some complexity researchers including **Jeffery Goldstein** have indicated that self-organization (order for free) is not the only process that drives emergence. For instance, in human organizations frictional effects (relational friction) are always present during self-organization, and this effect is not homogenous — its space-time distribution is not the same everywhere. Instead, self-transcending constructions has been proposed, and it involves some form of 'driving' mechanisms (presence of latent impetus), and a host of structuring operations (that is, order is not totally for free — presence of self-organizing capacity that can be elevated). In the intelligent organization theory, the emergent process is perceived to be constructional in time-space driven by individual intelligence (behavioral schemata) of the agents, and collective intelligence of the organization, with certain level of subtlety (associates with the intelligent person attributes and the intelligence leadership strategy that determines the rate/quality of self-transcending constructions). Thus, self-transcending constructions in a human organization can be accelerated by its collective intelligence, and its capability to explore the phase space. In the intelligent organization theory (**T.Y. Liang**, 2001), it encompasses four stages/states [1st degree self-organization/stcs, 1st degree emergence, S(1) to S(3), and 2nd degree self-organization/stcs, 2nd degree emergence, S(4)]. The process becomes/appears spontaneous when high collective intelligence, self-organizing capacity and emergence-intelligence capacity are nurtured/present so that 'spontaneous' self-organization/stcs could be activated at punctuation points. In human organizations, 'spontaneous' self-organization which is driven by individual intelligence (especially, through of the intelligence leadership) and collective intelligence is 'nurtured' self-transcending constructions [see constructionist hypothesis, reductionist hypothesis, hierarchical decomposition, behavioral schemata, collectiveness capacity, principle of locality, self-organization, punctuation point, emergence, self-powered, intelligent organization theory, intelligence, collective intelligence, phase space, self-organizing capacity, emergence-intelligence capacity, S(1)-S(4), self-organizing governance, intelligence leadership, latent leadership and emergence].

Small world network — A small world network is a type of real world network in which most nodes are connected to all other nodes [high clustering effect (clustering coefficient), high degree nodes — many connections, short path length (the maximum length of the shortest path length is the diameter of the network)] — possessing the $L \propto \log N$ relationship, where L is the distance between two randomly selected nodes, and N is the number of nodes in the network — the diameter is small relative to N (examples are neural networks, gene networks and social networks). Thus, the small world theory is a subset of network theory that focuses on real world networks (complex networks and complex adaptive networks => small world networks and scale free networks) where a small percentage of randomly selected links will be sufficient or good enough to generate the characteristics/impact of the entire network — a small world effect/phenomenon (strength of weak ties, 80/20 rule). In fact, as the networks involved get larger the percentage of links gets smaller to achieve the same effect. [Graph theory (in mathematics) deals with random networks (not all nodes are connected to one another)]. Network theory, in particular, small world theory reveals that real world networks are not random but followed a predictable pattern of order and growth, and preferential attachment. [Real world networks possess scale free and Pareto distribution characteristics as well. They form clusters and grow, and early nodes possess preferential attachment — first mover advantage. Their links are differentiated as strong ties and weak ties, and the latter provides a high percentage of contribution to the entire network (first discovered by **Mark Granovetter** (1943–present) in 1973, in his paper entitled 'The strength of the weak ties')] — [see graph theory, network theory, complex networks, complex adaptive networks, scale free network, S(1)-S(4), emergence, self-organizing governance, self-organization, scalability, power law, power law phenomena and Pareto distribution].

Smarter evolver — In the evolution theory, an evolver (besides natural selection) normally try to achieve short-term goal using a trial-and-error approach (blind variation), and does not possess longer-term goal. However, a smarter evolver (confined only to human agents with intense intelligence and consciousness — evolving beyond natural selection and blind variation — the intelligent person model — higher adaptive capacity and greater anticipative ability) is willing to endure short-term losses for a larger long-term gain. Such an evolver recognizes the characteristics of the rugged/fitness landscape, and that the latter is changing continuously. Such an evolver also possesses other characteristics as stipulated in the intelligent person model, such as better awareness and mindfulness, inherent self-powered capacity, intrinsic leadership capability, orgmindfulness, higher innovation and creativity, and higher quality self-organizing and emerging ability (self-organizing capacity, emergence-intelligence capacity and emergent strategist). In addition, a intelligent person is complexity-centric and recognize the continuous presence of the rugged landscape and red queen race — (see evolution, nonlinearity, natural selection, intelligence/consciousness-centric, complexity-centric, intelligence, consciousness, information decoder, exaptation, rugged landscape, self-powered, adaptive capacity, global optimality, intrinsic leadership, self-organization, self-transcending constructions, intelligent person, self-organizing capacity, emergence-intelligence capacity, emergent strategist, constructionist hypothesis, broken symmetry, rugged landscape, red queen race, network theory, emergence, futurology and sustainability).

Space of complexity — This space exists in all CS/CAS (order and complexity co-exist), including the humanity and its organizations. It is a space with uncertainty to a certain extent, but it has a surface pattern, although the dynamical details are not known. Traditionally (with the Newtonian mindset), there is a tendency that such spaces human organizations are avoided. However, some spaces of complexity (as perceived in the intelligent organization theory) are embedded with 'gold nuggets'. The first person/organization to venture into such a space (with the right thinking and appropriate knowledge, and concentrated calmness), and observes the surface pattern will reap the rewards — first mover advantage. These spaces also possess characteristics that overlap with the concept of edge of chaos ('old', in the US complexity approach) in complexity theory. It is important to note that not all spaces of high complexity are punctuation points (no suddenness or surprises, for examples, highly complex bio-technology and ICT R&D spaces are not punctuation points — the two terms are intentionally differentiated in the intelligent organization theory). In fact, in human organizations complexity is relativistic (relativistic complexity, **T.Y. Liang,** in 2013) due to the high mental dimension (3rd order stability), and a space of complexity can be perceived as a space of relativistic order — depending on the intensity of intelligence, conscious-ness and knowledge of the agents, and the collective intelligence, org-mindfulness and org-awareness of the organization — a new opportunity/niche, better risk management, and intelligence advantage will emerge (complexity management <=> risk management <=> intelligence advan-tage) — (see space of order, complexity, nonlinearity, uncertainty, edge of order, edge of chaos (old), edge of emergence, stasis, punctuation point, butterfly effect, intelligence, consciousness, collective intelligence, org-mindfulness, complexity management, space of relativistic order, relativ-istic complexity, first mover advantage, intelligence advantage and intelligent organization theory).

Space of order — The space that is orderly, and it is therefore linear and predictable (events are more easily understood). To the extreme the space is in static equilibrium. Most human beings are more comfortable in this space (at least mentally so, stability-centric). However, such a space in human organizations (and its environment) does not provide a niche as it encompasses nothing new (no innovation and creativity, also associated with comfort and complacency). An organization that exists in a pro-longed space of order will disintegrate quickly (space-time constraint). In this respect, the space of order is different from the space of relativistic order, and relativistic static equilibrium in relativistic complexity (see order, static equilibrium, stability, stasis, dynamical equilibrium, space of complexity, stability, stability-centric, relativistic complexity, relativistic static equilibrium and space of relativistic order).

Space of relativistic order — This is a space of complexity in human organizations that appears to be relative orderly to certain interacting agents and their system due to their intense intrinsic intelligence, collective intelligence, and knowledge available — a term coined by **T.Y. Liang** in 2013 — relativistic complexity. (The ability to transform a space of complexity into a space of relativistic order is a new niche in the current knowledge intensive and fast changing world — first mover advantage, a new innovation/technology/market, and further enhancing intelligence advantage.) In this case, the dynamic at dynamical equilibrium appears to be in relativistic static equilibrium — that is, in a better position to observe the surface pattern first. Thus, it is a 'perceived' space (unique to human agents/organizations due to their intense intelligence/consciousness-centricity, also associated with concentrated calmness) that could give the interacting agents/organization that perceived it a higher intelligence advantage (see space of order, space of complexity, intrinsic intelligence, intelligence/consciousness-centric, collective intelligence, complexity management, relativistic complexity, first mover advantage and intelligence advantage).

Stability — According to the intelligent organization theory, stability (stability-seeking, stability-centric) is a primary attribute that initiates the creation of the physical matter world, as well as the biological world, including human beings and their organizations. Stability exists at three different levels namely, 1st order stability (physical — due to the proto-intelligence in the matter world), 2nd order stability (physical and biological — due to the basic life-intelligence), and 3rd order stability (physical, biological and mental — due to the intense intelligence and consciousness of human beings). The presence of the matter world and the existence of life are created by this fundamental characteristic that defies universal expansion (morphogenesis). In the human world, the third-dimension of mental stability emerges because of the presence of the intense intelligence and consciousness (confined only to humanity). The latter creates the unique mental space of the human agents that also leads to the emergent of relativistic complexity. In intelligent human organization, organizational mental cohesion and org-centricity are mutually enhancing — (see stability-centric, self-centric, autopoiesis, symbiosis, homeostasis, proto-intelligence, basic life-intelligence, intelligence, intelligence spectrum, mental cohesion, complexity approaches, morphogenesis, relative truth and relativistic complexity).

Stability-centric — Stability-centricity is a fundamental intrinsic property of the physical matter world, as well as all CAS (including human organizations) — as specified in the intelligent organization theory (stability-centricity and intelligence are positively correlated). The intention of achieving stability is self-centric (enhancing localized order — a confinement effect — creation of a localized space/network — principle of locality). Localized order at different level/scale (agent/network/organization) is associated with characteristics such autopoiesis, symbiosis, interdependency, ambidexterity, self-transcending constructions, networks, symmetry breaking, sustainability and emergence. The physical matter world exists because atoms that are not stable interact to form molecules (physical self-organization) that are more stable (1st order stability — physical stability). In human organizations, stability-seeking is a three-dimensional phenomenon, namely 3rd order stability (physical, biological, and mental) — involving mental self-organization/self-transcending constructions which much more complex. The dominant presence of spaces of mental complexity in humanity redefines the characteristics of complexity adaptive dynamic in human organizations — *i*CAD. Complexity in this case becomes relativistic (see stability, localized order, self-centric, intelligence, intelligence/consciousness-centric, consciousness, principle of locality, intelligence spectrum, autopoiesis, symbiosis, extropy, interdependency, self-organization, self-transcending constructions, *i*CAD, mental cohesion, broken symmetry, homeostasis, network theory, principle of locality, resilience, sustainability, law of complexity/consciousness, law of complexity/intelligence, law of consciousness/intelligence, feeling system and relativistic complexity).

Stasis — In CAS, stasis is a period of stability where the net effect of all 'forces' are balanced — order, or no change. In the intelligent organization theory, it is the period of linear and orderly changes (or at least perceived/construed to be so by the interacting agents — relativistic complexity) inbetween punctuation points, and hence the organization, as well as the interacting agents is usually affected minimally (stability) — can also be perceived as dynamical equilibrium (relativistic static equilibrium). All human organizations, including human civilizations move through continuous cycles of stasis and punctuated equilibrium. In-ability to manage the latter (space of in-deterministic chaos) leads to self-destruc-tion (see order, linearity, punctuation point, stability, space of order, space of complexity, static equilibrium, dynamical equilibrium, relativistic com-plexity, space of relativistic order and relativistic static equilibrium).

Static equilibrium — It is a state of order in a traditional linear system — no change. However, CS/CAS do not stay in such as state. CS/CAS in 'absolute' static equilibrium are unstable, and will disintegrate (equilibrium ≠ optimality). Instead, as CS/CAS are continuously changing, dissipative, and adaptive (CAS) they tend to maintain steady dynamic equilibrium. In relativistic complexity theory, relativistic static equilibrium (a term coined by **T.Y. Liang** in 2013) emerges from the close linkage between complexity and intense human intelligence/consciousness in a space of relativistic order. In addition, all CS/CAS exhibit far-from-equilibrium dynamic — (see order, adaptive, dissipation, dynamical equilibrium, far-from-equilibrium, com-plex systems, complex adaptive systems, space of complexity, relativistic static equilibrium, space of relativistic order and relativistic complexity).

Statistical mechanics — It is a general mathematical theory (developed by **Ludwig Boltzmann,** 1844–1906, a highly prominent physicist of the 19th century, conceived the entropy formula $S = k \log W$, and H-theorem) for closed highly DS (total randomness or infinite degrees of freedom) that shows how macroscopic properties (average value, for examples, heat, tem-perature, and pressure) arise from statistics of the mechanics (e.g., positions and velocities) of a large collection of microscopic components/properties (e.g., atoms and molecules) — ontological reductionism. [It uses probability theory (Maxwell–Boltzmann distribution, **James Clerk Maxwell**, 1831–1879) that focuses on the average behavior of random variables, stochastic processes, and events of large systems. The theory is commonly used in thermodynamics — the study of heat and thermal energy — kinetic theory of gases.) For instance, the statistics of positions and velocities of atoms/mole-cules give rise to the temperature and pressure of the system (infinite random-ness ≠ in-deterministic). Boltzmann also show that any gaseous systems always evolve into an equilibrium state (maximum entropy) independent of the starting state (second law of thermodynamics) (see disorded systems, order system, entropy, dimensionality, deterministic, in-deterministic, uncertainty, ontological reductionism, stochastic, entropy, predictability and second law of thermodynamics).

Stochastic — This term is used to describe an event/system that is unpredictable due to the presence of a random variable (there are at least several ways it can change). In probability theory, a stochastic system (infinite randomness) possesses a state (with probability distribution that can only be analyzed statistically) that can only be randomly determined but not predicted (stochastic systems <=> disordered systems) — (see deterministic, in-deterministic, predictable, uncertainty, statistical mechanics, power law, Pareto distribution and complexity theory).

Strange attractor — This is the 'third' attractor (relatively stable, and encompasses a large number of states in a confine space) of the four types of attractor of nonlinear dynamical systems (it was discovered last from the studies of chaos and complexity — by **Edward Lorenz** (1917–2008) in 1963 from his weather system, and by **David Ruelle** (1935–present) and **Floris Takens** (1940–2010) in 1971 in mathematics). A strange attractor only emerges in a nonlinear dynamical system. A strange attractor is chaotic attractor if it exhibits sensitive dependence on initial conditions characteristic (but not all strange attractors are chaotic attractor). Strange attractors appear in both continuous-time and discrete-time nonlinear dynamical systems. It has some kind of patterned order and boundary. When represented by a three dimensional phase diagram it (phase space trajectory) appears like an infinite line that never passes through the same point twice but continues indefinitely within a bounded space (far-from-equilibrium). Typically, it has a fractal structure (scale invariance) and a fractal dimension (strangeness <=> fractal). Thus, a strange attractor is a closed and bounded subset of the phase space. Some common examples of strange attractor are Lorenz attractor, logistic map, Henon attractor, and Rossler attractor. In mathematics, the evolving variables of an attractor are represented by an n-dimensional vector. A strange attractor is given the name 'strange' because it has a non-integer dimension (also because it possesses a fractal structure) — (see attractor, chaotic attractor, nonlinearity, far-from-equilibrium, bifurcation, phase transition, fractal, fractal dimension, dimensionality, Lorenz attractor, logistic map and phase space).

Structural capacity — The way a system is structured determines its robustness, rigidity or competitiveness. For a physical system (atom, molecule, crystal), its structure determines its stability and existence. It is also believed that all structures are embedded with information. For living systems (varying from a bee hive, to an ecosystem, to the entire humanity), its structure is also link to connectivity, interdependency and coherency, (collectiveness capacity and unifying capacity), competitiveness (adaptive capacity, self-organizing capacity and emergence-intelligence capacity), resilience and sustainability — initiated by its intelligence, and collective intelligence — intelligence-intelligence linkages. In this respect, how an organization is structured is vital and it manifests a correlation with the collective intelligence of the system (see stability, intelligence, collective intelligence, intelligence-intelligence linkage, interdependency, coherency, biotic macro-structure, agent-agent/system micro-structure, collectiveness capacity, adaptive capacity, self-organizing capacity, emergence-intelligence capacity, unifying capacity, network management, resilience and sustainability).

Super-system — It is a term used to denote a group of systems connected by different input–output relationships that forms a larger system (organizational network). If the super-system functions with sufficiently high coherency, it is regard as a system in its own right — a large scale integrated nested/composite system with the smaller systems as its subsystems (see complex adaptive systems, interdependency, network theory, complex network, composite CAS, upwards causation and downwards causation).

Sustainability — This term is commonly used after the publication of the United Nation World Commission on Environment and Development report — the **Brundtland report** (**Our common future**), in 1987. In general, the idea seeks a longer-term goal, especially with respect to humanity existence (longevity) and their environment. Conceptually, including in the intelligent organization theory, sustainability has two components namely, **instinctive sustainability** and **innovative sustainability**. Instinctive sustainability is present in most animal species, and the dynamic is highly autopoietic (self-centric, localized order). While innovative sustainability only emerge from an intense intelligence/consciousness source (human thing systems), and it encompasses better co-evolution (interdependency, ambidexterity) with other ecosystems, including the global ecosystem, Gaia (see agent, self-centric, symbiosis, localized order, interdependency, ambidexterity adaptive capacity, intelligence/consciousness-centric, nonlinearity, complexity management, network management, satisficing principle, intelligence/consciousness management, biosphere, biotic system, evolution, co-evolution, resilience, Gaia, sustainability revolution, futurology, *i*CAS and *i*CAD).

Sustainability revolution — Humanity is witnessing the initial stage of a new societal revolution likely similar in magnitude/scale and significance as the industrial revolution. There is a gradual shift from the 'economistic' industrial paradigm towards an intelligence/consciousness-centric sustainability paradigm (elevating 'sustainalization' of the entire Gaia). This sustainability revolution is a 'green' revolution — it is highly significant to recognize the interdependency of the social, political, economic, and environmental dimensions/perspectives, and their positive correlation with intelligence, consciousness (awareness, mindfulness), of human beings, and collective intelligence and org-consciousness of human organizations. A large number of people and organizations (business corporations, social communities, nations, and global institutions) are now investigating, conceptualizing, and adopting new thinking, knowledge, experience, goals, technologies, methods, and practices that support innovative environmental sustainability (green thinking, green values and green practices). Hopefully, the entire humanity is moving into a more comprehensive intelligence era — where new thinking, awareness, organizing, regulating, and standards are emerging — establishing a more direct link to the longevity of the homo sapiens sapiens (see intelligence/consciousness-centric, intelligence, awareness, mindfulness, collective intelligence, org-consciousness, intelligence era, intelligence mindset, global mindset, intelligence/consciousness management, complexity management, adaptive capacity, collectiveness capacity, co-evolution, Gaia, intelligent organization, governance system, resilience, sustainability, *i*CAS and *i*CAD).

Swarm Intelligence — Human collective intelligence and swarm intelligence are far from similar. Swarm intelligence (a lower form of collective intelligence) is an inherent integration (usually 'biologically/genetically' instilled) of very low levels basic life-intelligence sources, such as those observed in insect colony (ant colony — nest, bee colony — hive). The individual intrinsic intelligence of each of these insects is low, linear and orderly (very often such insects perform specific tasks, and they do not survive for long if they venture beyond their colony). However, when they are well-integrated (spontaneous and inherent) resulting in the emergent of swarm intelligence, it significantly increases the colony survival ability (the ratio of swarm intelligence and its individual intelligence is tremendously high — synergetic effect), high coherency but still low consciousness level (can be more easily captured in a mathematical model — artificial life). Comparatively, human intrinsic intelligence is highly intense. It is also highly nonlinear — resulting in subjectivity, perception, and innovation and creativity. Consequently, nurturing coherency and collective intelligence in human organizations is much more complex, and has to be managed subtly (enhancing intelligence-intelligence linkages, orgmindfulness, and intelligence/consciousness management, nurturing relational capacity, and orchestrating self-organization/self-transcending constructions — more often 'socially' instilled). The process is not spontaneous in totality due to many factors, including self-centricity, stability-centricity, emotions, network-centricity, org-centricity, autopoiesis, symbiosis, interdependency, high consciousness, and mental cohesion (most human beings are not fully network/organization dependent as ants or bees — they do not seize to exist when they leave a group/organization — independency/autonomous versus interdependency, autopoietic versus symbiotic, self-centric versus network-centric/org-centric). Thus, collective intelligence in the human world is different from swarm intelligence as the collective intelligence of a human organization is closely integrated with its org-consciousness (orgmindfulness, org-awareness and mental cohesion) — (see intelligence, intelligence spectrum, consciousness, awareness, mindfulness, nonlinearity, self-centric, stability-centric, intelligence-intelligence linkage, autopoiesis, symbiosis, interdependency, autonomous, coherency, synergetics, collectiveness capacity, relational capacity, collective intelligence, intelligence/consciousness management, orgmindfulness, self-organization, self-transcending constructions, self-organizing capacity, emergence-intelligence capacity, unifying capacity and mental cohesion).

Symbiosis — It refers to close and long-term biological interactions, including mutualistic relationships (more group associated, network-centric and org-centric). This term emerged when **Lynn Margulis** (1938–2011) introduced the endosymboisis theory in 1966, and later the theory of symbiotic relations (encompassing interdependency and co-evolution) — in the book *Symbiotic Planet: A New Look at Evolution,* in 1998. It is a more open form of 'self-focusing' (stability enhancing) dynamic than autopoiesis, and is more appropriate for describing human social dynamics. In this case, the 'boundaries' of the agent/network/system are also not so clearly defined. In the intelligent organization theory, autopoiesis is interpreted as highly self-centric, while symbiosis is more balancing between self-centric and network-centric/org-centric — (balancing autopoiesis and symbiosis <=> ambidexterity, self-centricity versus network-centricity versus org-centricity, and presence of unifying capability is vital. (Another terminology that has been used in CAS is heteropoietic — such a system is not sustainable — some human created systems are heteropoietic) — (see intelligence, autopoiesis, self-centric, stability-centric, principle of locality, org-centric, interdependency, coherency, network theory, network management, autonomous, self-organization, self-transcending constructions and unifying capacity).

Synergetics (synergy, synergetic effect) — The origin of this theory (linked to complexity) encompasses the empirical study of systems in transformation, and focuses on the fact that the total system behavior is not predictable from its individual components. Synergetics from **Hermann Haken** (1927–present) focuses on self-organization of patterns/structures in open systems far from dynamical equilibrium. In 1973, Haken developed his science of synergetics based on his lasers study demonstrating that an incoherent mixture of light waves with different frequencies and phases could self-organize into a coherent light with a single monochromatic wavelength — spontaneous transformation of incoherency to coherency. The common meaning of the word synergetic effect is the combined effect of the whole is greater than the sum of the effects of all the parts — for instance, in an ecosystem, what a wolf can achieve and what a pack of wolves can achieve collectively is significantly different. In addition, in the evolution dynamic, interaction is not a zero-sum-game. The gain of an agent is not the lost of another — presence of synergetic effect. In this respect, there is an advantage for collaboration. The term synergetics was earlier introduced by **Buckminster Fuller** (1895–1983), in 1975 — (see open system, complex adaptive systems, self-organization, self-transcending constructions, reductionist hypothesis, constructionist hypothesis, coherency and unifying capacity).

Systems spectrum — This spectrum (introduced in the intelligent organization theory, **T.Y. Liang**, 2001) encompasses the common systems in complexity theory and the exact sciences, including ordered systems (OS), deterministic chaotic systems (DCS), complex systems (CS), complex adaptive systems (CAS), and (infinite randomness) disordered systems (DS). The horizontal axis of the spectrum is dimensionality (varying from 1 to ∞). Thus, at the lower end the first category of systems is OS (low dimensionality, orderly, linear, deterministic and predictable), and the other extreme end is DS (infinite randomness, statistical mechanics, ontological reductionism, deterministic and predictable). Next, DCS are low finite dimensionality nonlinear dynamical systems (starting from dimension 1, discrete-time, continuous-time, deterministic, bifurcate, butterfly effect and unpredictable), while CS/CAS are high finite dimensionality nonlinear dynamical systems (in-deterministic and unpredictable). Finally, human organizations (high finite dimensionality, continuous-time, intelligence/consciousness-centric, uncertainty, and in-complete phase space) are CAS with additional intelligence/consciousness-centric characteristics (intelligence, consciousness, awareness, mindfulness, collective intelligence, org-awareness, orgmindfulness — IO <=> iCAS <=> rCAS). OS/DCS/CS/CAS can be captured mathematically [discrete-time (bifurcate, difference equations) or continuous-time (phase transition, differential equations)], while human organizations can only be captured as estimated mathematical models due to in-complete phase space (see dimensionality, ordered systems, chaos, deterministic, in-deterministic, bifurcation, butterfly effect, predictability, complex systems, complex adaptive systems, phase transition, uncertainty, DS, statistical mechanics, stochastic, ontological reductionism, human organization, intelligence, consciousness, awareness, mindfulness, intelligence/consciousness-centric, collective intelligence and orgmindfulness).

Notes: The five zones of the systems spectrum:

- **Order** — low dimension and linear — encompassing OS.
- **Chaotic** — low to finite high dimension and nonlinear — encompassing DCS.
- **Complex** — finite high dimension and nonlinear — encompassing CS/CAS and human organizations.
- **Disordered** — infinitely high dimension — infinite randomness (statistical/stochastic/probabilistic) — compassing DS.
- **In-deterministic chaotic** — any types of systems — catastrophic, towards disintegration.

Thought technology — It is a type of intangible/mental methodology that develops deeper deliberation and understanding within a group/team/organization. Thus, it is exploited for nurturing better connectivity, more truthful engagement, higher mutual understanding, collectiveness capacity, collective intelligence and mental cohesion through constant engagement (exploiting certain characteristics such as divergent conversation, better/longer thinking space, self-organization, and no immediate goal — also encompasses an orgmindful mindset). It engulfs methodologies such as dialogue, paper dialogue and visual thinking (see intelligence/consciousness-centric, Abilene paradox, phobic mindset, defensive routine, connectivity, nonlinearity, engagement, autopoiesis, symbiosis, self-organizing communications, collectiveness capacity, orgmindfulness, mindful culture, network theory, collective intelligence, self-organization, mental cohesion, dialogue and paper dialogue).

Tipping point — This term was first used by **Morton Grodzins** (1917–1964) in sociology (in the early 1960s) to indicate the event when a previously rare phenomenon suddenly becomes abundant — a threshold model of social behavior. This phrase was later popularized by **Malcolm Gladwell** (in his book *The Tipping Point: How Little Things can Make a Big Difference*, 2000). It is now commonly used to indicate the point (associated with critical point, threshold, turning point) in a process when there is a sudden tremendous increase in its rate abruptly and irreversible [in the intelligent organization theory (an additional interpretation) tipping point may have a historical perspective — hysteresis] — [see butterfly effect, phase transition, bifurcation, Pareto distribution, space of complexity, hysteresis, black swan, punctuation point (wicked problems) and hysteresis].

Topology — It is a branch of mathematics that study shapes and spaces (for example, mobius strips) whose properties are preserved under continuous deformation. It focuses on connectedness, continuity and boundaries — the invariant properties of certain object under certain kind of transformation. One of its subsets is **knot theory** that study mathematical knots (for example, trefoil knot). A mathematical knot is different from a 'common' knot because its two ends are joined and cannot be disconnected (see complexity, connectivity, fractal, self-similarity and scalability).

Uncertainty (I) — In quantum physics, there are two laws that are linked to the concept of uncertainty (point towards the in-deterministic nature of the Universe). The **Heisenberg's uncertainty principle** conceived (**Werner Karl Heisenberg**, 1901–1976, Nobel Prize in Physics, 1932; Max Planck Medal, 1933) in 1927 indicates that there is certain basic limit (no high precision) to which a pair of complementary variables (complementarity principle) when measured simultaneously ($\sigma_x \sigma_p \geq \hbar/2\pi$ where x is position, p is momentum, and $\hbar$ is reduced Plank constant — **Max Planck**, 1858–1947, Nobel Prize in Physics, 1918). This principle is inherent in the properties of wave-like systems — beyond observer effect. Next the **Born's rule** conceived by **Max Born**, 1882–1970, (Nobel Prize in Physics, 1954, Max Planck Medal, 1948) in 1926 is a law that indicates the probability to a measurement on a quantum system will yield a given result. [Thus, in certain physical systems, complexity is a measure of the probability of the state vector of the system. For example, the Schrodinger equation (a partial differential equation) of a quantum system describes how its quantum state changes with time. This state, known as the eigenstate (not a state with definite value but a state with in-determinate or partial uncertainty value — probabilistic value), is a wave function that provides a means for predicting a probability result (eigenvalue). The role and significance of the Schrodinger equation in the quantum world is very much similar to $F = ma$ in the mechanical world — establishing the foundation of the 'quantum mindset'. Thus, there is an overlap between the complexity mindset and quantum mindset when dealing with partial uncertainty — probabilistic value/result of state/output.] In other domains, uncertainty is associated with random observable. A common example of random process is Brownian motion (see complexity, predictability, non-linearity, statistical mechanics, deterministic, in-deterministic, stochastic and complexity mindset).

Uncertainty (II) — Uncertainties are also defined as 'unknown unknowns' — used with this meaning in the intelligent organization theory — the more we know the more we realized that we do not know). With uncertainties or undefined/unknown variables — (also due to onto-logical reductionism) the exact duplication of the system/organization by a mathematical model is not possible (dimensionality cannot be fully accounted for), and the phase space is also in-complete — that is, not all the states in the system are known. In this case, the output is in-determin-istic and unpredictable, thus, global optimality can never be achieved. Concurrently, in-determinism has also been perceived to deal with events that are not certain with respect to the fact that the outcome is a probabil-ity (related to chance, also link to Born's rule). Hence, recognizing the satisficing principle is significant for leaders in an IO/iCAS (see deter-ministic, in-deterministic, predictability, global optimality, nonlinearity, dimensionality, variable, statistical mechanics, complexity, ontological reductionism, phase space, global optimality, stochastic, satisficing prin-ciple, intelligence leadership and intelligent human organization).

Notes: **Relationship between Certainty/Uncertainty and Known/ Unknown:**

- **Known** = > (i) **'deterministic' known** — can be measured/calculated accurately (high certainty) — but if nonlinearity is also present the dynamic can still be chaotic (unpredictable), or (ii) **'in-deterministic known'** — cannot be measured/calculated accurately (presence of uncertainty, partial uncertainty) — value could be probabilistic or value is unknown — towards in-determinism and unpredictability — may be towards in-deterministic chaos.

- **Known unknowns** => can become 'known' through learning and knowledge acquisition — can be an existing space of complexity — futuristic, scenario planning can be executed — may be linked to better risk management (presence of uncertainty or partial certainty) — overlaps with 'in-deterministic known'.
- **Unknown unknowns** => currently not known (variable or event) — may appear suddenly with surprises — may be linked to punctuation points or crises (total uncertainty).

Universe — The Universe came into existence about 13.7 billion years ago after a big bang (big bang theory). It encompasses a huge collection of subsystems, including 'orderly' systems, (deterministic and in-deterministic) chaotic systems, complex systems, complex adaptive systems and 'invisible' systems. The dynamics are linear and orderly; nonlinear, chaotic and complex; with emergence and destruction — varying with the subsystems concerned. Currently, it is believed that its composition is about 4% atoms (physical matter), 23% cold dark matter, and 73% dark energy. The human world is within the atomic/physical/ biological world. The biological world encompasses intelligence/ consciousness sources (with intense self-centric and stability-centric characteristics). Thus, the Universe is intelligent, conscious, and is more a cosmic mind than just a huge machine (although, our understanding of the 'dark matter/energy world' is minimal) — (see order, linearity , nonlinearity, chaos, complexity, intelligence, consciousness, ordered systems, complex systems, complex adaptive systems, self-centric, stability-centric, biosphere, biotic system, Gaia, evolution, co-evolution and emergence).

Unifying capacity — This is a critical capacity of intelligent human organizations that is closely associated with many other attributes (interconnectivity, engagement, mutual trust, collective intelligence, coherency, ambidexterity, synergy, leadership, governance, mental cohesion), and capacities (structural capacity, relational capacity, collectiveness capacity, adaptive capacity, self-organizing capacity, emergence-intelligence capacity, leadership capacity and governance capacity). The quality of the unifying capacity determines the levels of consensus and collaboration of the agents, effectiveness of leadership and governance, and emergent of new attributes or capabilities (synergetic effect, constructionist effect, mental cohesion, higher robustness, resilience and sustainability of the organization) — (see intelligent human organization, collective intelligence, connectivity, coherency, synergetics, structural capacity, collectiveness capacity, adaptive capacity, self-organizing capacity, emergence-intelligence capacity, relational capacity, leadership capacity, governance capacity, mental cohesion, constructionist hypothesis, resilience and sustainability).

Notes: Significant capacities of intelligent human organizations:

- Intelligence/consciousness capacity (agent)
- Self-powered capacity (agent)
- Intrinsic leadership capacity (agent)
- Collective intelligence/org-consciousness capacity
- Structural capacity
- Collectiveness capacity
- Relational capacity
- Adaptive capacity
- Exploratory capacity
- Self-organizing capacity
- Emergence-intelligence capacity
- Economic capacity
- Leadership capacity
- Governance capacity
- Innovative and creative capacity
- Futuristic capacity
- Unifying capacity

Upwards causation — It indicates that the behavior of the whole (system) is determined or influenced by the characteristics (functions) of the entities/parts (networks/subsystems) — that is, the more elementary units normally impose certain coherency on their system and/or super-system — functional cohesion. The causal relation (cause-and-effect, condition-action) is determined by the goals of the agents, as well as their behavioral schemata. Thus, intelligence leaders must recognize that the local activities of agents (employees, citizens) produce collective (network/organizational) effect, and how the contributions of these local interactions can be elevated is vital (principle of locality, self-organizing capability) — (see super-system, complex adaptive systems, composite CAS, network theory, fundamentalism, reductionist hypothesis, constructionist hypothesis, synergetics, intelligence leadership, self-organization, self-transcending constructions, autocatalysis, circular causation, feedback, downwards causation, behavioral schemata, principle of locality, self-organizing capability and emergence).

Variable — It is a natural entity in the natural/exact sciences. The entire set of variables involved defined the boundaries of a domain/discipline/theory, as well as determines the dimensionality and phase space of the system studied. For instance, distance, time, and mass are examples of primary (physical) variables in Newtonian/classical mechanics. Some of the computed variables are speed, angular velocity, acceleration, and force. The non-sciences make use of artifacts as variables which are 'artificially' defined. For instance, in the general information theory the artifacts are data, information, knowledge, wisdom, information-coded energy quantum, and information-coded matter quantum. However, in the human world (human organizations, markets) not all variables are known. In this case, creating a complete mathematical model is not possible. (In mathematics, variables and parameters are different. For instance, in the equation $y = ax^2 + bx + c$, the variables are x and y, while a, b, and c are parameters; and a system can be chaotic if a parameter is nonlinear (for instance, logistic map) — (see basic entity, artifact, agent, dimensionality, attractor, phase space, deterministic, predictability, ontological reductionism, general information theory, human organization and Laplace belief).

Bibliography

1. Ahituv, N. (1987). A meta-model of information flow: A tool to support information systems theory. *Communications of the ACM*, 30(9), 781–791.
2. Allen, P. M. (2000). Knowledge, ignorance and learning. *Emergence*, 2(4), 78–108.
3. Allen, P. M. (2001). What is complexity science? Knowledge of the limits to knowledge. *Emergence*, 3(1), 24–42.
4. Allen, P. M. and Strathem, M. (2003). Evolution, emergence and learning in complex systems. *Emergence*, 5(4), 8–33.
5. Allen, P. M., Macguire, S. and McKelvey, B. (2011). *The SAGE Handbook of Complexity and Management*. Los Angeles: SAGE.
6. Anderson, P. W. (1972). More is different: Broken symmetry and the nature of the hierarchical structure of science. *Science*, 177 (4047), 393–396.
7. Anderson, P. W. (1999). Complexity theory and organization science. *Organization Science*, 10(3), 216–232.
8. Anderson, P. W., Arrow, K. J. and Pines, D. (1988). *The Economy as an Evolving Complex System*. New York: Addison-Wesley.
9. Andriani, P. and McKelvey, B. (2007). Beyond Gaussian averages: Redirecting organization science towards extreme events and power laws. *Journal of International Studies*, 38, 1212–1230.
10. Andriani, P. and McKelvey, B. (2009). From Gaussian to Paretian thinking: Causes and implications of power laws in organizations. *Organization Science*, 20(6), 1053–1071.
11. Andriani, P. and McKelvey, B. (2011). Using scale-free processes to explain punctuated-change in management-relevant phenomena. *International Journal of Complexity in Leadership and Management*, 1(3), 211–251.

12. Argyris, C. (1991). Teaching smart people how to learn. *Harvard Business Review*, May–June.

13. Arthur, B. (1990). Positive feedback in the economy. *Scientific American*, 262(2), 92–99.

14. Arthur, B. (1994). *Increasing Returns and Path Dependence in the Economy*. Ann Arbor: University of Michigan Press.

15. Ashby, R. W. (1956). *An Introduction to Cybernetics*. London: Methuen.

16. Ashby, R. W. (1962). Principles of the self-organizing system. In von Foerster, H. and Zopf, G. W. (Eds.), *Principles of Self-organization* (255–278). New York: Pergamon.

17. Axelrod, R. (1997). *The Complexity of Cooperation: Agent-based Models of Competition and Collaboration*. Princeton: Princeton University Press.

18. Baets, W. (2006). *Complexity, Learning and Organizations: A Quantum Interpretation of Business*. UK: Routledge.

19. Baets, W. (2010). The ecology of management: Cassandra, a holistic diagnostic for sustainable performance. *International Journal of Complexity in Leadership and Management*, 1(1), 37–54.

20. Bak, P. (1996). *How Nature Works: The Science of Self-organized Criticality*. New York: Springer-Verlag.

21. Bak, P., Tang, C. and Wiesenfeld, K. (1987). Self-organized criticality: An explanation of 1/f noise. *Physical Review Letters*, 59 (4), 381–384.

22. Bak, P., Tang, C. and Wiesenfeld, K. (1988). Self-organized criticality. *Physical Review A*, 38 (1), 364–374.

23. Bar-Yam, Y. (1997). *Dynamics of Complex Systems*. Reading: Addison-Wesley.

24. Baskin, K. (1998). *Corporate DNA: Learning from Life*. Boston: Butterworth-Heinemann.

25. Baskin, K. (2007). Ever the twain shall meet. *Chinese Management Studies*, 1(1), 57–68.

26. Battram, A. (1996). *Navigating Complexity*. London: The Industrial Society.

27. Begun, J. W. (1994). Chaos and complexity: Frontiers of organization science. *Journal of Management Inquiry*, 3(4), 329–335.

28. Beijerse, R. P. (1999). Questions in knowledge management: Defining and conceptualizing a phenomenon. *Journal of Knowledge Management*, 3(2), 94–109.

29. Bento, F. (2011). A complexity perspective towards leadership in academic departments: Investigating organizational changes in a Norwegian research-intensive academic department. *International Journal of Complexity in Leadership and Management*, 1(2), 116–132.

30. Bento, F. (2011). The contribution of complexity theory to the study of departmental leadership in possesses of organizational change in higher education. *International Journal of Complexity in Leadership and Management*, 1(3), 275–288.

31. Bohm, D. J. (2000). *On Dialogue*. New York: Routledge.

32. Boisot, M. and Child, J. (1999). Organizations as adaptive systems in complex environments: The case of China. *Organization Science*, 10(3), 237–252.

33. Boisot, M. and McKelvey, B. (2010). Integrating modernist and postmodernist perspectives on organizations: A complexity science bridge. *Academy of Management Review*, 35(3), 415–433.

34. Borge-Holthoefer, J. *et al.* (2013). Cascading behavior in complex sociotechnical networks. *Journal of Complex Networks*, 1(1), 3–24.

35. Broer, R. and Nieuwpoort, W.C. (1999). Hole localization and symmetry breaking. *Journal of Molecular Structure*, 458, 19–25.

36. Brown, S. L. and Eisenhardt, K. M. (1997). The art of continuous change: Linking complexity theory and time-based evolution in relentlessly shifting organization. *Administrative Science Quarterly*, 42(1), 1–34.

37. Churchman, C. W. (1967). Wicked problems. *Management Science*, 14(4), 141–142.

38. Cilliers, P. (2002). Why we cannot know complex things completely. *Emergence*, 4(1/2), 77–84.

39. Cleveland, H. (2002). *Nobody in Charge*. San Francisco: Josey-Bass.

40. Comfort, L. (1994). Self-organization in complex systems. *Journal of Public Administration Research and Theory*, 4(3), 393–410.

41. Conner, D. R. (1998). *Leading at the Edge of Chaos*. New York: Wiley.

42. Cox, T. (1993). *Cultural Diversity in Organizations: Theory, Research and Practice*. San Francisco: Berrett-Koehler.

43. Daly, H. (1996). *Beyond Growth: The Economics of Sustainable Development*. Boston: Beacon Press.

44. Davis, B. and Phelps, R. (2007). Participatory consciousness and complicity. *Complicity: An International Journal of Complexity and Education*, 4(1), 1–4.

45. De Geus, A. (1998). *The Living Company*. Cambridge, MA: Harvard Business School Press.

46. Dixon, N. M. (1998). *Dialogue at Work: Making Talk Developmental for People and Organization*. London: Lemos and Crane.

47. Dombkins, D. (2014). Realizing complex policy: Using a systems-to-systems approach to develop and implement policy. *Policy and Complex Systems*, (1)1, 22–60.

48. Duit, A. and Galaz, V. (2008). Governance and complexity — emerging issues for governance theory. *Governance: An International Journal of Policy*, 21(3), 311–335.
49. Ehin, C. (2000). *Unleashing Intellectual Capital*. Boston: Butterworth-Heinnmann.
50. Eigen, M. and Schuster, P. (1979). *The Hypercycle: A Principle of Natural Self-organization*. New York: Springer.
51. Einstein, A. (1954). *Ideas and Opinions*. New York: Crown Publishers.
52. Eldredge, N. and Gould, S. (1972). Punctuated equilibria: An alternative to phyletic gradualism, In Schopf, T. J. M. (Ed.), *Models in Paleobiology* (82–115). San Francisco: Freeman Cooper.
53. Ellinor, J. and Gerald, G. (1998). *Dialogue: Rediscovering the Transforming Power of Conversation*. New York: John Wiley and Sons.
54. Farmer, J. D., Ott, E. and Yorke, J. A. (1983). The dimension of chaotic attractors. *Physica D*, 7, 153–180.
55. Feigenbaum, M. (1983). Universal behavior in nonlinear systems. *Physica D*, 5, 16–39.
56. Fioretti, G. and Visser, B. (2004). A cognitive interpretation of organizational complexity. *Emergence*, 6(1/2), 11–23.
57. Fitzgerald, L. A. (2002). Chaos: The lens that transcend. *Journal of Organizational Change and Management*, 15(4), 11–23.
58. Fu, H. (2011). Anthropologizing the complexity of leadership: A holistic understanding of cross-cultural context. *International Journal of Complexity in Leadership and Management*, 1(4), 395–410.
59. Garvin, D. (1993). Building a learning organization. *Harvard Business Review*, July–August, 78–91.
60. Gell-Mann, M. (1994). *The Quark and the Jaguar*. Boston: Little Brown.
61. Gell-Mann, M. (1995). What is complexity? *Complexity*, 1(1), 16–19.
62. Ghemawat, P. (2005). *Strategy and the Business Landscape*. Upper saddle River: Prentice Hall.
63. Gladwin, M. (2000). *The Tipping Point: How Little Things can Make a Big Difference*. New York: Little Brown.
64. Gladwin, T. N., Kennelly, J. J. and Krause, T. S. (1995). Shifting paradigms for sustainable development: Implications for management theory and research. *Academy of Management Review*, 20(4), 874–907.
65. Gleick, J. (1987). *Chaos: Making a New Science*. London: Heinemann.
66. Glynn, M. A. (1996). Innovative genius: A framework for relating individual and organizational intelligence to innovation. *Academy of Management Review*, 21(4), 1081–1111.

67. Goldstein, J. (1988). A far-from-equilibrium systems approach to resistance to change. *Organizational Dynamics*, 17(2), 16–26.

68. Goldstein, J. (1999). Emergence as construct: History and issues. *Emergence*, 1(1), 49–62.

69. Goldstein, J. (2000). Conceptual snares emergence: A construct amid a thicket of conceptual snares. *Emergence*, 2(1), 5–22.

70. Goleman, D. and Boyatzis, R. (2008). Social intelligence and the biology of leadership. *Harvard Business Review*, September, 74–81.

71. Goleman, D., Boyatzis, R. and McKee, A. (2003). *The New Leaderships*. London: Time Warner.

72. Granovetter, M. (1973). The strength of weak ties. *The American Journal of Sociology*, 78 (6), 1360–1380.

73. Green, D. G. and Newth, D. (2001). Towards a theory of everything? — Grand challenges in complexity and informatics. *Complexity International*, 8, 1–12.

74. Gulick, D. (1992). *Encounters with Chaos*. New York: McGraw-Hill.

75. Haken, H. (1978). *Synergetics — An Introduction*. Berlin: Springer Verlag.

76. Haken, H. (1981). *The Science of Structure: Synergetics*. New York: Van Nostrand Reinhold.

77. Harvey, J. B. (1974). The Abilene Paradox: The management of agreement. *Organizational Dynamics*, 3, 63–80.

78. Hayes, R. M. (1993). Measurement of information. *Information Processing and Management*, 29(1), 1–11.

79. Hazy, J. K. (2011). Parsing the 'influential increment' in the language of complexity: Uncovering the systemic mechanisms of leadership influence. *International Journal of complexity in Leadership and Management*, 1(2), 164–191.

80. Hazy, J. K. (2012). Unifying leadership: Shaping identity, ethics and the rules of interaction. *International Journal of Society Systems and Science*, 4(3), 222–241.

81. Hazy, J. K. (2012). Leading large: Emergent learning and adaptation in social networks. *International Journal of Complexity in Leadership and Management*, 1(4), 52–73.

82. Heames, J. T. and Harvey, M. (2006). The evolution of the concept of the 'executive' from the 20th century manager to the 21st century global leader. *Journal of Leadership and Organizational Studies*, 13(2), 29–41.

83. Heyligen, F. (1992). Evolution, selfishness and cooperation. *Journal of Ideas*, 2(4), 70–76.

84. Heylighen, F., Cilliers, P. and Gershenson, C. (2007). The philosophy of complexity. In Bogg, J. and Geyer, R. (Eds.), *Complexity Science and Society* (117–135). Oxford: Radcliffe Publishing.
85. Holland, J. H. (1995). *Adaptation in Natural and Artificial Systems.* Cambridge: MIT Press.
86. Holland, J. H. (1995). *Hidden Order: How Adaptation builds Complexity.* Reading: Addison-Wesley.
87. Holland, J. H. (1998). *Emergence: From Chaos to Order.* Reading: Addison-Wesley.
88. Inguaggiato, C. and Occeli, S. (2014). Policymaking in an information wired environment: Religning government and governance relationships by complexity thinking. *Policy and Complex Systems,* 1(1), 77–92.
89. Juma, C. (2014). Complexity, innovation, and development: Schumpeter revisited. *Policy and Complex Systems,* 1(1), 4–21.
90. Kauffman, S. A. (1989). The evolution of economic webs. In Anderson, P.W., Arrow, K.J. and Pines, D. (Eds.), *The Economy as an Evolving Complex System* (125–146). New York: Addison-Wesley.
91. Kauffman, S. A. (1991). Antichaos and adaptation. *Scientific America,* 78–84.
92. Kauffman, S. A. (1993). *The Origins of Order: Self-organization and Selection in Evolution.* Oxford: Oxford University Press.
93. Kauffman, S. A. (1995). *At Home in the Universe: The Search for the Laws of Self-organization and Complexity.* New York: Oxford University Press.
94. Kelly, K. (1998). *New Rules for the New Economy.* New York: Viking.
95. Kelso, S. (1995). *The Self-organization of Brain and Behavior.* Cambridge, MA: MIT Press.
96. Kilmann, R. (2001). *Quantum Organizations.* Palo Alto: Davies-Black.
97. Klein, J. T. (2004). Interdisciplinary and complexity: An evolving relationship. *Emergence,* 6(1/2), 2–10.
98. Knowles, R. N. (2001). Self-organizing: A way of seeing what is happening in organizations and a pathway to coherence. *Emergence,* 3(4), 112–127.
99. Knowles, R. N. (2002). Self-organizing: A way of seeing what is happening in organizations and a pathway to coherence, Part II. *Emergence,* 4(4), 86–97.
100. Kowch, E. G. (2013). Conceptualizing the essential qualities of complex adaptive leadership: Networks that organize. *International Journal of Complexity in Leadership and Management,* 2(3), 162–184.
101. Krugman, P. (1996). *The Self-organizing Economy.* Cambridge, MA: Bradford Press.

102. Kuhn, T. S. (1970). *The Structure of Scientific Revolutions*. Chicago: University of Chicago Press.
103. Langloris, R. N. and Everett, M. J. (1992). Complexity, genuine uncertainty, and the economics of organization. *Human Systems Management*, 11, 67–75.
104. Langton, C. G. (1989). *Artificial Life*. New York: Addison-Wesley.
105. Levin, S. A. (1998). Ecosystems and the biosphere as complex adaptive systems. *Ecosystems*, 1, 431–436.
106. Levinthal, D. A. (1997). Adaptation on rugged landscapes. *Management Science*, 43(7), 934–950.
107. Levy, D. (1994). Chaos theory and strategy: Theory, application and management applications. *Strategic Management Journal*, 15, 167–178.
108. Lewin, R. (1993). *Complexity: Life at the Edge of Chaos*. New York: Macmillan.
109. Lewin, R., and Regine, B. (2000). *The Soul at Work: Embracing Complexity Science for Business Success*. New York: Simon & Schuster.
110. Li, T. Y. and Yorke, J. A. (1975). Period three implies chaos. *American Mathematics Monthly*, 82, 985–992.
111. Liang, T. Y. (1994). The basic entity model: A fundamental theoretical model of information and information processing. *Information Processing and Management*, 30(5), 647–661.
112. Liang, T. Y. (1996). The basic entity model: A theoretical model of information processing, decision making and information systems. *Information Processing and Management*, 32(4), 477–487.
113. Liang, T. Y. (1998). General information theory: Some macroscopic dynamics of the human thinking systems. *Information Processing and Management*, 34(2–3), 275–290.
114. Liang, T. Y. (2001). Nurturing intelligent human organizations: The nonlinear perspective of the human minds. *Human Systems Management*, 20(4), 281–289.
115. Liang, T. Y. (2002). The inherent structure and dynamic of intelligent human organizations. *Human Systems Management*, 21(1), 9–19.
116. Liang, T. Y. (2003). The crucial roles of the artificial information systems web in intelligent human organizations. *Human Systems Management*, 22(2), 115–124.
117. Liang, T. Y. (2004). Intelligence strategy: The evolutionary and co-evolutionary dynamics of intelligent human organizations and their interacting agents. *Human Systems Management*, 23(2), 137–149.
118. Liang, T. Y. (2004). Intelligence strategy: The integrated 3C-OK framework of intelligent human organizations. *Human Systems Management*, 23(4), 205–211.

119. Liang, T. Y. (2007). The new intelligence leadership strategy in *i*CAS. *Human Systems Management*, 26(2), 111–122.
120. Liang, T. Y. (2010). Innovative sustainability and highly intelligent human organizations (*i*CAS): The new management and leadership perspective. *International Journal of Complexity in Leadership and Management*, 1(1), 83–101.
121. Liang, T. Y. (2011). Emergence and the new intelligence leadership. *International Journal of Complexity in Leadership and Management*, 1(2), 192–207.
122. Liang, T. Y. (2013). Edge of emergence, relativistic complexity and the new leadership. *Human Systems Management*, 32 (1), 3–15.
123. Liang, T. Y. (2015). Relativistic complexity, adaptive governance and the intelligence leadership. *Human Systems Management*, 34(3), 201–223.
124. Lichtenstein, B. (2011). Levels and degrees of emergence: Toward a matrix of complexity in entrepreneurship. *International Journal of Complexity in Leadership and Management*, 1(3), 252–274.
125. Lichtenstein, B., Dooley, K. J. and Lumpkin, G.T. (2006). Measuring emergence in the dynamics of new venture creation. *Journal of Business Venturing*, 21, 153–171.
126. Lichtenstein, B. and McKelvey, B. (2011). Four types of emergence: A typology of complexity and its implications for a science of management. *International Journal of Complexity in Leadership and Management*, 1(4), 339–378.
127. Lichtenstein, B. and Plowman, D. (2009). The leadership of emergence: A complex systems leadership theory of emergence at successive organizational levels. *The Leadership Quarterly*, 20(4), 617–630.
128. Liebowitz, J. (1999). *Building Organizational Intelligence*. New York: CRC Press.
129. Lissack, M. R. (1997). Of chaos and complexity: Management insights from a new science. *Management Decision*, 35(3), 205–218.
130. Lissack, M. R. (1999). Complexity: The science, its vocabulary, and its relation to organization. *Emergence*, 1(1), 110–126.
131. Lorenz, E. (1963). Deterministic non-periodic flow. *Journal of Atmospheric Sciences*, 20(2), 130–141.
132. Love, J. (1988). *The Age of Gaia: A Biography of our Living Earth*. New York: W. W. Norton.
133. Low, D. and Vadaketh, S. (2014). *Hard Choices: Challenging the Singapore Consensus*. Singapore: NUS Press.

134. MacIntosh, R. and MacLean, D. (1999). Conditioned emergence: A dissipative structures approach to transformation. *Strategic Management Journal*, 20, 297–316.

135. Maguire, S. and McKelvey, B. (1999). Complexity and management: Moving from fad to firm foundations. *Emergence*, 1(2), 19–21.

136. Mahmud, S. (2011). Developing managerial understanding of self-organization. *International Journal of Complexity in Leadership and Management*, 1(2), 105–115.

137. Mandelbrot, B. B. (1982). *The Fractal Geometry of Nature*. New York: Freeman.

138. Mantegna, R. N. and Stanley, H. E. (2000). *An Introduction to Econophysics*. Cambridge: Cambridge University Press.

139. Marion, R. and Uhl-Bien, M. (2001). Leadership in complex organizations. *The Leadership Quarterly*, 12, 389–418.

140. Markus, H. and Kitayama, S. (1991). Culture and the self: Implications for cognition, emotion, and motivation. *Psychological Review*, 98(2), 224–253.

141. Maturana, H. and Varela, F.J. (1973). Autopoiesis: The organization of the living. In Maturana, H. and Varela, F.J. (Eds.), *Autopoiesis and Cognition: The Realization of the Living*. Boston Studies in the Philosophy of Science. Dordrecht: D. Reidel.

142. May, R. M. (1976). Simple mathematical models with very complicated dynamics. *Nature*, 261, 459–467.

143. McKelvey, B. (1991). Complexity theory in organizational science: Seizing the promise or becoming a fad? *Emergence*, 1(1), 5–32.

144. McKelvey, B. (1997). Quasi-natural organizational science. *Organization Science*, 8(4), 352–380.

145. McKelvey, B. (1999). Avoiding complexity catastrophe in co-evolutionary pockets: strategies for rugged landscape. *Organizational Science*, 10, 294–321.

146. McKelvey, B. (2001). Energizing order-creating networks of distributed intelligence. *International Journal of Innovative Management*, 5, 181–212.

147. McKelvey, B. (2008). Emergent strategy via complexity leadership: Using complexity science and adaptive tension to build distributed intelligence. In Uhl-Bien, M. and Marion, R. (Eds.), *Complexity and Leadership Volume 1: Conceptual Foundations*. Charlotte: Information Age Publishing.

148. McKelvey, B. (2010). Complexity leadership: The secret of Jack Welch's success. *International Journal of Complexity in Leadership and Management*, 1(1), 4–36.

149. McKelvey, B., Lichtenstein, B. and Andriani, W. (2012). When organizations and ecosystems interact: Towards a law of requisite fractality in firms. *International Journal of Complexity in Leadership and Management*, 1(4), 104–136.

150. McMaster, M. D. (1996). *The Intelligence Advantage: Organizing for Complexity*. Boston: Butterworth-Heinemann.

151. Merry, U. (1995). *Coping with Uncertainty*. Connecticut: Prager.

152. Mintzberg, H. and Waters, J. A. (1985). Of strategies, deliberate and emergent. *Strategic Management Journal*, 6(3), 257–272.

153. Morrison, K. (2011). Leadership for self-organization: Complexity theory and communicative action. *International Journal of Complexity in Leadership and Management*, 1(2), 145–163.

154. Ng, D. (2011). The entrepreneurship of nested systems: A socially complex approach. *International Journal of Complexity in Leadership and Management*, 1(4), 379–394.

155. Ng, P. T. and Liang, T. Y. (2005). Speaking the unspeakable: The paper dialogue approach. *International Journal of Human Resources Development and Management*, 5(2), 190–203.

156. Nicolis, G. (1989). Physics of far-from-equilibrium systems and self-organization. In Davies, P. (Ed.), *The New Physics*. Cambridge: Cambridge University Press.

157. Nicolis, G. and Prigogine, I. (1977). *Self-organization in Non-equilibrium Systems: From Dissipative Structure to Order through Fluctuations*. New York: Wiley.

158. Olmedo, E. (2010). Complexity and chaos in organizations: Complexity management. *International Journal of Complexity in Leadership and Management*, 1(1), 72–82.

159. Overman, E. S. (1996). The new science of management: Chaos and quantum theory and method. *Journal of Public Administration Research and Theory*, 6(1), 75–89.

160. Packard, N. (1984). Complexity of growing patterns in cellular automata. In Demongeot, J., Goles, F. and Tchuente, M. (Eds.), *Dynamical Systems and Cellular Automata*. New York: Academic Press.

161. Packard, N. (1988). Adaptation toward the edge of chaos. In Kelso, J., Mandell, A. and Schlesinger, M. (Eds.), *Dynamic Patterns in Complex Systems*. Singapore: World Scientific.

162. Pagels. H. R. (1988). *The Dreams of Reason*. New York: Simon and Schuster.

163. Pascale, R. T., Millemann, M. and Gioja, L. (2000). *Surfing the Edge of Chaos*. New York: Three Rivers Press.

164. Paul, C.N. and Soofi, E.S. (2012). Rare, outlier and extreme: Beyond the Gaussian models and measures. *International Journal of Complexity in Leadership and Management*, 1(4), 6–38.

165. Perry, T. S. (1995). Management chaos allows more creativity. *Research Technology Management*, 28(5), 14–17.

166. Pico, R. M. (2002). *Consciousness in Four Dimensions*. New York: McGraw-Hill.

167. Pirson, M. and Turnbull, S. (2015). The future of corporate governance: Network governance — a lesson from the financial crisis. *Human Systems Management*, 34(1), 81–89.

168. Popper, K. R. (1968). *The Logic of Scientific Discovery*. New York: Harper & Row.

169. Price, I. (2004). Complexity, complicatedness and complexity: A new science behind organizational intervention? *Emergence*, 6(1/2), 40–48.

170. Price, I. and Evans, L. (2003). Punctuated equilibrium: An organic metaphor for the learning organization. *European Forum for Management Development Quarterly Review*, 93(1), 33–35.

171. Prigogine, I. (1967). Dissipative structure in chemical systems. In Claessons, S. (Ed.), *Fast Reactions and Primary Processes in Chemical Kinetics*. New York: Elsevier Interscience.

172. Prigogine, I. (1980). *From Being to Becoming: Time and Complexity in the Physical Sciences*. San Francisco: Freeman.

173. Prigogine, I. and Prigogine, J. (1989). *Exploring Complexity: An Introduction*. New York: Freeman & Co.

174. Prigogine, I. and Stengers, I. (1984). *Order Out of Chaos*. New York: Battram Books.

175. Probst, G., Raub, S. and Romhardt, K. (2000). *Managing Knowledge*. West Sussex: John Wiley and Sons.

176. Richardson, K. A. and Lissack, M. R. (2001). On the status and boundaries, both natural and organizational: A complex systems perspective. *Emergence*, 3(4), 32–49.

177. Ruelle, D. and Takens, F. (1971). On the nature of turbulence. *Communications in Mathematical Physics*, 20(3), 167–192.

178. Sanders, T. I. (1998). *Strategic Thinking and the New Science*. New York: The Free Press.

179. Sawyers, K. (2005). *Social Emergence: Societies as Complex Systems*. New York: Cambridge University Press.

180. Scott, A. (2007). *The Nonlinear Universe: Chaos, Emergence and Life*. New York: Springer.

181. Senge, P. *et al.* (1994). *The Fifth Discipline: The Art and Practice of the Learning Organization*. London: Nicholas Brealey.

182. Shenhav, Y. (1995). From chaos to systems: The engineering foundations of organization theory, 1879–1932. *Administrative Science Quarterly*, 40, 557–585.

183. Siggelkow, N. (2002). Evolution toward fit. *Administrative Science Quarterly*, 46, 125–159.

184. Simon, H. A. (1962). The architecture of complexity. *Proceedings of the American Philosophical Society*, 106, 467–482.

185. Simon, H. A. (1969/1988). *The Sciences of the Artificial*. Cambridge, MA: MIT Press.

186. Simon, H. A. (1972). Theories of bounded rationality. In McGuire, C. B. and R. Radner (Eds.), *Decision and Organization: A Volume in Honour of Jacob Marschak* (161–176). Amsterdam: North Holland Publishing Company.

187. Simon, H. A. (1976). *Administrative Behavior: A Study of Decision-making Processes in Administrative Organizations*. New York: Macmillan.

188. Simon, H. A. (1989). Cognitive Science: The process of human thinking. Public Lectures by Professor Herbert A. Simon (Lee Kuan Yew Distinguished Visitor), National University of Singapore, 1–21.

189. Simon, H. A. (1989). Cognitive Science: The nature of economic reality. Public Lectures by Professor Herbert A. Simon (Lee Kuan Yew Distinguished Visitor), National University of Singapore, 22–43.

190. Snowden, D. J. and Boone, M. E. (2007). A leader's framework for decision making. *Harvard Business Review*, November, 68–76.

191. Stacey, R. D. (1991). *The Chaos Frontier: Creative Strategic Control for Business*. Oxford: Butterworth-Heinemann.

192. Stacey, R. D. (1992). *Managing the Unknown: Strategic Boundaries between Order and Chaos in Organizations*. San Francisco: Jossey-Bass.

193. Stacey, R. D. (1995). The science of complexity: An alternative perspective for strategic change processes. *Strategic Management Journal*, 16, 477–495.

194. Stacey, R. D. (1996). *Complexity in Creative Organizations*. San Francisco: Berrett-Kochler.

195. Stacey, R. D. (2001). The emergence of knowledge in organizations. *Emergence*, 2(4), 23–39.

196. Stacey, R. D. (2001). *Complex Responsive Processes in Organizations: Learning and Knowledge Creation*. New York: Routledge.

197. Stacey, R. D. (2005). *Experiencing Emergence in Organizations: Local Interaction and the Emergence of Global Pattern*. London: Routledge.

198. Stonier, T. (1990). *Information and the Internal Structure of the Universe: An Exploration into Information Physics.* London: Springer-Verlag.
199. Stonier, T. (1991). Towards a new theory of information. *Journal of Information Science,* 17(5), 257–263.
200. Stonier, T. (1992). *Beyond Information: The Natural History of Intelligence.* London: Springer-Verlag.
201. Sungalia, H. (1990). The new science of chaos: Making a new science of leadership? *Journal of Educational Administration,* 28(2), 4–23.
202. Sydanmaanlakka, P. (2002). *An Intelligent Organization.* Oxford: Capstone.
203. Taleb, N. N. (2007). *The Black Swan: The Impact of the Highly Improbable.* New York: Random House.
204. Taylor, J. B. (2006). *My Stroke of Insight.* USA: Viking.
205. Thietart, R. A. and Forgues, B. (1995). Chaos theory and organization. *Organization Science,* 6(1), 19–31.
206. Thietart, R. A. and Forgues, B. (1997). Action, structure and chaos. *Organization Studies,* 18(1), 119–143.
207. Uhl-Bien, M. and Marion, R. (2008). *Complexity Leadership.* Charlotte: Information Age Publishing.
208. Uhl-Bien, M., Marion, R. and McKelvey, B. (2007). Complexity leadership theory: Shifting leadership from the industrial age to the knowledge era. *Leadership Quarterly,* 18 (4), 298–318.
209. Urry, J. (2003). *Global Complexity.* Cambridge: Polity Press.
210. Vega-Redondo, F. (2013). Network organizations. *Journal of Complex Networks,* 1(1), 72–82.
211. Vinten, G. (1992). Thriving on chaos: The route to management survival. *Management Decision,* 30(8), 22–28.
212. Von Bertalanffy, L. (1968). *General Systems Theory.* New York: Braziller.
213. Waldrop, M. M. (1992). *Complexity: The Emerging Science at the Edge of Order and Chaos.* New York: Simon and Schuster.
214. Weeks, J. and Galunic, C. (2003). A theory of the cultural evolution of firm: An intra-organizational ecology of memes. *Organizational Studies,* 24(8), 1309–1352.
215. West, B. J. and Deering, B. (1995). *The Lure of Modern Science: Fractal Thinking.* Singapore: World Scientific.
216. Westley, F. and Vredenburg, H. (1997). Inter-organizational collaboration and the preservation of global biodiversity. *Organization Science,* 8(4), 381–403.
217. Wheatley, M. (1992). *Leadership and the New Science: Learning about Organization from an Orderly Universe.* San Francisco: Berrett-Koehler.

218. White, R. P. and Hodgson, P. (2003). The newest leadership skills. In Goldsmith, M., Govindarajan, V., Kaye, B. and Vicere, A. A. (Eds.), *The Many Facets of Leaderships*. Upper Saddle River: Prentice Hall.
219. Wiener, N. (1948). *Cybernetics*. Cambridge, MA: MIT Press.
220. Williams, D. (2005). *Real Leadership*. San Francisco: Berrett-Koehler.
221. Winter, S. G. (2000). The satisficing principle in capacity learning. *Strategic Management Journal*, 21, 981–996.
222. Wolfram, S. (2002). *A New Kind of Science*. Canada: Wolfram Media, Inc.
223. Wood, R. (2000). *Managing Complexity*. London: Profile Books Ltd.
224. Zeleny, M. (1985). Spontaneous social orders. *General Systems*, 11(2), 117–131.
225. Zeleny, M. (1987). *Autopoiesis. Systems and Control Encyclopedia* (393–400). New York: Pergamon.
226. Zeleny, M. (1989). Knowledge as a new form capital, Part 1: Division and re-integration of knowledge. *Human Systems Management*, 8(1), 45–58.
227. Zeleny, M. (1989). Knowledge as a new form of capital, Part 2: Knowledge-based management systems. *Human Systems Management*, 8(2), 129–143.
228. Zeleny, M. (1990). Amoeba: The new generation of self-managing human systems. *Human Systems Management*, 9(2), 57–59.
229. Zeleny, M. (2005). *Human Systems Management*. Singapore: World Scientific.

***Notes*: Some 'interesting' terms and their reference sources:**

- Broken symmetry, constructionist hypothesis — Anderson (1972).
- Increasing returns — Arthur (1994).
- Cybernetics — Ashby (1956); Wiener (1948).
- Self-organizing criticality — Bak, Tang and Wiesenfeld (1987).
- Wicked problem — Churchman (1967).
- Hypercycle — Eigen and Schuster (1979).
- Dialogue — Ellinor and Gerald (1998).
- Chaotic attractor — Farmer, Edward and Yorke (1983).
- Bifurcation — Feigenbaum (1983); May (1976).
- Tipping point — Gladwin (2000).
- Self-transcending constructions — Goldstein (1995).
- Synergetics — Haken (1978, 1981).
- Abilene paradox — Harvey (1974).

- Self-organization, order for free — Kauffmann (1993).
- Strange attractor — Li and Yorke (1975).
- Stability-centricity, self-centricity — Liang (2001, 2002).
- Intelligent person (model) — Liang (2004).
- Relativistic complexity, edge of emergence — Liang (2013).
- Sensitive dependence on initial conditions — Lorenz (1963).
- Fractal — Mandelbrot (1982).
- Autopoiesis — Maturana and Varela (1973).
- Intelligence advantage — McMaster (1996).
- Uncertainty — Merry (1995).
- Paper dialogue — Ng and Liang (2005).
- Edge of chaos — Parkard (1988).
- Edge of order, dissipative structure — Prigogine (1967).
- Bounded rationality, administrative man (model), satisficing principle — Simon (1989).
- Information decoder — Stonier (1990).
- Black swan — Taleb (2007).

About the Author

 LIANG Thow Yick (1953–present) holds two first degrees in Mathematics and Physics (1977), First Class Hon in Physics (1978), MSc in Remote Sensing/Computer Image Processing (1980), and PhD in Particle Physics (1985). The two first degrees were acquired concurrently from 1974 to 1977. He completed the Mathematics degree course (University of London, external) through self-study when he was with the National University of Singapore (then University of Singapore). At the moment, he teaches the course Intelligent Organizations (Complexity Intelligence Strategy) at the Singapore Management University.

Liang is the Founding Chief Editor of the *International Journal of Complexity in Leadership and Management* (Inderscience). He is also a member on the Editorial Board of Human Systems Management (IOS Press), and the International Journal of Quality and Innovation (Inderscience). His publications spread over a diversification of journals, including *Journal of Mathematical Physics, Physical Review D, Nuovo Cimento, Information Processing and Management, Human Systems Management, Information and Management, Behavior and IT, International Journal of Complexity in Leadership and Management,* and *International Journal of Human Resources Development and Management.* He has also been invited to contribute articles (general information theory) to the *Encyclopedia of Computer Science and Technology,* and the *Encyclopedia*

in Library and Information Science. Currently, his primary research interest focuses on complexity theory, and relativistic complexity in intelligent human organizations, in particular the redefined intelligence leadership, self-organizing governance, intelligent person attributes, biotic systemic transformation (*i*CAS, multi-layer structure, network organization), intelligent complex adaptive dynamic (*i*CAD) and the holistic (integrated deliberate and emergent) strategy.

Finally, Liang is a cancer survivor since April 2000. A significant portion of his research in complexity theory (and the intelligent organization theory) is accomplished after his encounter with cancer. The works/contents on the analysis, inference, and conceptualization of this book are consolidated over the last three years.

Printed in the United States
By Bookmasters

Printed in the United States
By Bookmasters